Aesthetic Science

Aesthetic Science

CONNECTING MINDS, BRAINS, AND EXPERIENCE

Edited by Arthur P. Shimamura and Stephen E. Palmer

OXFORD
UNIVERSITY PRESS

OXFORD
UNIVERSITY PRESS

Published in the United States of America by Oxford University Press, Inc.,
198 Madison Avenue, New York, NY, 10016
United States of America

Oxford University Press, Inc. publishes works that further Oxford University's
objective of excellence in research, scholarship, and education

Oxford is a registered trade mark of Oxford University Press in the UK
and in certain other countries

Library of Congress Cataloging-in-Publication Data

Aesthetic science : connecting minds, brains, and experience / edited by
Arthur P. Shimamura & Stephen E. Palmer.
   p. ; cm.
 Includes bibliographical references.
 ISBN 978-0-19-973214-2 (hardcover : alk. paper)
 1. Neuropsychology. 2. Visual perception. 3. Aesthetics--Psychological
aspects. I. Shimamura, Arthur P. II. Palmer, Stephen E.
 [DNLM: 1. Esthetics—psychology. 2. Neuropsychology. 3. Art.
4. Visual Perception. WL 103.5]
 QP360.A327 2011
 612.8—dc22   2010053137

1 3 5 7 9 10 8 6 4 2

Typeset in Minion Pro
Printed on acid-free paper
Printed in the United States of America

ACKNOWLEDGMENTS

We would like to thank the contributors of this volume for taking the time to consider the viability of aesthetic science. As we wanted this volume to be accessible to a broad audience, the authors confronted editorial demands to avoid jargon and specificities that only a professional in their respective fields would appreciate. We would also like to thank Catharine Carlin, Joan Bossert, and the editorial staff at Oxford University Press for making this project an enjoyable and feasible endeavor. Art would like to thank the John Simon Guggenheim Foundation for financial support during the preparation of this volume, and Steve would like to thank the National Science Foundation (Grant No. 0745820) and a gift from Google for financial support.

PREFACE

As academic scientists, we have both led rather typical lives. We have been immersed in our respective research programs, trained graduate students, taught undergraduate courses, and dealt with perhaps more administrative duties than we care to remember. In fact, the variety of roles that we play as academicians has provided extraordinary opportunities to explore diverse avenues of interest (particularly after tenure). It is in this intellectual atmosphere that we have considered, rather late in our careers, the nature of aesthetic experiences.

Coincidentally, both of us developed an interest in aesthetics through our love of photography. In pursuing our artistic inclinations, we gained some insight into the nature of aesthetics as we honed our skills in artistic composition, lighting, and printmaking. We also learned from people's responses to our images. We began to ask questions: How do such things as color, balance, and form affect aesthetic responses? How does an image create a point of view or communicate a thought? What attracts people to some images but not to others? These questions led us to connect our experiences in photography with our knowledge of cognitive science. Art began teaching a freshman seminar on the *Psychology of Art* (no pun intended), whereas Steve began teaching research seminars about *Color and Aesthetics*. Soon, we realized that much of what we thought could or should be known about the nature of aesthetic experiences was not known or at least not well developed.

Individually, we set out trying to make meaningful contributions in areas where we felt the gaps most deeply. Art delved into those Big Questions where mostly philosophers and fools rush in: What drives our aesthetic experiences? How does culture and personal knowledge influence the way we look at art? What can neuroscience tell us about aesthetic experiences? With the good graces of a John Simon Guggenheim fellowship, Art spent a sabbatical year considering these questions from his own viewpoint. The product of this endeavor is his forthcoming book, *Experiencing Art*. Steve, on the other hand, took the empirical front and initiated a research program that explores the quality and nature of aesthetic preferences, in particular preferences for colors and spatial compositions. The fruits of his research are described in Chapter 8 and have sparked considerable interest across many disciplines, including cross-cultural psychology and the aesthetics of Web-based design.

From our casual conversations about photography, art, and aesthetics, we felt we could contribute to the field by working together to develop a much broader knowledge base than what has previously been considered. We have called this approach *aesthetic science,* which takes its lead from cognitive science, the multidisciplinary approach that considers the nature of cognition. The goal of aesthetic science is to approach the issues by promoting meaningful dialogues among people in various disciplines, including psychologists, philosophers, neuroscientists, art critics, historians, anthropologists, and artists themselves. Such an endeavor is much easier to propose than it is to accomplish, because a real dialogue across disciplines requires a common language and some agreement as to what is being studied. Indeed, the very object of interest, *aesthetics,* is prone to heavy and serious debate.

Once we began to consider the breadth of disciplines that could make up aesthetic science, it became clear that the arena would include a realm of human endeavors broader than any scholastic field we have ever encountered. It would include (at least) the theory, history, and practice of the fine arts, as well as attempts to understand the creative process, such as painting, sculpture, film, theater, music, dance, literature, architecture, and of course many others. If one does not tether aesthetic experiences to art objects (and there are good reasons not to), then the way we decide what we like or dislike about any object could be worthy of investigation within the realm of aesthetic science. It is acknowledged that a full understanding of aesthetics requires a collaboration between scientists and non-scientists. We view this edited volume as an attempt to initiate a forum for such a multidisciplinary approach.

As an initial effort, we invited position papers from five philosophers (actually four philosophers and an art critic), five psychologists, and five neuroscientists. We asked these scholars to consider visual aesthetics from the beholder's perspective— that is, what aspects of the mind and brain drive our aesthetic experience? Is it even possible to consider a science of such complex experiences? By keying on the beholder's experience (and assuming that whatever the beholder is looking at is *art*), we avoid some very thorny issues: What is art? What is the nature of the artist's creative experience? Why do humans create art? Such questions are certainly relevant to aesthetic science, but we have put these issues aside in order to approach a somewhat more tangible issue. Yet even by focusing discussions on the beholder's (rather than the artist's) experience, there are still incredibly difficult questions to consider: Can a multidisciplinary approach advance our understanding of aesthetics, or will such an endeavor simply muddle the issues (will too many chefs spoil the consommé)? Must aesthetics be tethered specifically to art objects? Must experiences with art be tethered specifically to aesthetics? Can science help to connect mind, brain, and aesthetics? With these questions in mind, we offer these position papers as an invitation to begin a dialogue concerning the nature of aesthetics. We hope that readers will take our invitation and consider these issues from their own perspective.

CONTENTS

Contributors   xi

1. Toward a Science of Aesthetics: Issues and Ideas   3
   ARTHUR P. SHIMAMURA

PART I Philosophical Perspectives

2. The Philosophy of Art and Aesthetics, Psychology, and
   Neuroscience: Studies in Literature, Music, and Visual Arts   31
   NOËL CARROLL, MARGARET MOORE, AND WILLIAM P. SEELEY

3. Aesthetic Theory and Aesthetic Science: Prospects for Integration   63
   VINCENT BERGERON AND DOMINIC MCIVER LOPES

4. Triangulating Aesthetic Experience   80
   MURRAY SMITH

5. Art and the Anthropologists   107
   GREGORY CURRIE

6. Aesthetic Science and Artistic Knowledge   129
   BLAKE GOPNIK

PART II Psychological Perspectives

7. Empirical Investigation of an Aesthetic Experience with Art   163
   PAUL J. LOCHER

8. Hidden Knowledge in Aesthetic Judgments: Preferences for
   Color and Spatial Composition   189
   STEPHEN E. PALMER, KAREN B. SCHLOSS, AND
   JONATHAN SAMMARTINO

9. Processing Fluency, Aesthetic Pleasure, and
   Culturally Shared Taste   223
   ROLF REBER

10. Human Emotions and Aesthetic Experience: An Overview of
    Empirical Aesthetics   250
    PAUL J. SILVIA

11. Artistic Development: The Three Essential Spheres   276
    KIMBERLY M. SHERIDAN AND HOWARD GARDNER

PART III Neuroscience Perspectives

12. Neuroaesthetics: Growing Pains of a New Discipline   299
    ANJAN CHATTERJEE

13. The Modularity of Aesthetic Processing and Perception in
    the Human Brain: Functional Neuroimaging
    Studies of Neuroaesthetics   318
    ULRICH KIRK

14. Art Compositions Elicit Distributed Activation in
    the Human Brain   337
    ALUMIT ISHAI

15. A Cognitive and Behavioral Neurological Approach to Aesthetics   356
    ZACHARY A. MILLER AND BRUCE L. MILLER

16. Neurology of Visual Aesthetics: Indian Nymphs,
    Modern Art, and Sexy Beaks   375
    VILAYANUR S. RAMACHANDRAN AND ELIZABETH SECKEL

    Index   391

CONTRIBUTORS

Vincent Bergeron
Assistant Professor
Department of Philosophy
University of Ottawa
Ottawa, ON, Canada

Noël Carroll
Distinguished Professor
Graduate Center of the City University
    of New York
New York, NY

Anjan Chatterjee
Professor of Neurology University
    of Pennsylvania
Philadelphia, PA

Gregory Currie
Professor of Philosophy
University of Nottingham
Nottingham, UK

Howard Gardner
Hobbs Professor of Cognition and
    Education
Harvard Graduate School
    of Education
Cambridge, MA

Blake Gopnik
Special Correspondent, Arts
Newsweek
New York, NY

Alumit Ishai
Professor of Cognitive Neuroscience
Institute of Neuroradiology
University of Zurich
Zurich, Switzerland

Ulrich Kirk
Human Neuroimaging Laboratory
Virginia Tech University
Carilion Research Institute
Roanoke, VA, USA and
Centre for Addition and
    Mental Health
University of Toronto
Toronto, ON, Canada

Paul J. Locher
Professor Emeritus of Psychology
Montclair State University
Montclair, New Jersey, NJ

Dominic McIver Lopes
Department of Philosophy
University of British Columbia
Vancouver, BC, Canada

Bruce L. Miller
A.W. Clausen Distinguished Professor
    of Neurology
Director, Memory & Aging Center
University of California
    San Francisco
San Francisco, CA

Zachary A. Miller
Clinical Instructor
UCSF Memory and Aging Center
Department of Neurology
San Francisco, CA

Margaret Moore
Post-doctoral Researcher
Philosophy Department
University of Leeds
Leeds, UK

Stephen E. Palmer
Professor of the Graduate School
Psychology and Cognitive Science
University of California, Berkeley
Berkeley, CA

Vilayanur S. Ramachandran
Director, Center for Brain and
    Cognition
University of California, San Diego
La Jolla, CA

Rolf Reber
Professor of Cognitive Psychology
University of Bergen
Bergen, Norway

Jonathan Sammartino
Lecturer
Psychology Department
University of California, Berkeley
Berkeley, CA

Elizabeth Seckel
UCSD Center for Brain and Cognition
San Diego, CA

William P. Seeley
Visiting Assistant Professor
Department of Philosophy
Bates College
Lewiston, ME

Karen B. Schloss
Department of Psychology
University of California, Berkeley
Berkeley, CA

Kimberly M. Sheridan
Assistant Professor
College of Education and Human
    Development and
College of Visual and
    Performing Arts
George Mason University
Fairfax, VA

Arthur P. Shimamura
Professor of Psychology
University of California, Berkeley
Berkeley, CA

Paul J. Silvia
Associate Professor of Psychology
University of North Carolina
    at Greensboro
Greensboro, NC

Murray Smith
Professor of Film Studies
Director of Research, Humanities
University of Kent
Canterbury, Kent, UK

Aesthetic Science

Toward a Science of Aesthetics

ISSUES AND IDEAS

Arthur P. Shimamura

What happens when we experience a work of art? What does it mean to have an aesthetic experience? Can science help us derive general principles about aesthetics, or is there really "no accounting for taste"? Philosophers, psychologists, and recently neuroscientists have sought answers to these questions, with each group focused on specific issues. In this volume, an interdisciplinary approach is offered that draws on philosophy, psychology, and neuroscience, and considers the feasibility of an integrative science of aesthetics.

Historically, the term *aesthetics* has been linked to the way art evokes an emotional response. Alexander Baumgarten[1] coined the term in 1750 to advance his new philosophical approach, which was to study the "art of thinking beautifully" (*ars pulchre cogitandi*). He argued that the appreciation of beauty is the endpoint of an aesthetic experience. People sense beauty in many things, from natural objects to skillful artworks, and aesthetics is the study of how the mind beholds beautiful objects. Baumgarten posited that certain physical properties of an object may evoke feelings of beauty, but the experience itself is purely a mindful event. Many contend that the sole purpose of art is to create objects that evoke feelings of beauty—that is, to instill an *aesthetic* response.

Considering the many ways people experience art these days, Baumgarten's definition is certainly inadequate. Contemporary art critics and philosophers find the term outdated and irrelevant to the way people experience art today (see Chapter 6). For now, rather than dispensing with the term, a broadening of it will be considered. Art can arouse our emotions in many ways—from beauty to anger to horror or disgust. It may pique our sensory processes through artistic balance and form, remind us of our own past, or force us to think about the world in new ways. Rather than considering the *one and only* aesthetic experience as that overwhelming sense of beauty people sometimes experience, perhaps while viewing Michelangelo's *David* or listening to Beethoven's *Ninth Symphony*, there are various kinds of aesthetic experiences, even ones that may be more focused on perceptual or conceptual features. Some may wince at a definition of aesthetics that is so broad that its experience is devoid of any emotional involvement. Indeed, it may be best to separate the notion of "aesthetics" from our experience with art altogether. Such issues will be addressed in the chapters to follow. At the outset, we will err on the side of inclusion rather than exclusion, and consider *aesthetics* as any "hedonic" response to a sensory experience. A hedonic response refers to a preference judgment: an object may be preferred or not, liked or not, interesting or not, approached or avoided. Artworks are prime objects for aesthetic evaluation, because for many their sole purpose is to instill an hedonic response. As such, this volume centers on the way we behold artworks, though hedonic responses may be elicited by any object.

The contributors of this volume were asked to address the potential of an *aesthetic science*. This chapter provides background material by briefly describing general issues of aesthetics from philosophical, psychological, and neurobiological perspectives. Other chapters delve further into these issues and even debate the plausibility of aesthetic science as a workable enterprise. The focus of the book is primarily on the visual arts, though many issues pertain to all traditions within the arts, including music, film, theater, dance, and literature. We also focus on the way art evokes aesthetic responses rather than how or why art is created—that is, the intent is to consider the nature of the beholder's experience rather than the artist's creative output. In this way, we hope to downplay such thorny issues as defining art (*What is art?*) and specifying its meaning within a culture (*Why do humans make art? What is its function in modern society?*).[2] By focusing on the beholder's experience, we hope to highlight the ways in which art is perceived, interpreted, and felt. In other words, we will explore what goes on in the mind and brain of the beholder.

Philosophical Approaches

Long before attempts were made to approach aesthetics scientifically, philosophers addressed the nature of aesthetic experiences. Their analyses have been and continue to be essential, as they define and sharpen essential issues concerning the quality of these experiences. Here we provide a brief overview of four philosophical approaches to aesthetics—mimetic, expressionist, formalist, and conceptual—each of which highlights different aspects of human psychological experiences.[3]

A MIMETIC APPROACH: SEEING NATURE THROUGH A WINDOW

In Plato's *Republic* (Book X),[4] art is defined as *mimesis* or imitations of reality. According to Plato's view of idealism, there exist ideal or pure forms, such as a perfect circle or a perfect bed. Such ideal forms cannot be realized by the hands of humans, because no one can draw a perfect circle or build a perfect bed. Plato denigrated art as intellectually distant from ideal forms. A carpenter's bed is a copy of the ideal form. A painting of a bed is even worse, because it is a copy of a carpenter's bed, and indeed a rather poor copy. It lacks the function of a bed, as one cannot sleep on it, and it is depicted from only one viewpoint. Thus, a painting grossly misrepresents the nature of objects, as it is at best twice removed from ideal forms. Plato was willing to banish all art from his Republic. Poets and dramatists were just as far from the truth as the lowly painter, because their works merely imitate human experiences and conditions. Even worse, art stirs emotions, thus clouding the ability to think rationally. According to Plato, artists are unworthy rivals of philosophers, because they try to reveal truth but manage only to create poor imitations of reality. Plato's negative view of art is certainly extreme. Yet his characterization of art as *mimesis*, as an imitation or representation of the real world, could be applied to much of Western art.

As in many philosophical issues, Aristotle offered a view that opposed Plato's position. In *The Poetics*,[5] Aristotle acknowledged that art is a form of mimesis, but viewed it as a natural form of pleasure instead of a perversion. We delight in listening to a poem or watching a good drama. Moreover, we can learn from art as imitations of reality. A dramatic play may depict what could happen just as much as what has happened. We learn from the mistakes or triumphs of fictional characters, such as the hero in a tragic drama. Indeed, art can depict and rarify essential universals of the human condition. Aristotle thus proposed that art should be valued, not vilified, as an imitation of reality.

Plato and Aristotle defined the Western approach to art as creating imitations of the real world. With respect to painting, the ability to do this accurately required extensive knowledge and technical skills that were not well developed until the 15th century, when Renaissance artists began to study the mathematics and scientific knowledge necessary to create realistic scenes. With this information, an artist could mimic with paint on canvas the sensory experience of viewing an actual scene. Indeed, the artist created a window through which the beholder could view nature.

Painting scenes accurately depends upon the representation of a three-dimensional (3-D) world onto a two-dimensional (2-D) surface. Interestingly, in every waking moment we perform this process, as our retina, that curved 2-D surface at the back of the eye, serves as the brain's canvas from which we derive and represent a 3-D world. Our brains transform these ever-changing upside-down and mirror-reversed images into spatial relations of objects in the real world, a feat accomplished with exquisite rendering of size, depth, and color. In paintings, artists create the *illusion* of objects in 3-D space, a feat that requires knowledge of how light is reflected off objects and projected to the eye.

Before the Renaissance, artists had acquired some skill in depicting 3-D objects. For example, early Greek and Roman artists were aware of the importance of shading and foreshortening to create the impression of depth. Yet it took Renaissance artists, such as Brunelleschi, Masaccio, and Leonardo, to conceptualize and implement the rules of linear perspective with mathematical and artistic acumen.[6] Another significant advance was the development of *chiaroscuro* (Italian for *light-dark*), a technique in which shading is used to heighten the perception of three dimensionality in objects. In the real world, contoured surfaces reflect light in various directions. Surfaces that reflect more light into the eye appear lighter than surfaces that reflect light away from the eye. Thus, information about the spatial orientation and depth of objects can be gleaned by changes in shading. Leonardo was a master of chiaroscuro, as can be seen in his study of drapery (Fig. 1.1). Note how the gradations of light and dark render exquisitely the contours of the folds. Leonardo's masterful application of chiaroscuro created the illusion of seeing 3-D forms in a 2-D drawing. The realism is so accurate that the drawing resembles a photographic image. Leonardo's artistry was grounded in knowledge about linear perspective and the way light reflects off surfaces.

FIGURE 1.1 **Leonardo da Vinci (1452–1519).** Drapery for a seated figure. *Distemper with white highlights. (Photo credit: Réunion des Musées Nationaux/Art Resource, NY.)*

In a mimetic approach to art, the beholder evaluates an artwork on the basis of how closely it resembles a view through a window onto a real-world scene. Renaissance artists advanced this approach with linear perspective and chiaroscuro. When we experience art today, we can appreciate the skill involved in creating such scenes. Indeed, much of Western art, particularly art up to the mid-19th century, was principally concerned with creating artworks intended to be experienced from a mimetic approach.

AN EXPRESSIONIST APPROACH: PERCEIVING WITH FEELING

Most museum-goers would say that art, while offering a window to the world, has its primary goal in expressing emotions. More specifically, they would concur with Baumgarten's thesis that art is meant to evoke feelings of beauty. We sense beauty in many things—in nature, in people, in ideas, and in art. Francis Hutcheson, in a treatise considered to be the "first modern essay in philosophical aesthetics,"[7] described art as instilling a sense of beauty and pleasure in the beholder.[8] He argued that when we behold a beautiful object we do so independently of the object's purpose or function. Hutcheson acknowledged that people have different opinions about what is beautiful, though he argued that there are absolute standards. He claimed that we all appreciate the beauty of a harmonic chord, an elegant mathematical theorem, or a well-composed painting.

The ancient Latin aphorism *De gustibus non est disputandum* ("About taste there's no disputing") sets the stage for David Hume's 1757 essay *Of the Standard of Taste*.[9] According to Hume: "Beauty is no quality in things themselves: it exists merely in the mind which contemplates them; and each mind perceives a different beauty." Hume advanced Hutchinson's argument by describing what seems to be a totally subjective view of taste: "a thousand different sentiments, excited by the same object, are all right: Because no sentiment represents what is really in the object." Nevertheless, Hume argued that there are universal standards by which we evaluate and judge beauty. Good taste depends upon expert knowledge, training, and having a "delicate" sense. Moreover, the ideal beholder avoids personal prejudices and cultural biases. With such rules for guiding one's aesthetic experiences, Hume asserted that there is a common basis (i.e., a standard) for evaluating beautiful objects.

From Hume, we advance to Immanuel Kant, whose viewpoint is often considered as the beginning of a *cognitive* approach to the mind. In *Critique of Pure Reason*[10] he wrote: "though all our knowledge begins with experience, it by no means follows that all arises out of experience." Kant argued that there is more to knowledge than just the sights, sounds, and smells that impinge on our senses. We interpret the world by linking sensory experience to pre-existing concepts or ideas. This interaction between experience and knowledge forms the basis for Kant's philosophy of aesthetics, which he described in *Critique of Judgment*.[11] Kant stated that judgments of taste are evaluations of pleasure (or displeasure) and that these evaluations are largely subjective. Many things elicit pleasurable feelings, such as fine food, a lovely home, and sex, but these things are also appreciated for other reasons, such as sustenance, shelter, and procreation. Kant identified three features of objects that give us pleasure: they are agreeable, good, and beautiful. Aesthetic judgments are specifically based on our evaluation of beautiful things. For Kant, beauty is an innate ideal that is shared among all individuals and is thus a universal concept. Thus, Kant echoed the sentiments of Hutcheson and Hume by arguing that aesthetic judgments are both subjective (based on experience) *and* universal (based on a pre-existing concept of beauty).

In addition to beauty, Kant considered *sublime* feelings. Whereas beauty refers to the quality of an object and is thus bounded by the object, the sublime refers to a feeling of overwhelming boundlessness. We experience the sublime when we consider the immensity of nature: galaxies of innumerable stars; the vast, seemingly unending expanse of the ocean; or the earth-shaking power of an erupting volcano. Unlike feelings of beauty, which are always pleasurable, the sublime may involve a sense of fear or pain, as when we compare the enormity of nature with the vulnerability and inadequacy of one's own being. Although many associate sublime feelings with religious or spiritual experiences, Kant took a decidedly secular viewpoint by referring to people's aesthetic response to nature. With respect to art, Kant argued that artworks themselves cannot be sublime, but in representing magnificent things or events, they can elicit sublime feelings.

For Kant, aesthetic judgments are not associated with an object's function or purpose. A sunrise is not beautiful because it offers warmth, nor is a painting of a woman beautiful because we desire to have amorous relations with her. Aesthetic judgments are made in an entirely *disinterested* manner (*ohne alles Interesse*). This term is rather misleading, as it should not be interpreted as meaning *without interest*. Instead, Kant meant that an object viewed aesthetically should be considered without reference to its function or other practical uses, such as satisfying one's hunger, physical comfort, or sexual desire. According to Kant, art accentuates reality by providing beautiful or sublime renderings of nature that are appreciated in a *disinterested* manner—without regard to the purpose, function, or desire of the objects portrayed. This notion is the basis for the common view of aesthetics as *art for art's sake*.

In the 19th century, *Romanticism* took hold by emphasizing emotional expressiveness in art. Art was not meant to represent mundane copies of the real world; rather, it was meant to be magnificently dramatic and heroic. At the Louvre museum in Paris, Théodore Géricault's *The Raft of the Medusa* (Fig. 1.2) illustrates an actual event, the aftermath of the wreck of the French naval ship *Méduse*, which ran aground off the West African coast. In this tragic event, a makeshift raft was constructed and of the 146 people aboard, only 15 were finally rescued. Géricault's painting depicts the moment when survivors see a boat that has come to their rescue. In *The Raft of the Medusa*, we witness a sublime moment filled with terror and awe. The painting inspires an *expressionist* approach, which follows the Kantian notion that art must arouse and excite our feelings of beauty and sublimity.

FIGURE 1.2 **Géricault, Théodore (1791–1824).** The Raft of the Medusa. *1819. Oil on canvas.* (*Photo credit: Réunion des Musées Nationaux/Art Resource, NY.*)

Throughout the 19th century and into the 20th century Western art was experienced from both a mimetic and expressionist approach. In *What is Art?*, Leo Tolstoy[12] argued that the essential success of an artwork is the degree to which the artist is able to communicate his or her feelings to the beholder. Philosophical theories under the rubric of *Expressionism* placed the emotional quality of an artwork at the forefront of all aesthetic experiences.[13] As exemplified by the 20th-century development of *Abstract Expressionism,* art could be the pure embodiment of emotion as depicted by splashes of colors, bold lines, and nondescript shapes. When asked about his view of art, Matisse pointed to a table and stated: "Well, take that table, for example . . . I do not literally paint that table, but the emotion it produces upon me."[14] For many artists, philosophers, and indeed most laypeople, the essential purpose, if not the only purpose, of art is to induce feelings in the beholder.

A FORMALIST APPROACH: ABSTRACTING SIGNIFICANT FORM

During the second half of the 19th century, a markedly different approach to art emerged. Artists began experimenting with the perceptual quality of their works and rejected the traditional approach of creating the *illusion* of 3-D scenes on canvas. Pictorial skills admired since the Renaissance, such as linear perspective and chiaroscuro, were viewed as old-fashioned tricks that artists applied to make scenes look realistic. Why should art be restricted to portrayals of the world as we see it? In his seminal treatise, *Modernist Painting*,[15] the noted art critic Clement Greenberg stated that the essence of modern art is its flatness. Rather than portraying 3-D objects in natural scenes, modern art is about the "flat surface" and the "properties of pigment."[16] Artists (and beholders) must recognize that the canvas is fundamentally a 2-D surface onto which paint is brushed, dripped, or smeared.

Greenberg identified Manet as the first Modernist painter, as his paintings did not include traditional finishing touches that created the illusion of 3-D space. His paintings were often rejected by the Académie des Beaux-Arts, the established organization that defined good and bad art, because his backgrounds were bare or roughly painted, and the application of subtle shading to create depth was missing. Critics at the time considered his paintings crude and unfinished. In hindsight, we now see the beginning of a bold form of painting. Manet accentuated the flatness of his canvas: gone is the strong sense of 3-D space attained by linear perspective, gone is the extensive use of chiaroscuro to enhance the three-dimensionality of objects, gone is the heavy glazing of paint to conceal brushstrokes. Manet emphasized the sensual quality of paint itself, thus foreshadowing Impressionism, the tradition he later embraced.

From Manet to other Impressionist artists, such as Monet and Renoir, one sees the application of color on canvas in a new and dynamic manner. The interpretation of form changes from mimetic depictions of realistic scenes to "impressions" of nature. At the time, Impressionist paintings were considered ugly, hardly worthy of consideration as art. The revolution they began was to use paint as light, creating form almost as a byproduct that emerged from rendering their impressions. In the paintings of these then-renegade Impressionists viewers now appreciate the sensual quality of their art. Post-Impressionist artists such as Van Gogh, Gauguin, and Cézanne experimented further with the dissolution of realism by distorting color, perspective, and form. It is virtually impossible to appreciate a Van Gogh painting without noticing the force of his brush strokes and his application of paint on canvas.

Clive Bell, the art theorist who, along with Clement Greenberg, helped define early-20th-century art, described the essence of the aesthetic experience as perceiving *significant form*. For Bell,[17] the actual content of a painting was irrelevant; instead it was critical that the artist magnify the sensual quality of lines, colors, and abstract shapes. This view of art forms the basis for *formalism*: the view that art should be appreciated solely on the basis of its sensory qualities. Formalism offers a means of interpreting abstract art, because the content and objects in a painting are irrelevant. With a formalist approach, the beholder considers an artwork purely on the basis of sensory features—that is, the aesthetic interplay of colors, lines, textures, and shapes.

What motivated the shift from a mimetic or expressionist approach to a formalist approach? Historians have suggested that the advent of photography acted as a catalyst for this change. Photography rendered mimetic paintings as inadequate or outdated. Why should an artist paint a realistic scene when a photograph could do the job with perfect depiction of perspective and shading? By the 1860s, photography was in the mainstream. People could pose at photography studios and obtain family portraits to send to family and friends. Landscape photographers, such as Carleton Watkins and Francis Frith, were showcasing magnificent scenes of distant lands. Given the popularity of photography, artists, such as the Impressionists, may have decided to create a style different from that offered by this new technology.

Interestingly, artistically inclined photographers during the 19th century de-emphasized the exquisite detail of their medium and tried to mimic the appearance of paintings. To give their work an "artistic" feel, soft, out-of-focus images were in vogue as they emulated oil paintings. Some scratched their prints with fine needles to mimic etchings. It was not until the 20th century that "straight" photographers, such Edward Weston and Ansel Adams, used the medium to its fullest. These two photographers were part of "Group f.64," an informal cadre of photographers who advocated sharp focus and detail of form (the term *f.64* refers to the smallest lens aperture available at the time, which afforded maximal sharpness through more extensive depth of field). These photographers developed a formalist approach as they discounted content and emphasized the interplay of lines, shades, and shapes. Consider Edward Weston's *Pepper No. 30* (Fig. 1.3). Such a common object is not depicted for its function or purpose. Weston photographed the vegetable to highlight the lines, contours, and shadings that give the object its form. There is, of course, an organic—some say erotic—quality to Weston's photographs. In his own words, however, he simply wanted to abstract the sensory quality of the object depicted—that is, he wanted to express aesthetic appeal in terms of significant form.

A CONCEPTUAL APPROACH: BELIEVING IS SEEING[18]

Long before artistic advances in linear perspective and chiaroscuro, in prehistoric cave paintings and ancient mummy portraits, artworks were meant to communicate concepts or messages, often to a higher being. In other words, the purpose of such "artworks" was to convey a conceptual point (e.g., a plea to the gods) rather than to present a realistic view of the world or to express feeling. When we search for the underlying meaning of an artwork we apply a conceptual approach to art. Contemporary art critics rely heavily on this approach, because art during the past 50 years has focused on the representation of conceptual statements. This contemporary view has its roots in Marcel Duchamp's 1917 piece *Fountain*, which was submitted to an art exhibition sponsored by the Society of Independent Artists, a group of avant-garde artists who eschewed juried exhibitions and awards. *Fountain* is actually a men's urinal turned on its back. Duchamp purchased it from the

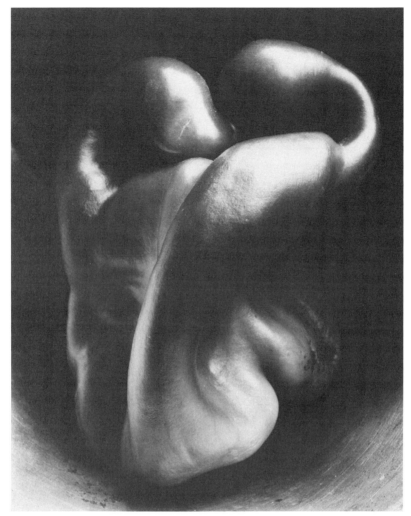

FIGURE 1.3 **Weston, Edward (1886–1958).** Pepper No. 30. *1930. Gelatin silver print, 9-7/16 ×
7-1/2". Gift of David H. McAlpin. (1913.1968) (Photo credit: Digital Image © The Museum of
Modern Art/Licensed by SCALA/Art Resource, NY.)*

J. L. Mott Iron Works in New York City, signed it "R. Mutt," and submitted it under
that pseudonym. Although the Society stated that they would show all submitted
works, *Fountain* was never exhibited, as some board members refused to consider
the piece as a work of art. Even if one claimed it was art, then Mr. Mutt must be
guilty of plagiarism, as the piece was obviously a commercial product.

Although the original *Fountain* was never exhibited, Duchamp later commis-
sioned several replicas, which are now displayed in prominent art museums.
In 2004, a survey of 500 art experts[19] voted *Fountain* as "the most influential

modern art work of all time," thus surpassing any work by Picasso, Matisse, or Warhol. Why? Clearly, in order to consider *Fountain* a work of art the actual concept of art needed to be radically changed. *Fountain* was (1) not created by an "artist," (2) not intended to express a sense of beauty, and (3) not intended to elicit a sense of significant form. Duchamp's intention was to make people *think* and question the very definition of art. You may find beauty and significant form in *Fountain*, but that certainly was not Duchamp's intention. His selection of a urinal was intended to disturb and disgust viewers, which adhered to his alliance with *Dadaism*, an art movement designed to shock and poke fun at the beholder.

One could view *Fountain* as an early example of *post-modern* art. The term has many meanings and has been bandied about in numerous ways. However, one attribute of *post-modernism* is the role of the artist as a conceptual theorist attempting to define the meaning of art itself. I will refer to this notion as *meta-art* or *art about art*.[20] Although some art historians would suggest that all art is essentially a comment about art, I view the strong notion of meta-art as an outgrowth of early modernist views, evidenced initially by Impressionist artists who experimented with the nature of the medium. Post-modernism continued the investigation by conceptualizing the process of creating art. A conceptual approach strives to extend the boundaries of art: Does art need to be created by an "artist"? Does it need to be beautiful or have significant form? What distinguishes art from non-art? Post-modernism intellectualizes the practice of art. It is thus anti-expressionist, anti-formalist, indeed some may even say anti-aesthetic. Issues of beauty, significant form, and other aesthetic experiences, such as the sublime quality of artworks, give way to conceptual statements about the meaning of art.

It took the art world several decades to appreciate fully the significance of *Fountain* as a harbinger of post-modernism. At the time, Duchamp's *Fountain* and his other offerings of everyday objects that he christened as "art" were generally considered Dadaist jokes, a way of teasing and rattling the art establishment. It was not until the latter half of the 20th century that many artists began to express themselves as conceptual theorists. The goal of the post-modern artists was essentially the goal of any philosopher of art: namely to define and characterize the nature of art. The post-modern artist, however, used art itself to describe a theoretical point rather than writing or talking about it. To interpret post-modernist works, one needs to understand the language of art. Nelson Goodman's *Languages of Art*[21] and Suzanne Langer's *Art in a New Key*[22] characterized this new approach, wherein artworks are viewed as conceptual interpretations or expressive symbols of thought. Pop Art, as exemplified by Warhol's paintings of Campbell's Soup cans, Lichtenstein's large renditions of comic strip panels, and Jasper Johns' painting of the American flag, depicts *symbols* or *icons* of popular culture that before were considered mundane, everyday objects.

A conceptual approach to art requires knowledge about the symbolic referents displayed in an artwork. To appreciate meta-art statements, it is necessary to have knowledge about art history and the various ways art has been defined.

For example, Joseph Kosuth's *One and Three Chairs* (1965) is a gallery installation that includes a real chair, a photograph of the same chair, and a dictionary definition of the word *chair*. This artwork is meaningful from a conceptual approach, as knowledge of art history, such as Plato's description of mimesis and Langer's notion of art as symbols, helps us understand the piece. Interestingly, for each exhibition of *One and Three Chairs*, Kosuth provides only an enlarged printout of the definition of the word "chair" and instructs the museum installer to select a real chair and display it and Kosuth's printout of the definition along with a life-sized photograph of the same chair. Thus, the actual chair that is used in each museum exhibition is different from previous ones and is selected by the installer rather than the artist. In this way, Kosuth seems to accentuate the conceptual rather than the formal or emotional nature of his artwork, as the objects themselves (the chair used and the photograph of it) change with each installation.

To summarize philosophical approaches, beholders over the centuries have considered artworks in terms of (1) how successfully they mimic the sensory experience of looking at the real world as if through a window, (2) how well they express feelings and a sense of beauty, (3) how well they create significant form, and (4) how well they convey conceptual statements. Each of these approaches highlights different aspects of the beholder's mental processes involved in the art experience: sensory processes with mimetic and formalist approaches, emotional processes with an expressionist approach, and semantic or cognitive processes with a conceptual approach. Today, pluralism is key, in the sense that anything goes, from retro artworks relying on mimetic representations to post-modern statements about art.

Empirical Approaches

What sets scientific analyses apart from other practices is its reliance on empirical research, which involves objective, systematic, and repeatable measurements. For over 125 years, aesthetic experiences have been studied scientifically using behavioral measures. Most of these investigations have been conducted under the rubric of psychological science. Recently, neuroscientists have begun to delve into the biological underpinnings of aesthetics by studying neurological patients with impairment in aesthetic experiences and applying neuroimaging methods to locate brain circuits that are active when we look at art.

PSYCHOLOGICAL SCIENCE

Psychological science has its roots in investigations of sensory processes. In 1860, Gustav Fechner offered a method for the scientific analysis of human sensation in his major treatise *Elemente der Psychophysik*[23] (*Elements of Psychophysics*). This new science of *psychophysics* considered the ways in which physical stimuli are registered by the mind. In 1876 Fechner published *Vorschule der Aesthetik* (*Primer of Aesthetics*),[24] which presented his seminal analysis of the psychophysics of aesthetics. Fechner suggested that aesthetics could be studied from the bottom up (*von Unten herauf*). In other words, rather than confronting complex philosophical concepts about beauty and sublimity, Fechner focused on analyses of elemental perceptual features. He studied preference judgments for basic shapes, such as rectangles of varying proportions, to determine which one was most appealing. He also studied preferences for colors. By understanding these basic elements of visual aesthetics, Fechner hoped to build a general understanding of the perceptual qualities that drive our aesthetic experiences.

Fechner paved the way for countless psychological investigations under the rubric of empirical aesthetics.[25] In these experiments, observers are shown various stimuli, such as a collection of shapes, colors, objects, or even actual paintings, and are asked to rate their preferences: that is, how much they like one stimulus over another. Fechner believed that by studying the building blocks of perception, such as basic shapes and colors, he could construct a general theory of aesthetic experiences. With this elemental, bottom-up approach—from basic sensory features to more complex representations—Fechner defined an empirical approach to the study of aesthetics that is still practiced today.

In the early 20th century, Gestalt psychology offered an alternative to the elemental, bottom-up approach exemplified by Fechner's psychophysical approach. Three German psychologists, Max Wertheimer, Kurt Koffka, and Wolfgang Köhler, were prominent in establishing this holistic approach to perception. They considered the visual scene as an organized grouping of features[26] and argued that perceptions could not be dissected into basic elements. This stance was inherent in their credo that the whole is different from the sum of its parts. The Gestalt psychologists developed the principle of *Prägnanz*, the notion that we organize our perceptions based on the simplest or most succinct interpretations. They acknowledged that the perceptual world is ambiguous and illusory. Thus, it is the organization of a visual scene that we interpret and not the elemental features themselves that make up a scene.

The psychologist Rudolf Arnheim applied Gestalt principles to the study of visual aesthetics. In his seminal book *Art and Visual Perception*,[27] Arnheim analyzed the ways in which artworks conform to Gestalt principles of perceptual organization. He described paintings with respect to the "perceptual forces" that artists induced through balance, harmony, and object placement. These forces give rise to aesthetic experiences, such as a sense of calm or tenseness. For example, a circle placed at the center of a rectangle is balanced and reduces tension, whereas a circle moved to one side of a rectangle is unbalanced and thus heightens tension. Arnheim's writings on visual aesthetics offered a theoretically motivated approach to the psychology of art. His Gestaltist interpretations stressed the manner in which the organization and dynamics of perceptual features act to create interesting works of art.

Whereas Fechner and Arnheim were primarily interested in perception, other psychologists studied how art influences the beholder's emotions. Daniel Berlyne[28] developed a theory about the way artworks arouse feelings. Consider a painting that you have never seen before. A painting that does little to arouse you or one that causes minimal tension will lead you to be indifferent to it. On the other hand, a painting that is so terribly arousing or causes so much tension will be overpowering and likely cause confusion or displeasure. According to Berlyne, optimally pleasing artworks are those that create some arousal or psychological tension but not so much that they become disturbing. He suggested that arousal is determined by specific features of artworks, such as novelty, complexity, surprisingness, uncertainty, and incongruity. He called these features "collative" properties because they must be put together (i.e., collated) in order to drive one's emotional experience. The greater the number of collative properties in an artwork, the greater our arousal.

According to Berlyne, we prefer some novelty, surprise, or incongruity in artworks, but too much will lead to a negative response. Notice that the features Berlyne defines are not, strictly speaking, properties of the artwork itself, but instead related to the beholder's past experience. How novel or surprising a painting is for a given viewer depends on that viewer's past experiences and knowledge. Thus, Berlyne's model can explain why individuals differ in their appreciation of artworks, and how appreciation can change over time. Consider the mid-19th-century beholder who has seen only realistic (mimetic) and romantic art. Impressionist paintings may have been considered too surprising or incongruous and thus be considered disturbing or odd. With our 21st-century eyes and brains, we have been exposed to all kinds of abstract forms, not only in art museums but also in television commercials and magazine ads. As a result, Impressionist paintings may be just complex and incongruous enough to be pleasing and moderately arousing. Experience with post-modern works may allow one to garner positive feelings from 20th-century styles such as Cubism, Abstract Expressionism, Surrealism, and Minimalism.

Since Fechner's seminal treatise, the empirical analysis of aesthetics has undergone periods of growth and stagnation. Arnheim, Berlyne, and others stimulated interest and offered important theoretical frameworks,[29] yet many have questioned the value of the methods and theories developed by these pioneers of aesthetic science. Even among psychologists, the study of aesthetics has generally been viewed as a "fringe" topic. Moreover, many philosophers have ignored or rejected empirical approaches, and likewise, psychologists have typically discounted philosophical notions. The insular nature of these disciplines has thus limited progress in aesthetic science.

COGNITIVE SCIENCE

Cognitive science is a outgrowth of experimental psychology. It seeks to understand mental processes such as perception, memory, language, emotion, and reasoning through an interdisciplinary approach.[30] Several features distinguish cognitive science from traditional psychological science. First, cognitive science incorporates findings and perspectives from many practices outside of psychology, including philosophy, computer science, anthropology, linguistics, and neuroscience. Second, it draws heavily on computer-based models of how the mind works. Although cognitive scientists do not believe that the brain *is* a digital computer, they often adopt the analogy of the mind as a computational mechanism that manipulates information and has its own input, storage, and output devices. Third, a prominent concern is how information in the mind/brain is *represented* or stored. Cognitive scientists rely on an *information processing* approach originally developed in computer science. The goal of this approach is to characterize the way sensory signals act as information that is encoded, interpreted, and represented.

One particularly important distinction is between *bottom-up* and *top-down* processing.[31] Bottom-up processing refers to the route of information processing from sensory signals to knowledge. Top-down processing refers to the use of knowledge to direct what we perceive. Thus, *bottom* refers to low-level sensory processes, whereas *top* refers to knowledge. Consider the drawing in Figure 1.4a by psychologist Roger Shepard, entitled *Sara Nader*. If you focus on the black region, you see a silhouette of a man playing the saxophone. However, if you focus on the white region to the right of the man, you see a woman's face. Now that you know that both objects exist, you can guide your perception by "seeing" the saxophonist or the woman's face. Thus, knowledge guides your sensory processes and orients you to critical features. This is top-down processing—knowing is seeing.

Figure 1.4b shows the inter-relationship between top-down and bottom-up processing. Early cognitive approaches, such as Fechner's psychophysical approach,

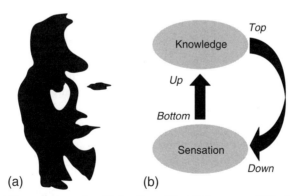

FIGURE 1.4 *(a) Shepard, Roger.* Sara Nader *(from* Mind Sights, *1990, W. H. Freeman and Co., New York). (b) Bottom-up processing describes the way we acquire knowledge from sensations, whereas top-down processing describes the way knowledge can influence sensations.*

were based primarily on bottom-up processes, as it was thought that perceptual elements (e.g., shape, color) could be constructed to derive meaning (e.g., recognizing objects). Indeed, it was once thought that engineers could build robots that could identify objects in a visual scene based purely on bottom-up information, such as the kind of information recorded from a video camera. Although such robots could function in very restricted environments, it soon became apparent that humans rely heavily on top-down processes to interpret complex visual scenes. In other words, we apply our knowledge of the world to interpret what we see.

The noted art historian Ernst Gombrich was the first to consider top-down processing as an integral part of aesthetic experiences. In *Art and Illusion*, Gombrich argued that an artist "begins not with his visual impression but with his idea or concept."[32] This point is equally important for the experience of the beholder. Based on our personal and cultural knowledge, the beholder forms expectations that help interpret an artwork and direct viewing to salient features. Just as the image of *Sara Nader* is ambiguous, Gombrich suggested that all art is illusory and we must build an interpretation of what an artwork represents based on existing knowledge—or what he (and cognitive scientists) call *schemata* or, more simply, *schemas*. Schemas are conceptual frameworks that people use to form expectations. For example, as you enter a restaurant you apply a *restaurant* schema that sets up expectations that include sitting at a table, ordering from a menu, enjoying a meal, paying for the meal, and leaving a tip. We also have a *museum* schema that includes walking through galleries, developing preferences about artworks, and considering what the artist is trying to communicate. Past knowledge and experiences determine the nature of these expectations. Gombrich integrated psychology, art history, and philosophy in an analysis of the art process (both in making and viewing art). He adopted a cognitive science approach, suggesting that artworks act as symbols that describe or represent real-world objects and experiences.

The cognitive science approach to aesthetics has gained in interest recently with the commercial importance of digital animation and web design. For example, computational analyses of chiaroscuro, or what computer scientists call *shape from shading*, have provided extraordinarily realistic computer-generated animations. With respect to web design, commercial ventures depend on attracting and maintaining clients to their websites. People tend to dislike modifications in the color and organization of favorite websites. Web designers now take this tendency into account and often apply findings from cognitive science to reduce the impact of design alterations. For example, a finding called "change blindness"[33] shows that alterations in a visual display can go unnoticed when they are done gradually, one feature at a time or in small increments of single features, such as color or texture. In 2008, Yahoo.com gradually introduced a new look to their homepage across days. Similarly, eBay.com took 30 days to change its background from gray to white. It is likely that many did not notice these changes.

NEUROSCIENCE

Can the complexities of aesthetic experiences be understood by examining brain mechanisms? Neuroscientists have studied the workings of the brain from many levels of analysis—from analyses of individual brain cells (i.e., neurons) to the study of neural activity in the human brain. By the late 19th century, staining techniques were developed that enabled scientists to visualize individual neurons so that their shape, size, and connectivity could be examined. In 1909, Korbinian Brodmann published a seminal atlas of the human cerebral cortex based on his detailed anatomical studies.[34] We now know that the cerebral cortex is a thin sheet of interconnected neurons that has expanded considerably during evolution, in fact so much so that it has become enfolded within the human skull, thus giving its appearance of many ridges (gyri) and valleys (sulci). If the cerebral cortex were flattened, it would be equivalent in area to the size of an extra-large (very thin) pizza (about 20 inches in diameter, 2 mm thick). Brodmann compared the cellular structure of neurons in different parts of the cerebral cortex. He defined 52 distinct areas, ZIP codes if you will, on the basis of physical features, such as size, shape, and density. We refer to these regions as Brodmann areas, which are still used today to identify regions of the human cerebral cortex.

Neural circuits have been identified that pertain to various mental capabilities, such as vision, memory, language, emotional drive, and motor control.[35] Both structural (anatomical) and functional (brain activity) analyses have been used to investigate the neural correlates of human cognitive function. With respect to anatomical landmarks, Figure 1.5 shows the *lateral* (side) surface of the left cerebral cortex. The *medial* surface is hidden from view as it sits flat against the other cerebral cortex. The initial input of visual information into the cortex occurs at the most posterior region of the occipital lobe, an area called the *primary visual cortex.* From this point, visual information is processed along two major paths. The dorsal or "where" path courses up to the parietal lobe and processes spatial information, whereas the ventral or "what" path courses down through the temporal lobe and processes object information.

The most anterior region of the frontal lobes is called the *prefrontal cortex* (PFC). It receives inputs from other brain regions and sends projections back to these regions. In this way, the PFC coordinates and controls neural processing. If one considers the multitude of neural signals active at any given moment, it becomes obvious how important it is for us to have a mechanism that orchestrates this cacophony of brain activity. Our ability to focus attention to specific sensory signals or retrieve specific memories depends on the PFC to monitor and control neural activity, just as an orchestral conductor must control the activity of a group of musicians in order to present a smooth performance. The PFC's role in monitoring and controlling neural activity forms the basis for top-down processing as it guides and selects sensory signals. Various terms, such as *executive control* and

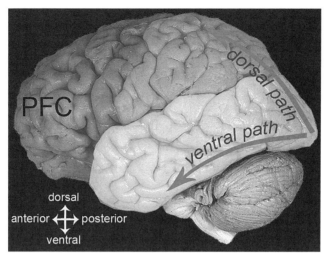

FIGURE 1.5 The lateral surface of the cerebral cortex. *Visual processing begins at the most posterior part of the occipital lobe (green) and courses through the temporal lobe (yellow) via the ventral path and through the parietal lobe (pink) via the dorsal path. At the most anterior part of the frontal lobe (purple) is the prefrontal cortex (PFC), which acts to monitor and control cortical activity in posterior regions. (Brain images reprinted with permission from* Digital Anatomist Interactive Atlas, *University of Washington, Seattle, WA, copyright 1997.)*

metacognition, have been used to describe the role of PFC in supporting top-down processing.[36]

Before the advent of neuroimaging techniques such as fMRI (functional magnetic resonance imaging), neuroscientists studied human brain function by observing the way damage to different parts of the brain disrupts cognitive function.[37] Such *neuropsychological* investigations offered insights into the organization of the human brain, as discrete damage often led to rather discrete behavioral disorders. For example, patients with damage along the dorsal visual pathway exhibit deficits in spatial ability, whereas those with damage along the ventral pathway exhibit deficits in object recognition. From such studies, the neural underpinnings of mental abilities, such as perceiving, reading, remembering, and even appreciating art, have been analyzed (see Chapters 12 and 15).

With respect to emotions, we know that the ventral (lower) region of the PFC, an area called the *orbitofrontal cortex*, is important for the control and regulation of emotions. This fact became quite apparent from studies of the now-classic neurological case of Phineas Gage.[38] Gage was a railroad foreman for the Rutland and Burlingame Railroad. On September 13, 1848, he was working with explosives to clear a rail path through a rocky area in Vermont. This procedure involved the use of an iron rod, called a tamping iron, to compress explosive powder into a bored hole. Gage was using his tamping iron when it inadvertently struck the side of the hole, causing a spark that ignited the explosive powder. The explosion sent the rod, harpoon-like, up through Gage's left cheekbone, through his frontal lobes, and out the top of his skull. Amazingly, Gage survived the accident and lived for another 11½ years. Although he did not appear to exhibit intellectual impairment, his emotional disposition changed. Prior to his accident, Gage was known to be a good foreman and friendly with the other workers. After the accident, the physician who treated Gage, John Martyn Harlow, stated that Gage was "fitful, irreverent, indulging at times in the grossest profanity (which was not previously his custom)."[39]

Contemporary analyses of patients with orbitofrontal damage have affirmed the role of the orbitofrontal cortex in emotional control (see Chapter 15). It is as if these patients act out their feelings and desires without considering the consequences of their actions. If they feel angry, they may become violent; if they are sexually aroused, they may immediately act out their feelings. In a recent case, Samantha Fishkin was ejected out the window of an overturning pickup truck as her boyfriend swerved to avoid another vehicle. She hit a concrete embankment, which fractured her skull and caused severe frontal lobe damage. In a *New York Times Magazine* article about Samantha's injury,[40] the author, Peter Landesman, wrote: "the new Samantha was savagely disinhibited. Breaks in her neural web had erased all sense of social convention. She couldn't control her desire to talk, her anger, her sexual urges." Patients with orbitofrontal damage often exhibit emotional outbursts, inappropriate social behavior, risk-taking behavior, and obsessive-compulsive disorder.[41]

Since the 1990s, neuroimaging techniques have given neuroscientists a window to the workings of the human mind in a way that would have been considered science fiction only 20 years ago. With the development of fMRI, neuroscientists can assess brain activity in specific regions, virtually on a moment-to-moment basis. In fMRI, the same scanner used in hospitals can be tuned to detect subtle changes in blood flow that occur when a brain region becomes active. At any given moment, however, tens of thousands of neurons are active just to keep us alive, such as maintaining heart rate, respiration, body temperature, and general conscious awareness. Other brain activity occurs in response to whatever we are doing at the moment, such as listening to a lecture, remembering a past event, or viewing a painting. An image of the brain's activity at any moment would not be very informative, as we would not know which areas are active in response to a specific event and which areas are active merely to keep us alive. Thus, neuroscientists obtain scans from one condition and compare them to scans from another. For example, one could scan subjects when they have their eyes open and compare the scans to moments when they have their eyes closed. By subtracting the eyes-open scans from the eye-closed scans one can assess brain activity that is specific to having the eyes open. All other brain activities would be canceled out because they occur in both conditions. This *subtraction method* has allowed neuroscientists to identify brain areas that are related to particular mental events.

With the advent of human neuroimaging techniques, particularly fMRI, studies of the brain's response to art have been conducted (see Chapters 13 and 14). In this burgeoning field of *neuroaesthetics*,[42] the orbitofrontal cortex has been shown to be particularly active during emotional responses to art. Kawabata and Zeki[43] presented realistic and abstract paintings that participants had previously rated as ugly, neutral, or beautiful. The orbitofrontal cortex was active when subjects were presented with paintings that they rated as beautiful compared to those rated as neutral. In another study,[44] the orbitofrontal cortex was active while listening to classical music that was rated as intensely pleasurable (e.g., Rachmaninoff's *Piano Concerto No. 3 in D Minor*, Opus 30). These findings show that the orbitofrontal cortex is involved in the evaluation of beautiful works of art.

It is important to note, however, that complex mental processes activate broad neural networks that are important for a multitude of functions. To appreciate a painting numerous brain regions are working together to process sensory signals, connect sensory information with what we know, and derive emotional significance. In the Kawabata and Zeki study, the orbitofrontal cortex was particularly involved when the viewing of beautiful paintings was compared with the viewing of neutral paintings. Thus, the study isolated a particular feature of the brain's response to paintings—namely the judgment of beauty. Many other brain regions were active, such as those involved in perceiving and conceptualizing paintings, but these activations would have occurred for both sets of paintings and were thus subtracted out in the analysis. Other studies have focused on sensory or conceptual aspects of aesthetic experiences (see Chapter 16). Thus, it is important to keep in mind that we are not dealing with a form of neural phrenology, linking one brain area with one mental function. Instead, many brain regions are involved in aesthetic experiences, and the goal is to understand the dynamic interactions across these brain regions.

Issues for Aesthetic Science

DEVELOPING A FRAMEWORK FOR EMPIRICAL ANALYSES

Philosophical approaches offer guidelines for scientific investigations of aesthetics. Mimetic and formalist approaches key on perceptual qualities and stimulate questions such as: What does it mean to interpret a painting as a window to the real world? What perceptual processes are involved in experiencing realistic scenes versus abstract art? How do lines, colors, shapes, and scenes influence our aesthetic experiences? Expressionist approaches consider the manner in which perceptual features evoke emotions. Since Berlyne's seminal work[45] on the way emotional arousal influences aesthetic responses, scientists have considered both psychological and neuroscientific factors associated with an expressionist approach (see Chapter 10).

Relatively few empirical studies have addressed conceptual approaches to art. The role of knowledge in our art experience has often been downplayed, as many feel that art should be experienced directly, from perceptual qualities to emotions, as if knowledge could only detract from our aesthetic experiences. It is clear, however, from cognitive science, and particularly in the writings of Gombrich,[46] that knowledge plays a significant role, particularly in guiding top-down processes. Also, when we try to grapple with the way we experience post-modern art, it becomes imperative to consider the role that knowledge plays in our analysis of such works (see Chapter 6).

The promise of an interdisciplinary aesthetic science is motivated by an interest from a growing number of philosophers, psychologists, and neuroscientists who feel a need to bridge resources and form a more comprehensive analysis of art and aesthetics (see Chapters 2, 3, and 5). The goal is analogous to the tradition of cognitive science, in which many disciplines are valued and considered in the service of understanding cognition. What is needed is a way of triangulating information from many perspectives (see Chapter 4). In aesthetic science, many disciplines must be included and valued. In particular, philosophers, psychologists, anthropologists, historians, artists, and neuroscientists must consider the many ways we experience and value art.

This introductory chapter provided a brief background of philosophical and scientific approaches to art. Aesthetic experiences are captured in the ways we approach art, which include: (1) a mimetic approach (how well does an artwork portray a realistic scene?), (2) an expressionist approach (how well does an artwork drive emotional experiences?), (3) a formalist approach (how well does an artwork enhance sensations?), and (4) a conceptual approach (how well does an artwork communicate meaningful statements?). The beholder may experience art from any or a combination of these approaches. Moreover, some artworks may lend themselves better to one approach than another.

Figure 1.6 diagrams a componential framework of the art experience. It is purported that *The Artist* intends to offer an *Artwork* for aesthetic judgment. Definitions of "The Artist" and "Artwork" could be discussed *ad infinitum*; we will simply assert that *The Artist* is a human and *The Artwork* must be sensed.[47] Our essential concern is how we experience art—that is, the beholder's aesthetic experience. I propose that the beholder's experience is best understood by considering the ways in which an artwork influences three primary mental functions: sensation, knowledge, and emotion. These psychological functions relate directly to the philosophical approaches that we have considered. Mimetic and formalist approaches emphasize sensation, conceptual approaches emphasize knowledge, and expressionist approaches emphasize emotion.

This framework is called *I-SKE* in reference to the four critical features—the artist's *intention* to offer an artwork for aesthetic evaluation and the beholder's three mental components, *sensation*, *knowledge*, and *emotion*. With respect to the beholder, sensory and emotional factors are rather obvious, as they have been

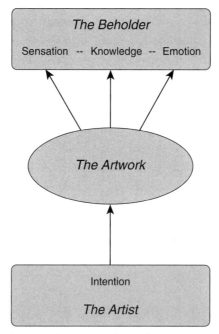

FIGURE 1.6 **The I-SKE framework acts as a schema for experiencing art.** The Artist *intends to create* The Artwork, *which is experienced by* The Beholder, *who uses sensations, knowledge, and emotion to generate an aesthetic experience. These three components of the beholder's psyche drive the art experience.*

considered in both early philosophical and more recent empirical analyses. Knowledge refers to world (i.e., semantic) knowledge, personal knowledge, and cultural knowledge (including knowledge about art history and art practices). These aspects of knowledge influence how we interpret and appreciate art (see Chapter 11). According to the I-SKE framework, sensation, knowledge, and emotion all contribute to aesthetic experiences, though one or two of these components may be more emphasized than others. I propose that the fullest aesthetic experience is one that heightens all three components.

By keying on these three components, a more balanced approach to aesthetic science may be developed. The preponderance of studies in aesthetic science has been directed toward sensory aspects of aesthetics (see Chapters 7 and 8). Recently, research has considered ways in which artworks drive emotional responses (see Chapter 10). The I-SKE framework suggests that knowledge plays just as important a role in our aesthetic experiences as sensation and emotion. Only a few investigators have considered ways in which knowledge drives our art experience (but see Chapter 9). Finally, it is clear that various approaches to art can be taken— from appreciating realism to delving into conceptual, social, or political responses to art. Art may or may not induce strong emotions; it may or may not refer to objects in the real world.

WHAT, THEN, IS THE PHENOMENON OF INTEREST?

It is clear that meaningful advances in aesthetic science must first develop an appropriate and workable definition of the phenomenon of interest—namely, what is *aesthetics*? If we consider a very narrow definition, such as the one proposed by Baumgarten and echoed by Kant, then the phenomenon of interest would focus specifically on disinterested feelings evoked by beautiful objects.[48] As stated in the beginning of this chapter, Baumgarten's definition is much too narrow. One issue is whether aesthetic science should be tied specifically to the study of artworks. It is certainly useful to broaden the concept and include aesthetic responses to any object, including natural ones and ones not intended to be *art*. This broadening of the objects of interest is particularly prudent for our understanding of art, because what is defined as "art" is always changing. The broadening of acceptable objects raises interesting questions. Does our "aesthetic" experience differ when we appreciate a painting, say of a waterfall, as opposed to the way we appreciate natural phenomena, such as an actual waterfall? Does an object's presence in an art museum create a different kind of experience?

Another way to broaden the definition of "aesthetics" is to consider how objects evoke different kinds of emotional responses, including humor, sadness, horror, and disgust. Many postmodern works are intended to shock or disgust the beholder. Should all emotions be considered as relevant for aesthetic science? It is clear that conceptual approaches to art demand a non-emotional, even anti-aesthetic, analysis of art (see Chapter 6). One could consider broadening the concept of "aesthetics" to include completely non-emotional aspects of the art experience, though such a stance may go too far. If we, as many art critics suggests, consider the art experience as going well beyond what many consider an "aesthetic" experience, it may be prudent not to "tether" aesthetic science to art (see Chapters 3).

As proposed earlier, we might tie aesthetic science to our understanding of the *dimension* of hedonics, from very positive (beautiful) to very negative (disgusting) or from very interesting to not at all interesting (see Chapter 8). From this perspective, we could consider any object and derive an explicit preference or interest judgment: we like it or we don't, it's interesting or it's not. Such preferences could be mapped onto emotional (pleasant or not) or conceptual (interesting or not) aspects, and aesthetic science could address the reasons why certain objects are more pleasant or interesting than others. Hedonic responses could be related to evolutionary factors, such as analyses about the ways in which objects evoke an approach vs. avoidance response (see Chapter 5 and 8). Of course, artworks have often been created for the sole purpose of eliciting "disinterested" hedonic responses (i.e., art for art's sake), and thus it is not unreasonable to consider the psychology of art as a prime subarea within aesthetic science. Yet many objects not considered as art (e.g., foods, people, locations) evoke strong hedonic responses and these responses may be mapped onto psychological processes, such as motivation, drive, arousal, and pleasure. Moreover, underlying brain responses associated with these processes are relevant to aesthetic science. As such, research in such diverse areas as affective neuroscience (e.g., neural basis of empathy), neuroeconomics, and theory of mind (e.g., mirror neurons) is important for aesthetic science to consider.

The ideas discussed in this chapter provide a foundation for building a multidisciplinary approach to the science of aesthetic experiences. The following chapters address the viability of aesthetic science and discuss possible avenues of interest. Philosophical, psychological, and neurobiological approaches are considered here, with the intention of initiating a discussion concerning the beholder's experience.

Acknowledgments

I would like to thank the John Simon Guggenheim Memorial Foundation for financial support during the preparation of this chapter. I would also like to thank Helen Ettlinger, Blake Gopnik, Julian Hochberg, Rich Ivry, Jerry Levinson, Steve Palmer, and Leslie Zemsky for helpful comments on earlier drafts.

Endnotes

1. Baumgarten, A. G. (1961/1750). *Aesthetica*. Olms, OK: Hildesheim.

2. For analyses of these issues, see Dissanayake, E. (1992). *Homo aestheticus*. Seattle, WA: University of Washington Press; Dutton, E. (2009). *The art instinct*. New York: Oxford University Press; and Turner, M. (Ed.) (2006). *The artful mind*. New York: Oxford University Press.

3. More extensive analysis of these approaches can be found in Beardsley, M. D. (1966). *Aesthetics from classical Greece to the present*. Alabama: University of Alabama Press; Graham, G. (2000). *Philosophy of the arts: an introduction to aesthetics* (2nd ed.). New York: Routledge Press; Shimamura, A. P. (in press). *Experiencing art: explorations in aesthetics, mind, and brain*.

4. Plato. (2003). *The Republic*. New York: Penguin Books.

5. Aristotle. (1996). *Poetics*. New York: Penguin Books.

6. See Alberti, L. B. (1991/1436). *On painting*. New York: Penguin Books; Panofsky, E. (1991/1927). *Perspective as symbolic form*. New York: Zone Books.

7. Beardsley, 1966.

8. Hutcheson, F. (2003/1725). *An inquiry into the origin of our ideas of beauty and virtue*. London: Kessinger Publishing.

9. Hume, D. (1898/1757). Of the standard of taste. In T. H. Green & T. H. Grose (Eds.), *Essays moral, political and literary*. London: Longmans, Green.

10. Kant, I. (2008/1781). *Critique of pure reasoning*. New York: Penguin Books.

11. Kant, I. (2007/1790). *Critique of judgment*. New York: Oxford University Press.

12. Tolstoy, L. (1995/1898). *What is art?* London: Penguin Books.

13. See Collingwood, R. G. (1963/1938). *Principles of art.* London: Oxford University Press; and Croce, B. *Aesthetic as science of expression and general linguistic* [Online] Rev. Sept. 19, 2003. Available: http://www.gutenberg.org/etext/9306.

14. Flam, J. (1995). *Matisse on art* (p. 66). Berkeley, CA: University of California Press.

15. Greenberg, C. (1965). Modernist painting. *Art and Literature, 4,* 193–201.

16. Greenberg, 1965, p. 194.

17. Bell, C. *Art* [Online] Rev. Oct. 21, 2005. Available: http://www.gutenberg.org/etext/9306.

18. The term "conceptual" is used here to include all *knowledge-based* approaches to art, rather than referring specifically to the genre of *conceptual art.*

19. Duchamp's urinal tops art survey, *BBC News* [Online] Rev. Dec. 1, 2004, Available: http://news.bbc.co.uk/2/hi/entertainment/4059997.stm.

20. A similar usage of the term *meta-art* can be found in Piper, A. (October 1973). In support of meta-art. *Artforum, 12,* 79–81. Also relevant is the analysis by Kosuth, J. (1975). 1975, *The Fox,* 1, 87–96.

21. Goodman, N. (1976). *Languages of art.* Indianapolis, IN: Hackett Publishing Co.

22. Langer, S. (1942). *Philosophy in a new key.* Cambridge, MA: Harvard University Press.

23. Fechner, G. (1860). *Elemente der Psychophysik.* Leipzig, Germany: Breitkopf and Hatrtel.

24. Fechner, G. T. (1876). *Vorschule der Aesthetik.* Leipzig, Germany: Breitkopf and Hatrtel.

25. For review, see Funch, B. S. (1997). *The psychology of art appreciation.* Denmark: Museum Tusculanum Press; Kreitler, H., & Kreitler, S. (1972). *Psychology of the arts.* Durham, NC: Duke University Press; Reber, R. (2008). Art in its experience: can empirical psychology help assess artistic value?" *Leonardo, 41,* 367–372; Solso, R. L. (1994). *Cognition and the visual arts.* Cambridge, MA: The MIT Press; and Winner, E. (1982). *Inverted worlds: the psychology of the arts.* Cambridge, MA: Harvard University Press.

26. Koffka, K. (1922). Perception: an introduction to the Gestalt-theorie. *Psychological Bulletin, 19,* 531–585; Wertheimer, M. (1932). Untersuchungen zur Lehre von der Gestalt II. *Psycologische Forschung, 4,* 301–350. Translation published in W. Ellis (Ed.) (1938). *A source book of Gestalt psychology* (pp. 71–88). London: Routledge & Kegan Paul.

27. Arnheim, R. (1974). *Art and visual perception.* Berkeley, CA: University of California Press.

28. Berlyne, D. E. (1971). *Aesthetics and psychobiology.* New York: Appleton-Century-Crofts.

29. See Funch, 1997; Kreitler & Kreitler, 1972; Reber, 2008.

30. See Gardner, H. (1987). *The mind's new science.* New York: Basic Books; Miller, G. A. (March 2003). The cognitive revolution: a historical perspective. *Trends in Cognitive Science, 7,* 141–144; and Norman, D. A. (1980). Twelve issues for cognitive science. *Cognitive Science, 4,* 1–32.

31. Solso, R. L. (1996). *Cognition and the visual arts.* Cambridge, MA: MIT Press.

32. Gombrich, E. H. (1960). *Art and illusion* (p. 73). Princeton, NJ: Princeton University Press.

33. Rensink, R. A., O'Regan, J. K., & Clark, J. J. (1997). To see or not to see: the need for attention to perceive changes in scenes. *Psychological Science, 8,* 368–373.

34. Brodmann, K. (1989). *Vergleichende Localisationslehre der Grosshirnrinde in ihren Prinzipien dargestellt auf Grund des Zellebaus.* Leipzig: Barth. See also Annese, J. (2009). In retrospect: Brodmann's brain map. *Nature, 461,* 884.

35. See Gazzaniga, M. S., Ivry, R. B., & Mangun, G. R. (2002). *Fundamentals of cognitive neuroscience.* New York: Norton.

36. Shimamura, A. P. (2008). A neurocognitive approach to metacognitive monitoring and control. In J. Dunlosky & R. A. Bjork (Eds.), *Handbook of metamemory and nemory* (pp. 373–390). New York: Psychology Press.

37. Luria, A. R. (1974). *Working brain.* New York: Basic Books; Milner, B., Squire, L. R., & Kandel, E. R. (1988). Cognitive neuroscience and the study of memory. *Neuron, 20,* 445–468.

38. For a detailed description of Gage's life, see Macmillan, M. (2000). *An odd kind of fame: stories of Phineas Gage.* Cambridge, MA: The MIT Press.

39. Harlow, J. M. (1868). Recovery of an iron rod through the head. *Publications of the Massachusetts Medical Society, 2,* 327–347.

40. Landesman, P. (Sept. 17, 2000). Speak memory. *New York Times Magazine,* 74–79.

41. To see what happens when an artist incurs orbitofrontal damage, read the story of the 19th-century photographer Eadweard Muybridge in Shimamura, A. P. (Winter 2002). Muybridge in motion: travels in art, psychology, and neurology. *History of Photography, 26,* 341–350.

42. Zeki, S. (1999). *Inner vision.* New York: Oxford University Press; and Skov, M., & Vartanian, O. (Eds.) (2009). *Neuroaesthetics.* Amityville, NY: Baywood Publishing Co.

43. Kawabata, H., & Zeki, S. (2004). Neural correlates of beauty. *Journal of Neurophysiology, 91,* 1699–1705.

44. Blood, A. J., & Zatorre, R. J. (2001). Intensely pleasurable responses to music correlate with activity in brain regions implicated in reward and emotion. *Proceedings of the New York Academy of Sciences, 98,* 11818–11823.

45. Berlyne, 1971.

46. Gombrich, 1960.

47. *The Artist* is a human because intention is a human characteristic (though a human could offer for aesthetic evaluation an artwork created by some other person, an animal, or a computer). *The Artwork* must be sensed and thus cannot be a thought or dream (though a written or visual description of a thought or dream would suffice as an artwork).

48. Baugarten, 1961/1750; Kant, 2007/1790.

{ PART I }

Philosophical Perspectives

The Philosophy of Art and Aesthetics, Psychology, and Neuroscience

STUDIES IN LITERATURE, MUSIC, AND VISUAL ARTS

Noël Carroll, Margaret Moore, and William P. Seeley

Introduction

Aesthetics was born as a branch of philosophy in 1735 with Alexander Baumgarten's use of the term "aesthesis" in his *Meditationes Philosophicae de Nonnullis ad Poema Pertinentibus* (*Philosophical Meditations Pertaining to Some Matters Concerning Poetry*).[1] Baumgarten used the phrase *episteme aisthetike* to mean the science of what is sensed and imagined, in contrast to the science of what is known through rational thought. In his incomplete *Aesthetica*, Baumgarten further defined the terms as follows: "Aesthetics (the theory of the liberal arts, the logic of the lower capacities of cognition [*gnoseologia inferior*], the art of thinking beautifully, the art of the *analogon rationis*) is the science of sensible cognition."[2] Contained in this definition are the roots of many 21st-century topics in the philosophy of art. Indeed, the 18th century is important to the history of aesthetics for introducing a range of enduring questions whose provenance can ultimately be traced back to an interest in the sensory grounds for perceptual knowledge. These topics include the analysis of our judgments of beauty, which involves an account of the faculties of the judging subject and the qualities judged in the object; an explanation of our aesthetic preferences or the standards of taste; the role of the imagination in presenting sensory appearances; our experience of artworks as objects suited for detection of beauty or perfection; as well as the relationship between aesthetic pleasure and the domain of morality. However, it is only with the advent of cognitive science in the late 20th century that Baumgarten's vision of aesthetics as a science of sensory cognition, including the study of our engagement with artworks, has become truly possible.[3]

Aestheticians since Baumgarten have addressed these topics, sometimes in slightly altered form, but typically without any concern for a scientific solution. The relevant judgments about, and responses to, artworks are *too* subjective, the argument goes, to admit of scientific study. The extreme expression of this view can be found in the Logical Positivists approach to knowledge in general. The positivists argued that the only genuine candidates for knowledge are those that admit of verification through empirical observations. Rather than seek a scientific account of every domain of human knowledge following an 18th-century model—the projects of Hume and Kant include morality and aesthetics as well as mathematics and natural science—the Positivists preferred to exclude anything that involves subjective feeling from the general domain of knowledge. It was not just that a complete account of aesthetics had to wait for the development of psychology and neuroscience; rather, the Positivists argued that there was a complete divorce between what science could deliver and what aestheticians would ask. Science could not, *in principle*, have any bearing on questions about the nature of art, beauty, or aesthetic appreciation.

This view has remained influential throughout the 20th and into the 21st century. Thus, despite the historical connections between the study of perception and aesthetics, analytic philosophers have been generally skeptical about the relevance of psychology to the philosophy of art and aesthetics. The types of concerns raised in these contexts fall into three general categories: concerns about the relevance of psychology to our understanding of aesthetic appreciation; concerns about the relevance of psychology to our understanding of aesthetic properties; and general concerns about the possible utility to aesthetics of understanding how artworks function as perceptual stimuli. Concerns about the relevance of psychology to aesthetic appreciation can be traced back to arguments in Ludwig Wittgenstein's *Lectures in Aesthetics* and George Dickie's "Is Psychology Relevant to Aesthetics."[4] Wittgenstein writes:

> 7. People have the idea that psychology is one day going to explain all of our aesthetic judgments, and they mean experimental psychology. This is very funny—very funny indeed. There doesn't seem any connection between what psychologists do and any judgment about a work of art. We might examine what sort of thing we would call an explanation of an aesthetic judgment.[5]
>
> 8 . . . The question is whether this is the sort of explanation we should like to have when we are puzzled about aesthetic impressions, e.g., there is a puzzle—"Why do these bars give me such a peculiar impression?"[6]

Wittgenstein is not particularly forthcoming in these lectures about the nature of his reservations. However, a plausible interpretation is that he does not think that psychological studies of beholders' *particular subjective responses* to artworks will help us understand the *general nature* of either aesthetic appreciation or aesthetic properties.

Dickie argues that the sorts of questions asked in aesthetics differ in logical form from the sorts of questions asked in psychology, so that when we answer aesthetic questions with data concerning the behavioral responses of participants to particular artworks we are committing a category mistake—we confuse a logical problem for a scientific one. Consider two examples that Dickie offers: studies that involve adjective matching and studies that involve preference orderings. In the first case, participants are asked to match musical compositions to a range of adjectives (e.g., *stately, sprightly, wistful,* etc.) that expert judges have identified as appropriate to the works. Dickie argues that these data—agreement among subjects—are beside the point. Just as agreement among children about the meaning of a nonsense word is not evidence that a word is meaningful, what matters in the case of our responses to music is whether the formal composition of the work—in this case, the syntactic features of compositions that constitute a musical language—is adequate for the attribution of the aesthetic feature in question. And this, Dickie argues, is a matter of convention rather than psychological causation—a matter of the rules of the particular language game appropriate to the production and appreciation of the category of music used as the stimulus.

Dickie's second case is analogous to the first. In preference-ordering studies participants are asked to rank a set of works from best to worst. Again, Dickie argues that these data are not logically appropriate to the question. What matters is the criteria that determine what constitutes good compositional structure, and agreement among novices is not appropriate evidence in this context. Rather, what is important are the rules of the appropriate language game—conventions that are embedded in our common linguistic practice and revealed in the *a priori* judgments of experts. Again, questions of psychological causation are said to be irrelevant to the investigation of these conventions. Thus, Dickie argues that psychology is not relevant to aesthetics.

Neither the claims of Wittgenstein nor the arguments of Dickie strike us as ultimately compelling. Wittgenstein's position represents an extremely narrow conception of the domain of philosophical aesthetics. He appears to have presupposed that all questions of aesthetics are connected to rendering aesthetic judgments (a.k.a. appreciating an art work) from the inside (of a language game). But there is a larger view of the philosophy of art and aesthetics—one that regards as germane to the field any and all questions about the construction and reception of artworks and other aesthetic objects. Questions about the origins as well as the nature of aesthetic experience belong to this broader conception of the philosophy of art. Likewise, confronting the theoretical problems provoked by our standing language games with respect to art also belongs to the philosophy of art, properly construed (e.g., as we shall see in the next section, certain psychological conceptions of the emotions may help us dissolve longstanding issues such as the paradox of fiction).

But it may also be the case that psychology—by elucidating the dynamics of the audience's response to artworks—can help readers, viewers, and listeners sharpen those responses to greater effect. In other words, by understanding the psychology that underpins our appreciative responses, we can self-consciously hone in on the pertinent variables, and thereby enhance our understanding and appreciation of artworks by making those responses more focused than they would be without a sense of the psychology of appreciation—that is, by understanding how the psychology of appreciation works, we can help it along. In the next section, we will see how Jenefer Robinson's account of our emotional response to certain kinds of literature encourages us to monitor our reactions in ways that make appreciation more complete and more vivid. Thus, *pace* Wittgenstein, psychology need not be denied a role in the philosophy of art and aesthetics.

Turning from Wittgenstein's arguments to Dickie's, we note that recent imaging studies involving adjective matching and preference orderings support Dickie's observations but challenge his assessment of the relevance of psychology to aesthetics.[7] Calvo-Merino compared ratings of discrete dance movements along five aesthetic dimensions (simple–complex, dull–interesting, tense–relaxed, weak–powerful, and like–dislike) with fMRI recordings collected while participants watched the same dance movements in a separate session. Individual differences among preference ratings generally preclude projecting aesthetic preferences back to common features of the stimulus space (e.g., formal and compositional features of the works) in these types of studies. Therefore, there is an underlying assumption that the behavioral results do not generalize to the perceived features of artworks.[8] However, correlations among Calvo-Merino' imaging results revealed common cortical networks subserving participants' aesthetic judgments. Discussions of the functions of these cortical networks suggest that aesthetic judgments within a medium are realized by a unique set of psychological processes. This, in turn, demonstrates that psychological studies can contribute to our understanding of the underlying structure of aesthetic judgments. Therefore, although adjective-matching and preference-ordering studies do not, as Dickie argues, contribute to our understanding of the nature of artworks, they do contribute to aesthetics, broadly construed.

Finally, Dickie concedes that psychology can help unpack art critical judgments about the way particular artworks work to produce artistically salient effects and therefore might be useful in art criticism. However, he argues that these types of results cannot contribute to the sorts of conceptual, or definitional, questions traditionally asked in the philosophy of art. Questions about the nature of art and the character of aesthetic experience are prior logical questions about the use of a language (e.g., What do we mean when we use terms like *dynamic*, *stately*, *wistful*, or *beautiful* to refer to the perceived attributes of aesthetic features of artworks? What are the syntactic characteristics of musical compositions that enable them to represent emotions and events? What do we mean when we call the experience involved in engaging with an artwork an *aesthetic experience*?). Questions about our engagement with artworks, so the argument goes, are questions about the way particular artworks and experiences exemplify aesthetic concepts embedded in our ordinary discourse about art, but they do not elucidate our understanding of either the structure of these concepts or the properties they refer to. If sound, this objection would challenge the utility of psychology to philosophical questions about art.

However, one can argue against Dickie that our use of aesthetic concepts in ordinary language draws on, reflects, or perhaps even itself constitutes an underlying tacit theory about the nature of art and the character of aesthetic experience. This "theory" is grounded in a range of conventions that we bring to bear in aesthetic judgments, conceptual biases about the nature of art and aesthetic experience whose validity depends on facts about the way viewers actually engage with artworks. In this regard, our systematic use of aesthetic terms in ordinary language should yield testable predictions about the nature of art and the character of aesthetic experience. These predictions can, in turn, be explored and evaluated either experimentally or through case study approaches analogous to the method of counterexample employed in the philosophy of art. Therefore, even if, as Dickie suggests, the philosopher of art is concerned with language games, a language game can be studied empirically.

Dickie's reservations stem from a philosophical view, by now controversial, that takes the boundary between philosophy and science to be stark. But philosophers are no longer so convinced of such a sharp division between philosophy and empirical science. They are, as a result, increasingly turning to psychology and neuroscience as a resource. In the remainder of this essay, we explore significant interactions between philosophy and psychology with special regard to the arts of literature, music, and visual art.

Literature

Philosophers of literature have paid scant attention to developments in psychology and neuroscience. One exception to this tendency is Jenefer Robinson's *Deeper than Reason: The Emotions and their Role in Literature, Music and Art*.[9] This is recognized as an important book and, for this reason, is likely to change the attitude of many philosophers of literature with regard to the relevance of psychology and neuroscience to their research. In this section, we will discuss Robinson's treatment of literature, the art form with which she opens her discussion of aesthetics proper and the art form to which she devotes (marginally) the most space.

Throughout her book, Robinson is at pains to simultaneously align her position with cutting-edge empirical work in psychology and neuroscience and solve longstanding problems in the philosophy of art. Her embrace of contemporary psychology is perhaps most evident in the view of the emotions that she takes on board. It is roughly a form of non-cognitivism that we can call neo-Jamesianism (in honor of William James).[10] This is a very distinctive stance. Philosophers have, until recently, tended to shun James's approach to the emotions in favor of various types of cognitive accounts. On James's view, it is physiological change that is essential to an emotion. When we perceive something that causes fear, for example, that perception directly causes bodily changes. In James's words, "our feeling of the same changes as they occur *is* the emotion."[11] Where philosophers of art have been explicit about their conception of the emotions, they generally appear to buy into one or another cognitive theory of the emotions rather than adopting a Jamesian view (e.g., Noël Carroll and Berys Gaut).[12]

The cognitive theory of the emotions to which Robinson is most opposed is what she labels *judgmentalism*. This is the view that an emotional state is essentially a judgment. To be afraid of the puff adder, to steal an example from Darwin, one must judge the snake to be dangerous to oneself. If I realize that the glass between myself and the snake is sufficient to protect me from it and, in consequence, I judge that the snake is not dangerous, then I will feel no fear. According to Robinson, judgmentalists, such as the late Robert Solomon, will count a mental state as an emotion even if the pertinent judgment is not accompanied by any feelings (whether phenomenological or physiological).[13] Judgmentalists maintain that one of the strengths of their view is that it solves the problem of how to finely individuate emotional states. In other words, putatively many emotional states are indistinguishable from each other in terms of the way in which they feel. The feeling qualities (or *qualia*) of certain forms of fear are not all that different, it is said, than certain forms of anger. Likewise, it may be difficult to feel the difference between joy and admiration, on the one hand, and indignation and contempt, on the other. So, how do we differentiate between emotional states if not on the basis of *qualia*? The judgmentalist answers: in terms of their animating judgments.

Robinson argues that most philosophers of literature buy into judgmentalism, or something very like it. This is especially apparent when one contemplates one of the leading problems in the philosophy of literature, namely the paradox of fiction. This paradox raises the question of how it is possible for us to respond emotionally to fictions. The quandary here is that emotional responses allegedly require a belief in the existence of whatever engenders the emotional state in us; *but* we do not believe in the existence of Godzilla or Tess of the D'Urbervilles; so how can we fear Godzilla or feel sorrow for Tess? The crux of this paradox is also the leading tenet of judgmentalism. A judgment is an assertion and an assertion entails that we believe its propositional content. Therefore, the judmentalist holds that in order for an emotion to take hold, it is necessary that we have certain beliefs.

Robinson rejects judgmentalism. Her rejection is based upon a combination of considerations—some philosophical, some psychological, and some neuroscientific. The philosophical argumentation takes the form of a series of thought experiments. Robinson invites us to imagine certain kinds of states of affairs—for instance, to entertain the thought that I am accidentally slicing my finger in half lengthwise. In such cases, we notice that one can make herself shudder as a result of merely contemplating this prospect. We need not believe it is transpiring in the here and now. Imagining it—entertaining it as a proposition or situation type held before the mind as unasserted—is sufficient for emotional uptake. Therefore, emotions can, contrary to the claims of judgmentalism, erupt *sans* beliefs. Consideration of additional thought experiments indicates that emotions can be ignited by states

that are even less cognitively contentful, including ones involving aspect perception and attention to patterns of salience.

Robinson supports her philosophical arguments with psychological research
from Robert Zajonc and Paul Ekman. Zajonc has demonstrated that, at least in
primitive episodes of emotional response such as the startle reaction, affect can
obtain without being caused by any cognitive state. Further, Zajonc and his
colleagues have established that people form preferences for stimuli to which they
had been previously exposed, but that were presented to them at rates too fast to
allow conscious recognition.[14] Thus, affective appraisals were marshaled where
there were no previous cognitions. In a similar experiment, happy and angry faces
projected too quickly for conscious recognition nevertheless primed the subjects'
affective appraisals of a sequence of Chinese ideographs.[15] Zajonc also re-interpreted
the earlier "subception" experiments of Richard Lazarus and Robert McCleary in
which subjects registered greater affective reactions to words, again projected too
quickly for conscious recognition, that had been accompanied on earlier exposure
with the administration of electrical shocks.[16] This reaction recurred even though
no such shocks were applied during the experiment in question. Finally, Paul
Ekman's studies of facial communication demonstrate that exposure to a happy
face can make me happy. Your smile disposes me to smile, and the alteration in my
facial musculature causes the sort of changes in my autonomic nervous system
that are characteristic of joy. There need be no thought here, merely changing
facial expressions. Therefore, your facial expressions can directly induce converging affective states in me without cognitive intervention (a phenomena known as
emotional contagion). This latter phenomenon also gives us some reason to think
that some emotions may be differentiated in light of the distinctive ways in which
they feel, as opposed to the way we cognitively appraise them.

Robinson believes that changes in the facial musculature and the corresponding
alterations of the autonomic nervous system provide some grounds for discriminating between the so-called basic emotions (e.g., *anger, disgust, fear, joy, sadness,*
and *surprise*). However, she also maintains, as do the judgmentalists, that it is
primarily the cognitive processing that attends the emotion that fixes the identity
of the affective state. The way in which Robinson differs from the judgmentalist in
this regard lies in where and when she locates the cognitive interlude. On the judgmentalist picture, the emotional state begins with a conscious judgment—an evaluation or appraisal of the stimuli in terms of whether it abets or impedes my
interests. This causes a feeling state in me that puts me on the lookout for more
relevant information and primes my behavioral response. For Robinson, in contrast, our initial appraisal of the stimuli is non-cognitive; it is of the nature of a
perception—the system signals "Danger" or "Look out" before we have even identified the nature of the potential threat. This triggers the physiological response
that gears us up for action. Nevertheless, cognition kicks in at this point in the
process, monitoring the earlier stages of the process and either endorsing them

(and the associated behavioral response) or modifying them (as when cognition evaporates our negative-fear appraisal when we recognize that the puff adder is securely behind a thick wall of glass). The cogitations here are what classify my affective state as anger when I assess the stimulus of my original, non-cognitive appraisal as genuinely being a wrong done to me or mine. But in Robinson's account, those cognitions—the cognitive monitorings—come toward the end of the process, not at the beginning. For Robinson, the paradigmatic emotional response is something like the startle response. This may strike readers as initially very strange when you recall that Robinson intends to employ this account of the emotions to our emotional responses to literature. For reading a novel seems to be nothing like the experience of being taken aback by a sudden loud noise. Reading a novel would appear to be quintessentially cognitive. So the question immediately arises: how will Robinson negotiate this anomaly?

Some emotions look like they require a lot of cognition in the form of some antecedent deliberation. For example, it may take a great deal of conscious reflection in order to locate our position in the corporate pecking order in such a way that I become stricken with envy. Absorbing literature emotionally seems more like the sort of affect that is born of reflection than like a non-cognitive reflex such as the startle response. Movies and plays may literally startle, although it seems beyond the power of a novel or a lyric poem to secure that kind of affect. So has Robinson endorsed a model of the emotions that is at odds with her aims? In effect, Robinson denies that cognition or deliberation itself causes the physiological changes that prime the pertinent behavioral tendencies. She argues that things are more complicated than they seem. What happens is that the reflection in question activates our emotional memory system by recalling a certain type of situation that, in turn, prompts an appropriate non-cognitive appraisal and puts in motion the relevant physiological changes and associated behavioral dispositions (i.e., we respond as if directly confronted by the recalled event type). On this account, it is still the non-cognitive appraisal that kick-starts the core emotional process, which is then followed by cognitive monitoring.

Robinson sees emotional responses as involving two different stages. The first stage is the immediate appraisal of a stimulus whose identity need not be consciously recognized, but that nonetheless gives rise to physiological and behavioral tendencies. The second stage occurs later when the earlier stage is monitored cognitively. Robinson bolsters her hypothesis concerning the different stages of the emotional process by reference to research by the neuroscientist Joseph LeDoux.[17] On the basis of his studies of fear in rats, LeDoux concluded that "[O]n the one hand, there is a 'quick and dirty processing system,' which responds very fast, warns the organisms that something dangerous may be around without identifying it very carefully, and gets the organisms to respond appropriately to whatever it is. And, on the other hand, there is a slower, more discriminating processing system which operates through the cortex and figures out whether the thalamo-amygdala affective appraisal is appropriate or not."[18] The "quick and dirty system" activates the amygdala directly, but then that system is checked by processes operating in the frontal cortex. The former processes, of course, correspond to Robinson's non-cognitive appraisals, while the latter are the neural basis for what she calls cognitive monitoring.

Robinson applies this model of the emotions to literature in a fairly straightforward manner. Reading a fiction prompts our memory system to recall event types like the ones in the story that provoke immediate, non-cognitive, affective appraisals, and thereby activate physiological changes and behavioral tendencies; this then is cognitively monitored, leading to an adjustment of our appraisal of the situation, refining our understanding of it. For instance, Robinson cites an exchange in Henry James's *The Ambassadors* in which we chuckle at Lambert Strether.[19] That chuckle signals our initial appraisal of Strether as a faintly comic character, which causes a feeling of levity and inclines us toward sympathy for Strether. When we cognitively monitor our responses to this incident, we are able to clarify our conception of Strether, finding that faint amusement to be grounded in our perception of his incongruous combination of good-naturedness and priggishness.

Robinson's account of our emotional response to literature enables her to resolve several longstanding questions in the philosophy of literature. One is the issue that we have already encountered—the paradox of fiction. In other words, how can it be that we respond emotionally to fictions, given that emotional responses require a belief in the existence of their objects, and we don't believe in the existence of Scarlett O'Hara, Rhett Butler, Ashley Wilkes, Tara, etc.? Robinson answers: Emotions are essentially non-cognitive appraisals that provoke physiological changes and behavioral tendencies. Emotions do not require beliefs (cognitions) in order to explode; so the paradox dissolves.

A second recurring question that Robinson addresses is: How can we learn from fictional literature? Many philosophers are skeptical of the longstanding belief that we can learn from fictions. How, for example, could we learn general propositions from fictions? Fictions typically involve only one or two cases of whatever problem they explore and, to make matters worse, the cases are rigged to support the thesis they advance. Robinson outflanks this sort of objection by arguing that it is not, first and foremost, propositions that we learn from fictions. The learning is emotional, what she calls a sentimental education. She conjectures that we respond to fictional characters as we do to people in everyday life. Thus, by responding emotionally to fictional characters, we learn how to respond to people who inhabit the world outside fiction. Emotional learning is prompted in the sense that we may acquire a broader emotional repertoire by encountering events and individuals outside our daily experience. Further, as we cognitively monitor our responses to fictional characters, we may gain insight into what features make our responses to fictional characters appropriate ones, thereby refining our emotional sensitivity. This entails that by monitoring our emotional responses to literary characters, we may also gain insight into ourselves. Therefore, the case of emotional learning dodges longstanding skeptical arguments about the impossibility of learning general propositions from fiction.

Robinson also believes that our emotional responses to literature can help us understand many literary works, especially the ones she calls realist. She makes this claim with varying degrees of strength. Sometimes she suggests that understanding the works in question, like *Anna Karenina*, requires an emotional response, but, at most other times, she claims only that it can help our understanding. For example, by reflecting on our response to Strether—by cognitively monitoring that chuckle—we become aware of important features of Strether's character. We come to understand Strether better. Our emotional response to Strether enables us to interpret him better. Indeed, for Robinson, cognitively monitoring our emotional responses to characters is a crucial part of what it is to interpret them. So, Robinson concludes, cognitively monitoring our emotional responses to literature can provide the foundation of our interpretive response.

These arguments provide a way of meeting the objection, sketched in the last section, that psychology doesn't guide us in our understanding of how to appreciate art. In clarifying the psychological processes that subserve our emotional responses to literature, and articulating the ways these processes contribute to interpretation and narrative appreciation, Robinson implicitly points out the importance of cognitive monitoring to a successful engagement with a type of realistic literature. In effect, she is advising readers about the way in which understanding and reflecting on our emotions will help us realize our aesthetic aims. Her account of the psychology of literature helps us to become more sensitive readers by educating us about the nature of our emotional responses to literature and their relation to emotional understanding. Therefore, psychology is anything but irrelevant to the philosophy of art: it both contributes to our understanding of and enhances our capacity for narrative appreciation.

Robinson has advanced our grasp of the emotional understanding of literature appreciably. However, before concluding this section, certain reservations need to be voiced. In particular, we wish to question the thoroughgoing non-cognitivism of her account. As stressed, she thinks of the response to literature as rather like that of a startle response. She appears to deny that deliberation and reflection can give rise to the physiological changes that appear to mark emotional episodes. She deals with apparent counterexamples—cases where protracted thinking (as might occur in response to a complex fiction) give rise to emotions—by asserting that their contribution is only indirect. They call forth memory types that prompt a non-cognitive appraisal, and *that* is where the emotion process begins. However, this strikes us as exceedingly *ad hoc*. What, apart from a commitment to complete non-cognitivism, warrants the addition of this epicycle—the mobilization of the memory type—to the emotional process?

Perhaps Robinson feels that she is entitled to this move on the basis of her earlier objections to William Lyons's theory of the emotions.[20] Lyons holds a cognitive theory of the emotions, although he is not a judgmentalist. On his account, an emotional state involves an initial cognitive state—an evaluation or appraisal—that causes a bodily alteration that is generally connected to some behavioral tendency. This sort of theory would fit with what many suppose our ordinary experience of literature to be. We read, we contemplate, we form appraisals of the various characters and events, and this causes physiological changes in us. But Robinson objects to this sort of account because she maintains that Lyons fails to account for situations where we make a certain cognitive evaluation—so-and-so has wronged me—but do not suffer the physiological perturbations that are a necessary constituent of the emotion of anger. She says, "The trouble with this suggestion [Lyons's] is that it does not explain why sometimes an evaluative judgment leads to physiological change and hence emotions, while at other times what appears to be the same evaluative judgment *fails* to lead to physiological change and emotion."[21] Thus, she seems to surmise that it is never viable to suppose that the first stage of an emotion process can be a cognition, such as reflecting upon a character.

But if this is Robinson's argument, it does not seem consistent with the rest of her theory. One problem is that she maintains that cognitive monitoring can affect and modify the earlier stages of the emotional process. So, if it has that causal power at one stage of the process, why doesn't it have that power at an earlier stage? Surely, we are owed an explanation of this. Second, Robinson concedes that even on her account of the emotions, I may sometimes render negative appraisals of a person or a situation but not be thrown in physiological consternation, whereas at other times, given a comparable situation, I will be. Robinson has various explanations of this, including that I may not take the situation as seriously relevant to my interests, I may be distracted, I may not be in a state of bodily readiness, and I may not be in a suitable mood.[22] These, of course, all seem like plausible explanations. But the problem is that they are equally available to people like Lyons for meeting Robinson's challenge to them.[23] Consequently, Robinson has not thoroughly defeated every version of the cognitive theory of the emotions, especially as a rival account to the question of our emotional response to literature. Perhaps with respect to this matter, a hybrid combination of a neo-Jamesianism approach with some version of a cognitive theory of the emotions may provide the most comprehensive model for our emotional responses to literature. Nonetheless, Robinson's use of psychology to clarify the nature of our emotional engagement with literature offers promising solutions to both the paradox of fiction and difficult questions about the issue of learning from literature, while also affording a model for how readers understand, interpret, and appreciate.

Music

There is a longstanding connection between the psychology of music and philosophical theories of musical understanding and appreciation. The very earliest philosophical discussion of music in Plato's *Republic* draws on the Aristoxenean theory that music in different modes affects our mental states in different ways (e.g., the Lydian mode has a calming, softening effect, while the Dorian instills the courage and self-control befitting a warrior).[24] Plato stresses the way "rhythm and harmony permeate the inner part of the soul"[25] and likens hearing music to "pouring those sweet, soft, and plaintive tunes . . . through his ear, as through a funnel."[26] The assumption behind Plato's tactile physiological metaphors is that music is something we make direct physical contact with; the emotional and aesthetic effects of music are directly caused by the physical properties of musical sounds.[27] Therefore, even as early as Plato, there is an implicit appeal to speculative psychology in philosophical discussions of music. The following section will review some of the connections between the philosophy and psychology of music, and then discuss musical imagery as a case study of the way in which results from psychology and neuroscience can shed light on the way we understand music.

Music aesthetics has explored questions involving our psychological response to music in the centuries since Plato, despite, and in large part without any concern for, a lack of empirical grounding in knowledge of the mind's inner workings. The most often discussed problem has been our emotional responses to music, followed closely by the question of whether music can or should represent non-musical ideas. These issues gained new prominence with the publication of Eduard Hanslick's *The Beautiful in Music*.[28] Hanslick argued that our affective responses to music could not involve genuine emotions, for an emotional response is not possible unless its object has some semantic content. This issue is closely related to the theory of judgmentalism with respect to emotions in fiction discussed earlier. However, Hanslick makes a weaker claim than the judgmentalists: whether or not an emotion is a judgment, an emotion must take an object, and if music is to represent that object, it must do so in terms of a concept.

For Hanslick, in order for us to be saddened by music, the music would have to depict some particular thing that we recognize and react to in a canonical way. But music does not have the semantic resources of a language. Therefore, Hanslick argued that it could not depict the appropriate objects of genuine emotional responses. Peter Kivy has likewise argued that those who believe music arouses or expresses genuine emotions are confused.[29] People often say either that the slow movement of Beethoven's *Symphony No. 3* "Eroica" is sad, or that it makes them sad, but, according to Kivy, neither the music nor the listener is actually sad. Instead, the music has certain melodic and harmonic features that make it expressive of sadness. It is not literally sad; nor is what we feel genuine sadness. If we are aroused by music, what we feel is better described as a kind of awe in response to the music itself.[30]

The inability of music to express emotion literally is a conceptual claim for Kivy—it ultimately rests on our definition of the nature of emotion and the nature of music. At issue in these cases, as in the discussion of Dickie's claims about the relevance of psychology to art, is whether, and if so how, empirical studies can help to elucidate our understanding of the nature of our affective responses to music. This question is not limited to the relationship between music and the emotions, of course; it also bears generally on questions about musical understanding and appreciation. Empirical data are relevant to several points related to these questions. First, music is something we normally have access to only through the perceptual modality of hearing. Music is, as Edgar Varèse has asserted, organized sound.[31] It is the science of acoustics that studies the physics of sounds. Therefore, the science of acoustics is relevant to an analysis of the musical object. Furthermore, the study of how we perceive sounds involves both auditory perception and psychoacoustics. Therefore, perceptual psychology will contribute important data as well. More concretely, questions about musical emotions are also questions about our emotions in general. In these contexts, psychology and affective neuroscience will be relevant. Finally, claims about musical understanding often involve explicit or implicit comparisons with other types of understanding (e.g., understanding sentences or pictures). In these contexts, the study of music will draw on data from the study of cognition in general. In sum, both musical understanding and appreciation involve a relation between a perceiving subject and a physical object. The sciences that study the listening subject as well as the musical object may have quite a bit to tell us about the interaction between subject and object. Philosophers would do well to recognize that although questions about the nature of music or emotions may be partly conceptual questions, they are also empirical questions. Indeed, even where they are conceptual questions, our concepts continue to evolve as they are influenced by scientific developments.

The relevance of music cognition to both the philosophy of music and aesthetics is exemplified in the study of musical imagery and its relation to the variety of faculties and processes that have been termed "the imagination" over the centuries. Imagination is related to music in a number of respects: we often imagine music silently in our minds, just as we imagine visual scenes. We refer to composers, especially the most highly regarded ones, as extraordinarily imaginative. We claim that composers are able to be imaginative *in virtue of* imagining music internally. However, philosophers have resisted an imagistic, or experiential, account of musical imagination. It was an anathema to speak of any entities existing inside the mind, whether pictures or sounds, for many 20th-century philosophers—notably Wittgenstein, Ryle, and Scruton.[32] Instead, imagining is simply an attitude we take. Rather than *believing* that we hear a melody when there is no actual sound present, we merely *imagine* the sound. For instance, Scruton argues that in imagination we conceptualize, or entertain the idea of particular sounds; however, doing so does not involve commitment to the existence of any actual internal perceptual representation or experience of these sounds.

The difficulty with Scruton's account is that it does little to explain the phenomenology of our experiences of musical imagery. We would like a theory of the musical imagination that does justice to the fact that the experience of imagining sound feels like an experience of actual sounds in important respects. The term "imagination" is currently used to refer to any one of several related concepts: imagination as the production of mental imagery; imagination as a faculty that organizes percepts for coherent cognition (the constructive imagination); imagination in the sense of being imaginative or creative; and imagination as a propositional attitude taken towards fictional or imaginary propositions.[33] The neurophysiological processes that underwrite our experience of musical imagery can be said to be a kind of imagination in *several* of these senses. Certainly, there is an explanation of imagination as the *capacity for musical imagery*, and this can easily be linked to the *capacity for creativity*. Furthermore, an explanation of the experience of musical imagery also involves the constructive imagination in the sense discussed below (i.e., the general capacity to organize and manipulate percepts in the service of *cognition*). It turns out, therefore, that any coherent experience of music at all must draw on imagination in this sense.

It is necessary to review a bit of history in order to see how the different senses of imagination are related and have come to be at the heart of aesthetics. The 18th century's contribution to the conceptual development of the imagination takes the form of a complicated synthesis of three senses of imagination.[34] In Hume's *A Treatise of Human Nature*, the imagination is a storehouse of ideas derived from past perceptions.[35] Cognition is a capacity that always involves the imagination, since it involves the comparison of present perceptions to past perceptions, or the application of general concepts, which are formed by the imagination. Having an image of something not present also involves the imagination, since this involves either the recall of a past idea from the imagination, or the construction of a new idea out of past ideas. To be imaginative in the sense of being creative, then, is to be especially innovative in constructing new ideas, whether these ideas are imagistic (i.e., sensory) or abstract. Artistic creation is a product of this type of imaginative activity. Kant argues that the imagination is responsible for shaping sensory information from perception so that it is available to our understanding, or coherent to us.[36] In the case of music, we are able to hear music as an ordered succession of sounds through time precisely because the imagination structures auditory sensory input so that this is possible.[37] Further, Kant argues that visual aesthetic judgments arise from the harmony between the imagination and the understanding as they work together in the perception of a beautiful landscape or painting.[38] Kant's definition of the imagination as the grounds for the possibility of sensory cognition in general is, therefore, also the root of his theory of aesthetic experience. So, the idea that the imagination is a productive, creative capacity that also constructs coherent sensory cognition and grounds our aesthetic judgments was present in, and has been inherited from, 18th-century theories of aesthetics.

Visual imagery has dominated mental imagery research in the late 20th century. These studies have demonstrated that imagery preserves key metrical properties of perceptual representations in a target modality, that it draws on the same neurophysiological processes as perception in a target modality, and that the capacity for imagery is disrupted by both focal damage and the application of repetitive transcranial magnetic stimulation (rTMS) to the discrete brain regions that realize these perceptual processes.[39] For instance, Kosslyn, Ball, and Reiser demonstrated that differences in the time it takes to answer questions about the presence of targets on a memorized map are proportional to the distances one would have to scan to locate them on the original.[40] This suggests that visual images are things that can be scanned, or have constituent spatial properties that can be explored and evaluated. Similarly, Shepard and Metzler demonstrated that differences in the time it takes for participants to evaluate whether an object is identical to a target in mental rotation studies are proportional to the distance the former would have to be rotated to match the latter.[41] This suggests that mental images are things that can be rotated, or that the constituent spatial properties of visual images can be mentally manipulated. Further, imaging studies demonstrate that visual imagery tasks employ the same areas of the cerebral cortex that are involved in ordinary perception and derive their modality-specific metric properties from the functional organization of these brain regions.[42] Behavioral evidence from studies of patients with focal lesions that affect perceptual systems supports these conclusions. For instance, Bisiach and Luzzatti demonstrated that the perceptual effects of hemifield neglect, a syndrome in which selective damage to one side of the cerebral cortex causes patients to fail to perceive objects in associated areas of the visual field (i.e., the right or left side of the visual field), generalize to visual imagery.[43] Patients asked to visualize that they were in a familiar location and report what they could see consistently omitted familiar objects and locations in the "blind" hemifield, regardless of which spatial perspective they adopted. Finally, Kosslyn and his colleagues have demonstrated that the use of rTMS to disrupt activity in areas of the cerebral cortex involved in the encoding of sensory information in visual experience also disrupts the capacity in normal perceivers to use imagery and visualization to make spatial comparisons among the parts of recollected visual stimuli.[44]

These observations about visual imagery generalize to auditory imagery. The perceptual features of auditory experience occur along three dimension: pitch, meter (or rhythm), and timbre. Auditory imagery experiments confirm that these metric properties of auditory perception are preserved in auditory imagery, that auditory imagery draws on the same neurophysiological processes in the auditory cortex as ordinary hearing, and that focal damage to these areas disrupts auditory imagery.[45] For instance, Halpern asked participants to identify whether a lyric was part of a song or not. Those asked to mentally play through the song took longer to respond than those who were not, and differences in their response times were proportional to the musical time between the target lyrics.[46] Typically, participants reported that they needed to "play through" the song from the beginning. In a second experiment, Halpern asked participants to identify whether a note corresponding to a lyric was higher or lower in pitch than the starting note. Some subjects could not do this at all. However, those with musical training were better than non-musicians, and differences in response times were more pronounced than in the previous experiment. These data provide further evidence to suggest that participants use a modality-specific representation of the musical elements of pitch and tempo rather than conceptual knowledge of a tune in musical imagery tasks.

Halpern's claims are modest: she states that her results show that auditory imagery is a "strong subjective experience," and at least partly quantifiable. "People indeed behave as if they were running songs through their heads. That is, the evidence seems to point towards a representation that codes extension in time, that unfolds in real time, that has strong links between adjacent elements, and that is unidirectionally ordered."[47] This isn't to say that we don't also encode melodies in other ways (e.g., to know that a piece starts on F♯ requires conceptual encoding of the music-theoretical category "F♯"), but it is to insist that the metric qualities of musical imagery that are unique to the modality of hearing must be represented in ways that are sensitive to just these qualities. Nonetheless, Halpern's results support our phenomenological intuitions about musical imagery as a productive capacity to generate auditory images. We experience "inner tunes" not merely as having *some* pitch, but as having *particular identifiable* pitches. Furthermore, we can scan melodies by playing them in our heads, demonstrating that these representations encode temporal features of their targets. Finally, lesion studies of focal brain damage and imaging studies of normal subjects demonstrate that auditory imagery exploits the same sets of neurophysiological processes as ordinary auditory experience.[48] Overall, these studies in psychology and neuroscience support the hypothesis that "parts of the cortex specialized for processing actual sound are also recruited to process imagined sound."[49] This, in turn, lends support for the phenomenological intuition that the experience of imagery is importantly like the experience of perception. Halpern describes musical imagery as follows:

> the "tune inside the head" is in some ways an apt description of the representation of familiar tunes. These tunes seem to be stored with much exact or analogue information . . . [Moreover], real time passes while auditory images are activated, and the representations apparently include the fairly absolute perceptual information of tempo and pitch, in addition to the relative information of note and harmony relationships.[50]

What philosophical purpose does a discussion of these results from the cognitive neuroscience of music serve? It supports the intuition that experiences of musical imagery have a perceptual basis, and thus contributes to debates about the nature of musical understanding. Musical sounds, especially pitches of instrumental sounds, are not the sorts of thing that we can comprehend through multiple sense modalities. If we are to imagine musical sounds, and not just imagine that there are musical sounds, or that something is true of a musical sound, this imagination must be, contrary to Scruton's claims, perceptual, and it must be specifically auditory.[51] This opens the way for specifically perceptual cognition, and demonstrates that the propositional imagination cannot coherently explain imagined content that has a perceptual, as opposed to propositional, structure. Thus, shedding light on the neural underpinnings of auditory imagery provides support for the claim that there is something that performs the functions of the musical imagination, and elucidates an important component of the musical listening experience. Auditory memories seem to be stored as past auditory percepts, and can be recalled in a way that reproduces the pitch and temporal details of the original auditory experience. Zatorre and Halpern review evidence that suggests that it is plausible to think that composers who report "hearing" their compositions internally are drawing on the same capacity for auditory imagery used to rehearse a remembered piece of music.[52] In addition, gifted composers are likely to have this capacity developed to a high degree—a link between one sort of imagination and creativity. Musicians who "rehearse" pieces internally are also reporting vivid imagery experiences. Hearing a piece that one already knows involves reviving an auditory image of that piece, drawing upon memory stores that function as a kind of constructive imagination.[53] All of these are functions of the imagination as that concept developed in the 18th century.

Finally, these studies can contribute to our understanding of musical appreciation. Cognitive neuroscience demonstrates that musical capacities are highly variable, and that both listening to and performing music seems to alter the very structure of the brain.[54] Arguably, what is happening is the formation of aural/musical categories for the components of music as well as for entire compositions. As a result, it may not be advisable to give a univocal philosophical account of musical understanding. This variability in musical imagery capacities might explain why non-experts tend to understand music through various non-musical aids, while highly trained musicians and musical formalists insist that it is improper to summon visual pictures to accompany one's experience of purely instrumental music. Further, if it is the case that the musical ability relevant to music listening can be developed later in life, then those who insist on formalist listening are not asking the impossible. If, however, there are limits to what listening capacities many people can develop, whether or not audiences appreciate complex, abstract, atonal music is not merely a matter of conservative or progressive tastes. Rather, most people simply have not developed the musical categories needed in order to hear this music as coherent, let alone enjoyable.[55] The studies and results discussed in this section demonstrate that cognitive neuroscience can help determine whether philosophical paradigms of music listening are consistent with physiological facts about the psychological processes that underwrite our engagement with performances of musical compositions, and, as a result, contribute to aesthetic issues related to musical understanding and appreciation.

Visual Art

Current research in the cognitive neuroscience of visual art lies at the confluence of two broad research strategies: *empirical aesthetics* and *aesthetic experimentalism*.[56]

Empirical aesthetics is a field of research that traces its roots to the beginnings of experimental psychology in the late 19th century.[57] The central claim of the field is that we can learn about the nature of art and associated aesthetic experiences by using the methods of psychology and related fields to examine behavioral responses to artworks. Aesthetic experimentalism is the view that visual artists develop formal and compositional vocabularies by trial and error, or through a systematic exploration of the perceptual effects of different sets of marks, color schemes, and compositional arrangements.[58] The central claim of aesthetic experimentalism is that we can learn about the operations of perceptual systems by examining the productive strategies of artists (e.g., the way visual artists develop and use formal techniques to convey information in their works). A general model for the cognitive neuroscience of visual art emerges from the rapprochement between these two research strategies. Cognitive science, in the broadest sense, is the study of the way organisms acquire, recognize, manipulate, and use information in the production of behavior. Visual artworks are stimuli intentionally designed to trigger ordinary perceptual, affective, and cognitive responses in spectators. Questions about the understanding and appreciation of visual artworks are, as a result, questions about the way viewers acquire, represent, and manipulate information embedded in the formal and compositional structure of artworks in order to recognize and evaluate their content. Cognitive neuroscience is a tool that can be used to investigate and model these processes. Therefore, cognitive neuroscience is a tool that can be used to investigate and model the cognitive and perceptual processes subserving our engagement with artworks. Data collected in these types of studies can be used to confirm art critical judgments about particular paintings and, as discussed above in the cases of narrative fiction and music, adjudicate between competing theories in philosophical debates about the nature of art and the defining characteristics of aesthetic experience.

This model for the cognitive neuroscience of visual art rests on the assumption that correlations between the formal features of artworks and basic neurophysiological mechanisms in the visual system can be used to explain how visual artworks work as perceptual stimuli.[59] This assumption is, in turn, grounded in the following argument. The input to the visual system is replete with information about the local environment. However, only a small fraction of this information is *diagnostic* for the identity of an object, action, or event at any given time.[60] In this regard one can think of the visual system as a set of evolved biological mechanisms whose function is to select information from sensory inputs that is sufficient for visual recognition and action. Artists' formal methods and vocabularies are tools for culling features sufficient for object, action, and event recognition (or in the case of abstract visual art features sufficient for figure–ground segregation and form recognition) from ordinary perceptual experience and rendering them in a medium. These productive strategies work because artists' formal strategies and vocabularies are directed at just those sets of environmental features that trigger the ordinary operations of perceptual systems. Therefore, the success of a visual artwork, its capacity to convey its content to viewers, depends on productive relationships between its formal features and the operations of the visual system. A good deal of research in the cognitive neuroscience of visual art is dedicated to searching out and explaining these relationships between the formal strategies employed by artists and the operations of the visual system.[61]

Philosophers have been generally skeptical whether these types of perceptual explanations of artworks can contribute to our understanding of the nature of art or the character of aesthetic experience.[62] What one needs in order to answer these skeptics is an argument that ties explanations of the way artworks work as perceptual stimuli to explanations of their artistically salient features (e.g., perceptual features responsible for the aesthetic effects and semantic associations constitutive of their status as artworks). A first pass at such an argument is forthcoming in the analysis of artists' productive practices. Consider the case of realistic landscape painting. Painters engage in formal studies (e.g., drawing studies) in order to recover sets of environmental features sufficient for naturalistic depiction. However, there is no single, ideal set of formal cues necessary for rendering these environmental features. Even in the case of highly realistic portraits and landscape paintings, any of a broad range of formal vocabularies and compositional strategies will suffice. This suggests that artists choose the formal and compositional strategies they use relative to the aesthetic effects and semantic associations they intend a particular work to produce. Artworks can, in this context, be thought of as artifacts intentionally designed to direct attention to their artistically salient features.[63] Cognitive neuroscience can contribute to explanations of the ways particular artworks work to direct attention and produce perceptual, expressive, and cognitive effects. These explanations can, in turn, provide data to clarify whether our best theories of art are consistent with the psychological processes that underwrite our engagement with artworks. Therefore, explanations of how visual artworks work as perceptual stimuli can contribute to our understanding of how they work as artistic stimuli. In what follows we discuss three case studies that illustrate this model for the cognitive neuroscience of visual art: Richard Latto's discussion of the use of *irradiation* in Georges Seurat's *Bathers at Asnières*, Margaret Livingstone's discussion of Mona Lisa's elusive smile, and Lizann Bonnar, Frédéric Gosselin, and Phillipe Schyns's discussion of Salvador Dalí's disappearing portrait of Voltaire.[64]

Georges Seurat used a formal technique called *irradiation* to enhance edges and amplify figure–ground segregation in *Bathers at Asnières* (Fig. 2.1).[65] Irradiation is derived from the observation of *Mach bands* in ordinary perception. Mach bands are perceived light and dark stripes that occur at luminance boundaries in the visual field.[66] However, these image features do not correspond to any objective features of the distal environment. They are instead artifacts of the way the visual system initially encodes the information contained in the light that impinges on the retina. Interestingly, although the scientific discovery of Mach bands is attributed to Ernst Mach in the mid-19th century, painters have copied this feature of

FIGURE 2.1 **Seurat, Georges (1859–1891).** Bathers at Asnières, *1884. Oil on canvas, 201 ×*
300 cm. (Photo credit: Copyright © National Gallery, London/Art Resource, NY.)

ordinary appearances into their paintings since at least Robert Campin (1406–
1444),[67] and Leonardo (1452–1519) described the utility of this technique in his
writings on artists' formal methods.[68] The presence of Mach bands in the visual
field is explained by *lateral inhibition* in the retina, an architectural feature
of neural networks that enables cells to modulate the outputs of their nearest
neighbors.[69] A ganglion cell in the retina receives *excitatory signals* from photore-
ceptors and *inhibitory signals* from other ganglion cells that surround it. The outputs of retinal ganglion cells are determined by the sum of their *excitatory* and
inhibitory inputs. Ganglion cells that respond to discrete regions of a homogenous
light field receive identical excitatory and inhibitory inputs. Therefore, the outputs
of these cells are identical. However, imagine a border between two homogenous
fields of different luminance. Ganglion cells along the bright side of the border
between these regions receive less inhibition from their neighbors on the dark
side. The overall response of these cells will therefore be higher than their neighbors in the "bright" field. The converse is true for the cell along the dark side of the
border. As a result, lateral inhibition generates illusory light and dark stripes along
the boundaries between regions of different luminance that do not match the
intensity of light received from the environment.

The visual system interprets sharp variations in luminance to indicate boundaries
between discrete surfaces that define objects in the visual field. Lateral inhibition

enhances luminance contrast along these edges. Therefore, one function of lateral inhibition is to amplify the intensity of a feature of the sensory input that defines the boundaries between objects in perception. This in turn contributes to form recognition by enhancing the contrast between figure and ground.[70] Irradiation involves copying Mach bands onto the canvas at critical object boundaries in order to amplify the effects of lateral inhibition in our perceptual interactions with a painting. The resultant glowing, irradiated edges draw attention to object boundaries, amplify the luminance contrast between a figure and its surround, and so sharpen the perception of depth in the picture plane (e.g., the contour defining the back of the seated figure in the center foreground in *Bathers at Asnières*.[71] Therefore, irradiation is an explicit feature of artists' formal vocabularies whose utility in paintings is explained by its resonance, or close coupling, with discrete neurophysiological mechanisms in the visual system.

Latto argues that irradiated edges are *aesthetic primitives* or features of a work that viewers experience as aesthetically pleasing because of their resonance with the basic operations of the visual system. However, there is a difficulty for this interpretation. Stimuli like the luminance ramps used to illustrate Mach bands are intentionally designed to optimally stimulate these basic neurophysiological mechanisms.[72] Further, Mach bands, as artifacts of the way lateral inhibition contributes to figure–ground segregation in all ordinary perceptual contexts, are ubiquitous in the visual environment (e.g., we see Mach bands at shadow boundaries because lateral inhibition is finely tuned to this type of environmental feature). If Latto's model were correct we should find luminance ramps and shadow boundaries to be deeply compelling aesthetic stimuli—but we do not. Therefore, although this case study demonstrates that cognitive neuroscience can contribute to our understanding of the way paintings work as perceptual stimuli, it does not establish irradiated edges as artistically salient features of *Bathers at Asnières*. This objection reflects a common problem for any theory that proposes to explain art in terms of ordinary cognitive processes: if the nature of art can be explained in terms of ordinary psychological processes subserving our engagement with artworks, one needs an additional explanation to determine what, if anything, differentiates artworks from ordinary artifacts.

It has been argued that the artistic value of Leonardo's *Mona Lisa* emerges from the way he used *sfumato* to render the dynamics of the figure's facial expression.[73] Sfumato is a formal technique in which artists blur the sharp edges that define object features in a painting so that these boundaries disappear into soft, "smoky" shadows. Leonardo used this technique to render the critical facial features that define Mona Lisa's expression, the corners of her mouth and eyes. Gombrich argues that these sfumato contours introduce a degree of ambiguity into the painting that forces viewers to use their imagination to interpret an expression that cannot ever be discretely resolved. The dynamics of the composition, on his account, emerge from these imaginative events, and are enhanced by spatial inconsistencies in the background landscape that alter the way viewers perceive the posture and relative size of the figure as they scan the painting. The net result is an elusive, lifelike expression that is indicative of the ebb and flow of an ordinary individual's mental states and enhances the qualitative character of our imaginative engagement with the subject of the painting.

Livingstone has demonstrated that differences between the spatial resolution of *peripheral* and *foveal* vision explain how sfumato works to generate the dynamics of Mona Lisa's expression.[74] We are able to discern remarkably fine-grained visual detail in the central, or foveal, region of the visual field. However, foveal vision is nearly blind to visual features defined by coarse-grained image information. Conversely, peripheral vision is tuned to coarse-grained image features at the expense of fine-grained visual detail. Livingstone filtered a reproduction of Leonardo's painting in order to separate out the low-, middle-, and high-spatial-frequency information used to depict Mona Lisa's face (Fig. 2.2). The difference between low/middle- (coarse-grained) and high (fine-grained)-spatial-frequency information is roughly analogous to the difference between the use of shading or discrete narrow lines to depict object boundaries in a drawing. The sfumato contours that define Mona Lisa's smile were more apparent in the images representing low- and middle-spatial-frequency information in the painting than the sharp lines of the high-spatial-frequency image. For instance, the slight upturn of the corner of her mouth, which is extended and exaggerated into the hollows of her cheek by the coarse-grained image features in the low- and middle-frequency images, is nearly invisible in the fine detail of the high-frequency image. Therefore, critical formal features defining Mona Lisa's smile are depicted only in low- and middle-spatial-frequency information.

The spatial resolution of human vision decreases dramatically as one moves from the center of the visual field towards the periphery. For instance, Livingstone

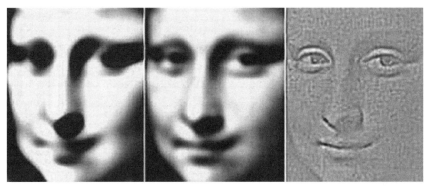

FIGURE 2.2 *A detail of the* Mona Lisa's *smile depicted with coarse, low spatial frequencies (left panel), medium spatial frequencies (middle panel), and high spatial frequencies. Livingstone's analysis of these images suggests that the smile is driven largely by medium- and low-spatial-frequency information. (Figure from Livingston [2002] with permission by the author.)*

reports that the spatial resolution of normal vision diminishes by a factor of 10 just 7 degrees from the central fixation point of one's gaze. This difference in spatial resolution between central, or *foveal*, and *peripheral* vision is explained by the fact that the receptive fields of peripheral retinal neurons are dramatically larger than those of their foveal counterparts.[75] The result is that foveal neurons are sensitive to sharp, narrow-luminance boundaries that carry high-spatial-frequency information, but are unable to register coarse, broad-luminance gradients, like contours rendered in sfumato, that carry low- and medium-spatial-frequency information. Conversely, the wider receptive fields of neurons in the peripheral field are well suited to record the latter category of contours, but are nearly blind to high-spatial-frequency information. As a result, when one foveates on, or directs one's attention to, Mona Lisa's smile it disappears. However, the smile reappears in a viewer's peripheral field when he or she looks away. Therefore, the dynamics of Mona Lisa's expression emerge from the differential sensitivity of foveal and peripheral vision to low-spatial-frequency information in the painting.

Livingstone's discussion of the *Mona Lisa* provides another example of the close coupling between the operations of the visual system and the formal strategies of artists. Further, the identification of a mechanism that underwrites the dynamics of the depicted expression both clarifies and improves upon Gombrich's discussion of the painting. If sound, Gombrich's account would entail that a viewer's interpretation of Mona Lisa's expression should vary with his or her state of mind, or with the qualitative character of his or her imaginative engagement with the painting.[76] In this sense, the depicted expression need not necessarily be dynamic at all. If Mona Lisa's mental state remains stable in a viewer's imaginative engagement with the painting, so will her expression. Livingstone's explanation, to the contrary, demonstrates that the depicted expression varies systematically with the eccentricity, or distance, of one's focus of attention from the center of Mona Lisa's face. This explanation accounts for the robustness and elusiveness of Mona Lisa's expression. It also attributes a more explicit directive role to the sorts of compositional choices Leonardo made in constructing the background landscape: spatial discrepancies in the landscape draw viewers' attention away from the figure (e.g., the discrepancy between the position of the horizon on the left and right side of the painting); the depicted expression is revealed as one looks away to explore these spatial discrepancies; it changes systematically as one scans the painting; and it disappears as one returns his or her attention to the face to resolve it.

It is important to note, however, that this case study does not itself establish that the elusiveness of Mona Lisa's smile is an artistically salient aesthetic effect of the painting. Sfumato works to produce the effects it does in the painting because it yields the same types of facial cues that the visual system uses to recognize and interpret facial expressions in ordinary, non-aesthetic perceptual contexts.[77] Nonetheless, the case study does confirm the art critical claim that Mona Lisa has a dynamic expression and explains the sorts of formal choices that Leonardo used to guide viewers' attention and produce this central feature of the work. In this regard, Livingstone's discussion contributes evidence in support of a particular hypothesis about the aesthetic quality of the painting. This in turn demonstrates that these types of case studies can contribute to art critical discussions about particular artworks. Further, theories about the nature of art and aesthetic experience rest ultimately on their consistency with facts about the way we engage with particular artworks. Therefore, case studies like Livingstone's, case studies that are focused on understanding the way we acquire, represent, manipulate, and use artistically salient information carried by a painting, can potentially provide data to help adjudicate among competing positions in theoretical debates about difficult aesthetic problems.

Bonnar, Gosselin, and Schyns' discussion of Salvador Dalí's *Slave Market with the Disappearing Bust of Voltaire* demonstrates that the differential use of low- and high-spatial-frequency information to convey information in a painting generalizes to other cases. Dalí's painting is a bistable ambiguous image (e.g., a Necker cube or the duck/rabbit image) whose central feature is perceived as either two figures walking arm in arm or a large marble bust of Voltaire (Fig. 2.3). The bistability of the image is an artistically salient feature of the painting that generates both the perceptual ambiguity and the range of semantic associations that are constitutive of its identity as an artwork. Bonnar and her colleagues used a technique called *frequency-specific adaptation* to demonstrate that this high- and low-spatial-frequency information was selectively used to drive the perception of either the nuns or the bust of Voltaire in the painting. They first filtered a cropped reproduction of the work into six different spatial scales in order to separate out low- and high-spatial-frequency information diagnostic for the perception of either the two figures or the bust of Voltaire. Although there was some overlap, the nuns were more apparent in the high-spatial-frequency images and the bust of Voltaire was more apparent in the low-spatial-frequency images. Frequency-specific adaptation can be used to desensitize the visual system to the particular spatial-frequency information presented in a stimulus. Bonnar and her colleaguess predicted that if high- and low-spatial-frequency information is used selectively in the Dalí painting to drive the perception of either the nuns or the bust of Voltaire, then participants adapted to high-spatial-frequency information should see the bust of Voltaire and participants adapted to low-spatial-frequency information should see the two nuns. Participants viewed an animation constructed of either high- or low-spatial-frequency dynamic noise, after which they were shown a hybrid image composed of just the high- and low-spatial-frequency information diagnostic for the nuns and the bust of Voltaire. The results of the experiment confirm this prediction.

These results demonstrate that Dalí used different types of spatial-frequency information to carry different artistically salient information in *Slave Market with Disappearing Bust of Voltaire*. The background under the arch behind the two nuns is colored brown as if filled in with a wall. However, the cut-out windows resemble the shapes of clouds, which is consistent with the open-air arch to its left. In the latter context the occlusion boundary that defines the top of Voltaire's head has the

FIGURE 2.3 **Dalí, Salvador.** Slave Market with the Disappearing Bust of Voltaire, *1940. Oil on canvas, 18-1/4 × 25-3/8 inches. (Copyright © Fundación Gala-Salvador Dalí [Artist Rights Society], 2010. Collection of the Salvador Dalí Museum, Inc., St. Petersburg, FL, 2010.)*

appearance of a rough-hewn open arched doorway through which the nuns have entered the market. These ambiguities in the identity of the background draw viewers' attention to the top of the doorway and the cloud/windows, and, in the process of doing so, reveal the coarse-grained visual information diagnostic for the bust of Voltaire (i.e., the heads of the nuns become his eyes, their interlocked arms his nose, and their aprons his chin).[78] The play of these two discrete perceptual resolutions of the work, in turn, generates the contrasting interpretations that are constitutive of its artistic salience.

The three case studies discussed here provide a promising model for how to pursue research in the cognitive neuroscience of art more generally. They suggest that we can come to understand the nature of art and aesthetic experience by tracking the relationship between the formal and compositional structure of particular artworks and viewers' behavioral responses. The model that emerges defines artworks as attentional strategies intentionally designed to direct attention and enhance the perception of features diagnostic for their artistically salient aesthetic (e.g., Mona Lisa's elusive smile) and semantic (e.g., the bistable ambiguous content of Dalí's painting) content.[79] These case studies each demonstrate a role for exogenous, stimulus-driven attentional processes in our engagement with artworks. However, attention is also endogenously driven by knowledge and expectations. The influence of knowledge and expectations in perception is mediated by frontoparietal attentional networks that are employed to shift attention and prime the firing patterns of networks of neurons in the visual system to the presence of expected objects and features at particular locations. These feedback projections influence visual processing as early as the lateral geniculate nucleus.[80] Although there is not space to discuss these processes here, research suggests that artworks are attentional strategies that harness both basic formal features and viewers' semantic knowledge, including art historical knowledge of the unique sets of formal strategies used to categorize artworks as belonging to artistic types (e.g., the works of particular artists, schools, or epochs), to convey their content.[81]

What, if anything, can all of this contribute to the philosophy of art? First, it suggests that some of the philosophical difficulties associated with the cognitive neuroscience of art can be attributed to the growing pains of an evolving field of interdisciplinary research. The various disciplines involved in interdisciplinary endeavors each bring prior theoretical and practical biases with them to the table, biases that can initially cut at cross-purposes to one another. In the case of cognitive science and aesthetics we see that there is often a difficulty clarifying (and agreeing upon) the appropriate targets for perceptual explanations of artworks, or identifying which exactly are the artistically salient features towards which research in the cognitive science of art ought to be directed. In this regard more work needs to be done to determine how to isolate and model the types of aesthetic and semantic effects used to categorize artifacts as artworks.[82] Second, we often make reference to the *formal structure* of artworks in explanations of the nature and function of art. In its broadest, most comprehensive sense the term denotes all of the individual parts of an artwork and the relations among them (e.g., the lines, color patches, and shapes, as well as the objects, their parts, and the relations among them in a painting). However, this *descriptive* sense of artistic form is not particularly useful in explaining art. What one needs is a way to constrain our understanding of formal structure to just those features and relations that contribute to the function of an artifact as an artwork. An account of this *functional* sense of artistic form is transparent in the definition of visual artworks that emerges from the discussion of the cognitive neuroscience of visual art. Works of visual art are artifacts intentionally designed to direct attention to the features responsible for their artistically salient effects. The formal structure of an artwork can thereby be understood as the sum total of the formal and compositional choices directed towards the production of these effects.[83]

Finally, the account of formal structure that emerges from this discussion can contribute to debates about the role that artists' intentions play in the determination of the content of a work of art. On the one hand it seems beyond question that the intentions of an artist play a significant role in our determination of the content of an artwork (skeptics need only consider how the meaning and artistic value of a particular work would change with the discovery that it is a forgery, or that the artist intended it as a piece of unappealing political propaganda). Many, if not all, artworks are occasions for communicative events in which artists express ideas and emotions. In this context it seems that our interpretation of the content of an artwork is constrained by the intentions of the artist in ways that are analogous to our interpretation of the use of metaphors in ordinary conversation. However, we rarely, if ever, come to a work of art with explicit knowledge of the actual intentions of the artist. Rather, it would seem that we treat the artist as a hypothetical agent, or infer the most plausible set of intentions from the best available evidence. On the account that we have provided, visual artworks are attentional strategies that carry information sufficient to enable viewers to recover their content from their perceptible surfaces. In this regard the formal choices made by an artist direct attention to the work's semantically salient features, and so constrain the set of available, appropriate interpretations. This in turn provides a principled means not only to recover the content of the work without demanding explicit prior knowledge of an artist's actual intentions, but also to evaluate the adequacy of competing interpretations of those intentions.[84]

Conclusion

In this chapter we have provided counterarguments to philosophical skepticism about the relevance of results of psychology and neuroscience to aesthetics, maintaining that philosophical skeptics who hold this view have an overly narrow conception of the problems of aesthetics. Artworks are, ultimately, artifacts intentionally designed to direct attention to the features responsible for their artistically salient aesthetic and semantic effects. In this regard, questions about the nature of our understanding and appreciation of art are questions about the ways in which we cognitively engage (broadly construed to include perception) with art, questions that ultimately depend on an understanding of our psychological interactions with particular artworks. Therefore, we have claimed that cognitive science has bearing on a variety of topics relevant to aesthetics. We have focused on three sets of examples from different art forms. First, we showed that recent research on the emotions elucidates our responses to fiction. Second, we argued that studies of musical imagery shed light on both the way we hear and understand music and the cognitive and neural processes that account for some of our experiences of sensory imagination. Finally, we argued that explanations of how visual artworks work as perceptual stimuli can contribute to our understanding of how they work as artistic stimuli. These discussions point towards the continuation of the rich and productive rapprochement between aesthetics and psychology originally envisioned in works of 18th-century philosophers like Alexander Baumgarten.[85]

Endnotes

1. For a general discussion of 18th-century aesthetics see Guyer, P. (1996). *Kant and the experience of freedom.* Cambridge: Cambridge University Press. See also Guyer, P. (2007).

18th-century German aesthetics. In E. N. Zalta (Ed.), *The Stanford encyclopedia of philosophy.* [online] Available: http://plato.stanford.edu/archives/fall2008/entries/aesthetics-18th-german/ [accessed June 24, 2010]; and Guyer, P. (1998). Alexander Gottlieb Baumgarten. In M. Kelly (Ed.), *Encyclopedia of aesthetics* (pp. 227–228). Oxford: Oxford University Press.

2. Guyer, 2007; translated from Alexander Gottlieb Baumgarten, *Aesthetica*, partial Latin text and German translation in Schweizer, H. R. (1973). *Ästhetik als Philosophie der sinnlichen Erkenntnis* (§1, 107). Basel: Schwabe.

3. See Seeley, W. P. (2006). Naturalizing aesthetics: art and the cognitive neuroscience of vision. *Journal of Visual Arts Practice, 5*(3), 195–213.

4. Wittgenstein, L. (1966). *Lectures on aesthetics, psychology, and religious belief.* Berkeley: University of California Press; and Dickie, G. (1962). Is psychology relevant to aesthetics. *The Philosophical Review, 71*(3), 285–302.

5. Wittgenstein, 1966, pp. 19–20.

6. Wittgenstein, 1966, p. 20.

7. Calvo-Merino, B., Jola, C., Glaser, D. E., & Haggard, P. (2008). Towards a sensiromotor aesthetics of performing art. *Consciousness and Cognition, 17,* 911–922; Jacobsen, T., Schubotz, R. I., Höfel, L., & von Cramon, D. Y. (2006). Brain correlates of aesthetic judgment of beauty. *NeuroImage, 29*(1), 276–285; and Cela-Conde, C. J., Marty, G., Maestú, F., Ortiz, T., Munar, E., Fernandez, A., Roca, M., Rosello, J. & Quesney, F. (2004). Activation of the prefrontal cortex in the human visual aesthetic perception. *Proceedings of the National Academy of Science, 101*(16), 6321–6325.

8. One goal of Calvo-Merino and coworkers' study is to develop a methodology to resolve this difficulty with preference-ordering studies.

9. Robinson, J. (2005). *Deeper than reason: the emotions and their role in literature, music, and art.* Oxford: Oxford University Press.

10. James, W. (1894). The physical basis of emotion. *Psychological Review, 1,* 516–529.

11. Robinson, 2005, p. 28.

12. Carroll, N. (1990). *The philosophy of horror, or paradoxes of the heart.* London: Routledge; and Gaut, B. (2006). *Art, emotion, and ethics.* Oxford: Oxford University Press. But see Prinz, J. J. (2004). *Gut reactions: a perceptual theory of emotions.* New York: Oxford, for an influential neo-Jamesian approach to emotions within philosophy.

13. Solomon, R. (1976) .*The passions: emotions and the meaning of life.* Garden City, N.Y.: Anchor-Doubleday.

14. Kunst-Wilson, W. R., & Zajonc, R. B. (1980). Affective discrimination of stimuli that cannot be recognized. *Science, 207,* 42–56.

15. Murphy, S. T., & Zajonc, R. B. (1993). Affect, cognition, and awareness. *Journal of Personality and Social Psychology, 64,* 723–739.

16. See Lazarus, R. (1991). *Emotion and adaptation.* Oxford: Oxford University Press.

17. Ledoux, J. (1996). *The emotional brain.* New York: Simon and Schuster.

18. Robinson, 2005, p. 50.

19. Robinson, 2005, pp. 112–113.

20. Robinson, 2005, p. 16; Lyons, W. E. (1980). *Emotion.* Cambridge: Cambridge University Press.

21. Robinson, 2005, p. 16.

22. Robinson, 2005, pp. 95–96.

23. Robinson, 2005, p. 16.

24. Plato. (1992). *The Republic* [trans. G. M. A. Grube] (pp. 398e–399c). Indianapolis: Hackett.

25. Plato, 1992, p. 401d.

26. Plato, 1992, p. 411b.

27. Plato, of course, also followed the belief attributed to the Pythagoreans that music is a manifestation of mathematical ideas. It is only music in its earthly manifestation that has a direct effect on human psychology. For a more detailed discussion of these distinctions see Hamilton, A. (2007). *Aesthetics and music.* London: Continuum; and Barker, A. (2004). *Greek musical writings, vol. 2: Harmonic and acoustic theory.* Cambridge: Cambridge University Press.

28. Hanslick, E. (1986). *On the musically beautiful* [trans. G. Payzant]. Indianapolis: Hackett.

29. Kivy also endorses the Dickie-style arguments discussed above. He has written that he is skeptical of any claims made in philosophical contexts that begin with the phrase, "As psychologists have shown." See Kivy, P. (2007). Moodophilia: a response to Noël Carroll and Margaret Moore. *Journal of Aesthetics and Art Criticism, 65*(3), 323–329; see also Kivy, P. (2006). Critical study: deeper than emotion. *British Journal of Aesthetics, 46*(3), 287–311.

30. Kivy, P. (2009). *Antithetical arts: on the ancient quarrel between literature and music.* Oxford: Oxford University Press.

31. This is not to claim that a work of music is *nothing but* organized sound; surely it is a cultural object as well.

32. Wittgenstein, L. (1972). *Philosophical investigations* [trans. G. E. M. Anscombe]. Oxford: Basil Blackwell; Ryle, G. (1984). *The concept of mind.* Chicago: University of Chicago Press; and Scruton, R. (1997). *Art and imagination.* South Bend, IN: St. Augustine's Press.

33. See Strawson, P. F. (1974). Imagination and perception. In *Freedom and resentment and other essays* (pp. 50–72). London: Methuen.

34. See Brann, E. (1991). *The world of the imagination.* Savage, MD: Rowman & Littlefield; and Warnock, M. (1976). *Imagination.* Berkeley: University of California Press.

35. Hume, D. (2000). *A treatise of human nature* (D. F. Norton & M. J. Norton, eds.). Oxford: Oxford University Press.

36. Kant, I. (1998). *The critique of pure reason* (P. Guyer, ed.). Cambridge: Cambridge University Press.

37. See Husserl, E. (2008). *On the phenomenology of the consciousness of internal time* [trans. J. Barnett Brough]. Norwell, MA: Kluwer.

38. Kant, I. (1953). *The critique of judgment* (J. C. Meredith, ed.). Oxford: Oxford University Press.

39. For an alternative interpretation of these data concerning mental imagery see Pylyshyn, Z. (2003). Return of the mental image: are there really pictures in the brain. *Trends in Cognitive Sciences, 7*(3), 113–118.

40. Kosslyn, S. M., Ball, T. M., & Reiser, B. J. (1978). Visual images preserve metric spatial information: evidence from studies of image scanning. *Journal of Experimental Psychology: Human Perception and Performance, 5,* 47–60.

41. Shepard, R. N., & Metzler, J. (1971). Mental rotation of three-dimensional objects. *Science, 171,* 701–703.

42. For a review see Kosslyn, S. M., Thompson, W. L., & Ganis, G. (2006). *The case for mental imagery.* New York: Oxford. This observation generalizes to motor imagery, which

employs the same areas of the motor cortex involved in planning and preparation for the imagined types of actions in ordinary contexts. These areas are also activated when expert musicians listen to music, suggesting that motor simulation plays a productive role in musical understanding. See Decety, J., & Grèves, J. (2006). The power of simulation: imagining one's own and others' behaviour. *Brain Research, 1079,* 4–14.

43. Bisiach, E., & Luzzatti, C. (1978). Unilateral neglect of representational space. *Cortex, 14,* 129–133.

44. Kosslyn, S. M., Pascual-Leone, A., Felician, O., Camposano, S., Keenan, J. P., Thompson, W. L., Ganis, G., Sukel, K. E., & Alpert, N. M. (1999). The role of area 17 in visual imagery: convergent evidence from PET and rTMS. *Science, 284,* 167–170.

45. Halpern, A. R. (1992). Musical aspects of auditory imagery. In D. Reisberg (Ed.), *Auditory imagery* (pp. 1–28). Hillsdale, NJ: Lawrence Erlbaum Associates; Halpern, A. R., Zatorre, R. J., Bouffard, M., & Johnson, J. A. (2004). Behavioral and neural correlates of perceived and imagined musical timbre. *Neuropsychologia, 42,* 1281–1292; and Zatorre, R. J., & Halpern, A. R. (2005). Mental concerts: musical imagery and auditory cortex. *Neuron, 47,* 9–12.

46. Halpern, A. R. (1984). The organization of memory for familiar songs. *Journal of Experimental Psychology: Learning, Memory, and Cognition, 10,* 496–512.

47. Halpern, 1992, p. 10.

48. See Zatorre, R. J., & Halpern, A. R. (1993). Effect of unilateral temporal-lobe excision on perception and imagery of songs. *Neuropsychologia, 31,* 221–232; and Halpern et al., 2004, 1289–1291.

49. Halpern, A. A. (2001). Cerebral substrates of musical imagery. *Annals of the New York Academy of Sciences: The Biological Foundations of Music, 930,* 190.

50. Halpern, 1992, p. 25.

51. But see fn. 40. See also Zatorre and Halpern, 2005, pp. 10–11. This is a claim about the failings of propositional accounts of musical imagery and understanding, not a skeptical claim about multisensory integration in auditory perception.

52. See Zatorre and Halpern, 2005, p. 10.

53. See Huron, D. (2006). Chapter 7 in *Sweet anticipation: music and the psychology of expectation.* Cambridge, MA: MIT Press.

54. Pascual-Leone, A. (2007). The brain that makes music is changed by it. In I. Peretz & R. J. Zatorre (Eds.), *The cognitive neuroscience of music* (pp. 396–409). Cambridge, MA: MIT Press.

55. Huron, 2006, 344.

56. Rollins, M. (2004). What Monet meant: intention and attention in understanding art. *Journal of Aesthetics and Art Criticism, 62*(2), 175.

57. Fechner, G. T. (1876). *Vorschule der Aesthetik.* Leipzig: Breitkopf & Hartël.

58. Gombrich, E. H. (1960). *Art and illusion.* Princeton, NJ: Princeton University Press.

59. Latto, R. (1995). The brain of the beholder. In R. Gregory, J. Harris, P. Heard, & D. Rose (Eds.), *The artful eye* (pp. 66–94). New York: Oxford University Press; Livingstone, M. (2002). *Vision and art: the biology of seeing.* New York: Harry N. Abrams; and Zeki, S. (1999). *Inner vision.* New York: Oxford University Press.

60. Diagnostic features are defined as sets of image cues that are sufficient to determine the identity of a stimulus or to perform an action. See Schyns, P. G. (1998). Diagnostic recognition: task constraints, object information, and their interactions. *Cognition, 67* (1–2),

147–179; Seeley, W. P., & Kozbelt, A. (2008). Art, artists, and perception: a model for premotor contributions to visual analysis and form recognition. *Philosophical Psychology, 21*(2), 1–23.

61. See, for instance, Livingstone, 2002; Cavanagh, P. (2005). The artist as neuroscientist. *Nature, 435,* 301–307.

62. See, for instance, Currie, G. (2003). Aesthetics and cognitive science. In J. Levinson (Ed.), *The Oxford handbook of aesthetics* (pp. 706–721). New York: Oxford University Press.

63. See Rollins, 2004, pp. 182–186; Calvo-Merino et al., 2008, p. 911, make an analogous claim about choreographers and the compositional structure of dance.

64. Latto, 1995; Livingstone, 2002; Bonnar, L., Gosselin, F., & Schyns, P. G. (2002). Understanding Dalí's *Slave Market with Disappearing Bust of Voltaire*: a case study in the scale information driving perception. *Perception, 31,* 683–691.

65. See Riley, B. (1999). *The eye's mind: Bridget Riley* (R. Kudielka, Ed.; pp. 174–182). London: Thames and Hudson, Ltd.; Latto, 1995, pp. 72–75; Ratliff, F. (1992). *Paul Signac and color in Neo-Impressionism* (pp. 92–97). New York: Rockefeller University Press.

66. For an illustration see "Mach Bands," available: http://www.yorku.ca/eye/machband.htm [June 28, 2010].

67. Ratliff, 1992, p. 94.

68. See Leonardo Da Vinci. (1989). *Leonardo on Painting* (M. Kemp, Ed.). New Haven: Yale University Press.

69. Palmer, S. E. (1999). *Vision science* (p. 116). Cambridge, MA: MIT Press.

70. See Palmer, 1999, p. 282.

71. In fact, Seurat used irradiation to amplify contours defining figure–ground relations throughout the painting.

72. See fn. 66.

73. Gombrich, E. H. (1950). *The story of art* (pp. 300–303). New York: Phaidon Press.

74. Livingstone, 2002, pp. 68–73.

75. The *receptive field* of a neuron within the visual system is defined as either the discrete area of retinal stimulation that results in the reaction of that neuron or the projection of that area of the retinal image onto the visual field. See Kandel, E. R., Schwartz, J. H., & Jessel, T. M. (2000). *Principles of neural science* (p. 418). New York: McGraw-Hill; and Palmer, 1999, 116.

76. Livingstone, 2002, p. 71.

77. Livingstone, 2002, p. 73.

78. Dalí's painting is replete with these types of perceptual ambiguities. For instance, the two bodies embracing one another on the right side of the painting are depicted with inconsistent postures and orientations that also serve to draw a viewer's attention away from the center of the painting.

79. See also Rollins, 2004, pp. 185–185; Carroll, N. (1999). *The philosophy of art* (pp. 142–152). New York: Routledge; and the discussion of peak shift effect in Ramachandran, V. S., & Hirstein, W. (1999). The science of art: a neurological theory of aesthetic experience. *Journal of Consciousness Studies, 6*(6–7), 15–51.

80. See Kastner, S. (2004). Attentional response modulation in the human visual system. In M. I. Posner (Ed.), *Cognitive neuroscience of attention* (pp. 144–156). New York: The Guilford Press.

81. See Kastner, 2004; Koivisto, M., & Revonsuo, A. (2007). How meaning shapes seeing. *Psychological Science, 18*(10), 845–849; Schyns, P. G., & Olivia, A. (1999). Dr. Angry and Mr. Smile: when categorization flexibly modifies the perception of faces in rapid visual presentations. *Cognition, 69,* 243–265.

82. See Skov, M. (2009). Neuroaesthetic problems: a framework for neuroaesthetic research. In M. Skov & O. Vartanian (Eds.), *Neuroaesthetics* (pp. 9–26). Amityville, NY: Baywood Publishing Company, Inc.

83. See Carroll, 1999, pp. 137–144, for a discussion of the distinction between descriptive and functional accounts of artistic form.

84. See also Rollins, 2004, pp. 185–186.

85. Baumgarten, *Aesthetica*; see also Mendelssohn, M. (1997). On the main principles of the fine arts and sciences. In D. O. Dahlstrom (Ed.), *Philosophical writings* (pp. 169–191). New York: Cambridge University Press.

Aesthetic Theory and Aesthetic Science

PROSPECTS FOR INTEGRATION

Vincent Bergeron and Dominic McIver Lopes

Researchers from different disciplinary backgrounds often propose competing explanations of such phenomena as emotion, consciousness, or aesthetic response. Though sometimes heated, this kind of disagreement is not fundamental. Fundamental disagreement occurs when researchers from different backgrounds have different, even incompatible, conceptions of the phenomenon to be explained. Disagreements about how to explain a phenomenon are not fundamental; disagreements about what is to be explained are fundamental. There is currently a great deal of fundamental disagreement in research into aesthetic response. The remedy is ideally integration, wherein researchers converge on a common conception of what they are trying to explain, even if they continue to disagree about how to explain it. In other words, the remedy is to work towards a theoretical concept of aesthetic response that serves explanations in the different aesthetic sciences and non-scientific studies as well. An integrated concept has potential benefits for all kinds of scholars whose subject is aesthetic response.

The Aesthetic Sciences

Quite independently of the need for a theoretical concept of aesthetic response that is common to the sciences and the humanities, there is also a need for integration within the aesthetic sciences themselves. On the one hand, an examination of the recent literature in different sciences on aesthetic responses to visual stimuli indicates that investigators may not be getting at the same phenomenon in their explanations. Aligning the aesthetic sciences with each other may prove beneficial. On the other hand, these investigations range over different levels of analysis, from the neurobiological to the psychological, and a common conception of what is to be explained may be useful to understand how explanations at these various levels of analysis cohere and reinforce each other.

To begin with, different groups of investigators have, over the past few decades, studied what we may think of as different parts of aesthetic responses to visual presentations. It makes sense to expect that any aesthetic response (e.g., when looking at a painting) will comprise several different processes that vary in number and kind depending on the nature of the stimulus as well as on the subject's particular "aesthetic sensibility," and the physical and social setting in which the subject experiences the stimulus (see Locher, Chapter 7, this volume). These processes might be organized into stages, such as a basic perceptual analysis, a series of intermediary cognitive operations (e.g., implicit memory, explicit classification, affective appraisal), and finally an evaluation.[1] Or perhaps it is better not to think of the many processes involved as occurring in a series of stages but rather in parallel, as proposed by Shimamura in Chapter 1 of this volume. Either way, one goal of aesthetic science is to explain how these processes contribute, individually and as a whole, to our aesthetic responses.

To see how different groups of investigators differently conceptualize aesthetic response in their explanations, consider the case of aesthetic pleasure. Several investigators associate aesthetic response with pleasure or reward and have set out to identify the mechanisms underlying this pleasure. For example, Ramachandran and Hirstein present a theory of aesthetic experience by stating several general principles deployed by artists (either consciously or unconsciously) to "titillate the visual areas of the brain."[2] Chief among these principles is the peak shift effect, which takes place when a subject responds more strongly to an amplified version of a previous stimulus, and the hypothesis is that strength of response can underlie pleasure. Similarly, Martindale and Moore argue for a theory of aesthetic preference according to which "the amount of pleasure elicited by a stimulus is a positive function of how activated the internal representations or cognitive units that code it are," so that stimulus preference is positively related to prototypicality.[3] In the same vein, but at a different level of analysis, Biederman and Vessel propose a neurobiological mechanism for perceptual pleasure according to which the greater the activity in visual association areas, the greater the amount of perceptual pleasure generated in the viewer.[4] Finally, Leder and colleagues propose a multistage cognitive model aimed at explaining the hedonic and self-rewarding character of our aesthetic responses to art.[5]

It is important, however, to be aware that explanations of aesthetic pleasure may not be full explanations of aesthetic response. To be sure, targeting the pleasurable or rewarding aspects of aesthetic response allows room to address other parts of aesthetic response in more complete explanations, and it may also turn out that mechanisms such as prototypicality and the peak shift effect explain different components of aesthetic response. In that case, thought should be given to the specific role of explanations of aesthetic pleasure in a fuller understanding of aesthetic response. Moreover, as an added complication, aesthetic pleasure can be understood in different ways. For example, studies that set out to explain the pleasurable aspect of aesthetic response often use preference as an indicator of pleasure,[6] even though it is not clear how well preference indicates pleasure.

Some researchers are more explicit about the scope of their research. For example, Reber, Schwarz, and Winkielman limit their analysis of aesthetic response to beauty, which they define as "a pleasurable subjective experience that is directed toward an object and not mediated by intervening reasoning."[7] Distinguishing beauty and aesthetic pleasure on one hand from aesthetic value on the other, they understand aesthetic response as unrelated to aesthetic value. Taking a different approach, the parallel architecture proposed by Shimamura in Chapter 1 allows pleasure to be an optional part of an aesthetic response.

Even this rapid survey of the literature shows that it is an open question what features of aesthetic response need to be explained. Candidate features include pleasure or reward, evaluation, classification, affective appraisal, emotion, and combinations of these features. It is also an open question whether any or some of these features are essential to aesthetic response, are typical to it, or accompany it sometimes. How is the choice to be made?

Part of what is at stake is an implicit assumption about what objects evoke aesthetic responses. For example, if some works of art have great aesthetic value and yet evoke no pleasure, but we assume that pleasure is a component of aesthetic response, then it follows that aesthetic response and aesthetic evaluation may dissociate. However, we need not reason this way. One alternative is not to assume that pleasure is essential to aesthetic response, so the value of these unpleasant works may be understood in terms of the aesthetic responses they evoke. Yet another option is to assume that pleasure is essential to aesthetic response but artistic value is not the same as aesthetic value. In this case, the unpleasant works may have artistic value and not aesthetic value. In other words, an unpleasant work may have high artistic value and, because it is unpleasant, have little or no aesthetic value. These considerations suggest that focusing on art in an attempt to explain aesthetic response[8] might not be the best way to achieve integration. As we argue in the next section, there are good reasons to dissociate aesthetic response from art.

For another way to see how different groups of investigators differently conceptualize aesthetic response in their explanations, consider the phenomenal character of aesthetic response. Here the studies seem to fall into three categories. Some studies set out to identify mechanisms of aesthetic response to which we have no conscious access. One example is the mere exposure effect,[9] where nonconscious, repeated exposure to various kinds of stimuli (e.g., paintings) helps shape preferences for them.[10] Another example, mentioned earlier, is the neurobiological mechanism for perceptual pleasure proposed by Biederman and Vessel in order to account for the apparent link between the amount of activity in visual association areas of the brain and the amount of perceptual pleasure that is generated in the viewer.[11]

Other studies set out to identify mechanisms that take place at the "fringe" of consciousness—that is, mechanisms that have a direct effect on consciousness though we have no conscious access to their particular workings. For example, Reber, Schwarz, and Winkielman explain aesthetic response in terms of processing fluency.[12] Aesthetic pleasure, they argue, is a positive function of the experience of the ease with which the perceiver processes a stimulus. Yet perceptual fluency depends on several underlying mechanisms, such as perceptual priming and mere exposure, to which we have no conscious access.

A third category of studies set out to explain the more explicit side of aesthetic response. Thus, the cognitive model proposed by Leder and coworkers explains "aesthetic experiences," at least in part, in terms of higher-level cognitive mechanisms such as explicit classification, cognitive mastering, and evaluation, of which we are at least partially conscious.[13]

In contending with the phenomenal character of aesthetic response in different ways, these kinds of studies bring to light another integration challenge for aesthetic science, namely the problem of keeping track of what is to be explained across different levels of analysis ranging from the neurobiological to the cognitive. This vertical integration challenge can be distinguished from the horizontal integration challenge, the challenge of integrating the wide range of current conceptions of aesthetic response. If aesthetic response is a complex process, then the concept of aesthetic response will be maximally explanatory if it integrates both horizontally and vertically.

Achieving integration at the level of what is to be explained is not the same as achieving integration at the level of explanations. Both are important. What appear to be competing explanations of aesthetic response might turn out to be parts of a more complete theory. For example, Reber, Schwarz, and Winkielman propose that several mechanisms of aesthetic pleasure (e.g., mere exposure, prototypicality) can be unified in terms of the effects they have on processing fluency.[14] However, integration of theories is easier once we agree on what the theories aim to explain.

Philosophical Theories of Aesthetic Response

Faced with the need to converge upon an integrated concept of aesthetic response, scientists might turn to philosophers for help. Thus Reber suggests that "art theorists . . . define the criterion of what the [aesthetic] experience is expected to be; scientists . . . provide a test of whether this criterion is fulfilled."[15] Some philosophers would agree that a collaboration between scientists and philosophers is a division of labor wherein philosophers define the nature of a phenomenon like aesthetic response, leaving scientists to discover the mechanisms by which it is realized. Maybe it is sometimes useful to divide labor along these lines, but not when it comes to research on aesthetic response.

It is true that one task of philosophy is to provide a theory of what it is for a psychological state to be an aesthetic response; however, philosophy does not operate in a vacuum. To be satisfactory, a theory of aesthetic response should model and make sense of the role played by the concept in certain contexts where it is used. The same goes for many other philosophical theories. A philosophical theory of time will treat the concept of time as a component of hypotheses in physics. Philosophical theories of personhood treat the concept of a person as one that plays a fundamental role in folk psychology and legal reasoning, especially in connection with attributions of responsibility. In the same way, a theory of aesthetic response should model and make sense of the work that the concept is expected to perform in certain contexts.

Which contexts? Traditionally, philosophers have analyzed aesthetic response as it is conceptualized in critical practice and in historical and cultural studies of critical practice.[16] Those who have had an interesting aesthetic response routinely tell others about it so as to guide them towards having a similar experience,[17] not only by saying where they can get the experience (from that movie) but also how (by attending to its overt use of jump cuts). This basic level of critical activity is normally built up into more elaborate forms such as published reviews, exhibition design, and even art education; and changes in critical practices across time and culture are tracked by historians, anthropologists, and sociologists. Philosophers try to make sense of aesthetic response as playing a fundamental role in the many practices of criticism that envelop and shape our encounters with works of art and natural beauties.

However, a flaw in this traditional methodology stems from historical circumstances. Since the eighteenth century, thought about aesthetic response has come to be intermeshed with thought about art. Indeed, "criticism" now seems to be synonymous with "art criticism." For example, Noël Carroll describes his book *On Criticism* as "an exercise in the philosophy of criticism . . . a branch of the philosophy of art (or aesthetics) that takes as its object of inquiry the criticism of the arts."[18] This historical intermeshing of aesthetic response with art threatens to distort philosophical theories of both.[19]

To explain, historians have shown that a major shift took place between the Renaissance and the eighteenth century in how we think about art.[20] Activities such as painting, architecture, music, and poetry had been practiced for thousands of years. What was new was the classification of these activities together in a group, the arts, which was clearly distinguished from groupings of other activities—the crafts or applied sciences and also the liberal arts and sciences. Shiner provides a striking illustration of this shift to a new conceptual scheme in the frontispieces of two encyclopedias published a few decades apart in the mid-eighteenth century.[21] Both use tree diagrams to show genetic and similarity relationships among various human endeavors. Whereas in the earlier diagram the arts scatter across the tree's branches, in the later diagram they cluster together on one branch representing the arts.

This shift had a profound effect on conceptions of aesthetic response. Premodern thought mostly focused on aesthetic response either to nature or to the specific arts, as in Aristotle's *Poetics*. Later philosophy showed two trends. First, aesthetic responses to natural objects and scenes were downplayed (until the very recent revival of environmental aesthetics[22]). Second, philosophers increasingly sought theories of aesthetic response having enough generality to apply to all works in all of the different art forms—albeit in different ways in the different arts.[23] A land-mark event in this history was Charles Batteux's formulation of a single theory of aesthetic response as common to works in all the arts.[24] Batteux's enterprise was inherited in the twentieth century by theorists and philosophers like Monroe Beardsley.[25]

The flip side of defining art in terms of aesthetic response is the need to under-stand aesthetic response as suitable to define art. Beardsley, for example, defines a work of art partly as an item that functions to afford "an experience with a marked aesthetic character."[26] It follows that an experience with a marked aesthetic charac-ter is one that may be elicited by any work of art whatsoever. If Monet's paintings of lily ponds, Mozart's *Requiem*, T. S. Eliot's "Wasteland," John Cage's *4´33˝*, *Citizen Kane*, Martha Schwartz's *Bagel Garden*, and some Balanchine choreography are works of art, then they all afford experiences with a marked aesthetic character. Aesthetic response stretches across an incredible variety of phenomena.

The outcome can be seen in the parade of philosophical theories of aesthetic response that have been toppled one after another by counterexamples of artworks that do not fit the going theory. It should be no surprise that a theory meant to cover a huge variety of phenomena should be vulnerable to counterexamples. Batteux's imitation theory of art claims that works of art imitate beauty in nature so as to give rise to an experience of that beauty, but some works of art do not imitate beauty in nature (e.g., pure music), so aesthetic responses to works of art go beyond responses to beauty in nature. Tolstoy's expression theory of art claims that works of art transmit individualized feelings of their makers enabling their beholder to have the same feelings,[27] but some works of art (Mondrian's grid paintings) transmit no feelings, so aesthetic responses to works of art go beyond emotional responses. Formalist theories of art[28] claim that works of art evoke responses to their purely compositional features, such as their colors and shapes, in the case of painting, but some works of art have no compositional features—for example, Cage's *4´33˝*, which consists in a pianist playing no notes for about four and a half minutes. What one philosopher called "the very expansive, adventurous character of art"[29] is too much for aesthetic response to contain.

The final step was the creation of art that neither provokes nor was intended to provoke any interesting aesthetic response. Cage's *4´33˝* is an example. A more recent example is the 2001 Turner Prize winner, Martin Creed's *Work No. 227, the lights going on and off*, which consists in an empty, drab gallery where the lights switch on and then off every 5 seconds. Champions of aesthetic theories of art may either insist that these works provoke interesting aesthetic responses or deny that they are art.[30] However, the consensus is that they are art although they do not do much aesthetically, so we must abandon aesthetic theories of art.[31] Jerrold Levinson perfectly sizes up the situation:

> if one reflects on the varieties of art and art making in the past half century, one cannot help but be struck by the fact that, intrinsically speaking, there

are simply no holds barred. Anything, seen from the outside as it were, can be art .... the return to a traditional notion of aesthetic aim or aesthetic experience seems blocked by the undeniable evolution of art beyond the contemplative, perceptually based conception.[32]

After 300 years, works like Creed's and Cage's sunder theories of art from theories of aesthetic response and cast aside theories of aesthetic response as not essentially tied to theories of art. So first we stretch aesthetic response impossibly thin by using it to try to explain too much, and then we discard it when it fails. The focus is now really on art rather than aesthetic response.

This story about the tethering of theories of aesthetic response to theories of art teaches three lessons that are particularly useful to keep in mind while seeking an integrated conception of aesthetic response. First, if the tethering has hobbled theories of aesthetic response since the eighteenth century, then it will not help those who are studying aesthetic response to rifle through the classic texts. These texts may confuse matters that are better kept apart. In particular, they may deploy conceptions of aesthetic response that are thinned out so as to cover all art, and they may shift the focus from aesthetic response to art.

Second, anyone who wishes to study aesthetic response should leave open the question of whether art is best understood as functioning to elicit aesthetic responses. Many works of art do elicit aesthetic responses (especially those created by artists who believed aesthetic theories of art). Yet maybe some do not. Dissociating aesthetic response from art might allow for richer conceptions of aesthetic response. To be prudent, we had better not confuse responses to art with aesthetic responses. In other words, if aesthetic response is the phenomenon to be studied, then art should be treated as an independent, possibly confounding, factor. Aesthetic science is not about art, except incidentally.

This does not mean that understanding aesthetic response tells us nothing about some works of art, and it does not mean we cannot look to works of art for examples of aesthetic response. After all, as noted, many works of art do elicit aesthetic responses. However, if art and aesthetic response are dissociable, then aesthetic science is not *ipso facto* the science of art.

Third, if philosophers aim to analyze the concept of aesthetic response as one that plays a role in certain contexts, then those contexts surely include scientific explanations. Aesthetic science is as much a source for a philosophical theory of aesthetic response as is critical practice.

The Fragility of Aesthetic Response

Science surprises. For hundreds of years, it has adopted methods (e.g., controlled experiments) that are designed to protect against reinforcing our false beliefs, even beliefs held most dear. Anyone who reads aesthetic science with an open mind will be surprised time and again by what it tells us about our responses and the mechanisms behind them. Two examples are the effects on aesthetic preferences of mere exposure and the rule of thirds. These two phenomena illustrate how science can pay off for non-scientists: the promise of such payoffs is a good reason to seek to integrate how scientists and non-scientists conceptualize aesthetic response.

Hundreds of studies identify a number of factors that help determine aesthetic responses to images. One is the mere exposure effect. According to the textbook definition, the effect occurs when "a condition which just makes the given stimulus accessible to the individual's perception" is "a sufficient condition for the enhancement of his attitude towards it."[33] The effect has been found for many different kinds of stimuli, including sounds, nonsense words, shapes, drawings, and photographs.[34] How strong the effect is depends on a variety of conditions, including length and frequency of exposure, and whether or not the stimulus is recognized.[35] Counterintuitively, the effect is weakened by stimulus recognition—that is, there is a greater tendency to respond positively to a stimulus when one is exposed to it and yet one is unaware of having come across it before.

It might seem as if the mere exposure effect is a laboratory phenomenon that tells us nothing very interesting about what is going on when we look at and richly respond to images in real life. What light could it possibly shed on how a visitor to the Louvre stands captivated by one of its Chardins? The Louvre is not the sterile atmosphere of the laboratory, and looking at a Chardin is not much like responding to cardboard rectangles on a seven-point scale.[36] Aesthetic response is culturally freighted: it expresses and depends on structures of knowledge and critical practice in a culture, and laboratory phenomena like the mere exposure effect barely scratch its surface.

In an elegant series of studies of the Impressionist canon, the Cornell psychologist James E. Cutting brings out just how hasty is this kind of complaint.[37] Most people first see Impressionist paintings through reproductions, and these appear in different kinds of cultural outlets: art history courses, museums, books, and advertisements. Cutting first found out how frequently each work belonging to a large Impressionist collection appeared in books in the Cornell University library, and he established that these data provide a representative sample of the Impressionist canon. Given the assumption that the more frequently images of paintings appear, the more likely it is that people will see them, Cutting then measured preferences for Impressionist paintings and was able to draw several conclusions about the factors that determine variances in these preferences. He found, in particular, that the preference for a work was not explained by its inclusion in the influential collection of Gustave Caillebotte, by its display in the Musée d'Orsay, by its prototypicality as an Impressionist work, by the number of art history courses subjects had taken, or by their recognizing the work. Rather, preferences were in part a function of simple frequency of appearance. In fact, Cutting was able to undo subjects' preferences by changing frequencies of appearance in their local environment.

As Cutting sums up, "it is not where an image is, or who bought it, but how often it appears that affects public appreciation."[38] He adds that "we digest images voraciously, even without noticing. A very small proportion of these images are from the Impressionist corpus and canon. Nonetheless, we respond to their occurrence in our future interactions with Impressionism. We like the ones we have seen before."[39]

Stepping back from the details of this study, two broad lessons come into view. First, we should be skeptical of the somehow compelling idea that we are fully aware of the reasons for our aesthetic responses. We know that sometimes explicit reasoning about a choice interferes with making the choice that fits one's actual aesthetic preferences.[40] Perhaps we are better off responding without reasoning. Cutting's findings help to explain why, if part of what drives aesthetic responses to images is mere exposure, independent of aesthetic quality. This is a lesson about the fragility of aesthetic response, its vulnerability to rationally irrelevant factors. A second lesson may be useful to scholars who already downplay the efficacy of critical reasoning in aesthetic response and who take aesthetic response to be "socially constructed." If Cutting is right, appearance is one of the mechanisms by which aesthetic culture is transmitted and entrenched. Formal education, curatorial practices, and art criticism transmit and entrench aesthetic culture at least in part through this mechanism. This is important to correctly weighing the role of different social institutions in aesthetic response.

Cutting's data do not go so far as to show that aesthetic response is wholly determined by mere exposure, and some of the variance in responses to different Impressionist paintings may reflect differences in their aesthetic quality. Aesthetic responses arguably fall under norms. Our aesthetic responses to works ought to fit, ought to be true to, their aesthetic quality. If the frequency of a work's appearance is independent of its quality and if appearance biases aesthetic response, then we will tend to fall short of meeting our norms. Again, aesthetic response is fragile. That is no surprise, though: after all, we fail to meet many of our norms—moral norms, for example.[41] This means only that a significant part of understanding aesthetic response focuses on its normative dimension, and actual aesthetic responses tell us little about what aesthetic responses ought to be. Science informs us about our actual responses. Can it contribute to an understanding of aesthetic norms?

Consider the rule of thirds. Images are composed within frames, and some compositions are better than others, but young artists are not left on their own to figure out what works: they are explicitly or implicitly taught certain traditional wisdom. According to the rule of thirds, the principal object shown in an image should not be located at the image center. Rather, the surface should be divided into thirds vertically and horizontally, with the principal object placed along the dividing lines or at their intersection. This rule of thirds is widespread and well known: a Google search nets thousands of pages of explanation and illustration. Some professional cameras have an option to display a grid of thirds.

Palmer, Gardner, and Wickens recently published the results of some experiments suggesting that the rule of thirds does not drive aesthetic response in appreciating or making images of common objects.[42] The experiments reveal a more subtle interaction between the framing of an object and its orientation in the scene. There are strong biases to situate forward-facing objects at the center of the frame and not to situate left-facing objects on the left and right-facing objects on the right, but instead to place left- and right-facing objects just off center, facing toward the center. These biases are inconsistent with the rule of thirds.

So long as we can be mistaken about our norms, there is evidence that the rule of thirds is not in fact a norm and that we are not aware of the more subtle norm we do follow. Can science show us to be mistaken about our norms? A compositional rule is an aesthetic norm only if we follow it when we are given a chance and are not constrained by interfering factors. After all, an artist composing an image follows rules like the rule of thirds on the assumption that doing so is a way to achieve a desired result—a certain response. The artist has every reason to reject a norm if it turns out that it does not perform as promised.

As self-deceived as we humans admit ourselves to be, we too often assume that our aesthetic responses and their causes are transparent to us. How could a face but be attractive for its blue eyes if it seems attractive for its blue eyes? The methods of science are designed to steer us to the truth when things are not as they first appear. They are extremely useful tools if aesthetic responses and their causes are not, after all, quite so transparent to us.

A Critical Contribution

It takes two to integrate. What can approaches to aesthetic response in the humanities bring to scientific approaches? Nobody is very sure. Perhaps the blame goes to a confusion, described earlier, between aesthetic response and other phenomena, notably art. There is a danger of a missed opportunity.

To see what is at stake, consider what it would be like for science to go it alone and pay no heed to non-scientific studies. Scientific methods and explanations are not the same as historical, anthropological, or philosophical ones—indeed, psychological methods and explanations are not even the same as neurophysiological ones. So integration is not the same as convergence on a unified theory of aesthetic response. It does not even require that scholars from different disciplines share the same interests or vocabulary. It requires only that they seek to understand the same phenomenon. Therefore, science goes it alone when the phenomenon that it attempts to understand is not the phenomenon that others have in mind.

Some of the work of the esteemed vision scientist Semir Zeki illustrates how elusive can be the goal of integration, for integration eludes him although he is a scientist with a fine critical sensibility who knows a great deal about art, the writings of artists, and the history of art, and who takes pains to weave what he knows about these into what he knows about vision.

Zeki[43] begins with a hard-won achievement of recent vision science, an understanding of how the brain processes different components of the visual scene (such as orientation, motion, and color) separately and then combines these processing streams to represent the stable characteristics of objects. Inspired by this vision of the brain, he proposes that visual aesthetic response has an analogous functional specialization.[44] This gives him a definition of art:

> the general function of art [is] a search for the constant, lasting, essential, and enduring features of objects, surfaces, faces, situations, and so on, which allows us not only to acquire knowledge about the particular object, or face, or condition represented on the canvas but to generalize, based on that, about many other objects and thus acquire knowledge about a wide category of objects or faces.[45]

Given this definition, the idea is that art's search for the enduring features of objects requires artists to discover representational techniques that specifically exploit the various components of visual processing in the brain. It turns out that, in a slogan, "artists are neurologists."[46]

Note the structure of Zeki's proposal. He defines a phenomenon, art, as serving to represent the constant features of things. He then supplies an explanation of this phenomenon. Art represents the constant features of things by exploiting the functional specialization of the components of vision. In brief, his proposal has two parts: a specification of what is to be explained and then an explanation.

The question is whether Zeki's conception of what is to be explained integrates with that of other scholars. Zeki defends his definition of art in two ways. The first strategy is to cite philosophers and artists whose views are consistent with his conception of art—Schopenhauer and Hegel, Constable and Cézanne, Mondrian and Malevich, for example. The problem is that each authority who agrees with Zeki is counterbalanced by another who can be found to disagree. Thus his more compelling strategy is to survey major developments in the history of art and to show how each one reflects the discovery of a new way to exploit some component of visual processing in order to represent stable realities. For example, the emphasis on pure line in some modern art targets and activates the areas of the brain that are responsible for processing orientation, and kinetic art, such as Calder's mobiles, activates areas of the brain responsible for processing motion.[47] In this way, the specifics of how visual processing is broken down into components explain episodes in art's quest to represent the essential features of things.

Admittedly, it is unclear how ambitious Zeki's proposal is meant to be. At one point he sums up his project by observing that "aesthetics, like all other human activities, must obey the rules of the brain of whose activity it is a product, and it is my conviction that no theory of aesthetics is likely to be complete, let alone profound, unless it is based on an understanding of the workings of the brain."[48] This suggests a view that almost nobody would deny. If we respond aesthetically to color, for example, then a complete explanation of aesthetic response must include a description of the neural processing of color. (Just as a complete explanation of human social behavior must include a description of the brain's facility for face recognition.) Obviously, a fact that is merely a part of a complete explanation may do relatively little of the explaining. The more ambitious idea is that art's search to reveal the essential features of things is largely explained by the fact that vision processes features by components. Art performs its function by taking advantage of the modularity of visual processing. Only this more ambitious idea raises questions about integration.

If Zeki is right to foreground his functional definition of art as characterizing what aesthetic science needs to explain, then his explanation is probably quite powerful. That leaves open the question whether his definition of art does in fact provide the right approach to characterizing what aesthetic science needs to explain.

The power of Zeki's explanation might be enough by itself to convince us that he has successfully zeroed in on what needs to be explained. Specifications of what is to be explained are rarely fixed in stone while we go searching for an explanation. The search for explanations, discarding less adequate ones while homing in on better ones, quite often serves to refine or radically revise our understanding of what needs to be explained. Having a very powerful explanation that happens to require a new specification of what is to be explained is reason to adopt the new specification. Perhaps, at the end of the day, Zeki's specification of what is to be explained—his conception of the function of art—is justified by the virtues of the explanation he proposes.

Yet the costs of accepting Zeki's specification of what is to be explained must be counted, and some of these costs can be seen quite clearly if we think of aesthetic response in the context of critical practice. True, art critics and art theorists dispute the details of how criticism is and should be conducted—witness the recent quarrels between formalist, Marxist, psychoanalytic, feminist, postmodernist, and now postcolonial schools of criticism. Within philosophy, there are debates about the objectivity of critical verdicts, the relationship between criticism and interpretation, and the proper role of references to artistic intentions in criticism. Nevertheless, all this hubbub masks consensus on some basic features of criticism.

One feature of critical practice that is taken for granted by critics, historians, and philosophers is that the standard object of criticism is the individual work, in all its individuality. Even if two works are fairly similar, our responses to them may differ markedly. Presumably the various determinants of aesthetic response interact in highly complex ways.[49] Indeed, as a result of this kind of interaction, a feature (e.g., symmetry) that promotes a positive response in one work can ruin another work. For this reason, criticism is specific and detailed about the features of works and how they interact with each other. However, this is not something that can be explained by Zeki's proposal: every Calder exploits the component of vision that processes motion information in the same way as any other Calder.

Some of the individuality of a work flows from the fact that it is an artifact made by someone who is using available materials in order to realize some goal or goals. We respond to images as achievements. Two works that look a lot alike can represent quite different achievements because the same materials are used to realize different goals. This again is something that informs criticism and so seems to be an element of aesthetic response. Perhaps a few artists have set themselves the goal of trying to discover the architecture of visual processing, but the number is small, and criticism focuses on quite different kinds of achievements.[50]

A third observation about critical practice expands on the first two. If the aim of criticism is to communicate how to see a work so that others can have an aesthetic response, and if criticism is at least partly successful in achieving this aim, then criticism reflects some of the factors driving aesthetic response. From that perspective, it is important to see that most criticism focuses on bringing out such features of images as being elegant, chilling, provocative or consoling, original or derivative, structured or chaotic, dynamic or serene. This list indicates that images may evoke aesthetic responses in different, perhaps incommensurable, ways. This is not something that can be explained on the view that artworks function to detect and trigger functionally specialized components of the visual system.

Those impressed by the elegance and simplicity of Zeki's model may say that it explains art as Zeki defines it, and so they may set aside these three observations as irrelevant to their research goals. That is a case of science going it alone, and sometimes science is right to go it alone. One price of fixing on different conceptions of what is to be explained is that there can be no expectation that different explanations should fit together, and that means conceding that scientific results should be of little relevance to non-scientific research. The alternative is to acknowledge that aesthetic response is embedded in critical practice, about which non-scientists have a lot to say.

Fifty years ago a commentator assessing the prospects for integration commented that "some of my friends in the humanities were hostile to the very idea of subjecting questions of aesthetic theory to empirical inquiry. On one of those occasions a friend showed me a quotation from Aristotle that settled the matter for him. It was heresy when I suggested that we knew more about this problem than Aristotle."[51] This caricatures both the scientist and the humanist: humanities research does not consist in citing ancient authorities, as many scientists know perfectly well.

Towards Integration

To summarize, convergence among scholars in different disciplines on a shared conception of aesthetic response as a target of explanation is not required, but it may have benefits. The recent scientific literature suggests that some apparently incompatible hypotheses can be fit together if they are seen as explaining different parts of aesthetic response. Moreover, there is reason to think that the results of scientific inquiry into aesthetic response can enrich and be enriched in turn by humanistic studies of aesthetic response as grounding critical practices and norms—as long as scientists and non-scientists are studying the same phenomenon. Sometimes philosophy can specify, top-down, the nature of a phenomenon for empirical study. However, for historical reasons, philosophical ideas may replicate and not reconcile[5] the tensions in our thinking about aesthetic response that hinder integration. In the circumstances, integration is likely to occur only because of its perceived benefits for researchers of different stripes and only through a bottom-up, negotiated process. We close with a few pointers.

The different scientific, philosophical, and humanistic studies point to the complex nature of aesthetic response, and each cluster of disciplines is in a good position to contribute to a more complete understanding of this complexity. With that in mind, it makes sense to aim for an account of aesthetic response that is structured to accommodate each of these contributions. A good start might be to sketch an account of aesthetic response in terms of a small number of main components. To this end, we propose an integration-friendly working conception of aesthetic response as comprising affective, evaluative, and interpretative components.

Consider first the aesthetic sciences, where several groups of investigators have focused their efforts on the affective component. As a result of these investigations, we now have a better understanding of some of the mechanisms underlying aesthetic preference and aesthetic pleasure (e.g., prototypicality, mere exposure, peak shift). Other studies, for example in the psychology of music perception,[52] have even begun to elucidate our emotional responses to works. Aesthetic science is not, however, the only discipline capable of contributing to our understanding of the affective component. For example, Jenefer Robinson's philosophical theory of emotion[53] provides a detailed analysis of emotion in aesthetic engagement.

Nor is the affective component the only target of explanation in the aesthetic sciences, as some studies also set out to explain the evaluative and interpretative components of aesthetic response—that is, judgments of quality or achievement and attempts at understanding ("it's a Picasso," "it represents a face," or "it's about light"). For example, in the multistage cognitive model of aesthetic response proposed by Leder and his collaborators,[54] three of the five stages—explicit classification, cognitive mastering, and evaluation—directly refer to these two other components.

Humanistic studies of aesthetic response may prove especially useful at probing the roles of and interactions between components of aesthetic response as they are manifest in conscious experience of aesthetic response to particular works. Critical discourse draws attention to aesthetic features by pointing to the perceptible features that realize them.[55] Thus studies of critical practices attempt to tease out the apparent contributions of various components of aesthetic response as we experience and articulate it. The subtleties of writing in the humanities are no barrier to integration so long as they zero in on interaction effects that are built up out of affect, evaluation, and interpretation.

Although it might turn out to be a good strategy to think of aesthetic response as comprising affective, evaluative, and interpretative components, this does not mean that all three components must be represented on every occasion—and it is an empirical question if they are dissociable or merely distinct. It could be that none of these three components will turn out to be a necessary part of aesthetic response. To give an intuitive example, one may feel unmoved by an artwork but at the same time may engage with it on an interpretative or even evaluative level. We all have experiences of understanding a work and seeing its value, yet not liking it. In such a scenario, the presence of an interpretative or evaluative component (or both) may be enough to consider it a case of aesthetic response.

To put the point another way, we should not expect a conception of aesthetic response that is productive for research across disciplines to be given a precise *a priori* definition. The multidisciplinary nature of the task of making sense of aesthetic response in all its complexity requires some flexibility. Integration must come from the bottom up, as a result of give and take among researchers whose training enables them to propose different kinds of hypotheses as part of a larger picture.

Acknowledgments

We would like to thank Natalie Forssman for research assistance and Art Shimamura and Paul Locher for helpful criticisms and suggestions.

Endnotes

1. Leder, H., Belke, B., Oeberst, A., & Augustin, D. (2004). A model of aesthetic appreciation and aesthetic judgements. *British Journal of Psychology, 95,* 489–508.

2. Ramachandran, V. S., & Hirstein, W. (1999). The science of art: a neurological theory of aesthetic experience. *Journal of Consciousness Studies, 6,* 17.

3. Martindale, C., & Moore, K. (1988). Priming, prototypicality, and preference. *Journal of Experimental Psychology: Human Perception and Performance, 14,* 661.

4. Biederman, I., & Vessel, E. A.. (2006). Perceptual pleasure and the brain. *American Scientist, 94,* 247–253.

5. Leder, Belke, Oeberst, & Augustin, 2004.

6. Martindale & Moore, 1988; Ramachandran & Hirstein, 1999.

7. Reber, R., Schwarz, N., & Winkielman, P. (2004). Processing fluency and aesthetic pleasure: is beauty in the perceiver's processing experience? *Personality and Social Psychology Review, 8,* 365.

8. Zeki, S. (1998). Art and the brain. *Daedalus, 127,* 71–103; Ramachandran & Hirstein, 1999; Leder, Belke, Oeberst, & Augustin, 2004.

9. Zajonc, R. B. (1968). Attitudinal effects of mere exposure. *Journal of Personality and Social Psychology Monographs, 9,* 1–27.

10. See Cutting, J. E. (2003). Gustave Caillebotte, French Impressionism, and mere exposure. *Psychonomic Bulletin & Review, 10,* 319–343, for a striking demonstration of this phenomenon in paintings.

11. Biederman & Vessel, 2006.

12. Reber, Schwarz, & Winkielman, 2004.

13. Leder, Belke, Oeberst, & Augustin, 2004.

14. Reber, Schwarz, & Winkielman, 2004.

15. Reber, R. (2008). Art in its experience: can empirical psychology help assess artistic value? *Leonardo, 41,* 367.

16. Beardsley, M. C. (1982). *Aesthetics: problems in the philosophy of criticism* (2nd ed., p. 299). Indianapolis: Hackett.

17. Isenberg, A. (1949). Critical communication. *Philosophical Review, 57,* 330–344.

18. Carroll, N. (2009). *On criticism* (p. 1). London: Routledge.

19. Lopes, D. M. (2008). Nobody needs a theory of art. *Journal of Philosophy, 105,* 109–127.

20. Kristeller, P. O. (1951-2). The modern system of the arts. *Journal of the History of Ideas, 12,* 496–527 and *Journal of the History of Ideas, 13,* 17–46; Shiner, L. (2001). *The invention of art: a cultural history.* Chicago: University of Chicago Press.

21. Shiner, 2001.

22. See Carlson, A. Environmental aesthetics. In E. N. Zalta (Ed.), *Stanford encyclopedia of philosophy.* [Online] Available: http://plato.stanford.edu/entries/environmental-aesthetics.

23. Schaeffer, J. (2000). *Art of the Modern Age: philosophy of art from Kant to Heidegger* [trans. S. Rendall]. Princeton: Princeton University Press.

24. Batteux, C. (1746). *Les beaux-arts réduits à un même principe.* Paris.

25. Beardsley, M. C. (1981). *Aesthetics: problems in the philosophy of criticism* (2nd ed.). Indianapolis: Hackett, and Beardsley, M. C. (1982). *The aesthetic point of view.* Ithaca: Cornell University Press.

26. Beardsley, 1982, p. 299.

27. Tolstoy, L. (1978) *What is art?* [trans. A. Maude]. Indianapolis: Bobbs-Merrill. See also Carroll, N. (1999). *Philosophy of art.* London: Routledge.

28. Bell, C. (1914). *Art.* London: Chatto and Windus.

29. Weitz, M. (1956). The role of theory in aesthetics. *Journal of Aesthetics and Art Criticism, 15,* p. 32.

30. Beardsley, 1982.

31. Dickie, G. (1984). *The art circle.* New York: Haven; Gaut, B. (2000). Art as a cluster concept. In N. Carroll (Ed.), *Theories of art today.* Madison: Wisconsin University Press; Carroll, N. (2001). *Beyond aesthetics.* Cambridge: Cambridge University Press.

32. Levinson, J. (1989). Refining art historically. *Journal of Aesthetics and Art Criticism, 47,* 22.

33. Zajonc, 1968, p. 1.

34. Bornstein, R. F. (1989). Exposure and affect: overview and meta-analysis of research, 1968–1987. *Psychological Bulletin, 106,* 269–270.

35. Bornstein, 1989, pp. 271–275; Bornstein, R. F., & D'Agostino, P. R. (1992). Stimulus recognition and the mere exposure effect. *Journal of Personality and Social Psychology, 63,* 545–552.

36. Morgan, D. N. (1953). Psychology and art today: a summary and critique. In: E. Vivas & M. Krieger (Eds.), *Problems of aesthetics* (p. 45). New York: Holt, Rinehart, and Winston; Jacobsen, T. (2006). Bridging the arts and sciences: a framework for the psychology of aesthetics. *Leonardo, 39,* 156–157.

37. Cutting, 2003.

38. Cutting, 2003, p. 335.

39. Cutting, 2003, p. 335.

40. Wilson, T. J., Lisle, D. J., Schooler, J. W., Hodges, S. D., Klaaren, K. J., & LaFleur, S. J. (1993). Introspecting about reasons can reduce post-choice satisfaction. *Personality and Social Psychology Bulletin, 19,* 331–339.

41. Doris, J. (2002). *Lack of character.* Cambridge: Cambridge University Press.

42. Palmer, S. E., Gardner, J. S., & Wickens, T. D. (2008). Aesthetic issues in spatial composition: effects of position and direction on framing single objects. *Spatial Vision, 21,* 421–449.

43. Zeki, S. (1993). *A vision of the brain.* Oxford: Blackwell.

44. Zeki, 1998, p. 75.

45. Zeki, 1998, p. 76.

46. Zeki, 1998, p. 77.

47. Zeki, 1998, pp. 92–95.

48. Zeki, 1998, p. 99.

49. Sibley, F. (2006). *Approach to aesthetics.* Oxford: Oxford University Press.

50. Ione, A. (1999). An inquiry into Paul Cézanne: defining the role of the artist in studies of perception and consciousness. *Journal of Consciousness Studies, 7,* 64–74.

51. Quoted in Dickie, 1984, p. 286.

52. Krumhansl, C. (1997). An exploratory study of musical emotion and psycho-physiology. *Experimental Psychology, 51,* 336–352; Vines, B., Krumhansl, C., Wanderly, M., & Levitin, D. (2006). Cross-modal interactions in the perception of musical performance. *Cognition, 101,* 80–113.

53. Robinson, J. (2005). *Deeper than reason.* Oxford: Oxford University Press.

54. Leder, Belke, Oeberst, & Augustin, 2004.

55. Sibley, 2006.

{ 4 }

Triangulating Aesthetic Experience
Murray Smith

> To study Metaphysic, as they have always been studied, appears to me to be like puzzling at Astronomy without Mechanics. - Experience shows the problem of the mind cannot be solved by attacking the citadel itself. - The mind is a function of the body. - We must bring some *stable* foundation to argue from.
>
> —CHARLES DARWIN[1]

> I can calculate the motion of heavenly bodies but not the madness of people.
>
> —ISAAC NEWTON[2]

There are many concepts and phenomena within the domain of aesthetics that one might approach in a scientific spirit: aesthetic form, style, and value might all be tackled in this way, as might the very existence of beauty and aesthetic activity as fundamental features of human life. Depending on the particular focus of our inquiry, the methods of various particular scientific disciplines will come to the fore. In this essay, I will be concerned with the prospects for a scientific approach to *aesthetic experience*, which I take to be a defining feature of the aesthetic domain: to engage in an aesthetic activity, whether as a creator of art or as an appreciator of nature or art, is to engage in an activity that is consciously experienced, in an important sense; indeed, when such experiences go well, they are not merely *had*, but *savored*. They become the object of a particular kind of self-consciousness. Taking aesthetic experience as our point of departure is, for this reason, doubly interesting: not only is aesthetic experience a *sine qua non* of the domain of aesthetics, but insofar as it is a type of conscious experience, it would be regarded by many as one of the least scientifically tractable dimensions of the field of aesthetics. If, as many hold, consciousness in general is not amenable to scientific study, what hope is there that a sub-species of conscious experience will be any different? Taking the art of film as my primary example, I will argue that, on the contrary, we have good cause to be optimistic.

With aesthetic experience in our sights as the particular target of our investigation, how do we go about approaching it? One of the problems with "experience" as a phenomenon, of course, is that it is precisely not physical—at least not in the sense that we can measure and hold it. In this respect, note how aesthetic experience throws up a very different, and arguably stiffer, challenge than aesthetic form and style, both of which are physically instantiated. We can begin by considering some basic aspects of film form: all films have a particular duration and a particular aspect ratio (that is, relative length to height), both of which we can sense approximately, and measure precisely. Different styles of filmmaking will employ editing to a greater or lesser degree, a fact that (at least) informed and observant spectators will register, and that can be quantified exactly through edit counts and average shot lengths (produced by dividing the duration of the film by the number of shots within it). But aesthetic *experience* would appear to be just the point at which scientific methods lose their grip. How are we going to measure and compare, in a scientific sense, my experience of *Avatar* (James Cameron, 2009) as exhilarating with your experience of it as disorienting? Or, for that matter, my exhilarating experience with your exhilarating experience? For even where there is agreement about the kind of experience a work of art seems to prompt, it is difficult to see how one goes about investigating the experience scientifically. On one view, this is where the purely qualitative, descriptive, and interpretive work of film (and, more generally, art) criticism assumes control. Indeed, on a traditional view, such criticism kicks in much earlier in the proceedings, allowing scientific methods at most a negligible role. Critical interpretation, from this perspective, is the method that refreshes the parts other methods cannot reach.

How, if at all, can we vault this barrier lying between the tangible and the experienced? A clue lies in what has already been said. In describing film duration and aspect ratio, I made coordinated mention of both concrete features and experienced qualities: watching *Avatar*, we "sense"—that is, we know from our experience—that we are watching a widescreen film of long duration; and we will also know from experience whether we are watching the 2-D or the 3-D version. But it will take a stopwatch to establish the exact duration of the film, a ruler to calculate the precise aspect ratio, and quite a bit more empirical research to learn about the differences between 2-D and 3-D filming and projection. The key point here, though, is that the evidence of experience, and the evidence that can be gleaned from scientific quantification of duration, aspect ratio, and "dimensionality," cohere with one another. In each case, what we "sense" to be the case is confirmed, and given more precise form, by the empirical techniques. I do not mean to suggest that experience and measurement can never come apart, and that human perception and cognition are infallible. Optical illusions are the clearest counterexamples to any such claim, but there are many less dramatic instances. We might, for example, significantly misjudge the actual duration of a film, or we might find it difficult to gauge, just by looking at it, the exact aspect ratio of a given film (Fig. 4.1).

The epistemic limitations of human perception and cognition will be vital in what
follows (and are important in the more general case for an aesthetics aided and
informed by scientific methods).[3] But the fact that experience and physical form
(as established through empirical methods) can and perhaps usually do resonate
with one another gives us a starting point for our assault on Mount Experience.
How, though, do we get beyond the foothills?

FIGURE 4.1 **Aspect ratios.** Top: /Mad Detective /(Johnny To, 2007; aspect ratio 2.35:1),
Middle: /Der Stand der Dinge/ (Wim Wenders, 1982; aspect ratio 1.77:1), and Bottom:
Werckmeister Harmóniák (Béla Tarr, 2000; aspect ratio 1.66:1). Seen in isolation, viewers
may find it difficult to judge the precise aspect ratio in which a given film is projected.

Triangulation, the "Natural Method"

Here I want to draw on an approach advanced by Owen Flanagan in relation to the more general problem of consciousness—the problem, that is, of explaining the existence, nature, and function of consciousness within the natural order. Flanagan calls his approach the "natural method," and in passing uses the metaphor of "triangulation" as a way of characterizing it.[4] As a first approximation, we can think of such triangulation as a refined version of the simple, two-part schema I've sketched, in which perceptual and cognitive experience on the one hand, and the physical form of the stimulus on the other hand, are mapped onto one another.

At the heart of triangulation is the principle that at the outset of enquiry we take seriously not just two but *three* factors—three levels of analysis with their attendant types of evidence—that we have at our disposal with respect to mental phenomena: the phenomenological level (what, if anything, it feels like when we undertake some mental act), the psychological level (what sorts of psychological capacities and functions our minds seem to possess), and the neurological level (what seems to be happening in the brain when we exercise these capacities or have these experiences). In other words, we have evidence pertaining to our *experience* of mental phenomena; the *information* processed by mental activity; and the physical *realization* of the mental. Having put these varieties of evidence on the table, we then attempt to "triangulate" the object of enquiry. Triangulation involves locating or "fixing" the object in explanatory space by (to follow the metaphor) projecting lines from each body of evidence, and following them to see where they intersect. Where any two, or all three, forms of evidence mesh in this way, so each of them is corroborated. Finally, however, and very importantly, Flanagan argues that "[a]s theory develops, analyses at each level are subject to refinement, revision, or rejection."[5] According to Flanagan, then, no item within these bodies of evidence is insulated from revision or rejection, so elimination of even long-established, cherished beliefs and theories is certainly possible. Moreover, no straightforward methodological hierarchy among the three levels of analysis is established: no one of the three types of evidence necessarily overrules the others.[6] Rather, the assumption is made that while *particular* posits within each level may be shown to be false or faulty, the three levels themselves are interdependent and thus all necessary in a comprehensive investigation of the mind. Something like Neurath's boat comes to mind. Otto Neurath likened scientists to "sailors who on the open sea must reconstruct their ship but are never able to start afresh from the bottom. Where a beam is taken away a new one must at once be put there, and for this the rest of the ship is used as support. In this way, by using the old beams and driftwood, the ship can be shaped entirely anew, but only by gradual reconstruction."[7] In a similar fashion, researchers working on the mind can move around among the three levels, and they can reconstruct (question, reconceptualize) particular items at a given level while "standing" on other assumptions made at the same time, on the other levels.

Flanagan initially presents triangulation as a methodological principle, staying true to the spirit of Flanagan's argument, I will stick my neck out by suggesting that this is, if not quite the *only* way psychologists and philosophers of mind can proceed, then certainly the most powerful. Let us consider each of the three levels of triangulation more fully in this light, beginning with the phenomenological. While noting the limitations of phenomenology as a method of exploring consciousness, Flanagan suggests that "it is incredible to think that we could do without phenomenology altogether."[8] As we've already noted, our experience of things may be misleading. Based on experience, we ordinarily think that our visual system affords us a uniformly colored and detailed visual field. Careful testing shows this is wrong: only a small fraction of our visual field is in sharp focus at any given moment, and at the extreme peripheries our visual system represents the world in monochrome.[9] We are also subject not only to "change blindness," an inability to spot changes in our visual field not in the spotlight of focused attention, but also to "change blindness blindness"—that is, we are resistant to accepting the reality of change blindness even when presented with evidence of it.[10] So, odd as it may seem, we can be wrong not just about the world, but our experience of it. The general impression I have of my visual perception misleads me with respect to the perceptual skills I actually do possess, when examined closely.[11] So phenomenological evidence is fallible; but it does not follow that it is wholly false. In any event, whether our experience is veridical or otherwise, *the experience itself still needs explaining*. To discard phenomenal evidence of conscious mental experience would be tantamount to discarding a key dimension of the *explanandum*—that is, the very thing that we want to explain. So we can neither do without phenomenological evidence, nor treat it as infallible and absolutely authoritative.

Explanations on the level of psychological function are, similarly, important but limited when viewed in isolation, because "[t]here are always more functional hypotheses compatible with the facts than can be true."[12] Flanagan offers the case of "auditory splitting" as an example.[13] In the relevant experiments, subjects hear distinct audio streams in their left and right ears, but they are told to pay conscious attention to the left audio stream. Subsequent testing shows that subjects do "take in" and process information from the right audio stream, even though they have no conscious experience or memory of doing so. The orthodox psychological explanation is that information from the left channel is both decoded semantically and retrievable from memory because we attended to it consciously, while information from the right channel is decoded but enters our mental economy non-consciously, and is thus not available for conscious memory retrieval. Our auditory system is sufficiently complex that auditory inputs may be processed and memorized in a variety of ways. Flanagan points out, however, that there are other possible psychological explanations: perhaps we do consciously experience both left and right audio streams when they occur, but the directive to pay attention to the left channel results in our *forgetting* our fleeting conscious experience of the right channel stream. We do, after all, routinely forget events that we were

conscious of at the time of their occurrence. On this analysis, it looks like conscious attention comes with semantic decoding, since we are said to be conscious
at the time that we hear the right channel stream (in contrast to the orthodox
explanation, according to which we decode right channel information without
awareness); but consciousness has a weaker relationship with episodic memory
(having consciously attended to something does not guarantee that we will be able
to recall having the experience, or retrieve how we came to possess the information encoded in the memory). Our functional mental economy, in terms of the
relations among hearing, decoding, and memorizing, looks different on the two
interpretations. *Some* explanation of auditory splitting, whether one of these two
or some other account, must be correct, but analysis at the level of information
processing alone will not determine which is correct.

Neuroscience may play a vital role here, in pushing us towards one of the two
(or more) psychological explanations on offer for any given mental phenomenon.
Pursuing the example of auditory splitting, Flanagan imagines the point at which
neuroscience is able to detect a distinctive pattern of neural activity subtending
auditory consciousness for each ear. Running the experiment again, we find the
pattern present for both ears. The neural evidence would thus, in this scenario,
favor the second hypothesis, suggesting that the unattended sound in the right
channel is consciously experienced for a moment, but no memory of the momen-
tary episode is formed (even though the information contained in the right channel is processed semantically, and in that sense enters semantic memory). In this
way, the findings of neuroscience are able to constrain and direct psychological
theorizing. Just as, in Darwin's words, Newtonian mechanics provided a stable
foundation for astronomy, so neuroscience may prove to be such for psychology.

Neuroscientific evidence, however, does not straightforwardly trump phenomenological or psychological evidence. "The study of the brain alone will yield
absolutely no knowledge about the mind unless certain phenomena described at
the psychological or phenomenological level are on the table to be explained,"
Flanagan notes. "Imagine an utterly complete explanation of the brain framed in
the languages of physics, chemistry, and biochemistry. What has one learned about
mental function? The answer is nothing, unless one's neuroscientific inquiry was
guided in the first place by the attempt to map certain mental functions onto the
brain."[14] In the case of auditory splitting, neuroscience comes into play on the heels
of phenomenal and psychological phenomena—evidence that while we consciously experience only the left channel, we process information from both channels. We have something on which to hang our neuroscience; we are not blinding
poking around in the brain for just any flashing synapses.

This is not to suggest that there cannot be cases *led by* neuroscientific data. For
example, there is some evidence that the perception of left facial profiles triggers
brain activity that is not triggered by right profiles.[15] But what are we to make of
this in *mental* terms, if not by asking whether there is any phenomenal, psychological, or behavioral evidence with which the brain activity meshes: Does anyone

experience the left profile of a face differently from the right profile? Is there any evidence for greater perceptual acuity with respect to left over right profile perception? Is there any evidence of practices of perception or representation in which there are marked preferences or differences of treatment in relation to left and right profiles? Or, to take a better-known body of research that I discuss at length below, the discovery of mirror neurons – neurons that are active both when a subject performs and observes an action – was an accident. Vittorio Gallese and his colleagues were undertaking experiments on the premotor cortex of macaque monkeys, focusing on how the neurons in this brain region respond to objects of different sizes and shapes. Evidence that the neurons discriminated for movements and actions arrived, so to speak, uninvited.[16] Once discovered, hypotheses were formulated concerning the functions of these neurons, and their possible links with aspects of experience. In short, in cases where unanticipated data about brain activity emerges, the evidence pushes us to make functional psychological and phenomenal hypotheses, without which the neural activity remains theoretically "meaningless"—that is, it remains just a description of brain activity. Not for nothing have neuroscientists labeled one major type of brain scanning *f*MRI— *functional* MRI.[17] In sum, then, the method of triangulation makes an important ontological assumption. While any particular phenomenological, psychological, or neurological claim may be overturned, and while not all mental activity has a phenomenological character, none of the *levels* can be eliminated.

As we have seen, Flanagan characterizes his approach as the "natural" method— and it certainly is a natural and appropriate method for physicalists, for whom the mind emerges from, or supervenes upon, in one sense or another, the brain. We can see this even more clearly in the case of color perception, as it has been discussed by one of the original and staunchest of "neurophilosophers," Paul Churchland. Indeed, Churchland does not merely analyze human color perception as an instance of triangulation; he advances it in support of the still stronger *identity theory*—the idea that mental activity just is neural activity. Churchland begins by describing our current understanding of the color visual system in neurological and psychological terms. According to the Hurvich-Jameson opponent-process theory, our color vision depends on the functioning and interaction of neurons in the visual pathway, located both on cones in the retina and in parts of the brain. These neurons calculate or "code for" particular colors according to the wavelength information that they receive. The specific arrangement of cones and neurons that characterize the human visual system gives rise to a "spindle" of colors—that is, a graphic representation of the relations of similarity and dissimilarity among the colors that humans can perceive (Fig. 8.2 shows a related representation of the array and relations of colors perceivable by humans; for details see Chapter 8).[18] The Hurvich-Jameson theory explains why it is that our visual system "codes" for color in this way. But where, you may ask, is our *experience* of color in this scheme of explanation?

FIGURE 4.2 Timecode *(2000), directed by Mike Figgis, includes auditory splitting at transitional points, where the sound shifts from one visual quadrant to another.*

Our experience of ordinary colors is the form in which we humans register (not infallibly, but generally reliably) the complex of light waves hitting objects in our visual field; that we have such conscious, qualitative experience of light-wave length is no more (or less) mysterious than the fact that we possess consciousness at all. Churchland introduces his most intriguing twist at this juncture, however. The Hurvich-Jameson theory implies—indeed, *predicts*—that there are types of color experience that will not be triggered by ordinary perception, but that are possible given the physiological design of our system of color perception. These "rogue sensations"[19] can be triggered only by rare—and usually artificially induced—visual cues, and include our experience of "impossible," "self-luminous," and "hyperbolic" colors. The sensation of "impossibly" dark blue can, for example, be induced by focusing visual attention on a yellow patch for a sustained period (at least 20 seconds) and then shifting attention to a black patch. We will then experience an afterimage distinctly blue in hue, but as dark as the surrounding black— even though, in ordinary visual experience, anything with a hue must be lighter than pure black. Here we see "a color that you will absolutely never encounter as an objective feature of a real physical object, but whose qualitative character you can nonetheless savor in an unusually produced illusory experience."[20] Like other illusions, these "chimerical" color experiences do not veridically represent objects in the world, but arise from the layout of our visual system. If stressed or stretched in particular ways, these are the color *qualia*—the qualities characterizing our perceptual experience—that arise. From the point of view of the informational function of perception—the provision of accurate knowledge of the external world—non-veridical color experience is nothing more than noise in the system; but artists have been exploiting the characteristics of our perceptual systems for millennia.

Churchland's argument, then, is relevant for us in two ways. Although the identity theory remains controversial, Churchland's analysis supports the more modest thesis of triangulation: that our understanding of conscious experience will be advanced by seeking convergence among our three levels (the phenomenological, the psychological, and the neurological). Color qualia have been one of the prime examples used to undermine the possibility of a science of consciousness,[21] yet Churchland manages to derive predictions from neural evidence that, it appears, are borne out at the phenomenological level. Moreover, as with the example of auditory splitting, "chimerical color" experience is particularly pertinent for aesthetics. Film in particular—and the visual and aural arts more generally—trades in the creation of audiovisual experience. We might expect to find filmmakers exploiting these features of our perception, and we do. Many films briefly combine multiple, competing streams of speech or other sound, sometimes split between channels, sometimes flowing together in a monophonic field of sound. Overlapping dialogue is something of a trademark in the work of both Orson Welles and—heightened by the emergence of multichannel sound—Robert Altman. Mike Figgis' four-screen *Timecode* divides our visual and at points our aural attention, though it generally uses the sound mix to direct the viewer's attention to one of its four visual quadrants (Fig. 4.2). More stridently experimental filmmakers, including Jean-Luc Godard, Paul Sharits, and Alexander Sokurov, have created more sustained passages in which our auditory attention is torn between multiple streams of sound (Fig. 4.3a). (Outside of film, a very lengthy example of auditory attention split between two verbal streams is found in the Velvet Underground song "The Murder Mystery."[22]) Sharits is also one of a small group of filmmakers who have explored afterimage effects through the use of "flicker," the rapid alternation of frames dominated by contrasting hues (Fig. 4.3b). Other filmmakers who have worked with this method include Peter Kubelka, Stan Brakhage, Robert Breer, and Tony Conrad. The interests and achievements of Brakhage in particular, in films such as *Rage Net* (1988) (Fig. 4.3c) and *Glaze of Cathexis* (1990) as well as in his theoretical writings, are founded to some degree on an elaborate play with color perception, evoking many of the fleeting, otherworldly color experiences Churchland describes.[23] In various works by these filmmakers, we see both *representations* of phosphenic, non-veridical color experience (where imagery on the screen depicts such experience) and *representation-by-enactment* of such experience (where the film is designed to actually trigger afterimages and other entoptic phenomena).

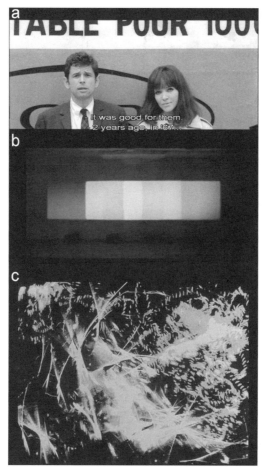

FIGURE 4.3 *(a) Godard launches two simultaneous streams of speech at the spectator in* Made in USA *(1966). (b) "Flicker" in* Shutter Interface *(1975) by Paul Sharits, an installation using four overlapping images and four separate, simultaneous streams of sound. (c) Imagery evocative of non-veridical, phospenic color imagery in Stan Brakhage's* Rage Net *(1988).*

To summarize, then, the three types of evidence at our disposal do not exist in a simple hierarchy, but rather in a tail-chasing form of interdependence. Many (but by no means all) mental activities are consciously experienced; this experience makes these mental phenomena salient, and provides some evidence of their character. Psychological evidence—evidence for the existence of both conscious and non-conscious mental capacities—points us towards the functional specification and explanation of the human mind. Phenomenology and psychological theory can both be mistaken, however, and neuroscience is one important resource for either cross-confirming and corroborating, or highlighting problems with, these other forms of evidence. Each level of analysis taken alone is vulnerable: phenomenology is elusive and intangible; psychology ungrounded and unconstrained; neuroscience blind and inert.

Triangulation, then, is more than mere pluralism, since it goes beyond the idea that the complexity of the world—and human experience of the world—must be explored through a variety of methods. It might be regarded as a particular form of *consilience*—that "jumping together" of separate bodies of evidence that reinforces the plausibility of each taken individually.[24] What distinguishes triangulation as a form of consilience is that it occurs across distinct types of evidence and levels of enquiry, rather than meshing together different bodies of evidence on a single level—as one might, say, in seeking to integrate neural accounts of the perceptual and emotion systems; or psychological theories of memory and imagination. Note also that the division of labor among the three types of scholars contributing to this volume—art theorists, psychologists, and neuroscientists—across the three strands of triangulation is not as straightforward as it might appear. Art theorists certainly frequently advert to phenomenological evidence in setting out their arguments. But they also engage in psychological theorizing, seeking to place aesthetic cognition within human cognition more generally, and they often draw upon psychological and neuroscientific evidence.[25] In addition, in the close analysis of works of art, art theorists are themselves pursuing a kind of empirical research (mostly qualitative, but sometimes quantitative), a point that is often insufficiently appreciated. It would be thus a gross caricature to think of art theorists (as a group) working narrowly with the evidence of introspection and intuition. And the same is true for psychologists and neuroscientists: while each "stands" in a particular part of explanatory space and attends especially to the requisite type of evidence, each typically engages with one or both of the other levels of enquiry.

Tracking Suspense

Let me turn now to the first of my two main examples, in which we explore the potential of triangulation to illuminate particular types of aesthetic experience: the case of *anomalous suspense*.[26] Suspense is an emotion typical of an important class of narratives, where our attention is focused on, and we experience anxiety about, the outcome of the narrative (or some part of it). Watching *Speed* (Jan De Bont, 1994) for the first time, I wonder how on earth Jack Traven (Keanu Reeves) is going to get the passengers off the rigged bus alive, and fear that he won't; suspense is just this blend of *hope* for an outcome with *fear* of its opposite. So far, so familiar. But what about those occasions where we experience suspense in full possession of knowledge of the outcome? Think of the many contexts in which this is a factor—not only repeat viewings of fiction films, but occasions when we've learned the outcome in advance through a conversation or "spoiler," and historical narratives where we already know the outcome, as for example with *Titanic*

(James Cameron, 1997) and *United 93* (Paul Greengrass, 2006). If suspense is premised on ignorance of an outcome, how can suspense arise in contexts where we seem to know the outcome? Such suspense is "anomalous" with respect to the standard case, and in need of an additional or alternative explanation.

There are several possible responses to the anomaly. Perhaps it isn't really suspense we are experiencing in these cases? We can still be gripped by sympathy for the passengers on the doomed flight even if we know the outcome, appalled at what they had to live through. Watching Roman Polanski's *Macbeth* (1971), I know just where this story is headed because I studied the play *ad nauseam* in high school—and in any case, tragedies depend upon a sense of inevitability. In cases where we know that the outcome of a suspenseful narrative is bad, our emotional state has this character: grim fascination with the unfolding of a tragic, horrific, or otherwise undesirable sequence of events. And in cases where we know that a suspense narrative turns out well, perhaps the emotion we feel is a form of occurrent, empathic suffering with the central character(s). (We will look at empathy itself in more detail below.) Knowing that things will end happily does not simply erase or neutralize unhappy events as they happen: we might empathize with Jack Traven and his fellow passengers as the bus hurtles along, even if we know that they will all survive. (Compare: when I visit the dentist, I loathe the experience even if I know that the visit will not last forever.) On this theory, then, our fallible phenomenology gets revised: we may think initially that we are experiencing suspense, but further reflection on the work of art itself and our response to it reveals that it is not suspense as we have defined it, but rather appalled fascination or empathy with the current state of a character. Our understanding of our experience is revised in the light of a fuller appreciation of the psychological possibilities: suspense is not the only candidate on the table.

Neuroscientific evidence suggests a different possible solution to the anomaly. Our perceptual and cognitive skills can broadly be divided into those that are fast, bottom-up, and "informationally encapsulated"—that is, largely immune to the influence of our existing beliefs—and those that are deliberative, top-down, and thus heavily inflected by what we already believe.[27] If we think of suspense only in relation to our deliberative, top-down cognition, anomalous suspense seems like an intractable problem—for if suspense responses are dependent on integration with our existing background knowledge, and we know the outcome of a story, how can we experience suspense in relation to it? But if we think of suspense as largely, or at least in some significant measure, dependent on bottom-up processes, then it is really no mystery at all that our minds continue to process the narrative as suspenseful and we continue to experience suspense even in cases where we know the outcome. Bold emotional expressions, fast cutting, rousing music, and clearly delineated actions stir up our senses, generating suspenseful anxiety even as we may say to ourselves, drawing on those other, top-down mental capacities, "He doesn't fall down the cliff" or even "It's only a movie." The screeching violins, stabbing motions, and the terrified faces of Janet Leigh and Vera Miles still work

on the umpteenth viewing of *Psycho* (Alfred Hitchcock, 1960) (Fig. 4.4). As David
Bordwell has put it, it is as if our senses are always "seeing the movie for the first
time."[28]

The distinction between fast, bottom-up processes and slower, top-down processes is a classic functional distinction, but it is backed up by neuroscience that
confirms that different types of cognition are subtended by specific patterns of
neural activity. Neuroscientific research on suspense should, in principle, be able
to discover what sorts of cognition come into play when readers or viewers engage
with suspenseful narratives, and crucially, whether and where there are differences
in the profile of cognitive activity for perceivers knowing the outcome on the one
hand, and those ignorant of the outcome on the other. This might point us in the
direction of either one of the two theories of anomalous suspense canvassed here:
if knowledge of the outcome of a narrative results in a marked decrease in the
intensity of bottom-up processing, or if there is some other strong contrast in the
overall profile of cognitive activity, we would have reason to favor the theory that
something other than suspense—in the prototypical sense—is occurring. However
things actually might fall out, the crucial point to appreciate here is the power of
triangulation as a method: we are most likely to solve the problem of anomalous
suspense by examining the way in which *all three* layers of evidence—experiential,
informational, and "realizational"—come together. No one of these levels is sacro-
sanct, or capable of delivering an authoritative answer on its own; but neither
should the implications of any one of them be discarded too swiftly. As Flanagan
notes, triangulation involves finding a kind of "reflective equilibrium" among the
three layers.[29]

FIGURE 4.4 *Anomalous suspense and 'bottom-up' emotion in Alfred Hitchcock's* Psycho *(1960).*

Fixing Empathy

My second example of triangulation in action concerns *empathy*. Understood as the process of "feeling into" (from the German *Einfühlung*) another person or object, empathy has been widely referenced as an important constituent of our experience of certain types of art. The concept is invoked most commonly in relation to narrative film and literature, in both informal and formal theoretical contexts. Often it is claimed that empathy with characters is either essential for, or typical of, a full appreciation of at least certain kinds of narrative. In its original context, however, as a term of art in German psychology and art history, empathy had more to do with a kinesthetic "feeling into" geometrical forms and architectural structures, like arches. If we add to this the fact that long before the coining of the term *empathy*, the same or very similar phenomena had been noted by earlier philosophers using other terms (notably David Hume and Adam Smith), one gets a sense of the central place that empathy and related phenomena have held within philosophy and psychology in general, and aesthetics in particular.

The investigation of empathy is particularly ripe for triangulatory treatment. Anecdotal, phenomenological evidence on the idea of empathy abounds; people frequently talk about feeling the feelings of others, and "empathy" is one of the words they use to label this experience. At the psychological level, over the past 20 years we have witnessed the development of a debate between those who ascribe our ability to attribute states of mind to others to an implicit "theory of mind," and those who ascribe that ability to an empathic or "simulative" capacity whereby we "try on" and seek to elaborate those states.[30] And most recently evidence for a neural "mirror system" in humans has been advanced, which many have taken as relevant for theories of empathy. The existence of a rich (if recent, in the case of the debates around simulation and mirror neurons) body of evidence and theorization across all three levels makes the concept of empathy an ideal candidate for at least attempted triangulation.

How exactly are mirror neurons relevant to the project of triangulating empathy? As I noted in passing above, mirror neurons are neurons that fire both when a subject *executes* and *observes* an action, and appear to be present in both humans and many other primates. The existence of a neural "mirroring system" in humans is significant because it provides evidence in support of the psychological theory of simulation, and the phenomenological intuition that we sometimes share the emotional states of others. In other words, there is a certain kind of psychological state in which we do not merely *feel for* a fellow human being, but *feel with* him or her. In contemporary psychological and aesthetic theory, this is the contrast between sympathy and empathy. While many have doubted the existence of empathy, questioning the reliability of our phenomenology, and the coherence of the psychological theories that posit such a state, mirror neurons specify a neural mechanism that may underpin the experience of empathy and the psychological function it performs.

According to one influential account, mirror neurons furnish us with a special route to understanding a range of motor and emotional states experienced by others, one that depends upon the "direct mapping" of neural activity from an observed to an observing person.[31] What makes such understanding "special"? In ordinary cognition, we grasp the states of others, including their motor intentions and feelings, through inference: we see a smile and recognize it as an expression of happiness; we witness someone reaching to grasp an object and we recognize their intention to pick it up. Such "cold" cognition contrasts with the "hot" cognition enabled by the mirror system, where the neural mirroring response triggered by the sight of the smile or the grasping gesture involves a kind of imaginative mimicking or simulation of the action, rather than a mere categorization of it. In each case, further downstream, the understanding of the gesture or expression, whether derived from the mirror system or "cold" inference, will be integrated with other background information we already possess about the context of action.

Mirror neurons do not provide *direct* evidence for the existence of empathy and the truth of the simulation theory. When we look at brain scans showing the mirror system in action, we are not seeing empathy. But insofar as we hold to the assumption that neural activity subtends mental activity—that the brain is the engine of perception, emotion, and cognition—we can reasonably assume that the neural activity underpins important cognitive work. And when we integrate the data concerning mirror neurons with what neuroscience tells us about those parts of the brain involved in motor activity and emotion, we can conclude that we have reason to believe in the reality of empathy, understood as a state of emotional matching and mirroring between human subjects. If the psychological hypothesis of simulation calls for further evidence to substantiate, elaborate, and refine it, research on and evidence of the mirror system is the response to that call. The case is by no means closed, but the intersection of phenomenological, psychological, and neural evidence strengthens the case for empathy. Empathy and simulation theory gain plausibility, and the burden of argument falls on the skeptic to provide some alternative explanation of mirror neuron evidence, perhaps by showing how this evidence knits as well or better with an alternative combination of psychological hypotheses and experiential intuitions. Note that in this case, even if the apparent convergence of empathy with the mirror system turns out to be wrong, triangulation as a method still holds. As in the case of anomalous suspense, the point of triangulating the phenomenological, the psychological, and the neural is to examine the extent to which a given hypothesis is or is not supported by a convergence of evidence across the three levels.

The Brain and the Body

There is a second area of neuroscience that potentially sheds light on empathy, much less remarked upon than the discovery of mirror neurons: the body of research on the brain's mapping of bodily image, vividly explored in V. S. Ramachandran's *Phantoms in the Brain*.[32] One of the exemplars of Ramachandran's "phantoms" are those ghostly limbs that amputees continue to sense after they have been removed. The significance of such phantoms extends well beyond the case of the amputee, however: on the one hand, some individuals born without particular limbs nevertheless sense the presence of a limb (suggesting a genetic basis for normal human body image), and, on the other hand, clinical and experimental evidence shows that the brain's map of the body can be redrawn, reflecting either permanent changes in the topography of the body or illusions that mislead our senses with respect to the extension and boundaries of the body (suggesting that there is a considerable degree of elasticity and plasticity to the neural map). Once more we encounter the fallibility, though not the chronic unreliability, of human (self-)perception.

This second point, concerning the plasticity of our neural body maps, probably accords with what most of us would expect: our brains possess generally accurate maps of our bodies. A neural body map is broadly isomorphic with the body that it represents; the boundaries of the body are as the map represents them. This map may be partly innate, but it is modified by the reality of the body we come to possess, a body that changes, usually gradually, over time. Thus, for example, our neural map adjusts to reflect increasing physical height (otherwise we would routinely misjudge our height relative to the height of potential obstacles—not good for surviving or thriving).[33] Common sense does not seem to accommodate, however, evidence that the neural map of the body is so plastic that, at least given the right conditions, our image of the body can extend well beyond the actual physical boundaries of the body, either giving us the impression that particular body parts are dramatically distended relative to their real size, or, equally intriguingly, that inanimate objects can in some sense be assimilated within our body image. It is this latter possibility that takes us closer to empathy.

Ramachandran has discussed two sorts of case that are relevant here. The first concerns experiments he has undertaken that show that many human subjects can be led to *sense* a table at which they are sitting as if the table were a part of their own body.[34] In one such experiment, subjects sit at a table, with their arms under the table and concealed from their view by a screen immediately in front of them. The subject's vision is, instead, directed towards the table, which is tapped and stroked by an experimenter. At the same time, one of the subject's arms, under the table, is also tapped and stroked by the experimenter, the rhythm and intensity of the two sets of movements being synchronized and matched as closely as possible. The effect on roughly half[35] the subjects tested is that they come to locate the sensation of tapping and stroking at the point where the table is being stroked and tested, rather than where their arm literally lies.[36] To eliminate the possibility that subjects reporting this effect were simply using language in metaphorical fashion, or were exaggerating the character of the experience—"confabulating" their experience,[37] perhaps out of a desire to please the researcher and themselves—Ramachandran employed galvanic skin response (GSR) measures to gain quantifiable, objective data that might go some way towards corroborating the evidence from introspection. And he discovered that GSR responses to sharp blows to the table were commensurate with those that would be expected if such blows were directed against the actual body of the subject. Ramachandran comments:

> It was as though the table had now become coupled to the student's own limbic system and been assimilated into his body image, so much so that pain and threat to the dummy [the table] are felt as threats to his own body ... perhaps it's not all that silly to ask whether you identify with your car. Just punch it to see whether your GSR changes. Indeed the technique may give us a handle on elusive psychological phenomena such as the empathy and love that you feel for your child or spouse. If you are deeply in love with someone, is it possible that you have actually become part of that person?[38]

Note that Ramachandran is, in effect, putting the method of triangulation into practice here. Although he has not set out to examine empathy, the convergence of phenomenological and physiological evidence leads him to the psychological concept of empathy, which might be explained in part by the plasticity of neural body mapping.

More recent research in a similar vein has thrown up even more remarkable results. Valeria Petkova and Henrik Ehrsson have demonstrated in a series of experiments that it is possible to displace a subject's overall sense of bodily location into the body of an alternate subject—a dummy or another person—by combining synchronous tactile stimulation of the type used by Ramachandran with the visual point of view of the alternate (relayed by cameras on the head of the alternate to the subject via a head-mounted display). In other words, subjects do not merely sense an object as if it were part of their body; rather, their sense of what body they occupy has been relocated. The effect is sufficiently robust that it persists even when subjects view their own actual body (via the relayed visual perspective of the alternate). Differentiating this experience from the experience of recognizing oneself in a mirror or other visual representation, Petkova and Ehrsson note that "in the body-swap illusions, the visual, tactile and proprioceptive information [from the alternate] is mapped directly onto the multisensory neuronal populations that represent one's own body in ego-centric coordinates."[39] Once more we see a process of "intermapping" between experience, psychological function, and neural realization.

The final sentence in the quotation from Ramachandran above takes us to the second kind of case discussed by him which may be relevant to empathy. In the cases discussed so far, the bodily image of the self is extended to assimilate objects that are not literally part of the self (plastic arms, tables, cars, and at the limit other selves). There is a "melding" of the physical self with some other bit of the world, but the literal, physical self remains the center of gravity. In the second kind of case, by contrast, the self is not only extended to some other chunk of the world, but is remodeled around it. The relevant example here from Ramachandran concerns men who suffer from "so-called sympathetic pregnancy or *couvade* syndrome," a condition that can include all the changes associated with actual pregnancy, "including abdominal swelling, lactation, craving for strange foods, nausea, even labour pains."[40] In such cases, "I" have made way for "you"—the literal self remodels itself, as far as possible (which, it seems from this case, is a remarkably long way!), on the self who constitutes the "target" of empathy. Perhaps, though, it makes more sense to think of the difference between the two kinds of case as a difference in degree rather than kind. If we are capable of assimilating tables and cars into our bodily self-image, the integrity of the self as traditionally conceived may be a misleading idea. In place of a unified self with fixed and permanent boundaries, we have a self whose sense of physical and psychological extension may vary.

What bearing does all of this have for our experience of art, and of film in particular? With the more detailed and materially grounded account of empathy enabled by triangulating phenomenological, psychological, and neural evidence in place, we are in a better position to propose and explore hypotheses concerning the functioning of empathy in artistic experience. It is plausible to suppose that filmmakers may exploit our empathic capacities in the way that they represent action and emotional expression. Alfred Hitchcock, in particular, sought empathic effects through precisely wrought renderings of gesture and facial expression (Figs. 4.4 and 4.5). More generally, many films create one or more "scenes of empathy," scenes in which viewers are exposed to sustained close-ups of emotive facial expressions, often combined with aural affective cues, apt to elicit empathic feelings via the mechanism of mirror neurons.[41] It is important to recognize, however, that the proposal here is *not* that empathy amounts to a wholesale "identification" with an empathic target character, in which the spectator loses his or her sense of self for the duration of the experience. The experiences of bodily extension and swapping revealed in the experiments discussed above require the combination of very specific, highly coordinated visual *and tactile* cues, which we do not find in cinema as we know it. And the still more outlandish cases of empathic transfer, like phantom pregnancy in men, are clearly even more complex and require extraordinarily specific conditions to arise. These more radical instances of identity transformation via empathic responsiveness to the condition of another thus have less direct pertinence for our understanding of film spectatorship, and our experience of artworks more generally.

Neural Behaviorism

It is important to stress here that neural evidence, whether pertaining to neural mirroring, body maps, visual attention, suspense, or whatnot, does not speak for itself. We must triangulate this evidence with phenomenological and psychological

FIGURE 4.5 *Grasping and grimacing as cues for empathy in Alfred Hitchcock's* Strangers on a Train *(1951).*

data bearing on our understanding of the actions, emotions, and intentions of others. An experiment on the perception of that great American institution, the Super Bowl ads, reveals some of the problems that can arise from overheated interpretation of neural evidence, without due regard for the two other levels of analysis. A team of neuroscientists, led by Marco Iacoboni, conducted fMRI scans on viewers as they watched ads for the 2006 Super Bowl and conducted interviews with them afterwards.[42] In his commentary on the experiment, Iacoboni first notes that parts of the mirror system were strikingly active during a Michelob ad, leading him to suggest that "[t]he activity in these areas may represent some form of empathic response," or perhaps "the simulated action of drinking a beer." "Whatever it is," he concludes, "it seems a good response to the ad." Presumably Iacoboni means that the neural evidence shows that the subjects were in some sense "taking on" the actions depicted in the ads (and the ads are thus "good" in the sense that they appear to be fulfilling their function).

But on the account developed here, all the neural evidence suggests is that the subjects *understood* the action depicted (in part) through that "direct mapping" onto the premotor cortex that can be described, psychologically, as simulation. It is a big further step to suggest that such understanding affects our *desires*. And the neural evidence presented tells us nothing of the total pattern of neural activity or, at the psychological level, of the relation between understanding-through-simulation and other dimensions of the cognizing of the ad: granted that the evidence suggests that subjects understood the actions in the ad in a "direct experiential" fashion, we don't know from this evidence whether they were delighted by the thought of drinking beer, indifferent, or hostile to it; nor whether they might have found the ad itself—as distinct from the action it depicts—amusing, uplifting, manipulative, or clichéd. The neural evidence here, at least as presented, is too limited and far too coarse-grained for any judgment to be made beyond that concerning understanding-through-simulation.

The problem is repeated in even more egregious form later in the commentary, when Iacoboni suggests that the validity of negative verbal reports of female subjects to "ads using actresses in sexy roles" was undermined by scans showing the mirror systems of these subjects firing up "quite a bit, suggesting some form of identification and empathy." Again Iacoboni assumes that the mirror system response goes beyond understanding and indicates an endorsement of the desires and values implicit in the "sexy roles." It is at least equally plausible that the negative verbal reports provide a valid indication of the subjects' moral stance towards the actresses—as valid as the neural evidence is for the "direct understanding" of the actions of the actresses. Iacoboni is quite right to note that when interviewed, people often "say what they [believe they] are expected to say"—we have already encountered the possibility of such confabulation in discussing Ramachandran's experiments. But Iacoboni has no grounds for the claim that the neural evidence he reports shows us that the brains of these female interviewees "seem to say the opposite" of what the women state verbally.

There is still another example of over-interpretation of the neural data in the essay. Iacoboni discusses a third ad, for FedEx, in which a caveman is crushed by a dinosaur towards the end of the ad, noting that activity in the amygdala – a brain region associated with emotional responses, in particular fear – spikes dramatically at the moment the caveman is flattened. "The scene looks funny and has been described as funny by lots of people, but your amygdala still perceives it as threatening, another example of disconnect between verbal reports on ads and brain activity while viewing the ads." Surely a more plausible interpretation of the data is that the activity of the amygdala provides us with only part of the overall story. How is the activity of the amygdala related to the activity of other parts of the brain? Iacoboni doesn't tell us. The fact that the amygdala lights up when watching a representation of a fearful event is significant, suggesting as it does that at least aspects of our emotional responses to actual events carry over directly to responses to fictional representations. But the verbal reports that stress the humor of the ad may still be fundamentally accurate—statements that describe the overall phenomenal experience created by the global activity of the brain. Again, the problem is not just the slender amount of neural evidence presented, but the very idea that brain activity speaks for itself—a fallacy that we might label *neural behaviorism*.[43]

Concluding Remarks

One other important point arises from the cases of anomalous suspense and empathy. In setting up the former, I posed the question: "What about those occasions where we appear to experience suspense in full possession of knowledge of the outcome?" Once we take into account the heterogeneity of our mental capacities—the mix of fast and slow, bottom-up and top-down—it should be apparent that there is no simple *I* who could be in *full possession* of the knowledge. We do exist as persons—that is, as more or less coherent, goal-oriented, conscious entities—but the capacities we recognize as typical of persons are built up from a host of *subpersonal* processing capacities, capacities whose investigation is the province of physiology and psychophysiology, using such techniques as eye-tracking (saccadic eye movement), electromyography (muscle movement), GSR, and, not least, fMRI and other kinds of brain imaging.[44] Most of the time, these subpersonal processes are integrated effectively enough that we can function as purposeful creatures. Sometimes the system of orchestration falls apart, however, and even when it doesn't, if we look closely enough, we can see the strains in the system—as when the sudden sight of the shark in *Jaws* (Steven Spielberg, 1975), compounded by a musical "stinger" in the score for the film, makes me jump out of my skin, even as another part of my mind recognizes that it's just a piece of rubber (Fig. 4.6).[45] Or, to refer to some examples we've already encountered, when my body gets agitated with suspenseful anxiety over the fate of a character, even though I know, having seen the film before, that character will live happily ever after; or when I experience

FIGURE 4.6 *Rubber or reality? Steven Spielberg's* Jaws *(1975).*

a chimerical color as a result of pushing my visual system in unusual ways, knowing all the while with another part of my mind that the color is an artifact of my visual system and does not correspond to light waves in the world. So our traditional conception of selfhood is misleading in two ways: it is neither as *internally unified* nor, as we saw above in the discussion of bodily self-image being extended and relocated, is it as *spatially contained* as we are inclined to think. A naturalized understanding of the self, which accepts and embraces these facts as they are revealed by scientific investigation, can also lead us to a more nuanced conception of aesthetic response and experience, which pushes beyond the purely conceptual, and sometimes sterile, debate that has dominated the field of aesthetics historically.

We cannot pick up my experience of red, or your experience of the peculiarly horrible dilemma facing the central characters in *The Wind that Shakes the Barley* (Ken Loach, 2006), with tweezers and weigh them on a set of scales. But then, neither can we directly observe subatomic particles or extinct species. Much of what we readily acknowledge as science depends on inference and reconstruction. To appreciate properly the prospects for a scientifically informed aesthetics, we need to work with a more capacious and sophisticated definition of science than high-school biology and chemistry—the dissected frog and magnesium over the Bunsen burner—afford us. To be sure, the inaccessibility of conscious experience to direct observation is of a particular kind that can't simply be assimilated with the other cases I allude to here. But setting consciousness, and our conscious experience of aesthetic objects, into this context appropriately deflates the sense of implausibility that may initially strike us when we contemplate approaching aesthetic experience scientifically. Scientific practice long ago came to encompass the unobservable and the indirect; without such elusive phenomena, we would not have the science and the scientific history that we do in fact possess. Triangulating the phenomenological with the psychological and neural may yet allow us scientific insight into the "madness" of people to match our understanding of the motion of heavenly bodies.

Acknowledgments

My thanks to Uri Hasson and to the editors for feedback on earlier drafts of this chapter, to Dominic Topp and members of the Filmies e-mail list for discussion of the use of auditory splitting and afterimages in film, and to Dom Lopes for a masterstroke in academic networking.

Endnotes

1. Darwin, C. (1987). Notebook N. In P. Barrett, P. Gautrey, S. Herbert, D. Kohn, & S. Smith (Eds.), *Charles Darwin's notebooks, 1836–1844* (p. 564). Cambridge: Cambridge University Press.

2. Quoted in Marcus, G. (2008). *Kluge: the haphazard construction of the human mind* (p. 144). London: Faber.

3. An entertaining and wide-ranging discussion of this theme can be found in Chabris, C., & Simons, D. (2010). *The invisible gorilla: and other ways our intuitions deceive us.* New York: Crown Publishers.

4. Flanagan, O. (1992). *Consciousness reconsidered* (pp. 11–20). Cambridge, MA: MIT Press.

5. Flanagan, 1992, p. 11.

6. This is distinct, of course, from the question as to whether there is an *ontological* hierarchy among the three levels. Here I make the common physicalist assumption that psychological and phenomenological phenomena emerge from, and are in that sense dependent on, neural phenomena. In that sense there is an ontological hierarchy among the three levels, though it does not follow, on my view, that (say) perception, or the distinct qualia associated with perceiving a particular low-pitched but harmonically complex sound, are any less *real* than the neural activity underlying them. For if we go down that particular reductionist path, we will need to say that neural activity is itself less real than the biochemical domain on which it, in turn, depends. And so on, as low as we can go...

7. Neurath, O. (1921) *Anti-Splenger.* Available in translation in M. Neurath & R. S. Cohen (1973). *Empiricism and sociology* (p. 199). Dordrecht: D. Reidel Publishing Company, 1973. Quine, W. V. O. (1960). *Word and object.* Cambridge, MA: MIT, alludes to the passage, and notably adds: "The philosopher and the scientist are in the same boat" (p. 3).

8. Flanagan, 1992, p. 12.

9. Dennett, D. C. (1991). *Consciousness explained* (pp. 53–54). Boston: Little, Brown, and Company.

10. Chabris and Simons, 2010, pp. 54–5.

11. I cannot be wrong about my *impression*: if it seems to me the world or my perception of it is thus and so, then so be it. But an impression is, precisely, a diffuse and vague apprehension of something, and impressions can mislead us. Daniel Dennett puts it this way: "subjects are unwitting creators of fiction, but to say that they are unwitting is to grant that what they say is, or can be, an account of *exactly how it seems to them*. They tell us *what it is like* to them to solve the problem [etc.]. . .but then it follows that what it is like to them is at best an uncertain guide to what is going on in them" (Dennett, 1991, p. 94). See also

Schwitzgebel, Eric (2011). *Perplexities of Consciousness.* Cambridge, Mass.: MIT. Schwitzgebel emphasizes the unreliable and incomplete nature of phenomenological evidence.

12. Flanagan, 1992, p. 12.

13. Flanagan refers to Lackner, J., & Garrett, M. (1973). Resolving ambiguity: effects of biasing context in the unattended ear. *Cognition, 1,* 359–372.

14. See also Schwitzgebel, 2011, pp. 98, 114–5. Note also that, in the proof, a space is missing after this sentence Flanagan, 1992, p. 12; see also Schwitzgebel, Eric (2011). *Perplexities of Consciousness* (pp. 98, 114–5). Cambridge, Mass.: MIT. Flanagan writes of an imagined "complete explanation of the brain framed in the languages of physics, chemistry, and biochemistry." But I wonder if the brain (let alone the mind) *can* be fully *explained* in these languages alone, because the concepts available within these sciences would not enable us to capture the purposes of the brain (whether or not we conceive of these purposes as simply a matter of biological evolution, or of the cultural extension of brain capacities beyond those for which it evolved). Restricting ourselves to the concepts and language of physics, chemistry, and biochemistry, we would at most be able to forge a complete *description* of the brain and its activities at the level of these sciences.

15. James Kilner, Wellcome Trust Centre for Neuroimaging, University College London, personal correspondence.

16. See Alison Motluk, 'Read My Mind,' *New Scientist* 2275 (27 January 2001), p. 23.

17. See Chapter 1, this volume.

18. For studies of color preferences, see Chapter 8, this volume.

19. Churchland, P. (2007). Chimerical colours: some phenomenological predictions from cognitive neuroscience. *Neurophilosophy at work* (p. 161). Cambridge: Cambridge University Press.

20. Churchland, 2007, p. 183. Churchland's essay is also available online, and includes various demonstration charts, enabling readers to test out his predictions: http://web.gc.cuny.edu/cogsci/private/Churchland-chimeric-colors.pdf

21. Jackson, F. (1982). Epiphenomenal qualia. *Philosophical Quarterly, 32,* 127–136, is the most famous instance; see also Levine, J. (1983). Materialism and qualia: the explanatory gap. *Pacific Philosophical Quarterly, 64,* 354–361.

22. On *The Velvet Underground* (1969).

23. Brakhage, S. (1963). Metaphors on vision. *Film Culture, 30* (special issue). Compare, for example, Brakhage's (1963) interest in "hypnagogic" colors, with Churchland's (2007, p. 182) discussion. For an analysis of the attempt to represent phosphenes and other non-veridical visual phenomena in Brakhage's work, see Wees, W. C. (1985). Chapters 3 and 4 in *Light moving in time: studies in the visual aesthetics of avant-garde film.* Berkeley: University of California Press.

24. See Whewell, W. (1840). *The philosophy of the inductive sciences: founded upon their history.* London: J.W. Parker; Wilson, E. O. (1998). *Consilience: the unity of knowledge.* London: Little, Brown, and Company; and Churchland, 2007, viii.

25. See Rollins, M. (forthcoming, 2011). Neurology and the new riddle of pictorial style. In E. Schellekens & P. Goldie (Eds.), *The aesthetic mind: philosophy and psychology.* Oxford: Oxford University Press, for a particularly systematic example of triangulation, applied to Monet's *Poppy Field Outside of Argentueil* (1873). Rollins shows how our impression of movement and spatial imprecision in the painting arises from a deliberate challenge to our perceptual ability to locate objects in space. That challenge is realized through a deployment

of contrasting but "equiluminant" hues in the foreground and background, which has the effect of defeating the neural system that normally deals with spatial location, leaving our color processing system to do the job. The "failure" of our visual system to place objects in the painting with precision leads to the sense of movement, and is, of course, anything but a failure in the aesthetic context.

26. The phrase was coined by Gerrig, R. (1993). *Experiencing narrative worlds: on the psychological activities of reading.* New Haven: Yale University Press.

27. Fodor, J. A. (1983). *Modularity of mind: an essay on faculty psychology* (p. 41ff). Cambridge, MA: MIT Press.

28. Bordwell, D. (Sept. 24, 2007). This is your brain on movies, maybe. Available: http://www.davidbordwell.net/blog/?p=300. Bordwell's title and thesis in this piece is inspired by Levitin, D. (2007). *This is your brain on music: understanding a human obsession.* London: Atlantic Books.

29. Flanagan, 1992, p. 11.

30. See, for example, Currie, G., & Ravenscroft, I. (2002). *Recreative minds: imagination in philosophy and psychology.* Oxford: Oxford University Press.

31. Gallese, V., Keysers, C., & Rizzolatti, G. (2004). A unifying view of the basis of social cognition. *Trends in Cognitive Science, 8/9,* 396–403; Rizzolatti, G. & Sinigaglia, C. (2006). *Mirrors in the brain: how our minds share actions and emotions* (F. Anderson, Trans.). Oxford: Oxford University Press. I should note that research in this area is still at an early stage, and many aspects of the theory and research methodology have been questioned. For a sympathetic but critical overview, see Dinstein, I., Thomas, C., Behrmann, M., & Heeger, D. J. (Jan. 8, 2008). A mirror up to nature. *Current Biology, 18*(1), R13–18.

32. Ramachandran, V. S., & Blakeslee, S. (1998). *Phantoms in the brain: human nature and the architecture of the mind.* London: Fourth Estate.

33. Here I take issue with the philosophical spin that Ramachandran puts on the material under discussion. "*Your own body* is a phantom," he writes, "one that your brain has temporarily constructed purely for convenience" (emphasis in the original, p. 58); and earlier on the same page he states that "pain itself is an illusion—constructed entirely in your brain like any other sensory experience." But the force of the "phantom" metaphor—and the casting of pain as an "illusion"—applies properly only to cases where there is a more or less dramatic inconsistency between what is sensed and what is physically the case, as in the classic case of a phantom limb: I still sense an arm even though it has been amputated. The "convenience" of which Ramachandran writes is, of course, largely a matter of negotiating the physical world, and generally speaking, a rather high degree of veridicality of perception (and neural mapping of the body) is essential for such negotiation. In short, the seed of philosophical idealism is present in the extension of the "phantom" metaphor from the exceptional to the standard cases of perception, which flies in the face of the multifaceted realism I argue for here. Such idealism is also at variance with much else in Ramachandran's own perspective on the brain, though I will not pursue this point here.

34. Ramachandran & Blakeslee, 1998, pp. 58–62.

35. Not a very compelling proportion, you say? What the results suggest is that susceptibility to impressions of extended bodily selfhood is variable. Some of us are more disposed than others to this experience. And it may be that there are patterns to the dispositional variation, just as there is evidence that women are, on average, more psychologically empathic than men. Just how widespread the phenomenon is, and whether there are patterns of sus-

ceptibility within and among populations, is a matter for further empirical research. On gendered patterns of empathy in relation to film, see Kramer, M. (November 2004). The mating game in Hollywood cinema. *New Review of Film and Television Studies, 2*(2), 137–159.

36. Ramachandran argues that experiments of this sort illustrate "the single most important principle underlying all of perception—that the mechanisms of perception are mainly involved in extracting statistical correlations from the world to create a model that is temporarily useful" (p. 59).

37. Nisbett, R. E., & Wilson, T. D. (1977). Telling more than we can know: verbal reports on mental processes. *Psychological Review, 84*, 231–259.

38. Ramachandran & Blakeslee, 1998, p. 61.

39. Petkova, V. I., & Ehrsson, H. (December 2008). If I were you: perceptual illusion of body swapping. *PloS ONE, 3*(12), p. 7.

40. Ramachandran & Blakeslee, 1998, p. 218. A recent study is reported in "Men suffer from phantom pregnancy," http://news.bbc.co.uk/1/hi/6751709.stm?lsm

41. On empathy and related effects in the work of Hitchcock, see Smith, M. (1995). *Engaging characters: fiction, emotion, and the cinema* (pp. 95–106). Oxford: Clarendon Press; and Empathy, expansionism, and the extended mind (pp.99–117). In A. Coplan & P. Goldie (Eds.) (forthcoming 2011). *Empathy: philosophical and psychological perspectives.* Oxford: Oxford University Press. On the "scene of empathy," see Plantinga, C. (2009). *Moving viewers: American film and the spectator's experience* (pp. 125–128). Berkeley: University of California Press.

42. Iacoboni, M. (2006). Who really won the Super Bowl? Available at: http://www.edge. org/3rd_culture/iacoboni06/iacoboni06_index.html (accessed Feb. 12, 2010). Iacoboni is a major figure in mirror neuron research—see Iacobini, M. (2008). *Mirroring people: the new science of how we connect with others.* New York: Farrar, Straus & Giroux. I should note that Iacoboni's Super Bowl experiment was not published in a peer-reviewed scientific journal, and he does not present it as a polished, fully fledged piece of research; he rather jokingly refers to it as a piece of "instant science." So I do not wish to imply that it is representative of the quality of Iacoboni's research in general. Nevertheless, since the essay was (and remains) posted on a respected website and thus exists in the public domain, and argues for a particular view of the value of neuroscientific evidence, it is fair game for comment.

43. There is evidence that certain basic features of perception, such as edge detection, can be reliably read off from neural data. The neural signature for such mental activity is sufficiently consistent and reliably correlated with the perceptual activity in question that we can treat it in this way. It remains an open question—empirically, and arguably also philosophically—as to whether neural evidence will ever be sufficiently fine-grained to be able to read off more complex cognitive states from it. Crucially, however, in such cases— whatever the degree of complexity of the cognitive state—there must be a point early on in the process where the relevant patterns of neural activity are correlated with psychological and/or phenomenological evidence that a certain type of mental activity is at stake. Without such an evidential context, the neural behavior will remain quite meaningless. For discussion, see Dennett, 1991, Flanagan, 1992, pp. 14–15, and Schwitzgebel, 2011, pp. 98, 114-5; on neural evidence of edge detection, see Kamitani, Y., & Tong, F. (May 2005). Decoding the visual and subjective contents of the human brain. *Nature Neuroscience, 8*(5), 679–685.

44. For an analysis of the way in which emotions, in the familiar folk psychological sense, emerge out of a number of component subpersonal processes, see Ellsworth, P. (1994). William James and emotion: is a century of fame worth a century of misunderstanding? *Psychological Review, 101,* 222–229, discussed in Robinson, J. (2005). *Deeper than reason: emotion and its role in literature, music, and art* (pp. 76–77). Oxford: Clarendon Press.

45. Barratt, D. H. (2004). *The paradox of fiction revisited: a cognitive approach to understanding (cinematic) emotion.* PhD thesis, University of Kent. Barratt posits a general theory of film spectatorship integrating low-level subpersonal responses with higher-level cognitive awareness.

5

Art and the Anthropologists
Gregory Currie

I saw among them wonderful works of art and marvelled at the subtle
ingenuity of people in strange lands.

—ALBRECHT DÜRER[1]

To recognise another's material culture as worthy of the highest treatment
our society accords artifacts—that is, to consider them art and
display them in art museums—is to honour and esteem
not just the artifacts but also their makers.[2]

We are familiar with the idea that a cow may be a work of art—when preserved in
formaldehyde. What about living cows? Not those that might be herded into the
Tate Gallery in search of prizes, but uncurated cows, grazing peacefully in places
with few institutions to constitute an art world, no prizes to be had, and no general
term in use that translates naturally as "art." The Dinka people, along with other
Nilitic groups with whom they share a common history, are cattle breeders. They
are highly appreciative, apparently, of the colors, patterns, and shapes their cattle
provide them with. And this is not wholly a matter of the appreciation of nature
rather than artifact, though it may be that there is a higher degree of recognition
of the natural in their responses to cattle than we associate with Old Master paintings. Breeds of cattle are, surely, artifacts. They are things we make, in the sense
that we govern, to a considerable extent, both their production and their characteristics. We do not make them in the ways that we make stone tools or computers;
we exploit natural patterns of reproduction to do the post-selection work for us.
But a dependence on natural processes of causation need not compromise our
claim to make art; think of the action of acid in etching.

Anthropologists say that the Dinka do not breed for the prized colors and
patterns—the patterns not being predictable—and that a bull with the right kinds
of markings is often castrated. But they do ensure that plain black and red are used
as stud bulls, trusting that this will result occasionally in the piebald form. Other
aspects of the cattle's appearance are aesthetically important and are more obviously a result of intentional manipulation: horns are cut in distinctive ways so as to

encourage increased size as well as regrowth in desirable patters, for which there is
a special set of terms; they are further emphasized by hanging buffalo-tail hair tas-
sels from them.[3] The castration of piebald bulls makes salient their nonfunctional
status and results in increased size and a more glossy coat, rendering these animals
even more aesthetically desirable.[4] It is stressed that "bigness and fatness are not
appreciated because they will lead to a better price at market, or to a larger meal on
the death or sacrifice of the animal: cattle are primarily a feast for the eyes, and
only secondarily a feast for the stomach."[5] Evans-Pritchard tells us that a large
hump that wobbles when the animal walks is much admired, and to exaggerate
this feature owners often manipulate the hump shortly after birth.[6] While cattle
are vital commodities for these people, a great deal of attention seems to be
paid to their aesthetic refinement, and not merely as a byproduct of other
concerns.

That attention is reflected in a complex critical vocabulary. Jeremy Coote quotes
a slightly earlier opinion on the connoisseur-like reflection of Nilitic people on
their biological artifacts:

> When discussing the colour pattern of an animal—as they do for hours—the
> Dinka sound more like art critics than stockbreeders. For instance, when
> does *mathiang*—dark brown—become *malual*—reddish brown? If the
> animal has brown patches, are they large enough to make it *mading* or are
> they the smaller mottling that identifies *malek*?[7]

Appreciation of the cattle helps to enrich the aesthetic and imaginative activity
of these people in other ways: their cattle's appearance is celebrated in song; they
delight in, and elaborate on, connections between the cattle and the owner-maker
in ways that involve complex patterns of metanomic transfer wherein makers are
ascribed characteristics by virtue of the quality of their products:

> . . . amongst the Western Dinka . . . a man with a black display ox may be
> known not only as *macar* 'black ox', but also as, for example, *tim atiep*, "the
> shade of a tree"; or *kor acom*, "seeks for snails", after the black ibis which
> seeks for snails.[8]

Personal ornaments imitate the shape of horns, while certain bodily attitudes
regarded as graceful are imitations of the rearing horns or slow gallop. Clay models
of their cattle, sometimes quite abstractly fashioned, serve in the pretend play of
children.

Universal Art

So, are the Dinka cattle works of art? There are choices open to us in answering that
question and I'll consider them later. But it's worth noting that those around in
the early days of systematic anthropology were struck by the apparently universal

impetus to aesthetic activity in humankind, and took a very inclusive view of what counts as art. Once convinced that biological things can also be artifacts, it would not be much of a stretch for them to include the Dinka cattle.[9] Franz Boas, a founder of social anthropology, is sometimes cited as an advocate—indeed, as the inventor—of cultural relativism. Yet his book *Primitive Art* (1927) sounds a strongly universalistic note:

> In one way or another esthetic pleasure is felt by all members of mankind. No matter how diverse the ideals of beauty may be, the general character of the enjoyment of beauty is of the same order everywhere . . . [10]

Nor was Boas a relativist about aesthetic merit, content to say that the works of art of all communities are good in their own ways. While he praised the work of most "uncontaminated primitive manufacturers" to the extent that "most objects of everyday use must be considered as works of art" he remarked on the lack of skill shown by painters in Tierra del Fuego and the "imperfect control" exhibited in Melanesian painting and carving (1927, pp. 23–24). Boas felt able, it seems, to apply his own taste to the products of diverse cultures, delivering judgments, at least in broad terms, of their quality. And that, despite the warnings of more recent anthropologists, is what large numbers of people interested in the artifacts of other cultures do, and have done at least since Roger Fry's admiring commentary on African sculpture.[11] We might treat this as evidence of our own uneducable crassness, our insatiable appetite for cultural appropriation, our insensitivity to cultural difference—or as an indication that there is, after all, something genuinely universal to the aesthetic values and interests of human kind. The latter view (I'll call it *Universalism*) is suggested by the philosopher John McDowell when he says that "it is remarkable, and heartening, to what extent, without losing hold of the sensitivities from which we begin, we can learn to find worth in what at first seems too alien to appreciate."[12] Art, we may say, is not merely universal, it is *open*: appreciating the art of societies radically different from our own does require effort, sympathy, and a desire to know how other people live; it does not require a fundamental shift in our vision or values.

The doctrine of Openness is not concerned only with our efforts to comprehend the art of alien societies; it's a general claim about the passage from untutored looking to moderately or highly appreciative engagement. As Chris Janaway puts it: "The untutored judge and the expert critic are on a continuum. The elaborations of critical discourse enable one to see and judge beauty more finely and in more challenging material, but should not be mistaken for an acquisition of the capacity to apprehend beauty."[13] Just as a young person in our own society, knowing nothing yet of Western art history but struck by the beauty of an early Renaissance painting, may be drawn into the world of art, learning more and appreciating better as time goes by, so someone who knows nothing of the culture of a contemporary society very different from our own is not thereby precluded from beginning a journey of aesthetic discovery. That's the view I want to defend.

Before I do, I should make some clarificatory points. On the formulation I just gave, there seem to be two components to the view: one (Universalism) says that art is everywhere, while the other (Openness) says that we are able, in principle, to appreciate it anywhere we find it. Is there really a difference between them? One reason for doubting that there is a difference would be the belief that each entails the other, making them logically equivalent. In fact, neither entails the other. Openness does not entail Universalism; Openness means simply that people have some capacity to appreciate art from wherever it may come; Universalism claims additionally that it may come from any culture. Does Universalism entail Openness? Some people, touched, perhaps, by the philosophical doctrine called verificationism, will argue that the truth of Universalism requires the truth of Openness. For it makes no sense, they say, to claim that there is art in that culture over there of which I have no artistic appreciation whatever. For what then would support my claim that the stuff in question is art? I reject this argument, claiming that we might have good reasons for thinking that something is art without being able to bring to it any of our art-relevant responses. We might, for example, identify it as art on functional grounds, noting that the stuff in question functions in that society much as art functions in ours: it gets displayed and discussed, prizes are awarded, the people of that society claim to get pleasure from its contemplation, etc. That said, I'll be arguing mostly for Openness; that seems to me to be the idea that has caused the most controversy in anthropology.

Secondly, my ambition here is not to establish the truth of the doctrine of Openness in all its generality. Thus stated, it may well be false. My position will not collapse if that is so. My point is that Openness is much closer to the truth than alternative doctrines we hear much about, according to which art and aesthetics are concepts that do not travel beyond the boundaries of recent and contemporary Western societies. It's not quite true that the Earth is spherical, but someone who believes it is has a much better grip on reality than someone who thinks it is a cube. The right way to proceed, once we have seen how attractive Openness is, is then to decide what adjustments we need to make to Openness in order to get to the truth. This will be no trivial undertaking (determining the exact shape of the earth wasn't easy either). And making the adjustments may tell us interesting things about the real limits of aesthetic generality. But I will not have space to attempt that task here.

Third, Universalism is a claim about all societies, not about all individuals. No doubt there is a good deal of variation among the individuals in any given society in terms of sensitivity to and interest in art. Perhaps some individuals have no such sensitivity or interest. Correspondingly, Openness is not the claim that all individuals are open to the art of other cultures—some may indeed not be open to the art of their own culture.[14]

Fourth, the doctrine of Openness sounds like good news: there is a whole world of art out there, and we may look forward to enjoying it. But a sensible defense of Openness will insist that this optimism needs significant qualification, at some of which I have already hinted. We can't appreciate Yoruba sculpture or Inuit face masks or Nilitic cattle to the fullest, or even to a satisfactory extent, without the training provided by substantial acquaintance with the works concerned, substantial knowledge of the techniques involved, and a good deal of insight into the broader role of these activities in the societies that nurture them. That's true of the art of our own past and present, and it's a truth that puts severe practical limits on our capacities to appreciate that art. In thinking seriously about the relative merits of the plans of Ghiberti and Brunelleschi for the Florence Baptistery doors, we would not give weight to the opinion of someone with no knowledge of the work of either artist, no understanding of church architecture, and no acquaintance with biblical stories or Renaissance history.[15] If we want help in tuning our own aesthetic responses we look to people who score highly on all these dimensions of expertise. But for all that, we don't insist that people take art history courses before they are allowed into art galleries; we don't think that this kind of instruction is a precondition for *any* appreciation of art. We accept that there is a pathway to the appreciation of artworks that moves gently uphill from wholly untutored looking through to curatorial levels of expertise, with convenient stopping-off places along the way. The doctrine of Openness says that such pathways exist, connecting any culture with any other. There are no sheer aesthetic cliffs that require heroic endeavors before we can glimpse the riches above us.

The Argument

What reasons are there for believing Openness? The primary reason I shall offer is a simple and perhaps naïve one: that it seems to be the case that people appreciate the art of other cultures, and the best explanation for this is that they do, in fact, appreciate those arts. I'll call this the argument from appearances. I admit that arguments like this need to be treated with care. We must be wary of endorsing widely held beliefs that are said to be "obviously true" and that their advocates claim to be verified in everyday experience; we need to look closely at what the supposed evidence actually is, and at anything that looks like counter-evidence, and to consider how easily the view in question sits with the rest of our knowledge, especially that which has a high degree of systematic verification through experiment and reflective theory construction.[16] But I believe one would have to work very hard to persuade a rational agent not to believe in Openness, given the extent to which it appears to be true. Simply attend any of the many museums that display the artifacts of other cultures, and see large numbers of people apparently appreciating the objects on display. You may have doubts about the motives of those attending; you may suspect that they are there because they feel somehow they ought to be and that they are merely faking an interest in and enjoyment concerning these objects. But you have, presumably, equal reason to doubt the sincerity of those attending a concert of Western classical music at the Wigmore Hall or an exhibition at the Tate Modern. No doubt there are people in all these groups who attend without enjoyment. But is it plausible that most do? And if you acknowledge that there is some degree of genuine enthusiasm for Bach or Beuys at these events, are you able to give any reasons why we should not conclude the same about attendees at ethnographic exhibitions? Do they more obviously give off signs of boredom or bad faith? And what about your own case? Unless you exercise a good deal of willpower to suppress the tendency, you will very likely observe yourself appreciating the exhibits, admiring such things as simplicity of line, apt choice of materials, unity of parts, witty representations of facial expression, etc. All this, I say, is indicative of the extent to which it seems that we appreciate the art of other cultures.

Perhaps it will be said that, in the case of the ethnographic exhibition-goers, the aesthetic delight is real enough, *qua* subjective experience, but that it is illusory: people think that they are responding to, making contact with, properties of the works themselves, but in fact are not. This is also implausible. People are able, to some admittedly limited degree, to say what it is they like about these objects, to point to particular features they find interesting or pleasing, to make comparative judgments between particular objects and between particular styles of objects. I do not think that people untutored in art history behaving comparably in front of artworks from the Western canon would be accused of undergoing purely illusory experiences of aesthetic appreciation. To think that would be a very obvious kind of art snobbery. A proper response would surely be to see the behavior as a promising beginning: worthy of encouragement, along, no doubt, with the helpfully critical attitude we apply to any learning process. To repeat: the initial capacity of most people to appreciate the art of other cultures is limited, sometimes very limited. But, and this is another repetition, exactly the same can be said about the majority of attendees at the Tate Modern. The issue before us is not whether cultural and artistic neophytes could appreciate these things better—that is true in virtually all cases—but whether they appreciate them at all.

A further response to Openness says that Western appreciators of traditional art are suffering a different kind of illusion: they are finding things to be beautiful (or in some other way aesthetic) that are beautiful, but that were not intended to be so; they are admiring qualities that they think of as intentionally imposed by the objects' makers when they were not. I admit it is possible that these objects are, as it were, merely accidentally fitted to appeal to Western sensibilities, and that they were not intended to have the properties that people find appealing. But this, too, is extremely implausible. Who would suppose, in advance of the facts, that the artifacts of many non-Western societies would, just by accident, appeal to the aesthetic sensibilities of contemporary Westerners? Did God arrange things so that objects not intended by their human makers for aesthetic delight just happen to delight us? There is something outrageously Eurocentric in the idea that we have been singled out for this special benevolence. Furthermore, the testimonial evidence we have—and I admit the inconclusiveness of such testimony—goes against the hypothesis. A number of careful and sensitive studies indicate that while the aesthetic conversations of traditional, small-scale societies are carried on in ways very different from our own, respect for skill and attention to the aesthetic effects skill can achieve—effects, that is, we recognize as aesthetic—are generally present.[17]

Of course there can be mistakes, especially when we start to move upwards towards a properly culturally informed appreciation of artifacts: we can miscategorize particular works, misunderstand the defining features of particular genres, think that an element is functional or meaningful when it isn't. These are all mistakes we have made and continue to make about art within the bounds of our own cultural history; it doesn't show that the project of trying to understand these things is hopeless or vicious.

Now I admit that, in one respect, the kind of aesthetic attention that artifacts of traditional societies are likely to get from a Western audience is distorted, if by that we mean that it is a different kind of attention from that which these objects would generally get as situated in their home communities. For it will be an attention that gives a concentrated and perhaps exclusive focus to the aesthetic properties of these things, and it may well be that they were not designed with the intention that their (intended) aesthetic properties would be attended to in so concentrated a fashion, and that may also not be the way in which people in the society that is home to these artifacts would normally or perhaps even ever attend to them. But this argument from the balance of attention, while probably correct in its factual claim, should not be allowed to unsettle our conviction that we Western observers are thereby making genuine contact with these works. It is of the nature of connoisseurship to focus attention on elements within a work that, while having been placed there intentionally, were probably not placed there with the intention that they be focused on with that degree of attention. Critics draw attention to the aptness of a Shakespearean metaphor, the balance of a line, the precise ways in which a speech expresses the disordered mind of the speaker. When we learn about these things, we focus on them to a degree vastly greater than anyone in the audience of a production would have the opportunity to do; and if they did do that, it would compromise their engagement with the play as a whole. We do this in a reflective mode that Shakespeare was not catering for and probably never foresaw. But in doing it, we are finding ways to engage more deeply with the work; why should it be different in the case of the artifact of the traditional society? Anyway, the argument from the balance of attention, if it had any merit, would apply to all sorts of interests we might take in these artifacts, including the interests that anthropologists regularly do take. When Alfred Gell, a theorist much opposed to the idea of any role for aesthetic considerations in anthropology, asks us to reflect on the fear-inducing qualities of the Asmat shield, he is not thrusting us into battle to face one: he is asking us to think about how fearful this *would be* in those circumstances, which is as alien as anything could be to the intended purpose of the artifact.[18]

Much of the weight of the distortion argument falls on the institution of muse-ums and galleries, which are said to present their artifacts in inappropriate ways, wrenching them from their proper cultural contexts.[19] But this claim cannot be treated as an independent move in the argument; it works only for those already profoundly skeptical of Openness. Those of us who think that there is a universal aesthetic sense may endorse the practice of museum display on the grounds that it is well suited to the bringing out of aesthetic qualities that, in other contexts, would be occluded or at least dampened by attention to factors such as practical use, religious ceremony, warlike intent, or competition for status. Museums can be more or less well suited to the display of these artifacts, their exhibitions more or less sympathetic to and informative concerning the symbolic, technical, and his-torical situations of their making. But they cannot reasonably be criticized for pro-moting a selective attention to certain aspects of these artifacts; concentrated attention is always selective.[20] In this connection it is worth quoting the reaction of Kwame Anthony Appiah to the exhibition *Africa: Art of a Continent* that appeared at the British Academy and at the Guggenheim, New York, in the mid-1990s:

> There *was* too much to see; the labels *were* too cryptic; some of them, I fear, *were*, as we happened to know, plain wrong. But the consensus over lunch was that the show was wonderful; and what made it wonderful was that the eye could linger with pleasure on the forms, the shapes, and the surfaces, the patination and the pigment, and engage each object with whatever we happened to know of its materials, its history, its origin. In short, we found ourselves responding naturally to these African artifacts *as* art.[21]

Appiah, I think, is as aware as anyone of the distance between the museum display and the home culture of these objects, and as anxious as anyone that their cultural context be understood. But he also, and consistently, delights in the oppor-tunity for the kind of selective focus, where "the eye could linger with pleasure on the forms," that the exhibition provides. And, says Appiah, "to take these African artworks seriously does not require us to take them as their makers took them."

Art and the Philosophers

The argument from appearances is my first and primary argument for Openness. In developing it I have not appealed to any specialized philosophical theory about art and the aesthetic, of which there are many. But anthropologists opposed to the category of the aesthetic often object that talk of art and the aesthetic is embedded in the rarified and highly prescriptive theorizing of modern Western philosophy, the unrestricted application of which distorts our understanding of other cultures and their artifacts.[22] We ought to consider this claim, especially since the present essay comes, suspiciously, from someone who earns a living by the profession of philosophy.

Openness is the claim that there is a more or less universal sensitivity to the aesthetic properties of artifacts. It is not an attempt to characterize, in the manner of philosophical analysis, what aesthetic sensitivity is, whether it is principled or rule-governed, whether aesthetic judgment brings objects under concepts, or to settle any other outstanding philosophical issue. It is like the claim that cricket balls are apt to break windows—a claim we are all able to agree on without needing to analyze the notion of causation, or defeat Humean skepticism, or take a view about whether causal transactions always involve energy transfer. Nor does practical skill generally improve with philosophical understanding. We don't hope to be better at causing things to happen by reading about the philosophy of causation, and few people are better appreciators of art through reading Kant's *Critique of Judgment*, a work often cited by opponents of Universalism as an indication of the narrowness and unportability of Western conceptions of the aesthetic. At the level of abstraction Kant favored, it is unlikely that anything he said would be of much use to someone interested in either Renaissance painting or Sepik River carving. While Kant is perhaps an extreme example, Western aesthetic writing generally is unhelpful if one wants to have a more discerning eye for, or a better understanding of, art.

So Openness does not bring to the conversation any heavy-duty philosophy of art, and the claim of some anthropologists that the aesthetic is an invention of modern Western philosophy confuses a phenomenon with philosophical attempts to analyze that phenomenon.[23] But it is worth saying in addition—though this is by no means a claim essential to the defense of Openness—that philosophical theories of art and the aesthetic may give us valuable and quite general insights into the nature of aesthetic appreciation, in much the way that linguistic theories give us insight into language production. Theories of grammar are not understood by competent speakers; if they were, progress in the construction of theories of grammar could be made simply by consulting the opinions of native speakers about why certain strings are acceptable and others are not.[24] But theories of grammar may yet help us understand the processes of language use, if the distinctions made within the theory correspond to causally effective distinctions within the mechanisms of speech comprehension and production—mechanisms to which speakers do not have personal access. A philosophical theory of the aesthetic is not the same sort of thing as a theory of grammar. A theory of grammar looks for an account of the causal structure of language comprehension and production; a philosophical theory of the aesthetic seeks an account of the conceptual structure of art and the aesthetic. But they are similar in this: neither is limited in its ambitions by the thought that its deliverances do not correspond to the intuitive understanding of those who engage in the corresponding activity.

I shall not, I repeat, appeal here to philosophically inspired analyses of such concepts as art, beauty, the aesthetic, or attention; my strategy throughout is to pay regard instead to common practices visible among Western audiences who regularly do take an interest, apparently aesthetic, in the artifacts of other cultures, to take my lead from those practices in identifying the sorts of artifacts that we ought to consider, which apparently give pleasure to audiences who attend to and reflect on such things as color, form, quality of making, elegance of design, strikingness of expression in a represented face: the sorts of properties that, considered in connection with a gallery object in our own culture, would count as unproblematic instances of attention to the aesthetic. But one philosophical commitment I will sign up to, as a decision on this issue is crucial to avoiding the accusation that an aesthetic approach to artifacts is a kind of pure, context-free—and hence culture-free—looking. There are suggestions of this view—the one I am going to reject—in various philosophically influenced systems: one thinks in this context of such notions as aesthetic distance, disinterested contemplation, the independence of aesthetic judgment from concepts, and the supposed dependence of aesthetic features on such "appearance properties" as color and shape, volume, and texture.[25] Within the world of art theory and practice something like this view was pressed by Clement Greenberg as part of his advocacy of abstract expressionism; Greenberg especially emphasized the idea of taste as a kind of context-free sensitivity to the appearances of things. This view, often called *formalism*, offers a relatively thin account of the aesthetic domain: it says that once you know exactly what the object looks like, you know everything on which its correct aesthetic characterization depends. According to formalism, what is available to be appreciated in art is entirely a function of what can be seen in it.[26] Thus a popular response to the discovery of forgery in art is to declare those who would remove the offending item from the gallery walls to be snobs, on the grounds that the work "does not look any different after the discovery from the way it looked before." Generalizing formalism about the visual arts to other areas, we may say that what matters in music is the notes played and how they are sounded, not who wrote the piece, when, and under what circumstances; what matters for the novel is the words on the page, not the genre to which it belongs or the literary influences on its author.

The formalist will say that the act of looking or hearing or reading is something that involves attention, concentration, and acuity, and so is a matter of improvable skill; we are not all, automatically, highly competent interpreters and judges of art, even on the minimalist account. But those with normally developed senses and, for literature, basic literacy count at least as beginners in the looking, hearing, or reading stakes, and we are all thus provided with a ticket for entry into the world of art, as Openness requires. So formalism sounds like a good bet for anyone keen to promote Openness. Indeed, Arthur Danto argues that formalist thinking in the 20th century was influential in creating a more inclusive idea of aesthetic activity, de-emphasizing the ideas of canon and tradition that previously isolated Western art from the arts of other cultures, and encouraging the inclusion of those arts within the horizon of taste.[27]

But the cost of this formalist justification for openness is the severing of art from its religious, symbolic, and sometimes utilitarian background—a pretence that artworks are "pure appearances" made wholly for appearance's sake. And the effect of that is an impoverishment, not an enhancement, of the work's aesthetic richness. Of course there is something true in the formalist's claim. On anyone's account, the look of the picture, the sound of the symphony, the text of the novel are highly important to appreciating the work. Let's say that acquaintance with these things is acquaintance with the *appearance* of the work, where the appearance, overall, of the work is given by the totality of its *appearance-properties*— properties such as color and shape properties for painting, and word order and spelling for literature. Acquaintance with the appearance of the work is a necessary condition for appreciation. It can be rational to believe that a painting you have never seen is beautiful—you might have been told that it is by an extremely reliable judge of these matters, and in this area as in others, knowledge can be transferred by testimony. But belief is not appreciation; to appreciate the work, you have to see it. The question at issue is whether appearance *on its own* determines the aesthetic properties of the work.[28]

Surely it does not. As people have often pointed out, it's possible (I emphasize the word "possible"; it certainly isn't likely) for a paint spillage to result in something visually indistinguishable from an Old Masters painting, or perhaps (a bit more plausibly) a Morris Louis abstract. The paint spillage that looked exactly like a work of art would be astonishing and no doubt the source of endless interest; it might even be beautiful in the way that a sunset or landscape is for those of us who don't see the Maker's hand in nature, though it is more likely to be regarded as simply bizarre. But it would not be a work of art, and it would not have the kind of aesthetic appeal that we associate with art rather than with nature. In particular, it would not be in any sense an achievement, and I believe that the idea of achievement is fundamental to our most basic and most universal sense of value in art. Artworks are essentially vehicles for the manifestation of skill, imagination, insight, and other admired traits; that is why we are often concerned with expression in art, for we recognize art as a pre-eminently efficient means by which a person's qualities and dispositions are expressed.[29] The psychologist Nick Humphrey puts the point well:

> We love beauty through the medium of our senses, but at the same time what we love is obviously *not merely the sensory stimulus as such*. With cheesecake, we have only to have the stimulus on our tongue and the right affective buttons will be pressed. But with beauty it's not so straightforward. For a start we often need to be told that this *is* beauty, before we will respond to it at all. . . We care deeply about *genuineness and authenticity*. While we find a copy of a slice of cheesecake just as tasty as any other version, we find a reproduction of a Rembrandt less valuable—and surely less beautiful— than the original. While we enjoy the cheesecake for its gustatory qualities without thinking to ask who or what made it, we marvel at the cave paintings at Lascaux only because we believe they were made by human beings— and if it were to turn out they'd been created by a freak flood they'd become merely quaint.[30]

It would be wrong to conclude from this that artworks are merely instruments by which we gain access to the really valuable personal qualities they express. We do value the work itself.[31] There is a difference between purely instrumental value and the derived but intrinsic value I claim is possessed by artworks. Consider a poorly composed, dark, and out-of-focus photograph of a loved one. In such a case the photograph is of instrumental value only, and is considered a mode of access to the really valuable thing, the person. Works of art, by contrast, are objects that have their own value, but it is value they have by virtue of the activity that went into their production, and if it turns out that they are natural or accidental products they cease to be accorded that kind of value, whatever other value they may have. (I'll say more about photographs in this connection later.) To understand such varied qualities as artistic vision, originality, sensitivity to tradition, and respect for the medium, we have to do more than simply be exposed to the work's appearance, even if we know already that it is a work, and not a spillage. We need to know a great deal about its art historical context: its genre, its place in historical development, its role in a magical or religious belief system, its place in the artist's oeuvre, what the artist was trying to do, the techniques available to him or her. That in broad outline is the contextualist's position, and I agree with it.

Artworks as Traces

It is these historical-cultural aspects of context that philosophers have so rightly emphasized recently.[32] But this emphasis might be taken to imply that works are closed to us when we lack this kind of specialized knowledge, which is not after all easily come by, and hence as an indication that Contextualism is inconsistent with Openness. This, I will argue, is an unnecessarily pessimistic conclusion. While it is true that one cannot arrive at an excellent critical grasp of a work and its qualities without this sort of historically and culturally specific understanding, there is a more broadly human context in which we as observers participate by virtue of our common bodily nature. This participation does not depend on propositional knowledge: knowing that such-and-such is the case. Rather, it provides the scaffolding around which our propositionally represented understanding and appreciation of artworks may grow. Many linguists say that for all the apparent divergence between human languages, they actually have a good deal in common, since all must conform to the constraints set by our first-language acquisition mechanism. This is a controversial view, but I suggest that something like it can be said of human aesthetic sensibility: while it is a response to forms that seem bewilderingly varied, it is constrained by universal facts about our bodily constitution; Martians with quite different bodies may have aesthetic experiences and values that are closed to us, while ours are unavailable to them.[33] The connection with art that this provides—preconceptual, bodily based, and partly invisible to consciousness—is enough, I think, to allow us to say that the arts of cultures of which we know little or nothing are, while not immediately transparent, also not locked in a safe marked "do not open before passing Ethnography 401."

How does this pre-theoretical engagement with the work operate? In the arts I am considering here, where our focus is on physical artifacts, visual engagement is primary: we see the object, and in typical museum conditions we are unlikely to get further than seeing. But what we see is not simply patterns of color and shape. We see traces of human activity. Western art-historical scholarship has long recognized something of this, notably the power of the drawn line as a mark or trace of the artist's activity, a power that has encouraged talk of the line as emblematic of the artist's genius.[34] But in most plastic art-making practices we see traces of the artist's activity, most obviously in brushstrokes, or marks on surfaces that record the process of shaping of solid material (an issue I'll return to when I consider the origins of aesthetic activity), or in the pattern of a woven basket, blanket, or rug, all of which, being three-dimensional structures rather than mere patterns on a surface, provide a detailed record of the maker's activity.[35]

What, then, is our response to the seeing of these traces of activity? It is a kind of bodily resonance with that very activity, what Vittorio Gallese, one of the discoverers of mirror neurons, calls "intercorporeity—the mutual resonance of intentionally meaningful sensory-motor behaviours."[36] It is not that we actually start to move our bodies in response to the sight of a striking artifact—or if we do, that is not the response I am indicating. The movements I am speaking of are sometimes said to be imagined, though this gives a misleading impression of control, clarity, and determinacy as to their nature. Neuroscientists, who have a great deal of interest in these processes, and well beyond the aesthetic realm, sometimes call them implicit or simulated movements. And neural mechanisms that underlie this are currently under investigation. Gallese has hypothesized that a related neural system, the so-called canonical neurons, is implicated in our responses to art. These neurons fire when we grasp an object, but also when we merely see an object that could be grasped. It seems that we respond to objects and the opportunities for action they present—their affordances, in Gibson's terms—by mentally simulating the grasping of them.[37] The pathology called utilization behavior, in which people will pick up and drink from a glass of water if one is presented, whether thirsty or not, is thought to result from a breakdown of the systems that normally keep these implicit graspings "off line."[38]

In addition to experiencing imagined (I'll go on using this not-quite-appropriate term in the absence of anything better) interactions with affordance-providing objects, we also, it seems, are capable of reliving the movements that shaped the object. Recent work in neuroscience confirms the idea that seeing the result of a person's behavior can provoke an imagined or simulated movement of a kind that reproduces the behavior. It has been shown that exposure to handwriting produces activation in areas of motor cortex that are used in the writing of letters; this activation constitutes a simulated movement that, if really executed, would produce the letter; this is part of the explanation of how, with surprising ease, we read words into very un-word-like squiggles. Gallese suggests that similar patterns of activation underpin our sense of the actions undertaken by artists—the work of Pollock and Giacometti being vivid examples.

This system of responses is one that allows development and training. Brain-scanning studies show that dancers respond more strongly in these ways to the sight of people dancing than do non-dancers, and a parallel point holds, not surprisingly, of the imagined movements we undertake when we hear a piano being played.[39] But the system itself is a primitive one in that it is (a) present to some degree in all normally developing subjects irrespective of the idiosyncrasies of upbringing, education, and experience and (b) apt to operate without initiation or control by the subject, though we can also initiate imagined movements at will, as when experimenters ask us to imagine moving our hands in certain ways, or tapping our fingers at a certain rate.

These imagined movements, while often acknowledged on reflection by sub-jects as part of their artistic experience, are generally recessive and hard to describe. They have been largely ignored through the last 100 years of otherwise strenuous aesthetic thinking, partly perhaps because they do not easily submit to articulation within a subtle language of criticism; witness Berenson's somewhat mechanical insistence on "tactile values" as the key to appreciating early Renaissance art.[40] A more austere mood has prevailed through most of the 20th century, exemplified in otherwise divergent theoretical stances: the varieties of formalism; the emphasis emerging in anthropology on an intellectualized notion of symbolic meaning; certain approaches to abstract expressionism that insisted—Greenberg again—on a purely visual engagement freed from the illusion of solid space. And, as I have noted, the philosophers' emphasis on context outlined above has been framed in terms of propositional knowledge rather than, as here, in terms of affinity of bodily disposition.

We await, I think, a serious empirical study of the role of these implicit move-ments on our aesthetic sense, but a reasonable projection from current research would be this: that they give rise, first of all, to a strong bodily sense of the artifac-tuality of the object and to a representation of its manner of making; to a sense—again preconceptual and nonpropositional—of the physical skills and levels of effort and concentration involved. In this way the object, through its retention of traces of making, is expressive of its maker's activity—an important feature, I have claimed, in our response to art and one that is, to some degree, independent of specialized knowledge.[41]

The idea that art's value partly resides in its being a trace of the maker's activity goes some way towards explaining the controversial status that photography has enjoyed, or suffered from, throughout its 170-year history. What is distinctive of photography, compared to painting, is that it collapses the distinction between representation and trace. A painting or other "hand-made" image is both a representation—in fact a depiction—of its subject and a trace of the artist's activity. Even where the picture is a self-portrait, there is a distinction to be made between the marks on the paper *qua* elements in the depiction of the subject, and those same marks *qua* traces of the artist's activity. But the relation between the trace-features of a photograph and what it represents is more intimate: the surface features of the photograph are traces of the person who stood in front of the camera, not of the photographer's activity, and the photograph represents whoever it does represent by virtue of being a trace of that person.

Art and the Extension of Agency

Suppose an anthropologist, previously hostile to the idea of a universal aesthetic sense, accepts my arguments. She might respond by saying that the conclusion just isn't of any interest to anthropology, since the concern of the anthropologists is with cultural difference. In response to this two things must be said. The first is that an interest in difference, legitimate though it may be, ought not to be built on a denial of universality, if the claim of universality is true. If something is true, it ought not to be denied. The second is that an interest in difference must also be an interest in sameness. One may be interested in the differences between triangles, but only so long as one is aware of the necessary similarities between them; it will be a waste of time to look for differences in number of sides, for instance. And if one is interested in difference, one is interested in the degree of difference. But that can be assessed only by having a view about the ways in which things are not different.[42]

But this is rather too abstract for comfort. Let us make the argument for the anthropological relevance of the aesthetic more concrete. Throughout, I've emphasized the connection between art objects and the agency behind the object, a connection described here largely in terms of expression. Our enjoyment and understanding of Renaissance painting, or Yoruba sculpture, or just about anything artifactual, depends on our sense—in its most basic form a bodily sense—that the object in question is the result of a deliberate and skilful act of making. I want now to connect this idea with another, which I take, paradoxically, from a determined opponent of the aestheticization of artifacts from non-Western societies, Alfred Gell. Gell argued that artworks need to be understood primarily as devices for extending the powers of agents.[43] This, as he sees it, is an alternative—a much better alternative—to the view that artworks should be understood, by the anthropologist, as aesthetic. I shall argue that Gell's case for the power of art objects as extensions of agency is made stronger by appeal to the ideas I have outlined concerning the expressive connection between art and artist, and that his case supports, rather than undermines, an aesthetic approach to art.

How are our views related? I have been saying something about the *input* side, while Gell is concerned with the *output* side. My thesis was that art attracts us because it is the upshot or terminus of the artist's activity; Gell is focusing on the way in which art is a cause rather than an effect, a cause that extends the powers of agents. But the connection here is not hard to see. For objects that are the outcomes of agency, and that are highly expressive of that agency, can be expected to carry with them some of the authority of the agent, and therefore to have, themselves, causal powers by virtue of their being thus expressive. Let us consider an example of how this works. Gell discusses the Asmat, a New Guinean tribe living in what is now Irian Jaya, whose warlike practices once involved the use of long, body-protecting shields covered with remarkable designs.

Gell says that such an object is "indisputably a work of art of the kind interesting to the anthropologist, but its aesthetic properties (for us) are totally irrelevant to its anthropological implications." For warriors were not interested in the aesthetics of an opponent's shield; it was there to frighten others. "Anthropologically, it is not a 'beautiful' shield, but a fear-inducing shield" (p. 6). But there is no contradiction in holding one and the same shield to be both beautiful and fear-inducing.[44] Indeed, it is a very natural thought that the shield is fear-inducing partly *because* it is beautiful (note that beauty is not the same as prettiness). Of course context matters a great deal here; the same design displayed in a harmonious situation would not be fear-inducing. The point is that the design is apt to induce fear in the right circumstances, and apt to do so because its design, particularly in regard to the use of jagged lines and strong verticals, is expressive of personal characteristics that, in the right circumstances, would be fearful.[45] Of course strong verticals and jagged lines don't automatically make for beauty; the beauty here is a function of the overall "skewed" symmetry of the piece, the evident quality of the craftsmanship, and other factors that, as always, are not easy to localize—we recognize beauty more easily than we are able to analyze it. But the beauty of the design and execution add to the sense of confidence and power the piece expresses, and hence contributes to its fearful impression. Gell seems to be close to making this point himself when he observes that "their [Asmat shield] designs seem to have been composed in a mood of terror" (p. 31). At least, he recognizes here that there is an importantly expressive element in the power of the work; for expression is generally a matter of something *seeming* to arise from a certain quality of mind or person, as sad music seems, at least, to emanate from a sad person, even though it probably didn't. But he is surely wrong to think that what is expressed is *terror*, and his efforts to bolster this hypothesis only make things worse. An attacking tiger, an enraged opponent, and an Asmat shield all look "terrified," he says, creating terror in the victims by convincing them that they see their own terror reflected back. It's surely much more plausible to say that the shield (as well as the opponent and the tiger) look *terrifying*, and so we are terrified by them. And the shield does that by seeming to be expressive of characteristics that, in the circumstances of a battle at least, would warrant terror.

This way of seeing the matter suggests that aesthetic considerations sometimes play a significant role in anthropological explanation; things are powerful, sometimes, partly because they are beautiful. More specifically, they are powerful partly because they have that peculiar beauty that is produced by skilful agency and that, through the exercise of that skill, manages to express personal qualities we associate with power.

Art: A Postscript

Throughout this essay I have used the word "art" without much thought as to the delimitation of its meaning, and merely in conformity with the admittedly very loose usage of Boas. But anthropologists opposed to an aesthetic approach to art sometimes take as liberal—or more liberal—an approach; Gell defines art as, roughly, an index of social agency. This would include any artifact and, he says, anything found but displayed.[46] We ought, surely, to do better than this.

While some categorizations seem too inclusive to be useful, it is unlikely that any one restriction will be uniquely best. One way "art" is currently used by philosophers is to name the domain of things that exist within a certain institutional setting, which they call the art world, and which contains many things that do not have, and were not intended to have, significantly aesthetic properties; this approach claims as an advantage for itself that it includes the work of conceptual artists (so-called) that an aesthetically based account of art would struggle with.[47] If we adopt the institutional theory, little of what I have discussed here counts as art. And much of what would then count as art would certainly provide counter-examples to Openness. I do not claim that someone from a culture very different from our own would have any initial access to what, if anything, is worth appreciating in the works of Joseph Kosuth or Robert Barry. These are, arguably, objects that depend for their interest wholly on a specific cultural background and do not appeal to an aesthetic sense. And while it is sometimes claimed that works of these kinds take their place within the domain of art by being counter-aesthetic works—works consciously and manifestly created as critical responses to the notion of the aesthetic—and hence as intimately related to the concept of the aesthetic, they would not be aesthetic works of the kind to which we are given the kind of intuitive and body-based initial access I have described; they are works whose relation to the aesthetic is argumentative, and for such works no such pre-theoretical access seems to be helpful.

But we can use the term "art" to tag items that *are*, to some significant degree, aesthetically fashioned. Going further, we might propose the following: we'll call things art when they are significantly aesthetic artifacts made within a social context that recognizes the practice of aesthetic production, thereby making a tradition of that practice; that is how, roughly speaking, the term is used in much anthropological discussion. That recognition may come about through the institutions of religion, through magical and symbolic practices, through the creation of a critical terminology, through the creation of an acknowledged class of artists, or in some other way. Such a definition would allow the Dinka's cows as art; their practices certainly seem to constitute a tradition. We can refine further: think of the emphasis I have given to the idea of aesthetic artifacts being expressive of their makers' qualities partly through their displaying traces of their makers' activities. Adding a clause to the effect that the artifacts concerned should bear significant expressive traces of making would get rid of the cows; they are just too "natural"-looking to meet this condition.

At this point we reach about as restrictive a definition as we could go for if we want a notion of art for which Universalism is true. Once we start requiring art be the object of disinterested attention, or to have been made with a purely aesthetic purpose, or to be the product of a person specially designated as an artist, we move into territory occupied by a very limited range of communities. There is no arguing, in the abstract, about which of these definitions is right; it depends on our purpose. The interest of Universalism and of Openness depends on the fact that—I claim—there are ways of conceiving art that make those claims true.

Acknowledgments

In writing this paper I have benefited from discussions with Andrew Hirst, and from a reading of Peter Lamarque's Palaeolithic cave painting: a test case for transcultural aesthetics, in T. Heyd & J. Clegg (Eds.), *Aesthetics and rock art*. Ashgate, 2005. I am also grateful for the comments of Howard Morphy, Arthur Shimamura, and an anonymous referee.

Endnotes

1. On seeing works sent by Moctezuma to Charles V; quoted in Danto (1998). *After the end of art* (p. 109). Princeton, NJ: Princeton University Press. As I write, some of the same objects are on display in the British Museum's exhibition, *Moctezuma: Aztec Ruler*.

2. Eaton, A. W., & Gaskell, I. (2009). Do subaltern artifacts belong in museums? In J. Young & C. Brunk (Eds.), *The ethics of cultural appropriation*. Malden, MA: Wiley-Blackwell.

3. Coote, J. (1994). "Marvels of everyday vision": the anthropology of aesthetics and the cattle-keeping Nilotes. In J. Coote & A. Shelton (Eds.), *Anthropology, art, and aesthetics* (Oxford Studies in the Anthropology of Cultural Forms, p. 253). Oxford: Clarendon Press.

4. Coote, 1994, p. 252.

5. Coote, 1994, p. 254.

6. Evans-Pritchard, E. E. (1940). *The Nuer: a description of the modes of livelihood and political institutions of a Nilotic people*. Oxford: Clarendon Press.

7. Ryles, J. (1982). *Warriors of the White Nile: the Dinka* (p. 92). Amsterdam: Time-Life. Quoted in Coote, 1994, p. 251.

8. Coote, 1994, p. 256, citing Lienhardt, G. (1961). *Divinity and experience: the religion of the Dinka*. Oxford: Clarendon Press.

9. Though that modern universalist about art, Denis Dutton, says, "The Dinka of East Africa have almost no visual art, but have a highly developed poetry, along with a

connoisseur's fascination with the forms, colours and patterns of the natural markings on the cattle they depend on for their livelihoods." Dutton, D. (2009). *The art instinct* (p. 30). Oxford University Press.

10. Boas, F. (1928). *Primitive art* (p. 9). Harvard University Press.

11. See Fry, R. (1920). Negro sculpture. In R. Fry. *Vision and design*. Fry's essay was written in response to an exhibition of African sculpture seen in London in 1920 and was very influential. Items from Fry's own collection of African and Oceanic works may be seen in the Courtauld Gallery, London.

12. McDowell, J. (1983). Aesthetic value, objectivity and the fabric of the world. In E. Schaper (Ed.), *Pleasure, preference & value* (p. 3). Cambridge University Press.

13. Janaway, C. (1997). Kant's aesthetic and the "empty cognitive stock." *Philosophical Quarterly, 47,* 459–476.

14. On this see Buller, D. (2005). Chapter 8 in *Adapting minds.* Cambridge, MA: MIT Press.

15. For the view that the aesthetic opinions of experienced judges converge, and an argument from this to the objectivity of aesthetic attributions, see Slote, M. (1971). The rationality of aesthetic value judgments. *Journal of Philosophy, 68*(22), 821–839.

16. Note in this connection the work of social psychologists who have challenged the very widespread (perhaps universal) belief in personal character and its role in explaining behavior. For references and discussion relating character to the literary arts, see Currie, G. (2010). Chapters 10 and 11 in *Narratives and narrators.* Oxford University Press.

17. See, for example, Howard Morphy's study of the Yolngu concept of *bir'yun* (Morphy, H. [1992]. From dull to brilliant: the aesthetics of spiritual power among the Yolngu. In J. Coote & A. Shelton [Eds.], *Anthropology, art and aesthetics.* Oxford University Press); on delicacy, proportion, and other aesthetic criteria among the Yoruba, see Thompson, R. F. (1973). Yoruba artistic criticism. In W. d'Azevedo (Ed.), *The traditional artist in African societies.* Bloomington: Indiana University Press. See also Coote, 1994, on *dheeng,* a concept with broad, partly aesthetic connotations for the Dinka.

18. See Gell, A. (1998). Chapter 1 in *Art and agency.* Oxford University Press. As Howard Morphy reminds me, Gell's position is not representative of much anthropological opinion.

19. See, for example, Price, S. (1989). *Primitive art in civilized places.* University of Chicago Press. Much of Price's argument, highly critical of Western curatorial and interpretive practices, can be read as an argument for a universal aesthetic, or at least as countering certain anti-universalistic presumptions, though Price might not see it that way. She points, for example, to the invocation of images of the primitive, the erotic, the symbolically charged, and the anonymously collective that serve to distance the aesthetic of people in small-scale societies from our own (see discussion of the Maroons in Price, S. [2001]. *Primitive art in civilized places,* ed. 2. University of Chicago Press).

20. For an excellent defence of the display of artifacts from other cultures in museums, see Eaton & Gaskell, 2009.

21. Appiah, K. A. (April 24, 1997). *New York Review of Books,* pp. 46–51

22. See, for example, Gell, who tells us that the " 'aesthetic attitude' is a specific historical product of the religious crisis of the Enlightenment and the rise of Western science . . . [that brought about] the separation between the beautiful and the holy" (Gell, 1998, p. 97).

23. This point is well made by Coote, 1994, p. 248.

24. Chomsky has claimed that grammar is "tacitly" understood by speakers, that they have "unconscious" knowledge of the principles of grammar (see, e.g., Chomsky, N. [1986]. *Knowledge of language* [p. 270]. New York: Praeger). Chomsky would not claim that speakers are thereby able to articulate those principles. In my view subjects equipped with normal aesthetic sensitivities do not even have tacit knowledge of the principles (if any) that underlie their responses. For the view that it is the same with language, see Devitt, M. (2006). *Ignorance of language.* Oxford University Press.

25. This last doctrine is often associated with the philosopher Frank Sibley (see, e.g., Walton, K. [1970]. Categories of art. *Philosophical Review, 79,* 334–367). For Sibley's own exposition see Chapters 1 and 3 of Sibley, F. (2001). *Approaches to aesthetics* [J. Benson et al., eds.]. Oxford University Press.

26. There are other versions of formalism, and not all are committed to this principle.

27. "Modernism enfranchised 'exotic art' by liberating its viewers for the obligation to narrativise it" (Danto, 1998, p. 110). It is partly this formalist denial of context that Sally Price is responding to—very negatively—in *Primitive art in civilized places* (see especially Chapter 1). Howard Morphy relates how the Yolnhu artist Narritjin Maymuru's interest in the art and way of life of the Abelam people challenged his (then) modernist picture of the "unreflective primitive artist locked into his own world of conservative tradition" (Morphy, H. [2007]. *Becoming art* [p. 112, see also p. 120]. New York: Berg; Morphy is speaking of the late 1970s).

28. Aesthetic properties are generally divided into thick and thin. Thick properties are those like *being expressive in a certain way, having a certain sort of elegant design, effectively embodying certain sorts of skills.* Thin aesthetic properties are the properties of *being beautiful* or *being ugly*, or *aesthetically pleasing* or *displeasing.* Thin aesthetic properties are said to be dependent on thick ones in that, once we have assigned thick aesthetic properties to a work, the distribution of thin properties to it is thereby determined. Two works cannot differ in their thin properties without differing in their thick properties. Anthony Shelton (Shelton, A. [1994]. Predicates of aesthetic judgement: ontology and value in Huichol material representations. In J. Coote & A. Shelton [Eds.], *Anthropology, art, and aesthetics* [Oxford Studies in the Anthropology of Cultural Forms, p. 210]. Oxford: Clarendon Press), citing Wittgenstein, notes that "beautiful," or terms that can be translated into it, are rare in aesthetic discourse; thick aesthetic predicates are more informative, and hence more often used, their use generally implying one or another thin attribution, which rarely needs to be stated.

29. There is something of this idea in Gregory Bateson's claim that universality in art depends on the expression of grace, though I think Bateson does not quite acknowledge the extent to which grace is to be understood as a personal quality (Bateson, G. [1973]. Style, grace and information in primitive art. In A. Forge (Ed.), *Primitive art and society.* Oxford University Press).

30. From the outline of a book (never written, I regret to say) that argues for the essentially social nature of our interest in art: http://www.humphrey.org.uk/papers/2004Beauty'sChild.pdf. But Humphrey is surely wrong to contrast art and food; we do care deeply about how our food gets to taste the way it does, and something with the same taste might prove utterly abhorrent if its production violates a cultural or religious norm.

31. In earlier work I have taken a somewhat unorthodox view of the nature of artworks, one according to which the artwork itself is the action performed by the artist in making it

(see Currie, G. [1989]. *An ontology of art.* London: Macmillan); a related view is also urged by Davies, D. (2004). *Art as performance.* Blackwell. The points I am making above are ones that, I hope, could be agreed to by people who think, more conventionally, that the work is, at least in the case of the visual arts, the physical artifact that results from that act of making.

32. For arguments of this kind see, for example, Walton, 1970; Levinson, J. (1980). What a musical work is. *Journal of Philosophy, 77,* 5–28; and Currie, G. (1989). *An ontology of art.* London, Macmillan.

33. I consider the ways in which aesthetic values are contingent on facts about our biological evolution in Chapter 13 of Currie, G. (1994). *Arts and minds.* Oxford University Press. The fact that Martian aesthetic experience might be unavailable to us while being none the worse for it is one reason we need to maintain a distinction between the doctrines of Universality and Openness.

34. See Rosand, D. (2005). *Drawing acts: studies in graphic expression and representation.* Cambridge University Press. See also Maynard, P. (2005). *Drawing distinctions: the varieties of graphic expression.* Ithaca, NY: Cornell University Press.

35. Some art forms effectively remove the more obvious traces of the artist's activity, as with the smooth sculptural forms of Canova, and in such cases one may require knowledge of the process of making in order to connect with that activity; such objects provide, most immediately, a sense of mystery as to their making. Significantly, certain communities produce art that itself represents traces of other activities, as with central Australian Aboriginal culture: "The essence of the style is the representation of the marks left by people and animals as they move across the landscape" (Layton, R. [1994]. Traditional and contemporary art of Aboriginal Australia: two case studies. In Coote & A. Shelton [Eds.], *Anthropology, art, and aesthetics* [Oxford Studies in the Anthropology of Cultural Forms, p. 138]. Oxford: Clarendon Press). See also Shelton on the extent to which Huichol artifacts are considered the "manifestation" of deities (Shelton, A. [1994]. Predicates of aesthetic judgement: ontology and value in Huichol material representations. In J. Coote & A. Shelton [Eds.], *Anthropology, art, and aesthetics* [Oxford Studies in the Anthropology of Cultural Forms, p. 240]. Oxford: Clarendon Press).

36. Gallese, V. (2009). The two sides of mimesis: Girard's mimetic theory, embodied simulation and social identification. *Journal of Consciousness Studies, 16,* 21–44.

37. See Freedberg, D., & Gallese V. (2007). Motion, emotion and empathy in esthetic experience. *Trends in Cognitive Sciences, 11,* 197–203; and Gallese, V., & Freedberg, D. (2007). Mirror and canonical neurons are crucial elements in esthetic response. *Trends in Cognitive Sciences, 11,* 411.

38. See L'hermitte, F. (1983). Utilisation behaviour and its relation to lesions of the frontal lobes. *Brain, 106,* 237–255.

39. See News and comment, *Trends in Cognitive Science,* Oct. 6, 2002; Calvo-Merino, B., et al. (2005). Action observation ad acquired motor skills: an FMRI study of expert dancers. *Cerebral Cortex, 15,* 1243–1249; also Haueisen, J., & Knosche, T. (2001). Involuntary motor activity in pianists evoked by music perception. *Journal of Cognitive Neuroscience, 13,* 786–792.

40. For remarks on a school of thinkers I call the empathists, who did take bodily involvement seriously, including brief comments on Berenson, see Currie, G. (2010). Empathy for objects. In A. Coplan & P. Goldie (Eds.), *Empathy: philosophical and psychological essays.* Oxford University Press.

41. The editors sensibly queried this claim, pointing to the practice of artistic "ready-mades" such as Duchamp's bottle rack. I follow here the tradition of regarding such activity as parasitic in the sense that it can be countenanced as art only by dint of its commenting on, challenging, or otherwise engaging with a more conventional artistic practice that involves making.

42. On commonalities and differences between cultures and their relation to aesthetic universals, see Chapter 21 in Boyd, B. (2009). *On the origin of stories.* Cambridge, MA: Belnap Press.

43. The idea that art extends agency is surely right. It is not even clear that anyone would disagree with this: artworks affect people in certain ways, and if your aim is to affect them in those ways, making an artwork may enable you to do that. Gell himself focuses on ways in which art enhances power. Who would dispute that art extended the power of the Renaissance church and its priests? And why, by the way, is the extension of agency thesis inconsistent with thinking of art as symbolic? Gell describes the construction of the Maori meeting house thus: "The ridge pole objectifies the genealogical continuity of the chiefly line . . . while the descending rafters indicate the proliferation of cadet lines on either side" (Gell, 1998, p. 253). Surely it is only by convention that there are these associations between poles/rafters and lines of descent. Symbols certainly add to the power of an individual or institution. Even ordinary communicative uses of artifacts extend our powers in various way; we communicate with people because we want to produces changes in their beliefs, their desires, or their behavior. I happen to agree with Gell that art need not be symbolic, but I am puzzled as to where he thinks the argument for this, based on the efficacy of art, comes from.

44. Boris Wiseman says, "From an 'aesthetic' point of view, the Asmat shield can be *at once* a beautiful shield *and* a fear-inducing shield" (Wiseman, B. [2007]. Introduction to *Levi-Strauss, anthropology, and aesthetics.* Cambridge University Press). Howard Morphy, generally a friend of the aesthetic approach to the anthropology of art, says, "In the case of Yolngu art, what Europeans interpret as an aesthetic effect Yolngu interpret as a manifestation of ancestral power emanating from the ancestral past" (Morphy, H. [1992]. From dull to brilliant: the aesthetic of spiritual power among the Yolngu. In J. Coote & A. Shelton [Eds.], *Anthropology, art, and aesthetics* [Oxford Studies in the Anthropology of Cultural Forms, p. 183]. Oxford: Clarendon Press). Once again, I see no inconsistency in supposing that these aesthetic effects are part of what explains the capacity of the objects concerned to manifest this connection with an ancestral past.

45. I have in mind here the shield that Gell himself chose to illustrate his point; the designs vary somewhat.

46. Gell, 1998, Chapter 2.

47. See, for example, Dickie, G. (1974). *Art and the aesthetic: an institutional analysis.* Ithaca, NY: Cornell University Press, and Dickie, G. (1997). *Art circle: a theory of art.* Chicago: Spectrum Press. For a recent defense of the aesthetic approach to art see Zangwill, N. (2007). *Aesthetic creation.* Oxford University Press.

6

Aesthetic Science and Artistic Knowledge
Blake Gopnik

The scientific method is a wonderful thing. It has given us insights into the least "scientific" of problems: it has told us about irrational economic behaviors, how blind people draw, and why bronze-medal winners are happier than athletes who win silver.

I believe strongly that science can yield equally crucial knowledge of art objects. I have written on what science has told us about the relationship between vision, viewpoint, and perspective and about the scientific calculation of sources of light in a painting by Caravaggio.[1]

But the new field of aesthetic science often wants to go further than such "incidentals." It wants to account, in a much more direct way, for the fundamentals of what it is to look at art. At its most ambitious, aesthetic science almost wants to practice a kind of art criticism and interpretation, helping all of us to be better art lovers by getting us to understand what's most basic to appreciating art. If that's the goal, any art critic, and many an art lover, would want that science to give insight into problems such as:

How Renaissance art could make Ottoman turbans, Byzantine icons, and medieval buildings all count as powerful revivals of the culture of ancient Greece and Rome[2]

How radical Dada sculpture, by such 20th-century masters as Marcel Duchamp and Man Ray, depends for much of its meaning on the early history of retailing[3]

How one work of video art can be valued for what it tells us about the clichés of television culture, and another, not all that different-looking, can be admired for its insights into real-world social interactions[4]

Those are the kinds of questions that those who contemplate art the longest and most passionately want answered about it. For art's most expert informants, artistic images don't only trigger perceptions or cause emotions, the usual subjects of aesthetic science. They also carry content. In fact, that may be the most important thing they do. For such people, the particulars of how art addresses the kind of "semantic" questions listed above make up much of what art *is*.

No one would deny that the formal and affective qualities of art objects, and our responses to them, have always played a role in how those objects work for us; everyone ought also to acknowledge that content has always mattered at least as much, and probably more, in making art meaningful, important, and useful. A concentration on content isn't by any means a *recherché* position, recently dreamed up by a few postmodern scholars or avant-garde conceptualists. Content is fundamental to the nature and understanding of art, and always has been.

If the scientific study of the artistic experience can't deal with issues of content, doubts spring up about its long-term leverage on the realities of art. If it willfully ignores such central issues, it has a problem on its hands. And if it doesn't even know such issues are out there, at the heart of how many people talk and think about art—at the heart, in fact, of how most people have *always* spoken and thought about art—then it's a field that is in crisis, even if it doesn't know it.

Science and Artistic Expertise

It is an admittedly distressing fact that, for years, art historians and critics have ignored what experts on vision and the psychology of representation have discovered about the scenes artworks can show, and how they can show them.[5] It's at least equally lamentable that so many aesthetic scientists feel free to ignore what art experts believe about the very nature of the artistic experience—including the role content plays in it. Look at any of a number of recent introductions to aesthetic science, and you'll be lucky to find a single citation to art history or criticism.[6] Yet it hardly seems radical to imagine that, in defining their novel field of study, aesthetic scientists would want to pay close attention to a large community of scholars who have spent decades thinking about nothing other than what matters most in art, and what counts as the most informative, insightful commentary on it.

Later in this chapter, I'll also be suggesting that, in certain cases and cultural contexts—possibly in most of them—what count as the salient features and effects of works of art are in fact determined by the judgments of experts and elites. A scientist, that is, may need to pay attention to what art experts say because the nature of our entire artistic experience trickles down from them. The art experts don't deserve anyone's attention because of their professional authority; they deserve it because their influence can be so profound that it shapes the very essence of a culture's experience of art. I will be arguing that art is such a peculiar, and peculiarly cultural, phenomenon that there can be no "natural," untutored set of reactions to art objects, or none at least that are reliably relevant to those objects' value as art. Elites and experts of one kind or another, from mothers to priests to art critics to college professors—even some scientists—may be almost entirely responsible for what an artwork makes us feel, think, and say at any given time.

Surveying the literature of aesthetic science, it is striking how much of it depends on notions of art that date back decades, or even centuries, and that haven't been in play among experienced viewers for almost as long.[7] Aesthetic science often elides the distinction between artistic excellence and realistic representation, or between art and technical skill, or art and stylistic virtuosity—yet these are distinctions that have always been crucial, and that recent art has made especially evident. To cite the "sudden emergence of *artistic* talent" (my emphasis) with dementia,[8] or to affirm that the drawings of a modern child with autism are "almost as aesthetically pleasing as those of Leonardo da Vinci,"[9] calls on such outdated and questionable notions of "artistic talent" and "aesthetic pleasure" that it's as though 20th-century art, and 20th-century research into the art of the past, had never happened.

In art-world terms, scientific accounts often seem built less on considered accounts of what matters in art than on a set of long-abandoned clichés: on ideas of the naturally "gifted" genius, of "appealing form," of the "expressive" hand or eye; on claims that "an outline drawing . . . is more effective as 'art' than a full color photograph,"[10] that artists aim "to depict objects as they are,"[11] or that "art reflects the inner life of the artist."[12] Art professionals who hear such ideas invoked by scientists feel the same discomfort that brain scientists do when they hear art-world babble about the "unconscious," the "superego," or the creative "right brain." Imagine an art historian invoking "the neurons in the brain that register the Oedipal complex"—scientists' worst accounts of the art they want to explain can be as jaw-dropping as that. If scientists want their accounts to be taken seriously, they will need to take the time to find out what kinds of talk have panned out best for talking about art, and which kinds have proved flawed. Otherwise, they risk remaining in the situation they find themselves in now: working hard to produce results that are systematically ignored among precisely those people who study art most closely and committedly.

This isn't about patrolling the borders of art history's academic fiefdom; it's about encouraging scientists to go to an important source of knowledge in a field that's new to them. To succeed, the scientific study of artistic phenomena will need true cross-disciplinarity. It's not enough for scientists to cross over into artistic subject matter, or for historians and critics to borrow a stray concept or finding from scientists. The best scientists and the best thinkers about art will need to work hand in hand to satisfy the criteria for excellence in all the fields involved, and to avoid having to groan at each other's mistakes.

Getting these interactions right matters more for aesthetic science than for many other scientific crossovers. Normally, when scientists decide to study complex human behaviors—scientific reasoning itself, perhaps, or our economic intuitions—they don't also see themselves as engaging in the behavior they're studying. Psychologists, that is, could study how a physicist thinks, or even how a brain lights up when it's considering a physics problem, without ever imagining that they're thereby *doing* physics. The unique thing about aesthetic science is that it often seems to be both studying how we interpret and elucidate art, and actually engaging in such interpretation and elucidation. The goal of aesthetic science often seems to be to figure out what a work of art is and why it works and what might make it good—a goal it shares, pretty much, with the art lovers it purports to be studying. When aesthetic science fails, it's often because it fails to yield cogent insights into art. In contrast, the psychology of physics doesn't fail by failing to predict the orbits of planets.

Toward the end of this chapter, I'll even be proposing that the central role of any professional who analyzes art, whether from a science or humanities perspective, is not merely to determine truths about a set of fixed relationships between viewers and art objects. It is to help viewers relate to art in fertile new ways that have not been available before—much as a talented theater director would want to establish new meanings and impacts for *Hamlet*, rather than confirm what his audience already thinks and feels about the play. The most useful and powerful claims to make about the Mona Lisa might not relate to confirming and fleshing out the old clichés about her supposedly enigmatic smile. They might, instead, direct viewers' attention to some completely different, previously unattended aspect of the picture—to fractals in the landscape, or to calculable inconsistencies in the picture's light, or to what it might mean that we've chosen a brunette, rather than a blonde, to be the most famous woman in Western art. A truly ambitious aesthetic scientist attending to a viewing subject's brain, that is, might want to come closer to getting the art to stimulate new areas in it than to studying or reinforcing stale reactions that have been triggered by earlier experts' ideas. A scientist analyzing the enigma behind Mona Lisa's smile may be making precisely as great a contribution to artistic knowledge as an art historian would make to physics by studying the way apples fall from trees.

Science, Aesthetics, and the Nature of Art

What is art? Before aesthetic science can get off the ground, it has to address that question. What is the phenomenon that the field imagines it should study? Or, more vexingly, the question might be, Can we even be sure there is such a thing as a stable artistic phenomenon, to which humans have the kind of generalized responses that science might set out to examine? As I've suggested, and will go on to flesh out, art may be such a peculiar, flexible, culture-bound activity that it does not present—perhaps cannot present—the kind of invariants that science is best equipped to study. The objects artists produce may indeed have features that stay the same across time, and reliably trigger certain responses (neural or otherwise) in their viewers. The problem is that it's very hard to know, at any given moment in the life of our artistic culture, which of those features will count as contributing to an object's specifically *artistic* interest or importance. There might be moments in the history of culture where the artfulness of objects resides in the emotions they trigger, but where their compositional features are not relevant to their reception as art. At other moments, the objects that are most salient as works of art may be all about the political positions they communicate; their ability or failure to tug at heartstrings might not be something worth attending to. For a scientist to discover that one of these "political" works reliably triggers neural activity in the limbic system, and that another doesn't, might be both perfectly true and quite irrelevant to their relative status, worth, and meaning as art at the moment they were made.

It's obvious that not every perceivable, brain-stimulating feature of an art object is relevant to its aesthetic status. What a painting tastes like when licked would (usually, but perhaps not always!) count as not worth studying. It is not at all clear that even the visual features of works of visual art, or the invariant responses to them that science might study, are all guaranteed to be much more relevant to what makes them count as artful. After all, not all viewable objects are art, so there have to be criteria that determine which objects, and which qualities in those objects, count as artistically charged at any given time. As noted earlier, the biggest challenge facing aesthetic science may be to deal with the extreme cognitive and cultural variability that is at the heart of the art experience—that may be almost constitutive of it, and that may make it worth attending to at all.

This chapter will propose another possibility that is even more ominous for the scientific aesthetician: it may be that one of the crucial functions of truly great art objects is to rewrite which qualities in any object, and in our reactions to it, we ought to count as artistic. Just when our poor scientist thinks she's got a handle on which of our reactions to art are worth studying, and which are incidental and irrelevant, some genius artist comes along and makes work that asks us to pay attention to a whole new set of features when we look at art.

Yet rather than acknowledging, let alone tackling, the extreme flexibility that characterizes our responses to art, so far aesthetic science has tended to concentrate on a tiny subset of features and reactions, and has acted as though they were constitutive of the entire art experience. And the subset scientists have preferred to study is one that many art professionals practicing today might have much less interest in. In fact, aesthetic scientists' assumptions about what they need to explain, in order to explain art, have almost nothing to do with what most art experts imagine might need to be studied. Those experts would barely recognize the "art" aesthetic science takes as its subject. (If, that is, scientists want to make claims about art at all. A science of "aesthetic" experience could be something quite separate from a science of art, as a few thinkers have already acknowledged. If you define "aesthetics" as consisting of affective responses to perceptual stimuli of any kind, an aesthetic scientist could study preferences in hamburgers or flowers, without ever imagining that the findings would be especially relevant to the more complex, even arbitrary activities normally called "art."[13])

As an outsider encountering a range of topics in aesthetic science, I find a field that's dominated by the view that art, and the art experience, is primarily about something called "beauty," and about the emotions that "beautiful" (or even just "excellent") pictures reliably trigger in their viewers. Yet the very idea of the "aesthetic," the evident backbone of the "aesthetic response" that scientists claim to be studying, has little currency in art writing today, and is certainly not one of its central, inescapable concepts. In the nearly 500 articles I've written for the *Washington Post*, I've almost never used the term to account for what is going on in a work of art, and the concept itself is largely irrelevant to most analyses by today's leading art historians. As philosopher Peter Osborne has put it, "the aesthetic (a reflective judgement of taste) appears to capture so little of what is significant and challenging about specific works of modern art that it often seems to drop out as a meaningful factor in their analysis."[14] Most art historians would say the same about the place of the aesthetic in understanding a lot of earlier art.

If nothing else, the fact that thousands upon thousands of art professionals now study and enjoy art *without* ever thinking or talking about "aesthetics" or "beauty" means that the concepts are not necessary, and certainly not sufficient, to what constitutes an art object or its understanding. (Unless one were willing to make the strange, surely counterintuitive claim that the responses of throngs of art-loving, dedicated professionals are irrelevant to the study of artistic responses.) It also suggests at least the possibility that those thousands of influential voices could convince everyone else to jettison such notions, and make the study and appreciation of art a beauty-free zone, right across the culture. If that's not impossible to imagine, it means that the aesthetic can't be as necessary to art as science sometimes makes it out to be.

In much of aesthetic science, a work of art is treated as just another stimulus in the environment; its human viewers react to it in predictable ways, which a scientist can study to "see what they find pretty" or what "instantly evoke[s] an emotional response."[15] And, most importantly, according to such thinkers these almost automatic, predictable reactions *are* the art experience itself—the crucial thing to get at if you're going to account for art.

This view of what art is and how it works dates back barely 200 years, to the specifically "aesthetic" theories of Kant and his contemporaries. It did not dominate before then; it has little currency today, at least among art's most committed observers. Judging by the historical evidence, it hasn't been what most art viewers have ever focused on when they've expressed their thoughts and feelings about art.

In the Middle Ages, and well into the modern era, "beauty" and "pleasure," or even more general ideas about "aesthetic satisfaction" (the kinds of ideas that might, for instance, justify an interest in the ugly and extreme in art), took a distant second place to the ritual and magic functions of art works—to what a picture could literally make happen in the world, or in the afterlife.[16] In religious terms, an old and "ugly" painting of the Virgin Mary might work better (it might count as absolutely better art, that is) than something newer and far more "attractive." Many Renaissance altarpieces were "spoiled," in purely aesthetic or stylistic terms, by having a crude but miraculous image stuck into their middle.

Even when the Renaissance seems to be trying on more modern ideas about art and what looks good, pictures and sculptures are as likely to be discussed in terms of *what* they show, and what those subjects signify, than in terms of how "pleasing" they might be to human senses. Giorgio Vasari, founder of art history, was far more likely to catalogue the subjects of a painting than to spend time on its "aesthetic" merits. In 1568, his unusually detailed account of Leonardo da Vinci's large-scale drawing of the Virgin Mary and Saint Anne, now in London, is framed as though it were describing the contents of a real scene rather than the aesthetic features of an artifact. Leonardo wanted, Vasari says, "to reveal the modesty and humility of a Virgin completely contented by the happy sight of her beautiful son, whom she tenderly holds in her lap . . . as well as the smile of a St. Anne who, full of happiness, sees that her earthly progeny has become heavenly."[17]

In those cases where artworks were discussed in terms that might have ignored the details and significance of subject matter, the primary criterion for admiration wasn't "aesthetic" in anything like modern terms. Approval for a work of art wasn't built around a notion of perceivable beauty and the emotions it induced. Instead, by far the dominant criterion for judgment was an artwork's "realism." As Ludovico Dolce put it in 1557, "The duty of the painter is to use his craft to paint something so much like the various works of nature that it seems to be real. That painter whose works lack this resemblance, is no painter; whereas the more closely a painter's pictures resemble real things, the more skillful and excellent a painter he will be."[18] Then that mimetic criterion got grafted onto judgments of beauty, which was more a generic term of approbation than a specifically aesthetic concept. For Vasari, a drawing that looked convincingly three-dimensional was also, and necessarily, "most beautiful."[19] And, crucially, what counted as "lifelike" turns out to have been almost as variable, across time and place, as such culture-bound phenomena as what respectable female behavior might be.[20] Even ideas of "excellent realism," that is, though built on a substrate of measurable advances in representational techniques, could be full of culture-specific meaning, and could depend on cultural context. They did not depend on the kind of stable percepts and affective responses that experimental science would be likely to get at.

Well after the birth of the Enlightenment's aesthetic approaches to art, pictures were still more likely to be described, and judged, in terms of their depicted content, and its meaning and significance, than in terms of how that content looked or the emotions it induced. That was true as late as 1884, when the Pointillist Georges Seurat painted his great *Afternoon at the Island of the Grande Jatte*, now one of the most appreciated pictures at the Art Institute of Chicago. That picture might seem the perfect example of an "aesthetic" and "perceptual" exercise, and has often been discussed as such. It seems to be all about a new way of depicting the world that relies on bright colors, new conceptions of pleasing light, and novel ways of breaking up the picture surface. It seems plausible to imagine that it's all about finding new ways to please the eyes of its audience, and that studying the ways that subjects' visual brains are tickled by it would get to the heart of its matter.

But look at some of the first reactions to the painting, and instead you get a story of what the picture means: "Monsieur Seurat's idea comes out clearly: The painter wished to show the tedious to-and-fro of the banal promenade of these people in their Sunday best . . . Maids, clerks, troopers move with the same slow, banal motions, all alike, which certainly conveys the character of the scene."[21]

Today's most important art historians have suggested that we need to pay close attention to such historical evidence in our own readings and appreciation of these pictures. They suggest that much of the import of Seurat's *Grande Jatte*—of what makes it valuable as a great work of art—depends on what it tells us about humans and their social world. A large part of a picture's greatness, that is, lies in how a picture reacts to and shapes the ideas we think and talk about. The almost standard view of today's most expert lookers is that the cognitive and semantic specifics of art objects, rather than their perceptual or emotional effects, are what is central in them. Or, more accurately, that percepts and affects are likely to be in the service of content.

Throughout the history of art, aesthetics—understood as "pleasing the eye" or "triggering emotions"[22]—have tended to play a subsidiary role in the functioning of art objects. Portraits could commemorate an event, or a relationship, or a death; narrative art could shore up power and political legitimacy; public monuments could display wealth and civic commitment; religious art could reinforce dogma or repudiate heresy. To the extent that pictures were made to "please" at all, the kinds of pleasure they provided would be dependent on how they succeeded in their goals.

In the words of philosopher Jonathan Rée, reliance on a sense-based, aesthetic model can "obliterate the space in which art is able to do its work—its probing, disturbing, challenging and rearranging of the terms of our shared engagements with reality."[23]

Brains, Perception, and the Stuff in the World

Semir Zeki, in one of the founding documents of neuroaesthetics, said that "the overall function of art is an extension of the functions of the brain," and that may be close to right.[24] But the central function of the brain, as many philosophers and psychologists have pointed out, is not to contemplate or analyze its own inputs, percepts, affects, and states. It is to build a picture of a rich world beyond the brain that humans move through and interact with. For philosopher Alva Noë, even that may not be going far enough. According to his recent work, the world itself, and our interaction with it, may even be as constitutive of human consciousness as anything that happens in our brains.[25] This leaves vision, even artistic vision, as being much less about sight than about stuff—all the stuff that matters to us out there in the world, in all its full complexity.

So the question then becomes, how much can aesthetic science help to account for the "stuff" that art deals with? Even if you reject Noë's "immersive" view, and claim that our consciousness of art can be reduced to some correlated state of affairs in our brain, you've got a problem: there may not be any realistic chance that such complex neural or psychological states could ever be deciphered. The eminent art historian John Onians, one of a few recent converts to aesthetic science, has suggested that neurology is the place to go to unlock many of the secrets of culture and biography. The "subjectivity of the individual," he writes, is "embodied in the brain . . . and since all the experiences a person has during their life are liable to affect the formation of their neural networks, to the extent that those experiences can be reconstructed, the subjectivity they produce can also be reconstructed hundreds or even thousands of years after the person in question has died."[26] I wonder how many neuroscientists would want to be saddled with the task of accounting for the individual subjectivities even of living people—for who they are and how they think and whether, on seeing *Hamlet*, they believe that its hero is to be held responsible for his fatal indecision, or excused as the victim of a constitution that prevents him from being decisive.[27] And even if one could read the entire neural coding that accounted for such thoughts, it's not at all clear, from an epistemological point of view, that such low-level deciphering would yield useful insights into the higher-level semantic phenomena at stake. As recently suggested to me by philosopher Dominic Lopes, also writing in this volume (Chapter 3), "it may be that textuality, in the broadest sense—the content of our reactions to the world—can't be studied experimentally."[28] Many art historians would agree with that intuition.

If the complexities, and especially the actual *content*, of "semantic" responses to works of art are out of reach of experimentation, does aesthetic science then have to confine itself to what it *can* study? Are scientists limited to studying stable preferences, pleasures, predictable emotional triggers and perceptual responses to artistic stimuli? And, if that's the case, are they getting at art, at all?

Object Features versus Art Features

The responses that aesthetic science gets from its experimental subjects may have less to do with the "art" side of the stimuli that it presents than with other features that they share with many other non-art objects in the world.

Scientists often study certain very narrow aspects of artistic production and reception—our ability to make and see realistic representations, to create and enjoy color harmonies, to express and respond to emotions—as though they are getting at art itself. They often fail, that is, to acknowledge the crucial difference between techniques and tools that have, at various times, been recruited in the making of art (and at other times not) and the art itself that gets made. To discover, for instance, that a brain injury or illness increases certain people's representational skills tells you very little about their potential role in the art of the 21st century. It is much like discovering that an increase in finger strength or fine-motor neurons helps sculptors cut marble: it is true, but almost irrelevant to the worth of their art. Art requires such a complex and variable set of skills and intelligences that it's a mistake to study a small set of them as indicative of the whole artistic endeavor. It's a notable fact that savants with a huge increase in any single skill have very rarely made objects that have contributed to the larger artistic culture.

In some deep sense, the "pure" perceptual and affective stimuli presented by works of art—and most likely to be facilitated by single skills and techniques—may have *least* to do with how works function as art, or with what they are as *art* objects. It may simply be false to imagine that "visual art is largely, though not exclusively, the product of the activity of the visual brain."[29] Rather, as I suggested at the start of this chapter, studying the non-discursive, non-semantic, perceptual qualities of art objects may be rather like studying what people say, or how their brains light up, after they've licked a painting. It tells you something about human "reactions" to a work of art, but nothing that you much want to know about it, as art.

All you have to do is switch art forms, and this set of claims seems almost obvious. If it makes sense to discuss literature as an art form—and it's hard to think of any *a priori* reason not to—then it seems clear that, in very many cases, the subtleties of what a work is *about* matter as much as how it is put together, its "pleasing" use of language or the emotions it triggers. At very least, you'd want to say that its language and structures, even its emotions, very often subserve its content and ideas.

Take *King Lear*. It's hard to imagine any significant account of the play that wouldn't somewhere acknowledge that the complex things it has to say about family, jealousy, age, power, and betrayal are constitutive of its excellence. The raw fact of the aesthetic "pleasures" or emotions induced by *Lear* seem obviously inadequate to account for what is important about it. It's not at all hard to imagine that the emotional states produced by *Lear* could also be produced by any number of other texts or stimuli; a useful account of *Lear* would need to talk about what's special about *it*, as a vehicle for content, and not about the generic emotions it triggers.

To properly get at Shakespearean aesthetics using fMRI, that is, a scan would have to yield data about the actual mental contents of our brains, not just about affective or perceptual states. It wouldn't even be enough to learn about the neurocognitive mechanisms that underlie our understanding of the play's contents; *King Lear* matters, as art, for the specific things it has to say about specific things that happen in the world. It's hard to imagine any aesthetic model for the study of Shakespeare that wanted to be taken seriously and that turned out to be incapable of coping with the content of his works, or that did not at very least acknowledge the very severe limitations of studying them as meaning-free perceptual and emotional stimuli.[30]

And yet that seems close to what happens in many scientific studies of the visual arts. The capacity of pictures to carry important, complex ideas about the worlds depicted in them, much like *King Lear* does, is systematically slighted in favor of their status as "pure" and stable visual stimuli and emotional triggers.[31]

    Part of the problem may be that scientifically minded thinkers are being led astray by a false analogy between the psychology of vision, one of their classic and most productive areas of study, and the "perception" and interpretation of art. Because artistic pictures seem to resemble other visual stimuli out there in the world, the assumption is that the same investigative tools will be suitable for both. But the fact that experiences of art enter the brain through the eyes does not mean that their final goal is to "optimally titillate the visual areas of the brain"[32]—their targets may be far, far upstream from there. Such a claim seems obvious when it comes to literature: the discoveries of psychologists and neurologists who work on audition, or even on language—or for that matter on vision, since we can as easily take in a Shakespearean text through our eyes as through our ears—will not get us far at all in understanding Shakespeare in any way that will make his art substantially more meaningful to us. And that's the crucial point: fine accounts of art objects will yield important new insights into them, as art, not simply true facts about them, as objects.

    What we care about, when we think of art as art, is what differentiates *King Lear* from a phone call or computer manual, or from an episode of "Lost"—or even from an almost-as-good play by Ben Johnson—and what sets Seurat's *Grande Jatte* apart from a cruise-ship ad or Uncle Bill's watercolors. The difference between art and non-art, or between important art and the expendable, is as likely to be found in what an artwork has to say, in a particular cultural context, as in what it looks or sounds like, or the raw emotions it triggers.

    If any purportedly "aesthetic" analysis gets only as far as the perceptual or affective substrate an art form is built on, and never rises to the level of meaning, then there seems a good chance that it is barely an aesthetic analysis at all, if by that we mean an analysis of how art actually works.[33] After all, one of the most notable features of artistic culture is that it can use a single, apparently stable stimulus to achieve the most varied goals and mean a vast number of things. A scene of blood and guts might very well trigger reliable emotions of disgust in viewers in a psych lab, or with their heads in a scanner. In the real world where art is consumed, however, though it might indeed be used as a turn-off (in an image of a body snatcher, say), similar imagery could also be used to evoke feelings and ideas of religious transcendence (in a gory Spanish crucifixion), of humor (in a Dutch butcher scene), of intellectual curiosity (in an anatomy lesson), or of stylistic accomplishment (in a Francis Bacon side of beef). And all those, depending on the context they are made and viewed in, can be judged successful and interesting or worthless and banal—obviously good, or evidently, unquestionably bad.

    The same is true of stimuli that experiments might conclude to be "beautiful" and "pleasurable." They are as likely to be found in objects widely judged to be weak art or kitsch as in objects treasured in the world's great museums. The purely experiential and emotional reactions to the stimuli themselves tell us surprisingly little about the artworks they come packaged in. As Jonathan Rée has put it, "A work of art that is not worth recalling is not worth anything, however much pleasure it may have provided. If a work of art fails, it is not because it disgusts us . . . but because—whether through its fault or our own—it has proposed nothing interesting for our consideration."[34]

Content and Art History

A content-based approach to art comports with the most basic thinking of today's experts in the field—who happen to be labeled "art historians," but whose true remit is explaining art, rather than uncovering the historical facts surrounding it.

The simplest art historical account of a Picasso still life, say, would begin with identifying the absinthe spoon and playing cards and furniture it shows, and would go on to uncover the full cultural import of all these at the time that it was made.[35] Any account that did not get even that far in responding to the content of the work, and saw it as having only "visual appeal,"[36] would barely register as an "account" at all, or would have to be acknowledged as a very partial one.

A more sophisticated art historical explanation would be likely to go a step further than such identification. In the case of the accumulated junk in a Dada assemblage, for instance, it might start by recognizing the nature of the department-store objects it was made from, then go on to relate them to the new culture of mass retailing that the artworks come out of, and that they therefore speak about.[37]

Even works of abstract art, whose analysis one might imagine doing in purely formal and perceptual terms, have recently been shown to have meanings and values specific to the cultural moments of their birth. It is not necessarily enough to recognize the formal qualities and virtues in one of Morris Louis's veils of colored paint; those works take on added meaning and heft when understood as playing to an original audience caught up in the Camelot moment of John F. Kennedy's administration.[38] A successful account of Louis's colored washes might want to describe them as unsaturated, soft-edged—and *liberal*.

Lately, there has grown up an entire category of artworks that are aimed at accentuating their documentary, content-carrying functions, while downplaying or even eliminating any "distracting" aesthetics. "Artistic practice is being acknowledged as the production of knowledge," writes theorist Irit Rogoff.[39]

The slide shows and photographic portfolios of leading American artist Alan Sekula, for instance, document subjects such as the history of the union movement, or the nature of international shipping, with an absolute minimum of formal elaboration; his photos would be far too foursquare for *National Geographic*, and even a maritime newsletter might be disappointed in their aesthetics. That is what gives them their force as art. The same is true of Polish video artist Artur Zmijewski, one of today's most important younger figures—the Museum of Modern Art recently gave him a show—who simply puts people in distressing situations, then records the results as straightforwardly as possible. (One piece consisted in staging and recording a tweaked version of the famous Stanford prison experiment.) Such works are meant to be read as entirely as possible in terms of, and for, the content they present. Their ostensive function, the goal of pointing to certain features of the world, is what they are all about. To read them in terms of their aesthetics, or even for their lack of good looks—as interestingly ugly—is to miss their point.

Sekula's photos and Zmijewski's videos shouldn't be confused with some non-art documents they might resemble—with a newsletter's illustrations or a psych lab's videos of subjects. They are clearly art, circulating through the same art-world channels as more evidently "attractive" works whose goals might be formal and aesthetic. The only difference is that, right now at least and among some of the art world's most influential viewers, the content-rich photos and videos of these two figures count as the better, more important, and more stimulating art.

Part of the problem facing aesthetic science may be that good art has always had a tendency to break free of the traditional categories and concepts used to think about it—to stay one step ahead of the critics, art historians, and theoreticians who come up with such categories and concepts, after the fact, by looking at already existing works of art.[40] That means the best new art is likely to be at least two steps ahead of many aesthetic scientists, who often seem to get their ideas about the nature of art at second hand—by a kind of cultural osmosis, through the most informal channels and with a very long delay—from people in the arts. The job of all those who want to talk about art, including scientists, will always be to catch up as quickly as they can to the new frameworks that the art works themselves insist on or create. A content-only approach is one such framework. It may be novel in its purity, but it points to an option that's always been available in art.

The Non-Aesthetic Everyman

I have suggested that no scientific approach to aesthetics can afford to ignore what artworks do to, and for, today's most expert and experienced viewers. It seems likely that any realistic, real-world definition or account of art will come at least in part from looking at the place it plays in such circles, as I argue in detail below. But even if you imagine, as many scientists do, that art is constituted by lay reactions, a content-based approach will still be crucial to "getting" what art is all about.

All you have to do is spend a few minutes in any museum, and you see that most neophyte approaches to its works of art center on the things they show. "Why is that woman carrying her breasts on a tray?" is what you'll most often hear in front of any Renaissance image of Saint Agatha. "Isn't that little girl darling?" is a standard response to *The Railway* by Manet, even though art historians would insist that her cuteness is a small part of what is going on. Or even, "I don't like pictures without a subject," overheard from an older viewer of the Hirshhorn Museum's attractive abstractions by Morris Louis—making clear, in that rejection, how much subjects, in general, matter to her feelings about art.

On a recent visit to the Museum of Modern Art in New York, I overheard a mother and son looking at a painting titled *Child With Doll* (c. 1884), by the Belgian artist James Ensor, whose *fin-de-siècle* aesthetics are as peculiar and noteworthy as could be. Yet their comment on the painting dwelt on the objects represented in it: "What the heck is that thing leaning on the table? An umbrella? It looks like an axe," said mother to son.

Simple ostension—"to make absent things present," in a phrase that dates back to antiquity—has always been an absolutely central function of representational art in the West. Even medieval Christian icons, which we now tend to admire for their striking looks, could originally function as catalogs of information, rather than as unique objects defined by style and aesthetics: icons that look very different could count as artistically equivalent and almost interchangeable, so long as they shared and preserved and transmitted a few crucial features, such as the pose of a figure or a cast of sacred characters.[41] It can't make sense to downplay art's ostensive function, and the actual content such a function is in aid of, in favor of a limited, Enlightenment notion of sense-based aesthetics. Any wall text or docent's tour is far more likely to dwell on what an artwork shows than on its "aesthetic" worth. To the extent that people declare an art work "beautiful"—and thereby invoke an "aesthetic" analysis—their declaration is as likely to be a generic way of praising it as to be an account of what's of interest to them in the work itself.

An Inconstant Beauty

Even if you did believe in the central significance of judgments of "beauty"—or of the generic praise I believe it stands in for—you'd have a problem in its scientific study. There's not much historical evidence that such judgments have the kind of stability that you need in a phenomenon to make it suit the experimental method. Consistent results in experiments conducted today might not tell us as much as we think.

Vermeer, now seen as an undeniably "great" master and the maker of the ultimate in pleasing art (the crowds for his shows have been steadily growing), was seen as nothing special for almost two centuries after his death. His art was there to be viewed: he counted as one of many minor masters of the Dutch interior, and was bought and sold and collected as such. But it didn't register as especially significant until after the advent of photography, when his proto-photographic style came to seem obviously great and also evidently pleasing, and worth paying very close attention to.[42]

Just when Vermeer was on the rise, the first paintings of Renoir and Monet, which we now judge to be just as evidently, effortlessly "beautiful" as the Dutch master's, were meeting with almost universal ridicule and hatred. Well into the 20th century, Americans who hated any of the "moderns"—artists such as Matisse and Picasso, for instance—continued to describe them as "those horrible Impressionists."

Even such seemingly obvious purveyors of "beauty" as Fra Angelico or Sandro Botticelli were discounted as unpalatably "primitive," or at least as appealing only to the most esoteric and capricious of tastes, until well into the 19th century—until the moment when their "primitive" use of line and color came to be seen as aesthetic virtue rather than vice. Believe it or not, you had to learn to like Botticelli's *Birth of Venus*.

There are also plenty of reverse cases where the instability of aesthetic judgments shows up as a fall from grace. Artists once see as patently "great," such as Guido Reni, who painted figures in Bologna and Rome in the early 17th century, or Salvator Rosa, who painted landscapes and satires just a little bit later, have much less appeal today. You have to imagine that the brain of a modern viewer of such pictures would react quite differently to them than the brain of one of their erstwhile admirers. Any scientific study that did not pick out that difference would have to count as not getting at the art that's in the objects, or at our specifically artistic responses to them. There are no stable features that make these artworks count as "good" or "bad," which are the two most basic, classically "aesthetic" judgments people make about a work of art. The specifically aesthetic valence of these works depends heavily on cultural and historical context.

There's surprising instability even in the reading of a superstar masterpiece such as the Mona Lisa that has never counted as anything but "beautiful" and popular. (Although the picture's current status as *the* iconic masterpiece came only very late in its life, after 1913, when its theft from the Louvre and subsequent return had given it two sets of headlines, and two sets of reproductions, in the newly photo-heavy newspapers.)[43]

Praise for the Mona Lisa may indeed have been almost constant from soon after it was made. But the *terms* of that praise are so varied as to make one doubt there's a way to nail down any objective excellence in the painting, at least experimentally. The Mona Lisa has been judged great because of the demure beauty of its sitter; or because of the perfect realism of Leonardo's craft; or because of its subject's power as a *femme fatale*; or because of her mysterious or androgynous smile.[44] Martin Skov, a neurologist who specializes in aesthetic preference formation, cites Mona Lisa's "enigmatic" smile as an exemplary case of the kind of stable artistic "puzzle" that his field needs to address[45]—apparently unaware that for most of that picture's early history that smile was seen as a perfectly transparent, delightful expression of pleasure. Vasari describes it as "tremendously pleasing," and explains it with a tale of how Leonardo got entertainers to keep his sitter amused as he painted.[46]

The Art of Change

The obvious scientist's reaction to such shifts is to imagine that "natural," perceptual responses to works of art are being overridden by social factors—the way that one might argue that a "natural" aversion to the smell of rot is being overcome by people who enjoy the French cheese known as *époisses*. But in fact it seems quite possible that the specifically *artistic* features of art objects—the ones that actually constitute their art-ness—are precisely the ones that are most deeply embedded in culture, and that change most with time and place and social context. To paint in a Cubist style now would be a different artistic act, with different effects and meanings, than it was in 1912. When you study those aspects of responses to a work that *don't* change from viewer to viewer, from era to era, and that leave art historical opinions behind, it could be that you are studying the non-artistic aspects of the work. You are doing the equivalent of studying how a painting tastes.

Recent neuroscience emphasizes the extreme plasticity of the brain and the vast amount of top-down processing that goes on in it. Isn't that likely to mean that in order to get at "aesthetic cognition," a fine-grained view of the brain's neuroaesthetic activity would have to be able to register the neural effects of context and culture—and that any view or scan that doesn't register such effects is insufficiently informative to be of any use? In other words, a neural situation isn't in fact aesthetic at all unless it registers context, at its most complex.

None of this is meant to argue for relativism in the study of art; it doesn't imply that anything that anyone could ever say about a work of art would be equally true, valid, and interesting. (A relativist wouldn't last long as an art critic.) It simply claims that the crucially *artistic* aspects of art works are the kind of painfully complex cultural and cognitive phenomena that are likely to escape experimental study, at least for the foreseeable future.

Art shouldn't be thought of as playing out in some uniquely complex, high-flown, culture-bound arena, protected by obscurantist artsies waving signs that say "Scientists Keep Out" and "Reality Is A Fiction." Art is right down there beside us in our normal everyday, alongside lots of other facets of experience that science can barely get at. Even such basic features of being human as having a belief or desire with a particular content may prove resistant to scientific analysis. Which experiments or brain scans are likely to get at what's involved when someone says something as simple as "I believe my mother is an atheist" or "I want to be a better person"? Now imagine the obstacles confronting any scientist who wants to study an activity like art, which piggybacks on our basic beliefs and desires and concepts, but wants to twist and play with them.

If nothing else, scientists who want to study art would need to develop a good, informative account of the gap between any stable responses they might identify under controlled conditions, and the varied responses that art history's more "ecological" research reveals. In other words, any stability you find in the objects as perceptual or even cognitive stimuli would need to be reconciled with how they function as works of art in a culture. Without that reconciliation, you aren't studying art, you're simply studying neural and psychological responses that artworks share with other kinds of non-art objects.

I've been acting as though the extreme variability of our reactions to art is a problem—as it might prove to be for many scientific approaches. But in our actual encounters with great works of art, that variability may be a crucial virtue of these objects, and of our reactions to them. Art historian T. J. Clark reports, and supports, the 19th-century critic Paul Valéry's view that "a work of art is defined by the fact that it does not exhaust itself—offer up what it has to offer—on first or second or subsequent reading." As Clark puts it, "art-ness is the capacity to invite repeated response."[47] Those responses don't stay the same from encounter to encounter and from viewer to viewer; their virtue lies in how much they change. Look at responses to any great work of art—or even at the entire canon of great art and what we think about it—and what you'll notice most is variation. As I suggested earlier, readings of art, and especially our most valued readings of art done by our most valued readers, are like a theater director's interpretation of *Hamlet*: they are most admirable when they come up with new things to say. As the philosopher Arnold Isenberg put it in 1949, a critic is "one who affords new perceptions and therefore new values."[48]

Recent research by the art historian Joshua Shannon, for instance, forces us to recognize that when Jasper Johns cast his bronze beer cans in 1960 he was engaging in a particular kind of nostalgia, which is thus part of what the objects are about. Viewers in the 21st century wouldn't have registered or appreciated that nostalgia before the expert's intervention, and no brain scan, even with the sensitivity of a Vulcan mind-meld, could therefore have picked it out.[49]

A critic, that is, gets most kudos for *changing* readers' perceptions and understandings of a work of art, or their emotions upon seeing it, rather than for "discovering" or reinforcing or predicting thoughts and feelings they will automatically have.[50] The "resilient, stable and cumulative quality" of scientific knowledge may be precisely what we don't want from works of art. We want the knowledge and effects they provide to be frangible, labile, and particular—not formless or infinitely elastic, but suited to a large range of purposes and contexts, and to repeated, and repeatedly fertile, viewing.[51]

And yet aesthetic science consistently favors precisely those "stable" artistic readings that would count as weak and hackneyed if presented in the context of an actual encounter with the work of art—in a graduate class on art or literature, say, or even in a popular review or docent's talk.[52] To discover that kinetic art is an art of motion, and that it triggers motion sensors in the visual cortex, or that the Fauves were colorists, and (guess what) made art that especially triggers color sensors—both are barely caricatures of some claims made by neuroaestheticians—adds almost nothing that wasn't already obvious about those movements.[53] In fact, it confirms clichéd and shallow readings of them.

You'd imagine that you'd want some overlap between good criticism and the readings studied by good aesthetic science, but not much seems to favor that outcome. The kinds of complex, subtle, eye-opening readings that are most important to the culture at large have precisely the kind of idiosyncrasy that aesthetic science tends to shy away from—may *have* to shy away from, given the conceptual framing of the field.

A strong reading can do even more than change viewers' understanding of a work's specifics, and their reactions to them. It might even succeed in transforming readers' postures toward the work. It could turn artworks from excellent to horrible or vice versa, transforming pleasure to misery or discomfort to appeal.

It's not at all inconceivable that the millions who now flock to a Monet show and profess admiration for his art—for the most varied of reasons—could someday stop flocking or admiring. As I've already suggested, such things have happened before: Caravaggio fell almost completely out of view for more than 300 years before being suddenly reclaimed in a show in 1951. They might happen again. In my own writing, I have questioned the assumed, "timeless" excellence of pictures by Vermeer. I'd be happy if, over the long term, attention was redirected from him to other more neglected artists. If I could get a handful of powerful curators and fellow critics to join in my campaign, I might achieve that goal—and wouldn't it be likely, then, that scientific study of reactions to the newly discounted painter from Delft would yield absolutely new results? And if it didn't, would not that itself show that the science was having trouble getting at some of art's fundamentals?

Art and its Umpires

Aesthetic science often has the goal of discovering what the "normal" responses to art might be, across average populations or even our entire species. Yet, given the kind of changes that I've outlined in the historical record of such responses, even in the single culture of the West, it is credible to imagine that art—how it feels, what it means, what it *is*—is constituted, and has always been constituted, by a changing series of decisions reached by a small, insider elite, which are then passed on to a larger community of viewers. Psychologist James Cutting has presented evidence that the works of art the public prefers are also those that feature most often in expert publications. That suggests the unsurprising notion that the art historical canon trickles down, with varying efficiency, from experts into the culture at large.[54]

Discussing Picasso's pioneering *Demoiselles d'Avignon,* Semir Zeki denies the relevance of a claim that a crucial feature of the painting is that it "rejects the spirit of humanism and naturalism"—a claim almost every Picasso scholar would see as so basic as to be almost a truism—because that claim demands a knowledge of Western art that "the average viewer . . . does not possess."[55] He fails to consider the near certainty that the painting, like almost all paintings, assumes a community of non-average viewers with precisely such knowledge, and that its "art" depends on it.

To imagine that the most relevant results for aesthetic science can be had, as Colin Martindale once suggested, from studying those who have not been "brainwashed" by artistic knowledge (in his example, into liking "naturally detestable" Cubist painting) may do violence to how artistic culture pans out in real life.[56]

The brain may not have any artistic views for someone to interfere with, until they've been put there by artistic initiates.[57]

Alva Noë has argued that "the question of consciousness" arises for living beings as they interact with their environments, rather than for brains in skulls.[58] It may also be true that the "question of artistic consciousness" properly arises only for a certain kind of "artistically informed being" encountering art in a specific cultural environment, rather than for any brain in any skull confronting any work of art.

When notions of art resembling our own first emerged, in the 16th century in Italy, it was a largely elite activity. Almost all the Renaissance pictures we most admire today were deluxe commodities intended for the wealthy and powerful. Working in tandem with the artists they employed—who were, culturally at least, part of that same elite—the powerful decided what made for a successful picture and what did not. The mass of people may have had access to at least some of these objects, but they had almost no say in the decisions that brought them into being. It wasn't merely that the masses didn't have the power to make their views heard; they may not have had any views at all on an activity that took place in a different sector of society. A Renaissance farmer or tinker was unlikely to have any more idea of what might count as a "good" painting than he would have of what counted as a well-turned phrase in Latin rhetoric.

Someone's simple presence before a work of art—in front of the original in a museum, or viewing a tiny reproduction in an fMRI machine—doesn't automatically make that person part of its true and intended audience; the responses of such a non-audience member aren't necessarily relevant to the object's existence as art. Thus, a paint scientist reflecting on the condition of the surface of a Monet, or a museum guard reflecting on the difficulties involved in keeping it safe, would obviously not count as relevant to understanding it as an "aesthetic" or "artistic" object. Any non-insiders' views might count as almost equally irrelevant to such an understanding. The pleasure or annoyance they might get from a work would simply be separate from its standing as art—though those reactions might have everything to do with an object's standing as room decor, or as memorabilia or even as a pleasant regulator of mood.

The true and ideal goal of a museum, or of an art history class—or of some art reviews, for that matter—may not be merely to put artworks before a larger audience and imagine that they'll have a set of "natural" responses to them. (That was in fact the 19th-century "aesthetic" view of things.) It may be to take as big a pool of outsiders as possible, and introduce them to the insider views and tastes and procedures that define the field.

Those views and tastes—the rules of the game of art—will change over time. Just as, in baseball, a stolen base that once counted as an excellent play now doesn't count at all, so a once-desirable move in art (the achievement of near-photographic realism, say) can come to be negligible. In either case, only the people who make and change the rules, or play by them, or at least who watch the game, are in a

position to judge a move's excellence and relevance. The views of an absolute outsider to the game barely mean a thing. In a situation such as this, there may be no
"natural" state of affairs suited to scientific study. "The difficult question of what
distinguishes great art from merely good art" may in principle not be resolvable, at
least in terms that science can address.[59]

The "elitism" I'm invoking is not (or should not be) built around class or wealth,
power, or social position. It's an elitism of expertise and community—the same
elitism that makes connoisseurs of baseball cards, or of heavy-metal rock, the
only communities that count for understanding which features matter in those
aesthetic disciplines.

It is a striking fact that just about any of the standard accounts that laymen give
of works of art can be traced back to some long-ago expert who first came up with
it. Enjoy the pyramidal composition in a Leonardo? You're echoing formalist
approaches from the 1920s, which no one seemed to care for before then. (And
maybe your brain will activate its shape-processing systems when you busy yourself with that reading.) Appreciate the expressionist angst in El Greco? You learned
to do that from another set of critics, circa 1910. (In his own day, El Greco was more
likely to have been seen as an elegant stylist than as an emotional extremist.)[60]

We are surrounded by images of art from very early childhood, and we learn to
recognize and imitate what others say about them. To the extent that we haven't
heard a thing about a certain kind of art, or spent time studying examples of it,
we're probably like an expert at checkers presented with a chess set: we're left mute
and uncomprehending, without anything like natural instincts or reactions to fall
back on.

Of course, unlike in the case of chess, there's no rulebook for neophyte art lovers
to consult. Instead, they are in the position of someone encountering a language
they've not heard before: it takes time, and deep immersion, before conceptions of
its grammar and usage start to kick in.

Conceptual Art, Now and Always

Some philosophers and scientists acknowledge that certain forms of "conceptual"
art, by figures such as Marcel Duchamp and Hans Haacke, can properly be thought
of as non-aesthetic, rule-bound games of the kind I've been describing. But they
see such forms as marginal, occupying an avant-garde of "baffling" work that is a
very special case, and that has little to do with the more aesthetic, perceptual,
affective models that apply to "normal" art. To almost anyone operating within
today's art world, however, that distinction does not ring true.

For such people, there is no stable category of "baffling" or "perverse" or
"unnatural" art, out on the cutting edge, that needs to be considered separately
from the more "straightforward" and aesthetic art of the past. As a working critic,
writing in a newspaper with a mass audience, I encounter the full range of art, and

don't feel or see a fundamental difference in the strategies I use for talking about Old Masters or Duchamp—or a difference any greater than might apply in talking about, say, a religious sculpture from 1100 and a secular painting of a nude from 1600.

A picture such as the great *Las Hilanderas* ("The Spinners"), painted circa 1657 by Diego Velazquez, might seem at first to be as straightforward—and straightforwardly beautiful—as any traditional painting could be (Fig. 6.1). In the foreground, it shows a wonderfully believable scene of five servant women carding and spinning wool, complete with the first-ever substantially illusionistic image of a spoked wheel in motion. In the background, an immaculately rendered beam of light illuminates the fine ladies whom, one imagines, have instructed the servants to spin, as well as the deluxe tapestry that hangs on the wall behind them and that must depend on the spinners' skills. Study an average modern viewer using fMRI, and the painting's realistic imagery and rendering would be sure to cause a spike in regions that process light, motion, and object and scene recognition; one might also imagine all sorts of pleasure centers lighting up at the simple scene.

What scanning that viewer's brain would miss, however, would be the complexities of subject matter that are central to how *Las Hilanderas* actually functions as a work of art. Velazquez's "realistic" domestic scene in fact contains an incontestable web of references to classical mythology: those well-dressed figures in the background are Minerva and Arachne, borrowed from a story about art and originality told by Ovid.[61] *Las Hilanderas* has an equally complex web of references to the history of European art: the tapestry depicted in its interior is based on the *Rape of Europa*, a painting by Titian, Velazquez's most influential predecessor, that was then in the Spanish royal collection and that treated the same subject as a tapestry woven by Arachne in her legend; Velazquez's entire painting echoes the subject of a picture by his great rival Rubens, also owned by the Spanish royals. *Las Hilanderas* makes such intricate claims about the nature and capacities of Velazquez and his art that it makes Duchamp's urinal-as-art *Fountain* read like Dick and Jane. A "direct" response to the painting, as an uncomplicated perceptual stimulus, is at very least inadequate, and might distort the very nature of the piece.

(At the same time, any "semantic" understanding needs to take into account the way Velazquez's ideas are camouflaged behind what seems to be a normal scene, relying on normal perceptual processes and representational frameworks. The painting's initial invitation for us to view it naïvely and perceptually—to study the brain states it generates, for instance—is part of its sophisticated play of ideas. Similarly, Duchamp capitalizes on standard reactions to a urinal to give his *Fountain* meaning. Much "conceptual" art in fact depends on a strong visual or material component, just as a great deal of older, more "visual" art has a significant conceptual aspect—the two kinds of art are almost as much alike as different.)

Las Hilanderas, along with any number of similar pictures, also demolishes a common notion that an interest in "art about art" is peculiar to 20th-century "radicals," and can therefore be discounted in the scientific study of more "normal" art

FIGURE 6.1 **Velazquez, Diego Rodriguez (1599–1660).** The Fable of Arachne *(Las Hilanderas), 1657. Canvas, 220 × 289 cm. Cat. 1173. (Photo credit: Erich Lessing/Art Resource, NY)*

that's about beauty, pleasure, perception, and emotion. Not surprisingly, artists have always made art that is at least in part, and sometimes largely, about the achievements and limits of their discipline, and how what they've done is different, more complex, more sophisticated, more knowing that what other artists did before.[62]

No art has ever simply been about pleasing the senses, triggering emotions, and setting brains aglow. It has acquired much of its cultural meaning from the games it has played and the rules it has broken. Any account of art that hopes to be at all wide-ranging or ambitious, that is, cannot afford to set aside a conceptual dimension that has maybe been brought into focus in some 20th-century art, but that was always there.

Art, as understood in the West for the past five centuries or so—and that's the notion of art that aesthetic science is almost always working with—is such a peculiar phenomenon that almost all of it feels hopelessly obscure and perverse, even to a full-time art critic, while also, eventually, yielding dividends to those who persist in finding (or even crafting) rules it seems to follow, or that help in its deciphering. The "baffling" art of the 20th-century avant-garde isn't the exception; it is the norm. Older art seems straightforward only when you mistakenly imagine that you're finished with it once you've settled on a single interpretative model. For scientists, that's often an aesthetic and perceptual model, but any single approach, whether symbolic, semiotic, or social-historical, would be equally misleading if it proposes itself as the "straightforward" or "normal" or "necessary" view.

In fact, there's little sign in the historical record of a moment when art yielded transparent readings or uncomplicated reactions—where a single take was all it took to deal with it. Read Vasari, and there's often every sign that he's perplexed or bemused by the very pictures he likes best. The notable feature of art writing through the ages has been its very evident, often self-acknowledged failure to do justice to its subject.[63] Some level of incomprehension seems always to have been typical of Western art; it's not a 20th-century invention.

Some of the most valued art of the past 500 years has started out by fully baffling its viewers, leaving them imagining that it broke all "normal" rules of art making—that it was "just" some kind of perverse play, without grounding in the normal, natural ways that art achieves success. It seemed to appeal to the minds of contrarians, rather than to normal eyes or natural good taste.

The visible brushwork invented by Titian was received that way, though it went on to be the source of so much later art. Patrons rejected his most brushy paintings as simply unfinished—there was no place for them in the standard aesthetics of his day. Titian's paintings weren't merely ugly or un-aesthetic, that is: they didn't even count as works of art ready for viewing. Vasari suggested looking at Titian's pictures from so far away, their brushwork would become imperceptible. He was eager to praise someone who was clearly a major figure, but he could find his way to doing so only by entirely eliminating a crucial feature that made Titian stand out. Titian's avant-gardism had to be neutralized, set aside—rendered invisible, in fact—for him to be accepted in the canon of his time.

Caravaggio, another figure also seen as evidently great today, had equal problems with his first patrons, who rejected work they had paid him to paint. The "ugliness" of his figures seemed a deliberate affront to canons of good taste and propriety—to the fundamentals of what made art, art. (Rembrandt sometimes suffered similar reactions.) Like Titian, that is, Caravaggio wasn't seen as merely failing at the standard tasks of art. He was purveying non-art—empty, naughty gestures of rebellion that took on the name of art, but that lacked the crucial features that could make them live up to the name. Very similar claims—that new art is in fact a *non*-art game of purified nose-thumbing—accompanied the work of Turner, of Whistler, of the Impressionists, of the Fauves, of the Cubists and of the earliest abstractionists, and of course of Dada and conceptual artists, all now accepted into the canon of how "normal" art should function and look.

Let's not forget that when our toddlers are taught art, they're now taught to cut up magazines to make collages and to glue found objects together into assemblages—two art forms that were once seen as so baffling as to barely count as art at all. When they grow up to go to college, our children decorate their rooms with posters of abstractions that were once considered shockingly un-artful. (Rothko's a current favorite, according to the firms that sell such posters.)

As recently as the 1960s, the new Minimalist sculptures of figures such as Donald Judd and Robert Morris were seen as so peculiar, so anti-art in their essence, as to operate purely on a conceptual level, without any appeal to the senses or traditional aesthetics. Even their supporters felt that way about them. And now such art is widely seen as coming too close to prettiness and stylish elegance for its own good—as too easy on the eyes.

In the 21st century, freshmen begin art school fully expecting to do performance pieces, the way students 30 years ago expected to paint abstractions and 60 years ago expected to draw from the model. Judging from the positive response that the Museum of Modern Art got to its recent retrospective of performance artist Marina Abramovic, it looks as though one of the most seemingly peculiar, unaesthetic, anti-material, and extreme of art forms is on its way to being fully normalized.

If you do set vast swaths of modern art aside as different from what "real" art is, and as somehow "unnatural" and therefore unsuited to scientific study, you're slighting the real interests and affections of huge numbers of art lovers, both expert and novice. A recent show exploring the Dada movement of the teens and twenties of the last century, whose leaders such as Duchamp and Man Ray produced some of the most purportedly "baffling" art of all time, drew enthusiastic crowds in Paris, Washington, and New York.[64] The popularity of "baffling" works by Damien Hirst, such as his embalmed shark and diamond-encrusted skull, has made him one of Britain's wealthiest men. When his first retrospective launched in Kiev, Ukraine, of all places—hardly a bastion of art-world sophisticates—the exhibition was mobbed.[65] I am not at all sure that conceptual art now suffers from a greater "appreciative failure" than many other forms have done, at one time or another, with one or another of the many audiences that encounter art they don't appreciate.[66]

A Place for Science

The fundamental claim I'm making is that fine art, as understood for something like the past 500 years of Western culture, is such a weird, near-functionless phenomenon that it has no definable qualities that can be taken for granted in its scientific study. The "essence" and aim of an artwork can be defined only in terms of all the very different things that people have got out of it, or used it for. At certain moments, that has included perceptual pleasures and emotional effects. But it has also almost always involved semantic content, as well as a "baffling" conceptual component, that have been at least as important as aesthetics and often more so.

Aesthetic science can't choose to privilege one very limited, historically specific version of art and think it's getting close to the essence of the whole phenomenon. At very least, it has to acknowledge just how constrained its purview is likely to be.

I realize that I began this chapter praising the explanatory power of science, and it may seem that I've been back-pedaling ever since. But even if I'm right that art is too semantic and conceptual and culture-bound for aesthetic science to get much purchase on it, that doesn't mean there isn't a whole lot science can tell us about the *pictures* and *objects* a culture builds its art around. Pictures and objects and our reactions to them aren't art—to the extent that aesthetic science thinks they are, it goes astray—but art is nothing without them.

Art depends on objects or actions that have certain perceivable qualities— ostensive, representational, formal, affective—and we need to go to science to find out what those qualities might be. In other words, when it comes time for art critics or historians to enumerate the features of the work that their semantic explanation will account for, they need to know just what those features are. Art experts get it wrong when they think that such enumeration is easy or obvious. The pastis bottle in a still life by Picasso, for instance, may be immediately recognizable as such to any viewer with the knowledge to identify the real thing in life, no science required. But there's more to the bottle than *what* it is. Even a Cubist picture, despite its perspectival confusion, makes implicit claims about where a bottle is in space in relationship to other features in the scene, and to an assumed viewer of it. It makes claims about the bottle's transparency or lack of such, about the light that strikes it and its relationship to other lights implied by other objects in Picasso's café. If the cultural meaning and artistic sense of Cubism depend on breaking up the normal world, we need to understand how the world of Cubism strays from normalcy. A science of pictorial perception, built on a science of visual cognition—perhaps with some neuroscience thrown in—can get at precisely such features. It can tell us, that is, what it is we're seeing in a Picasso still life, beyond just what we think we're looking at. And then more fully semantic accounts of those features can kick in.

This doesn't only apply to "difficult" world-building such as we see in Picasso. For all their stunning illusionism, even the great interiors and cityscapes of classic Dutch art don't offer up their contents to us at all transparently, as art historians often seem to assume. I've argued elsewhere that the viewing habits of modern art historians and critics have blinded them to the "what" of these pictures, so that their higher-level readings of them fail as well.[67]

Vermeer's great *View of Delft*, for instance, has often been described in formal terms as being composed in a series of horizontal strips of sky, cityscape, and water that descend the picture plane. But view the picture from very near and far off to the left, as I believe it was originally meant to be viewed—and as perspective science indicates it was constructed—and that is not at all the impression you get. The picture plane becomes nearly invisible, the sky looms overhead, the city reaches out and wraps almost around you (it isn't a "strip" on a surface but a looming presence that approaches), and the water sits in a plane below your eyes. There is no "what" in this picture, even in terms of the most surface reading of it, which can be considered apart from how it shows its scene, and how our eyes and brain can take it in. Both of the latter need the help of vision science to be properly spelled out, in Vermeer's *Delft* and in almost any picture you could name.

An art historian named Lorenzo Pericolo, in his research into the theological import of the 1599 *Calling of Saint Matthew* by Caravaggio, has long been interested in which figures in the depicted scene can see Christ, and which cannot. He is currently collaborating with scientist David Stork, whose computer simulations of the scene implied in Caravaggio's painting promise to answer questions about these issues.[68] Just knowing where figures are looking, in a random sampling of pictures, is of no interest; the result may be scientific, but it doesn't answer questions that are worth asking. Coupled to the right, semantically rich question, however, the science begins to pan out.

Attending a conference on neuroaesthetics a few years ago, I suggested that the discipline was bound to fail if its brain scans could not account for the difference between a urinal as seen in a plumbing supply store, and the identical one to be seen in Duchamp's *Fountain*, sometimes rated as the most influential work of the past 100 years. I was told the example was irrelevant, because *Fountain* wasn't the kind of "real," "normal," "natural" art—an art of aesthetics and emotions—that the discipline was there to serve. There was a better, more ecologically correct rebuttal to my claim. It's true that the brain state of someone seeing the urinal is bound to be the same as that of someone seeing Duchamp's work—that the brain state alone won't tell you why one is for peeing and the other is art. However, seeing a urinal is likely to produce different brain states than seeing a side of beef, say, or a machine gun, and the meaning of the artwork is likely to revolve around manipulating such differences, which can be studied scientifically. There is no stable, "natural" aesthetic or artistic reading of a urinal—or of any other object or picture one could name. So there's little there for science to get at. But once an object gets pulled into the game of art, the nature of that object shapes what can be done with it. In other words, there are things to say and claims to be made about the objects shown or used in a work of art that are separate from the artistic status and meaning of the work itself. And those are the claims that can, at least in theory, be tested scientifically.

Endnotes

1. Gopnik, B. (April 26, 2009). Shedding new light: David Stork uses science to see a world of art through old masters' eyes. *Washington Post*.

2. Nagel, A., & Wood, C. (2010). *Anachronic Renaissance*. New York: ZONE Books.

3. Molesworth, H. (2005). Rose Sélavy goes shopping. In L. Dickerman with M. S. Witkovsky (Eds.), *The Dada seminars* (pp. 173–189). Washington and New York: National Gallery of Art and D.A.P./Distributed Art Publishers.

4. Compare, for instance, the 1998 video by the Canadian artist Stan Douglas called *Win, Place or Show* with the 2005 video called *Repetition* by Polish artist Artur Zmijewski.

5. In an otherwise insightful essay on Cézanne—Shiff, R. (2009). Lucky Cézanne (Cézanne *Tychique*). In *Cézanne and beyond* (pp. 55–101). Philadelphia: Philadelphia Museum of Art—the great art historian Richard Shiff discusses the relationship between mark and subject matter in the painter's works but gives no sign of having consulted the important literature on that topic in the psychology and philosophy of representation. The same lack leaves a major recent book on photography by the eminent art scholar Michael Fried—Fried, M. (2008). *Why photography matters as art as never before.* New Haven and London: Yale University Press—full of errors about the nature of vision and representation.

6. Look, for example, at the works cited—or rather, not cited—by Martin Skov in Skov, M. (2009). Introduction: what is neuroaesthetics? and Neuroaesthetic problems: a framework for neuroaesthetic research. In M. Skov & O. Vartanian (Eds.), *Neuroaesthetics*. Amityville, NY: Baywood. The chapter in that same book by Anjan Chatterjee, "Prospects for a Neuropsychology of Visual Art," is equally free of art historical citations. A distracting side effect of this neglect are art historical howlers such as the claim (in Zeki, S. [1999]. Art and the brain, in *Art and the Brain* [special issue]. *Journal of Consciousness Studies, 6,* 84) that "Piero della Francesca introduced perspective into painting" (it was introduced while Piero was still a small child) or the claim (in Ramachandran, V. S., & Hirstein, W. [1999]. The science of art: a neurological theory of aesthetic experience. In *Art and the brain* [special issue]. *Journal of Consciousness Studies, 6,* 16) that "in Western art, the 'discovery' of non-representational abstract art had to await the arrival of Picasso," though that artist in fact professed contempt for abstraction.

7. Zeki, 1999, supports his position (p. 90) that "the artist is trying to represent the essentials of form as constituted in his visual perception" by quoting a series of formalist texts from the early 20th century, texts that have long since been found wanting as general accounts of art. This is like an art historian supporting a behaviorist account of representation by appealing to the authority of Piaget.

8. Ramachandran & Hirstein, 1999, p. 15.

9. Ramachandran & Hirstein, 1999, p. 24.

10. Ramachandran & Hirstein, 1999, p. 24.

11. Zeki, S. (1999). *Inner vision* (p. 12). Oxford: Oxford University Press.

12. Zaidel, D. W. (2005). *Neuropsychology of art: neurological, cognitive and evolutionary perspectives* (p. 171). Hove: Psychology Press. Zaidel is one of the few neuroaestheticians who acknowledges that "art is a human-made creation with a social anchor that communicates ideas, concepts, meanings and emotions," although that acknowledgment has almost no effect on the perceptual and neural accounts that make up the bulk of her book.

13. Reber, R., Schwarz, N., & Winkielman, P. (2004). Processing fluency and aesthetic pleasure: is beauty in the perceiver's processing experience. *Personality and Social Psychology Review, 8,* 365, discuss how "beauty" and "aesthetic value" (i.e., the value of an experience or object as art) are unrelated in their research. As the authors say, "since the emergence of modern art, a piece of art can have aesthetic value . . . without producing an experience of aesthetic pleasure." But they are wrong to imagine that this is a situation unique to modern art, as I will show.

14. Introduction: from an aesthetic point of view. In P. Osborne (Ed.) (2000). *From an aesthetic point of view: philosophy, art and the senses* (p. 7). London: Serpent's Tail.

15. Ramachandran & Hirstein, 1999, pp. 31–32. That "objectivist" view dominates the field, but there are other options. Reber, Schwarz, and Winkielman, 2004, suggest an

"interactionist" view that leaves some room for factors external to the immediate relationship between an object and its observer at the moment of interaction. They are unwilling, however, to allow prolonged thought or complex content, both typical of profound artistic experiences, much of a role in the equation that defines "aesthetic pleasure."

16. Freedberg, D. (1989). *The power of images*. Chicago and London: University of Chicago Press.

17. Vasari, G. (1962–6). *Le vite de' più eccellenti pittori scultori e architettori* [A. Rossi et al., Eds.] Milan: Club del Libro, 3:402. All translations are my own unless otherwise noted.

18. Dolce, L. (1968). Dialogo della pittura di M. Lodovico Dolce intitolato l'Aretino. In M. W. Roskill (Ed.), *Dolce's Aretino and Venetian art theory of the cinquecento* (p. 96). New York: New York University Press.

19. Vasari, 1962–6, 1:123.

20. Gopnik, B. (1995). *Pictorial mimesis in cinquecento Italy, 1500–1568: texts, visual rhetorics, and a Roman test-case*. PhD dissertation, University of Oxford.

21. Alfred Paulet, writing in 1886, quoted in T. J. Clark (1985). *The painting of modern life* (p. 264). London: Thames and Hudson.

22. Lopes, D. M. (2005). *Sight and sensibility*. Oxford and New York: Oxford University Press, proposes a much enlarged "interactionist" model of aesthetics that includes (p. 130) the "cognitive merits" of pictures. But that is not the model normally invoked in aesthetic science.

23. The aesthetic theory of the arts. In P. Osborne (Ed.) (2000). *From an aesthetic point of view: philosophy, art and the senses* (p. 68). London: Serpent's Tail.

24. Zeki, 1999, p. 76. More recently, in Zeki, S. (2009). *Splendors and miseries of the brain*. Chichester: Wiley-Blackwell, Zeki proposes (p. 1) that "the central and primordial function of the brain is the seeking of knowledge," but this does not lead to neuroaesthetic analyses that are at a much higher level of semantic sophistication than in his earlier work. They still focus on "emotional states" (p. 2) and "the appreciation of beauty" (p. 3).

25. See Noë, A. (2004). *Action in perception*. Cambridge, MA: MIT Press, and Noë, A. (2009). *Out of our heads*. New York: Hill and Wang.

26. Onians, J. (2007). *Neuroarthistory: from Aristotle and Pliny to Baxandall and Zeki* (pp. 14–15). New Haven and London: Yale University Press. Onians posits a neural substrate for his historical accounts of art historians and their ideas about art, simply by adding the phrase "as caused by certain neural states" to all his accounts of their behaviors and ideas. He does not, however, explain how that advances our knowledge beyond what the same accounts would yield without his new phrase attached. When the Renaissance writer Leon Battista Alberti noted that the first representational sculptors might have noticed the resemblance between knots in trees and human faces, it is not correct—or at best tautologically so—to say, as Onians does (p. 43), that Alberti's insights into this "mental activity" on the part of the sculptors also means that he had insight into the "neural events" that caused them. Similarly, in *Inner Vision* (p. 3) Zeki says that an artist adjusts a picture "until it pleases them, which is the same thing as saying it pleases their brains"—but it isn't the same thing at all. For one thing, any philosopher would insist that a brain can't be "pleased," only a person can, and for another, knowing that someone is pleased by a picture actually tells you almost nothing about the state of their brain; if it did, neuroscience would be unnecessary.

27. In Zeki's *Inner Vision*, the book that more or less launched neuroaesthetics, Zeki admitted (p. 2) that he chose to concentrate on works of modern art because he was

unwilling to imagine that his field could get at "the relationship between brain physiology and the perception of some of the more complex, narrative and representational works," let alone at the rich and varied meanings that a narrative or scene might convey.

28. Personal communication, Aug. 4, 2009.

29. Zeki, 1999, 8.

30. When neuroaesthetic models are applied to literary texts, it is notable that they seem incapable of dealing with actual matters of content, and focus instead on issues of structure, rhetorical devices, and emotion. In other words, to the extent that they adequately account for any responses to literary artworks, they miss out on some of the very most important ones. See, for example, Miall, D. S. (2009). Neuroaesthetics of literary reading. In M. Skov & O. Vartanian (Eds.), *Neuroaesthetics* (pp. 233–247). Amityville, NY: Baywood.

31. Onians, 2007, p. 179 and passim, rejects "cognitive" readings of art in favor of readings that privilege (p. 2) feeling, emotion, intuition, and sensation.

32. Ramachandran & Hirstein, 1999, p. 15.

33. Reber, R. (2008). Art in its experience: can empirical psychology help assess artistic value? *Leonardo, 41,* 367–372, is an unusually measured and careful analysis of the field where he proposes an approach to the art experience that includes "cognitive, perceptual, emotional and imaginative processes." But he also insists, in almost contradictory terms, that the experience must be "immediate, without the intervention of reason," which seems to rule out higher-level cognition and most kinds of artistic content, not to mention the normal cogitation that goes on when any serious art lover spends time taking in an important work. Reber ends his analysis with the caveat that his suggestions for the empirical study of the art experience may have limited applicability to "the actual practice of art"—a fact that puts the entire discipline in doubt.

34. The aesthetic theory of the arts. In P. Osborne (Ed.) (2000). *From an aesthetic point of view: philosophy, art and the senses* (p. 67). London: Serpent's Tail.

35. See T. J. Clark's analysis of a Picasso still life, as reported in Gopnik, B. (March 22, 2009). Shades of meaning at first blush. *Washington Post*. See also *Picasso and Truth*, Clark's six talks on Picasso for the 58th annual Mellon Lectures at the National Gallery of Art in Washington, D.C., March 22 to May 3, 2009, whose publication is forthcoming.

36. Ramachandran & Hirstein, 1999, p. 30. The authors align the Picasso with other supposedly "visual" objects such as "a Rodin, or a Chola bronze," and oppose it to the "semantics" of Surrealism.

37. See Molesworth, 2005.

38. Nemerov, A. (2006). Morris Louis: court painter of the Kennedy era (pp. 21–38). In *Morris Louis now*. Atlanta: High Museum of Art.

39. What is a theorist. In M. Newman & J. Elkins (Eds.) (2008). *The state of art criticism* (p. 97). Routledge: New York and Abingdon.

40. The best art, that is, has often put pressure on art's definitions, ontologies, and art-form boundaries. On these categories, see Lopes, D. (2007). Conceptual art is not what it seems. In P. Goldie & E. Schellekens (Eds.), *Philosophy and conceptual art* (pp. 238–256). Oxford: Oxford University Press.

41. Maguire, H. (1996). *The icons of their bodies: saints and their images in Byzantium* (pp. 33–34). Princeton: Princeton University Press.

42. Zeki, 2009, pp. 4–5, assumes the stability of judgments about the official "masterpieces" of Western art by such figures as Dante, Michelangelo, and Wagner.

(Wagner's name, especially, will come as a surprise to the many art lovers, past and present, displeased by his work.) Their "universal" works deserve (p. 5) "to be studied therefore for the light they may shed on common brain processes." In *Inner Vision*, pp. 22–29, Zeki discusses Vermeer as a similar example of an artist of unrivaled "psychological power," one of those who (p. 2) "understood something fundamental about the psychological make-up of man which depends upon the neurological organization of the brain."

43. Sassoon, D. (2001). *Becoming Mona Lisa: the making of a global icon* (pp. 171–220). New York: Harcourt.

44. Sassoon, 2001, passim.

45. Skov, M. (2009). Neuroaesthetic problems: a framework for neuroaesthetic research. In M. Skov & O. Vartanian (Eds.), *Neuroaesthetics* (p. 9). Amityville, NY: Baywood.

46. Vasari, 1962–6, 3:403.

47. Clark, T. J. (2006). *The sight of death: an experiment in art writing.* New Haven and London: Yale University Press (p. 115).

48. Quoted in Lopes, D. M. (2005). *Sight and sensibility* (p. 165). Oxford and New York: Oxford University Press. Lopes also quotes Stuart Hampshire, writing a decade later, saying that "one engages in aesthetic discussion for the sake of what one might see on the way, and not for the sake of arriving at a conclusion."

49. Shannon, J. (2009). *The disappearance of objects: New York art and the rise of the postmodern city.* New Haven and London: Yale University Press.

50. Reber, R. (2008). Art in its experience: can empirical psychology help assess artistic value? *Leonardo, 41,* 368, insists on accounts of art that *predict* most viewers' responses, ignoring the possibility that the "art experience" he wants scientists to study might, in the best cases, be *caused* by significant acts of criticism or interpretation.

51. The quote on the nature of science is from Goguen, J. A. (1999). Art and the brain: editorial introduction. *Art and the Brain* [special issue]. *Journal of Consciousness Studies, 6.*

52. See Miall, D. S. (2009). Neuroaesthetics of literary reading. In M. Skov & O. Vartanian (Eds.), *Neuroaesthetics* (pp. 233–247). Amityville, NY: Baywood. When Miall discusses a subject's interpretation of a short story by Irish author Sean O'Faolain, one notable feature that he doesn't dwell on is how weak those interpretations are, as reactions to a work of art. " 'Smooth, sinewy branches': That's very poetic, I like that," is not necessarily the kind of aesthetic reaction you want to hold up as exemplary, or worthy of study. In general, neuroaestheticians never seem to spell out which reactions, of the almost infinite number possible for any work of art—from those that are trivial, derivative, purely idiosyncratic, or even moronic to ones that are brilliant, insightful, and original—will count as relevant to the discipline, and which will not. If they favor "average" readings, as sometimes seems to be the case, are they then willing to rule out the study of precisely those innovative readings that will go on to shape artistic culture?

53. On kinetic and Fauve art, see Zeki, S. [1999]. Art and the brain, in *Art and the Brain* [special issue]. *Journal of Consciousness Studies, 6,* 90–94.

54. See Cutting, J. E. (2003). Gustave Caillebotte, French Impressionism and mere exposure. *Psychonomic Bulletin and Review, 10,* 319–343. I disagree with Cutting, however, when he implies that artists whose works do *not* trickle down into the culture at large might not count as part of the canon. That would leave as uncanonical crucially important and influential figures such as Correggio and Nicolas Poussin who, for complex and contingent

reasons, have not been embraced by the public. This seems to do violence to normal notions of what it means for an artistic figure to be canonical.

55. Zeki, S. (1999). *Inner vision* (p. 51). Oxford: Oxford University Press.

56. Martindale, C. (1999). Peak shift, prototypicality and aesthetic preference. In *Art and the Brain* [special issue]. *Journal of Consciousness Studies, 6,* 54. Note that the last time Picasso's "unpleasing" art was shown in Paris, hordes of people waited hours in the winter cold to get in.

57. This is known as the "institutional" theory of art. If there are questions about its applicability to the art of all cultures, at all times, it seems relatively safe to apply it to current Western conceptions of fine art. See Lopes, D. M. (2007). Art without "art." *British Journal of Aesthetics, 47,* 1–15.

58. Noë, A. (2009). *Out of our heads* (pp. 46–47). New York: Hill and Wang.

59. Goguen, J. A. (1999). Art and the brain: editorial introduction. *Art and the Brain* [special issue]. *Journal of Consciousness Studies, 6,* 12.

60. Gopnik, B. (Oct. 26, 2003). Stretching the truth: El Greco's artistic twist. *Washington Post.*

61. For an account of this picture and its meanings, see Alpers, S. (2005). *The vexations of art: Velazquez and others* (pp. 135–180). New Haven and London: Yale University Press. It is also an example of the kind of transformative, sophisticated reading that aesthetic science needs to take into account if it is going to account for the reality of what happens when people look at pictures.

62. For a 16th-century example, see Gopnik, B. (1997). Physiognomic theory and a drawing by Baldassare Peruzzi. *Konsthistorisk Tidskrift, 6,* 133–141.

63. See De Clercq, R. (2000). Aesthetic ineffability. In *Art and the Brain Part II* [special issue]. *Journal of Consciousness Studies, 7,* 87–97.

64. Ramachandran, V. S., & Hirstein, W. [1999]. The science of art: a neurological theory of aesthetic experience. In *Art and the brain* [special issue]. *Journal of Consciousness Studies, 6,* 16, simply dismiss Dada art as irrelevant to their concerns.

65. Pancake, J. (May 10, 2009). The art world's shark man, still in the swim. *Washington Post.*

66. On appreciative failure and conceptual art, see Lopes, D. (2007). Conceptual art is not what it seems. In P. Goldie & E. Schellekens (Eds.), *Philosophy and conceptual art* (pp. 238–256). Oxford: Oxford University Press. Lopes does not, however, believe that the appreciative failure he posits as particular to conceptual art indicates its larger failure as an artistic practice. The failure is in the inappropriate criteria that disappointed viewers bring to judging what is actually an impressively new art form.

67. Gopnik, B. Ken Burns's "Baseball" and Vermeer's "View": A Much Closer Look at Dutch Art. Paper presented at the conference titled *Pictures in Art, Science, and Engineering,* Berkeley, CA, March 23–25, 2007. See also Gopnik, B. (Feb. 3, 2009). The 'Golden' Compass: Dutch cityscapes point to liveliest of details. *Washington Post.*

68. Gopnik, B. (April 26, 2009). Shedding new light: David Stork uses science to see a world of art through Old Masters' eyes. *Washington Post.*

{ PART II }

Psychological Perspectives

Empirical Investigation of an Aesthetic Experience with Art

Paul J. Locher

Investigations of visitors in art museums reveal that their viewing behaviors are not random.[1] As visitors move from one artwork to another in a gallery, the time they spend looking at a painting varies from little more than a quick glance at it to 17 seconds (the median time) in front of a work that an observer finds particularly interesting and/or pleasing. Whether one decides to ignore a painting on the basis of a single brief glance at it, or take some time to "savor" it, the aesthetic experience is driven by a complex interaction among characteristics of the artwork and of the viewer. For example, a painting's pictorial features, structural organization, artistic style, and thematic content all contribute to its aesthetic appeal. Simultaneously, a visitor's characteristics, such as his or her personal history, personality, cognitive abilities, and knowledge about art, contribute to the aesthetic experience. It has also been shown that the physical (e.g., the museum setting) and social contexts (e.g., visiting alone or with friends or family) of a museum visit influence the event. These same factors contribute to an experience with art when it is viewed in different reproduction formats (e.g., art seen on a computer screen or in a printed format), as discussed below.

The many factors that contribute to an aesthetic experience are included in Jacobsen's[2] framework for the psychological study of aesthetic processing of artworks. The framework consists of seven multilevel and highly interrelated vantage points or factors from which an aesthetic experience should, according to Jacobsen, be investigated. These include (1) the *Body* or biology's contribution to our understanding of aesthetics revealed chiefly by recent advances in cognitive neuroscience; (2) the structural qualities, or *Content,* of the artifact; (3) the *Person's* individual processing characteristics and preferences; (4) the time and place at which an aesthetic experience occurs—that is, the *Situation*; (5) changes in aesthetic behavior over time (*Diachronia*) from the perspective of evolutionary biology and cultural and ontogenetic development; (6) the vantage point of comparisons within a given time segment (*Ipsichronia*) with focus on social processes, cultures, and sub-cultures, and (7) the *Mind*, as represented by contemporary psychological theories and models accounting for aesthetic experience with art, such as those presented in this chapter.

Because of the many factors that contribute to the cognitive and emotional experience of an artwork, one might assume it would be very difficult, if not impossible, for science to subject aesthetic phenomena to rigorous experimental scrutiny and identify the underlying processes involved. However, researchers working in this field have made substantial strides in recent years in doing just that. The primary purpose of this chapter is to provide an overview of research findings reported in the past decade that have contributed to our understanding of one's aesthetic experience with art. A secondary purpose is to acquaint the reader with the variety of methodological procedures and techniques used to acquire this information. Given the enormous corpus of recent literature related to the focus of this chapter, and the limited space available herein for its presentation, the topics presented will of necessity be selective and determined by my own interests and research activities in this field. I have, however, endeavored to ensure that the contents of the chapter and the research cited provide a comprehensive overview of the component processes that underlie an aesthetic experience from a viewer's initial contact with an artwork to the end of the episode.

The aesthetic experience with art has been shown to occur in two phases,[3] as is generally believed to be the case when one encounters a visual stimulus of any kind. Upon exposure to an artwork, the viewer spontaneously generates a global impression (or gist) of the work that can be acquired with the first glance at it. As described in detail below, one's first impression includes a sense of the work's pictorial content, its overall structural organization, its semantic meaning, and an initial affective response to it. Everyday observations of museum visitors' behaviors show that they very rapidly decide not to stop to view some works of art as they pass through a gallery. When, however, gist information perceived in a painting is deemed to have sufficient interest to an observer, the second phase of aesthetic processing ensues. This consists of focal exploration of the image to expand knowledge concerning the relationship between interesting pictorial features and their structural organization to satisfy cognitive curiosity and to develop aesthetic appreciation of the artwork. Leder, Belke, Oeberst, and Augusten[4] have published a detailed multicomponent information-processing model of the sensory, perceptual, and cognitive processes that occur across the two phases of an aesthetic experience with abstract art. Briefly, the model comprises a sequence of five processing stages: perceptual analyses, implicit memory, explicit classification, cognitive mastering, and evaluation. The two outputs of the model are aesthetic emotions and aesthetic judgments, which are the endpoints of aesthetic experience.

This chapter presents the findings of recent empirical investigations of the factors and perceptual/cognitive processes described above that underlie an aesthetic experience with art. It is divided into six sections: (1) the contribution of an artwork's pictorial composition and format to the experience; (2) an observer's reaction to a painting at first glance; (3) what focal exploration of a painting adds aesthetically to this initial reaction; (4) the contribution of viewer characteristics to the experience; (5) the influence of contextual factors in which an aesthetic

experience is embedded; and (6) psychophysiological approaches to the investigation of aesthetic experience.

An Artwork as Stimulus

We begin with the source of stimulation in an aesthetic experience, the artwork
itself—the *Content* factor in Jacobsen's[5] framework. A visual art form is built up of
three types or levels of perceptual organization. At the lowest level of stimulation
are the individual fundamental or first-order pictorial elements of a painting such
as line, texture, color, and shape. At the next higher level of structural organization
are the holistic perceptual qualities (such as complexity, contrast, and balance)
synthesized from these elements, and at the highest level pictorial elements
organize themselves into a composition that conveys the semantic meaning of
the work. Tinio and Leder[6] have proposed a taxonomy of image manipulation
procedures relevant for aesthetics research that corresponds to these three levels
of pictorial composition, namely surface-level manipulations, composition-level
manipulations, and semantic-level manipulations. It is important to remember
that fusion of visual information makes it difficult to isolate pictorial elements and
themes in aesthetics research. For example, in their writings about the contribution of color to the perception and evaluation of a work of art, Kreitler and Kreitler[7]
repeatedly emphasize the point that "in a picture, as in daily life, colors are bound
up with forms, objects, meanings, situations, and memories, any or all of which
may determine the pleasure or displeasure we feel when seeing colors." Despite the
high degree of interaction among levels of compositional components, researchers
have devised methodologies to investigate the contribution of pictorial elements
in their simplest or first-order form to aesthetic perception and pleasure, which is
the subject of the next section.

THE LINE: A PERCEPTUAL PRIMITIVE OF ART

The importance of line has been central in the theoretical writings about artistic
design for centuries. Early and contemporary research findings have demonstrated
that line is the most powerful aesthetic pictorial primitive that contributes to the
perception and preference for visual art of all artistic styles and degrees of structural complexity. Two properties of line that have been subjected to considerable
investigation are angularity (curved vs. angular) and orientation (vertical vs. horizontal vs. oblique). Nevertheless, there is still much to be learned about line as an
aesthetic primitive with the use of research perspectives that improve upon the
flawed designs and stimulus materials of past studies. For example, Silvia and
Barona[8] recently conducted two studies of the contribution of the angularity of lines
to aesthetic preference while controlling potentially confounding variables not
addressed in previous research, namely balance, symmetry, and prototypicality of

stimulus displays. They also sought to extend past research by examining the influence of artistic expertise on aesthetic perception and preference for line angularity. The stimuli employed in Silvia and Baron's first study consisted of black-on-white displays composed of either seven circles or seven hexagons that varied in size and distribution within a display. These manipulations produced three levels of structural imbalance of the pictorial elements: low, medium, and high. In addition, the fact that each display was composed of an equal number of circles or hexagons at each level of balance controlled for typicality—that is, neither shape was seen more frequently than the other in the stimulus set. University students, who differed in degree of self-reported training in the visual arts, saw each stimulus array for 2 seconds, after which they rated its pleasingness. Silvia and Barona found that, overall, subjects preferred the displays composed of round circles more than the angular hexagons, and this was the case regardless of the level of balance of the arrays. However, expertise moderated the effect of angularity in that angularity reduced preference only for participants with lower levels of expertise. As expertise increased, the effect of angularity decreased.

The stimuli in Silvia and Barona's[9] second study consisted of black-on-white angular asymmetrical polygons that were structurally more complex than the displays employed in Study 1. A curved version of each shape was created by digitally rounding its sharp angles. Since all of the stimuli were asymmetrical, the factor symmetry, which has been shown to influence aesthetic preference, was controlled as a potentially confounding variable in this study. Students completed a self-report measure of expertise in the arts and then were given unlimited viewing time to rate either the rounded or angular version of the 12 polygons for pleasingness and complexity. Results revealed that participants with low levels of art expertise preferred the rounded and angular polygons equally, whereas those with high degrees of expertise preferred the curved over the angular polygons. These preference patterns appeared across all levels of shape complexity. Thus, expertise once again moderated the effect of angularity on preference, but the pattern of the interaction was different for the two experiments. Silvia and Barona offer possible explanations for this discrepancy (e.g., the stimuli in Study 1 were less complex as a set than those in Study 2; the range of expertise of the sample of university students probably only extended to moderate levels), and they see their findings as demonstrating the need for continued study of line angularity, one of the oldest stimulus variables in the empirical study of aesthetics, to provide a more comprehensive understanding of the contribution of line angularity to the aesthetic quality of art.

With respect to the perceptual salience of lines in visual displays due to their orientation, there is a considerable body of psychophysical experimentation that demonstrates the oblique effect phenomenon. This is the principle that perception of oblique or diagonal lines is inferior to that of vertical and horizontal lines due, in part, to the privileged access that vertical and horizontal lines have to the visual system.[10] Latto, Brian, and Kelly[11] have shown that the psychophysical oblique effect gives rise to what they have termed an aesthetic oblique effect, which is manifest by the preference for horizontal and vertical lines over oblique lines in art. They used as their stimuli eight of the grid-based abstract paintings created by the artist Piet Mondrian. Each of these works is composed of high-contrast vertical and horizontal black lines extending either to the edge of the pictorial field or to another black line, and a red, blue, and yellow solid-color area on an off-white background. Mondrian's paintings of this style have been used as stimuli by many other researchers, some of whose work is described later, because they lend themselves to a wide range of experimental manipulations for use in aesthetics research.

Latto and his colleagues[12] showed college students with no training in the visual arts a set of stimuli that consisted of eight original paintings created by Mondrian, four with horizontal/vertical orientation formats and four with oblique (i.e., lozenge) formats; additionally, each original was shown rotated seven times at 45-degree intervals. Half of the rotations resulted in horizontal/vertical orientations of the paintings' component lines and the other half resulted in oblique component lines. Participants rated each of the 64 pictures for aesthetic pleasingness after viewing it for 5 seconds. Latto and coworkers found that, consistent with the notion of an aesthetic oblique effect, paintings presented with their component lines in a horizontal or vertical orientation were rated as more aesthetically pleasing than when their lines were in an oblique orientation. This effect was enhanced when the lines were parallel to a picture's format orientation (e.g., vertical lines in a vertically oriented painting), demonstrating that the orientation of a picture contributes to the salience of line orientation within a pictorial field and to its aesthetic value. Additionally, the overall rating for the originals was slightly higher than that for all the rotated versions. Recently, Plumhoff and Schrillo[13] replicated Latto and coworkers' experiment exactly and obtained comparable results, namely that art-naïve observers rated the paintings composed of horizontal/vertical lines as more aesthetically pleasing than pictures composed of oblique lines.

Latto and Russell-Duff[14] provide empirical evidence that artists are aware intuitively of the aesthetic oblique effect and preferentially use lines in their compositions oriented in the horizontal and vertical directions rather than the oblique. They measured the proportion of the three types of lines (operationally defined in detail by the researchers) in a representative selection of 88 20th-century paintings in the Israel Museum, Jerusalem, that varied in painting styles (e.g., abstraction, landscapes, self-portraits). The artists were found to overwhelmingly use vertical and horizontal lines as contrasted with oblique lines (45%, 31%, and 24%, respectively) to construct their compositions. There was a format effect such that the artists used more vertical lines within a portrait format and more horizontal lines within landscape formats.

HIGHER-LEVEL PERCEPTUAL QUALITIES OF ART: BALANCE AND THE "POWER OF THE CENTER"

The primary informational units of an artwork like those discussed above organize themselves through structural coupling into higher-level perceptual qualities, such as balance, symmetry, complexity, density, and continuity. Balance has long been considered by artists in most painting traditions and by writers on Western art to be the primary overriding design principle for unifying structural elements within a composition, and there is considerable empirical evidence[15] that balance influences the immediate and sustained perception of an artwork as well as its perceived aesthetic qualities. A balanced composition results when its structural elements and their qualities are arranged in such a way that their perceptual forces, or perceived weights, compensate one another about a balancing point or center. A balanced composition appears anchored or stable; it appears to be visually right (i.e., "good") with respect to its structural organization.[16] The perceived weights of pictorial elements within a painting are determined by such characteristics as their size, shape, location within the composition, and implied "directionality." Additionally, artists have known for a long time that the juxtaposition of colors within a composition is a major contributing factor to its balance or harmony. One general principle concerning the use of color found in treatises on composition and documented by a long history of experimental investigations involving the spatial balance of color pairs is that a large area of a dull, unsaturated color can be balanced by a small area of a highly saturated color.[17] This color-weight principle of color balance was quantified by Munsell[18] over a century ago in his law of inverse ratios of areas, which states that the areas of color used in combination should be inversely proportional to the product of their values (brightness) and chromas (saturation).

Everyday color displays, such as pictures, paintings, and computer images, typically contain more than two colors. In such images the perceived structural weight of each color component and the location of the composition's balance center are functions of the relationship among all of the colors and the areas they occupy. Piet Mondrian addressed the compositional issue of color balance "experimentally" in the non-objective grid-based paintings he produced in the 1920s through the 1940s. His search for the fundamental visual elements of abstraction and a universal design principle of order is manifest in his creation of a large number of abstract paintings, each of which, as previously described, is composed of three different-sized rectangular color areas (either red, yellow, or blue) within a lattice of horizontal and vertical black lines on an off-white background. Mondrian is known to have studied and revised some of his paintings over very long periods of time in order to achieve his goal of optimizing balance in each composition.[19] His abstract artworks have been used as art stimuli in many experimental aesthetics investigations of aesthetic primitives[20] because his compositions are relatively simple geometrical patterns and because the associative effects of the color planes with things of reality are controlled, or at least minimized, thereby excluding the semantic level of processing from investigations of compositional-level structural properties.

Locher and colleagues[21] used abstract paintings by Mondrian to investigate the contribution of color to pictorial balance in structurally more complex stimuli than had been previously studied (i.e., color pairs). They created their set of stimuli by experimentally changing the colors in the three color areas (red, yellow, or blue) of six original works by Mondrian so that the resulting five variations and their original constituted the six possible spatial arrangements of the three colors in the three locations. The size of the color planes varied across the set of originals. In Experiment 1, design-trained and untrained university students were given unlimited viewing time to determine the location of the perceived balance center of each composition seen in a random order on a computer screen and then to rate the apparent weight or heaviness of its three color areas.

The perceived weight of a color in an artwork was found to vary reliably for both trained and untrained viewers as a function of the size of the area it occupied, with red consistently being perceived as heavier than blue, which was perceived as heavier than yellow. Additionally, the balance centers of the originals were perceived to be located at or near the geometric or physical center of all compositions by both groups of participants, demonstrating the power of the center of a composition to function as the anchor point of its structural organization.[22] There was greater scatter of the perceived balance centers about the geometric centers of the perturbed versions compared to the originals, indicating that manipulation of color within the compositions disrupted the balance structure. Shifts in balance centers between the originals and their five variations were reliable, however, only for the trained participants, demonstrating their superior sensitivity to the contribution of color to balance structure compared to the untrained viewers.

Additional empirical support for the power of the center of a visual display is provided by the findings of a series of experiments conducted by Palmer, Gardner, and Wickens[23] that investigated university students' aesthetic preferences as a function of the horizontal position and facing direction of single, directed meaningful objects within a surrounding rectangular frame. Objects in their first three experiments were of two types: those that can in reality move in a particular direction (viz., a man, woman, car, boat, and cat) and those that can merely face in a particular direction (viz., a chair, teapot, flower, windmill, and telescope); only the forward-facing or front view of objects was used in this study. The researchers hypothesized that a moving object might exhibit a naturally stronger directional bias to take it toward the center of the frame than objects that were typically stable. The influence of the height-to-width aspect ratio of the images (two tall, thin vertical objects [a man and a flower]; two short, wide horizontal objects [a wolf and a sheep]; and two objects equal in height and width [a teapot and a rocking horse]) on shape-based directional effects was also examined. Objects were placed individually at one of either three or seven positions equally spaced along the horizontal axis of the frame in Experiments 1 and 2, respectively, and directed objects faced either to the right or left of the frame. In both experiments participants were shown two pictures simultaneously that differed only in the spatial framing of an object and asked to select the picture they preferred. In the third experiment, participants used a computer mouse to move the object along the horizontal midline of the frame until they found the most aesthetically pleasing position. People were given a camera in a fourth experiment and asked to take the most aesthetically pleasing picture they could of a teapot, a tape dispenser, and a steam iron under instructional conditions that imposed no constraints on the position/ location of the images in the picture produced, or they were given instructions that constrained the composition of the photo taken to conditions examined in the first three experiments.

Palmer and colleagues'[24] findings were similar across all four experiments. Viewers' aesthetic preferences were consistently greatest when front-facing objects were located at or near the center of the frame and decreased with distance to the right and left from the center. This "symmetrical center bias" provides strong additional evidence for the visual and aesthetic importance of the center in spatial composition. Additionally, the researchers reported that participants exhibited a stronger preference for directed objects that face into rather than out of the picture frame, and right-facing objects were preferred over left-facing ones (labeled the "inward bias" and "rightward bias," respectively, by the authors). These preference biases contributed considerably less to aesthetic preference for the objects studied than did the center bias. Palmer and colleagues conclude that their combined findings, which were obtained for the simple compositional properties investigated, affirm the power of the center of a pictorial display and facing direction of objects within the display in viewers' appreciation of visual art.

THE INFLUENCE OF PICTURE FORMAT ON THE AESTHETIC EXPERIENCE

When it comes to experiencing great art, most museum professionals assert that "there is nothing like the original." The aesthetic adequacy of reproductions of original artworks continues to be the focus of much discussion among theoretical aestheticians[25] and art educators.[26] Most people see the works of renowned artists in some form of reproduction, either as images on a computer screen, in printed pictures, or as slide-projected images. Given the widespread use of reproductions of art in aesthetics research, one would suspect a great many investigations about what is lost, or possibly gained, in an aesthetic experience when a viewer interacts with an original work in a museum by a renowned artist as compared with reproductions of it in different image formats. (The museum setting as a contributing context factor to an aesthetic experience is discussed later in this chapter.) In fact, very few studies of this sort have appeared in the literature over the years, and early studies of this type were conducted before new imaging technologies emerged that produce high-quality digital images of original artworks that seem to capture somewhat faithfully their physical properties.

Locher, Smith, and Smith[27] addressed the question of image and aesthetic adequacy of reproductions of art in a study conducted at New York's Metropolitan Museum of Art. Specifically, they sought to determine the influence of image

format on viewers' perception and evaluation of the pictorial and aesthetic qualities of paintings viewed in one of three different formats within the museum: the
originals seen in the museum galleries, slide-projected images, or images viewed
on a computer screen. Participants were adult art-naïve or sophisticated museum
visitors who volunteered approximately 1 hour of their visit for the study. They
rated each of nine paintings by renowned artists on 16 measures of physical and
structural characteristics, novelty of content, and aesthetic qualities. In a related
study Locher and Dolese[28] had art-trained or naïve university students perform
the same rating task with postcard images of the nine artworks in a laboratory
setting.

Results of the two studies revealed that ratings of the adjective pairs assessing
qualitative (items: patterned/random, homogeneous/heterogeneous, symmetrical/
asymmetrical, continuous/intermittent) and quantitative (items: crowded/
uncrowded, simple/complex, homogeneous/heterogeneous) stimulus properties
of the compositions were remarkably similar across the original and three reproduction formats for both naïve and sophisticated individuals. Moreover, sophisticated individuals consistently rated the paintings across all formats as more
complex, varied, asymmetrical, and contrasting than did unsophisticated visitors.
Thus, with respect to the physical and structural properties of the art, the four
presentation formats exhibited "pictorial sameness." However, in terms of the
observers' evaluative judgments, the majority of the artworks studied (those by
Chardin, Christus, Giotto, Rembrandt, van Eyck, and Vermeer) were rated significantly more surprising, interesting, and pleasant in the original than in reproduction by both groups of participants; ratings by the sophisticated visitors were
significantly higher than those of the naïve participants across formats, but no
interaction effect was obtained. These findings suggest that when it comes to experiencing the pleasure of art, there may, in fact, be nothing like the original. It
should be noted, however, that the format did not reliably influence either group's
ratings of the interest and pleasingness across formats for the works by Bruegel,
El Greco, or van Ruisdael, making it clear that much more research is required to
identify the characteristics of paintings that contribute to the hedonic value of a
composition in the original compared to reproductions of it.

Additional insights into the influence of presentation format on an aesthetic
experience are provided by Hubard,[29] who recorded the responses of 14-year-olds
to a Renaissance painting by the artist Petrus Christus entitled *A Goldsmith in His
Shop, Possibly St. Eligius* (1449) viewed in one of four conditions. Participants saw
the work as an original in New York's Metropolitan Museum of Art or as a postcard
or on a computer screen at their school, or they saw the works counterbalanced in
all three conditions. Participants observed each image for 20 minutes, during
which time they responded to a structured interview (which was taped) designed
to engage the students in dialogue with the contents of the work. Comparisons of
the response content across the four viewing conditions revealed that considerable
commonality in response content was observed across formats for issues related to

color, detail, clothes worn by the persons depicted, their socioeconomic differences, and the narrative to which the work alludes. There were two areas in which responses to the originals differed from those of both types of reproduction. The large scale, visual clarity, and richness of the original led to more accurate identification of scene components (e.g., the central figure was seen, correctly, as a goldsmith and not as a scientist, a carpenter, or a father, as was commonly the case in reproduction conditions) and in more complex interpretations of the painting than those suggested by its reproductions. Furthermore, the narratives of those who saw the original were more consistent with the one described in the wall label by the Museum. Additionally, all of the students who saw the work in three formats preferred the original to the reproductions. They volunteered that this was because of the size of the painting and the clarity of the smallest detail and because they were viewing "the real thing," which made them feel that they had access to something unique and valued. Hubard concluded that the students' preferences were shaped not only by the physical qualities of the images but also by their notions of the cultural status of originals compared to reproductions. The importance of the social context in which an aesthetic experience with art takes place is discussed later.

Another limitation to most experimental aesthetics research is the fact that the art reproductions used as stimuli are either almost always smaller (computer screen images) or sometimes larger (projected images) in size than the originals. Locher and colleagues[30] addressed this issue in a second experiment in their investigation of the contribution of color to pictorial balance described above. They sought to determine the ecological validity of findings obtained from the smaller computer screen images used in their first study by comparing them to findings obtained while participants viewed projected images in the second study that were the actual size of the originals. Differences in size of a reproduction may be a particular problem when abstract artworks are under investigation because many abstract painters effect both a spatial and a temporal organization in their artworks. As a viewer scans the structure of a large abstract painting in a museum setting, it is possible that the temporal or successive contrast effects of the colors on each other may change the perceived weight of the elements, which in turn will modify its balance structure.[31] In other words, perception of the color of one area may influence physiologically perception of the color in the next area fixated. In Locher and colleagues' Experiment 2, untrained participants performed the same tasks as in Experiment 1 (locating the balance center of each composition and rating the weights of its color areas) while viewing projected images of the art stimuli that were the actual size of the originals (ranging from 18 to 22 inches [45.7 to 56 cm] on a side). It was found that the perceived weights and the location of the perceived balance centers were very similar to those observed in Experiment 1, in which the art stimuli were presented as approximately 7-inch-square (17.8 cm) images on a color monitor. This finding provides additional empirical evidence for the "structural similarity" of certain types of pictorial features of artworks across viewing formats observed by Locher, Smith, and Smith.[32]

Locher and associates[33] speculate that while looking at the reproduction of a painting, people are able to adjust to the fact that they are viewing a reproduction and "look past" the limitations of the medium. Simply put, when one is looking at a Vermeer painting on a computer screen, for example, one accommodates to the screen image and focuses attention on the accomplishments of Vermeer. Participants' incidental comments while viewing reproductions during the experiment were almost exclusively related to the art and not the medium. Locher and associates speculate that even when looking at a reproduced image of a painting, people are able to immerse themselves in the composition and respond to many of its properties and qualities in a fashion similar to what their reactions would be if they encounter the original. They labeled this phenomenon *facsimile accommodation* and speculate that a viewer's immersion in an art facsimile may be likened to the sense of "presence" reported by users of virtual environment systems—to their perceptions of being enveloped within a virtual system.[34] Additional research is required to investigate the contribution of format characteristics of art to the aesthetic perception of visual art to test the limits of structural similarity.

The Aesthetic Experience "At First Glance"

As mentioned above, upon exposure to an artwork, the viewer spontaneously generates an initial global impression (or gist) of the work that is acquired with the first glance, or at most the first few glances, at it. Research has demonstrated that one's first impression of an artwork includes a sense of its pictorial content and structural organization, the semantic meaning conveyed, and an initial affective response to it. For example, Locher and colleagues[35] performed two experiments during which university students with no training in the visual arts were shown eight paintings by renowned artists representing a range of styles along an abstract (Klee's *Temple Gardens*)–representational (Vermeer's *Young Woman with a Water Pitcher*) continuum. In Experiment 1 participants saw a brief flash presentation of each artwork lasting 100 milliseconds, after which they immediately wrote five descriptions and/or impressions of the painting they would tell someone who had never seen it in an attempt to describe the work to that person. After completing this task, the eight artworks were presented individually a second time for 100 milliseconds in the same order, and participants rated the pleasingness of each artwork. In the second experiment another group of participants was given unlimited time to view each painting and evaluate it for pleasingness; their eye movements *and* verbal reactions to the artworks were recorded continuously as they completed the task.

The five statements about each painting obtained in Experiment 1 were classified in terms of six types of reactions that reflect a qualitative continuum of response ranging from attention to individual physical properties and pictorial elements of the compositions, to two or more elements described as a perceptual unit, to more holistic properties and characteristics of the compositions, including their realism, beauty, expressiveness, style, and form. Locher and associates[36] found that few of the respondents' first reactions to the paintings or their additional four comments (2% and 4%, respectively) reflected attention to single compositional elements (e.g., There is a boat in the picture). Rather, the majority of participants' initial and later reactions to the artworks were evenly distributed among statements that reflect attention to a group of pictorial elements perceived as a compositional unit (e.g., There is a woman reading a book), to the expressiveness of the whole composition (e.g., There is an intense dark feeling conveyed), or to its artistic style (e.g., The painting is very abstract) and form (e.g., The elements are just all over the place).

In the unlimited viewing time study (described later in greater detail), it was observed that participants began to describe holistic characteristics of the artworks of the type described above approximately 2 seconds after the onset of a pictorial display. These were likely based on the content of at most the first few glances at an artwork, given that the average duration of a fixation in aesthetics research is typically 300 milliseconds. Additional evidence that a global impression of an artwork is achieved at first glance is provided by the finding that the pleasingness ratings of the paintings obtained following the brief presentation correlated 0.73 with ratings obtained following unlimited viewing in the second experiment. This similarity suggests that the evaluation of an artwork's pleasingness can be made rapidly, as is typically observed in the viewing behaviors of museum-goers. However, it must be noted that the average pleasingness ratings for the set of paintings for Experiments 1 and 2 were 4.59 and 6.17, respectively, on a 10-point scale, demonstrating that the stimuli were evaluated as significantly more pleasing when participants had unlimited time to view them.

Additional support for a global response component to the aesthetic experience is provided by Smith, Bousquet, Chang, and Smith's[37] investigation to determine if the length of viewing time and presence of a label affect the perception and appreciation of a painting. University students unsophisticated in the visual arts viewed four paintings under a label or no-label condition and in a 1-second, 5-second, 30-second, or 60-second time condition. Each participant saw the four artworks on a computer screen in only one combination of conditions. The paintings were two works by Impressionists (Cézanne's *Still Life with Apples* and Monet's *Garden at Saint-Adresse*) and two modern works (Davis' *Report from Rockport* and Mondrian's *Composition with Red, Yellow and Blue*). After viewing each painting participants responded via computer to 24 adjective pairs of a semantic differential scale comprising three subscales: an *evaluative scale* (e.g., items pleasant/unpleasant, appealing/unappealing, interesting/uninteresting), an *activity scale* (e.g., items dynamic/calm, intense/relaxed, active/passive), and a *potency/structure scale* (e.g., items simple/complex, structured/unstructured, weak/powerful). A series of analyses revealed that the perception and evaluation of a given painting were not influenced by the length of time a viewer spent looking at it or by the presence of a label—that is, ratings obtained for the 1-second time condition did not reliably differ from the ratings obtained for the other time conditions. As would be expected, the ratings were dependent on the work of art itself, as evidenced by the large differences of participants' evaluations across the four paintings. For example, the abstract paintings by Mondrian and Davis were rated as reliably higher on items of the *activity* subscale than the Impressionist works by Cézanne and Monet.

Taken together, the findings obtained by Locher[38] and Smith[39] and their colleagues support the view that their participants' initial reactions to the artworks were based on stimulus information distributed across the pictorial field and that they responded to it in a holistic or global fashion. Furthermore, the findings demonstrate that the gist reaction to an artwork consists of more than just the immediate perception of pictorial properties such as a painting's symmetry, balance, or complexity of structural features, which research has shown can be detected with little more than a 50-millisecond glance at an artwork.[40] Moreover, they are consistent with Rasche and Koch's[41] explanation of the nature of a gist response and the neural mechanisms responsible for it.

Visual Exploration of an Artwork

As mentioned, if the content of a painting available in the initial global impression of it is deemed by a viewer to be worthy of continued attention, the second phase of aesthetic processing ensues. This consists of focal scrutiny of the image to acquire detailed perceptual and semantic information about the painting to satisfy cognitive curiosity and to develop aesthetic appreciation of it. In the field of experimental aesthetics, as in many other areas of research interest, the study of eye movements has proven to be a very useful tool to reveal the perceptual and cognitive component processes that underlie an aesthetic experience with visual art.[42] As an observer looks at a painting, his or her eyes move in rapid jumps or saccades followed by pauses or fixations. In general, one's eyes move three or four times per second during visual search. The number, duration, and location of the fixations used to scrutinize a work are determined by the interactions among the many factors mentioned by Jacobsen.[43] By superimposing a viewer's eye movements over an image of a display he or she has examined, one can map out the location and sequence of fixations, called a scanpath, and identify the pictorial features of it that raised the viewer's interest and invited exploration. A scanpath provides a graphic record of how information from an artwork was selected and processed by a viewer across the time course of an aesthetic experience with it. However, as Treisman[44] cautions, "the window of attention set by the parietal scan can take on different apertures, to encompass anything from a finely localized object to a global view of the surrounding scene." Thus, scanpaths provide accurate information about fixations but do not always lead to correct conclusions regarding the viewer's focus of attention and the underlying cognitive processes involved.

The study by Locher and associates[45] discussed above included two experiments that together were designed to obtain additional support for the two-phase processing model of aesthetic experience. In the second experiment, the eye positions of university students untrained in the visual arts were recorded as they viewed reproductions of eight masterpieces one at a time on a computer monitor for as long as they wished before rating each one for pleasingness. The eye-tracking system used sampled eye position every 1/60 of a second with a high degree of accuracy (i.e., to less than 1 degree of visual angle). As participants viewed each art stimulus they talked out loud about their reactions and thoughts about each painting; their verbal protocols were recorded simultaneously with their eye movements, a procedure not employed in previous eye-movement studies in this field.

For purposes of data analyses, the aesthetic episode was divided into three time periods: the first 3 seconds of viewing, from 3 seconds to 7 seconds of viewing, and the total viewing period, which averaged 30 seconds across the stimulus set. These time periods were used because it was found that in almost all cases participants began to speak about a composition between 2 to 3 seconds after it appeared on the screen, and 98% of all initial verbal reactions were completed within the first 7 seconds of exploration. As reported above, the overwhelming majority of participants' initial reactions to the artworks in both the limited and unlimited viewing time conditions (i.e., Experiments 1 and 2) were evenly distributed among statements that reflected attention to a group of pictorial elements perceived as a compositional unit, to the expressiveness of the whole composition, or to its artistic style and form. Furthermore, the distribution among the various types of responses did not change reliably following a viewer's first full statement about a work until he or she provided a pleasingness rating when finished looking at it.

The eye-fixation pattern for each participant for each painting was quantified for each time period by superimposing a 5 × 5 grid over the pictorial field and measuring the percentage of total fixation time in each grid location. These data were used to examine the nature of the coverage of the pictorial field. For example, if a participant directly fixated pictorial elements in 5 of the 25 grid cells of an artwork during the first 3 seconds of exploration, initial coverage of that artwork would be 20%. It was found that participants' initial responses to an artwork, which were begun approximately 2 seconds after its onset and were overwhelmingly holistic in nature, were generated from direct fixation of compositional elements contained in approximately one fourth (27% on average across the stimulus set) of the pictorial field. By the time viewers completed their first statements about an artwork they had significantly expanded their coverage to 38%, on average, of the painting. Coverage during the second focal exploration stage of processing increased to 46%, on average, a nonsignificant increase over coverage at 8 seconds. (There were no significant differences in average coverage obtained among the three time periods for the eight stimuli.) Furthermore, the regions of the pictorial field that received direct fixation were located in the center of the composition, and grid locations in the outer regions of each painting were not directly fixated or did not receive sustained fixation, a consistent finding in eye-movement studies carried out with reproductions of artworks. Presumably, information in the peripheral region of many compositions serves as the backdrop for the pictorial elements of central interest, and this region therefore receives little or no direct fixation unless the structural organization of the painting is deliberately designed to invite sustained attention there.

The fixation data were also used to identify which pictorial features in each composition drew viewers' attention across the time course of the aesthetic experience. Locher and coworkers[46] had five artists and five researchers engaged in experimental aesthetics investigations identify the locations of three pictorial elements or regions of each composition they considered to be the principal contributors to the structural organization and semantic meaning of the work. Consistent with the notion of the power of the center of visual art, almost all of the elements identified by the experts were located in the middle cells of the virtual grid employed for analyses. It was found that before verbalizing their initial reactions to the artworks, participants had directly fixated at least two major structural components identified by the experts during 67% of all trials, and this value increased to 85% by the time participants had verbalized fully their initial reactions to the artworks.

It was also found that the distribution of short-dwell and long-dwell fixations across the pictorial field remained very similar during the focal stage of exploration. Based upon their investigation of the role of formal art training on the perception and aesthetic judgment of artworks that differed in experimentally manipulated balance, and drawing upon Berlyne's[47] theoretical framework for relating perceptual analysis of artworks to their aesthetic judgment, Nodine, Locher, and Krupinski[48] distinguished between two types of exploratory behavior during an aesthetic experience: diversive exploration and specific exploration. Diversive exploration is carried out by short-dwell fixations (durations less than 300 milliseconds), which are used to scan the pictorial field to locate attractive, informative, interesting features. Periodically, as these features are discovered, long-dwell gazes (greater than 400 milliseconds) are directed to them to resolve questions of meaning and significance to the overall compositional theme, which is the purpose of specific exploration. As mentioned, Locher and associates[49] observed that the scanpaths of the untrained viewers in their study exhibited a fairly even distribution of both types of exploration, suggesting that their attention to pictorial details seemed to be guided fairly evenly by stimulus properties and cognitive curiosity in judging the aesthetic value of the paintings. Nodine and colleagues observed the same scanning strategy for individuals untrained in art who viewed original artworks and a less or more balanced altered version of each one as they selected the version they preferred. Trained participants, on the other hand, engaged in more specific and less diverse exploration, indicating that they were more sensitive to and devoted more time to the compositions' structural designs and less to pictorial detail.

Locher and associates'[50] findings for Experiments 1 and 2 demonstrate that major compositional elements of the paintings drew naïve viewers' interest at the earliest stage of exploration and likely contributed to their global impressions of the art. Furthermore, attention during the second phase of the experience remained directed for the most part to these pictorial features, presumably to satisfy cognitive curiosity about the contents of the artwork and develop more fully an aesthetic appreciation of it. This assertion is supported by the finding mentioned above that the average pleasingness rating for the set of paintings in the unlimited viewing condition was significantly higher than that generated from the global percept acquired with the brief 100-millisecond glance.

A more recent eye-movement study conducted by Kapoula, Daunys, Herbaz, and Yang[51] provides additional insights into the nature of the interaction of stimulus-driven influences (the degree of abstractness of a painting) and cognitively driven influences (manipulation of information concerning a painting's title) on an aesthetic experience. The art stimuli employed were three Cubist paintings by Fernand Léger: *The Wedding* (composed of fragments of human faces, limbs, and arbitrary pictorial fragments), *The Alarm Clock* (composed of pictorial fragments creating the perception of a person), and *Contrast of Forms* (consisting of forms and cylinders). Art-naïve adults explored each artwork either without knowing its title (called the spontaneous condition by the researchers), with the instruction to invent a title for each artwork (the active condition), or knowing the actual title of the work before viewing it (the driven condition). Participants' eye movements were recorded as they examined for an unlimited time each of the three paintings presented on a computer screen, after which they were interviewed about their perception and comprehension of each artwork.

Kapoula and colleagues[52] observed both commonalities and differences in visual encoding of the artworks during the first and last 5 seconds of exploration across the three paintings and three title conditions. Specifically, the center of a virtual grid superimposed on the images to quantify eye-movement behaviors received more fixation time than any other grid location for all conditions during both the initial and final phases of exploration, once again demonstrating with the "power of the center" notion. Additionally, fixations were more highly concentrated in the central area of each painting during the first 5 seconds than the last 5 seconds of exploration, which the authors suggest demonstrates the important contribution of information in the central area of the compositions to observers' initial impressions of the artworks. Moreover, participants tended to focus their gaze along the central vertical axis of each painting, about which the important structural components of each composition are located.

Differences in exploratory behavior were also observed as a function of title condition and artwork. Fixation durations were significantly different, on average across all paintings, among the three title conditions: durations were longest in the driven condition, shorter in the active condition, and shortest in the spontaneous condition. Kapoula and associates[53] suggest that this is due to the different levels of cognitive activity required by the three tasks. For example, they speculate that being given the actual title of a painting in the driven condition caused viewers to implement a search strategy to fit the contents of the painting to its title, which engaged a deeper level of semantic analysis, and correspondingly a greater number of long-dwell fixations, than used in the other two task conditions. The specific pictorial content of the paintings also contributed in a differential fashion to the participants' visual exploration. For example, *The Wedding* produced smaller sac-cade sizes (i.e., the distances between fixation locations) in the active and driven conditions than was the case for the other two paintings, presumably due to visual aspects of the composition (i.e., the high density of small pictorial fragments) and to the detailed semantic analysis required by the many real human faces and limbs contained in this composition. Collectively, Kapoula and associates' findings dem-onstrate the complex interaction of bottom-up (stimulus-driven) and top-down (cognitively driven) influences on visual exploration during an aesthetic experi-ence and the contribution that eye-movement research makes to the study of the processes involved.

The Viewer's Contribution to the Art Experience

The viewer brings individual processing characteristics and preferences to an expe-rience with art that are derived from the many components of his or her develop-ment. This section focuses on two key viewer characteristics that influence the art experience, namely expertise in the visual arts and the personality trait "openness to experience"—examples of Jacobson's[54] *Diachronia* and *Person* factors, respectively.

AESTHETIC FLUENCY

Training in art has consistently been shown to influence the processes underlying an aesthetic experience with art as well as emotional responses to it. Examples of the influence of this factor have been described in several studies presented thus far in this chapter. In general, it is typically found that artistically sophisticated people view artworks differently than do naïve individuals, and they have a greater tendency to find complex artworks more interesting and pleasing than naïve indi-viduals. The effects of training in art on aesthetic phenomena have been explained by a number of recent theories, including the processing fluency model of Reber, Schwartz, and Winkielman;[55] Axelsson's[56] scheme theory; and Silvia's[57] appraisal theory. Most researchers who have evaluated the contribution of expertise to aesthetics have contrasted the reactions to art between groups of novices and experts, usually those who self-report no formal education or training in the arts or art-related fields with those who have had training. There are two important limitations to this methodology: (1) art expertise has been shown to develop along a continuum (e.g., Parson's[58] stage model of art appreciation) and should not, therefore, be treated as a nominal variable with two levels, as has typically been the case, and (2) art expertise is not acquired just by direct instruction, but it is also achieved through experience with art in museums, in galleries, in school, by reading books, and increasingly on the Internet.

Smith and Smith[59] introduced the notion of aesthetic fluency to address these limitations. They define aesthetic fluency as the knowledge base that one has about art and aspects of life closely related to art that facilitates aesthetic experience in individuals, and they developed the Aesthetic Fluency scale to measure it. The scale, which provides a continuous measure of sophistication, was generated from the responses of a large sample of visitors to New York's Metropolitan Museum of Art to a survey that asked them to rate how much they knew about five artists (Mary Cassatt, Isamu Noguchi, John Singer Sargent, Alessandro Boticelli, and Gian Lorenzo Bernini) and five ideas in art (Fauvism, Egyptian funerary stelae, Impressionism, Chinese scrolls, and Abstract Expressionism). In addition, participants were asked a number of demographic questions, and questions concerning their museum visitation history, overall educational level, and training in art history. A series of analyses revealed that aesthetic fluency, as measured by the Aesthetic Fluency scale, develops gradually and broadly across areas of art, evidenced by the observed continuous distribution of knowledge on the 10 items of the scale across the sample of museum-goers in the study. Furthermore, it was found that aesthetic fluency is greatly influenced in a positive way by frequency of museum visitation, age, and training in art history (but not educational level).

Additionally, Silvia[60] reports that university students' levels of aesthetic fluency were highly correlated with the Openness to Experience scale of the Big Five dimensions of personality (discussed in the next section), but not to the Neuroticism, Extraversion, Agreeableness, or Conscientiousness scales. People high in aesthetic fluency were not generally found by Silvia to be smarter, as assessed by several measures of fluid intelligence. Thus, use of the Aesthetic Fluency scale in future investigations of the contribution of art sophistication to the aesthetic experience addresses limitations of previous studies in this field by providing researchers with a continuous quantitative measure (the scale's Likert rating format) of a viewer's knowledge about the arts rather than his or her informal, self-reported level of expertise.

RELATING PERSONALITY TO AESTHETIC REACTIONS

Traits and personality characteristics vary greatly among individuals, yet a considerable body of research shows that certain basic components of personality are related to aesthetic reactions and preferences. Feist and Brady[61] observed that the most consistent and robust findings of studies focused on the characteristics of observers that determine their aesthetic responses to art show that one's cognitive and dispositional flexibility, as well as openness to experience, are correlated with various aspects of aesthetic preference. Feist and Brady contributed to this literature with a study in which they sought to identify the psychological and social attitude profile of persons who prefer the generally unappreciated form of art, abstract art. College student volunteers completed two openness to experience scales and an experience-seeking scale; they responded to questions related to political liberalism and tolerance of substance abuse, and provided demographic information pertaining to their age, gender, race, and income; the political and religious affiliations of their parents; and their class and major in school. They also were given 5 seconds to rate their preference for each of 15 realistic, 15 abstract, and 15 ambiguous forms of art presented in a random order.

Feist and Brady[62] found that, overall, participants preferred realistic to abstract art, and this effect was most pronounced for individuals low in openness to experience. On the other hand, open participants preferred every style of art presented, and their preference increased as the art became more abstract. Additionally, those students who held attitudes that were more tolerant of political liberalism and drug use preferred abstract art the most. None of the demographic variables were significantly associated with preferences for abstract art. Feist and Brady argue from an evolutionary perspective that moderate levels of openness to experience, non-conformity, and risk taking have been adaptive in human evolution, and that a subset of humans has always been more receptive and open to novel experiences, whether in nature or manmade, as in the case of abstract art. They conclude that, consistent with the findings of other studies in this area of research, openness to experience is the personality trait that is most consistently associated with aesthetic appreciation, even if art is very abstract. This finding was replicated for museum-goers recently by Mastandrea, Bartoli, and Bove,[63] who reported that visitors to both the Braschi Museum for Ancient Art and the National Gallery of Modern and Contemporary Art in Rome achieved high scores on the Big Five Openness to Experience personality measure, with no significant differences between the two groups of visitors on this measure. Additionally, visitors to the modern and contemporary art collection scored significantly higher in sensation seeking than did those who viewed the Braschi collections.

The Influence of Context on the Aesthetic Experience

Every art experience, whether in a museum or gallery, on the Internet, or with printed matter, is embedded within a variety of contexts, which collectively constitute the *Situation* factor in Jacobsen's[64] framework. In the past 10 years there has been a considerable increase in audience-based investigations of the factors that contribute to museum experience and learning with respect to the interplay of three contextual factors: physical, personal, and social. This is because museum culture has made a major shift from its traditional roles of focusing on collection, scholarship, and preservation of artifacts to museums as public educational institutions. To organize a museum's holdings in such a way so as to foster visitor learning experiences, Chang[65] points out that a museum must know who is visiting, why they are visiting and with whom, what they do and see in the museum, and how all of these factors interact and interrelate. The following describes several examples of the interactive influence of contextual factors on an aesthetic experience in a museum setting.

Art museums themselves are imbued with high social status by most members of society because they contain artifacts of high social value—an *Ipsichronia* factor in Jacobsen's[66] framework. It is believed that the cultural notions about the value of "high art" lend a certain positive aura to a museum experience, although this author knows of no study that has sought to determine just how much additional positive valence the museum adds to the aesthetics of the artifacts within. As one informal example, however, recall that the adolescents in Hubard's[67] study who experienced only the original Renaissance painting by Petrus Christus and those who saw the original and two forms of reproduction reported that they preferred the original because it was "the real thing," which made them feel that they had access to something unique and valued. Recently, Mastandrea and colleagues[68] reported that the number-one reason given by visitors for their attendance at the National Gallery of Modern and Contemporary Art in Rome was to see the artworks in the original.

This ties into the great ongoing theoretical debate concerning the question of whether a painting on a museum wall, widely admired and praised as a masterpiece by art critics, loses some or all of its aesthetic value when it is confirmed to be a fake, as was the case when several paintings believed in the art world to have been painted by Vermeer were discovered to be the work of Han van Meegeren.[69] The acceptance of his paintings as genuine Vermeers was so complete that when he confessed that they were forgeries, no one believed him. There was certainly no difference in the monetary value between original paintings by Vermeer and van Meegeren's "visually indistinguishable" forgeries, for which van Meegeren earned the equivalent of $50 million. But how might the aesthetic value of the paintings have changed after they were accepted as forgeries? This is a fascinating issue that has yet to be subjected to empirical scrutiny (but see the study by Leder[70]). Would a collection of paintings by world-renowned artists displayed in a shopping mall and identified as the works of local artists receive the same aesthetic evaluations as when they are experienced in a museum and correctly identified? For the obvious practical limitations, a research study of this type is most unlikely to be completed.

There is an interesting paradox associated with the social context of a museum demonstrating the complex nature of contributing factors to an aesthetic experience.

It has been found[71] that museums' social status reinforces feelings of exclusion for some while strengthening feelings of belonging by others. What keeps non-visitors from art museums are their perceptions that museums are formal, formidable places that are for the upper class only; that those who visit museums are knowledgeable about art; and that they dress up for their visit. Thus non-visitors see museums as inaccessible to themselves because they feel they do not have sufficient background of the type they think necessary to interact with high art. Even on days when there is free entry, such individuals remain non-visitors to a great degree. In fact, the perceptions of non-visitors are supported by visitor studies that consistently show that, demographically, art museum visitors, on average, are well educated (55% have some graduate school education), Caucasian, mainly professional people with incomes greater than $50,000, and are central city residents who frequently visit museums and galleries. The many educational programs for children's groups conducted by museum staff are attempts to make the museum experience more meaningful to populations not now in attendance.

Social contexts within a museum also influence the way visitors engage with the art and how much they learn and remember about the contents of the collection. Differences in social context are linked to their personal agendas for the visit (e.g., enjoyment, socializing, discovery, relaxation). As one example of a social process factor, it is well documented[72] that the majority (frequently reported as high as 85%) of adult visitors to art museums come in the company of a partner, friend, or family group. Studies show those who visit alone have a higher need for cognition than those who visit in groups, spend more time reading labels, are much more likely to use audio guides, and demonstrate greater learning. Nearly 50% of couples attending the museum do not talk to each other while viewing the art and experience it in very much the same way as those who visit alone. The number and duration of social interactions among pairs who are experiencing the museum "together" varies as to the time spent looking at works, discussing their content, and reading text, all of which influence the nature of the experience. The art styles of the collection housed within a museum also attract different types of visitors in terms of the motivation for their visit. Mastandrrea, Bartoli, and Bove[73] report that visitors to the Museum Borghese of Rome (ancient art collection) were intent upon learning about and understanding the art and its history, whereas visitors to the Peggy Guggenheim Collection of Venice (contemporary art) took an emotional and pleasure-seeking approach to their experience.

Psychophysiological Approaches to the Investigation of the Aesthetic Experience

Neuroscientists working within the emerging discipline known as neuroaesthetics have in recent years made considerable progress toward an understanding of the brain areas and mechanisms that underlie a viewer's aesthetic processing and preference for the visual arts, referred to as the *Body* or biology's contribution to our understanding of aesthetics in Jacobsen's[74] framework. This area of research and knowledge obtained are described in much detail in the chapters in the third section of this volume, making it unnecessary to present any of this literature here (see also Skov and Vartanian[75] for a review of this literature).

Measurement of the changes in pupil size of an observer as he or she looks at a painting is another psychophysiological approach to the understanding of the aesthetic experience. This is because task-evoked pupillary responses have been shown to be reliably sensitive to cognitive aspects of information processing as well as affective components of emotional processing. A recent study by Kuchinke, Trapp, Jacobs, and Leder[76] demonstrates the potential for the application of this technique to the study of art appreciation. They examined the relationship between the ease of processing of the content of abstract Cubistic art (i.e., processing fluency) and positive aesthetic emotion. Specifically, the task for art-naïve university students was to press a mouse button at the moment they recognized a concrete object depicted in an abstract painting. The paintings differed across three levels of increasing content accessibility (low, medium, or high). For example, the face of the woman in Picasso's *Femme et Pot de Moutarde* was readily apparent in this high-processing-fluency painting, whereas the boats in George Braque's *Fishing Boats* were low in visual accessibility. The time needed to recognize a depicted object and the viewer's pupillary response following the point of recognition were recorded. Participants also rated each painting's complexity, familiarity, and their preference for it following the first phase of the study. As Kuchinke and associates anticipated, the time to recognize a depicted object was shortest for high-processing-fluency paintings, which were also rated highest in preference. Additionally, higher processing fluency was associated with larger pupil dilation following the point of recognition of an object. Moreover, pupil dilation following participants' behavioral response was positively related to individually rated preferences of the abstract paintings. The researchers interpreted their findings as supporting the "hedonic fluency model,"[77] which predicts higher processing fluency of paintings being associated with positive aesthetic affect.

Conclusion

The research findings described in this chapter demonstrate that substantial strides have been made in the past few years in illuminating the complex interaction of the many factors and processes that underlie an aesthetic experience with art. At the same time, this body of knowledge makes clear the need for much additional research employing the many different techniques currently in use in this field before a scientifically comprehensive theory and model of how art provides an observer with an aesthetic experience can be achieved.

Endnotes

1. See Smith, J., & Smith, L. (2001). Spending time on art. *Empirical Studies of the Arts, 19*, 229–236, and Chang, E. (2006). Interactive experiences and contextual learning. *Studies in Art Education, 47*, 170–186.

2. Jacobsen, T. (2006). Bridging the arts and sciences: a framework for the psychology of aesthetics. *Leonardo, 39*, 155–162.

3. See Locher, P. (2006). The contribution of eye-movement research to an understanding of the nature of pictorial balance: a review of the literature. *Empirical Studies of the Arts, 14*, 143–163, and Locher, P., et al. (2007). Visual interest in pictorial art during an aesthetic experience. *Spatial Vision, 21*, 55–77.

4. Leder, H, et al. (November 2004). A model of aesthetic appreciation and aesthetic judgments. *British Journal of Psychology, 95*, 489–508.

5. Jacobsen, T. (2006). Bridging the arts and sciences: a framework for the psychology of aesthetics. *Leonardo, 39*, 160.

6. Tinio, P., & Leder, H. (2009). Natural scenes are indeed preferred, but image quality might have the last word. *Psychology of Aesthetics, Creativity, and the Arts, 3*, 52–56.

7. Kreitler, H., & Kreitler, S. (1972). *Psychology of the arts* (p. 33). Durham, NC: Duke University Press.

8. Silvia, P., & Barona, C. (2009). Do people prefer curved objects? Angularity, expertise, and aesthetic preference. *Empirical Studies of the Arts, 27*, 25–42.

9. Silvia, P., & Barona, C. (2009). Do people prefer curved objects? Angularity, expertise, and aesthetic preference. *Empirical Studies of the Arts, 27*, 35.

10. See Latto, R. (1995). The brain of the beholder. In R. Gregory et al. (Eds.), *The artful eye* (pp. 66–94). Oxford: Oxford University Press.

11. Latto, R., Brian, D., & Kelly, B. (2000). An oblique effect in aesthetics: homage to Mondrian (1872–1944). *Perception, 29*, 981–987.

12. Latto, R., Brian, D., & Kelly, B. (2000). An oblique effect in aesthetics: homage to Mondrian (1872–1944). *Perception, 29*, 982–983.

13. Plumhoff, J., & Schrillo, J. (2009). Mondrian, eye movements, and the oblique effect. *Perception, 38*, 719–732.

14. Latto, R., & Russell-Duff, K. (2002). An oblique effect in the selection of line orientation by twentieth-century painters. *Empirical Studies of the Arts, 20*, 49–60.

15. See review by Locher, P. (1996). The contribution of eye-movement research to an understanding of the nature of pictorial balance. *Empirical Studies of the Arts, 14*, 143–163.

16. Locher, P. (2003). An empirical investigation of the visual rightness theory of picture perception. *Acta Psychologica, 114*, 147–164.

17. See Locher, P., Overbeeke, K., & Stappers, P. J. (2005). Spatial balance of color triads in the abstract art of Piet Mondrian. *Perception, 34*, 169–189.

18. Munsell, A. (1905). *A color notation.* Boston, MA: George H. Ellis Company.

19. McManus, I. C., Chemma, B., & Stoker, J. (1993). The aesthetics of composition: a study of Mondrian. *Empirical Studies of the Arts, 11*, 83–94.

20. For example, Latto, R., Brian, D, & Kelly, B. (2000). An oblique effect in aesthetics: homage to Mondrian (1872–1944). *Perception, 29*, 981–987, reported earlier.

21. Locher, P., Overbeeke, K., & Stappers, P. J. (2005). Spatial balance of color triads in the abstract art of Piet Mondrian. *Perception, 34*, 169–189.

22. See Rudolf Arnheim's classic book on spatial composition in the visual arts: Arnheim, R. (1988). *The power of the center.* Berkeley, CA: University of California Press.

23. Palmer, S., Gardner, J. & Wickens, T. (2008). Aesthetic issues in spatial composition: effects of position and direction on framing single objects. *Spatial Vision, 21,* 421–449.

24. Palmer, S., Gardner, J. & Wickens, T. (2008). Aesthetic issues in spatial composition: effects of position and direction on framing single objects. *Spatial Vision, 21,* 421–449.

25. See Currie, G. (1985). The authentic and the aesthetic. *American Philosophical Quarterly, 22,* 153–160.

26. See Hubard, O. (2007). Originals and reproductions: the influence of presentation formats in adolescents' responses to a Renaissance painting. *Studies in Art Education, 48,* 247–264.

27. Locher, P., Smith, J., & Smith, L. (2001). The influence of presentation format and viewer training in the visual arts on the perception of pictorial and aesthetic qualities of paintings. *Perception, 30,* 449–465.

28. Locher, P., & Dolese, M. (2004). A comparison of the perceived pictorial and aesthetic qualities of original paintings and their postcard images. *Empirical Studies of the Arts, 22,* 129–142.

29. Hubard, O. (2007). Originals and reproductions: the influence of presentation formats in adolescents' responses to a Renaissance painting. *Studies in Art Education, 48,* 247–264.

30. Locher, P., Overbeeke, K., & Stappers, P. J. (2005). Spatial balance of color triads in the abstract art of Piet Mondrian. *Perception, 34,* 179.

31. Wurmfeld, S. (2000). Color painters/color painting. In S. Davis (Ed.), *Color perception: philosophical, psychological, artists and computational perspectives* (pp. 31–51). Oxford: Oxford University Press.

32. Locher, P., Smith, J., & Smith, L. (2001). The influence of presentation format and viewer training in the visual arts on the perception of pictorial and aesthetic qualities of paintings. *Perception, 30,* 449–465.

33. Locher, P., Smith, J., & Smith, L. (2001). The influence of presentation format and viewer training in the visual arts on the perception of pictorial and aesthetic qualities of paintings. *Perception, 30,* 450.

34. See Witmer, B., & Singer, M. (1998). Measuring presence in virtual environments: a presence questionnaire. *Presence, 7,* 225–240.

35. Locher, P., et al. (2007). Visual interest in pictorial art during an aesthetic experience. *Spatial Vision, 21,* 55–77.

36. Locher, P., et al. (2007). Visual interest in pictorial art during an aesthetic experience. *Spatial Vision, 21,* 66.

37. Smith, L., et al. (2006). Effects of time and information on perception of art. *Empirical Studies of the Arts, 24,* 229–242.

38. Locher, P., Overbeeke, K., & Stappers, P. J. (2005). Spatial balance of color triads in the abstract art of Piet Mondrian. *Perception, 34,* 169–189.

39. Smith, L., et al. (2006). Effects of time and information on perception of art. *Empirical Studies of the Arts, 24,* 229–242.

40. Locher, P., & Nagy, Y. (1996). Vision spontaneously establishes the percept of pictorial balance. *Empirical Studies of the Arts, 14,* 17–31.

41. Rasche, C., & Koch, C. (2002). Recognizing the gist of a visual scene: possible perceptual and neural mechanisms. *Neurocomputing, 44–46,* 979–984.

42. See reviews of this literature by Locher, P. (2006). The contribution of eye-movement research to an understanding of the nature of pictorial balance: a review of the literature. *Empirical Studies of the Arts, 14,* 143–163, and Nodine, C., & Krupinski, E. (2003). How do viewers look at artworks? *Bulletin of Psychology and the Arts, 4,* 65–68.

43. Jacobsen, T. (2006). Bridging the arts and sciences: a framework for the psychology of aesthetics. *Leonardo, 39,* 156.

44. Treisman, A. (2006). How the deployment of attention determines what we see. *Visual Cognition, 14,* 411–443.

45. Locher, P., et al. (2007). Visual interest in pictorial art during an aesthetic experience. *Spatial Vision, 21,* 55–77.

46. Locher, P., et al. (2007). Visual interest in pictorial art during an aesthetic experience. *Spatial Vision, 21,* 69.

47. Berlyne, D. (1971). *Aesthetics and psychobiology.* New York: Appleton-Century-Crofts.

48. Nodine, C., Locher, P., & Krupinski, E. (1993). The role of formal art training on perception and aesthetic judgment of art compositions. *Leonardo, 26,* 219–227.

49. Locher, P., et al. (2007). Visual interest in pictorial art during an aesthetic experience. *Spatial Vision, 21,* 72.

50. Locher, P., et al. (2007). Visual interest in pictorial art during an aesthetic experience. *Spatial Vision, 21,* 66.

51. Kapoula, Z., et al. (2009). Effect of title on eye-movement exploration of Cubist paintings by Fernand Léger. *Perception, 38,* 479–491.

52. Kapoula, Z., et al. (2009). Effect of title on eye-movement exploration of Cubist paintings by Fernand Léger. *Perception, 38,* 486–487.

53. Kapoula, Z., et al. (2009). Effect of title on eye-movement exploration of Cubist paintings by Fernand Léger. *Perception, 38,* 489.

54. Jacobsen, T. (2006). Bridging the arts and sciences: a framework for the psychology of aesthetics. *Leonardo, 39,* 158 and 160.

55. Reber, R., Schwartz, N., & Winkielman, P. (2004). Processing fluency and aesthetic pleasure: is beauty in the perceiver's processing experience? *Personality and Social Psychology Review, 8,* 364–382, and Chapter 9, this volume.

56. Axelsson, Ö. (2007). Individual differences in preferences to photographs. *Psychology of Aesthetics, Creativity, and the Arts, 1,* 61–72.

57. Silvia, P. (2005). Cognitive appraisals and interest in visual art: exploring an appraisal theory of aesthetic motivation. *Empirical Studies of the Arts, 23,* 119–133, and Chapter 10, this volume.

58. Parsons, M. (1987). *How we understand art: a cognitive developmental account of aesthetic experience.* Cambridge: Cambridge University Press.

59. Smith, L., & Smith, J. (2006). The nature and growth of aesthetic fluency. In P. Locher, C. Martindale, & L. Dorfman (Eds.), *New directions in aesthetics, creativity and the arts* (pp. 47-58). Amityville, NY: Baywood Publishing Company.

60. Silvia, P. (2007). Exploring aesthetic fluency. *Psychology of Aesthetics, Creativity, and the Arts, 1,* 247–249.

61. Feist, G., & Brady, T. (2004). Openness to experience, non-conformity, and the preference for abstract art. *Empirical Studies of the Arts, 22,* 77–89.

62. Feist, G., & Brady, T. (2004). Openness to experience, non-conformity, and the preference for abstract art. *Empirical Studies of the Arts, 22,* 83.

63. Mastandrea, S., Bartoli, G., & Bove, G. (2009). Preferences for ancient and modern art museums: visitor experiences and personality characteristics. *Psychology of Aesthetics, Creativity, and the Arts, 3,* 164–173.

64. Jacobsen, T. (2006). Bridging the arts and sciences: a framework for the psychology of aesthetics. *Leonardo, 39,* 161.

65. Chang, E. (2006). Interactive experiences and contextual learning. *Studies in Art Education, 47,* 181.

66. Jacobsen, T. (2006). Bridging the arts and sciences: a framework for the psychology of aesthetics. *Leonardo, 39,* 159.

67. Hubard, O. (2007). Originals and reproductions: the influence of presentation formats in adolescents' responses to a Renaissance painting. *Studies in Art Education, 48,* 262.

68. Mastandrea, S., Bartoli, G., & Bove, G. (2009). Preferences for ancient and modern art museums: visitor experiences and personality characteristics. *Psychology of Aesthetics, Creativity, and the Arts, 3,* 168.

69. Wynne, F. (2006). *I was Vermeer.* New York: Bloomsbury.

70. Leder, H. (2001). Determinants of preference: when do we like what we know? *Empirical Studies of the Arts, 19,* 201–211.

71. Chang, E. (2006). Interactive experiences and contextual learning. *Studies in Art Education, 47,* 173.

72. See Ballantyne, R., & Packer, J. (2005). Solitary vs. shared: exploring the social dimension of museum learning. *Curator, 48,* 177–192.

73. Mastandrea, S., Bartoli, G., & Bove, G. (2007). Learning through ancient art and experiencing emotions with contemporary art: comparing visits in two different museums. *Empirical Studies of the Arts, 25,* 173–191.

74. Jacobsen, T. (2006). Bridging the arts and sciences: a framework for the psychology of aesthetics. *Leonardo, 39,* 160.

75. Skov, M., & Vartanian, O. (2008). *Neuroaesthetics.* Amityville, NY: Baywood Publishing Co.

76. Kuchinke, L., et al. (2009). Pupillary responses in art appreciation: effects of aesthetic emotions. *Psychology of Aesthetics, Creativity, and the Arts, 3,* 156–163.

77. Reber, R., Schwartz, N., & Winkielman, P. (2004). Processing fluency and aesthetic pleasure: is beauty in the perceiver's processing experience? *Personality and Social Psychology Review, 8,* 364–382; and Chapter 9, this volume.

{ 8 }

Hidden Knowledge in Aesthetic Judgments

PREFERENCES FOR COLOR AND SPATIAL COMPOSITION

Stephen E. Palmer, Karen B. Schloss, and Jonathan Sammartino

Aesthetic science is intended to be an interdisciplinary enterprise in which people from a wide variety of fields—including art practice, design, philosophy, psychology, art criticism, neuroscience, art history, sociology, cultural anthropology, and others—engage in a meaningful scholarly exchange aimed at understanding aesthetics and its role in the human condition throughout history. A natural starting point would be to provide a working definition of *aesthetics*. Much has been written on this subject, but there seems to be surprisingly little agreement. For purposes of the present chapter, we take *aesthetics* to be the study of that dimension of human experience anchored at the positive end by feelings that would elicit verbal expressions such as, "Oh wow! That's great! I love it!" and at the negative end by "Ugh! That's awful! I hate it!"

Clearly, it would be preferable somehow to ground such a definition in the external world, but doing so is surprisingly difficult. In defining more "objective" experiential dimensions, such as *redness*, one can augment a subjective definition by pointing to easily identifiable, prototypical examples: *Redness* is that chromatic experience common to the visual appearance of ripe strawberries, fresh blood, Coca-Cola cans, fire hydrants, and so forth, when viewed under standard daylight conditions. Unfortunately, this strategy is not available for aesthetics simply because people's aesthetic responses to such putative prototypes are too variable. If one were to claim, for instance, that aesthetics refers to the kind of experience that is common to one's perceptions of Van Gogh's *Starry Night*, Michelangelo's *David*, Beethoven's *Ninth Symphony*, Frank Lloyd Wright's Fallingwater, a perfectly shaped rose, etc., at least two important problems arise. One is that people's aesthetic responses differ so greatly that there may be some individuals who have strongly negative aesthetic experiences to all of the supposedly positive prototypes. The lack of agreement about aesthetic response even to such prototypes effectively derails the "exemplar" strategy.

Another problem is that aesthetic response, at least in our view, does not refer just to positive experiences or even just to extreme experiences. We assume that everyone has some sort of aesthetic response to everything he or she encounters (see also Chapter 9). It may be embedded only in the "fringe" of consciousness,[1] but it is there, nevertheless. Aesthetic response can come into focal consciousness in a variety of circumstances: when the aesthetic response is extreme (e.g., seeing something so wonderful or so terrible that it calls attention to itself on purely aesthetic grounds), when one's attention is directed to aesthetic response by context (e.g., viewing paintings in a museum or shopping for home furnishings in a store), or when one is given explicit instructions to do so (e.g., in the aesthetic ratings tasks researchers give participants in laboratory experiments).

In this chapter we address two principal questions about human aesthetic experience: How are aesthetic responses related to stimulus dimensions, and what causes people to have them in the first place? We will address these issues as concrete, well-defined empirical problems that can be approached using the standard tools of scientific research: formulating hypotheses about how the visual system works and/or why it works that way, doing experiments designed to test these hypotheses, interpreting the results in light of them, and formulating further hypotheses to be tested in the next iteration of an ongoing hypothesis-testing cycle.

Although we find it fairly obvious that aesthetic response can be studied scientifically, others may not. Indeed, some would claim that aesthetic science is not only impossible but oxymoronic, presuming that science and aesthetics are somehow inherently contradictory and incompatible concepts. Science, for example, is supposedly lawful and objective, whereas aesthetics is claimed to be whimsical and subjective. We acknowledge that there is a logical possibility that aesthetic science might fail if there were *no* systematic commonalities among different people's aesthetic preferences, but this is an empirical issue. Below we report several results that provide significant insights into aesthetic questions using rigorous experimental methods.

The two domains we have been studying are aesthetic preferences for color and spatial composition. Other than the fact that color and spatial structure are both visual features potentially relevant to aesthetic response, they seem to have little in common, being distinct aspects of vision that diverge within the visual nervous system right in the retina and appear to stay separated through much of early cortical processing.[2] Nevertheless, aesthetic responses to chromatic and spatial structure seem to have a surprising high-level commonality in that both are strongly influenced by implicit statistical knowledge of the observer's ecological niche. Below we review our reasons for coming to this conclusion.

Color Preferences

Most people have relatively strong and pervasive aesthetic preferences among colors. Although such preferences can differ quite dramatically across individuals, there do appear to be regularities. In modern Western cultures, for example, more people name blue as their favorite color than any other.[3] A century of scientific investigation has taught us a great deal about *which* colors people like, on average,[4-5] but there has been surprisingly little work on *why* people like the colors they do. In the first half of this chapter, we describe our attempt to fill this gap. The answer we propose, which we call the *ecological valence theory* (or EVT),[6] is relatively straightforward: people like colors to the degree that they like the environmental objects that are that color. If true, the EVT implies that the human brain contains statistical information about the overall affective valence (liking to disliking) of interactions with colored objects. Some of this knowledge may come genetically through the evolutionary history of the species, but some of it is surely specific to the autobiographical history of the individual. We first describe the EVT in the context of other theories of color preference. We then present experimental results that measure color preferences. Finally, we present data that test the theories, and we argue that the data strongly favor the EVT.

THEORIES OF COLOR PREFERENCE

Given the importance of the question, surprisingly little has been written about why people like the colors they do. Most of the literature on color preference consists of psychophysical experiments that simply describe preferences without explaining them.[7-8] This is, of course, an essential first step in understanding color preferences, but going on to answer the *why* question is the important next step, which has seldom been taken.

One approach was suggested by Nicholas Humphrey,[9] who proposed that color preferences arise because of the different signals that colors convey to organisms in nature. He argues that colors can send "approach" signals, such as the colors of flowers that attract pollinating bees, or "avoid" signals, such as the colors of poisonous toads that warn off potential predators. The underlying idea is that because colors carry information about which kinds of objects an organism should or should not interact with, it would be beneficial if the organism "liked" the colors that send approach signals and "disliked" the ones that send avoid signals, as these aesthetic experiences will lead the organism to behave adaptively. The bottom line is that the relevance of chromatic information for the organism's health and well-being makes it beneficial for the organism to behave in accord with such color preferences.

A related idea is proposed in Hurlbert and Ling's evolutionary theory, in which they suggest a neural mechanism for color preferences based on hard-wired, cone-opponent responses that arose from natural selection.[10,11] The physiological aspects of their theory are based on well-understood mechanisms in the first few synapses of the human color vision system (see Palmer, pp. 107–121,[12] for a summary). Hurlbert and Ling[13] found that 70 percent of the variance in their preference data could be explained by contrasts between the outputs of these cone-based systems in response to a color relative to its surrounding color. Among their findings was a gender difference on which they based their evolutionary hypothesis: females tended to prefer redder colors, whereas males tended to prefer colors that were more blue-green.[14]

Hurlbert and Ling[15] attributed this gender difference to evolutionary adaptation within prehistoric hunter-gather societies. They conjectured that females like redder colors because their visual systems were selected for finding ripe red fruit. They mentioned only this one example, however, and did not speculate on why males might prefer colors that appear more blue-green or why both genders prefer colors that are more blue-violet than those that are more yellow-green. By extrapolation, there should be evolutionarily good reasons for these other preferences as well, depending on which colors are most adaptive for members of the species, but the authors did not elaborate on such matters. Genetic modifications would presumably have accrued over an evolutionary time scale such that the members of the species came to be tuned to the most adaptive color preferences, whatever those might be.

There is a variant of this theory that has the same conceptual foundation but is based on a higher-level set of color dimensions. At some (as yet unknown) level of the visual nervous system, the representation of color in humans appears to undergo a transformation into a different set of three dimensions: hue (consisting of red-versus-green and blue-versus-yellow), brightness (how light or dark colors are), and saturation (how intense or vivid colors are). This set of dimensions is historically associated with the color theory of Ewald Hering[16] and is most closely aligned in modern times with the Natural Color System specified by Hård and Sivik.[17] We call this theory the "color appearance theory" simply because its dimensions correspond more closely to people's conscious experiences of color appearance than the outputs of the cone systems.[8]

Another approach to answering the *why* question is based on the emotional content of colors. Ou and associates[18,19] proposed and studied a set of "color-emotions," which they defined as "feelings evoked by either colors or color combinations." They did not actually propose it as a theory of *why* people prefer the colors they do, but it can readily be interpreted containing such a theory with a few additional assumptions. They proposed that people's experiences of colors include nine emotion-like dimensions: *warm–cool, heavy–light, modern–classical, clean–dirty, active–passive, hard–soft, tense–relaxed, fresh–stale, masculine–feminine*. They measured people's responses to colors in terms of these color-emotion dimensions and performed a factor analysis of these data. Sixty-seven percent of the variance in their color preference data could be explained by three factor-analytic dimensions: *active–passive* (active preferred), *heavy–light* (light preferred), and *warm–cool* (cool preferred). They did not speculate on how color-emotions arise nor why some color-emotions predict preferences better than others. It is unclear, for example, why *happy–sad* was not included as a color-emotional dimension; as perhaps the most evaluatively polarized emotion of all, it would seem to be relevant, but it does not seem to fit the obvious prediction that happy colors should be well liked and sad colors poorly liked. Our own data show that most shades of yellow are rated as happy colors and many shades of blue as sad colors, yet blues are among the most preferred colors and yellows among the least preferred (see Fig. 8.1C).

To extend the color-emotion theory to account for *why* people like the colors they do, one simply needs to assume that people like colors to the degree that they like the color-emotions produced by or consistent with viewing those colors. Because people like *active*, *light*, and *cool* colors better than *passive*, *heavy*, and *warm* ones, this hypothesis predicts that they should also tend to find *active*, *light*, and *cool* feelings more desirable than *passive*, *heavy*, and *warm* feelings. In a small study, we found that the first two dimensions of their three-factor model are appropriately aligned with this prediction, because people do rate *active* and *light* feelings as more desirable than *passive* and *heavy* ones, but we also found they generally rate *warm* feelings as more desirable than *cool* ones, which is inconsistent with the prediction.

The EVT that we propose as a framework for understanding color preferences in some sense unites and extends these previous approaches. It is based on both an evolutionary premise that color preferences are fundamentally adaptive and an emotional premise that affective valences (positive to negative evaluations of experiences) underlie them. The primary difference is that the EVT proposes it is not people's responses to the colors themselves that determine preferences, but their affective responses to the objects that are those colors.

In general, the EVT posits that people's health and well-being are likely to be improved if they are attracted to things whose colors "look good" to them and avoid things whose colors "look bad" to them. We thus view color preferences as providing a kind of steering mechanism roughly analogous to that provided by taste preferences in eating. Generally speaking, people's health and well-being are likely to be improved if they eat things that "taste good" to them and avoid eating things that "taste bad" to them. The rationale is that the tastes people tend to like (e.g., sweet fatty substances) are correlated with high-calorie content and those they tend not to like (e.g., bitter sour substances) are correlated with toxic content. The analogous ecological heuristic underlying the EVT will be similarly adaptive if how "good" versus "bad" colors look to people correlates with the degree to which things that characteristically are those colors are advantageous versus disadvantageous to their health and well-being.

The EVT makes a clear empirical prediction: average preferences for any given color over a representative sample of people should be highly predictable from average emotional responses (positive to negative) of similar people to the set of correspondingly colored objects. In other words, people should generally like colors associated with objects that tend to elicit positive affective reactions (e.g., blues and cyans with positively valued clear sky and clean water) and dislike colors associated with objects that tend to elicit negative reactions (e.g., brown and olive colors with negatively valued biological waste products and rotting food). We test this central prediction of the EVT in Experiment 2 and compare its predictions for color preferences with the predictions of theories based on cone contrasts,[20] color appearances,[21] and color-emotions.[22]

Feedback from color-relevant experiences can influence color preferences in at least two ways. First, it could shape genetically based preferences for evolutionarily advantageous colors over evolutionarily disadvantageous ones, as Humphrey (1976) and Hurlbert and Ling (2007) suggest. These preferences would presumably reflect universal biases in the ecological statistics of color within the human ecological niche (e.g., blue skies and brown feces). Similar principles might also hold for other species, but we will restrict our attention to people, who are much easier to study. Second, learning mechanisms could tune an organism's color preferences during its own lifetime based on environmental feedback such that it comes to like the colors it has found to be associated with advantageous outcomes and dislike colors it has found to be associated with disadvantageous outcomes. To the extent that people prefer more advantageous outcomes, they should learn to prefer the colors associated with those outcomes.

The best evidence for innate color preferences in humans comes from measurements of looking preferences in infants. Researchers measure either how much time infants spent looking at each color in comparison with white during a series of fixed-duration trials or the percentage of trials on which infants look first at each color in comparison with white. Figure 8.1A shows data adapted from Teller, Civan, and Bronson-Castain[23] for the first-look preferences of 12-week-old infants viewing pairs of six colors. The general shape of this function, with a peak at blue and valley around yellow-green, is surprisingly similar to the average hue preferences we find in adults (Fig. 8.1B,C). Although the infant preference function may of course reflect learning during the first 12 weeks of life, it may also include a strong innate component.

The EVT assumes that learning mechanisms modify color preferences from the inborn starting point, leading eventually to adult preference functions that reflect many diverse influences. Through interactions with objects in the environment, people learn valences for particular objects depending on the pleasantness/ unpleasantness of their experiences with them. For example, biting into a delicious red apple or diving into a refreshing blue lake should produce an increment of positive affect to corresponding red and blue colors, whereas smelling feces or tasting rotten fruit should produce a decrement in positive affect to the corresponding brown and olive colors. Colors thus accumulate increments and decrements in aesthetic valence by association with the corresponding objects, such that color preferences come to reflect the overall desirability of things associated with that color.

The EVT implies several levels at which environmental factors might influence color preferences. First, average color preferences from large, diverse samples of people across the world should reflect universal trends in colored object valences.

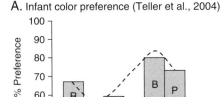

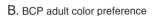

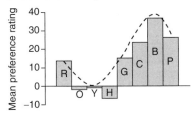

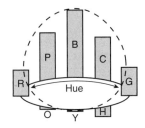

FIGURE 8.1 **Hue preference functions for saturated colors in infants and adults.**
(A) Infants most prefer looking at blue and least prefer looking at yellow (Teller et al., 2004).
(B) Preference patterns in aesthetic ratings for saturated colors by adults in the Berkeley
Color Project (BCP). (C) Data in B plotted in circular coordinates to highlight the difference
between blue–yellow versus red–green dimensions. Dashed curves indicate the overall
similarity of the functions (A and B) and how they translate into circular coordinates (C).

Presumably nearly everyone in every culture likes clear sky and clean water, but dislikes feces and rotten food. If similar trends hold for the valences of other objects of these colors, there should be a general liking of blues and cyans and a disliking of browns and olives that largely transcend culture. Second, systematic differences between color preferences in different cultures should co-vary with corresponding cross-cultural differences. There could be differences in color–object associations (e.g., Japanese observers may associate a certain shade of reddish orange with Shinto shrines, whereas observers from the United States would not) and/or differences in object valences (e.g., people in Japan may like eel, where it is considered a culinary delicacy, much more than people in the United States do). Third, systematic sub-cultural influences should also arise from individuals' associations with various societal groups with strong color associations, such as sports teams, universities, religions, and/or gangs. Other sub-cultural effects could arise from beliefs about what colors complement (versus clash) with one's eye, skin, and hair color. Fourth, truly idiosyncratic effects should also be present. The color of grandmother's rocking chair, for example, might have a positive effect on an individual's aesthetic response to that color if he or she loved sitting on grand-mother's lap in that chair as a child, but a negative impact if he or she loathed and dreaded those experiences with grandma. It would be impossible to tease apart all such idiosyncratic influences for any single individual, but some of them can be effectively isolated and studied, as we will explain later in this chapter.

We should also note that color preferences may change systematically over time on a scale from weeks to years within individuals and from years to centuries within cultures. Color fashions in the modern clothing industry change seasonally in fairly consistent ways and annually in less predictable ways. Even more dra-matic are cultural sea-changes in color preferences that have occurred over peri-ods of decades or longer, such as the ones Pastoureau[24] has documented for blue. Surprisingly, blue was the least favored color in ancient Rome, probably because blue was so prized by their arch-enemies, particularly the Celts and Germans, who painted themselves in blue for battle. Pastoureau posits that blue rose to favor in part via its association with the Virgin Mary within the increasingly dominant Catholic church.

One of the great virtues of the EVT is that all of these factors—universal, cultural, sub-cultural, idiosyncratic, and even dynamic—can potentially be accom-modated within its scope. That is not to say that it is so amorphous that it fails to make testable predictions: as we will show, numerous tests are possible, not only of its basic predictions across large samples of people, but also of more specific predictions that should hold with carefully selected subsets of individuals who share specific cultural and even personal experiences.

AVERAGE COLOR PREFERENCES IN THE UNITED STATES

The 32 colors we studied were systematically sampled over the three most salient dimensions of color appearance: hue, saturation, and brightness (Fig. 8.2). We effectively based our sampling on the structure of the Natural Color System.[25] We began by choosing highly saturated colors of the four Hering[26] primaries (approx-imating the unique hues[27] of red [R], green [G], blue [B], and yellow [Y]) and four well-balanced binary hues (orange [O], purple [P], cyan [C], and chartreuse [H]). We then defined four "cuts" through color space that differed in their saturation and lightness levels, as follows. Colors in the "saturated" (s) cut were defined as the most saturated color of each of the eight hues that could be produced on our mon-itor. The eight colors in the "muted" (m) cut were those about halfway between the

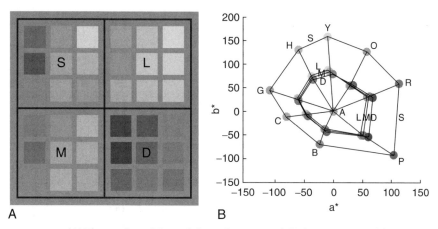

FIGURE 8.2 *(A) The 32 colors of the Berkeley Color Project. (B) The projections of these colors onto an isoluminant plane in CIELAB color-space.*

s color and neutral gray, those in the "light" (*l*) cut were those about halfway between each *s* color and white, and those in the "dark" (*d*) cut were those about halfway between each *s* cut and black. This set comprised the 32 chromatic colors that were studied. We also included five achromatic (A) colors—white, black, and the three grays whose luminance was the average luminance of the eight hues in the *l*, *m*, and d cuts—but we report results just for the 32 chromatic colors in this chapter. Colors within cuts were not constant in saturation or luminance, because we wanted to include highly saturated unique colors, which are not equivalent in either luminance or saturation. Unique yellow and blue, for example, vary dramatically in luminance, with unique saturated yellow being much lighter than unique saturated blue.

Forty-eight individuals from the San Francisco Bay area with normal color vision participated in 30 different tasks as part of the Berkeley Color Project. We will discuss only a small subset of these results here: preference ratings of individual colors, ratings of color appearance dimensions (*red–green, blue–yellow, light–dark*, and *high–low saturation*), and ratings of the three factor-analytic dimensions of color-emotions (*active–passive, heavy–light*, and *warm–cool*). All ratings were made using a continuous line-mark scale with explicit points at the middle and both ends.

Average preference ratings showed relatively strong effects of hue in the *s*, *l*, and *m* colors, producing approximately parallel hue functions with peaks at blue and troughs at chartreuse (Fig. 8.3). *s* colors were preferred to *l* and *m* colors, which did not differ from each other. Hue and cut did not interact across the *s*, *l*, and *m* cuts, but they did interact for the *d* cut versus the other three. In particular, dark-orange (brown) and dark-yellow (olive) were less preferred than other oranges and yellows, whereas dark-red and dark-green were more preferred than other reds and greens. (See Palmer and Schloss[28] for statistical and methodological details.)

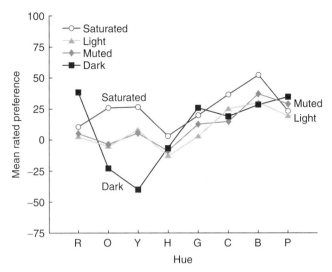

FIGURE 8.3 **Results of Experiment 1.** *Color preference ratings are plotted as a function of hue—red (R), orange (O), yellow (Y), chartreuse (H), green (G), cyan (C), blue (B), and purple (P)—for saturated, light, dark, and muted colors.*

We used multiple regression techniques to fit the models from the previously described theories to these data. The predictors for the cone-contrast model were computed from the cone contrasts of the 32 tested colors against the gray background, plus CIELUV saturation, as specified by Ling and Hurlbert.[29] These four predictors together accounted for just 37% of the variance in the preference data. The three predictors for the color appearance theory (our participants' ratings of *red–green, blue–yellow, light–dark,* and *low–high saturation*) performed better, accounting for 60% of the variance in the preference data. The predictors for the color-emotion theory (our participants' ratings of *active–passive, heavy–light,* and *warm–cool*) accounted for 55% of the variance. Clearly, the lower-level cone-contrast theory does not fit as well as the higher-level color-appearance and color-emotion theories, but the latter two are nearly indistinguishable in terms of their ability to account for the data. Next, we attempted to fit the data using a model from the EVT, but doing so required a much more complex experimental procedure to estimate the relevant predictor variable.

WEIGHTED AFFECTIVE VALENCE ESTIMATES (WAVES) OF COLORS

Experiment 2 was designed to test the principal assumption of the EVT: that color preferences should largely be predictable from the average valences of people's affective reactions to objects with corresponding diagnostic colors. Doing so required us to collect data from three different tasks: object associations, object valence ratings, and color–object match ratings.

Object Association Task

We collected object associations for each of our 37 colors by showing them to a separate group of 74 observers and asking them to describe as many things of that color as they could in 20 seconds. They were asked to describe only things whose colors would be known by most other people from their verbal description. Responses were eliminated if they (a) could be any color (e.g., crayons, shirts), (b) were abstract concepts instead of objects (e.g., winter, Christmas), (c) were color names instead of objects (e.g., "Cal Blue," "teal"), (d) were very dissimilar to the presented color (e.g., "grass at noon" for dark purple), or (e) were provided by only a single participant across all colors. The remaining descriptions were then categorized to reduce their number. Those that were judged to be essentially the same were combined into a single category (e.g., *algae* included the descriptions "algae," "algae water," "algal bloom," "algae-filled fish bowl," and "algae floating on top of water"). The net result was a list of 222 objects with diagnostic coloration.

Object Valence Ratings

The resulting 222 descriptive categories were then shown in black-on-white text to 98 different participants, who were asked to rate the affective value of the referent object (i.e., how positive or negative they felt about it) using the same line-mark rating scale as in Experiment 1. These ratings were averaged over participants, resulting in 222 object valence ratings.

Object–Color Match Ratings

Finally, we showed a third independent group of 31 participants each of the 222 object descriptions paired with each of the 32 colors for which it had previously been given as a description, one pair at a time. Participants were asked to rate how well the color of the described object category matched the color on the screen (e.g., strawberries together with a homogeneous square of saturated red) using the same line-mark rating scale. The average color–object match ratings were then used to weight the average affective valence rating for each object–color pair, such that the valences of the descriptions that better matched the color on the screen were weighted more heavily. We call this measure the "weighted affective valence estimate" (WAVE) of the color.

The fit of the WAVE to the preference data is impressive, producing a correlation of +0.89, which accounts for 80% of the variance. This level of fit to the data is considerably better than any of the other three theories tested, even though the WAVE model uses a single predictor variable, rather than the three or four used by the other three theories. Even the WAVE's weighting factor based on the object–color match ratings (which is not a free parameter because it is taken directly from the ratings our participants made in this task) is relatively unimportant, because the unweighted average valence ratings are almost as highly correlated with preferences ($r = 0.83$) as the WAVEs are.

The average WAVEs for our 32 chromatic colors are plotted in Figure 8.4, which the reader should compare with the average preference ratings shown in Figure 8.3. In addition to a better quantitative fit, the WAVEs also better capture the qualitative structure of the preference functions: the broad, pronounced peak at blue, the trough at chartreuse, higher preference for saturated colors, and the steep global minimum around dark yellow. Its main deficiencies lie in under-predicting the aversion to dark-orange (largely because chocolate is rated as quite appealing) and under-predicting the positive preference for dark-red (largely because blood is rated as unappealing).

Equally important is the fact that the EVT, from which the WAVE measure was derived, answers the *why* question: color preferences are *caused* by average affective responses to correspondingly colored objects. Although the present evidence is correlational, we find it unlikely that causation runs in the opposite direction, at least for diagnostically colored objects. It seems unlikely that preferences for these objects are caused by people's color preferences because there are such clear counterexamples. Chocolate and feces, for instance, are quite similar in color but dramatically opposite in valence. This should not happen if color preferences caused object preferences. Some third mediating variable could conceivably be at work, but it is unclear what that might be.

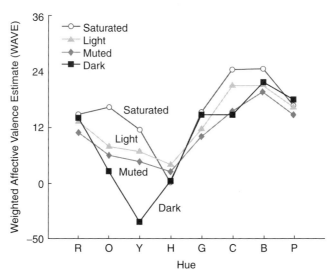

FIGURE 8.4 **Results of Experiment 2.** *Weighted affective valence estimates (WAVEs) are plotted for the 32 chromatic Berkeley Color Project colors as a function of hue—red (R), orange (O), yellow (Y), chartreuse (H), green (G), cyan (C), blue (B), and purple (P)—for saturated, light, dark, and muted colors.*

FURTHER TESTS OF THE ECOLOGICAL VALENCE THEORY

We are currently testing the implications of the EVT in a variety of ways. Below we sketch its predictions and, where available, describe pilot results that are relevant.

Cultural Commonalities and Differences

Critical tests of the EVT will come from cross-cultural studies of color preferences and their relation to corresponding WAVE data. The EVT clearly implies that the WAVE data generated by members of one culture will predict that culture's color preferences better than it will predict another culture's color preferences. We are currently working with collaborators in Japan, Mexico, India, and Serbia on collecting both color preference functions and WAVE functions within each culture. We now have color preference data from Japan and Mexico, but do not yet have their WAVE data.

Sub-cultural Differences

The EVT also predicts that if people have highly positive (or negative) emotional investments in a social institution that has strong color associations (e.g., an athletic team, gang, religious order, university, or even holiday) they should come to like the associated colors correspondingly more (or less) than the rest of the population, such that there will be a positive correlation between their liking/disliking of the institution and their liking/disliking of the associated colors. Preliminary results with university colors support this prediction: among students at the University of California, Berkeley, the amount of self-rated school spirit correlates positively with their preference for Berkeley's blue and gold relative to preference for the cardinal red and white colors of Stanford University, an arch-rival institution. The opposite pattern of results is found at Stanford. These findings support the prediction that sociocultural influences affect color preferences to a degree that depends on people's affective valence toward the institution. It also provides evidence of the direction of causation because it is wildly improbable that students' choice of and their attitude toward universities are caused by their color preferences: students who like Berkeley do not do so because they like blue and gold; they like blue and gold because they like Berkeley.

Individual Differences

The same logic described for using culture-specific WAVEs to test the EVT's ability to account for culture-specific color preferences also holds for any lower-level factors that might also influence color preferences. Thus, the EVT provides a theoretical framework for accounting for individual color preferences, provided that the WAVEs of colors can be accurately assessed for individuals. We are currently extending the basic WAVE procedure described above in two ways. One way is to have each observer make his or her own valence ratings of the "standard" set of objects for his or her culture (i.e., the 222 object descriptions compiled from other

U.S. participants[8]). If Jack loves lemons and Jill detests them, for example, then (all else being equal) Jack's personal WAVE for saturated yellow should be greater than Jill's personal WAVE for that color, and Jack's preference for saturated yellow should be higher than Jill's. The crucial test of the EVT for individuals is whether individuals' personal color preferences are correlated more highly with their own personal WAVEs than other people's WAVEs. The second way is to include idio-syncratic colored objects in the analysis, which the EVT predicts should further improve the fit of their personal WAVEs to their personal color preferences. We can then test whether this truly idiosyncratic WAVE component produces a significant increment to the correlation with their personal color preferences.

Although the EVT focuses on the effects of object preferences on color prefer-ences, we do not claim that color preferences have *no* influence on object prefer-ences. Clearly they do, especially for functionally identical artifacts that come in many colors, such as cars, clothes, appliances, and personal electronics. Widespread (and presumably effective) market research on color preferences for specific prod-ucts presupposes that such effects exist. Notice, however, that these effects too are compatible with the EVT: to the extent that people end up liking something that they bought, made, or chose initially because they liked its color, their preference for that color will be reinforced via positive feedback, provided that they continue to enjoy it. Color preferences will thus tend to be self-perpetuating until other factors, such as boredom, new physical or social circumstances, and/or fashion trends, change the dynamics of aesthetic response, as indeed they inevitably do.

Perhaps the most interesting implication of the EVT is that, if it is true and if there are indeed universal, cultural, sub-cultural, and idiosyncratic influences, then the human brain appears at some level to contain a statistical summary of the consequences of one's interactions with colored ecological objects. We did not ini-tially expect this to be the case, because we came into the study expecting that color appearance measures would provide the best predictors. Why else would people like a color than according to how it looks (appears) to them? Although the EVT's fundamental claim (i.e., that implicit statistical knowledge of the outcomes of interactions with colored objects is the basis for color preferences) is retrospec-tively plausible, it was by no means obvious at the outset. We therefore view it as a genuine discovery that color preferences are largely determined by ecological sta-tistics about the emotional valences of the colored objects one has encountered.

Spatial Composition

The second aesthetic domain we are studying is spatial composition. Painters, photographers, graphic designers, and other visual artists who work in two-dimensional media continually face the problem of how to position the subjects of their creations in aesthetically pleasing ways within a rectangular frame. We pose the problem like this: How should the to-be-depicted object(s) be situated within

a rectangular frame so that viewers, on average, have the most aesthetically pleasing experience? We avoid content issues (i.e., what particular objects or parts are
depicted) by measuring people's aesthetic responses to different compositions of
the same object viewed from the same perspective.

There are several ways in which our research on this topic differs from the usual
tradition in the analysis of art, which is for experts to introspect about their
aesthetic reactions to real paintings (e.g., Arnheim[30] and Gombrich[31]). First, we
collect data about the behavior of other people rather than relying on our own
introspections. This decision is critical to a scientific approach, because behavioral
measurements in a well-defined task can be confirmed by others. Second, we rely
on the reactions of "average" viewers, rather than a designated elite, such as art
critics, museum curators, patrons, and/or the artists themselves, because the elite
often have very specific training about what is (or should be) aesthetically pleasing. Third, rather than studying the composition of complex art objects, such as
actual paintings, graphic designs, and photographs, we study simple pictures that
nobody would claim as art. Real paintings vary from each other in so many ways ✗
that it is nearly impossible to determine why aesthetic responses differ. Using
simple, well-controlled visual displays allows us to understand aesthetic response
from first principles to get a clear notion of which perceptual factors matter. Below
we summarize an extensive series of experiments using a variety of tasks and
measurements that reveal several simple, yet robust, compositional biases of
average viewers.

HORIZONTAL PLACEMENT OF A SINGLE OBJECT

In the first experiment we will describe, participants performed a constrained
adjustment task.[32] They saw pictures of a single object against a minimal background (a black ground-plane and white wall-plane) and were asked to use a computer mouse to drag the object back and forth along the horizontal midline to find
the most aesthetically pleasing position. They clicked the mouse when the object
was at the best position. Each object was shown in three poses relative to the
viewer: facing leftward, facing rightward, and facing forward. We measured the
percentage of trials on which the object's center fell into each of seven equal-sized
horizontal bins.

The results of this experiment are plotted in Figure 8.5 for the left-, right-, and
forward-facing images, averaged over the 10 objects we studied. Large, systematic
interactions between facing direction and horizontal position are clearly evident.
Forward-facing objects were strongly preferred at or very near the center of the
frame, whereas left-facing objects were strongly preferred on the right side of the
frame, and right-facing objects were strongly preferred on the left side of the frame.
We believe that two strong aesthetic biases are at work: a *center bias* and an *inward
bias*.[33] The center bias alone acts on the forward-facing objects to produce the symmetrical distribution with clear spike at the center. Both a center bias and an

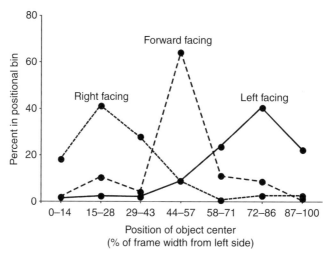

FIGURE 8.5 **Results of Experiment 3.** *Percentages of trials on which the object's center was placed in each of seven equal-sized positional bins along the horizontal dimension for forward-, left-, and right-facing objects.*

inward bias seem to operate on the left- and right-facing objects to produce strongly asymmetrical distributions with pronounced maxima on the right and left sides of center, respectively.[34] If the inward bias were operating alone, without the additional influence of the center bias, we presume that the most extreme left and right positions would be most preferred for the right-facing and left-facing objects, respectively. By this logic, it seems likely that the center bias is at work for all three facing directions, with the inward bias operating only for the left- and right-facing objects.

We believe that the center bias is essentially due to the structure of the frame itself. Arnheim[35] argued that a square has the "structural skeleton" illustrated in Figure 8.6A, with a clear singularity at the center. Indeed, his belief in the potency of this position is reflected in the title of one of his excellent books on spatial composition: *The Power of the Center.*[36] Experimental results by Palmer[37] and Palmer and Guidi[38] using a "goodness of fit" rating task support the validity of this belief. Their results are consistent with rectangles having the structural skeleton shown in Figure 8.6B, in which the single most potent structural element of the frame is its center, the point at which its vertical and horizontal axes of symmetry intersect. In this sense, the center bias does not depend on any particular knowledge about the object, except the location of the object's own center, which can be computed just from its visually evident contours.

The inward bias, however, is object-dependent and knowledge-based because it requires the perceiver to know which side of the object constitutes its front, and this depends on more than just the shape of the object. We do not yet know exactly

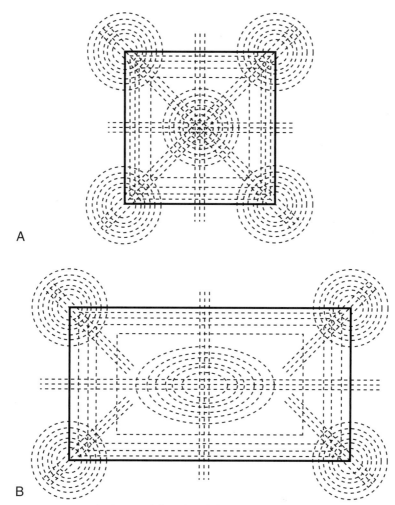

FIGURE 8.6 **Framing the frame.** *(A) Arnheim's diagram of the structural skeleton of a square was derived from his theories. (B) This diagram of the structural skeleton of a rectangle is based on data from Palmer and Guidi's empirical studies of goodness of fit (Palmer & Guidi, in preparation).*

why it arises. It could be due to the high perceptual salience of the features on the fronts of objects and/or to expected forward motion of objects (although we did not find significant differences between objects that were capable of movement and objects that were not when we examined this factor explicitly). Alternatively, it may reflect asymmetries in the functional *affordance space* around an object. The notion of an affordance space is derived from J. J. Gibson's[39] notion of *affordances* and specifies the local area around an object where it typically interacts with humans and other environmental objects. Our untested conjecture is that there is generally a much greater area in front of an object that is of functional interest to an observer than behind it, and no difference between the left and right sides, at least for bilaterally symmetrical objects. If so, it is possible that the best location for the different views of the same objects is that for which its affordance space, rather than its actual physical extension, is centered in the frame.

We have studied aesthetic biases in the horizontal position of single objects in several other ways,[40,41] including two-alternative forced choice (2AFC) psychophysical methods, free-choice photography of everyday objects (a steam iron, a teapot, and a tape dispenser), and analyses of the positions of objects in single-object stock photographs from a commercial database (corel.com). All methods show essentially the same effects, although to different degrees: We always find a clear center bias for forward-facing objects, and a combination of center and inward biases for left- and right-facing objects. Interestingly, when we looked for the effect with novel, letter-like, two-dimensional patterns containing a highly articulated side that we presumed people would see as its front, we did not find evidence of an inward bias.

VERTICAL PLACEMENT OF SINGLE OBJECTS

Another series of experiments examined aesthetic biases in the vertical position of single-object pictures.[42] This topic turned out to be somewhat more complex. One set of expected issues related to the role of the horizon and gravitational support in vertical placement. Unlike horizontal placement, there are severe gravitational constraints on where an object can be located vertically relative to a supporting horizontal surface. Unexpectedly, however, we also found effects of object-specific world knowledge that we term *ecological biases*: effects due to the typical position of the objects relative to human observers. In one experiment we studied vertical preferences in the position of a bowl that was supported by a horizontal surface below it and a light fixture that was attached to a horizontal surface above it. We independently varied both the vertical position of the object itself and the vertical position of the back edge of the horizontal supporting surface.

Examples of the displays in which the object and horizontal edge coincide are shown in Figure 8.7 below the graph. The solid line and large data points at the top indicate the results for the displays shown directly beneath them; the other lines and points show the corresponding data for displays in which the horizontal edge was above the bowl or below the light fixture. Two facts are particularly noteworthy. One is that the most preferred position of the horizontal edge is always at the same height as the object. Displacing the horizontal edge so that it was above the bowl or below the light fixture caused preference to decrease monotonically as distance increased. This result may occur because when the object is at the same height as the horizon edge, the object occludes (covers) part of the edge and therefore most clearly indicates that the object is closer than the horizontal edge.

Evidence of ecological biases comes from a clear lower bias for the bowl and an equally clear, and almost exactly opposite, upper bias for the light fixture. This pattern

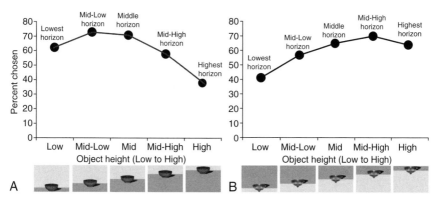

FIGURE 8.7 **Preference for vertical position in images of a bowl and a light-fixture.** *The average percentages of trials on which each picture was chosen in all possible pairs as a function of the vertical position of the bowl (A) or light fixture (B) and the vertical position of the horizon.*

of results for vertical position is so similar to the center and inward biases for horizontal position of left- and right facing objects that we currently believe them to be, in effect, corresponding phenomena in the vertical dimension. The bowl and light fixture do not have a "front" and "back" in the vertical dimension, of course, but it is easy to see by analogy that the top of the bowl and the bottom of the light fixture are their most salient functional parts. Indeed, if one were to draw their "affordance spaces," it seems likely that the bowl's would extend much further upward than downward and that the light fixture's would extend much further downward than upward. This asymmetry is virtually guaranteed by the fact that these objects are attached to support planes below and above them, respectively. Thus, we believe that these compositional biases in the vertical dimension may be analogous to those in the horizontal dimension.

There are further uncertainties about the interpretation of these vertical biases, however. They might also be due to a *perspective bias*, since the bowl is depicted from slightly above, so that its upper lip is visible, and the light fixture is shown from slightly below, so that its bottom is visible. Perhaps people like objects viewed from above to be lower in the frame and objects viewed from below to be higher in the frame. Such a perspective bias would provide redundant information about the viewpoint from which the object is being viewed, such that its preferred position correlates (negatively) with the perspective from which it is depicted (i.e., higher perspective views positioned lower in the frame and lower perspective views higher in the frame). Another potential factor is an *ecological bias*. Viewers might prefer the bowl to be low (and the light fixture high) in the frame because bowls are generally below (and light fixtures generally above) our vantage point. We conducted further experiments to test these possibilities.

Ecological Biases in Vertical Position

One problem with the bowl and the light fixture is that, when they are supported in the usual way (by a plane below and above them, respectively), they are not visible from certain viewpoints: the bowl is not visible from below its horizontal surface of support, nor the light fixture from above. We eliminated this problem in the next experiment by using pictures of objects that could, in principle, be seen from any viewpoint. For an object that is typically positioned above human viewers we chose a flying eagle, and for an object that is typically positioned below human viewers, we chose a swimming stingray. If the vertical position effects in the previous experiment are due to perspective effects, then we should see corresponding biases with both the eagle and stingray: when either object is viewed from above (as the bowl was), there should be a lower bias for both, and when it is viewed from below (as the light fixture was), there should be an upper bias for both. If the vertical position effects are due to ecological height, however, the flying eagle should produce an upper bias for all views because it is generally located above human viewers, and the stingray should produce a lower bias for all views because it is generally located below human viewers. It is important to note that these factors are not mutually exclusive: both perspective and ecological effects might operate at the same time, in which case some combination of the two patterns should occur together.

The other conditions we included in this study were designed to look for an analogue of the striking center bias we found in the first experiment we described about horizontal placement. When symmetrical objects were facing directly forward, people preferred them in the center of the frame. For the eagle and the stingray, we therefore included views from directly above and directly below to test for the existence of a corresponding vertical center bias.

We expected the results for the directly above and directly below conditions to produce a symmetrical center bias. The data, shown in Figures 8.8A and C for the eagle and 8.8B and D for the stingray, show a broad center bias, presumably due to the symmetry of the projections of these objects (and/or their affordance spaces) as viewed from directly above and below. However, it is an asymmetrical center bias, in which the eagle also exhibits a distinct upper bias and the stingray a somewhat less pronounced lower bias. These asymmetries are consistent with an ecological bias, because flying eagles are above earthbound observers, and swimming stingrays are below them. It is not consistent with a perspective bias, however, which implies that the eagle from directly below should exhibit an upper bias (which it does), whereas an eagle from directly above should exhibit a lower bias (which it does not), and vice versa for the stingray. It is worth mentioning that independent groups of observers saw the eagle pictures and the stingray pictures, because this fact eliminates the possibility that observers were responding to a "demand characteristic" of the experiment that might have arisen if the same observers had seen both the eagle and the stingray pictures.

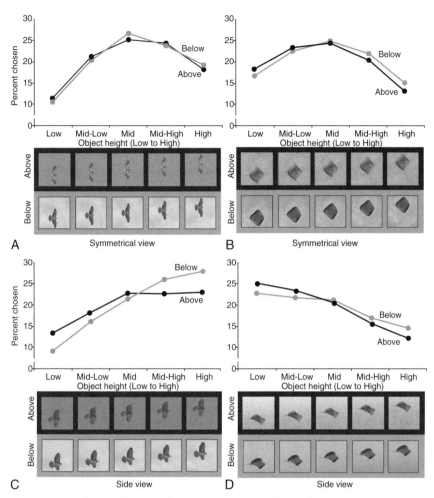

FIGURE 8.8 **Preference for vertical position in images of an eagle and a stingray.** *Displays and results for the directly above and directly below views of the eagle (A) and stingray (B), and for the side-above and side-below views of the eagle (C) and stingray (D).*

The results for the side views reveal stronger ecological biases. Both side views of the eagle exhibit a strong upper bias, presumably because flying eagles are generally above us in the environment, whereas both views of the swimming stingray exhibit a lower bias that is almost as strong, presumably because stingrays are generally below us in the environment. Notice, however, that there is also a smaller, but consistent, perspective bias: the upper bias for the eagle is stronger for the side-below view than for the side-above view, and the lower bias for the stingray is stronger for the side-above view than for the side-below view. These patterns are just what would be expected from a perspective bias: objects seen from below are preferred to be higher in the frame and objects seen from above to be lower in the frame. These biases are analogous to the inward-facing bias we found in horizontal compositions, except that here they are combined with a strong ecological height bias.

OTHER ECOLOGICAL BIASES

Ecological biases imply that people prefer pictures of a focal object in which its known spatial characteristics within the environment are consistent with corresponding spatial characteristics of their depicted two-dimensional framed images. Such effects are not restricted to height within the frame, however, as we will now consider for the domains of ecological perspective, size, and orientation.

Previous research by Palmer, Rosch, and Chase[43] on perspective effects in object perception identified a phenomenon that they called *canonical perspective*: certain views of objects are systematically rated as "better" pictures of the object in the sense that some perspective views "look more like the depicted object" than others. Palmer and colleagues showed that the better (more canonical) perspective views allowed the depicted object to be more quickly recognized and that people more often reported imagining the object from more canonical perspectives. Figure 8.9A, for example, shows the "best" perspective views of 4 of the 12 objects Palmer and colleagues studied in terms of having the highest ratings among the nine perspective views they studied. Figure 8.9B shows several perspective views of the horse that vary from best (left) to worst (right).

More recently Khalil and McBeath[44] reported the results of a study in which they explicitly asked their participants to rate their aesthetic judgments of different perspective views. These aesthetic preferences generally corresponded well with

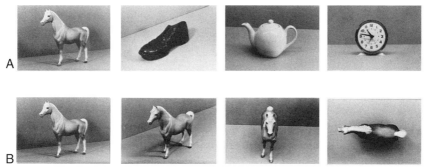

FIGURE 8.9 **Canonical perspective images (Palmer, Rosch, & Chase, 1981).** *(A) shows the "best" perspective views chosen by participants for four objects, and (B) shows four examples of different perspective views of the horse.*

the results reported by Palmer, Rosch, and Chase.[45] Ecological perspective biases associated with canonical perspective thus reflect another way in which people's aesthetic preferences reveal implicit knowledge about objects in the world: people like pictures of objects that make them most recognizable by showing their most informative parts and interrelations.

Recent research by Konkle and Oliva[46] has made a corresponding case for a phenomenon in the size domain that they call *canonical size*. Certain sizes of two-dimensional framed images of objects are rated as better depictions, are better recognized, and are more frequently drawn than other image sizes within the same rectangular frame. Moreover, these sizes are systematically related to the relative sizes of the objects: the "best" picture of an elephant, for example, is bigger than the "best" picture of a mouse, and the optimal size of the object relative to the frame is a function of the logarithm of the object's actual size. Linsen, Leyssen, Gardner, and Palmer[47] found similar results in people's choices of the most aesthetically pleasing picture of objects at different sizes.

Another ecological bias that is perhaps so obvious that it scarcely seems worth mentioning is canonical orientation. Many, if not most, real-world objects have canonical orientations within the environment—their "upright" orientations—that are dictated largely by gravitational stability and functional constraints. Dogs, chairs, cars, trees, and people are among the multitude of commonplace objects that have clear canonical orientations. Such objects are most easily recognized in their canonical upright orientations, and, roughly speaking, larger deviations from upright lead to more difficulty in recognizing them.[48] Although we know of no aesthetic research that has specifically addressed this question, it is intuitively obvious that most people will find pictures of such objects most aesthetically pleasing when they are depicted in their canonical, upright orientations.

The center bias excepted, all of these biases in spatial composition—the inward bias, the perspective height bias, and ecological biases in position, perspective, size, and orientation—depend strongly, but implicitly, on statistical knowledge about the properties of the depicted object. The inward bias, for example, depends on the observer knowing that the object has a distinguished front and a back, and prefers the front to be closer to the center. Ecological biases in position are based on knowing where objects are typically located relative to human observers; ecological perspective biases depend on observers knowing which surfaces of objects are most informative; and ecological size biases depend on the observer knowing how big objects are. In each case, people tend to prefer pictures in which their knowledge of these object properties is reflected in corresponding properties of its image within the picture frame.

MERE EXPOSURE, FLUENCY, AND FIT

Now that we have some clear idea about *what* spatial compositions people find aesthetically appealing, we can ask *why* people might prefer those compositions.

Perhaps the most obvious explanation is that the biases we find result from "mere exposure" effects:[49] people might prefer images with such compositions simply because they have seen more pictures composed in these ways than in other ways. The problem with this account is that, by itself, it suffers from infinite regress and thus fails to answer the *why* question. You might prefer the compositions that you have seen most frequently in the past, but why did the people who created those images use those compositions? The mere-exposure explanation requires that the bias was caused by those people preferring the compositions that they saw most frequently in their viewing histories. But why did they prefer those compositions they did? The obvious problem is that the mere-exposure explanation thus must be applied endlessly, always appealing to what the previous generation of image creators experienced most frequently and never "cashing out" the explanation in terms other than frequency-of-viewing histories. This is not to say that mere exposure has no effect on aesthetic preferences—see Cutting[50] for an interesting analysis of its impact on the canon of Impressionist paintings—but only that its explanatory value in answering the *why* question is limited to preserving a status quo that arose for some reason other than frequency-of-viewing histories.

The fluency theory of aesthetic preference, as outlined by Reber (Chapter 9 of this volume) and colleagues (e.g., Winkielman[51]), provides a far more satisfactory account. Its basic claim is that any factor that allows a picture to be perceived more easily (or "fluently") enhances a viewer's aesthetic experience. Standard examples of fluency concern context-free image properties, such as having high degrees of clarity, figure–ground contrast, symmetry, and exposure frequency, all of which should make them easier to perceive, independent of their specific content. (Notice that although a fluency account includes exposure frequency as a factor, it actually explains exposure effects by appealing to their influence on how easily people can perceive the current exposure rather than simply appealing to the person's exposure history itself.)

The aesthetic biases discussed above are different from such basic fluency factors because the former are context-specific and depend importantly on specific knowledge about the kinds of object depicted in the image. Nevertheless, most of the biases we have discussed above are consistent with a fluency account because they all plausibly increase the ease with which the depicted object can be perceived and/or identified within the picture. The center bias locates the object at or near the center, where it is least susceptible to lateral masking and crowding effects arising from the borders. The inward bias puts the object in a location where its most important side (front, top, or bottom) is closest to the center and thus is most easily perceptible. The various forms of ecological biases place the object in a relation to the frame that is most consistent with our knowledge about the object's likely location, perspective, size, and orientation in the environment, so that its most informative parts, its typical size, and its typical position relative to a human observer are optimally represented when viewing the picture. Indeed, canonical perspective[52] and, more recently, vertical position relative to the observer[53] have already been shown to facilitate identification performance.

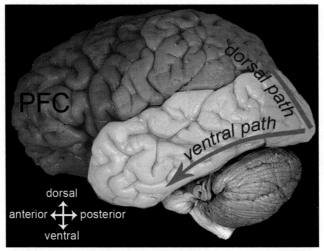

FIGURE 1.5 **The lateral surface of the cerebral cortex.** *Visual processing begins at the most posterior part of the occipital lobe (green) and courses through the temporal lobe (yellow) via the ventral path and through the parietal lobe (pink) via the dorsal path. At the most anterior part of the frontal lobe (purple) is the prefrontal cortex (PFC), which acts to monitor and control cortical activity in posterior regions. (Brain images reprinted with permission from* Digital Anatomist Interactive Atlas, *University of Washington, Seattle, WA, copyright 1997.)*

FIGURE 2.1 **Seurat, Georges (1859–1891).** Bathers at Asnières, *1884. Oil on canvas, 201 × 300 cm. (Photo credit: Copyright © National Gallery, London/Art Resource, NY.)*

FIGURE 2.3 **Dalí, Salvador.** Slave Market with the Disappearing Bust of Voltaire, *1940. Oil on canvas, 18-1/4 × 25-3/8 inches. (Copyright © Fundación Gala-Salvador Dalí [Artist Rights Society], 2010. Collection of the Salvador Dalí Museum, Inc., St. Petersburg, FL, 2010.)*

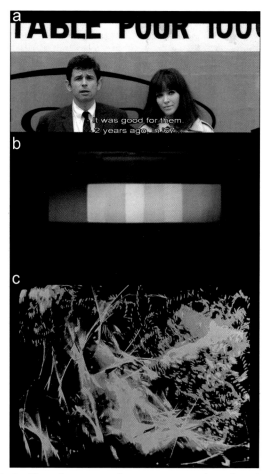

FIGURE 4.3 *(a) Godard launches two simultaneous streams of speech at the spectator in* Made in USA *(1966). (b) "Flicker" in* Shutter Interface *(1975) by Paul Sharits, an installation using four overlapping images and four separate, simultaneous streams of sound. (c) Imagery evocative of non-veridical, phospenic color imagery in Stan Brakhage's* Rage Net *(1988).*

FIGURE 4.6 *Rubber or reality? Steven Spielberg's* Jaws *(1975).*

FIGURE 6.1 **Velazquez, Diego Rodriguez (1599–1660).** The Fable of Arachne (Las Hilanderas), *1657. Canvas, 220 × 289 cm. Cat. 1173. (Photo credit: Erich Lessing/Art Resource, NY)*

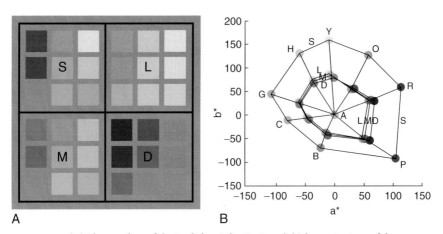

A   B

FIGURE 8.2 *(A) The 32 colors of the Berkeley Color Project. (B) The projections of these colors onto an isoluminant plane in CIELAB color-space.*

FIGURE 8.10 **Violating expectations for heightened aesthetic effect.** *This image (*Nature's Writing *from* Bodyscapes *by Jean-Paul Bourdier. San Rafael, CA: Earth Aware Editions, 2007) violates virtually every default bias discussed in this chapter, yet produces a highly pleasing aesthetic effect by doing so in a way that promotes a complex conceptual message about the relation between various aspects of a woman's body and the natural structure of the earth.*

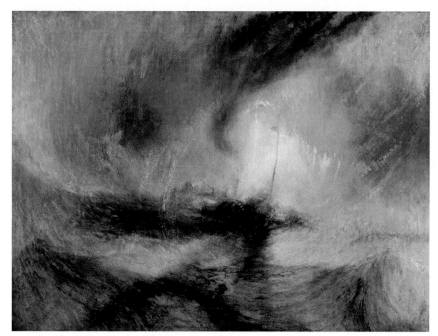

FIGURE 9.1 **Turner, Joseph Mallord William (1775–1851).** Snow Storm: Steam-Boat off a Harbour's Mouth. *Exhibited 1842. Oil on canvas, 91.4 × 121.9 cm. (Photo credit: Tate, London/Art Resource, NY)*

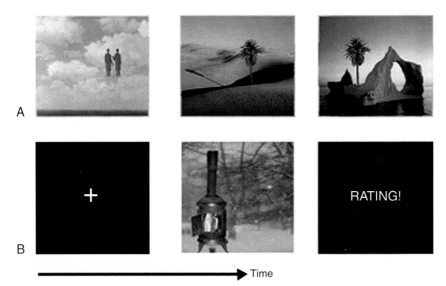

FIGURE 13.1 *(A) La Reconnaissance Infinie by René Magritte (1963; Leslie and David Rogath Collection). This work, among other Magritte paintings, served as inspiration for the stimulus development. Two examples of the stimuli used in the fMRI experiment are also presented: an object in its normal contextual setting and an object in an abnormal context. (B) Stimulus presentation paradigm. Subjects were asked to fixate (500 milliseconds) prior to a 3,500-millisecond stimulus presentation, followed by a rating period where subjects were required to make their aesthetic response via button press (2,000 milliseconds).*

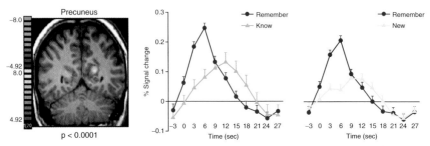

FIGURE 14.1 **Recollection and familiarity reflect memory strength.** *Subjects performed a flower detection task on portraits, landscapes, and abstract paintings, and 10 minutes later were surprised with a memory test. The previously seen paintings (old) were presented with new paintings that were either visually similar to or visually different from the old ones. For each painting, subjects had to report whether they remember it, it looks familiar, or it is new. Activation in the precuneus showed that correctly remembered old paintings evoked stronger activation than both paintings that looked familiar and new, never-seen-before paintings. It therefore seems that recollection reflects strong memories, whereas familiarity reflects weak memories.*

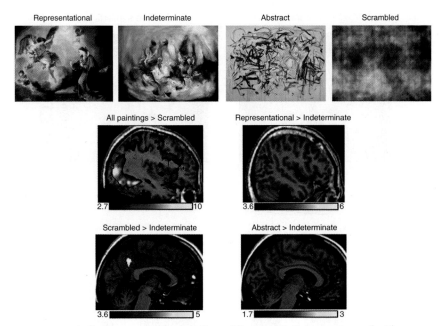

FIGURE 14.2 **Activation evoked by paintings.** *Viewing paintings as compared with scrambled pictures elicits activation in a distributed network of visual, limbic, parietal, and frontal regions. Comparing representational with indeterminate paintings revealed activation in the temporoparietal junction, a region that mediates the allocation of spatial attention across visual scenes. Comparing scrambled pictures with indeterminate paintings and abstract paintings with indeterminate ones revealed activation in the precuneus and medial frontal gyrus, regions that mediate the generation and maintenance of mental images from long-term memory. (Fairhall, Scott L., and Ishai, Alumit. (2008). Neural correlates of object indeterminacy in art compositions. Consciousness and Cognition. 17(3), 923–932. doi: 10.1016/J.CONCOG.2007.07.005. Used with permission of the publisher.)*

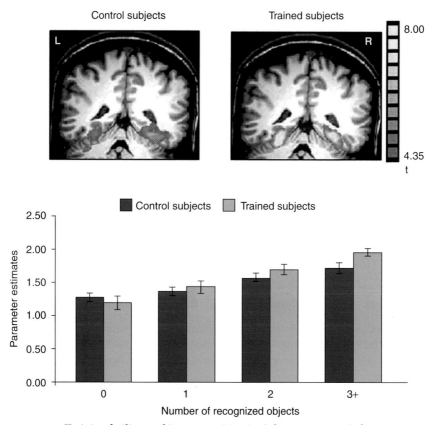

FIGURE 14.3 **Training facilitates object recognition in Cubist paintings.** *Subjects performed an object recognition task on Cubist paintings and indicated how many objects they recognized. Relative to the control group, the subjects who received a short training session on Cubism reported seeing more objects; activation in their parahippocampal cortex, a region that mediates contextual associations, was significantly stronger; and they showed a parametric increase in the amplitude of the fMRI signal as a function of the number of objects they recognized.*

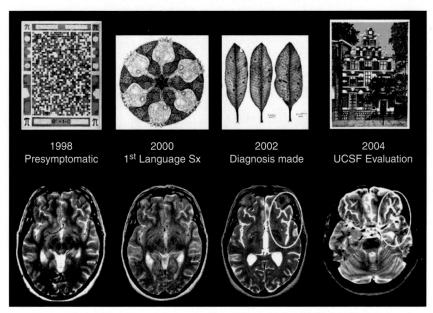

| 1998 | 2000 | 2002 | 2004 |
| Presymptomatic | 1st Language Sx | Diagnosis made | UCSF Evaluation |

FIGURE 15.3 **The progression of the patient's artistic style and disease.** *The paintings are paired with brain MRIs from that same year. The circled area reveals the significant atrophy pattern, which is most evident in the widening of the left sylvian fissure. The brain MRIs are displayed in the usual radiographic manner with the left side of the page referring to the right side of the brain, as if you were looking at the patient lying in the scanner with her feet towards you and her head in the scanner. Of note, the first image was obtained for reasons unrelated to and before the onset of her cognitive complaints and as such is considered presymptomatic. The titles of the paintings across the top from left to right are* pi, R, Arbutus, *and* Amsterdam. *Gouache. (Seeley, W. W., et al. [2008]. Brain, 131, 39–49; doi:10.1093/brain/awm270)*

FIGURE 15.4 **Unravelling Boléro.** *Gouache. (Seeley, W. W., et al. [2008]. Brain, 131, 39–49; doi:10.1093/brain/awm270)*

FIGURE 16.3 *Illustration of color grouping.*

Even so, we are not convinced that fluency theory provides a full and satisfying explanation of aesthetic response. The problem we see is that it is pitched at too low a level to explain many important aesthetic effects. It seems well equipped to explain the compositional effects we have just presented, which are relevant to understanding the aesthetic appeal of, say, high-quality stock photography or *National Geographic* images, in which the presumed intent is to create an image that depicts a particular object optimally. However, it seems problematic in dealing with the aesthetic appeal of less standard images in which there is some more complex perceptual, cognitive, and/or emotional message behind the image. Our view is that the compositional biases we have discussed thus far are essentially *default preferences* that apply when the conveyed meaning is essentially just the default message: "This is a picture of X," where X is the appropriate category of the portrayed object or situation. Under these conditions, optimality presumably means that the depiction is the most easily (or fluently) perceived image of that object or situation, and it is reasonable to suppose that it would be composed so that the focal object would tend to be centered, to be facing inward, and to reflect whatever ecological information is most relevant.

Nevertheless, there is often some deeper, less obvious, yet more important message that an image is intended to convey—or that it simply *does* convey to a particular viewer at a particular time, regardless of the creator's intentions. Such messages are often poorly served by adhering to default aesthetic biases such as the ones we have just described. A good example is shown in Figure 8.10. *Nature's Writing* is a striking photographic image by Jean-Paul Bourdier from his book *Bodyscapes*, in which he composes the female body within the frame so that it violates several default biases—including the center and inward biases both horizontally and vertically as well as ecological biases toward canonical perspective, orientation, and color—in ways that serve to convey the message that people's bodies are an integral part of the natural world and that even the boundaries between us and our environment are unclear and permeable. Clearly, a stock photograph of a woman standing on a sandy landscape would fail to convey such complex and subtle meaning.

Rather than trying to stretch the admittedly elastic concept of fluency to cover cases in which expectations have been violated in ways that create such obvious disfluency, we prefer to conceptualize aesthetic considerations in spatial composition in terms of what we have called "representational fit."[54] ("Fit" alone might be the more general and appropriate term, since "representational fit" is presumably relevant only to visual objects that qualify as representations, such as pictures or representational paintings.) The idea behind the "fit" hypothesis is that the aesthetic value of an image will vary with the extent to which the spatial composition of the image successfully conveys a meaningful message to a viewer. The content of this message might be sensory, cognitive, emotional, or any combination of these; ideally, it would encompass all of them together. It might be what the artist had in mind while creating the image or it might not, as viewers often generate meanings of their own when viewing such images.

FIGURE 8.10 **Violating expectations for heightened aesthetic effect.** *This image (*Nature's Writing *from* Bodyscapes *by Jean-Paul Bourdier. San Rafael, CA: Earth Aware Editions, 2007) violates virtually every default bias discussed in this chapter, yet produces a highly pleasing aesthetic effect by doing so in a way that promotes a complex conceptual message about the relation between various aspects of a woman's body and the natural structure of the earth.*

Within the "representational fit" framework, there is an effective default message, which is simply that the intent of the picture is to portray the object, scene, or situation it depicts in a perceptually optimal way. We take this to be the effective message of a stock photograph, for example, and it may be true, as fluency theorists propose, that under such an interpretation, the image is more aesthetically appealing to the degree that it is more easily perceived as that object, scene, or situation. But there are many more complex, meaningful, and emotional messages that an image can convey, and they are often carried at least in part by defying default aesthetic expectations, such as the center, inward, perspective, and the various ecological biases in spatial composition.

REPRESENTATIONAL FIT AND VIOLATING COMPOSITIONAL BIASES

To investigate this issue, we have begun to study how compositional preferences can be influenced by conceptual content. We do so by giving the same set of compositionally manipulated images different titles (meanings) and asking people to

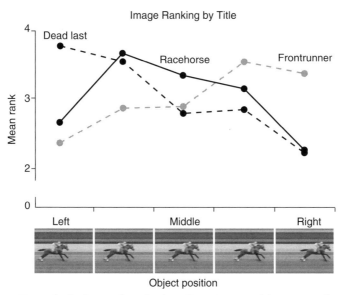

FIGURE 8.11 **Example displays and results from Experiment 5.** *The same racehorse is shown at five different positions for each of the three titles given to these images. Preference ratings are plotted as a function of horizontal position for the different title conditions.*

judge their relative aesthetic response to the different compositions. Figure 8.11 shows five compositions of the same racehorse against a uniformly motion-smeared background in which only the position of the racehorse varies. To manipulate the message, we gave the images three different titles. The default title was simply "Racehorse." Here we expected that the center and inward biases we found in our earlier studies would hold. We also used two titles that biased the composition in different and opposite ways. "Front Runner" was expected to bias the composition toward positions in which horse was, in effect, running out of the picture because the empty space behind it implies that it is far ahead of its (unseen) competition. "Dead Last" was expected to bias the composition toward positions in which horse was, in effect, running into the picture because the empty space ahead of it implies that it is far behind its (unseen) competition. Similar kinds of title manipulations were used with other images that implied the presence of other unseen objects either behind or in front of the depicted object (e.g., chasing versus being chased). Another set of images were based on a temporal metaphor in which empty space in the image could be seen as consistent with interpretations emphasizing different parts of a journey: for example, a man walking with the titles "Man Walking" (default), "Journey's End" (biasing images of him walking out of the frame), and "Starting Out" (biasing images of him walking into the frame).

In this experiment, the intended message of the images was provided by the title in the context of a brief cover story, in which participants were told to imagine that they were artists, who had decided on the title and the object for an image, and were now trying to decide on the composition of the image within a rectangular frame. They then ranked all the horizontal compositions for that title from most to least aesthetically pleasing. The results, plotted in Figure 8.11, show a very clear pattern that is consistent with our predictions. The default titles yielded aesthetic preferences like those we found in our previous experiments for facing objects: a clear center bias with an inward-facing asymmetry, peaking at the position in which the depicted object was close to the center, yet also clearly facing into the frame. The titles that biased non-standard interpretations, however, produced strikingly different preference functions. When the title promoted the idea that the depicted object was ahead of other implied objects or was at the end of a journey, the preference curve peaked at the two positions where it faced most clearly out of the frame. When the title promoted the idea that the depicted object was behind other implied objects or was at the start of a journey, however, the preference curve peaked at the two positions where it faced most clearly into the frame.

We interpret these results as supporting our notion that default compositional biases can be overridden by violations that fit (i.e., are consistent with) the message implied by the title. The aesthetic response to an image will thus be greatest when its spatial composition effectively conveys (fits) the message defined by the title it was given. It is possible that the results can also be interpreted as supporting a revised and expanded fluency account (see Chapter 9). The trick is to reinterpret the original notion that fluency reflects ease in *perception* of the focal object to encompass ease in some particular *conceptual interpretation*. The racehorse running out of the frame may not be the most easily perceived image of a racehorse, for example, but it might well be the easiest image to perceive as a *front-running* racehorse, where the additional conceptual content implies that the horse is ahead of the competition. The reason the two theoretical frameworks are consistent with each other is that a good fit between the title's meaning and the image should facilitate (make fluent) the apprehension of that meaning.

One problem that arises for fluency theories of aesthetics is that, despite its apparent flexibility, some kinds of expectancy violations necessarily make the image less, rather than more, fluently perceived or conceived by any reasonable understanding of fluency. Most problematic are cases in which the artist intentionally creates an image that is difficult to perceive and/or understand. Much of modern art, at least from Cubism on, poses challenges of this sort. It is even evident in the *Nature's Writing* image reproduced in Figure 8.10. Certainly part of the point of this image is to make the viewer scrutinize it carefully to try to find out what, if anything, is present in the picture other than a series of mounds of reddish earth. It is quite implausible, we think, to claim that its aesthetic value hinges on fluency of any reasonable sort. The most plausible argument would be that it is aesthetically pleasing because it is fluently perceived as disfluent. We find this move to be a perversion, if not an outright contradiction, of fluency theory.

Conjectures and Conclusions

When we began our studies of aesthetic response to visual displays, we naïvely expected that the underlying principles would be essentially knowledge-free. We thought, for example, that people's average color preferences would be largely explicable in terms of color appearances (i.e., the coordinates of colors in some appropriately structured color space) and that people's compositional preferences would be largely, if not completely, explicable in terms of the relation between objects and the structural skeleton of its rectangular frame (e.g., Arnheim[55]). In both cases, however, the results we obtained led us to a surprising conclusion: implicit knowledge of environmental objects and their relations to us appears to be absolutely central to people's aesthetic response in both domains. We initially avoided studying the aesthetic effects of specific content (i.e., the nature of the focal objects in a picture or scene) because we expected such considerations to involve strong, self-evident knowledge-based effects that would be difficult to study: people would like pictures of objects/scenes/situations that they liked for reasons quite independent of the picture's composition. Even when the displays consist of single colors or spatial compositions of the very same object in the very same pose, however, we are finding strong, and not particularly self-evident, effects of specific world knowledge. In the color domain, average preferences appear to reflect the statistics of how much people, in general, like the objects that are char- acteristically those colors. In the spatial domain, they appear to depend on people's knowledge of the salient characteristics of the objects depicted and how they relate to the observer.

Now that we have established that statistical world knowledge *is* relevant to aesthetic response, there is the deeper question of *why* this might be so. For the case of color, the EVT provides a plausible answer: preferences perform an adap- tive "steering" function, biasing sighted observers to approach objects that are likely to be beneficial and to avoid objects that are not. This explanation is satisfy- ing from an adaptive, evolutionary perspective because acting in accord with such aesthetic preferences would be beneficial for the organism to the extent that the preferences are correlated with (i.e., carry predictive information about) what is "good" versus "bad" for the observer.

It is not so obvious what adaptive function might be served by the spatial com- positional effects we have found: the center bias, the inward bias, and the various ecological biases. A central problem for any adaptive theory of these biases is that they all apply to framed representational visual displays that did not exist when humankind was presumably being shaped by evolution. Even in modern times, the composition of static, rectangular, framed images seem to be largely irrelevant to people's lives, at least outside the world of art, websites, and wall decorations. To be more generally relevant, the domain to which these principles apply would have to be broadened to include other, more adaptive decisions and behaviors.

One intriguing possibility is that the compositional biases we have found may be related to optimal eye fixations. People make thousands of eye movements every day, the purpose of which is to bring various ecological objects into view so that we can see them clearly and identify them efficiently. Perhaps the aesthetic effects we find in spatial composition are rooted in principles that people would use to optimize eye fixations.

The general idea is that if the composition of an image within a rectangular frame is conceived as roughly analogous to the position of objects within the visual field, it would be adaptive for people to make fixations that make the most important information about the relevant objects most available in the image. The center bias would be related to the strong foveation of retinal receptors and the cortical magnification of information at or near the central area of the visual field. The inward and perspective biases would similarly be related to putting the most important and informative parts of the focal objects at or near the foveal region. Ecological biases would be related to providing proximal image features that are consistent with distal object features, depicting small things as small in the frame, large things as large in the frame, high things as high in the frame, and low things as low in the frame.

There are differences between rectangular frames and the field of vision, to be sure. One is that the frame of a picture is explicitly visible whereas the boundary of the visual field is not, being defined merely by the absence of sensory input. Another is that the shape of the visual field is oval rather than rectangular. But, such relatively minor differences aside, the eye-fixation hypothesis provides a plausible, ecologically relevant rationale for why people might have these kinds of default biases.

The notion that these default expectations can be violated when some meaning other than the nature of the object or situation is foregrounded becomes analogous to an observer who is making eye fixations with some meaningful expectation about what the scene will contain. If the observer expects to see a front-running racehorse, then the best fixation might be behind the horse to look for the competition, whereas if the observer expects to see a racehorse that is dead last, the best fixation might be in front of the horse for an analogous reason. These ideas are mere hypotheses at this point, of course, but that is always precisely the starting point for the next round of experimental testing. They at least have the virtue of making a bridge between our aesthetic effects and adaptive properties of real-world perception.

We began by briefly outlining our conception of aesthetic science. We then went on to show that aesthetic response to both colors and spatial compositions is influenced by hidden knowledge about the observed colors and objects. We offer the research we have described essentially as an existence proof that scientific approaches to aesthetic questions are useful and productive. We freely acknowledge that our results to date have raised more questions than they have answered, but this is not at all uncommon in science, especially in the initial stages of investigating new phenomena. Even so, we are encouraged by the new questions our studies have raised, in large part because the answers we get when we examine them seem to fit together in an internally coherent and theoretically interesting way.

Acknowledgments

The authors wish to thank the members of PalmerLab (including Rosa Poggesi, Christine Nothelfer, Patrick Lawler, Laila Kahn, Cat Stone, Divya Ahuja, Jing Zhang, Eli Strauss, Will Griscom, Gary Hackett, Hye-Lim Jeon, Daisy Liu, Christopher Lau, and Jessica Jimenez) for their help and support in conducting the research reviewed in this chapter. This material is based upon work supported by the National Science Foundation under Grant No. 0745820, a Google Gift to the first author, and by a generous gift of product coupons from Amy's Natural Frozen Foods (Santa Rosa, CA) to the second author, with which we "paid" many of our participants in the research on color preferences. Any opinions, findings, and conclusions or recommendations expressed in this material are those of the author(s) and do not necessarily reflect the views of the National Science Foundation.

Endnotes

1. cf. Mangan, B. (1991). *Meaning and the structure of consciousness: an essay in psycho-aesthetics.* Ph.D. dissertation, University of California, Berkeley.

2. Livingstone, M. S., & Hubel, D. H. (November 1987). Psychophysical evidence for separate channels for the perception of form, color, movement, and depth. *Journal of Neuroscience, 7,* 3416–3468.

3. Eysenck, H. J. (July 1941). A critical and experimental study of color preference. *American Journal of Psychology, 54,* 385–391.

4. Granger, G. W. (1955). Experimental study of colour preferences. *Journal of General Psychology, 52,* 3–20.

5. Ling, Y. L., & Hurlbert, A. C. (2009). A new model for color preference: universality and individuality. *15th Color Imaging Conference Final Program and Proceedings,* 8–11.

6. Palmer, S. E., & Schloss, K. B. (May 2010). An ecological valence theory of human color preference. *Proceedings of the National Academy of Sciences, 107,* 8877–8882.

7. Eysenck, H. J. (July 1941). A critical and experimental study of color preference. *American Journal of Psychology, 54,* 385–391.

8. Guilford, J. P., & Smith, P. C. (1959). A system of color-preferences. *American Journal of Psychology, 73,* 487–502.

9. Humphrey, N. (1976). The colour currency of nature. In T. Porter & B. Mikellides (Eds.), *Colour for architecture* (pp. 95–98). London: Studio-Vista.

10. Hurlbert, A. C., & Ling, Y. (2007). Biological components of sex differences in color preference. *Current Biology, 17*(16), R623–625.

11. Ling, Y. L., & Hurlbert, A. C. (2009). A new model for color preference: universality and individuality. *15th Color Imaging Conference Final Program and Proceedings,* 8–11.

12. Palmer, S. E. (1999). *Vision science.* Cambridge: MIT Press.

13. Hurlbert, A. C., & Ling, Y. (2007). Biological components of sex differences in color preference. *Current Biology, 17*(16), R623–625.

14. This gender difference was reported in Hurlbert and Ling's (2007) initial study of color preferences, but a subsequent experiment failed to replicate it, as both males and females weighted negatively on the L–M axis, preferring colors that were more blue-green than red (Ling & Hurlbert, 2009). They did still find that females weighted *less negatively* than males on this axis, however.

15. Hurlbert, A. C., & Ling, Y. (2007). Biological components of sex differences in color preference. *Current Biology, 17*(16), R623–625.

16. Hering, E. (1892/1964). *Outlines of a theory of the light sense* [L. M. Hurvich & D. Jameson,trans.]. Cambridge, MA: Harvard University Press.

17. Hård, A., & Sivik, L. (March 1981). NCS, Natural Color System: a Swedish standard for color notation. *Color Research & Application, 6,* 129–138.

18. Ou, L. C., Luo, M. R., Woodcock, A., & Wright, A. (October 2004). A study of colour emotion and colour preference. Part 1: colour emotions for single colors. *Color Research & Applications, 29,* 232–240.

19. Ou, L. C., Luo, M. R., Woodcock, A., & Wright, A. (October 2004). A study of colour emotion and colour preference. Part 3: colour preference modelling. *Color Research & Applications, 29,* 381–389.

20. Hurlbert, A. C., & Ling, Y. (2007). Biological components of sex differences in color preference. *Current Biology, 17*(16), R623–625.

21. Palmer, S. E., & Schloss, K. B. (May 2010). An ecological valence theory of human color preference. *Proceedings of the National Academy of Sciences, 107,* 8877–8882.

22. Ou, L. C., Luo, M. R., Woodcock, A., & Wright, A. (October 2004). A study of colour emotion and colour preference. Part 3: colour preference modelling. *Color Research & Applications, 29,* 381–389.

23. Teller, D. Y., Civan, A., & Bronson-Castain, K. (May 2004). Infants' spontaneous color preferences are not due to adult-like brightness variations. *Visual Neuroscience, 21,* 397–401.

24. Pastoureau, M. (2001). *Blue: the history of a color.* Princeton: Princeton University Press.

25. Hård, A., & Sivik, L. (March 1981). NCS, Natural Color System: a Swedish standard for color notation. *Color Research & Application, 6,* 129–138.

26. Hering, E. (1892/1964). *Outlines of a theory of the light sense* [L. M. Hurvich & D. Jameson, trans.]. Cambridge, MA: Harvard University Press.

27. Unique hues are those hues that contain one and only one of the four chromatic primary hues: red, green, blue, or yellow.

28. Palmer, S. E., & Schloss, K. B. (May 2010). An ecological valence theory of human color preference. *Proceedings of the National Academy of Sciences, 107,* 8877–8882.

29. Ling, Y. L., & Hurlbert, A. C. (2009). A new model for color preference: universality and individuality. *15th Color Imaging Conference Final Program and Proceedings,* 8–11.

30. Arnheim, R. (1974). *Art and visual perception: a psychology of the creative eye.* Berkeley: University of California Press.

31. Gombrich, E. H. (1960). *Art and illusion.* London: Phaidon Press.

32. Palmer, S. E., Gardner, J. S., & Wickens, T. D. (2008). Aesthetic issues in spatial composition. *Spatial Vision, 21,* 421–429.

33. Palmer, S. E., Gardner, J. S., & Wickens, T. D. (2008). Aesthetic issues in spatial composition. *Spatial Vision, 21,* 421–429.

34. More precisely, the inward bias means that people prefer the object to be positioned so that the vector from its center to its front points in the same direction as the vector from its center to the center of the frame.

35. Arnheim, R. (1974). *Art and visual perception: a psychology of the creative eye.* Berkeley: University of California Press.

36. Arnheim, R. (1988). *The power of the center.* Berkeley: University of California Press.

37. Palmer, S. E. (1991). Goodness, Gestalt, groups, and Garner: Local symmetry subgroups as a theory of figural goodness. In G. R. Lockhead & J. R. Pomerantz (Eds.), *The perception of structure: Essays in honor of Wendell R. Garner* (pp. 23–39). Washington, DC: American Psychological Association.

38. Palmer, S. E., & Guidi (in preparation). Mapping the perceptual structure of rectangles through goodness-of-fit ratings.

39. Gibson, J. J. (1976). The theory of affordances. In R. Shaw & J. Bransford (Eds.), *Perceiving, acting, and knowing* (pp. 67–82). Hillsdale: Erlbaum.

40. Palmer, S. E., Gardner, J. S., & Wickens, T. D. (2008). Aesthetic issues in spatial composition. *Spatial Vision, 21,* 421–429.

41. Gardner, J. S., & Palmer, S. E. (May 2009). Representational fit in aesthetic judgments of spatial composition. Presented at the 9th Annual Meeting of the Vision Sciences Society, Naples, Florida.

42. Gardner, J. S., & Palmer, S. E. (in preparation). Aesthetic issues in spatial composition II: Effects of vertical position on framing single objects.

43. Palmer, S. E., Rosch, E., & Chase, P. (1981). Canonical perspective and the perception of objects. In J. B. Long & A. Baddeley (Eds.), *Attention and perception IX* (pp. 135–151). Hillsdale: Erlbaum.

44. Khalil, S., & McBeath, M. (June 2006). Canonical representation: an examination of preferences for viewing and depicting 3-dimensional objects [abstract]. *Journal of Vision, 6,* 267.

45. This *ecological* perspective bias should not be confused with the *positional* perspective bias described above. Ecological perspective biases are based on the aesthetic effects arising from different perspective views of the same object, in all of which the object is located at the same position within the frame (i.e., the center). Positional perspective biases are based on the aesthetic effects due to different positions for the same object within the frame, all of which are taken from the same perspective.

46. Konkle, T. & Oliva, A. (in press) Canonical visual size for real-world objects: Evidence from reconstructive memory, imagery, and perceptual preferences, *Journal of Experimental Psychology: Human Perception & Performance.*

47. Linsen, S., Leyssen, M., Gardner, J. S., & Palmer, S.E., (May 2010). Aesthetic preferences in the size of images of real-world objects. Presented at the 10th Annual Meeting of the Vision Sciences Society, Naples, Florida.

48. Jolicoeur, P. (July 1985). The time to name disoriented natural objects. *Memory & Cognition, 134,* 289–303.

49. Zajonc, R. B. (June 1968). Attitudinal effects of mere exposure. *Journal of Personality and Social Psychology, 9,* 1–27.

50. Cutting, J. E. (2005). *Impressionism and its canon.* Lanham: University Press of America.

51. Winkielman, P., Schwarz, N., Fazendeiro, T. A., & Reber, R. (2003). The hedonic marking of processing fluency: implications for evaluative judgment. In J. Musch & K. C. Klauer (Eds.), *The psychology of evaluation: affective processes in cognition and emotion* (pp. 189–217). Mahwah: Lawrence Erlbaum.

52. Palmer, S. E., Rosch, E., & Chase, P. (1981). Canonical perspective and the perception of objects. In J. B. Long & A. Baddeley (Eds.), *Attention and perception IX* (pp. 135–151). Hillsdale: Erlbaum.

53. Estes, Z., Verges, M., & Barsalou, L. S. (February 2008). Head up, foot down: object words orient attention to the objects' typical location. *Psychological Science, 19,* 93–97.

54. Gardner, J. S., & Palmer, S. E. (May 2009). Representational transparency in aesthetic judgments of spatial composition. Presented at the 9th Annual Meeting of the Vision Sciences Society, Naples, Florida.

55. Arnheim, R. (1974). *Art and visual perception: a psychology of the creative eye.* Berkeley: University of California Press.

9

Processing Fluency, Aesthetic Pleasure, and Culturally Shared Taste
Rolf Reber

Introduction

An age-old dream of researchers in empirical aesthetics has been to find the aesthetic formula. Although *the* aesthetic formula has never been found, it seems that people find certain objective attributes in a painting more beautiful than others. For example, people find symmetrical patterns more beautiful than asymmetrical patterns.[1] In the 16th century, the view that beauty depends on the right proportions was so dominant that artists introduced pattern books with pictorial elements that other artists could copy and combine to create beautiful artworks.[2] If beauty depended solely on objective features of objects, then every person would have the same taste. This apparently is not the case, as there are very different tastes for artworks across cultures and across individuals of the same culture.[3] Not only objective attributes of an artwork, but also subjective factors, like familiarity with the artwork, must play a role when people judge its beauty.

Indeed, viewers usually like the kind of paintings they have grown up with. For example, students from Cornell University preferred those Impressionist paintings that were most frequently depicted in books in the Cornell University Library.[4] Frequency with which depictions of paintings appeared was taken as a substitute for the frequency with which students had seen the painting in their lifetime. The same preference for more frequent paintings was found in older adults, but not in children, who obviously have not seen as many paintings as students or older adults. In a similar vein, people like the kind of music they grew up with. Sociologist Pierre Bourdieu observed that different social classes differ in their musical tastes because they grow up with different kinds of music in their homes.[5] What people like and find beautiful depends on what they have encountered before.

As both objective attributes and an individual's experience contribute to aesthetic preference, beauty must derive from the interaction between objective attributes of an artwork and the subjective experience of the viewer.[6] I am going to present a theory that helps explain why people find an artwork beautiful. Although beauty is not the only aesthetic quality,[7] it was a prominent one in the history of aesthetics,[8] and it remains an important notion in what laypeople think about art. The chapter has three main parts. The first part reviews the fluency theory of aesthetic pleasure, and evidence in its favor. The second part discusses challenges to the fluency theory: some findings apparently contradict the fluency theory, and some theories put forward mechanisms that could be alternatives to fluency. Another central challenge for every theory of empirical aesthetics is the question, what does it tell us about art? We shall see how the fluency theory can respond to those challenges. The final part builds on the work of sociologist Pierre Bourdieu and presents a fluency account of culturally shared taste that explains how individuals within a culture or social class develop the same taste and feel pleasure towards the same artistic objects.

The Fluency Theory of Aesthetic Pleasure

The basic idea of the fluency theory of aesthetic pleasure is simple: if people process information about an object *easily*, they feel positive affect, especially if ease of processing is unexpected.[9] This mild positive affect is experienced as beauty. Let me state at the outset that although the fluency theory covers some interesting phenomena, it does not cover all kinds of aesthetic experience, like emotions that go beyond mild positive affect,[10] or formal or stylistic judgments that promote aesthetic understanding.[11] Moreover, the fluency theory of beauty does not say anything about artistic value: there are beautiful paintings without artistic merit, and good art is not necessarily beautiful.

Before we discuss in more detail how processing fluency influences aesthetic experience, we have to define the terms *beauty*, *aesthetic pleasure*, and *processing fluency*, and to review the determinants and consequences of processing fluency.

BEAUTY AND AESTHETIC PLEASURE

A representative definition of beauty goes back to the philosopher George Santayana, who defined beauty as being value positive, intrinsic, and objectified.[12] *Value positive* means that it provides pleasure; *intrinsic* refers to the fact that this pleasure is immediate, without intermediate reasoning. This notion goes back to the medieval philosopher and theologian Thomas of Aquinas.[13] Finally, *objectified* means that the audience attributes the pleasure they experience to the object, unlike some cold drink on a hot day, where pleasure is due to palatability. Beauty can be felt only with a disinterested view on the object of pleasure.[14] This is the situation where the museum visitor looks at a painting and feels immediate pleasure that is attributed to the painting, not to one's own response. I use the term "beauty" when I refer to an aesthetic object, like a painting or a sonata, and the term "aesthetic pleasure" when I refer to the feeling of a person, but the two terms denote different aspects of the same interaction between person and object.

PROCESSING FLUENCY

Processing fluency, or simply fluency, is defined as the ease with which information flows through the cognitive system (which includes both perceptual and conceptual components). Processing is said to be fluent if the flow of information is fast and easy, and disfluent if the flow of information is slow and difficult. This feeling can be measured by asking people about the ease with which they can process information ("How easy is it to see this object?"; "How easy is this word to read?"), or by assessing the speed of the underlying cognitive processes.[15] There are several subcategories of processing fluency; for example, we call *perceptual fluency* experienced ease while processing input to the perceptual system, and *conceptual fluency* experienced ease while processing conceptual information. We deal mainly with perceptual fluency in this chapter. However, we shall see later that the ease with which people can process symbolic information from an artwork may also play a role in determining its aesthetic qualities.

DETERMINANTS OF PROCESSING FLUENCY

There are two main determinants of perceptual fluency. First, the architecture of the human mind facilitates processing of specific information, compared to other information. For example, symmetrical patterns are detected more easily than asymmetrical patterns;[16] high figure–ground contrast is perceived more easily than low figure–ground contrast;[17] and shapes with rounded edges are perceived more easily than shapes with jagged edges.[18]

Second, prior exposure to an object or event in the environment, in psychology called *stimulus*, changes the ease with which this stimulus can be processed. If a stimulus is repeated, it can be identified more quickly. Because the object itself does not change when a person is exposed to it, any change in mental processing is necessarily due to changes in the mind of the perceiver. What changes is the ease with which the object can be processed, which is independent of memory accuracy.[19] Exact repetition is not necessary in order to facilitate subsequent processing. People may see examples of sentences that follow the rules of a certain grammar or pictures that follow the rules of an artistic style, such that they are later able to identify whether new sentences follow the grammar or whether new pictures conform to the artistic style they saw previously.

In a seminal study, Arthur Reber showed that people were able to acquire information derived from an abstract grammar from exposure to stimuli that followed the rules of that grammar.[20] Specifically, he presented letter strings derived from a finite state grammar, which prescribed legal sequences of letters. Participants had to encode these letter strings. After this training phase, he presented new letter strings that followed the same grammar, and letter strings that did not. Participants had to classify the stimuli into those that followed the grammar and those that did not. Indeed, participants were able to classify the new letter strings at above chance without knowing the grammar. This is supposed to be similar to the process of language learning where infants and toddlers learn the rules of grammar without being able to state those rules. In a recent study, novices in dance have been exposed to sequences of classical dance movements that followed a rule. Despite lack of explicit knowledge, novice observers were able to distinguish dance movements as conforming or not conforming to the rule, suggesting that they have implicitly learned the rule behind the dance movement sequences.[21]

In a similar vein, people automatically extract prototypes from exemplars. When exposed to dot patterns that converged on a prototype, participants processed the prototype faster than non-prototypical patterns even when they never saw the prototype before.[22] In everyday life, people grow up seeing birds and then build up a representation of a typical bird, which is a prototype. People then classify a robin, which is similar to the prototype, more easily as a bird than for example a penguin.[23] Note that the resulting processing fluency is an interaction between the person and the situation: the person has a certain mental state that facilitates the processing of specific information. This state may emerge from both stimulus attributes (e.g., it is easier to process symmetrical stimuli) and experience with the situation (e.g., it is easier to process information one has encountered before). The situation provides information that fits the mental capabilities of the person to a greater or lesser degree, depending on both the stimulus and the person's prior experience. The better the fit between stimulus and processing capabilities, the more fluently the stimulus is processed, both in terms of speed of perception and subjective reports of ease of processing.

CONSEQUENCES OF PROCESSING FLUENCY

All the attributes listed in the previous section increase the positive evaluation of a stimulus: people like symmetrical stimuli more than asymmetrical ones,[24] simple shapes with high contrast more than simple shapes with low contrast,[25] shapes with rounded edges more than shapes with sharp-angled or jagged ones,[26] repeated visual stimuli more than novel ones,[27] letter strings following a rule more than irregular strings,[28] and prototypical stimuli more than non-prototypical visual stimuli.[29] In the latter study, perceptual fluency, as measured by response times in a classification task, mediated the effect of prototypicality on attractiveness, but there was a direct link from prototypicality to positive affect that fluency could not account for, suggesting that fluency accounted for part but not all variance of the attractiveness judgments.

In all these studies, participants in experiments were asked to judge their affective experience. Such judgments are susceptible to subtle influences, for example the order in which stimuli are given.[30] Therefore, researchers rely on psychophysiological methods to bolster questionnaire data by measuring bodily (physiological) processes that tell us something about psychological states. Indeed, psychophysiological findings support the notion that fluent processing is inherently positive.

In one study,[31] participants had to judge their positive and negative reactions to line drawings. Fluency was manipulated by presentation duration: the longer the drawings were shown, the more fluently they could be perceived. When the participants looked at the line drawings, activity of the zygomaticus major was measured. Activation of this muscle indicates positive affect because it is contracted when people smile. The result of the study was clear-cut: the more fluently a drawing could be processed, the more the zygomaticus major was activated, thus providing further support for the link between fluency and positive affect.

Why does fluent information processing result in positive affect? High fluency signals to the person that things are familiar and the ongoing cognitive processes are running smoothly,[32] whereas difficulty of ongoing processing signals that things are not going well. If fluency signals smooth interaction with the environment, then one would predict that fluency should influence processing style. As long as information can be processed fluently, everything appears to be fine, and the person should be more inclined to process information heuristically. If it becomes difficult to process information, however, this signals that something is going wrong, and a person has to attend closely to the situation, resulting in analytical processing. Indeed, this is exactly what has been found after presenting tasks where a spontaneous solution contradicted the right solution, which could be achieved by thinking harder. Song and Schwarz, for example, asked the question, "How many animals of each kind did Moses take on the Ark?" The spontaneous solution most people provide is two, but thinking harder makes them notice that it was Noah, not Moses, who took the animals on the ark. When the task was written in a difficult-to-read font people solved it better than when the task was written in an easy-read font. Presumably, the disfluent font slowed down ongoing processing and made people think harder, resulting in better performance.[33]

We have discussed fluency effects on affect. However, fluency influences variables other than affect, such as judged familiarity or judged truth. In one study on judged truth, we presented statements in the form "Osorno is in Chile" and instructed participants to indicate whether the judgment is true or not.[34] We manipulated fluency by whether a statement was shown in a color that contrasted strongly with the background, rendering statements well readable, or in a color that contrasted more weakly, rendering the statement moderately readable. We found that participants judged easily readable statements to be more likely true than moderately readable statements. This finding extended existing research that demonstrated that repeated statements were more likely to be judged true than new statements. Presumably, repeated exposure to statements facilitated their processing, increasing the experience of fluency while re-encoding the statements, and this ease of processing affected judgments of truth. Note that the findings discussed in this section demonstrate that processing fluency influences both positive affect and judgments of truth. This may help explain why mathematicians sometimes equate beauty with truth in that they find beautiful theories intuitively more plausible than theories that lack this sense of beauty.[35]

In sum, fluent processing feels positive because it signals that objects or events are familiar and the interaction with the environment is going smoothly. In addition, it has been shown that fluency has an impact on cognitive judgments, such as judged truth, suggesting that beauty and truth have some common underlying mechanisms. We are now ready to review the central assumptions of the fluency theory of aesthetic pleasure, to discuss some of the empirical evidence in favor of the theory, and to explore fluency and aesthetic pleasure outside the realm of art.

FLUENCY AND AESTHETIC PLEASURE

Processing fluency yields positive affect, but how does this positive affect translate into aesthetic pleasure? We made four assumptions.[36] First, as we have already seen, objects differ in the fluency with which they can be processed. Variables that facilitate fluent processing include stimulus features, like symmetry, and figure–ground contrast, as well as experience with a stimulus, such as repeated exposure or acquisition of prototypes. Second, fluency is itself hedonically marked, and high fluency results in positive affect. Third, fluency feeds into judgments of beauty because people draw on their subjective experience in making evaluative judgments, unless the informational value of the experience is called into question. This observation can be explained by the so-called affect-as-information framework. When people have to evaluate a stimulus, they may not assess stimulus content, but ask themselves, "How do I feel?" The resulting assessment of one's own feeling then feeds into the judgment at hand. Thus, if people can process a stimulus easily, this yields a positive affective feeling, which then is attributed to some aspect of the stimulus: its beauty in case of visual stimuli, or truth in case of a statement.

Fourth, we hypothesize that the impact of fluency is moderated by expectations and attribution. Presumably, fluency has a particularly strong impact on affective experience if its source is unknown and fluent processing comes as a surprise, in line with findings about fluency effects on judgments of truth.[37] If this were not the case, people would never prefer *Fugue No. 1 in C-major* by Bach to *Twinkle, Twinkle, Little Star*. When hearing a fugue from Bach, listeners do not easily recognize its structure, like they presumably do in a nursery rhyme. Therefore, high fluency comes as a surprise when hearing the fugue by Bach, which is predicted to yield special pleasure. On the other hand, the spontaneous, fluency-based affective experience is discounted as a source of relevant information when the perceiver attributes the experience to an irrelevant source. As we have seen, people like visual stimuli more if they encountered them repeatedly. However, if people notice that fluency stems from a salient pattern of repetition, they attribute fluency to repetition, which removes the positive affect due to fluency.[38]

EVIDENCE FOR THE FLUENCY THEORY OF AESTHETIC PLEASURE

There is a lively tradition to study aesthetic pleasure in empirical aesthetics. We discussed earlier two main determinants of processing fluency: stimulus attributes and prior exposure. We look at how the determinants of fluency influence aesthetic pleasure when perceiving artworks.

For effects of stimulus attributes, let us go back to the old dream of researchers to find the aesthetic formula. This research began even before the first official laboratory of experimental psychology was founded. In 1876, the German physicist Gustav Theodor Fechner published experiments performed in order to find laws of aesthetic. He presented students with rectangles of different proportions and asked them how beautiful they thought the presented stimulus was. He observed that the Golden Section is the proportion his participants perceived as most beautiful.[39]

It later turned out that there is no special preference for the Golden Section, and that Fechner's finding must have been a methodological artifact.[40] Although Fechner did not find a law of aesthetics, he ignited a search for such a formula that went well into the 20th century.[41] Mathematician George Birkhoff published a book titled *Aesthetic Measure* in which he approached aesthetics mathematically.[42] He thought that aesthetic measure is a ratio between complexity and order. In contrast, psychologist Hans-Jürgen Eysenck postulated, based on his own research, that it is not the ratio, but the product of complexity and order: the more complex and the more orderly (e.g., symmetrical) shapes were, the more they are preferred.[43] Eysenck concluded that "the pleasure derived from a percept as such is directly proportional to the decrease of energy capable of doing work in the total nervous system, as compared with the original state of the whole system."[44] This statement can be seen as an early formulation of the fluency theory of aesthetic pleasure.

There are today good arguments against the notion of an aesthetic formula. It has been shown that the objects that experts prefer are different from those novices prefer, rendering the search for one formula difficult.[45] Moreover, repeated exposure increases preference for an object without changing its physical features; an aesthetic formula would not cover changes in preference due to familiarity with the object. Therefore, there does not seem to exist "one formula that fits all" in aesthetic preference. Although all attempts at finding the aesthetic formula failed, the collected data showed that novices liked simple patterns,[46] and a recent study revealed that horizontal and vertical lines can be viewed more efficiently, an effect that contributed to aesthetic preference in Mondrian paintings.[47] Together with the other stimulus attributes that determine visual preference, like figure–ground contrast, roundedness of surface, and symmetry, this suggests that processing fluency is especially apt to explain the aesthetic preferences of novices. We shall later see how effects of conceptual fluency can explain the more complex preferences of experts.

After having explored stimulus attributes, we turn to the second determinant of processing fluency, prior exposure. As discussed above, the simplest way to make people familiar with an object is to expose them to it; people prefer repeatedly presented objects to new objects they have never seen before, which is the mere exposure effect.[48] From all determinants of fluency, effects of repeated exposure are the most-studied phenomenon in empirical aesthetics. In the research discussed in the introduction to this chapter, preference for paintings and music depended on frequency of exposure.[49] Recently, researchers showed acquisition of preferences from implicit learning of musical structure.[50] Although the nature of this learning has remained unclear, it became clear that participants were able to extract information from the musical excerpts that were composed in agreement with the 12-tone technique.

FLUENCY AND AESTHETIC PLEASURE OUTSIDE THE REALM OF ART

In the past century, physicist Hermann Weyl worked on a theory of gravitation called *Raum-Zeit-Materie*. His theory turned out to be wrong, but Weyl thought it was so beautiful that he did not wish to abandon it and kept it alive for the sake of its beauty. Much later, it turned out that Weyl's theory was useful—not as a theory of gravitation, but as a formal principle that could be incorporated into another theory, quantum electrodynamics. This anecdote suggests that even in rigorous sciences like mathematics and physics, aesthetic considerations can be important to assess a hypothesis or a solution to a problem.[51] Other examples of aesthetic pleasures in everyday life come to mind: looking at a beautiful landscape; children adoring the family's Christmas tree; a mechanic hearing the sound of a perfectly tuned Harley-Davidson. As philosopher John Dewey noted over 80 years ago, many of our everyday experiences outside art museums and galleries include an aesthetic component: "So extensive and subtly pervasive are the ideas that set Art upon a remote pedestal, that many a person would be repelled rather than pleased if told that he enjoyed his casual recreations, in part at least, because of their esthetic quality."[52] Dewey advocated bringing the aesthetic back from museums and galleries to the activities of everyday life. Indeed, applications of the processing fluency theory of aesthetic pleasure influenced theory and research in several scientific disciplines outside empirical aesthetics, including marketing,[53] finance,[54] archaeology,[55] and the cognitive psychology of mathematical intuition.[56] One of the promises of the fluency theory lies in the fact that it helps understand aesthetic pleasure observed both inside and outside the realm of art.

Challenges to the Fluency Theory

After having introduced the fluency account of aesthetic pleasure, the second part of this chapter begins with a discussion of empirical challenges to it before we turn to potential alternative mechanisms, and fluency and art.

EMPIRICAL CHALLENGES TO THE FLUENCY THEORY

Three challenges are going to be discussed in this section. First, some experimental results apparently cannot be explained by the fluency theory. Second, the inverted-U–shaped function of complexity on aesthetic pleasure apparently contradicts the notion that fluency influences aesthetic pleasure. Third, how does fluency influence the affective experience of emotionally negative content?

First, two studies revealed that their manipulation of the stimulus attributes influenced affective judgment, but not fluency; consequently, their effects could not be explained by fluency. The first study manipulated whether shapes were rounded or sharp-angled.[57] The stimuli were shown briefly and participants had to decide whether they liked or disliked the presented stimulus. Fluency was defined as the time it took to make the like/dislike judgment, and this response time measure did not differ between the two stimulus conditions. However, decision latency is inadequate to measure the ease with which rounded and sharp-angled stimuli can be processed; a proper test would be to assess perceptual fluency with some response time measure and with a subjective ease measure.[58] Indeed, a similar experimental manipulation revealed that rounded shapes were both easier to perceive and were judged more positively than shapes with jagged edges, supporting the fluency account.[59] The other study manipulated the quality of photographs and again used decision latency for liking ratings to measure perceptual fluency. As the authors found no difference for response times between high-quality and low-quality photographs, they concluded that fluency did not seem to influence the results.[60] Again, the proper assessment would have been related to the perception of the photograph, not to the affective decision. Of course, attributes other than fluency may influence affective judgments,[61] but only proper measurement of fluency can establish such a finding.

The second challenge is whether a stimulus could be too fluent to be attractive. For example, people may listen to a song dozens of times, but there comes a time when they get bored with it and no longer choose to hear it, even though this song certainly has become highly fluent. Would a fluency theory not predict that we like the same simple stimuli all the time? In one study that addressed this issue, participants saw Turkish words 3, 9, or 27 times. Study lists were long or short, containing few or many words. Of course, 27 presentations of the same word is much more salient when presented within a short list than within a long list. Then, participants were given a list composed of "old" Turkish words that had been presented before, and "new" Turkish words, and instructed to indicate how much they liked each word. It turned out that participants liked old Turkish words more under all conditions, with one exception: when Turkish words were presented for 27 times in a short list.[62] The authors interpreted their findings as support of their fluency-attribution framework: fluency due to repetition increases liking as long as the source of fluency is unknown. A decrease could be observed only when the source of fluency became salient. Moreover, each Turkish word was underlined during training in order to indicate how to pronounce the word. The authors manipulated fluency by consistency of pronunciation; they found that after 6 months, fluency due to consistency of pronunciation increased liking even in the salient conditions where words were repeated 9 or 27 times; consistency did not have an immediate effect. Presumably, participants did no longer think that the fluency they experienced was due to consistency of pronunciation and used fluency for their liking judgments. In sum, people do not base their affective judgments on fluency when they know where fluency comes from. When they do not know its source, fluency is positive.

This finding helps explain why people begin to like more complex artworks. As they hear the same piece of music dozens of times, or have seen the same simple paintings over and over again, people presumably attribute ease of processing to simplicity of the artwork, which undermines the affective experience. When viewers get familiarized with more complex music or paintings, it is unlikely that they attribute fluency to simplicity, at least for some time, so that fluency due to familiarity breeds positive affect.

The problem of boredom due to familiarity is related to the often-observed inverted-U–shaped curve that denotes aesthetic preference as a function of complexity:[63] preference increases from simple stimuli to stimuli with medium complexity and then decreases as the stimuli turn more complex. If fluency *per se* caused the effect, one would expect that simple stimuli are preferred most, and then preference decreases linearly with increasing complexity. There is an explanation, however, that is in line with the research on attribution of fluency in repeated exposure.[64] When complexity is low, the source of fluency is salient, and fluency is attributed to the simplicity of the stimulus. As complexity increases, the salience of the source of perceptual fluency decreases, and this enhances the perceived beauty of the object. Further increases in complexity will eventually reduce processing fluency, leading to a decrease in perceived beauty. These mechanisms would combine to form a U-shaped relation between complexity and beauty, as predicted and found by Berlyne and others. We have seen that there is some evidence for such attribution mechanisms, but to date there are no studies that show these effects in artworks.

The third challenge is the affective content of stimuli. It is conceivable that processing fluency increases positive affect in neutral stimuli and maybe positive stimuli, but what about negative stimuli? It may well be that fluent negative stimuli yield more negative feelings and are therefore aesthetically less pleasurable than disfluent negative stimuli. Research findings are scarce and mixed: one study on mere exposure showed that people liked negative stimuli more after repeated exposure,[65] whereas others found a decrease in preference.[66] In addition, prototypical negative stimuli, such as prototypical guns, are judged as being more attractive than guns that do not correspond to a prototype.[67] Further research may reveal the limiting conditions for beauty in negative stimuli. It may of course be that negative stimuli, like guns or spiders, look more beautiful when they can be processed fluently. However, this does not necessarily mean that people like them more. Moreover, extremely disgusting stimuli may be so negative that fluency manipulations cannot further influence the affective reactions unless the stimuli are shown at the limits of visibility, which usually is not the case in research on fluency and affect.

We discussed three empirical challenges. First, fluency has to be measured accurately when researchers want to exclude fluency as the mediating mechanism. Second, the fluency theory can explain boredom after numerous exposures and the inverted-U–shaped function of complexity on preference. Finally, it remains to be seen whether fluency is always positive or could lead to more negative evaluations of negative stimuli. Some other challenges remain. For example, not much empirical research has been done on the fluency theory of aesthetic pleasure with artworks as stimuli.[68] It is desirable that any theory that makes claims about aesthetic experience is supported by empirical evidence that includes artworks as stimuli.

POTENTIAL ALTERNATIVES TO FLUENCY

We are going to discuss two questions. First, is fluency nothing more than expectation? Second, could fluency be captured more precisely by inhibition of attention?

Response to music depends on whether a listener's expectations are fulfilled or violated.[69] In his book *Sweet Anticipation*, musicologist David Huron discusses how expectations in music yield affective responses. If listeners can accurately predict the continuation of a piece, they experience positive affect. An unexpected note yields surprise that could have different consequences, some of them negative, like the feeling that the tone is weird, and some of them positive, like laughter or awe, which may be a response derived from fear. According to Huron, surprise itself at first is negative because prediction failed;[70] however, the subsequent neutral feeling may contrast with the negative consequences of surprise and thus yield mild pleasure. When the predictability of the ensuing note is high, composers can create tension by slowing the tempo. The resolution of the tension then is positive.

Huron's theory of expectation in music is similar to the fluency theory of aesthetic pleasure introduced above. Could the fluency theory of aesthetic pleasure be discussed in terms of expectations? I do not think so: although Huron includes unconscious expectation, I think there are fluency effects where expectation does not play a role. Let us assume that Alma has once seen a reproduction of *The Yellow Cow* by Franz Marc in a book about art history. She visits her sister Sophie in her new apartment, and when she enters, she notices that Sophie has a poster of *The Yellow Cow* on the wall. Had she expected to see the painting, she may have felt pleasure at seeing that her prediction came true. However, Alma may feel pleasure at looking at the familiar painting even if she never had predicted to see the painting in Sophie's apartment. In cognitive psychology, this is the classical distinction between top-down and bottom-up processing. Top-down means that processing begins with a concept and goes into details. For example, if I know that the object I will see next is a car, this expectation will guide my processing of the details. Had Alma expected to see the painting by Franz Marc, she would have looked for detail information in order to confirm this expectation; this is typical for top-down processing. Bottom-up processing begins with the details: I see some elements of an object, like wheels, doors, and windows, and realize that this is a car. In a similar vein, Alma enters the apartment and suddenly sees details of a painting depicting a yellow cow. As she has encountered the painting before, she can process the details faster. In this example, having seen *The Yellow Cow* by Franz Marc does not create an expectation of what Alma might see in Sophie's new apartment; Alma, after all, may have seen thousands of other paintings. However, having stored a painting in memory means that whenever Alma sees the painting again, its processing is facilitated, even without having the expectation to encounter it. In my opinion, one would have to extend the definition of expectation in order to accommodate familiarity effects caused by bottom-up processing.

Does a fluency theory explain all effects of expectation? Presumably, expected events always are more fluent. Therefore, there is always a fluency component when explaining effects of fulfilled or disappointed expectation on affect. However, expectations may have cognitive components that are not covered by fluency theory, for example the creation of hypotheses that guide the perceptual process.[71] Huron's theory goes further than the fluency theory in that he discusses the consequences of surprise and the creation of tension. Whereas the negativity of surprise could be explained by a fluency theory, it remains to be shown whether fluency plays any role in the creation of tension where predicted events are postponed in order to create suspense.

The second theoretical challenge comes from a series of studies by Jane Raymond and her colleagues that supported a so-called attentional inhibition account of positive affect,[72] which could be seen as a competitor to the fluency theory. In a typical study, participants saw two patterns, a target pattern to which participants had to attend in order to give a response, and a distracter pattern that was ignored.[73] Afterwards, participants had to evaluate the distracter patterns and new patterns that had not been previously shown. The mere exposure account discussed above[74] would predict that the participants would evaluate distracters more positively than new items. In contrast to this prediction, distracter items were evaluated more *negatively* than new items. Raymond and colleagues argued that inhibition of attention, as in the non-attended distracter items, is affectively negative; that is why it is called the attentional inhibition account. This finding clearly is incompatible with the mere exposure effect—but is it incompatible with a processing fluency account? One could argue that if distracters are processed less fluently than new items, then one would expect distracters to be evaluated more negatively than new items. This is exactly what another study found: distracter items, though repeated, were processed more slowly and were evaluated more negatively than new items.[75]

Although the attentional inhibition account advocated by Raymond and her colleagues is compatible with the fluency theory,[76] the authors' research raises an important question: What are the mental and biological mechanisms underlying fluency effects on aesthetic pleasure? Fluency is an attractive concept because very different perceptual and cognitive processes contribute to this subjective experience, as discussed earlier. As this experience is grounded in mental and brain processes, it is interesting to know what these are. The attentional inhibition account presented by Raymond and colleagues may be interesting not only as an alternative account that replaces fluency as the variable that affects aesthetic pleasure,[77] but also as an account at a different level. If it could be shown that processing disfluency is caused by attentional inhibition, it would constitute a mechanism that underlies fluency effects on aesthetic preference. Other perceptual mechanisms relevant to the perception of art may be related to fluency as well.[78] In a similar vein, neuroanatomical[79] or neurochemical[80] accounts of aesthetic preference do not necessarily contradict the fluency theory, but may reflect the same mechanisms at a different level.

FLUENCY THEORY AND ART

Every psychological and neuroscientific theory of aesthetic preference has to meet two challenges. First, is there sufficient empirical evidence that supports the theory? Second, has the theory something to do with art? Whereas scientists are used to meeting the first challenge, they have more problems addressing the second one, as witnessed by criticism from philosophers[81] and art historians.[82] Although aesthetic experience is not necessarily about art *per se*, I assume that appreciation of art always includes aesthetic experience of some sort[83] and that any aesthetic experience outside art follows the same logic as aesthetic experience related to art.[84] Therefore, the validity of any theory of aesthetic experience critically depends on whether it is relevant to art. I here outline the challenges for the fluency theory of aesthetic pleasure and summarize recent theoretical work undertaken to meet this second challenge.[85]

A crucial consideration in such a discussion is that the fluency theory of aesthetic pleasure is not about art. George Dickie noted in the 1960s that research in empirical aesthetics, at least as it was conducted at that time, is not relevant to philosophical questions about aesthetics.[86] As the logic of empirical aesthetics has not changed much, Dickie's critique is still powerful,[87] and it parallels the criticism by philosophers[88] and art historians[89] of recent neuroscientific work.[90] Their argument is that empirical findings showing that some works of art have an effect on perception, judgment, or brain activity does not mean that scholars can draw any inferences about art from those observations. The effects one finds are not limited to art, for example. If research shows that processing fluency enhances positive affect, this finding is very general and not specific to art; it applies to any situation where there are differences in processing fluency. For example, lack of processing fluency has been invoked to explain why students do not study mathematical theories that are difficult to understand.[91] Here the relationship between lack of fluency and displeasure is clearly outside the realm of art. Moreover, some contemporary theories of aesthetics do not count pleasure as a defining feature of aesthetic experience,[92] which means that any empirical research on perceived beauty or affective reactions to artworks would not be about art.

A striking feature of modern art is that it is often difficult to understand or process. Nevertheless, some people like it, a phenomenon that directly contradicts the fluency theory of aesthetic pleasure. A revised version of the fluency theory of art is based on the psycho-historical theory of art[93] and further developed in Bullot and Reber.[94] The psycho-historical theory of art basically assumes that artworks are material traces of an artist's intention and of the historical, social, and cultural context in which the artwork was made. Proper appreciation of art means that the audience relies not on the visible traces of the artwork only, but also on knowledge about the artist's intentions and the context in which he or she worked. This knowledge, together with the material trace, determines aesthetic understanding.

This aesthetic understanding leads to proficiency with the artist's intention and the context, which increases fluency due to being better able to integrate the visible traces with what one knows. Fluency does not stem only from ease of perceiving attributes due to perceptual features or prior exposure to the artwork, but from greater semantic coherence due to proficiency, which leads to conceptual fluency. This helps explain the apparent paradox that on average, novices like simplicity whereas experts like more complex works of art.[95]

However, fluency does not have only affective consequences, and paintings often remain disfluent even for a knowledgeable audience. As people like apparently disfluent paintings, the fluency theory of aesthetic pleasure obviously is incomplete. Bullot and Reber discuss two functions of disfluency in paintings: first, the audience may draw inferences from disfluency about meaning with regard to content; second, disfluency may elicit analytical thinking.

Research has shown that people draw inferences from processing fluency, as an experiment by Hyunjin Song and Norbert Schwarz shows. They presented their participants with cooking recipes written in an easy-to-read font or a difficult-to-read font. The authors found that the participants judged the same behavior to take more time, effort, and skill when the print font of the instructions was difficult to read, with adverse effects on the willingness to engage in the behavior.[96] This finding demonstrates that processing fluency does not only have affective consequences, but also allows drawing inferences.

In a similar vein, the revised fluency theory postulates that perceivers of an artwork draw inferences from fluency and disfluency, and that artists may manipulate fluency as a strategy to express meaning. For example, disfluency in the painting *Snow Storm* by J. M. W. Turner (Fig. 9.1) allows the inference that it expresses chaos caused by the storm.[97] In a similar vein, disfluency in paintings by Robert Pepperell expresses uncertainty,[98] disfluency in paintings by Georg Baselitz meaninglessness.[99]

However, fluency as a cue to meaning is ambiguous: how does a viewer decide whether disfluency in the painting by Turner expresses chaos or meaninglessness?

FIGURE 9.1 **Turner, Joseph Mallord William (1775–1851).** Snow Storm: Steam-Boat off a Harbour's Mouth. *Exhibited 1842. Oil on canvas, 91.4 × 121.9 cm. (Photo credit: Tate, London/Art Resource, NY)*

As discussed above, the viewer may know some of the artist's intention, which in Turner's example is partly given by the title *Snow Storm*, which presumably is more associated with chaos than with meaninglessness. However, artists may intentionally leave the interpretation of disfluency ambiguous and thus enable multiple interpretations of an artwork.

Moreover, disfluency may make people think. Remember that people think harder when a task is given in a difficult-to-read rather than an easy-to-read font.[100] Decades ago, artists and art theorists like Shklovskij and Brecht must have had the same intuition when they introduced what is known as the alienation effect.[101] Brecht argued that the audience in theater automatically identifies itself with the characters in the play. This identification without reflection prevents the audience from seeing the reality as it is. To make the audience aware of the reality behind the situation depicted in the play, automatic identification has to be disrupted in order to make people reflect about what is going on. Brecht called this *Verfremdungseffekt*, often translated as *alienation effect*, and elaborated on such effects in Chinese drama and Flemish painting. By making a situation strange, the stream of events becomes disfluent, and people begin to analyze the situation. From a fluency point of view, alienation makes an artwork more difficult and thus less pleasurable; the pleasurable quality can be regained only if the artist can put into effect Brecht's dictum that the difficulties have to be resolved in the end and processing of the artwork as a whole has to be made easy.[102]

In sum, the psycho-historical theory of art allows adapting psychological theories in a way that they become relevant for art. Painters used disfluency strategically to provide expressive meanings that the audience can infer from disfluency. Moreover, knowledge about the historical context and the intentions of an artist increases the fluency with which the artwork can be experienced, and that, in turn, increases aesthetic pleasure even for perceptually disfluent paintings.

It is not only the fluency theory that can be adapted in that way. Research on the role of emotion in art has made some relevant contributions by using methods that take the artistic context of an artwork into account. Paul Silvia reported a study on reading an abstract poem in which the knowledge of the otherwise naïve participants was manipulated.[103] Participants' artistic understanding increased, and so did interest in the poem. In another study, Shigeko Takahashi asked art students to produce abstract line drawings that express certain emotion-related concepts, such as anger, joy, tranquility, or human energy. She then selected those drawings that students thought expressed a certain emotion best. Other students then had to rate the drawings and the related emotion words on a semantic differential, which assesses people's opinion on whether an object possesses certain attributes, such as Beautiful–Ugly, or Active–Passive. Although the students were not given any information about the underlying history of the drawings, and their relation to the emotion words were not mentioned, the students gave ratings that showed surprising conceptual agreement between drawings and the respective words.[104] Here, it has been shown that artists can communicate artistic intention by expressive means in their drawings. The two studies show that it is possible to do psychological research that takes artistic context into account.

Culturally Shared Taste

There is an apparent contradiction between the uniformity of musical preferences in infants and the differences of musical tastes in adults of different cultures. Infants prefer consonant melodies.[105] According to the fluency account, this is because infants share perceptual equipment that makes them process consonance in music more easily than dissonance. When children grow up, they are exposed to the music of their culture. This explains why individuals from different cultures have different musical tastes.[106]

So far, the fluency theory provides an explanation for the development of individual tastes. But how does culturally shared taste for music develop? To address this question, the work of Pierre Bourdieu becomes relevant. He observed that members of the same social class often share the taste for certain music; his explanation was that members of a social class learn what the taste of their class should be.[107] Especially the upper classes are socialized to have a "refined" taste. This taste pertains not only to art, but also to other, more mundane things like fashion, food, and furniture.[108] Refined taste is necessary to distinguish oneself from the lower classes that prefer "light" music or popular art. Music can even be devalued through popularization, like *The Blue Danube*. Members of the upper class thus undermine simple aesthetic tastes driven by familiarity and fluency, and they aim at getting accustomed to music that cannot be deciphered easily without musical training. The question emerges of whether people with refined taste really enjoy the art they have to prefer in order to demonstrate refined taste. According to Bourdieu, the pleasure does not always come from enjoying the artwork, but often from another source: it is the satisfaction of playing well the game that society poses.[109] This game means that one can distinguish the refined from the vulgar, the fine arts from popular art, and so on. In psychological terms, individuals may not feel pleasure from perceiving a beautiful object, but from pride that they have understood the societal game.

Culturally shared taste comes from the motivation to distinguish oneself from others—especially in the upper classes, where the "others" are presumed to have inferior taste. Bourdieu noted that there has been a debate between those who think that taste is a "natural gift" and those who claim that taste can be learned like any subject matter.[110] The upper classes defend the notion that taste is inborn and inherited: only by naturalizing taste can they justify the claim of their class for cultural leadership, because they always have had and always will have superior taste.

Members of a class learn through teaching or indoctrination what taste they are supposed to cultivate. Presumably, that is why researchers find prestige effects in aesthetic judgments: that is, people evaluating an artwork more positively if they are told that it is by a famous artist than when they are told that it is by an unknown artist.[111] To show refined taste, people would feel obliged to say that they like the work of a famous artist even when they do not feel positively about the work *per se*.[112] Bourdieu paints a cynical picture of the dominant classes that often do not really enjoy the art they expose themselves to, but know how to play the game when moving in society; their enjoyment lies in playing this game well. The relative uniformity of tastes within a society stems from the fact that this game is defined by the dominant classes and is valid for the whole society. Is it possible to paint a more optimistic picture where socially shared tastes emerge from enjoying art *per se*?

The fluency theory of aesthetic pleasure would predict that increasing fluency by exposing people to the music of their class not only teaches them how to play the game of society, but also yields genuine aesthetic pleasure. Children of a certain class listen to music at home; they become familiar with it. Upper-class children often have parents, at that time especially the mother, who played an instrument, and the children learned an instrument that suited their class, most often the piano.[113] This gave these children first-hand experience with music. This kind of mere exposure to music is different from those who later want to catch up with the taste of the dominant class, but have to learn a canon of what good taste is. They have to rely on knowledge, which does not have the same consequences as experience that comes from exposure to music.[114] In contrast to knowledge, repeated exposure yields positive affect; knowledge *per se* is not known to have the positive affective consequences that fluency has. Note that the mechanisms of exposing children to music are exactly those that, as discussed earlier, increase the ease of processing. Listening to *Fugue No. 1 in C-major* by Bach increases familiarity with this particular piece, but contributes also to implicit learning of tonality and temporal characteristics of this musical style. What in Bourdieu's otherwise comprehensive analysis is missing is the link between fluency from exposure and positive affect. When this link is added to Bourdieu's analysis, it becomes clear why offspring of the same social class have similar musical tastes: they are exposed to the music of their class, and that is why they may genuinely like this music.

This kind of cultural learning is quite passive and does not require active choice of music by the members of a social class. Active choice may help maintain musical tastes, as the notion of *identity motivation* suggests: people are motivated to behave in accordance to their class or culture of origin.[115] Either members of a social class may know what kind of style they are expected to like, or they were just exposed to a certain style. When many members of the same class actively seek out the same musical experience, they also share the experience of fluency when listening to this music; this shared fluency translates into shared taste in favor of that musical style. Musical taste of a group, such as social class or ethnicity, emerges from the fluency experiences of each individual because they expose themselves to the same musical style. Presumably, such shared fluency facilitates communication about music among members of the social group,[116] and both classical theories of interpersonal attraction[117] and the fluency theory would predict that mutual attraction among group members increases. As people who like each other imitate each other,[118] members of the same group are more likely to expose themselves to the same music, which then reinforces the shared taste. Moreover, shared knowledge may contribute to easier communication among group members that, as we have already seen, increases mutual attraction and liking. Note, however, that it is not the shared knowledge about music that increases shared taste, but the shared fluency that is inherently positive.

Fluency theory resolves the above-mentioned debate between those who think that taste is a "natural gift" and those who claim that taste can be learned like any subject matter.[119] According to fluency theory, taste is a "natural gift" insofar as perceptual equipment facilitates processing of certain kinds of stimuli, such as consonant music. As all healthy newborn children have the same perceptual equipment, and it never has been shown to depend on social class, inborn musical taste is likely to be universal. The differences between classes come from differential exposure to music, as described by Bourdieu; this exposure increases fluency, which in turn enhances positive affect.

Culturally shared aesthetic tastes pervade everyday life: We do not have taste only for music or art, but also for fashion, food, and furniture. Of course, the mechanisms that determine how people come to have shared tastes for scarves or sofas are supposed to be the same as for music. If a group is exposed to the same kind of sofas, be it through advertisements or simply through visiting friends, the group members become familiar with the sofas, which results in an experience of fluent processing that breeds positive affect attributed to the sofas.

Conclusion

We reviewed the processing fluency theory of aesthetic pleasure before we discussed challenges to this theory and finally an account of culturally shared taste. A challenge for the future is to examine the psychological and neurological mechanisms underlying processing fluency. We have seen that attentional inhibition explained devaluation of stimuli, and that a fluency theory can explain these findings. It will be interesting to examine whether some neurological mechanisms linked to aesthetic pleasure could be combined with fluency. For example, Biederman put forward a theory that endorphins (morphine-like substances released by the body known to provide pleasure or to relieve pain) play a crucial role in perceptual pleasure.[120] If so, does the release of endorphins result in more fluent cognitive processing? Other theories may complement a fluency theory of beauty. In a similar vein, theories that explain how artworks elicit emotions are independent of the fluency theory and do not contradict it;[121] they explain different phenomena related to the reception of art, and any overarching theory of art would have to integrate those theories built on single mechanisms (like fluency, or endorphins) or single constructs (like emotions, or cognitions).[122]

Finally, I presented a theory of culturally shared taste that is built on the assumption that people of a group develop culturally shared aesthetic pleasure when exposed to certain artworks. However, processing fluency influences not only affective processes, but also cognitive processes[123]—for example, judged truth,[124] and even moral evaluations, as recent research has shown.[125] Therefore, we predict that the ease of processing influences not only aesthetic pleasure shared within a group, but also cognitive judgments about art, or moral judgments connected to an artwork. As feelings exert most influence under uncertainty,[126] fluency may be well suited to explain phenomena in art, for art rarely deals with certainties.

Acknowledgments

I thank Jane Raymond, Arthur Reber, Hélène Reich Reber, and Sascha Topolinski for comments on earlier versions of this manuscript.

Endnotes

1. Jacobsen, T., Schubotz, R. I., Höfel, L., & von Cramon, D. Y. (2006). Brain correlates of aesthetic judgment of beauty. *NeuroImage, 29,* 276–285.

2. See Gombrich, E. H. (2000). Chapter 5 in *Art and illusion: the science of pictorial representation.* London: Phaidon.

3. For an example of cultural differences in music, see Huron, D. (2006). *Sweet anticipation: music and the psychology of expectation* (p. 53ff.). Cambridge, MA: MIT Press; cultural differences in visual preferences, Masuda, T., Gonzales, R., Kwan, L., & Nisbett, R. E. (2008). Culture and aesthetic preferences: comparing the attention to context of East Asians and Americans. *Personality and Social Psychology Bulletin, 34,* 1260–1275; interindividual differences, Furnham, A., & Walker, J. (2001). Personality and judgments of abstract, pop art and representational paintings. *European Journal of Personality, 15,* 57–72; and Jacobsen, T. (2004). Individual and group modeling of aesthetic judgment strategies. *British Journal of Psychology, 95,* 41–56.

4. Cutting, J. E. (2003). Gustave Caillebotte, French Impressionism, and mere exposure, *Psychonomic Bulletin & Review, 10,* 319–343.

5. Bourdieu, P. (1985). *Distinction: a social critique of the judgment of taste* [trans. R. Nice]. Cambridge, MA: Harvard University Press; for a review of psychological research on this topic, see Gaver, W. W., & Mandler, G. (1987). Play it again, Sam: on liking music. *Cognition and Emotion, 1,* 259–282.

6. Reber, R., Schwarz, N., & Winkielman, P. (2004). Processing fluency and aesthetic pleasure: is beauty in the perceiver's processing experience? *Personality and Social Psychology Review, 8,* 364–382.

7. For different kinds of aesthetic judgment, see Parsons, M. J. (1987). *How we understand art.* Cambridge: Cambridge University Press.

8. For example, Kant, I. (1987). *Critique of judgement.* [trans. W. S. Pluhar]. Indianapolis: Hackett; Gombrich, E. H. (1995). *A story of art* (16th ed., p. 475). London: Phaidon; Fechner, G. T. (1876). *Vorschule der Ästhetik.* Leipzig, Germany: Breitkopf & Härtel [online]. Available at: http://gutenberg.spiegel.de/fechner/vaestht1/vaesthi1.htm. Accessed September 23, 2009.

9. Reber, R., Schwarz, N., & Winkielman, P. (2004). Processing fluency and aesthetic pleasure: is beauty in the perceiver's processing experience? *Personality and Social Psychology Review, 8,* 364–382.

10. See Armstrong, T., & Detweiler-Bedell, B. (2008). Beauty as an emotion: the exhilarating prospect of mastering a challenging world. *Review of General Psychology, 12,* 305–329; for emotions in reading literature, see Feagin, S. L. (1996). *Reading with feeling: the aesthetics of appreciation.* Ithaca, NY: Cornell University Press; for emotions in music, see Juslin, P. N., & Västfjäll, D. (2008). Emotional responses to music: the need to consider underlying mechanisms. *Behavioral and Brain Sciences, 31,* 559–575; for emotions in visual art, see Silvia, P. J. (2005). Emotional responses to art: from collation and arousal to cognition and emotion. *Review of General Psychology, 9,* 342–357.

11. Parsons, M. J. (1987). *How we understand art.* Cambridge: Cambridge University Press.

12. Santayana, G. (1896/1955). *The sense of beauty.* New York: Dover.

13. For the reference to Aquinas, see Maritain, J. (1966) Beauty and imitation. In M. Rader (Ed.), *A modern book of esthetics* (3rd ed., pp. 27–34). New York: Holt, Rinehart & Winston.

14. For a discussion of disinterestedness, see Arthur P. Shimamura, Chapter 1 in this book.

15. For a discussion of the assessment of perceptual fluency, see Reber, R., Wurtz, P., & Zimmermann, T. D. (2004). Exploring fringe consciousness: the subjective experience of perceptual fluency and its objective bases. *Consciousness and Cognition, 13,* 47–60.

16. Reber, R., & Schwarz, N. (2006). Perceptual fluency, preference, and evolution. *Polish Psychological Bulletin, 37,* 16–22. Moreover, in a symmetry detection task, vertical symmetry was detected faster than horizontal symmetry, which, in turn, was detected faster than vertical symmetry; Palmer, S. E., & Hemenway, K. (1978). Orientation and symmetry: Effects of multiple, near, and rotational symmetries. *Journal of Experimental Psychology: Human Perception and Performance, 44,* 101–111.

17. Checkosky, S. F., & Whitlock, D. (1973). The effects of pattern goodness on recognition time in a memory search task. *Journal of Experimental Psychology, 100,* 341–348.

18. Reber, R., & Schwarz, N. (2006). Perceptual fluency, preference, and evolution. *Polish Psychological Bulletin, 37,* 16–22.

19. Jacoby, L., & Dallas, M. (1981). On the relationship between autobiographical memory and perceptual learning. *Journal of Experimental Psychology: General, 110,* 306–340.

20. Reber, A. S. (1967). Implicit learning of artificial grammars. *Journal of Verbal Learning and Verbal Behavior, 6,* 855–863.

21. Opacic, T., Stevens, C., & Tillmann, B. (2009). Unspoken knowledge: implicit learning of structured human dance movement. *Journal of Experimental Psychology: Learning, Memory, and Cognition, 35,* 1570–1577.

22. Posner, M. I., & Keele, S. W. (1968). On the genesis of abstract ideas. *Journal of Experimental Psychology, 77,* 353–363.

23. Rosch, E. (1975). Cognitive representations of semantic categories. *Journal of Experimental Psychology: General, 104,* 192–233. The experiments were conducted with native speakers of English for whom robins were more typical birds than penguins.

24. Jacobsen, T., Schubotz, R. I., Höfel, L., & von Cramon, D. Y. (2006). Brain correlates of aesthetic judgment of beauty. *NeuroImage, 29,* 276–285.

25. See Reber, R., Winkielman, P., & Schwarz, N. (1998). Effects of perceptual fluency on affective judgments. *Psychological Science, 9,* 45–48.

26. Bar, M., & Neta, M. (2006). Humans prefer curved visual objects. *Psychological Science, 17,* 645–648; Reber, R., & Schwarz, N. (2006). Perceptual fluency, preference, and evolution. *Polish Psychological Bulletin, 37,* 16–22.

27. Zajonc, R. B. (1968). Attitudinal effects of mere exposure. *Journal of Personality and Social Psychology, Monograph Supplement, 9,* 1–27.

28. Gordon, P. C., & Holyoak, K. J. (1983). Implicit learning and generalization of the mere exposure effect. *Journal of Personality and Social Psychology, 45,* 492–500.

29. Winkielman, P., Halberstadt, J., Fazendeiro, T., & Catty, S. (2006). Prototypes are attractive because they are easy on the mind. *Psychological Science, 17,* 799–806.

30. Schwarz, N. (1999). Self-reports: How the questions shape the answers. *American Psychologist, 54,* 93–105.

31. Winkielman, P., & Cacioppo, J. T. (2001). Mind at ease puts a smile on the face: psychophysiological evidence that processing facilitation leads to positive affect. *Journal of Personality and Social Psychology, 81,* 989–1000.

32. Winkielman, P., Schwarz, N., Fazendeiro, T. A., & Reber, R. (2003). The hedonic marking of processing fluency: implications for evaluative judgment. In J. Musch & K. C. Klauer (Eds.), *The psychology of evaluation: affective processes in cognition and emotion* (pp. 189–217). Mahwah, NJ: Lawrence Erlbaum.

33. Song, H., & Schwarz, N. (2008). Fluency and the detection of misleading questions: low processing fluency attenuates the Moses illusion. *Social Cognition, 26,* 791–799. This effect cannot be explained by longer reading time and therefore more time to answer the question. If the question was simple and undistorted, participants were more likely to give the accurate answer when the question was written in a fluent font. Presumably, fluency triggers the dominant response whereas disfluency encourages analytical thinking. For a similar study, see Alter, A. L., Oppenheimer, D. M., Epley, N., & Eyre, R. N. (2007). Overcoming intuition: metacognitive difficulty activates analytic reasoning. *Journal of Experimental Psychology: General, 136,* 569–576.

34. Reber, R., & Schwarz, N. (1999). Effects of perceptual fluency on judgments of truth. *Consciousness and Cognition, 8,* 338–342.

35. Reber, R., Brun, M., & Mitterndorfer, K. (2008). The use of heuristics in intuitive mathematical judgment. *Psychonomic Bulletin & Review, 15,* 1174–1178.

36. For a detailed discussion of these points, see Reber, R., Schwarz, N., & Winkielman, P. (2004). Processing fluency and aesthetic pleasure: is beauty in the perceiver's processing experience? *Personality and Social Psychology Review, 8,* 364–382.

37 . Hansen, J., Dechêne, A., & Wänke, M. (2008). Discrepant fluency increases subjective truth. *Journal of Experimental Social Psychology, 44,* 687–691.

38. Van den Bergh, O., & Vrana, S. R. (1998). Repetition and boredom in a perceptual fluency/attributional model of affective judgments. *Cognition and Emotion, 12,* 533–553.

39. Fechner, G. T. (1876). *Vorschule der Ästhetik.* Leipzig, Germany: Breitkopf & Härtel [online]. Available at: http://gutenberg.spiegel.de/fechner/vaestht1/vaesthi1.htm. Accessed September 23, 2009. The Golden Section is obtained if the ratio between the sum of the lengths of two adjacent sides of a rectangle to the length of the larger side is equal to the ratio between the lengths of the larger and the smaller side; this ratio is about 1.618.

40. Boselie, F. (1992). The Golden Section has no special aesthetic attractivity. *Empirical Studies of the Arts, 10,* 1–18; and Höge, H. (1997). The golden section hypothesis—its last funeral. *Empirical Studies of the Arts, 15,* 233–255.

41. McWhinnie, H. J. (1965). A review of some research on aesthetic measure and perceptual choice. *Studies in Art Education, 6,* 34–41.

42. Birkhoff, G. D. *Aesthetic Measure.* Cambridge, MA: Harvard University Press.

43. Eysenck, H. J. (1941). The empirical determination of an empirical formula. *Psychological Review, 48,* 83–92.

44. Eysenck, H. J. (1942). The experimental study of the 'Good Gestalt'—a new approach. *Psychological Review, 49,* 358.

45. McWhinnie, H. J. (1965). A review of some research on aesthetic measure and perceptual choice. *Studies in Art Education, 6,* 34–41.

46. McWhinnie, H. J. (1965). A review of some research on aesthetic measure and perceptual choice. *Studies in Art Education, 6,* 34–41.

47. Plumhoff, J. E., & Schirillo, J. A. (2009). Mondrian, eye movements, and the oblique effect. *Perception, 38,* 719–731.

48. Zajonc, R. B. (1968). Attitudinal effects of mere exposure. *Journal of Personality and Social Psychology, Monograph Supplement, 9,* 1–27.

49. Cutting, J. E. (2003). Gustave Caillebotte, French Impressionism, and mere exposure, *Psychonomic Bulletin & Review, 10,* 319–343; and Gaver, W. W., & Mandler, G. (1987). Play it again, Sam: on liking music. *Cognition and Emotion, 1,* 259–282.

50. Kuhn, G., & Dienes, Z. (2005). Implicit learning of non-local musical rules. *Journal of Experimental Psychology: Learning, Memory, & Cognition, 31,* 1417–1432.

51. For the anecdote about Weyl: Chandrasekhar, S. (1987). *Truth and beauty: aesthetics and motivations in science* (p. 65f). Chicago: University of Chicago Press; for beauty and truth in mathematics, see Hadamard, J. (1954). *The psychology of invention in the mathematical field.* Mineola, NY: Dover; and Stewart, I. (2007). *Why beauty is truth: a history of symmetry.* New York: Basic Books.

52. Dewey, J. (1934/2005). *Art as experience* (p. 4). New York: Perigee.

53. For examples, Lee, A. Y., & Labroo, A. A. (2004). The effect of conceptual and perceptual fluency on brand evaluation. *Journal of Marketing Research, 41,* 151–165; Janiszewski, C., & Meyvis, T. (2001). Effects of brand logo complexity, repetition, and spacing on processing fluency and judgment. *Journal of Consumer Research, 28,* 18–32.

54. Alter, A. L., & Oppenheimer, D. M. (2006). Predicting short-term stock fluctuations by using processing fluency. *Proceedings of the National Academy of Sciences of the U S A, 103,* 9369–9372.

55. Hodgson, D. (2009). Symmetry and humans: reply to Mithen's 'sexy handaxe theory.' *Antiquity, 83,* 195–198; and Reber, R. (2002). Reasons for preference for symmetry. *Behavioral and Brain Sciences, 25,* 415–416; for a discussion of art across cultures and times, see Gregory Currie, Chapter 5 in this book.

56. Reber, R., Brun, M., & Mitterndorfer, K. (2008). The use of heuristics in intuitive mathematical judgment. *Psychonomic Bulletin & Review, 15,* 1174–1178.

57. Bar, M., & Neta, M. (2006). Humans prefer curved visual objects. *Psychological Science, 17,* 645–648.

58. See Reber, R., Wurtz, P., & Zimmermann, T. D. (2004). Exploring fringe consciousness: the subjective experience of perceptual fluency and its objective bases. *Consciousness and Cognition, 13,* 47–60.

59. Reber, R., & Schwarz, N. (2006). Perceptual fluency, preference, and evolution. *Polish Psychological Bulletin, 37,* 16–22.

60. Tinio, P. P. L., & Leder, H. (2009). Natural scenes are indeed preferred, but image quality might have the last word. *Psychology of Aesthetics, Creativity, and the Arts, 3,* 52–56.

61. As discussed above, prototypicality has an effect in addition to the fluency effect; see Winkielman, P., Halberstadt, J., Fazendeiro, T., & Catty, S. (2006). Prototypes are attractive because they are easy on the mind. *Psychological Science, 17,* 799–806.

62. Van den Bergh, O., & Vrana, S. R. (1998). Repetition and boredom in a perceptual fluency/attributional model of affective judgments. *Cognition and Emotion, 12,* 533–553.

63. For the inverted-U–shaped function, see Berlyne, D. E. (1971). *Aesthetics and psychobiology.* New York: Appleton-Century-Crofts.

64. Van den Bergh, O., & Vrana, S. R. (1998). Repetition and boredom in a perceptual fluency/attributional model of affective judgments. *Cognition and Emotion, 12,* 533–553; for

the explanation of the inverted-U–shaped complexity-preference function, see Reber, R., Schwarz, N., & Winkielman, P. (2004). Processing fluency and aesthetic pleasure: is beauty in the perceiver's processing experience? *Personality and Social Psychology Review, 8,* 373.

65. Zajonc, R. B., Markus, H., & Wilson, W. R. (1974). Exposure effects and associative learning, *Journal of Experimental Social Psychology, 10,* 248–263.

66. For example, Brickman, P., Redfield, J., Harrison, A. A., & Crandall, R. (1972). Drive and predisposition as factors in the attitudinal effects of mere exposure. *Journal of Experimental Social Psychology, 8,* 31–44; for a summary, see Reber, R., Schwarz, N., & Winkielman, P. (2004). Processing fluency and aesthetic pleasure: is beauty in the perceiver's processing experience? *Personality and Social Psychology Review, 8,* 374f.

67. Halberstadt, J. (2006). The generality and ultimate origins of the attractiveness of prototypes. *Personality and Social Psychology Review, 10,* 166–183.

68. See P. J. Silvia, Chapter 10 in this book; artworks were used in research about prior exposure, e.g., Cutting, J. E. (2003). Gustave Caillebotte, French Impressionism, and mere exposure, *Psychonomic Bulletin & Review, 10,* 319–343, and about fluency and preference in Mondrian paintings, see Plumhoff, J. E., & Schirillo, J. A. (2009). Mondrian, eye movements, and the oblique effect. *Perception, 38,* 719–731.

69. Meyer, L. B. (1956). *Emotion and meaning in music.* Chicago: University of Chicago Press; Huron, D. (2006). *Sweet anticipation: music and the psychology of expectation.* Cambridge, MA: MIT Press.

70. Huron, D. (2006). *Sweet anticipation: music and the psychology of expectation* (p. 269). Cambridge, MA: MIT Press.

71. Neisser, U. (1976) *Cognition and reality: principles and implications of cognitive psychology.* New York: Freeman.

72. For example, Fenske, M. J., Raymond, J. E, & Kunar, M. (2004). The affective consequences of visual attention in preview search. *Psychonomic Bulletin & Review, 11,* 1055–1061; and Goolsby, B. A., Shapiro, K. L., & Raymond, J. E. (2009). Distractor devaluation requires visual working memory. *Psychonomic Bulletin & Review, 16,* 133–138.

73. Fenske, M. J., Raymond, J. E, & Kunar, M. (2004). The affective consequences of visual attention in preview search. *Psychonomic Bulletin & Review, 11,* 1055–1061.

74. Zajonc, R. B. (1968). Attitudinal effects of mere exposure. *Journal of Personality and Social Psychology, Monograph Supplement, 9,* 1–27.

75. Griffiths, O., & Mitchell, C. J. (2008). Negative priming reduces affective ratings. *Cognition and Emotion, 22,* 1119–1129.

76. But see Goolsby, B. A., Shapiro, K. L., & Raymond, J. E. (2009). Distractor devaluation requires visual working memory. *Psychonomic Bulletin & Review, 16,* 133–138. They found that devaluation effects disappeared under cognitive load. Fluency effects are supposed to be spontaneous and do not need cognitive resources. Therefore, fluency effects should not disappear under cognitive load. However, fluency has not been assessed in this study.

77. Let me note that Raymond and colleagues never claimed that their theory is a theory of aesthetic pleasure.

78. For theories of perceptual processing of art, see Kubovy, M. (1986). *The psychology of perspective and Renaissance art.* Cambridge, England: Cambridge University Press; and Leder, H., Belke, B., Oeberst, A., & Augustin, D. (2004). A model of aesthetic appreciation and aesthetic judgments. *British Journal of Psychology, 95,* 489–508.

79. Ramachandran, V. S., & Hirstein, W. (1999). The science of art: a neurological theory of aesthetic experience. *Journal of Consciousness Studies, 6,* 15–51; and Zeki, S. (1999). *Inner vision: an exploration of art and the brain.* Oxford: Oxford University Press.

80. Biederman, I., & Vessel, E. A. (May/June 2006). Perceptual pleasure and the brain. *American Scientist, 94,* 249–255.

81. For examples, see Hyman, J. (August 5–11, 2006). In search of the big picture. *New Scientist, 191,* 44–46; and Lopes, D. M. (2002). Review of *Inner vision: an exploration of art and the brain* by Semir Zeki. *Journal of Aesthetics and Art Critics, 60,* 365–366; see also V. Bergeron & D. McIver Lopes, Chapter 3 in this book.

82. Gombrich, E. H. (2000). Concerning 'the science of art': commentary on Ramachandran and Hirstein. *Journal of Consciousness Studies, 7,* 17.

83. Some philosophers claim that there is no such thing as aesthetic experience, most prominently Dickie, G. (1964). The myth of the aesthetic attitude. *American Philosophical Quarterly, 1,* 56–65; for a critique, see Wollheim, R. (1980). *Art and its objects, second edition with six supplementary essays* (pp. 157–166). Cambridge, MA: Cambridge University Press.

84. Reber, R., Schwarz, N., & Winkielman, P. (2004). Processing fluency and aesthetic pleasure: is beauty in the perceiver's processing experience? *Personality and Social Psychology Review, 8,* 365.

85. Bullot, N., & Reber, R. (submitted). *The Artful Mind Meets Art History: Toward a Psycho-Historical Framework for the Cognitive Science of Art.*

86. Dickie, G. (1962). Is psychology relevant to aesthetics? *Philosophical Review, 71,* 285–302.

87. For a discussion, see Reber, R. (2008). Art in its experience: can empirical psychology help assess artistic value? *Leonardo, 41,* 367–372.

88. Hyman, J. (August 5–11, 2006). In search of the big picture. *New Scientist, 191,* 44–46; and Lopes, D. M. (2002). Review of *Inner vision: an exploration of art and the brain* by Semir Zeki. *Journal of Aesthetics and Art Critics, 60,* 365–366.

89. Gombrich, E. H. (2000). Concerning 'the science of art': commentary on Ramachandran and Hirstein. *Journal of Consciousness Studies, 7,* 17.

90. Ramachandran, V. S., & Hirstein, W. (1999). The science of art: a neurological theory of aesthetic experience. *Journal of Consciousness Studies, 6,* 15–51; and Zeki, S. (1999). *Inner vision: an exploration of art and the brain.* Oxford: Oxford University Press.

91. McColm, G. (2007). A metaphor for mathematics education. *Notices of the American Mathematical Association, 54,* 499–502.

92. Carroll, N. (2002). Aesthetic experience revisited. *British Journal of Aesthetics, 42,* 145–168; see also B. Gopnik, Chapter 6 in this book.

93. Bullot, N. J. (2009). Material anamnesis and the prompting of aesthetic worlds: the psycho-historical theory of artworks. *Journal of Consciousness Studies, 16,* 85–109.

94. Bullot, N., & Reber, R. (submitted). *The Artful Mind Meets Art History: Toward a Psycho-Historical Framework for the Cognitive Science of Art.*

95. For preliminary evidence that understanding breeds pleasure, see Millis, K. (2001). Making meaning brings pleasure: the influence of titles on aesthetic experiences. *Emotion, 2,* 320–329. One could of course conceive of situations where understanding results in disappointment and more negative affect—for example, if one hears that an artwork is forged. Already children have a preference of authentic exemplars over duplicates; see Hood, B. M., & Bloom, P. (2008). Children prefer certain individuals over perfect duplicates. *Cognition, 106,* 455–462.

96. Song, H., & Schwarz, N. (2008). If it's hard to read, it's hard to do: processing fluency affects effort prediction and motivation. *Psychological Science, 19,* 986–988. For further examples of inferences from fluency, see Schwarz, N. (1998). Accessible content and accessibility experiences: the interplay of declarative and experiential information in judgment. *Personality and Social Psychology Review, 2,* 87–99.

97. Clark, K. (1961). *Looking at pictures* (p. 143ff). New York: Holt, Rinehart and Winston.

98. Pepperell, R. (2006). Seeing without objects: visual indeterminacy and art. *Leonardo, 39,* 394–400.

99. See Reber, R. (2008). Art in its experience: can empirical psychology help assess artistic value? *Leonardo, 41,* 367–372.

100. Alter, A. L., Oppenheimer, D. M., Epley, N., & Eyre, R. N. (2007). Overcoming intuition: metacognitive difficulty activates analytic reasoning. *Journal of Experimental Psychology: General, 136,* 569–576; and Song, H., & Schwarz, N. (2008). Fluency and the detection of misleading questions: low processing fluency attenuates the Moses illusion. *Social Cognition, 26,* 791–799.

101. Brecht, B. (1964). *Brecht on theatre: the development of an aesthetic* [Ed. and trans. J. Willett]. London: Methuen; and Shklovskij, V. (2004). Art as technique. In J. Rivkin & M. Ryan (Eds.), *Literary theory: an anthology* (pp. 15–21). Malden: Blackwell.

102. Brecht, B. (1964). *Brecht on theatre: the development of an aesthetic* [Ed. and trans. J. Willett, p. 174]. London: Methuen Brecht.

103. Silvia, P. J. (2005). Emotional responses to art: from collation and arousal to cognition and emotion. *Review of General Psychology, 9,* 342–357.

104. Takahashi, S. (1995). Aesthetic properties of pictorial perception. *Psychological Review, 102,* 671–683.

105. Zentner, M. R., & Kagan, J. (1996). Perception of music by infants. *Nature, 383,* 29.

106. For a discussion, see Reber, R., Schwarz, N., & Winkielman, P. (2004). Processing fluency and aesthetic pleasure: is beauty in the perceiver's processing experience? *Personality and Social Psychology Review, 8,* 364–382.

107. Bourdieu, P. (1985). *Distinction: a social critique of the judgment of taste* [trans. R. Nice]. Cambridge, MA: Harvard University Press.

108. Bourdieu, P. (1985). Chapter 3 in *Distinction: a social critique of the judgment of taste* [trans. R. Nice]. Cambridge, MA: Harvard University Press. Preferences for food are due to palatability and do not count as aesthetic preferences.

109. Bourdieu, P. (1985). *Distinction: a social critique of the judgment of taste* [trans. R. Nice, p. 498ff]. Cambridge, MA: Harvard University Press.

110. Bourdieu, P. (1985). *Distinction: a social critique of the judgment of taste* [trans. R. Nice, p. 74]. Cambridge, MA: Harvard University Press.

111. For a summary of effects of prestige and social class, see Crozier, W. R., & Chapman, A. J. (1981). Aesthetic preferences, prestige, and social class. In D. O'Hare (Ed.), *Psychology and the arts.* Brighton: Harvester.

112. Bourdieu, P. (1985). Chapter 6 in *Distinction: a social critique of the judgment of taste* [trans. R. Nice]. Cambridge, MA: Harvard University Press. For a summary of methodological problems related to prestige effects, see Reber, R. (2008). Art in its experience: can empirical psychology help assess artistic value? *Leonardo, 41,* 367–372.

113. Bourdieu, P. (1985). *Distinction: a social critique of the judgment of taste* [trans. R. Nice, p. 75]. Cambridge, MA: Harvard University Press.

114. Bourdieu, P. (1985). *Distinction: a social critique of the judgment of taste* [trans. R. Nice, pp. 74 and 328ff.]. Cambridge, MA: Harvard University Press; for the development of canons in painting, see Cutting, J. E. (2003). Gustave Caillebotte, French Impressionism, and mere exposure, *Psychonomic Bulletin & Review, 10,* 319–343.

115. For a recent discussion, see Oyserman, D. (2009). Identity-based motivation: implications for action-readiness, procedural-readiness, and consumer behaviour. *Journal of Consumer Psychology, 19,* 276–279.

116. This can be concluded from research that demonstrates that mere perception of other people leads to imitation of their behavior, which facilitates smooth interaction and increases liking; see Chartrand, T. L., & Bargh, J. A. (1999). The chameleon effect: the perception–behavior link and social interaction. *Journal of Personality and Social Psychology, 76,* 893–910.

117. Berscheid, E., & Walster, E. H. (1978). *Interpersonal attraction* (2nd ed.). Reading, MA: Addison-Wesley.

118. Stel, M., et al. (2010). Mimicking disliked others: effects of a priori liking on the mimicry–liking link. *European Journal of Social Psychology, 40*(5), 867–880.

119. Bourdieu, P. (1985). *Distinction: a social critique of the judgment of taste* [trans. R. Nice, p. 74]. Cambridge, MA: Harvard University Press.

120. Biederman, I., & Vessel, E. A. (May/June 2006). Perceptual pleasure and the brain. *American Scientist, 94,* 249–255.

121. Armstrong, T., & Detweiler-Bedell, B. (2008). Beauty as an emotion: the exhilarating prospect of mastering a challenging world. *Review of General Psychology, 12,* 305–329; Feagin, S. L. (1996). *Reading with feeling: the aesthetics of appreciation.* Ithaca, NY: Cornell University Press; Juslin, P. N., & Västfjäll, D. (2008). Emotional responses to music: the need to consider underlying mechanisms. *Behavioral and Brain Sciences, 31,* 559–575; and Silvia, P. J. (2005). Emotional responses to art: from collation and arousal to cognition and emotion. *Review of General Psychology, 9,* 342–357.

122. For a sketch of such a framework, see Jacobsen, T. (2006). Bridging the arts and sciences: a framework for the psychology of aesthetics. *Leonardo, 39,* 155–162.

123. For a review of recent research, see Oppenheimer, D. M. (2008). The secret life of fluency. *Trends in Cognitive Sciences, 12,* 237–241.

124. Reber, R., & Schwarz, N. (1999). Effects of perceptual fluency on judgments of truth. *Consciousness and Cognition, 8,* 338–342.

125. Laham, S. M., Alter, A. L., & Goodwin, G. P. (2009). Easy on the mind, easy on the wrongdoer: discrepantly fluent violations are deemed less morally wrong. *Cognition, 112,* 462–466.

126. Schwarz, N., & Clore, G. L. (2007). Feelings and phenomenal experiences. In E. T. Higgins & A. W. Kruglanski (Eds.), *Social psychology: handbook of basic principles* (2nd ed., pp. 385–407). New York: Guilford.

10

Human Emotions and Aesthetic Experience
AN OVERVIEW OF EMPIRICAL AESTHETICS
Paul J. Silvia

As staid as they seem, academic institutions have their fads, and these are known by their perky administrator-speak names. Recent decades have given us *the open university, service learning, self-directed learning, life-long learning, the e-college, community-based learning, global leadership,* and their ilk, all of them euphemisms of institutions that no longer merely teach but instead *enhance student outcomes.*

One fad that I'm glad is fading is the *interdisciplinary scholarship* fad, where Assistant Provosts for Something gush about how all work in the future will cut across obsolete disciplinary boundaries, creating a paradise where soil scientists, speech pathologists, ethnomusicologists, and bond-market historians collaborate to get millions of dollars in federal grants. This well-intentioned fad got in the way of the organic development of genuine connections between fields, which is as old as scholarship itself. Good work has always sought inspiration from outside, from without, as connoted by inspiration's literal meaning of breathing in. Cross-cutting work has to develop on its own: I haven't tried it, but I imagine that it's hard to force a collaboration between an item-response theorist and a historian of the ancient art of falconry.

Nevertheless, like shy teenagers at a dance, some fields of scholarship do seem to need a bit of a nudge before the magic can happen, and this book is a nice nudge for the different scholarly approaches to aesthetic experience. It's surprising that psychological aesthetics doesn't have more contact with philosophical aesthetics and art history, given that psychologists who study the arts, in my experience, tend to have backgrounds in the arts and humanities. In addition to writing mind-numbing articles packed with statistics, they also paint, write stand-up, play bass in a fusion band, and train falcons.

To help with the nudging, this chapter will review some of the major theories and themes in the psychological study of aesthetic experience, usually known as *empirical aesthetics.* I'll do so with a critical eye on the prevailing assumptions and methods of this field. Interdisciplinary work in psychology often means "You guys should pay attention to what we're up to in psych—it's good stuff." A more humble interdisciplinary approach should find value in the criticisms and contributions that come from without. Scholars in other areas find a lot of fault with the scientific study of aesthetics, and they're onto something.

The chapter starts with some background on what psychology usually means by *aesthetic experience* and why I think this meaning is limited and impoverished. After that, we'll review the most influential theories in empirical aesthetics and consider their shortcomings. Finally, I'll discuss an appraisal approach to aesthetic emotions. This model resolves some of the field's problems and affords stronger connections with other fields, but it doesn't yet address everything that a theory of aesthetic experience ought to address.

The Two Poles of Aesthetic Experience

To understand the culture of the psychology of aesthetics, we should examine a dimension that underlies how psychological, philosophical, and biological theories of aesthetics define aesthetic experience. On the one pole, aesthetic experience is an idealized, rare state, one that happens in special places (museums, amphitheaters, Edwardian drawing rooms) in response to special things (paintings, orchestral music) to special people (aesthetes and other sophisticates in the arts). There is a whiff of Victorian snobbery about this pole: it carves emotional life into the sacred states of aesthetic beauty and the profane states of normal emotions, and one suspects that book-writing, gallery-attending, NPR-supporting, Prius-driving, organic-leek-buying professors are conveniently among the kind of people to experience the sacred states. This pole is rare in psychological aesthetics; it strikes me as more common in art history and philosophy.

The other pole, in contrast, views aesthetic experience as "nothing but" normal emotional experience. Associated with most psychological theories and probably all biological ones, this approach is all profanity, much like an episode of *The Wire*. Models typical of this pole propose that the psychology of aesthetic experience is an instance of a broader psychology of something else, such as a psychology of perception, behavior, motivation, or emotion. If the first pole is too exclusive, the second is too ecumenical—almost anything is an aesthetic feeling. An implication of viewing aesthetic experience as a subset of typical psychological processes is that aesthetics can be studied using psychology's typical samples and methods. The research participants often have a startling ignorance and hostility toward anything that someone older than them would call "art"—if it won't fit onto an iPod or a dorm room wall, they aren't interested. And the research stimuli are often "art-ish"—they resemble art in some vague way, such as randomly generated polygons and dot patterns, but they are created by researchers to be displayed and rated, not by artists to be considered and appreciated.

We should consider the "nothing but" pole in more detail—unlike the first pole, which is a caricature of a sophisticated body of thought, the second pole really exists in its extreme form.[1] Why do psychologists, who are reasonable people, apart from their somewhat downscale dress and hygiene, do this kind of work? Why would someone think that studying how undergrads rate random polygons tells us anything about the human experience of the arts?

The typical defense for artificial laboratory research stems from the writings of Kurt Lewin, particularly his discussion of the Galileian mode of thought in psychology.[2] Lewin argued that scientists needn't replicate reality in all of its superficial features to understand and explain why reality works as it does. Instead, researchers can abstract the relevant conceptual variables, study them in controlled and contrived contexts, and then apply their findings in the real world. Conceptual realism, not superficial realism, is what matters. As Atkinson summarized it, researchers who wonder why boulders roll down mountains wouldn't build a true-scale replica of a mountain, complete with pebbles serving as boulders, in their dingy basement lab. Instead, they would recast the problem in terms of the basic conceptual dimensions and then conduct experiments with artificial stimuli, such as spheres and inclined planes.[3]

The mountain-in-the-lab argument is a good one; it captures why psychologists can and should conduct experiments that are flamboyantly detached from everyday reality. For example, it would be hard to understand how people perceive color, texture, and spatial perspective by studying only realistic, everyday visual scenes. Such scenes are chaotic, and it would take forever to disentangle the effects of the dozens of variables that are in play. Similarly, few people curl up with a good book while connected to an expensive eye-tracker, but studies of eye movements while reading have illuminated how the mind processes text and how some reading disorders work.[4] Laboratory research, like literature, is a lie that tells a truth.[5]

But the problem with the mountain-in-the-lab argument is that it presupposes that researchers already know what the conceptual variables are. Sometimes experimental methods are a lie that tells a lie, or at least that hems and haws evasively. It is easy for Atkinson, centuries after the fact, to equate boulders rolling down mountains and spheres rolling down inclined planes. It is harder to know what the conceptual variables might be in a new area of research. What variables are essential, and what variables can be left out? How do we abstract a model of a mystery?

I would suggest that empirical aesthetics has not yet figured out what its mountain ought to look like—we don't know what we can omit without gravely misrepresenting the real world of human aesthetic experience. Most theories of aesthetics agree on a few variables. For example, a family of variables related to novelty, complexity, typicality, and familiarity appears in most theories; we've got that one down. But is the aesthetic sophistication of the viewer a critical variable? Is this a conceptual variable that can be left out, thus allowing us to study only naïve undergraduates? Likewise, does it matter if the "stimuli" were made by someone who intended to create something called art and to share it with an audience? Is a randomly generated poem psychologically the same as a normal poem?

My point is not to force a firm yes or no answer to these questions. Instead, my broader point is that the Atkinson–Lewin model of experimental research is not as straightforward as it sounds. Knowing what the key variables are is not simply the starting point of research methodology—it is itself a major scientific accomplishment.

My own answer, though, would be no. Much of empirical aesthetics deserves the ridicule that is heaped on it by artists, art historians, and anyone with extra ridicule and a big heaper. Regarding samples, it is hard to agree that studies of naïve, disinterested college students capture all that we would want to know about aesthetic experience. People vary greatly in their expertise in the arts, their knowledge about the arts, and the values they bring to an aesthetic encounter. These differences really matter. Experts in the arts are not merely faster, smarter, or nerdier novices—their understanding of what art is, means, and does is qualitatively different.[6]

Regarding methods, it is hard to agree that art is just another stimulus. The study of aesthetics is the other side of the study of creativity. There is an intentionality to creative work that is absent, obviously, in randomly generated patterns and scenes. As an example, in a prior life (i.e., graduate school), I ran a small press devoted to experimental language art. Our meager post office box was deluged with poems and chapbooks, and each issue involved layers of hard creative decisions. Of all the poems someone wrote, only a few were submitted to us. Of all the poems we received, only a few were published. Of all the ways the poems could be arranged, only one layout was developed. Each issue was thus a complex collaboration involving authors, editors, and designers. Creative work is not worth doing if nothing differentiates a creative striving from random behavior.

To be credible, research on aesthetics should be persuasive to scholars outside of psychology, and the scoffing of art historians and philosophers shouldn't be dismissed as the scoffs of people who never took a class on research methods. Experimental aesthetics thus needs a third way, and it has had one for a long time. Some researchers have always insisted that the contexts, samples, and art objects under study matter. Many scholars have conducted research in realistic contexts, such as major museums.[7] Similarly, many researchers insist on using real works of art in their research, not contrived stimuli. Moreover, there is a growing interest in individual differences and expertise in the arts, which reflects an appreciation for how people bring different knowledge and values to aesthetic encounters.[8] If the field is still coming to know what its major variables are, then using realistic artworks and diverse samples will increase our chances of hiking up the right path.

A Look at Theories of Aesthetic Experience

How have psychological theories defined and explained aesthetic experience? This section reviews the theories that have attracted the most attention from researchers.

I don't mean to slight the omitted theories—some of them are much more promising than the ones covered here[9]—but the following three theories have attracted the most attention and best represent the methodological culture of experimental aesthetics.

BERLYNE'S PSYCHOBIOLOGICAL MODEL

Daniel Berlyne's psychobiological model of aesthetic experience, developed and tweaked over many years,[10] was a big deal for empirical aesthetics. It is common to hear that Gustav Fechner created the scientific study of aesthetics and that Berlyne revived it. This is broadly true, but arts researchers were not quite wandering the desert, searching for random polygons and semantic-differential scales, before Berlyne. There has always been a small, valiant band of arts researchers who attend the Division 10 sessions at the American Psychological Association conference, work under relative obscurity, and grumble about the abject lack of grants for basic arts research. Several books review the big body of interesting work published during the pre-Berlyne period.[11]

Nevertheless, Berlyne did transform empirical aesthetics, and he deserves his stature. His work attracted mainstream interest to aesthetic problems and injected a tough-minded empiricism into what had historically been a soft-minded area. Moreover, his search for a unified theory, one that would integrate aesthetic problems with the bigger problems of reward, motivation, and action, provided inspiration and coherence for an otherwise fragmented literature. Decades later, Berlyne's work remains a touchstone for modern researchers.

So what was his theory? Berlyne's work was the fusion of two trends in the 1950s. The first was the erosion of drive theory, embodied by Clark Hull's then-monumental theory of habits, drives, and reinforcement.[12] In brief, Hull argued that organisms preferred a low level of arousal. Stimuli impinging on the organism evoked a state of arousal, known as drive. Drive motivated activity diffusely; its energy was channeled by habits, which directed behavior. Reducing drive was rewarding, so the behaviors that reduced it were strengthened as habits. With this simple notion, accompanied by mathematical models and many motivated devotees, Hull launched a "drive reduction" revolution in motivation psychology. Hull's theory was pure and perfect in a way that only a misguided theory could be, and its rapid rise and swift collapse was one of 20th-century psychology's great spectacles.

The second trend was the emergence of theories of cognitive structure and conflict. Within early cognitive psychology, several researchers were applying information theory to represent concepts like uncertainty, conflict, and conceptual distance. The Gestalt tradition in psychology, particularly in social psychology, flourished in this time. Several major theories of how conflicting ideas motivate thought and action appeared, thus inspiring behaviorally trained psychologists to consider the motivational effects of thinking.[13]

The creative character of Berlyne's work comes from his innovative fusion of these trends. Motivation, in his view, was somehow tied to arousal and drive; whether people found something rewarding, such as whether they found a work of art pleasing, was thus ultimately a matter of the rise and fall of arousal. Furthermore, cognitive structure and conflict could influence arousal and drive. Taken together, these two trends yield a model in which objective, informational properties of objects impinge on the person and influence the level of arousal, which then motivates action (e.g., approach, avoidance, exploration) and creates a subjective experience of affect (e.g., pleasure, interest, discomfort).

The independent variables in Berlyne's model were cognitive variables, particularly a family of variables known as *collative variables*. This family includes states such as novelty, complexity, uncertainty, conflict, surprisingness, and unfamiliarity. The collative variables in some ways are one variable: they represent what happens when incoming information misfits with what people know or expect. As a behaviorist, Berlyne preferred that fanciful cognitive concepts like "uncertainty" and "conceptual conflict" be objective and quantitative, and information theory's family of concepts and equations worked nicely for this.[14]

The dependent variables in Berlyne's work were self-reports of preference, particularly a dimension called "pleasingness"; behavioral measures, particularly how long people chose to view or listen to something; and physiological measures, particularly measures of sympathetic arousal. And the typical participant, naturally, was an undergraduate student with no particular experience or interest in the arts.

The collative variables affected these outcomes by affecting the operation of neurological systems of reward. Figure 10.1 shows how Berlyne thought the systems worked; we'll use complexity as a proxy for the family of collative variables. As complexity increases, a primary reward system becomes increasingly active. This system generates positive affect and thus rewards exploring the object. Eventually, however, a second system activates—a primary aversion system, which generates negative affect as complexity increases and thus reinforces avoiding the object. The primary reward system plateaus but the primary aversion system does not, so the two systems create an inverted-U curve.

Berlyne and his group published a lot of work—they created an interest in empirical aesthetics through sheer volume. This tradition was the first to establish several findings that have inspired and bedeviled later researchers. Here's a sampling:

1. The family of collative variables hang together—as odd as it sounds, new things are also seen as complex, unfamiliar, and conflicted, complex things are also seen as novel, and so on. Many factor analytic studies have found that ratings of the collative variables load on the same factor.[15] Similarly, manipulating one of the variables tends to affect ratings of the others. Such findings suggest that the variables, as

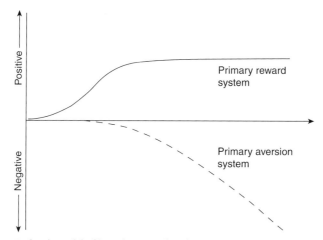

FIGURE 10.1 *Berlyne's model of how the reward and aversion systems generate affect.*

different as they seem, do share core characteristics, such as informational incongruity or processing dysfluency.

2. The collative variables have strong and consistent effects on people's
   judgments of objects as pleasing and interesting. Berlyne's predicted
   effects fall into the category of "good class project" effects—even hapless
   undergraduates can find these robust effects with their slapdash
   projects. The inverted-U effect, however, is tricky. Berlyne's group often
   found an inverted-U effect of the collative variables on pleasingness, but
   sometimes the effect was linear or asymptotically increasing. True
   inverted-U shapes are uncommon.

3. Pleasingness and interestingness are distinct responses. Berlyne found
   that finding something pleasing and finding something interesting had
   different effects. Interest strongly predicted behavioral exploration, such
   as measures of viewing time and listening time, and it loaded on the
   same factor as physiological arousal and the collative variables. This was
   awkward for Berlyne's model: pleasingness represented the rewarding
   and reinforcing actions of the neural systems believed to underlie
   preference, but interestingness was the experience associated with
   arousal and exploration. Berlyne lacked a good explanation for why
   pleasure and interest were so different, but he discussed these
   differences at length and laid the groundwork for a modern psychology
   of interest.[16]

4. Expertise in the arts affects people's feelings and judgments. In modern
   work, expertise is a central variable: it has widespread effects, but how
   expertise in the arts affects aesthetic experience is complex. Berlyne and
   his group conducted the first systematic studies that compared experts

and novices, and they found that experts, relative to novices, prefer works that are much more complex.[17]

5. Firm evidence for the psychobiology of aesthetic experience eluded Berlyne. His model of the neural systems that underlie reward failed to be supported by the growth of affective neuroscience. Instead, features like complexity and novelty themselves became the focus, and arousal was dropped as a moderator. Nunnally, for example, argued that the effects of information incongruity on preference and action were interesting in their own right and that arousal was immaterial.[18]

Berlyne's influence on modern research is both conceptual and methodological. Berlyne developed a set of causes (expertise, complexity, novelty, uncertainty, conflict, incongruity) and a set of effects (pleasingness, interestingness, exploration, arousal) that were sturdy, reliable, and robust. His model offered an easy way to understand how a new variable might affect preferences—for example, angularity might affect preferences because angular objects appear more complex than rounded objects[19]—so it afforded opportunities for later researchers. But by framing the outcomes in terms of arousal and reward, Berlyne decoupled his aesthetics model from the emerging science of emotion, which focused on different kinds of affective states. Even in the mid-1970s, when most behaviorists had resigned themselves to concepts like emotion, Berlyne was waving the Hullian banner.[20] Even in modern work, it is common to see "aesthetic experience" identified with simple feelings of pleasure.

Regarding methods, Berlyne anchored aesthetics research within the hardnosed discipline of experimental psychology, with all of its sophisticated statistics and entrenched prejudices. Berlyne's model fostered the view that art is just another stimulus, one with objective features that can be measured and with responses that can be observed. This view justified the use of "fake art," like randomly generated polygons and dot patterns, which makes sense only if one believes that art is merely another stimulus and that making art is merely another behavior.

PROTOTYPE PREFERENCE

It was natural, given the shifting tides of psychology, for Berlyne's behavioral model to be challenged by cognitive models. In the 1980s, prototype-preference theories positioned themselves as an alternative to Berlyne's collative theory. The best-known examples of this tradition are models associated with Martindale, who published a line of research using random polygons, color samples, and paintings,[21] and Whitfield, who studied responses to designed objects.[22]

A prototype-preference theory, stated simply, argues that people prefer objects that are typical of their categories. For Americans, for example, the prototypical member of the category "family car" resembles a 2002 Honda Accord more than a 1977 Datsun F-10 or a 2001 Pontiac Aztek (both considered to be among the ugliest cars in recent history). If an object is close to a category's central tendency—the category's prototypical object—then people prefer it more. A category's good members are thus more likable than its fringe members. Most of the support for a prototype-preference effect comes from research outside of aesthetics, which has found that people prefer typical faces, animals, colors, and objects,[23] but many strong studies have shown a prototype-preference effect in aesthetic contexts.[24]

An especially good example comes from a study by Farkas,[25] who formed of set of 40 surrealist paintings that varied in their typicality of surrealism as a style. Participants were shown 30 of the paintings many times: one group wasn't shown the 10 least typical paintings, and another group wasn't shown the 10 most typical paintings. At the end of the study, everyone viewed every painting and rated how much they liked each one. People liked the typical surrealist paintings, and disliked the atypical paintings, more than the rest of the set. Because the familiarity of the target paintings was held constant—they were equally novel and familiar—this study provides unusually good support for the prototype-preference approach.

The prototype approach to aesthetics, like any approach to anything in psychology, has its critics.[26] My own sense is that the prototype models—particularly Martindale's, which is the best-known one—haven't lived up to their promise of supplanting Berlyne's model. Typicality does affect liking, but the experience of pleasingness was only one part of Berlyne's work—interest was important, too. Berlyne never resolved why pleasingness and interestingness are different outcomes of the same collative processes, but he did document their differences in his usual exhaustive way. The prototype theories offer much less than Berlyne by focusing only on pleasing feelings—they propose only one cause (typicality) and one effect (pleasingness), so their scope seems small.

Moreover, if a theory is to have only one cause, that one cause should be easy to specify, describe, and measure. Berlyne's one cause—the family of collative variables—was easy to specify in experiments. The information-theory backdrop gave a specious sense of objectivity, but it was nevertheless a concrete way to depict what the theory meant by variations in complexity. But a prototype-preference theory's one cause—typicality—is hard to specify: an artwork could be typical or atypical on a range of categories, and it is hard to say ahead of time which ones people will use.

PROCESSING FLUENCY

A recent model proposes that processing fluency is the foundation of aesthetic pleasure. I won't review this theory in detail, given Reber's chapter in this volume (Chapter 9) and several recent reviews.[27] In brief, this line of work argues that the process of thought is hedonically marked. When stimuli are easy to process—by virtue of familiarity, figural goodness, perceptual contrast and clarity, or any other reason—positive affect is generated. The state of positive affect then acts as a metacognitive cue: people conclude that the stimulus is likely to be valid, familiar, and pleasant. The processing fluency model can thus be boiled down to this: processing fluency creates mild positive affect; aesthetic pleasure is mild positive affect; processing fluency thus enhances aesthetic pleasure.

The processing fluency model is a nice addition to empirical aesthetics. It offers some new findings—such as the links between fluency, liking, and the sense that something is true—and it integrates several classic findings. For example, it can explain why prototypicality affects preference, which was never handled well by theories of prototype preference. In a processing fluency account, central members of a category are easier to process than fringe members of a category and are thus liked more.[28] Likewise, processing fluency offers a good explanation for the mere exposure effect—the tendency to prefer things one has perceived before over wholly new things—because familiar objects are easier to process and categorize. Any theory that brings disparate findings together is welcome, given the somewhat scattered state of aesthetics research.

At the same time, I'm not sure that the processing fluency model is ready to be considered a proper model of aesthetic experience. The scope of the research doesn't map onto the scope of its claims. Essentially all of the studies use non-art or art-ish stimuli, such as dot patterns, images of simple objects, and so forth. Researchers interested in creativity, aesthetics, and the arts ought to insist on at least a few studies of real art. Armstrong and Detweiler-Bedell raise a similar criticism when they note that "those who champion the processing fluency account of beauty draw on studies of simple judgments even as they generalize their claims to more profound issues such as beauty's connection to truth."[29]

Indeed, Armstrong and Detweiler-Bedell have quite a bit to say about the limitations of a processing fluency account of aesthetic pleasure. In their lively and rabble-rousing article, they dismiss the effects of high processing fluency as mere prettiness as opposed to genuine beauty. In their view, high fluency creates mild, subtle feelings, such as the small pleasure of recognizing a familiar thing, but strong aesthetic feelings must entail more than merely recognizing, categorizing, identifying, or decoding something in front of one's face. As they put it, "the experience of beauty goes beyond recapitulating something already represented in the mind."[30]

I would add that the processing fluency model has a hard time explaining some findings that were found long ago. First, the Berlyne tradition yielded dozens of studies that showed that slightly complex images are preferred over simple images. The simple images are clearly easier to process, so it is odd that they are not the most preferred. I wonder what the processing fluency model would have to say about this easy-to-replicate finding. Second, it isn't yet known how processing fluency interacts with other evaluative processes. For example, repeated exposure generally increases liking, but it increases disliking for things that are initially disliked.[31] The processing fluency model would certainly not claim that fluency is the only cause of aesthetic pleasure, but more needs to be known about how it intersects with competing causes. Finally, interestingness and pleasingness consistently emerge as major dimensions of positive aesthetic experience, but the processing fluency account has had little to say about states other than mild pleasingness. Interestingness, however, is where much of the aesthetic action is—it predicts people's choices and actions better than pleasingness.

Subjectivity and Diversity in Aesthetic Experience

How might empirical aesthetics explain aesthetic experience without reducing it to mild pleasure? In this section, I describe the assumptions behind an appraisal approach to aesthetic experience.[32] Such a model does not explain everything that psychologists would like to explain about the human experience of the arts, but it does take the field in some new directions. In particular, an appraisal approach shows how empirical aesthetics can function without clinging to two unproductive assumptions: that objective stimulus features bring about feelings, and that mild positive affect is the defining aesthetic state. These two assumptions motivate an appraisal approach, so we'll consider them in detail before turning to the nuts-and-bolts of appraisals and emotions.

SUBJECTIVITY IN AESTHETIC EXPERIENCE

Much of empirical aesthetics has assumed that art objects have inherent features that evoke responses. This view started with the field's early work, such as Fechner's classic work on the golden section and other proportions.[33] Early textbooks that review early experiments reveal researchers' concern with simple forms and shapes and with variables like color, angularity, size, and proportion.[34] The eventual rise of behaviorism and of Berlyne's model calcified the objective approach, and the use of information-theory methods to generate and evaluate stimuli reinforced it further.

Perhaps the biggest reason for the success of the objectivist approach is that it fits a widely held human belief: that objects in the world exist as we perceive them, and that their properties directly bring about our experience of them. Known as the *nativist fallacy* in emotion psychology, the belief that objects and events in the world directly cause our feelings is generally untrue. The reasons for this are complex, but we can cover the ones most relevant to aesthetic experience here.

A first reason is that the meaning of an aesthetic object shifts over time. Consider, for example, Sherwood Anderson's *Winesburg, Ohio*, his best-known book to modern readers. When first published, the book provoked angry feelings for its depiction of twisted, thwarted people, including pedophiles and priests struggling with sexual desire. Literary critics, however, were impressed with its innovative structure: a set of loosely linked character portraits that revolve around the axis of the main protagonist. It remains a landmark in the history of American short fiction and in the canon of books to browbeat freshman composition students with.

But to modern readers, *Winesburg, Ohio* feels less modern: our jaded culture isn't surprised to hear that rural people can be pissed off and weird, and American literature has since seen a lot of books that develop a narrative via linked short stories. The meaning of the book also shifts in light of Anderson's later work: his best short story collections—*The Triumph of the Egg, Horses and Men*, and *Death in the Woods*—were yet to be published, and modern short fiction eventually emerged as a distinctly American contribution to world literature. Finally, those readers willing to dip into the critical literature will find many sophisticated critical treatments that will expand their construal and experience of the book. A modern reader with a first edition, complete with the typos and printing errors that serve as "issue points" for obsessive collectors, is reading the same literal object but isn't reading the same book.

Another example, one perhaps more worn around the edges, is the shifting meaning of artistic schools and genres. Impressionism was first "out" and then was "in," as in "in every dorm room." A sub-sub-genre of American literature known as "strike fiction," which concerns workers' struggles against evil industrialists and financiers, was popular during the 1920s and 1930s; it was probably angering then, but it means something different in light of the implosion of labor unions and the culture's acceptance of large-scale layoffs. Socially conscious rap music from the 1980s, such as Public Enemy's album *It Takes a Nation of Millions to Hold Us Back*, means something different to a culture that has embraced rap and hip-hop music and that has seen some striking successes and failures in race relations since then.

A second reason why the nativist fallacy is a fallacy is that people differ widely and obviously in their emotional responses to the same events and objects. Individual differences in emotions pose a huge challenge to theories that presume that objects cause feelings directly.[35] Nothing is pleasing, interesting, disgusting, surprising, confusing, saddening, angering, or contemptible to everyone. Although I don't like to dwell on the fact, there are people—tens of thousands, if not millions— who like the sappy landscapes of Thomas Kinkade and wish that more artists would paint like that instead of like East Coast snobs who hate America. Informed viewers feel anger and contempt at Kinkade's work, which seems like cynical pandering to a conservative fan base that has been failed by art education.

It is easy to demonstrate the breadth of people's emotional responses to the same objective thing. In one line of work, my colleagues and I have examined people's hostile feelings toward art.[36] Figure 10.2 shows how a sample of 200 people responded when asked to rate how angry they felt in response to Andres Serrano's photograph *Piss Christ*, perhaps the prototypical controversial work. Many people picked a 6 or 7, indicating that the photograph made them very mad, but many people picked a 1 or 2, indicating that they weren't mad at all. Obviously, a U-shaped pattern means that there's more to anger that the mere object itself.

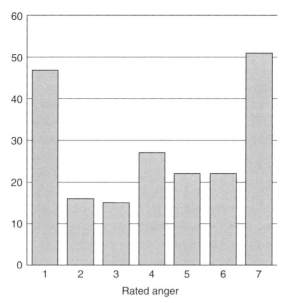

FIGURE 10.2 *Variability in rated anger in response to Andres Serrano's* Piss Christ.

The sources of individual differences are many and complex. Many personal differences—such as differences in values, beliefs, knowledge, abilities, interests, and expertise—influence how people can understand and appreciate the arts.[37] Many of these seemingly personal differences are really cultural: people are born into a particular point in time and onto a particular patch of the planet, and historical and cultural processes exert an enormous influence on people's mental models of what the world is like and how it ought to be.

In short, a theory of aesthetic emotions ought to recognize and explain the subjective origins of emotional experience. If different people have different emotions in response to the same work, then people's subjective understandings of the work deserve a closer look.

DIVERSITY IN AESTHETIC EXPERIENCE

Human emotions are complicated. I hope this claim needs no argument—if you have children, a real job, or some Russian novels, you're probably with me on this—but it is nevertheless important to assert. Empirical aesthetics has become increasingly narrow in its conception of aesthetic experience. Berlyne focused on pleasingness and interestingness; later theories focused on only one of these (pleasingness) and its one big cause (typicality or processing fluency). If a small sense of pleasure, a simple glow of the familiar, is all we mean by aesthetic experience, then psychology has accomplished the violent reductionism that its critics often accuse it of. People do have pleasant feelings, and they have them often, but if aesthetic experience is merely mild pleasure then I don't think it deserves the time and resources of a whole branch of psychology.

Artists hope to do much more than create a serene, mild state in their viewers. Much art aims to provoke, to confront, to inspire, to confuse, to intrigue. And it works. Some genres of popular music seek to create feelings of absorption, flow, and mania (club-friendly electronica); weepy melancholy (slow-core college rock); or anger and hostility (speed metal, although I may be reading too much into Pantera's song "Fucking Hostile"). The emotional aims of literature are many, such as humor, tragedy, suspense, and compassion. And much work has no obvious emotional target—creating a feeling in an audience is only one of many artistic goals, after all.

Some of the most interesting aesthetic feelings are negative. Sometimes art makes people angry, and angry people do mad things. Consider, for example, the many times when people have defaced, attacked, or stolen offensive works, sought to prosecute artists and curators for obscenity, and threatened to cut the funding of the pinko agitators who run the National Endowment for the Arts. What is behind this? Perhaps the clean-cut, family-oriented protesters outside the museum find Andres Serrano's photographs to be low in prototypicality or hard to process.

The study of aesthetic experience should expand, I think, to include states like anger, sadness, pride, confusion, awe, shame, and disgust. If people experience these emotions in response to the arts, a mature psychology of aesthetics ought to be able to say something about them. A common objection from psychologists, I have found, is that these states are not properly "aesthetic": they are emotions, to be sure, but they aren't "aesthetic emotions," a label reserved for beauty or for the sublime. This point of view doesn't appear in print often—the issue rarely comes up, given the dominance of the mild-pleasure view of aesthetic experience—but you will see it in the anonymous peer reviews if you submit articles about confusion, anger, and disgust to aesthetics journals.

Whether an emotion is an "aesthetic emotion" is a definitional issue and hence not especially important—understanding what we are studying is usually the end of research, not the start. We could define aesthetic experience as beauty, as sublime positive states, as emotions that are indifferent and selfless, or as anything else. Nevertheless, people experience a wide range of emotions in response to the arts, and artists have tried to evoke a wide range of emotions. The psychology of aesthetics does a disservice to both creators and audiences by excluding most of these feelings.

Appraisals and Emotions

If we agree that people differ widely in their experience of events and that aesthetic experience involves more than mere pleasure, then how do we explain both? Appraisal theories of emotion,[38] a mature family of theories in the psychology of emotion, can handle both problems—they can explain individual differences in emotions as well as how a wide range of feelings come about. As a result, they have a lot to offer empirical aesthetics, and scholars in several fields have applied aspects of these theories to aesthetic problems.[39]

Appraisal theories of emotion developed in reaction to behaviorism's views of motivation and emotion: they emphasize a view of humans as active, thinking, goal-directed creatures that find themselves in a complicated and dynamic world. Emotions arise when people appraise an event as impinging on one of their goals. This chapter can't cover the appraisal perspective on emotion in all of its vast, detailed glory, so we'll emphasize the aspects that are more relevant to aesthetics.

First, appraisal theories of emotion contend that emotions stem from people's subjective appraisals of what is happening in the world. The mind is continuously appraising whether what is happening bears on important goals, values, and concerns. If something relevant occurs, the event is appraised further, such as whether the event furthers or hinders a goal, whether it can be managed, and why it happened. These subjective appraisals, not objective features, create emotions. As a result, the world's objective features, such as they are, generally bring about emotions only indirectly. Emotions are thus closely tied to the subjective, personal meanings of events.

Second, appraisal theories of emotion expect vast individual differences in how people respond to events. If emotions stem from an event's subjective meaning, then differences in people's goals, values, and knowledge will translate into differences in their emotions. Furthermore, as a person changes over time, his or her emotional responses to an event will change, too.

Third, an appraisal approach explains aesthetic emotions without reducing art to just another stimulus. Because emotions come from subjective interpretations of the world, people's mental models and values related to art are pivotal to understanding their emotions. For example, most people's mental models of art include the concepts of intention (the artist meant to do something in one way and not in many others) and communication (the artist is trying to get something across to the audience). As a consequence, people can view works of art as having purposes and messages that differ from other areas of life, such as the natural world and random events. Furthermore, people can have goals, values, and concerns that are specific to the arts. Parsons, for instance, found that novices in the arts believe that paintings should create positive feelings and that art that doesn't do this is seen as falling short—it fails to meet people's goals and values relevant to the work.[40] As another example, many automotive interiors have artificial wood trim that eerily resembles the real thing but isn't. Some fans of the decorative arts believe that an object's materiality ought to be sincere—things should look like what they're made of, even if they're made of humble plastic and fiberboard. For people who value sincere materiality—a value unique to aesthetic contexts—plastic that looks like wood is unsatisfying: plastic that looks like plastic and exploits the aesthetic possibilities of plastic would be better.

Appraisals and Specific Emotions

How do appraisals work? Appraisal theories contend that each emotion can be defined by the appraisals that bring it about—the set of appraisals that cause and define an emotion is known as an *appraisal structure*. For example, the emotion of happiness involves appraising an event as relevant to a goal (viewed broadly as a goal, value, or concern) and as congruent with the goal. The emotion of fear, in contrast, involves appraising an event as relevant to a goal, as incongruent with the goal, and as difficult to manage, cope with, or prevent.[41]

These appraisals are abstract, in that they refer to broad interpretations of what is happening, not what is concretely happening. Many concrete events can bring about the same emotion because they share the same abstract, conceptual structure. For example, lots of things can make people happy—getting a good grant score, taking an especially nice loaf of sourdough bread from the oven, sitting in a well-crafted mid-century Danish armchair—and they're all appraised as goal-congruent. Likewise, many things can make people mad—getting cut off in traffic, finding a sticky juice-box on the couch, watching the wrong cable news network—and they're all appraised as goal-incongruent and as caused by a responsible agent.

In the following sections, we'll explore what appraisal theories have to say about a broad range of aesthetic emotions. For convenience, the emotions are sorted into families: knowledge emotions, positive emotions, hostile emotions, and self-conscious emotions. These labels are helpful for organizing the complicated world of emotion, but they're only one of many ways of classifying human feelings.

THE KNOWLEDGE EMOTIONS

The phrase *knowledge emotions* sounds odd in light of the antagonism between our cultural concepts of thinking and feeling, but some emotions arise in response to what is happening in the inner world of thought. People are creatures that know, believe, expect, and comprehend, so challenges associated with knowing and understanding can bring about emotions. The emotions of surprise, interest, and confusion are viewed as knowledge emotions because the appraisals that cause them are metacognitive: people are appraising what they know, expect, and understand.

Surprise, the simplest of the knowledge emotions, involves one basic appraisal—a novelty appraisal.[42] Novelty detection and expectancy violation are simple cognitive processes, but they are aesthetically interesting nevertheless, given that being new and different is central to creative work. In a fun line of research, Ludden, Schifferstein, and Hekkert have illuminated the role of surprise in people's experience of the decorative arts.[43] The researchers developed a set of consumer products that had conflicting visual and tactile properties, such as a cubic stool that looked like concrete but was soft and cushy. The objects' visual properties created a tactile expectation that was unmet, and users of the products were surprised as a result. The experience of surprise motivated people to explore the objects further, which in turn afforded other emotions (such as enjoyment and interest) to come about.

Interest, a related knowledge emotion, usually follows on the heels of surprise. When people appraise something as new, unexpected, conflicted, and unfamiliar, they then appraise their ability to understand the new thing. In appraisal theory, this appraisal is known as a *coping potential* appraisal—it entails evaluating whether one has the abilities and resources to manage a demand.[44] In the case of the knowledge emotions, the demands are epistemic (challenges to coherent representations) rather than physical (challenges to safety), but the abstract appraisal is the same. Appraising something as new and as comprehensible creates interest.

What I hope is a freakish amount of evidence supports this two-appraisal view of interest. In a line of work that has used classical paintings, experimental visual art, modern poetry, and film-festival submissions, my colleagues and I have found that interesting things are appraised as both new and understandable.[45] A special feature of this work is the use of multilevel models to estimate within-person relationships between appraisals and interest. Although I imagine that this makes no sense to readers who are not psychologists—and to some who are—the basic value of this method is that it essentially makes each participant a study unto him- or herself. As a result, the study's effects are not driven by confounding between-person variables, such as personality traits, expertise, and the like, and it is possible to see if the appraisals predicted emotions for each individual participant in the study.[46] As an example, Figure 10.3 depicts the individual regression effects for each person from a typical study.[47] There are 61 slopes, one for each participant, and the slopes show that the appraisals predicted interest as expected (i.e., positively) for nearly every person in the study.

Among other things, my line of work on interest has shown some ways in which expertise in the arts influences aesthetic experience. Given their training and knowledge, experts should appraise art differently than novices. In particular, experts should feel much more able to understand complex and challenging works, so they should be able to find things interesting that novices could not. In several studies, we have found that experts find challenging visual art and film more interesting than novices do, and that the reason seems to be that they feel more able to understand it.[48] For both experts and novices, appraisals of novelty and comprehensibility predict interest—experts are just more likely to appraise art in ways that foster interest.

Confusion is the ugly duckling of the knowledge emotions. Only a few studies on confusion have been conducted, and the notion of confusion as an emotion seems to make some psychologists strangely mad. Nevertheless, confusion has a subjective feeling state that is easy to describe and obvious expressive markers, particularly in the face.[49] I have speculated that confusion has the same two appraisals that interest has, except that confusion entails appraising an event as both new and as hard to understand.

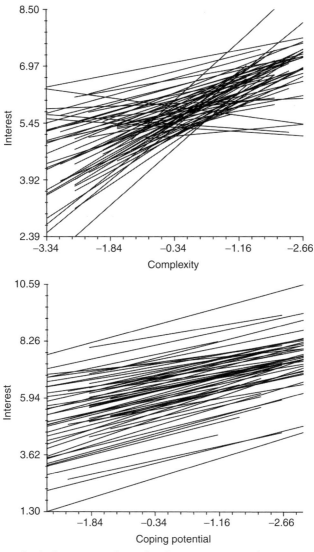

FIGURE 10.3 *Individual regression relationships between interest and its appraisals for a sample of 61 people.*

Several studies have found evidence for these predictions using within-person correlational designs. One study explored confusion in response to abstract visual art; another explored confusion in response to film clips from diverse genres. In the study of film, we found that experts in motion picture media (faculty and graduate students in media studies) found the film clips significantly less confusing (and more interesting) relative to novices, presumably because the experts were more able to understand the works. Furthermore, in an experiment, giving people information about a complex poem that made it easier to understand caused a decrease in confusion and an increase in interest, which is what ought to happen if appraisals of comprehensibility cause something to be confusing or interesting.[50]

THE POSITIVE EMOTIONS

By criticizing theories that concern only pleasant feelings, we don't want to dismiss the importance of enjoyment as an aesthetic state. People often seek out aesthetic contexts—movies, books, plays, music, built environments, and designed objects—because they want to experience positive feelings. Nevertheless, past models, particularly the prototypicality and processing-fluency models, make enjoyment seem curiously passive: people classify something as typical or find it easy to process, and that's that. In an appraisal approach, aesthetic enjoyment is active and trans-actional: it stems from people's idiosyncratic goals, values, and concerns and their construals of how events impinge on them.

An excellent example comes from a recent study of appraisals and emotions related to consumer products. Demir and coworkers conducted an experience-sampling study of people's emotional reactions to the products they interacted with in everyday life, and follow-up qualitative interviews explored the goals and appraisals that were involved. They found that people have a vast range of goals implicated in product use, such as abstract goals like social acceptance, safety, and intellectual stimulation and concrete goals like personal care and ease of operation. When products met or furthered these goals, people reported feeling happy, content, and satisfied.[51]

The goals, values, and concerns involved in aesthetic pleasure can be unique to aesthetics. In his classic work on aesthetic development, Parsons identified a series of stages in people's understanding of the arts.[52] These stages represent mental models of what art is and does, and they include value judgments of what makes art good and bad. For example, many people believe that art ought to depict reality and that its merit comes from its representational fidelity and what it depicts. Art that is abstract or that depicts unsavory things goes against this aesthetic value, so people in this stage of development don't enjoy it. In a later stage, people believe that art ought to express emotion, and art that evokes emotional experience is better than art that doesn't. The value shifts with development, but in each case the experience of aesthetic enjoyment comes from appraising a work as congruent with a value unique to aesthetics.

THE HOSTILE EMOTIONS

When artists seek to provoke, they often get more than they bargained for. Hostile feelings motivate aggressive, antagonistic behaviors, and art history has many flamboyant tales of angry audiences and mobs wreaking havoc on a creator's works. The hostile emotions—anger, disgust, and contempt—share the core appraisal of goal incongruence: something violates a goal, value, or standard of conduct. Anger, the most typical hostile emotion, further entails appraising an event as caused by a responsible agent—someone intended the event to happen.[53]

In one study, we examined anger and disgust as distinct emotional responses to the arts.[54] A sample of college students that varied in expertise viewed a wide range of photographs and paintings, which included some controversial, provocative, and homoerotic works. People rated the images for feelings of anger and disgust and for the appraisals believed to be important to hostile emotions. Within-person statistical models showed that anger was associated with appraising a work as incongruent with one's values and as intentionally offensive, and that disgust was associated with appraising a work as incongruent with one's values and as inherently unpleasant. In later work, we found that hostile feelings toward controversial photographs predicted antagonistic and rejecting behaviors, such as expressing punitive attitudes (e.g., a work shouldn't be shown in public or funded with taxpayer money) and rejecting the chance to take home a free postcard copy.[55]

As an aside, it's interesting to think about how people's hostile feelings toward single works can extend to broader practices and institutions, such as the world of art in general. I suspect that many people feel a sort of contempt for groups such as modern artists, whom they view as not sharing their values. People like Thomas Kinkade have made a lot of money by stoking the resentments of this group. Emotions toward institutions and their members might be outside of what people typically mean by aesthetic emotions, but they're relevant to the poor curators and NEA administrators who have to face the wrath of the anti-art crowd.

Hostile feelings needn't be as flamboyant as anger and contempt in response to obscene and blasphemous art. In their study of designed objects, Demir and coworkers found that people often got mad at the consumer products they interacted with.[56] People's goals for products go unmet when the objects malfunction, prove hard to use, or fail to live up to their promise. Despite the different goals and contexts, the appraisal structure for anger was the same—something conflicts with a goal, and some agent (an incompetent, corner-cutting designer) is responsible.

THE SELF-CONSCIOUS EMOTIONS

Our final cluster of emotions is the self-conscious emotions, such as pride, shame, guilt, and embarrassment. These feelings have received essentially no attention in empirical aesthetics, perhaps because they are as far from simple liking and simple displeasure as emotions can get. These are complicated feelings: they bind together people's goals, self-concepts, and moral judgments. Pride, for example, is rooted in appraisals that something good has happened to oneself or to a close person or group and that the agent is responsible for the event (i.e., a goal congruence appraisal and a responsibility appraisal). Shame, guilt, and embarrassment resemble pride, except that they involve appraising an event as goal-incongruent and as inconsistent with the self's or the group's moral standards of conduct.[57]

The self-conscious emotions are probably the most interpersonal and cultural of the emotions. People can experience these states due to their own actions as well as to the actions of members of their in-group, be that group their friends, family, nation, racial or ethnic group, region, gender, or school of thought. Furthermore, the events involved usually hinge on praise and blame from other people and on the standards held by the broader social group. Appraisal theories have been criticized for their focus on the individual thoughts of individual people and neglecting the social and cultural contexts of emotion.[58] There's something to be said for these criticisms, so self-conscious feelings offer an entrance for interpersonal and cultural approaches to aesthetic feelings.

Artists often wish to evoke self-conscious feelings, and people often feel them in aesthetic contexts. Making audiences squirm in guilt and embarrassment is a big part of confrontational, political, and challenging art, and making audiences feel proud is a big part of nationalistic and propagandistic genres. Moreover, the self-conscious emotions figure in artistic practices and institutions, such as galleries devoted to only a group's own artists and literary festivals devoted to a local author who made it big. It's a shame, though, that there's no research on self-conscious aesthetic feelings to review—graduate students desperate for dissertation ideas might find the self-conscious emotions to be good desperation relievers.

Wrapping Up: Unwrapping Aesthetic Experience

This chapter covered some of the assumptions, methods, and theories in empirical aesthetics. The field's roots in experimental psychology, particularly psychophysics and behavior theory, have had some unforeseen consequences for its models and methods. Showing contrived stimuli to abject beginners and measuring how much they like it strikes me as a poor paradigm for arts research. This approach has encouraged a class of theories that focus too heavily on pleasingness and overlook the range and complexity of aesthetic experience.

As an alternative, appraisal theories of emotion afford a lot to empirical aesthetics. They make predictions that can be tested with the nerdy lab-based methods that experimental psychologists know and love, but they don't reduce art to just another stimulus with objective parameters or aesthetic experience to just another fleeting feeling of liking. So far, enough research has been done to suggest that an appraisal approach to aesthetics can be fruitful.

An appraisal approach is neither the first nor last word, however. To date, most of the appraisal research has concerned visual art, poetry, and short films. It has had little to say about huge swaths of aesthetics, such as emotional responses to music, emotions arising from text-based narratives, and emotions due to fictional events.[59] Furthermore, the appraisal approach is probably more interested in variability—particularly variability between people and within an individual person—than in universality, such as things thought to be innately appealing to humans.[60]

I imagine that the broad appraisal approach could probably say something about some of these areas, but it seems unrealistic to think that the science of aesthetic experience could or should operate with only one big theory.

Endnotes

1. Berlyne, D. E. (1972). Ends and means of experimental aesthetics. *Canadian Journal of Psychology, 26,* 303–325.

2. Lewin, K. (1931). The conflict between Aristotelian and Galileian modes of thought in contemporary psychology. *Journal of General Psychology, 5,* 141–177.

3. Atkinson, J. W. (1964). *An introduction to motivation.* New York: Van Nostrand.

4. See Solso, R. L. (1994). *Cognition and the visual arts.* Cambridge: MIT Press, and Raynor, K., & Sereno, S. C. (1994). Eye movements in reading: psycholinguistic studies. In M. A. Gernsbacher (Ed.), *Handbook of psycholinguistics* (pp. 57–81). San Diego, CA: Academic Press.

5. Dufresne, J. (2004). *The lie that tells a truth: a guide to writing fiction.* New York: Norton.

6. Parsons, M. J. (1987). *How we understand art: a cognitive developmental account of aesthetic experience.* New York: Cambridge University Press.

7. For good examples, see Locher, P. J., Smith, J. K., & Smith, L. F. (2001). The influence of presentation format and viewer training in the visual arts on the perception of pictorial and aesthetic qualities of paintings. *Perception, 30,* 449–465; Mastandrea, S., Bartoli, G., & Bove, G. (2007). Learning through ancient art and experiencing emotions with contemporary art: comparing visits in two different museums. *Empirical Studies of the Arts, 25,* 173–191; and Mastandrea, S., Bartoli, G., & Bove, G. (2009). Preferences for ancient and modern art museums: visitor experiences and personality characteristics. *Psychology of Aesthetics, Creativity, and the Arts, 3,* 164–173.

8. Augustin, M. D., & Leder, H. (2006). Art expertise: A study of concepts and conceptual spaces. *Psychology Science, 48,* 135–156.

9. Konečni, V. J. (2005). The aesthetic trinity: awe, being moved, thrilled. *Bulletin of Psychology and the Arts, 5*(2), 27–44, and Leder, H., Belke, B., Oeberst, A., & Augustin, A. (2004). A model of aesthetic appreciation and aesthetic judgments. *British Journal of Psychology, 95,* 489–508.

10. Berlyne, D. E. (1960). *Conflict, arousal, and curiosity.* New York: McGraw–Hill; Berlyne, D. E. (1967). Arousal and reinforcement. *Nebraska Symposium on Motivation, 15,* 1–110; Berlyne, D. E. (1971). *Aesthetics and psychobiology.* New York: Appleton-Century-Crofts; Berlyne, D. E. (1974). The new experimental aesthetics. In D. E. Berlyne (Ed.), *Studies in the new experimental aesthetics: steps toward an objective psychology of aesthetic appreciation* (pp. 1–25). Washington, DC: Hemisphere.

11. Gordon, K. (1909). *Esthetics.* New York: Henry Holt; Valentine, C. W. (1913). *An introduction to the experimental psychology of beauty.* London: T. C. & E. C. Jack; and Valentine, C. W. (1962). *The experimental psychology of beauty.* London: Methuen.

12. Hull, C. L. (1952). *A behavior system.* New Haven, CT: Yale University Press.

13. Attneave, F. (1959). *Applications of information theory to psychology.* New York: Holt–Dryden; Festinger, L. (1957). *A theory of cognitive dissonance.* Stanford, CA: Stanford University Press; and Heider, F. (1958). *The psychology of interpersonal relations.* New York: Wiley.

14. Berlyne, D. E. (1957). Uncertainty and conflict: A point of contact between information-theory and behavior-theory concepts. *Psychological Review, 64,* 329–339.

15. Evans, D. R., & Day, H. I. (1971). The factorial structure of responses to perceptual complexity. *Psychonomic Science, 27,* 357–359.

16. Silvia, P. J. (2006). *Exploring the psychology of interest.* New York: Oxford University Press.

17. Hare, F. G. (1974). Artistic training and responses to visual and auditory patterns varying in uncertainty. In D. E. Berlyne (Ed.), *Studies in the new experimental aesthetics* (pp. 159–168). Washington, DC: Hemisphere; and Walker, E. L. (1980). *Psychological complexity and preference: A hedgehog theory of behavior.* New York, NY: Brooks–Cole.

18. Nunnally, J. C. (1972). A human tropism. In S. R. Brown & D. J. Brenner (Eds.), *Science, psychology and communication* (pp. 255–277). New York: Teachers College.

19. Bar, M., & Neta, M. (2006). Humans prefer curved visual objects. *Psychological Science, 17,* 645–648; and Silvia, P. J., & Barona, C. M. (2009). Do people prefer curved objects? Angularity, expertise, and aesthetic preference. *Empirical Studies of the Arts, 27,* 25–42.

20. Berlyne, D. E. (1975). Behaviorism? Cognitive theory? Humanistic psychology? To Hull with them all. *Canadian Psychological Review, 16,* 69–80.

21. Martindale, C., & Moore, K. (1988). Priming, prototypicality, and preference. *Journal of Experimental Psychology: Human Perception and Performance, 14,* 661–670; Martindale, C., Moore, K., & Borkum, J. (1990). Aesthetic preference: Anomalous findings for Berlyne's psychobiological model. *American Journal of Psychology, 103,* 53–80; and Martindale, C., Moore, K., & West, A. (1988). Relationship of preference judgments to typicality, novelty, and mere exposure. *Empirical Studies of the Arts, 6,* 79–96.

22. Whitfield, T. W. A. (1983). Predicting preference for familiar, everyday objects: an experimental confrontation between two theories of aesthetic behavior. *Journal of Environmental Psychology, 3,* 221–237; and Whitfield, T. W. A., & Slatter, P. E. (1979). The effect of categorization and prototypicality on aesthetic choice in a furniture selection task. *British Journal of Psychology, 70,* 65–75.

23. Halberstadt, J. (2006). The generality and ultimate origins of the attractiveness of prototypes. *Personality and Social Psychology Review, 10,* 166–183.

24. Hekkert, P., Snelders, D., & van Wieringen, P. C. W. (2003). "Most advanced, yet acceptable": Typicality and novelty as joint predictors of aesthetic preference in industrial design. *British Journal of Psychology, 94,* 111–124.

25. Farkas, A. (2002). Prototypicality-effect in Surrealist paintings. *Empirical Studies of the Arts, 20,* 127–136.

26. Boselie, F. (1991). Against prototypicality as a central concept in aesthetics. *Empirical Studies of the Arts, 9,* 65–73; and North, A. C., & Hargreaves, D. J. (2000). Collative variables versus prototypicality. *Empirical Studies of the Arts, 18,* 13–17.

27. Reber, R., Schwartz, N., & Winkielman, P. (2004). Processing fluency and aesthetic pleasure: is beauty in the perceiver's processing experience? *Personality and Social Psychology Review, 8,* 364–382; Chenier, T., & Winkielman, P. (2009). The origins of aesthetic pleasure: processing fluency and affect in judgment, body, and the brain. In M. Skov & O. Vartanian (Eds.), *Neuroaesthetics* (pp. 275–289). Amityville, NY: Baywood; and Alter, A. L., & Oppenheimer, D. M. (2009). Uniting the tribes of fluency to form a metacognitive nation. *Personality and Social Psychology Review, 13,* 219–235.

28. Winkielman, P., Halberstadt, J., Fazendeiro, T., & Catty, S. (2006). Prototypes are attractive because they are easy on the mind. *Psychological Science, 17,* 799–806.

29. Armstrong, T., & Detweiler-Bedell, B. (2008). Beauty as an emotion: The exhilarating prospect of mastering a challenging world. *Review of General Psychology, 12,* 307.

30. Armstrong, T., & Detweiler-Bedell, B. (2008). Beauty as an emotion: The exhilarating prospect of mastering a challenging world. *Review of General Psychology, 12,* 305.

31. Brickman, P., Redfield, J., Harrison, A. A., & Crandall, R. (1972). Drive and predisposition as factors in the attitudinal effects of mere exposure. *Journal of Experimental Social Psychology, 8,* 31–44.

32. Silvia, P. J. (2005). Emotional responses to art: From collation and arousal to cognition and emotion. *Review of General Psychology, 9,* 342–357; and Silvia, P. J. (2009). Looking past pleasure: Anger, confusion, disgust, pride, surprise, and other unusual aesthetic emotions. *Psychology of Aesthetics, Creativity, and the Arts, 3,* 48–51.

33. Fechner, G. T. (1876). *Vorschule der Ästhetik.* Leipzig: Breitkopf & Härtel.

34. Gordon, K. (1909). *Esthetics.* New York: Henry Holt; and Valentine, C. W. (1962). *The experimental psychology of beauty.* London: Methuen.

35. Smith, C. A., & Kirby, L. D. (2009). Putting appraisal in context: Toward a relational model of appraisal and emotion. *Cognition and Emotion, 23,* 1352–1372.

36. Cooper, J. M., & Silvia, P. J. (2009). Opposing art: rejection as an action tendency of hostile aesthetic emotions. *Empirical Studies of the Arts, 27,* 109–126; and Silvia, P. J., & Brown, E. M. (2007). Anger, disgust, and the negative aesthetic emotions: Expanding an appraisal model of aesthetic experience. *Psychology of Aesthetics, Creativity, and the Arts, 1,* 100–106.

37. Siemer, M., Mauss, I., & Gross, J. J. (2007). Same situation—Different emotions: How appraisals shape our emotions. *Emotion, 7,* 592–600.

38. Lazarus, R. S. (1991). *Emotion and adaptation.* New York: Oxford University Press; and Ellsworth, P. C., & Scherer, K. R. (2003). Appraisal processes in emotion. In R. J. Davidson, K. R. Scherer, & H. H. Goldsmith (Eds.), *Handbook of affective sciences* (pp. 572–595). New York: Oxford University Press.

39. Demir, E., Desmet, P. M. A., & Hekkert, P. (2009). Appraisal patterns of emotions in human–product interaction. *International Journal of Design, 3,* 41–51; Reddy, W. M. (2001). *The navigation of feeling: a framework for the history of emotions.* Cambridge, UK: Cambridge University Press; and Robinson, J. (2005). *Deeper than reason: Emotion and its role in literature, music, and art.* New York: Oxford University Press.

40. Parsons, M. J. (1987). *How we understand art: a cognitive developmental account of aesthetic experience.* New York: Cambridge University Press.

41. Roseman, I. J. (2001). A model of appraisal in the emotion system: Integrating theory, research, and applications. In K. R. Scherer, A. Schorr, & T. Johnstone (Eds.), *Appraisal processes in emotion: theory, methods, research* (pp. 68–91). New York: Oxford University Press.

42. Scherer, K. R. (2001). Appraisal considered as a process of multilevel sequential checking. In K. R. Scherer, A. Schorr, & T. Johnstone (Eds.), *Appraisal processes in emotion: theory, methods, research* (pp. 92–120). New York: Oxford University Press.

43. Ludden, G. D. S., Schifferstein, H. N. J., & Hekkert, P. (2008). Surprise as a design strategy. *Design Issues, 24*(2), 28–38; and Ludden, G. D. S., Schifferstein, H. N. J., & Hekkert, P. (2009). Visual–tactual incongruities in products as sources of surprise. *Empirical Studies of the Arts, 27,* 61–87.

44. Lazarus, R. S. (1991). *Emotion and adaptation.* New York: Oxford University Press.

45. Silvia, P. J. (2005). Cognitive appraisals and interest in visual art: exploring an appraisal theory of aesthetic emotions. *Empirical Studies of the Arts, 23,* 119–133; Silvia, P. J. (2005). What is interesting? Exploring the appraisal structure of interest. *Emotion, 5,* 89–102; Silvia, P. J. (2006). Artistic training and interest in visual art: applying the appraisal model of aesthetic emotions. *Empirical Studies of the Arts, 24,* 139–161; Silvia, P. J. (2008). Appraisal components and emotion traits: examining the appraisal basis of trait curiosity. *Cognition and Emotion, 22,* 94–113; Silvia, P. J. (2008). Interest—the curious emotion. *Current Directions in Psychological Science, 17,* 57–60; Silvia, P. J. (2010). Confusion and interest: the role of knowledge emotions in aesthetic experience. *Psychology of Aesthetics, Creativity, and the Arts, 4*(2), 75–80; Silvia, P. J., & Berg, C. (2011). Finding movies interesting: how expertise and appraisals influence the aesthetic experience of film. *Empirical Studies of the Arts, 29*(1), 73–88; Silvia, P. J., Henson, R. A., & Templin, J. L. (2009). Are the sources of interest the same for everyone? Using multilevel mixture models to explore individual differences in appraisal structures. *Cognition and Emotion, 23,* 1389–1406; Turner, S. A., Jr., & Silvia, P. J. (2006). Must interesting things be pleasant? A test of competing appraisal structures. *Emotion, 6,* 670–674.

46. Silvia, P. J. (2007). An introduction to multilevel modeling for research on the psychology of art and creativity. *Empirical Studies of the Arts, 25,* 1–20.

47. Silvia, P. J. (2010). Confusion and interest: the role of knowledge emotions in aesthetic experience. *Psychology of Aesthetics, Creativity, and the Arts, 4*(2), 75–80.

48. Silvia, P. J., & Berg, C. (2011). Finding movies interesting: how expertise and appraisals influence the aesthetic experience of film. *Empirical Studies of the Arts, 29*(1), 73–88; and Silvia, P. J. (2006). Artistic training and interest in visual art: Applying the appraisal model of aesthetic emotions. *Empirical Studies of the Arts, 24,* 139–161.

49. Craig, S. D., D'Mello, S., Witherspoon, A., & Graesser, A. (2008). Emote aloud during learning with AutoTutor: Applying the Facial Action Coding System to cognitive–affective states during learning. *Cognition and Emotion, 22,* 777–788; Rozin, P., & Cohen, A. B. (2003). High frequency of facial expressions corresponding to confusion, concentration, and worry in an analysis of naturally occurring facial expressions of Americans. *Emotion, 3,* 68–75.

50. Silvia, P. J. (2010). Confusion and interest: the role of knowledge emotions in aesthetic experience. *Psychology of Aesthetics, Creativity, and the Arts, 4*(2), 75–80; Silvia, P. J., & Berg, C. (2011). Finding movies interesting: how expertise and appraisals influence the aesthetic experience of film. *Empirical Studies of the Arts, 29*(1), 73–88.

51. Demir, E., Desmet, P. M. A., & Hekkert, P. (2009). Appraisal patterns of emotions in human-product interaction. *International Journal of Design, 3,* 41–51.

52. Parsons, M. J. (1987). *How we understand art: a cognitive developmental account of aesthetic experience.* New York: Cambridge University Press.

53. Kuppens, P., Van Mechelen, I., Smits, D. J. M., & Ceulemans, E. (2007). Individual differences in patterns of appraisal and anger experience. *Cognition and Emotion, 21,* 689–713.

54. Silvia, P. J., & Brown, E. M. (2007). Anger, disgust, and the negative aesthetic emotions: Expanding an appraisal model of aesthetic experience. *Psychology of Aesthetics, Creativity, and the Arts, 1,* 100–106.

55. Cooper, J. M., & Silvia, P. J. (2009). Opposing art: Rejection as an action tendency of hostile aesthetic emotions. *Empirical Studies of the Arts, 27,* 109–126.

56. Demir, E., Desmet, P. M. A., & Hekkert, P. (2009). Appraisal patterns of emotions in human–product interaction. *International Journal of Design, 3,* 41–51.

57. Tangney, J. P., & Dearing, R. L. (2003). *Shame and guilt.* New York: Guilford; Tracy, J. L., & Robins, R. W. (2007). Emerging insights into the nature and function of pride. *Current Directions in Psychological Science, 16,* 147–150; and Tracy, J. L., & Robins, R. W. (2007). The self in self-conscious emotions: A cognitive appraisal approach. In J. L. Tracy, R. W. Robins, & J. P. Tangney (Eds.), *The self-conscious emotions: theory and research* (pp. 3–20). New York: Guilford.

58. Parkinson, B. (2001). Putting appraisal in context. In K. R. Scherer, A. Schorr, & T. Johnstone (Eds.), *Appraisal processes in emotion: theory, methods, research* (pp. 173–186). New York: Oxford University Press.

59. Carroll, N. (1996). The paradox of suspense. In P. Vorderer, H. J. Wulff, & M. Friedrichsen (Eds.), *Suspense* (pp. 71–91). Mahwah, NJ: Lawrence Erlbaum Associates; Juslin, P. N., & Västfjäll, D. (2008). Emotional responses to music: The need to consider underlying mechanisms. *Behavioral and Brain Sciences, 31,* 559–575; and Miall, D. S. (2009). Neuroaesthetics of literary reading. In M. Skov & O. Vartanian (Eds.), *Neuroaesthetics* (pp. 233–248). Amityville, NY: Baywood.

60. Dutton, D. (2008). *The art instinct: beauty, pleasure, and human evolution.* New York: Bloomsbury.

11

Artistic Development

THE THREE ESSENTIAL SPHERES

Kimberly M. Sheridan and Howard Gardner

However seductive and current, evolutionary accounts of aesthetics provide little explanation for the particularities of the histories of any of the art forms. Nor do accounts based on biological predilections explain how individuals grow to understand and enjoy art across cultural context. We argue that meaningful accounts of arts learning and development need to integrate three spheres of psychological explanations of the arts: universal/evolutionary, cultural/contextual, and individual. To illustrate this integration, we discuss two examples: research on the reported U-shaped, rather than linear, pattern in artistic development, and the emergence of new types of artistic activity in the digital participatory cultures. In our view, artistic learning and development emerges as complex and not reducible to acultural, acontextual, non-idiographic accounts.

Introduction

Seeking understanding of how and why we (as *Homo sapiens*) develop the ability to make and appreciate art involves probing into processes long regarded as mysterious, if not intractable, by standard scientific methods of investigation. Whether we look at how the creative and expressive potential of each human infant develops over time into an adult with unique aesthetic perspectives; investigate how certain extraordinary individuals came to make works that continue to evoke powerful responses from audiences hundreds of years after their creation; or study how new styles and forms of art emerge and become appreciated by increasingly large circles, a developmental perspective on aesthetics is likely to expand our current methods of investigation and categories of explanation.

In this chapter, we attempt to be constructive; that is, we do not take a nihilistic, anti-scientific, or postmodern stance. However, we see important limitations in universal or evolutionarily oriented explanations' ability to explain what is most intriguing and most "special" about the artistic sphere. Our aim is more modest: to find some patterns, while recognizing the complexity; documenting meaningful variations on these patterns; and appreciating that any story of development will be continuously changing alongside inherently unpredictable cultural inventions, reactions, and trajectories.

To this end, we see the need for integration of three broad spheres of psychological explanations of the arts. The first sphere involves the universal, bio-psychological capacities and preferences that are generally shared by humans (and perhaps other higher primates) and underlie our varied aesthetic functions. This sphere identifies the broad constraints that guide our initial attention, preferences, and interests and may have some limited influence on the qualities of artistic inventions that tend to emerge and be valued across cultures and historical periods.

The second sphere is concerned with the cultural and technological innovations and qualities that shape and influence the manifestations of the art we make and value. This sphere represents the huge range of variations in the aesthetic realm documented to this point and continuously grows as artistic innovations expand our ways of perceiving the world and ourselves.

The third sphere involves variation at the individual level—how individual differences in temperament, personality, intelligence, perception, personal background, and experiences are reflected in the wide range of variation we see in artistic capacities and tastes.

Each of these spheres is "core" to developing theories of artistic development: how we develop from infants with a fairly general and circumscribed set of constraints on our aesthetic capacities, to diverse participants in the wide and ever-changing world of the arts. To be sure, this enterprise is dauntingly complex—as it should be. In 1967, when Nelson Goodman founded a research institution at Harvard University to look empirically at the nature of artistic thinking, how it develops, and how it might best be nurtured, he named it "Project Zero" to reflect the lack of systematic knowledge—whether scientific or humanistic—on the topic. Over 40 years later, due to work at Project Zero and of course many other sites, our state of knowledge is somewhat greater than zero, but our understanding of the enormity of the task has not diminished.[1]

But the study of artistic thinking, the varied ways it develops, and the factors that support its development, while interesting in what it adds to our knowledge of human psychology, also has a practical angle. As developmental researchers and as citizens, we know that regardless of how little is systematically known about learning and development in the arts, educators need to make decisions amid scarce resources of time and money about how much to educate in the arts, to whom, and in what ways. To be sure, most of these decisions involve questions of values that are unanswerable directly by science, and are guided by knowledge gleaned through the professional experiences of art educators. Nonetheless, as has been occurring in the areas of science and mathematics education, systematic studies of artistic thinking and development can and should contribute to the discussion.

An example. Suppose, as we discuss in greater detail later, researchers found points in development where children's expressive capacities decline, causing many children to "select out" of participation in the arts. Understanding when, on average, those points happen, identifying some of the causes, and describing the conditions where it does not happen may help educators to make decisions on how to educate. Of course, the scientific finding is not prescriptive: if a community decides the aim of aesthetic education is to identify the few most talented and committed arts students, this period of decline might be regarded as a helpful winnowing process allowing resources for art education to be allocated to those students whose interest persists despite the decline or whose decline is more or less precipitous than the norm for the cohort. Conversely, if the main aim is to develop the creative and expressive potential of all students, then additional resources and specifically targeted methods may be deployed at these key moments where development seems most likely to break down.

Education always involves decisions based on values: what is worth learning, in what ways, for whom, for what purposes. Applying scientific insight to education involves a shifting negotiation between what is known about how we learn with what we value to be learned. Thus our perspective needs to be sensitive to particulars of the contemporary context to which insights are applied and decisions are made.

Before proceeding, a word on terminology. First, rather than use the more narrow term of "aesthetics" (which has historical links to philosophy and emphasizes the perception and criticism of works of art), we think of development and education more broadly in terms of "art" and "the arts." This terminological preference fits with studies of the arts at Project Zero—studies that foreground the integrated nature of making, perceiving, and reflecting on art.[2]

While to even start trying to define "art" is beyond our scope here, we take a cue from Nelson Goodman.[3] Rather than trying to define art in terms of necessary and sufficient conditions, we identify a group of "symptoms" that tend to be present in art and think of the developmental picture of learning in the arts as things that work towards that cluster of symptoms. Some key aspects we focus on are that the arts may work in the area of things that are beautiful, interesting, memorable in the form in which they were created, and awe-inspiring.[4] But, for our purposes of talking about artistic development we can also be more pragmatic: art can encompass whatever parents and other adults value and whatever educators decide is important to learn in art classes. In terms of "development," we do not mean a universal, mainly endogenous process. We see artistic development—both the "endstates" identified as valuable and the trajectories by which individuals move towards them—as inextricable from the individual and cultural contexts in which it occurs.

Three Spheres Essential for Psychological Explanations of the Arts

In what follows, we outline three spheres of psychological explanations of the arts: universal/evolutionary, cultural/contextual, and individual differences. We argue that while currently scientific approaches to the arts are biased towards the universal aspects, all three spheres are core to understanding artistic development. We then discuss two research cases on aspects of artistic development to explore further the integration of these spheres: the debate around the U-shaped curve of artistic development; and an investigation of how the emergence of participatory culture/digital media influences how we conceptualize (and educate for) participation in the arts.

UNIVERSAL APPROACHES

The "problem" or "puzzle" of art has become alluring for those who like to think of human psychology in universal, evolutionary terms. It is no mean feat to explain, with the blunt evolutionary tool of natural selection, why something with as seemingly little biological function as art has been a part of the human experience for over 30,000 years, and in the visual realm alone encompasses the cave paintings of Lascaux, Renaissance art, the tadpole figures drawn by 3-year-old children, and the 20 hours of video currently uploaded to YouTube each minute.

Evolutionary Perspectives

Evolutionary approaches to understanding human aesthetics seek to explain why art exists, to characterize in what ways *Homo sapiens* are aesthetic creatures, and to identify the biological underpinnings of our specific aesthetic sensibilities and artistic production. The most direct connection to evolutionary history is through sex selection. Dating back to Darwin's own speculation, some evolutionary theorists of art tie key aspects of art, such as beauty, pleasure, and skill, primarily to the fact that those who demonstrated them would have been more likely to attract mates and propagate their genes.[5] Others include more indirect evolutionary pressures and adaptations. For instance, Dissanayake emphasizes art's connection to social bonds: the need for strong mother–child communication and attunement, social cohesion around shared needs, and the need for individuals to attach themselves to ideals that encourage them to pursue goals outside of their narrow, individual needs.[6] In his analysis of the time, location, and content of the cave paintings of Lascaux, Lewis-Williams focuses on the ritualistic nature of the paintings and argues for their reflection of a newly evolved consciousness among Paleolithic-era hominids. In his view, the paintings served a psychological need for Paleolithic-era hominids to capture and represent the mental imagery of their new consciousness. He also argues for a social purpose to the art: as a way to distinguish themselves from the coexisting Neanderthals who lacked this consciousness.[7] The shared work of all these evolutionary arguments is to identify and explore how different evolutionary pressures and our adaptations to them could have made us an art-making species.

But evolutionary psychologists also try to explain current aesthetic preferences in terms of evolutionary functionality. In particular, the two evolutionary functions of mate selection and habitat preference are considered key sources that reveal universal aesthetic preferences. For instance, the alertness to and preference for symmetry in faces and abstract figures is attributed to the fact that symmetry is a biological marker for health. Thus organisms with a preference for symmetry are more likely to choose reproductively successful mates and thus this preference becomes, over time, a species-wide trait that may have become generalized to aesthetic preferences more broadly beyond mate selection. Other models pose more complex processes working in sex selection; for instance we evolved to make a complex estimation of our own "mate value" and select optimally among mates of similar relative value, in order to ensure likelihood of access. Such estimations require interest in, the ability to discriminate between, and a preference for many visual perceptual cues, which then, it is argued, become incorporated into a set of universal constraints guiding human aesthetics.

Similar factors are argued to be at work in habitat preferences: greater awareness of, and emotional responsiveness to, subtle variations in properties of landscapes would likely provide survival advantages, as they would help our hunter-gatherer ancestors provide fertile and safe places to rest and live. Some studies look specifically at contemporary human preferences in artistic depictions of landscapes. For instance, some have demonstrated that we are consistently drawn to features that are characteristic of savannahs, regardless in what type of environments we grew up.[8] Others focus more on how evolutionary pressures may be reflected in the different moods and aesthetic associations evoked by depictions of landscapes.[9] To the extent that these preferences and associations exist cross-culturally, evolutionary psychologists argue that these can be considered adaptive, species-specific traits connected to a broader aesthetics.[10]

To be sure, most evolutionary psychologists would not claim that the vast array of taste in arts can be predicted fully by the need for our hunter-gatherer ancestors to find fit and fertile mates and homes; nonetheless they argue that these evolutionary adaptations provide the fundamental neurocognitive architecture that supports and constrains this vast range of artistic inventions and tastes.[11] In one sense, this is uncontroversial: our evolved neural architecture must support whatever it is we do with it. The controversy arises in terms of the extent to which one argues these universal traits explain what matters about art.

Experimental Psychology

In addition to explicitly evolutionary perspectives on the arts, experimental psychology also makes claims about universal aspects of aesthetics. The study of aesthetics and art was foundational in the history of experimental psychology; many early prominent scholars, including Gustav Fechner, G. Stanley Hall, and William James, saw it as central to understanding the human mind and behavior. Over time, it has become considerably less central to the field; however, it has occupied a consistent, productive niche.[12]

While most of these studies have been conducted with adults, infants represent the gold standard for such universal perspectives. Notwithstanding that even *in utero* environmental factors are inextricably intertwined with biological ones, the influences of culture are more limited in early infancy than in older children or adults. In recent decades, our view of infants has transformed from relative "blank slates" to organisms having content knowledge in areas such as number and physics, and powerful learning processes, such as those under girding language acquisition, categorization, and probabilistic judgments.[13] And infants also show ability to recognize artistic properties and show preferences for some over others. Through ingenious studies utilizing infants' limited communicative repertoire (i.e., measures such as comparisons of time spent looking, sucking, or shifting heads towards a referent), researchers assess which types of stimuli infants prefer and to which dimensions of these stimuli infants are alert. For instance, studies have found a robust correlation between faces infants prefer to look at and those deemed attractive to adults.[14] Very young infants are also sensitive to aesthetic features in forms beyond faces, such as patterns of symmetry, prototypicality, and coherence in forms, and can correlate patterns in one sensory modality with another.[15] Even the very processes on which many of these infant studies depend—infants' ability to initially recognize and prefer something familiar, become habituated to it, and then show a preference for something moderately novel—give insight into why our aesthetic preferences may shift over time rather than stay fixed.

However, infants pose some obvious limitations. To begin with, young persons haven't developed many of the capacities in which we are interested; second, among the capacities they do possess, it may be difficult to interpret what it is that they know. And, as with the evolutionary approaches, while the findings might be interesting psychologically, we should ask how meaningfully they relate to the broader world of art.

A good deal of the contemporary research of experimental aesthetics is influenced by a bio-psychological, evolutionary approach and seeks to minimize the influence of cultural, contextual, and individual factors. Thus it focuses on establishing principles around formal aesthetic properties, and developing strategies to distinguish between hard-wired predispositions and acquired preferences. There are also studies establishing processes such as optimal novelty for interest; role of protypicality in categorization and preferences; testing out the relative value of different principles through interactions (e.g., if we prefer balanced forms, but also novel forms, at what point do we switch from preferring a balanced, familiar form to an asymmetrical but novel form).[16]

Limitations to Universal Approaches

We see a basic limitation to purely universal approaches. The arts are about particularity, and the particularity of art history is inherently unpredictable in terms of broad universals. For instance, in the latter part of the 19th century, Cezanne and Pissarro were contemporaries who presented competing visions of art. At the time they were working, it was unclear whose vision would be more influential. As it happens, Cezanne prevailed and the history of modern art is as we now know it. But it easily could have been different, and that difference matters. Cezanne could have died early, Seurat's pointillism could have come into the ascendancy, Picasso and Braque might never have met, a French dictator could have ordered that all Impressionist works be burned. At about the same time, in 1889, young French composers Claude Debussy and Maurice Ravel happened to attend the Paris Exposition. For the first time, they heard native folk music from far-away countries, and these aural experiences decisively changed the way that they composed— and their influence on composers as disparate as Igor Stravinsky, Béla Bartók, and George Gershwin. Historical confluences such as the timing of wars, the inventions of new technologies, the sway of one political party over another, the state of the economy, the staging of a world exposition, the particular capacities, interests, and experiences of the artists working at the time, have little to do with our evolved aesthetic universals, yet all importantly—indeed, decisively—influence the particularities of what becomes made and valued as art.

Evolutionary theories of art sometimes avoid these complications of the history of art, by looking at more everyday artistic productions and tastes (as Pinker puts it, "think motel room not Museum of Modern Art,"[17] and Dutton's first chapter of *The Art Instinct* focuses on calendar art).[18] But even with this focus on "schlock" or "kitsch" (to use two highly technical terms), the story is not clear: schlock evolves as well. A pseudo-Impressionistic 1980s motel room painting would not be "schlocky" in the 1880s when the Impressionistic style was a new invention deemed radical and incomprehensible to viewers—and it might still be bothersome in a developing Asian or African context. Given time and familiarity, our cultural imagination accommodates innovations.

These universal, bio-psychological constraints may also be construed as <u>one</u> aspect of the medium in which artists work. Zeki, a neuroscientist specializing in visual perception, poses the view of the artist as a folk neurologist.[19] Artists investigate the qualities and explore and push the limits of our perceptual, cognitive, and affective systems. Just as a sculptor working with clay experiments with and pushes the range of possibilities offered by that medium, all artists work with the medium of the human brain. Our brains may set some general parameters on the type of art made (if we made art for dogs, there would likely be much more extensive artistic investigation of tonal variations in the 20,000- to 60,000-Hz range), but the more interesting bio-psychological story is how artists expand and refine what we perceive, feel, and think. It is difficult for us to imagine that 19th-century audiences of Impressionist paintings often found them not only ugly, but also incomprehensible. Sharing the same perceptual mechanisms, we instantly see and understand these paintings in ways they could not and value them differently (and even if we do not cherish them, we are more likely to view them as banal rather than ugly or confusing; but that is not what might happen in "less developed" regions of Paraguay, Vietnam, Somalia, or, for that matter, Europe or the United States).

From the perspective of education and development, these universal perspectives reiterate the fact that the arts are a universal and important part of the human experience, and may give us insight to what children hold as a sort of "folk aesthetic"—that is, what naïve children are likely to come to think and valorize in the arts due to their universal aesthetic birthright, which then is strengthened by that in culture designed to fit comfortably within this aesthetic, before nonconforming experiences and education in the arts challenge the intuitive conceptions and transform their understanding. (We limit our characterization to "naïve" children, because those raised in the homes of collectors of contemporary art are likely to exhibit quite different preferences.) Developmental psychology has frequently found that these intuitive folk conceptions are at odds with what we consider a mature understanding of a discipline or a domain.[20] For instance, we have a folk conception of physics that is built upon some evolved universals about how objects move. This folk conception works well enough for most of our everyday needs but stands in the way of more formal physics learning.[21] Therefore, when we think of the initial evolved aesthetics, it is merely a starting point that needs to be built up (and/or broken down).

CULTURAL/CONTEXTUAL SPHERE

Our second sphere operates in the world of cultural diversity and innovations. To be sure, as just reviewed, there may be some basic universals that set some constraints on what we initially find beautiful or ugly, interesting or not, and we have some ability to appreciate artworks from cultures and historical contexts other than our own (though never from a perspective unencumbered by our own socio-cultural-historical context). But we maintain that the variations and nuances of our socio-cultural-historical world and our responses to it could never be predicted by these universals. Each cultural innovation—social, technological, artistic—has the potential to bring to the fore new human capacities as central to the arts—and push others to the background. As we discuss later, with the participatory culture afforded by the Internet, children are creating and responding to art in a large public forum. This powerful trend brings to the fore a range of capacities around social cognition that were previously less emphasized in theories of children's artistic development.

Much of our knowledge and understanding of the cultural sphere comes from the humanistic scholarship: art history, cultural studies, and art criticism. Scholars in these fields document the nuances of the arts, interpret and evaluate works, and help us locate and understand them in cultural contexts. They help us to understand from whence Greek, Egyptian, Roman, medieval, and modern Western art emanated, how they evolved, and what happens, or does not happen, when these different cultural traditions abut one another. From a scientific perspective, however, these accounts are limited. Psychological explanations of the arts are needed to study how these patterns of culture may influence artistic thinking and development.

Psychological explanations can be built closely in response to claims of universal aesthetics, examining culture as a modulating influence on an evolved preference. For instance, given the theories on evolutionary origins of aesthetics as related to sex selection/mate value theory, male views of attractiveness in female body shape would be a likely candidate for having a strong universal basis. And numerous studies have found not only strong consistencies in the ideal waist to hip ratio (WHR) across the cultures and time periods measured, but also physiological reasons for believing that this preference has adaptive value (e.g., a lower WHR in women is associated with higher fertility and less chronic disease).[22] Male preferences for overall levels of body fat in women, however, shows greater variation between cultures, and a strong cultural preference for a certain body mass index (BMI) may supersede the WHR preference.[23] Thus even the strongest claims for aesthetic universals show evidence of being modulated by culture in some respects.

These instances where culture is shown to modulate of universal claims of aesthetic preferences are psychologically interesting. They help us understand the ways different influences and pressures interact to form certain aesthetic preferences. Still, their meaningful contribution to an understanding of art is fairly limited compared to the vast cultural differences in artistic traditions needing explanation.

From a developmental perspective, in this sphere, we consider how children learn to use and think with the artistic tools and conventions provided by their culture, and to embrace the aesthetic preferences and learn and value the artistic traditions of their particular culture. Sometimes these studies look explicitly at processes of enculturation. For instance, Rogoff and colleagues have examined differing roles of implicit observational learning and explicit teaching cross-culturally.[24] In a series of studies of traditional weaving cultures, Greenfield looked at factors such as the effects of schooling, exposure to novel patterns, and generational change to show how they related to the types of weaving patterns created and valued.[25]

Accounts of children's artistic development are also shaped by cultural differences in what adults view as a reasonable developmental endstate to measure in the arts. For instance, as we detail later, researchers find cross-cultural differences in the valuing of the expressiveness of young children's drawings versus those done by older youths, depending on the types of artworks the adults in that culture have tended to revere over time.[26] Also, researchers may examine how ill-defined concepts such as "artistic creativity" are used differently by different cultures, subcultures, artistic traditions, and disciplines, and how these differences affect artistic development. As an example, researchers have identified two types of creativity valued by different cultures or subcultures—horizontal, which values novelty and innovation within a domain, and vertical, which values more subtle variations within a constrained tradition. These differences result in different types of products created and valued, different types of education in the arts, and thus different trajectories in artistic development.[27] As we discuss later, this sphere also encompasses and probes how new technologies, such as the Internet and digital media, transform thinking and understanding and create new forms of cultural participation.[28] The aim of psychological work in this cultural sphere is to understand the processes by which these shared universals can transmogrify into the wide range of artistic activity seen thus far around the world.

SPHERE OF INDIVIDUAL DIFFERENCES

Even given similar cultural and educational backgrounds, there is much variety among individuals in both artistic production and taste. Psychological accounts of artistic development are not likely to make detailed predictions on the individual level, but importantly they identify patterns of differences among individuals that elude a model that encompasses just universal and cultural factors.

One clear area of difference is that a few people make extraordinary contributions to the arts. By studying these exceptional cases, we can gain insight into their traits and development. For instance, using comparative historical case studies, Gardner looked at eminent creators in domains including but not restricted to the arts, and found some common aspects in their histories and personalities as well as revealing differences.[29] Simonton explores larger samples more quantitatively, looking for historical patterns associated with people or works that have demonstrated genius, expertise, and creativity.[30] Scholars with humanistic and scientific grounding have provided fruitful insights into the creative process by focusing on Picasso's process of creation of a single important artwork—*Guernica*.[31] Through these diverse means, psychological study of clear examples of artistic achievements gives a unique vantage point into why and how we create art.

But even within the range of normal development, there are relevant individual differences as well. We come into the world with differences in terms of perceptual acuity, sensitivity to different types of stimuli, temperaments, and other aspects of cognitive, social, and affective processing. It appears that individuals are more "at promise" in the creative sphere if they exhibit the personality configuration termed neuroticism[32] or if they have a predisposition toward mania, or bipolar symptoms.[33]

Our lives are also made up of different experiences. One key experience researchers look at is the effect of explicit art education. In her investigation of the U-shaped curve as it resolves in pre-adolescence, Davis found different trajectories of expressive development for those who continued on in the arts versus those who did not.[34] Parsons poses a developmental sequence of modes of appreciating artwork, based on his analysis of how individuals ranging from preschoolers to art professors respond to representational paintings. He describes qualitatively different ways of interpreting and responding to art, with viewers at a relatively low level of development making simple, reflexive, and subjective responses of pleasure and associations, while more advanced viewers made intersubjectively based judgments that involve more in-depth inquiry and take into account perspectives outside their own immediate subjective response. Explicit education in the arts was more likely to encourage more advanced appreciation.[35] In her analysis of film fans, Sheridan takes a different stance on these subjective and intersubjective dimensions, construing them as modes of interpretation that viewers hold based on the types of understandings they seek from films rather than evidence of higher and lower development. Broadly speaking, film fans' tastes in film fall into two categories. Some individuals were oriented to subjective validity, justifying their tastes in terms of their subjective responses and connections to their own lives. Others were more oriented to intersubjective validity, justifying their tastes by making a case why they should be valued by others and drawing connections with the outside world. These differences were shown in the way the fans explained their tastes, interpreted films, and read criticism, and by their accounts of their history with films, but there was a wide variety of complexity of responses within each orientation.[36]

Regardless of the controversies involved in the details of developmental accounts, among any group of people we see vast differences in terms of mode and extent of involvement in the arts. Understanding how we move from members of a species with a basic capacity to make and appreciate art to this diversity of outcomes requires systematic investigation of individual differences.

Integrating these Spheres in Theories of Artistic Learning and Development

To understand how we ultimately exhibit varied ways of participating in the arts, we need to identify and then integrate insights from the universal, cultural, and individual spheres. As infants, we may begin with an evolved, common set of perceptual, emotional, and cognitive constraints that provide the basic capacities for making and appreciating art and may give an initial push to what we attend to and prefer. But the endstates of learning and development that are valued (e.g., an appreciation of an art form, eminence as an artist, creative expressiveness), and the processes by which individuals move towards these endstates, are profoundly shaped by culture and environment: general cultural contexts, specific contexts within specific subcultures, and individual experiences in the arts. A psychology of arts learning and development needs to explore processes of enculturation and cultural change, to examine how the effects of individual experiences and biopsychological profiles work in concert to produce learning that extends beyond simple expression of universal traits.

As developmental psychologists, we are interested in documenting the trajectories and the factors that influence them, as people learn and grow in the arts (or, less happily, fail to do so). Thus we need to traverse readily among the universal, cultural, and individual spheres as we form descriptions and explanations. To make this enterprise less abstract, in what follows we discuss this integration in two research examples: the U-shaped curve in artistic development, and arts learning in the participatory culture afforded by digital media and the Internet.

EXAMPLE 1: THE U-SHAPED CURVE IN ARTISTIC DEVELOPMENT

Child development is often conceptualized in terms of growth: as children grow older, they grow taller, acquire a larger vocabulary, are able to hold more items in short-term memory, and perform more sophisticated logical operations. Debates may ensue on whether to characterize this growth as steady and incremental or as qualitative shifts, but the underlying assumption of growth is rarely challenged.

In the arts, however, this expectation of growth is, in some important ways, upended. There has long been a conception that young children possess something we value in the arts that typically gets lost as they get older. This conception may have its roots in a general Rousseauian romanticization of the child, but it became more a central and explicit view in Modernist art, where the art of young children was valued and studied by prominent Western Modern artists, including Dubuffet, Klee, Picasso, and Miro.[37] Well-known quotes, such as Picasso's "Once I drew like Raphael, but it has taken me a whole lifetime to learn to draw like children,"[38] influence our cultural conception of child art.

In a series of studies, researchers at Harvard's Project Zero began investigating developmental processes in the symbolic capacities. Prior to age 5 children show steady growth in their mastering the basics of representational drawing, oral language, and musical composition. However, while some artistic capacities continued to grow as children got older, there were persistent findings of a decline in expressivity across different art activities. Children seemed to have a flowering of expressivity at around age 5: their drawings have an expressive immediacy, metaphors give their speech a poetic flair, they readily invent songs, and they envision rich stories through pretend play. Based on these findings, Gardner (1980) and Gardner and Winner (1982) proposed the construct of a U-shaped model of aesthetic development to describe the trajectory in artistry between age 5 and adulthood. According to this analysis, young children show an expressive fluency in their artistic productions in variety of domains—language, visual arts, music— that is gradually lost to a more literal approach to the arts over the school-aged years, which then, for some of those who continue to work in the arts, is gradually regained over time.[39]

Davis formally tested the U-shaped hypothesis in the visual arts, comparing the artworks of children ages 5, 8, and 11; 14-year-olds with and without art training; and adult artists and non-artists. She found support for the claim of a gradual decline in expressive development. This decline either persisted—adults with limited arts background having expressive skills at the 11-year-old plateau—or gradually rose with further education in the arts, where adult artists return to their early childhood expressive peak.[40] The finding invites questions, such as what is causing the decline. For instance, while this decline is seen in expressive production, in interpreting the expressiveness of artworks researchers find a more steady growth, and there is also a growth in the ability to critique one's own work—a growth that, lamentably, leads some older children to "opt out" of further arts participation.[41]

The proposal with respect to a U-shaped curve sparked debate. The most common critique is that the U-shape was more indicative of Modernist tastes of the researchers than of any "natural" developmental process.[42] Pariser and van de Berg investigated the U-shaped phenomenon cross-culturally, comparing the responses of Chinese judges and North American judges on the same artworks from different-aged children and adults. They found that while the North American judges replicated the U-shaped curve findings, Chinese judges were more apt to find a steady improvement with age.[43] Kindler and associates found an even greater range of patterns when using judges from three different countries, although again the U-shaped curve was a consistent pattern for a subset of the judges, even from other countries.[44] Other researchers focused less on the role of judges in evaluating the work. Instead they singled out the role of particular types of education both in encouraging the particular expressive style of young children at the preschool age and moving towards more literal, less formally expressive artworks during elementary school.[45]

From a purely Universalist stance, the "U-shaped curve" could be considered somewhat of an anomaly in a science of artistic development; after all, it does not hold cross-culturally and seems more tied to a particular culturally defined end-state of Modernistic expressive style rather than some universal, all-encompassing expressive capacity. Moreover, the whole process could be considered tainted because Modernist artists explicitly studied children's art.[46]

However, from the integrative perspective put forth in this paper, the theory of a U-shaped curve is an appropriately qualified account of development in the complex, historically situated, and evolving world of the arts. A valuing for the expressive properties of child art may be particularly highlighted in Modernist art and, in this sense, Modernist art widened our thinking on child development. Modernists created a new "endstate" for artistic development and education, one that involves integrating a more childlike and spontaneous expressivity and creativity into one's more intentional skilled adult work. According to this perspective, researchers have identified potential cultural influences and outlined some contexts under which these influences apply. The result is a mature understanding of both art and development, yielding a more meaningful contribution to education.

EXAMPLE 2: ARTISTIC DEVELOPMENT IN DIGITALLY MEDIATED "PARTICIPATORY CULTURES"

Over the past decade, the Internet, along with other advances in digital media tools and outlets, has dramatically reorganized our conceptions of cultural participation in many arenas, including the arts. In what Jenkins terms "digital participatory cultures,"[47] people are, in vast and growing numbers, creating, sharing, interpreting, and critiquing cultural content in a public, digital domain. This changing context is marked by a number of features important to our conceptions of artistic development and education. The role of gatekeepers in providing artists with access to audiences has greatly diminished. There are few barriers to entering the public sphere: anyone who wants to can publish (post) work in a wide range of online formats. And a great many persons are doing just that: in 2004, the Internet and American Life project found that 57% of surveyed teens (12 to 17 years old) had engaged in online content creation, and by 2006, 64% had. In 2004, one third of teens shared their artwork online; by 2006, 39% had.[48] Likewise, there are many forums for reading and writing criticism and interpretations of any art form of interest. In the domain of film alone, a plethora of review and criticism siteshost discussions on film, with tens of thousands of messages posted daily. People publish film journals documenting their interpretations and responses to everything they watch; they devise games to re-award the Oscars throughout history.[49] Boundaries separating cultures and age groups are blurred. The ease of creating, copying, and altering existing works encourages collaboration; creates many new sub-genres and styles; and raises issues around copyright, plagiarism, censorship, self-presentation, and appropriation. Social networks like Facebook and brief message transmitters like Twitter multiply the venues for distributing works, experiences, and discussions thereof.

The artistic capacities that we see expressed in all these digital participatory cultures are built upon the same basic motivations and capacities around social cognition, emotional sensitivity to imagery, imagination, and pleasure deemed part of our evolutionary heritage in the arts. However, these particular forms of expression were inconceivable 50 years ago, let alone 50,000. Our understanding of child development need to be revisited for the new roles (and anticipated future roles) children are assuming in this new context. The activities and concerns of the average child and adolescent, in terms of image creation, consumption, and criticism, are vastly different than they were even a generation ago.

An example. Kim Sheridan's 8-year-old son Anton has put his drawings, photographs, videos, poetry, and stories in a variety of public forums and has received feedback on them. He regularly is inspired by a site of posted Lego creations and designs made by other children (and adults) around the world and aspires to create and sell his own designs through the public sites. Co-creating animated movies with his friends is a common after-school activity. When Sheridan was 8, the school wall was the extent of her artistic exposure, and she only created art on her own. The artistic development, respectively, of Kim Sheridan and her son Anton will likely involve a different understanding of the function of an audience and a much more collaborative creative process than was the case in previous generations. These are not just differences of expanded opportunities; they represent qualitative shifts in the nature of participation in the arts.[50]

Educators struggle with how to conceptualize the skills needed for, and afforded by, these new forms of cultural participation, identify which connect with educational aims, and figure out new methods of instruction incorporating them.[51] Developmental psychologists studying these new forms of cultural participation are interested in understanding what it takes to learn to become an effective participant, and how new modes of communication and interaction may be transforming children's minds, development, and relationships. A theory of artistic development mindful of this participatory culture needs to foreground new skills; the culture creates a new developmental trajectory to be studied.

While understanding the interpretive process between artist and audience has always been a part of the arts, interpretation assumes a new form in digital participatory cultures. Children learn to interact with a large and diverse digitally mediated audience. They have more opportunities to become aware of how others interpret and perceive their work, learn to moderate their presentation in response to audience feedback, and evaluate different interpretations and critiques. They have the potential to engage in collaborations involving many individuals, including those whom they have never met face to face. They learn to put out fires if they happen to offend, and to better explain themselves if they happen to confuse.[52]

To make sense of artistic learning and development in this new media and cultural context, after identifying key qualities of these digital participatory cultures, we might consider the ways our evolved neurocognitive architecture is likely to align (or misalign) with the demands of this new context. Of course, humans are evolved to be highly social. Tomasello terms humans as "ultrasocial": not only do we exhibit social dynamics, but our sociality is also embedded in cultural objects and cultural learning. We imbue objects with thoughts, intensions, and meanings.[53] Art created and shared through digital participatory cultures reflects our drive to be social and a capacity for creating cultural objects. But in many ways there is a disjunct: we likely evolved to participate in smaller, more homogenous groups than we regularly encounter on the Internet.[54] We are suited for face-to-face interaction, with much of our thoughts and emotions communicated nonverbally; our evolutionary history gives us little insight into how we learn to do something as complex and nuanced as artistic collaboration in digitally mediated form, involving individuals who might be located at remote sites or who even put forth false and rapidly shifting identities. Moreover, the cultural objects created in the digital form are easily alterable, and lack physicality; as individuals who have evolved to deal with material objects obeying the laws of physics, how do we deal with a world that is increasingly virtual?

To be sure, thinking about universals and initial developmental trajectories that stem from them may yield insights. But our understanding will be limited to broad generalizations about capacities, without observing directly what is happening in the contexts and systematically analyzing patterns of participation in different subgroups and among different individuals. We can also gain insight by studying those particular individuals who are particularly attuned to and successful at exploiting the creative potential of this new context.

Just as Modern art highlighted a new endstate of expressiveness and altered our view of child art, these digital participatory cultures may challenge our view of artistic development in terms of individuals and direct our attention to collaborative processes. Digital artworks are easily shared and manipulated, and digital participatory culture encourages many new forms of collaborative art. We know little about the types of thinking involved in adding on, altering, adapting, and reappropriating others' artworks, as well as the larger-scale collaborative art projects, yet this is a major mode of artistic participation in this new culture.[55] Systematically examining questions like these will increase our understanding of human learning and development in ways that were not envisioned or highlighted before the Internet and its associated digital participatory cultures.

Conclusion

These two cases illustrate how artistic innovations and contexts reshape how we construe human development. The innovations of Modern art and Abstract Expressionism allow us to see more clearly the expressive capacities in the artworks of 4- and 5-year-olds and to posit and explore a U-shaped developmental trajectory. The technological innovations of digital media and the Internet reorganize our patterns of cultural and artistic participation and expand our thinking with respect to social cognition, collaboration, and the arts. To be sure, any artistic capacity that we come to express can be traced back to the evolved universals that undergird these capacities, and a reasonable *a posteriori* story can be fashioned to explain why we were evolved to work in this way. But this is of deceptive utility: predicting is impossible.

The scholarly tension lies in the extent to which one considers the diversity and innovations in the arts, the particulars of our cultural achievements, as *the* interesting story, or just another expression of this common set of aesthetic universals—the noise of extraneous factors such as social status and historical accident surrounding the clear signal of our evolutionary history.

In our view, each artistic innovation and achievement has the potential to expand our understanding of ourselves and the world. Artists explore and exploit the potential of their media—whether physical/digital material, concepts, or the minds of their audience. And as the arts expand our understanding, our theories of cognition and development need to keep pace. And while some of those artistic expansions are difficult to accommodate in our hunter-gatherer brains, and may make us want to run for the nearest savannah landscape painting, history repeatedly shows us that innovations can and do become a part of the general culture. Arts that were once difficult to comprehend or like become easier to understand

and enjoy. This accommodation can also be shown in our individual histories as well. While our tastes may change for a wide variety of reasons, some change is a result of greater understanding. As we become more experienced and knowledgeable in a particular artistic domain, we learn to make more fine-grained discriminations, learn to understand the languages and conventions of the art form, and can learn to understand and enjoy works that were initially unappealing.[56]

Even if it holds true that cross-culturally people are drawn to "savannah-like" landscapes (or any other particular finding of an aesthetic universal), and even if we accept that this preference is due to evolutionary pressures around habitat selection, this finding—and other findings about aesthetic universals—would do little to predict how particular artistic innovations will transform the cultural imagination and will lead to other particular artistic innovations, trickle down to even our more kitschy displays, and enable us to see the world in new ways. While each child may be granted the species birthright of an interest in and capacity for the arts, along with some initial more specific species-wide initial aesthetic interest and preferences, the story of the artistic development of all children is more importantly and more decisively shaped by their moment in history, their place in culture, and their individual bio-psychological profile, background, and experiences. Systematic psychological research of non-universals empowers one to make generalizations about the beautiful, important, and meaningful variations in the arts, and, accordingly, yields insight into how to educate. A psychology of the arts should not restrict itself to studying bio-psychological universals and then just offer an opinion-based argument about the extent to which culture and individual variation may matter. Systematic analyses of the rich interaction of the spheres, while messy and ever-changing, yield richer insights into how we all learn in the arts and how we might help others to learn more comprehensively in the future.

Endnotes

1. On Project Zero, see Gardner, H., & Perkins, D. (1989), *Monograph on Harvard Project Zero.* Urbana: University of Illinois Press, 1989; Perkins, D., & Leondar, B. (Eds.) (1977). *Arts and cognition.* Baltimore: Johns Hopkins University Press; and http://pzweb.harvard.edu.

2. Gardner, H. (1989). Zero-based art education: an introduction to Arts PROPEL. *Studies in Art Education, 30*(2), 71–83; Hetland, L., Winner, E., Veenema, S., & Sheridan, K. M. (2007). *Studio thinking: the real benefits of visual arts education* (pp. 15–20). New York: Teachers College Press.

3. Goodman, N. (1968). *Languages of art: an approach to a theory of symbols* (pp. 252–254). Indianapolis: Bobbs-Merrill.

4. Gardner, H. (2011). Truth, beauty, and goodness reframed: Educating for the virtues in the 21st century. New York: Basic Books.

5. Dutton, D. (2009). *The art instinct: beauty, pleasure and human evolution.* New York: Bloomsbury Press; and Miller, G. (2000). *The mating mind: how sexual choice shaped the evolution of human nature.* New York: Doubleday.

6. Dissanayake, E. (1988). *What is art for?* Seattle: University of Washington Press; Dissanayake, E. (1992). *Homo aestheticus: where art comes from and why.* New York: Free Press; and Dissanayake, E. (2000). *Art and intimacy: how the arts began.* Seattle: University of Washington Press.

7. Lewis-Williams, D. J. (2002). *The mind in the cave: consciousness and the origins of art.* London: Thames & Hudson.

8. Orians, G. H. (2007). Human behavioral ecology: 140 years without Darwin is too long. In J. H. Barkow, L. Cosmides, & J. Tooby (Eds.), *Evolutionary perspectives on environmental problems* (pp. 259–279). New Brunswick, NJ: Transaction Publishers; Orians, G. H., & Heerwagen, J. H. (1992). Evolved responses to landscapes. In J. H. Barkow, L. Cosmides, & J. Tooby (Eds.), *The adapted mind: evolutionary psychology and the generation of culture* (pp. 555–579). New York: Oxford University Press.

9. Appleton, J. (1988). Prospects and refuges revisited. In J. L. Nasar (Ed.), *Environmental aesthetics: theory, research, and applications* (pp. 27–44). New York: Cambridge University Press; Mealey, L., & Theis, P. (1995). The relationship between mood and preferences among natural landscapes: an evolutionary perspective, *Ethology and Sociobiology, 16*(3), 247–256.

10. For example, Dutton, D. (2009). *The art instinct: beauty, pleasure and human evolution.* New York: Bloomsbury Press; and Orians, G. H. (2007). Human behavioral ecology: 140 years without Darwin is too long. In J. H. Barkow, L. Cosmides, & J. Tooby (Eds.), *Evolutionary perspectives on environmental problems* (pp. 259–279). New Brunswick, NJ: Transaction Publishers.

11. Barkow, J. H., Cosmides, L., & Tooby, J. (Eds.) (1992). *The adapted mind: evolutionary psychology and the generation of culture* (pp. 19–136). New York: Oxford University Press.

12. Martindale, C. (2007). The foundation and the future of the society for the psychology of aesthetics, creativity and the arts. *Psychology of Aesthetics, Creativity and the Arts, 1* (3), 121–132.

13. Gopnik, A., Meltzoff, A. N., & Kuhl, P. K. (1999). *The scientist in the crib: minds, brains, and how children learn.* New York: William Morrow & Co.

14. For example, Rhodes, G., Geddes, K., Jeffery, L., Dziurawiec, S., & Clark, A. (2002). Are average and symmetric faces attractive to infants? Discrimination and looking patterns. *Perception, 31*(3), 315–321; Samuels, C. A., Butterworth, G., Roberts, T., & Graupner, L. (1994). Facial aesthetics: babies prefer attractiveness to symmetry. *Perception, 23*(7), 823–831; and Samuels, C. A., & Ewy, R. (1985). Aesthetic perception of faces during infancy, *British Journal of Developmental Psychology, 3*(3), 221–228.

15. For example, Bornstein, M. H., Ferdinandsen, K., & Gross, C. G. (1981). Perception of symmetry in infancy, *Developmental Psychology, 17*(1), 82–86; Bornstein, M. H., & Krinsky, S. J. (1985). Perception of symmetry in infancy: the salience of vertical symmetry and the perception of pattern wholes, *Journal of Experimental Child Psychology, 39*(1), 1–19; Spears, W. C. (1984). Assessment of visual preference and discrimination in the four-month-old infant, *Journal of Comparative and Physicological Psychology, 57*(3), 381–386; see Gopnik, A., Meltzoff, A. N., & Kuhl, P. K. (1999). *The scientist in the crib: minds, brains, and how children learn.* New York: William Morrow & Co., for a review.

16. Martindale, C. (2007). Recent trends in the psychological study of aesthetics, creativity and the arts. *Empirical Studies of the Arts, 25*(2), 121–141; and Winner, E. (1982). *Invented worlds: a psychology of the arts.* Cambridge: Harvard University Press.

17. Pinker, S. (1997). *How the mind works* (p. 526). New York: Norton.

18. Dutton, D. (2009). *The art instinct: beauty, pleasure and human evolution* (pp. 13–28). New York: Bloomsbury Press.

19. Zeki, S. (1999). *Inner vision: an exploration of art and the brain* (p. 10). Oxford: Oxford University Press.

20. Bruer, J. T. (1993). *Schools for thought: a science for learning in the classroom.* Cambridge, MA: MIT Press; and Gardner, H. (1991). *The unschooled mind: how children think and how schools should teach.* New York: Basic Books.

21. Schneps, M. H., & Sadler, P. M. (1985). *A private universe* [teacher workshop guide and video series]. Cambridge, MA: Harvard-Smithsonian Center for Astrophysics.

22. Lassek, W. D., & Gaulin, S. J. C. (2008). Waist-hip ratio and cognitive ability: is gluteofemoral fat a privileged store of neurodevelopmental resources? *Evolution and Human Behavior, 29*(1), 26–34; and Singh, D., & Luis, S. (1995). Ethnic and gender consensus for the effect of WHR on judgment of women's attractiveness. *Human Nature, 6*(1), 51–65.

23. Furnham, A., Moutafi, J., & Baguma, P. (2002). A cross-cultural study on the role of weight and waist-to-hip ratio on female attractiveness, *Personality and Individual Differences, 32* (4), 729–745; and Tovee, M. J., Maisey, D. S., Emery, J. L., & Cornelissen, P. L. (1999). Visual cues to female physical attractiveness. *Proceedings of the Royal Society of London, B, 226,* 2111–2118.

24. Rogoff, B. (1990). *Apprenticeship in thinking: cognitive development in social context.* New York: Oxford University Press; and Rogoff, B., Mistry, J., Goncu, A., & Mosier, C. (1993). *Guided participation in cultural activity by toddlers and caregivers.* Chicago: University of Chicago Press.

25 Greenfield, P. M. (2004). *Weaving generations together: evolving creativity in the Maya of Chiapas.* Santa Fe, NM: School of American Research Press.

26. Pariser, D. A., Kindler, A. M., & van den Berg, A. (2008). Drawing and aesthetic judgments across cultures: diverse pathways to graphic development. In C. Milbrath & H. M. Trautner (Eds.), *Children's understanding and production of pictures, drawings and art: theoretical and empirical approaches* (pp. 293–317). Ashland, OH: Hogrefe & Huber Publishers.

27. Keinänen, M., & Gardner, H. (2004). Vertical and horizontal mentoring for creativity. In R. J. Sternberg, E. L. Grigorenko, & J. L. Singer (Eds.), *Creativity: from potential to realization* (pp. 169–193). Washington, D.C.: American Psychological Association; Keinänen, M., Sheridan, K., & Gardner, H. (2006). Opening up creativity: the lenses of axis and focus. In J. C. Kaufman & J. Baer (Eds.), *Creativity and reason in cognitive development* (pp. 202–220). New York: Cambridge University Press; and Li, J. (1997). Creativity in horizontal and vertical domains. *Creativity Research Journal, 10,* 103–132.

28. For example, Jenkins, H. (Jan. 26, 2007). *Confronting the challenges of participatory culture: media education for the 21st century.* Occasional Paper for the MacArthur Foundation. [Online] Available: http://digitallearning.macfound.org/site/c.enJLKQNIFiG/b.2029291/k.97E5/Occasional_Papers.html. [accessed Feb. 10, 2010].

29. Gardner, H. (1993). *Creating minds: an anatomy of creativity as seen through the lives of Freud, Einstein, Picasso, Stravinsky, Eliot, Graham and Gandhi.* New York: Basic Books; and Gardner, H. (1997). *Extraordinary minds.* New York: Basic Books.

30. Simonton, D. K. (2000). Creative development as acquired expertise: theoretical issues and an empirical test. *Developmental Review, 20*(2), 283–318; Simonton, D. K. (2006). Creative genius, knowledge, and reason: the lives and works of eminent creators. In J. C. Kaufman & J. Baer (Eds.), *Creativity and reason in cognitive development* (pp. 43–59).

New York: Cambridge University Press; Simonton, D. K. (2008). Childhood giftedness and adulthood genius: a historiometric analysis of 291 eminent African-Americans. *Gifted Child Quarterly, 52*(3), 243–255; and Simonton, D. K., & Song, A. (2009). Eminence, IQ, physical and mental health, and achievement domain: Cox's 282 geniuses revisited. *Psychological Science, 20*(4), 429–434.

    31. Arnheim, R. (1962). *Picasso's Guernica.* Berkeley: University of California Press; Simonton, D. K. (2007). The creative process in Picasso's *Guernica* sketches: monotonic improvements versus nonmonotonic variants. *Creativity Research Journal, 19*(4), 329–344; Weisberg, R. W. (2008). On structure in the creative process: a quantitative case-study of the creation of Picasso's *Guernica. Empirical Studies of the Arts, 22*(1), 23–54.

    32. Eysenck, H. J. (1995). *Genius: the natural history of creativity.* Cambridge: Cambridge University Press.

    33. Jamison, K. R. (1993). *Touched with fire: manic-depressive illness and the artistic temperament.* New York: Free Press.

    34. Davis, J. (1997). Drawing's demise: U-shaped development in graphic symbolization. *Studies in Art Education, 38*(3), 132–157.

    35. Parsons, M. (1987). *How we understand art.* New York: Cambridge University Press.

    36. Sheridan, K. M. (2006). *Taste in film: subjective and intersubjective validity.* Doctoral dissertation, Harvard University; and Sheridan, K. M. (2008). Reading, writing and watching: the informal education of film fans. In J. Flood, D. Lapp, & S. B. Heath (Eds.), *Handbook on teaching literacy through the communicative, visual and performing arts* (2nd ed. pp. 259–270). Mahwah, NJ: Lawrence Erlbaum.

    37. Fineberg, J. (1997). *The innocent eye: children's art and the modern artist.* Princeton, NJ: Princeton University Press; and Gardner, H. (1980). *Artful scribbles: the significance of children's drawings.* New York: Basic Books.

    38. Quoted in de Meredieu, F. (1974). *Le dessin d'enfant* (p. 13). Paris: Editions Universitaires Jean-Pierre de Large.

    39. Gardner, H. (1980). *Artful scribbles: the significance of children's drawings.* New York: Basic Books; Gardner, H., & Winner, E. (1982). First intimations of artistry. In S. Strauss (Ed.), *U-shaped behavioral growth* (pp. 147–168). New York: Academic Press.

    40. Davis, J. (1997). Drawing's demise: U-shaped development in graphic symbolization. *Studies in Art Education, 38*(3), 132–157.

    41. Soep, E. (2006). Critique: assessment and the production of learning. *Teachers College Record, 108*(4), 748–777.

    42. Duncum, P. (1986). Breaking down the U-curve of artistic development. *Visual Arts Research, 12*(1), 43–54; Korzenik, D. (1995). The changing concept of artistic giftedness. In C. Golomb (Ed.), *The development of artistically gifted children: selected case studies* (pp. 1–30). Hillsdale, NJ: Lawrence Erlbaum Associates; Wilson, G., & Wilson, M. (1981). Review of *Artful Scribbles: The Significance of Children's Drawings* by H. Gardner. *Studies in Visual Communications, 7*(1), 86–89; and Wilson, B. (1997). Child art, multiple interpretations, and conflicts of interest. In A. M. Kindler (Ed.), *Child development in art* (pp. 81–94). Reston, VA: National Art Education Association.

    43. Pariser, D., & van den Berg, A. (1997). The mind of the beholder: some provisional doubts about the U-curved aesthetic development thesis. *Studies in Art Education, 38*(3), 158–178.

    44. Pariser, D. A., Kindler, A. M., & van den Berg, A. (2008). Drawing and aesthetic judgments across cultures: diverse pathways to graphic development. In C. Milbraith & H. M. Trautner (Eds.), *Children's understanding and production of pictures, drawings and*

art: theoretical and empirical approaches (pp. 293–317). Ashland, OH: Hogrefe & Huber Publishers.

45. Rostan, S. M. (1997). A study of young artists: the development of talent and creativity. *Creativity Research Journal, 10,* 175–192.

46. Fineberg, J. (1997). *The innocent eye: children's art and the modern artist.* Princeton, NJ: Princeton University Press.

47. Jenkins, H. (Jan. 26, 2007). *Confronting the challenges of participatory culture: media education for the 21st century.* Occasional Paper for the MacArthur Foundation. [Online] Available: http://digitallearning.macfound.org/site/c.enJLKQNIFiG/b.2029291/k.97E5/ Occasional_Papers.html. [accessed Feb. 10, 2010].

48. Lenhart, A., & Madden, M. (Nov. 2, 2005). *Teen content creators and consumers, Pew Internet and American Life Project* [Online]. Available: http://www.pewinternet.org/ Reports/2005/Teen-Content-Creators-and-Consumers.aspx. [accessed Aug. 9, 2010]; Lenhart, A., Madden, M., Smith, A., & Macgill, A. (December 2007). *Teens and social media, Pew Internet and American Life Project* [Online]. Available: http://www.pewinternet.org/ Reports/2007/Teens-and-Social-Media.aspx. [accessed Aug. 9, 2010].

49. Sheridan, K. M. (2008). Reading, writing and watching: the informal education of film fans. In J. Flood, D. Lapp, & S. B. Heath (Eds.), *Handbook on teaching literacy through the communicative, visual and performing arts* (2nd ed. pp. 259–270). Mahwah, NJ: Lawrence Erlbaum.

50. Gardner, H. (in press). *The true, the beautiful, and the good*; and Weigel, M., Davis, K., James, C., & Gardner, H. (October 2009). *New digital media: social institutions and the changing roles of youth, GoodWork Paper 61* [Online]: http://www.goodworkproject.org/ publications/papers.htm. [accessed August 9, 2010].

51. Weigel, M., Davis, K., James, C., & Gardner, H. (October 2009). *New digital media: social institutions and the changing roles of youth, GoodWork Paper 61* [Online]: http://www. goodworkproject.org/publications/papers.htm. [accessed August 9, 2010].

52. James, C. (2009). *Young people, ethics and the new digital media: a synthesis from the GoodPlay Project,* John D. and Catherine T. MacArthur Foundation Reports on Digital Media and Learning Series. Cambridge: MIT Press.

53. Herrmann, E., Call, J., Hernàndez-Lloreda, M. V., Hare, B., & Tomasello, M. (2007). Humans have evolved specialized skills of social cognition: the cultural intelligence hypothesis. *Science, 317*(5843), 1360–1366; Tomasello, M. (1999). *The cultural origins of human cognition.* Cambridge: Harvard University Press; Tomasello, M. (2009). Cultural transmission: a view from chimpanzees and human infants. In Ute Schönpflug (Ed.), *Cultural transmission: psychological, developmental, social and methodological aspects* (pp. 33–47). New York: Cambridge University Press.

54. Dunbar, R. I. M. (1992). Neocortex size as a constraint on group size in primates. *Journal of Human Evolution, 22,* 469–493.

55. Gardner, H. (in press). *The true, the beautiful, and the good.*

56. Gardner, H. (in press). *The true, the beautiful, and the good*; Goodman, N. (1968). *Languages of art: an approach to a theory of symbols* (pp. 252–254). Indianapolis: Bobbs-Merrill; Sheridan, K. M. (2006). *Taste in film: subjective and intersubjective validity.* Doctoral dissertation, Harvard University; and Sheridan, K. M. (2008). Reading, writing and watching: the informal education of film fans. In J. Flood, D. Lapp, & S. B. Heath (Eds.), *Handbook on teaching literacy through the communicative, visual and performing arts* (2nd ed. pp. 259–270). Mahwah, NJ: Lawrence Erlbaum.

{ PART III }

Neuroscience Perspectives

Neuroaesthetics

GROWING PAINS OF A NEW DISCIPLINE

Anjan Chatterjee

Introduction

Does neuroscience have anything useful to contribute to aesthetics? Neuroaesthetics is a new field that is gaining momentum. The field falls directly on the borders of art and science and brings with it the inherent tensions between these two human endeavors. Unresolved is the question of whether neuroaesthetics can be both true to its scientific roots and relevant to aesthetics. At this early stage it is worth examining the current state of neuroaesthetics while keeping in mind the principles that underlie this practice. In this chapter, I review briefly writings that fall under the rubric of neuroaesthetics. I offer suggestions of what might be needed if the field is to take itself seriously as a science, particularly as an experimental science. I then conclude with some cautionary notes about challenges that neuroaestheticians face.

The term *aesthetics* is used broadly here to encompass the perception of, production of, and response to art, as well as interactions with objects and scenes that evoke a response that might be considered aesthetic. I also restrict my comments to visual aesthetics, but the general principles would easily apply to music, dance, and literature. At the outset, I should be clear that neuroscience is not likely to offer much to discussions about definitions of art.[1] Some philosophers have claimed that defining art with necessary and sufficient conditions is not possible.[2] In response to such claims, recent theoreticians have defined art by its social and institutional[3] or its historical context.[4] Neuroscience is unlikely to address sociological or historical conceptions of art with any specificity. Neuroscientists are likely to avoid definitional issues and focus on accepted examples of artwork or properties of these works as probes for experiments.

Observations on Parallels Between Art and the Brain

With rare exceptions, most neuroscientists do not consider aesthetics worthy of inquiry. And some aestheticians probably consider neuroscientific inquiry into aesthetics trivial at best and more likely an abomination. Only recently has neuro-science joined a tradition of scientific inquiry into aesthetics dating back to Fechner in the 19th century.[5] There have been attempts to link aesthetic experiences to its biological underpinnings in the past. For example, Berlyne[6] emphasized the role of physiological arousal in aesthetic experiences. Similarly, Rentschler, Herzberger, and Epstein[7] edited the first book that explored links between beauty and the brain. However, it is the recent spate of writings on parallels between art and how the brain is organized that have garnered wide interest.

Zeki[8,9] argued forcefully that no theory of aesthetics is complete without an understanding of the role of the brain in aesthetics. He suggested that the goals of the nervous system and of artists are similar: both are driven to understand visual properties of the world. The nervous system decomposes visual informa-tion into attributes like color, luminance, and motion. Similarly, many artists, particularly within the past century, isolate and enhance different visual attri-butes. For example, Matisse emphasized color and Calder emphasized motion. Zeki suggests that artists endeavoring to uncover important distinctions in the visual world end up discovering modules that are recognized distinctly by the visual brain. Cavanagh[10] has similarly claimed that the artists' goals follow strate-gies used by the nervous system in enabling our perception. He observes that paintings often violate the physics of shadows, reflections, colors, and contours. Rather than adhering to physical properties of the world, these paintings reflect perceptual shortcuts used by the brain. Artists, in experimenting with forms of depiction, revealed what psychologists and neuroscientists are now identifying as principles of perception.

Livingstone[11] and Conway[12] focused on how artists make use of complex inter-actions between different components of vision in creating their paintings. The dorsal (where) and ventral (what) processing distinction is a central tenet in visual neuroscience[13] (see Shimamura, Chapter 1 in this volume, for a description of these processing streams). The dorsal stream responds to contrast differences, motion, and spatial location. The ventral stream responds to simple form and color. Livingstone suggests that the shimmering quality of water or the sun's glow on the horizon seen in some Impressionist paintings (e.g., the sun and surrounding clouds in Monet's *Impression Sunrise*) is produced by objects that can be distin-guished only by color and not by contrast differences. The dorsal stream is not aware of color differences. Since the dorsal stream senses motion (or the lack thereof) and spatial location, Livingstone argues that forms that reflect the same amount of light or have the same degree of contrast are not fixed with respect to motion or spatial location and are experienced as unstable or shimmering. Conversely, since shape can be derived from luminance differences, she argues that artists often use contrast to produce shapes, leaving color for expressive rather than descriptive purposes. Livingstone highlights the way that visual attributes combine in the construction of our visual perception. Artists make use of these combinations to produce specific aesthetic effects.

Ramachandran and Hirstein[14,15] proposed a set of perceptual principles that might underlie aesthetic experiences. For example, they rely on Tinbergen's[16] work to emphasize the "peak shift" phenomenon as offering insight into the aesthetics of abstract art. Tinbergen demonstrated that seagull chicks beg for food from their mothers by pecking on a red spot near the tip of the mother's beak. A disembodied long thin stick with three red stripes near the end evokes an exaggerated response from these chicks. Ramachandran and Hirstein propose that neural structures that evolved to respond to specific visual stimuli respond more vigorously (a shift in their peak response) to stylized versions of these stimuli. These stylized forms are referred to as "primitives." Their insight is that abstract art might be tapping into the responses to such visual primitives even if the viewer might not even be aware of the original stimulus from which the primitive is derived.

These examples of neuroaesthetics writings reflect recognition by neuroscientists that visual aesthetics are an important part of human experience. As such, this experience ought to conform to principles of neural organization. Intriguing parallels exist between the techniques and output of artists and the organization of the visual brain. The challenge for this approach to neuroaesthetics is to convert these observations into a systematic program of research. Can such observations motivate future experimental work? What would constitute falsifiable hypotheses?

A Framework for Neuroaesthetics

A cognitive neuroscience research program in visual aesthetics rests on two principles.[17] First, visual aesthetics, like vision in general, has multiple components. Second, an aesthetic experience arises from a combination of neural responses to different components of a visual object, along with the meanings and associations evoked by the image. The process by which humans visually recognize objects offers a framework from which to consider these components (Fig. 12.1). Investigations can focus on these components and on how they combine.

The nervous system processes visual information both hierarchically and in parallel.[18–20] The levels of this processing can be classified as early, intermediate, and late vision.[21] Early vision extracts simple elements from the visual environment, such as color, luminance, shape, motion, and location.[22,23] These elements are processed in different parts of the brain. Intermediate vision gives structure to regions in what would otherwise be a chaotic and overwhelming array of sensations. This structure is given by separating some elements and grouping others together.[24–27] Late vision scrutinizes these coherent regions as objects are recognized, meanings attached, and memories evoked.[20,28] These levels interact considerably, and the boundaries between higher levels of visual perception and conception may be not be completely clear-cut. However, these distinctions offer a framework from which to think about different aspects of artwork and our responses to them.

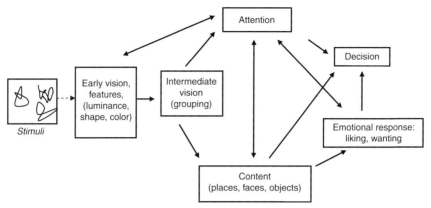

FIGURE 12.1 *A general information-processing model to guide research in neuroaesthetics. (Adapted from[29].)*

This way we process visual information is likely to be reflected in aesthetics[29] (for related models that include broader cultural concerns, see [30] and [31]). Any work of art can be decomposed into its early, intermediate, and late vision components. Aesthetic writings commonly distinguish between form and content (e.g.,[32,33]). Similarly, scientists observe that early and intermediate vision process form and later vision processes content. By *content* I mean the semantic content of an object—that is, its recognizable visual form as well as what the object is and the kinds of information it brings to mind and with which it is associated.

Figure 12.1 shows a model of how the neuroscience of visual aesthetics might be mapped. The early features of an art object might be its color and its spatial location. These elements would be grouped together to form larger units in intermediate vision. Such grouping occurs automatically. The neural basis of grouping is not well understood but likely involves extra-striate cortex (structures that are adjacent to cortical areas that first receive visual information from the eye).[24,25] Grouping creates "unity in diversity," a central notion that underlies compositional balance.

If compositional form is apprehended automatically by intermediate vision, then one might reasonably hypothesize that sensitivity to such form is also automatic. It turns out that people are sensitive to compositional form "at a glance" with exposures as short as 50 milliseconds.[34] Intriguingly, preference for form predominates when images are shown for short durations, while preference for detail predominates when images are shown for slightly longer times.[35] Combinations of early and intermediate visual properties (e.g., color, shape, composition) engage circuits in the frontal and parietal cortices that mediate attention. Attention modulates activity in early visual cortices[36–39] and is likely to contribute to a more vivid experience of the stimulus. The recognition of the object by higher vision then evokes its semantic associations.

Beyond perception and conception in visual aesthetics, two other aspects of aesthetics are important. The first is the emotional response to an aesthetic image; the second is the process of making aesthetic judgments. Parts of the temporal lobe (anterior medial) and frontal lobe (orbito-frontal) and other structures deep in the brain mediate emotions in general, and reward systems in particular.[40–45] Aesthetic judgments about images are likely to engage neural circuits that are distributed widely, particularly within the dorsolateral frontal and medial frontal cortices.

Empirical Evidence: Lesion Studies

Investigations of patients with brain damage have contributed greatly to our understanding of cognitive and affective systems. This approach offers substantial promise in advancing neuroaesthetics. Diseases of the brain can impair our ability to speak or comprehend language, to coordinate movements, to recognize objects, to apprehend emotions, and to make logical decisions. By contrast, while damage to the brain can certainly impair the ability to produce art, paradoxically in some cases art abilities seems to improve. Brain damage can create a disposition to produce visual art (for interesting speculations on how brain damage may have contributed to the oeuvre of the 19th-century photographer Muybridge, see[46]), provide artists with a unique visual vocabulary, add to artists' descriptive accuracy, and enhance their expressive powers. These paradoxical improvements offer unique insights into the creative underpinnings of artistic output, as reviewed elsewhere[47–50] (also see Chapter 15, this volume).

Studies of people with brain damage also can advance our understanding of the perception and experience of art. Some people with brain damage probably do not perceive art in the same way that non–brain-damaged individuals do, and their emotional responses to artwork may differ from those of people without brain damage. However, neuropsychological investigations of aesthetic perception to date are nonexistent. There are no adequate instruments to provide basic quantitative assessments of a person's apprehension of artwork. We have recently developed such a tool, The Assessment of Art Attributes.[51] This assessment assumes that the perception of art can be organized along different perceptual and conceptual attributes (Table 12.1). Using such an assessment, we have begun to investigate groups of patients to ascertain the relationship of brain damage to selective deficits or enhancements in art perception. Much remains to be learned if we can develop adequate methods and measurements for this line of inquiry.

Empirical Evidence: Imaging Studies of Beauty

Beauty is central to most people's concept of aesthetics.[52] Of course, not all art is beautiful and artists do not always intend to produce beautiful things.

TABLE 12.1 Form versus Content

Form	Content
hue	depictive accuracy
saturation	animacy
stroke/contour	emotionality
depth	abstraction
balance	fantasy
complexity	symbolism

A pervasive concern in empirical aesthetics has been
distinguishing between form and content of artwork. This list
of attributes represents one version of how this distinction
might be made in experimental studies.[51]

Current discussions by art experts rarely make mention of beauty (see Chapter 6, this volume). But beauty remains a central concept in lay discussions of aesthetic experiences. Understanding the neural basis of the apprehension of and response to beauty might offer insight into the apprehension of and response to visual art. Facial beauty has received most attention.

The response to facial beauty is likely to be deeply encoded in our biology. Cross-cultural judgments of facial beauty are quite consistent.[53–55] Adults and children within and across cultures agree in their judgments of facial attractiveness.[56] Similarly, infants look longer at attractive faces within a week of being born, and the effects of facial attractiveness on infants' gaze generalize across race, gender, and age by 6 months.[57,58] Thus, the disposition to engage attractive faces is present in brains that have not been modified greatly by experience. Some components of beauty are undoubtedly shaped further by cultural factors,[59] but the universal components are likely to have a common neural basis.

Several studies report that attractive faces activate reward systems in the brain. These systems include parts of the frontal cortex (orbito-frontal) and structures deep within the brain (the nucleus accumbens, the ventral striatum, and the amygdala).[60–65] Neural activity in these areas is interpreted as reflecting our emotional reactions to attractive faces.[66] The particular emotional reactions involve the desire to satisfy appetites. The notion that attractive faces are rewarding to look at, at least for men, is evident behaviorally. Heterosexual men are quite willing to sacrifice higher future rewards for smaller immediate rewards when looking at attractive female faces.[67] Presumably the patterns of neural activation to attractive faces are part of a system that helps us select mates.[63]

Perceptual features of faces, such as averageness, symmetry, the structure of cheekbones, the relative size of the lower half of the face, and the width of the jaw, influence people's judgments of facial beauty.[68–70] Winston and colleagues[65] found that activity in parts of the brain where the left occipital and temporal lobes meet was enhanced by facial attractiveness. Similarly, Kranz and Ishai[64] found more activity in a part of the ventral occipito-temporal region (the lateral fusiform gyrus) for attractive female faces than for unattractive female faces.

We conducted a study in which people looked at faces, and in one condition they judged the attractiveness of faces and in another they judged the identity of pairs of faces. Attractiveness judgments produced neural activity in a distributed network involving ventral visual association cortices and parts of posterior parietal and frontal cortices.[71] We suggested that the parietal and frontal activations represented the neural correlates of attending to faces and the process of deciding which faces they liked. We also found more neural activity within the insula (a structure underneath the frontal, parietal, and temporal lobes) and less activity within the anterior and posterior cingulate cortex (parts of the medial frontal lobes). We thought that these patterns represent the emotional reactions to attractiveness. Most important in this study, we found attractiveness continued to evoke neural responses in occipital lobe visual areas, even when subjects were judging the identity of faces and not their attractiveness. The degree to which these areas responded was no different than when they were considering beauty explicitly. We proposed that this visual region of the brain responds to beauty automatically.

Facial attractiveness is apprehended automatically[72,73] and has pervasive social effects beyond its specific role in mate selection. Attractive individuals are considered intelligent, honest, pleasant, natural leaders[74-76] and are viewed as having socially desirable traits, such as strength and sensitivity.[77] The cascade of events in the brain that end up with a bias in social judgments is likely to be triggered by an early perceptual response to attractiveness. We proposed that neural activity in ventral visual cortices that we found responding to facial attractiveness serves as the initial trigger for this cascade. The fact that this region of activation extended beyond parts of visual cortex especially sensitive to faces *per se* raises the possibility that this area may be responsive to attractive objects more generally.[71]

While studied less often than faces, human bodies also range in their beauty. Furthermore, many body proportions, such as the ratio of hip to waist diameter, can be quantified. People are quite consistent in the relative body proportions that they consider beautiful. This consistency gives rise to the idea that evolutionary selection pressures contribute to our standards of beauty.[78] Di Dio and colleagues[79] used images of western classical and Renaissance sculpture in an fMRI study to investigate neural responses to bodily beauty. They found that the right ventral occipital regions, parts of the frontal lobes, and the right insula were activated by images of the sculptures in their original form as compared to distorted views in which the proportions of the body were altered. Explicit judgments of beauty by the participants activated the right amygdala, an area deep in the anterior parts of the temporal lobe that has long been associated with emotional processing. The authors propose that the insula is responding to objective parameters of beauty (although a similar claim could be made for the ventral occipital regions that they found active, and we found active in our study on facial beauty described above) and the amygdala might be responding to subjective responses to beauty.

Empirical Evidence: Imaging Studies of Art

Very few studies have used art to examine the neural bases of aesthetics (see Chapters 13 and 14, this volume). While the goals in many of these studies are similar, their experimental approaches differ and the results at first glance appear bewilderingly varied. Kawabata and Zeki[80] asked participants to rate abstract, still-life, landscape, and portraiture paintings as beautiful, neutral, or ugly. The participants then looked at the same images in the scanner. Not surprisingly, they found that looking at portraits, or landscapes, or still-lifes evoked different patterns of activity within different parts of the ventral visual cortex. These patterns of activity represent different responses to the different content of these images. In contrast to these visual regions, they found more activity for beautiful than for ugly or neutral images in the undersurface of the frontal lobes (the orbito-frontal cortex). In the anterior cingulate and left parietal cortex, they found more activity for beautiful than for neutral stimuli. Only activity within the orbito-frontal cortex increased with the beauty of all the painting types. The authors interpreted this activity as representing the neural underpinnings of an aesthetic emotional experience of these paintings.

Vartanian and Goel[81] used images of representational and abstract paintings shown in different formats in an fMRI study. The images were of the originals, or they were altered or filtered. Each painting was presented in each of the three formats and participants reported their preferences for each image. In general, representational paintings were preferred over abstract ones. Representational paintings produced more activity than abstract paintings in the ends of the occipital lobes, the precuneus (a part of the parietal lobe that lies between both hemispheres), and the posterior middle temporal gyrus. Participants also looked longer at the images that they preferred. The authors also found more activity in the occipital gyri on both sides and the left anterior cingulate for images they liked. They also found that activity in the right caudate nucleus (a deep structure that is part of a neural system referred to as the basal ganglia) decreased as their liking for paintings decreased.

Cela-Conde and colleagues[82] used magnetoencephalography to record event-related potentials when participants viewed images of artworks and photographs. Magnetoencephalography is a technique of recording brain waves across different parts of the brain while a person is engaged in a specific task. In their study, participants looked at different kinds of art images, including abstract art, classical art, Impressionist art, post-Impressionist art, and photographs. They judged whether or not each of these images were beautiful. Beautiful images produced more neural activity than not-beautiful images over the left dorsolateral prefrontal cortex in a period of 400 to 1,000 milliseconds after the images were viewed. The authors infer that this region is involved when people make aesthetic judgments.

Jacobsen and colleagues[83] used a different strategy to investigate the neural correlates of beauty in an fMRI study. Rather than use actual artworks as their stimuli, they used a set of geometric shapes designed in the laboratory. Participants judged whether the images were beautiful or whether the images were symmetrical. Participants in general found symmetrical patterns more beautiful than non-symmetrical ones. When they made aesthetic judgments, the medial frontal cortex, the precuneus, and the ventral prefrontal cortex were active. Parts of the left parietal cortex (the intraparietal sulcus) were engaged by both symmetry and beauty. Both beauty and complexity of the images evoked activity in the orbito-frontal cortex. In a follow-up study using the same stimuli,[84] they found that beauty generated a brain wave, the lateral positive evoked potential, 360 and 1,225 milliseconds after they saw these images.

One might be disheartened that these studies investigating aesthetics report different patterns of activation. However, Nadal and colleagues[85] propose that the results of these studies are compatible within the general model (see Fig. 12.1) I proposed.[29] Engaging visual properties of paintings increases activity within ventral visual cortices.[81] Aesthetic judgments activate parts of dorsolateral prefrontal and medial prefrontal cortices.[82,83] And emotional responses to these stimuli activate the orbito-frontal[80,83] as well as anterior cingulate cortices.[80,81,86]

Why Aesthetics? A Neurobiological Proposal

Why are aesthetic experiences such a central feature of our lives? Any answer to such a question is necessarily speculative. I suggest that a drive to beauty and the propensity towards an aesthetic attitude might underlie the universality of making and appreciating art. Evolutionary biology may offer a general framework from which to consider why humans seem to be engaged in what seems to be such a pointless pursuit.

DRIVE FOR BEAUTY

Most people are drawn to beauty. As we have suggested in our own work, neural responses to attractive faces occur automatically, even when people are not explicitly judging beauty.[71] Three kinds of evolutionary arguments are made for the attraction to beauty. The first and most obvious is the way that beauty influences mate selection. With faces and bodies, the link between mate selection and beauty is clear.[87] Attractive features are physical attributes that are desirable in selecting mates, because they are clues to genetic health.[53,70,78,88–90] On this view, the nervous system has evolved to be attracted to specific configurations of facial features that signal "good genes." We have come to regard these features as beautiful. A variation of this view is the "costly signal" proposal.[91] Male birds attract female birds by using extravagant plumage or elaborate songs. These displays appear to be maladaptive insofar as they interfere with movement and attract predators. The costly signal proposal is that such displays advertise the unusual vigor of the displayer: he can afford these maladaptive indulgences because he is so fit to begin with.

Art-making requires considerable time and effort and, like a costly display, would similarly advertise one's fitness in the competition for mates.

Others have argued that thinking that art is derived from how we select mates is too narrow a view of how art might have evolved. Dissanayake[92] gathers considerable evidence for art's role in promoting social cohesion. She rejects relatively recent ideas that novelty or individual creativity is all that important. Rather, she takes an ethnographic view of the evolutionary significance of art to humanity. For her, the behavior of "making special" is critical to art. Ordinary objects, movements, patterns, and sounds are transformed into something extraordinary by exaggeration, repetition, embellishment, and so on.[93] This stylizing of visual forms is reminiscent of the peak shift idea emphasized by Ramachandran and Hirstein[14] in their discussions of the biology of aesthetics. Beauty, virtuosity, costliness, and emotional investment are all ingredients in the process of making something special. By focusing on the ritualistic nature of making and appreciating art she emphasizes the importance of art in enhancing cooperation and encouraging cohesion within local societies.

A different kind of argument for why we have come to regard things as beautiful has to do with how easily we apprehend objects.[94] On this account, preferences are a byproduct of a general information-processing mechanism. As mentioned before, one idea around for such a mechanism is the extraction of a prototype, or a typical member of a category. People prefer prototypes of different kinds of stimuli, such as color[95] and music.[96] Faces would presumably be another category of stimuli subject to this biased preference for prototypes.[97] A variation on the information-processing account for preference is the idea that people prefer to look at things that are processed "fluently." Fluency is the ease with which one processes objects. Specific physical features of objects themselves and their conceptual characteristics contribute to fluency. Features of the object, such as symmetry, and figure–ground relationships as well as the experiences of the viewer influence fluent processing. The important point is that processing fluency is associated with aesthetic pleasure.[98,99] People like what they see and recognize easily. Thus, familiarity as established by mere exposure, and as it contributes to processing fluency, influences people's preferences for simple displays in laboratories.[100] These influences also extend beyond the laboratory. Familiarity also influences which Impressionist paintings are regarded highly.[101]

Given that specific configurations of physical objects contribute to the experience of beauty, regardless of whether this contribution is driven by mating desires and rituals, promotes social cohesion, or facilitates processing, how do these experience relate to the aesthetic experience? Herein lies a paradox.

THE AESTHETIC ATTITUDE

Evolutionary arguments for the importance of beauty emphasize its significance in how humans have adapted to their environment. Mate selection, social cohesion, and better information processing all have utility. The point of adaptation is to be useful in propagating the species. This utilitarian view of aesthetics is at odds with an idea proposed in the 18th century[102] that the aesthetic attitude is one of "disinterested interest" (see Introduction, this volume). While Kant's idea is by no means agreed upon by all aestheticians, I base my speculations on its importance. Aesthetic pleasures are self-contained; they do not intrinsically evoke additional desires. That is not to say that an artwork cannot evoke utilitarian desires, such as the desire to own it or to display it to impress others. However, these rewards fall outside the aesthetic experience.

Tommaso and colleagues[86] found that gazing at beautiful paintings raised pain thresholds and at the same time inhibited a brain wave referred to as the P2 evoked potential. The P2 potentials are generated by the anterior cingulate cortex. These results suggest that beautiful paintings, even in the artificial laboratory setting, engage people enough to distract them from unpleasant experiences. This phenomenon may be related to the kind of aesthetic experience in which one is completely absorbed by the image, with little regard for anything else.

Can neuroscience contribute to a further understanding of disinterested interest? Berridge and colleagues have drawn a distinction between "liking" and "wanting" that may be relevant to this question.[45,103] Liking and wanting depend on different neural structures and different neurotransmitters. Liking seems to depend on specific parts of our rewards circuits (the nucleus accumbens shell and the ventral pallidum that uses opioid and GABA-ergic neurotransmitter systems) that differ from those structures on which wanting or satisfying our appetites depend (the mesolimbic dopaminergic system, which includes the nucleus accumbens core). Cortical structures such as the cingulate and orbito-frontal cortex further modify these liking and wanting experiences. This distinction between liking and wanting is made in rodents with experiments that use sweet and bitter tastes. Whether the organization of these neural systems also applies to humans and in response to visual images remains to be seen.

The idea that part of our reward systems are cleaved off those that deal with our appetites could be the neural basis for aesthetic disinterested interest. Perhaps the neural circuitry for liking grew out of more prosaic utilitarian reward systems—that is, liking was co-opted within our reward systems that began with clear utilitarian wanting to satisfy appetites. Perhaps the liking system evolved to allow humans to maintain some distance from the objects of desire and has now come to serve the aesthetic attitude. The fact that liking involves the opioid system might be a clue to the "inward" nature of the pleasurable experience.

Cautionary Coda

The neuroscience of visual aesthetics is in its infancy. With a field so wide open, progress in any direction would be an advance. However, I suggest that practitioners of neuroaesthetics should keep some concerns in mind. None of these concerns is unique to neuroaesthetics; rather, they have arisen in other domains within cognitive neuroscience. Neuroaesthetics can profit by being sensitive to these concerns as it matures.

1. RISKS OF REDUCTION

I argue that experimental neuroaesthetics needs to adhere to the constraints of any experimental science. In other words, experiments motivated by general frameworks are needed. And experiments should test falsifiable hypotheses. Such experimental work usually has two properties. First is that the domain in question can be broken down into more manageable components. Second is that the observations can be quantified. The analysis of specific components means tackling relatively narrow aspects of the broader universe of aesthetics. Such a componential approach is no different than how one tries to tackle any complex domain like language, or emotion, or decision-making. The complexity of the domain needs to be simplified in a way that offers some experimental control. While qualitative analyses can certainly provide important empirical information, quantification more easily provides ways to test hypotheses rigorously.

The risk of decomposition and quantification is that such reduction actually misses the very thing we are most interested in studying. Take the example of the aesthetic responses to beauty. Experimental aesthetics often addresses this issue by obtaining preference ratings from participants. In such a research program, one might ask methodologic questions about how best to capture people's preferences. One might ask whether judgments of interestingness are the same as judgments of preference. Or one might explore the relationship of complexity to either preference or to interest. These are all legitimate and important questions to be pursued. However, the pursuit of such questions might easily obscure the basic question of the relationship of preference to the aesthetic experience. Is preference simply a diluted version of the former? Or is that deeply moving experience that one might consider aesthetic qualitatively different? What do neuroscientists make of notions like the "sublime"? The sublime is a very special emotional experience and is mentioned frequently in aesthetics.[102] And yet, sublime is not talked about in affective neuroscience. When we reduce aesthetics to components that can be quantified we risk being diverted from the targets of our investigation.

A different risk of reduction is that what we study is simply not of much relevance to aesthetics. In other words, neuroaesthetics, by focusing on the perceptual and affective properties of artwork, misses what is most germane to contemporary discussions of art (see Chapter 6, this volume). Current discussions of art by critics make little reference to beauty. As I mentioned at the outset, neuroscience is less likely to contribute much to cultural and sociological aspects of art. This challenge might mean that the divide between what neuroscience can deliver and what is most important to aestheticians is too wide to traverse, and after a brief handshake, as represented by this volume, the disciplines will go their separate ways. In my view, such a conclusion would be premature: these are early days in a new discipline and future directions are difficult to predict. Nonetheless, neuroscientists should be sensitive to the proverbial problem of looking for the dropped coin under the lamp because that is where things are visible, even if the real action is elsewhere.

2. IS AESTHETICS USED AS A PROBE TO UNDERSTAND THE BRAIN, OR IS THE BRAIN USED AS A PROBE TO UNDERSTAND AESTHETICS?

Fechner, in *The Elements of Psychophysics*, distinguished between an outer psychophysics and an inner psychophysics. Outer psychophysics is the study of the relationship between human psychology and the physical properties of stimuli. This kind of study has been the main approach of empirical aesthetics over the past one and a half centuries. Inner psychophysics is the relationship between human psychology and the physical properties of the brain. Fechner recognized that such an inner psychophysics was possible in principle. We are now in a position to pursue an inner psychophysics. Modern neuroscience tools such as fMRI, ERPs, and transcranial magnetic stimulation do exactly that. However, it is worth being explicit about the triangular interactions between psychology and outer physics and inner physics.

Research that probes the relationship between outer and inner psychophysics without direct recourse to psychology is possible. In such experiments, finely controlled stimuli are related to the response properties of neurons in specific regions. Thus, one might find that parts of the ventral surface of the brain (the parahippocampal gyrus) respond preferentially to landscape depictions. Here the landscape images are being used to probe the properties of the brain. Do parahippocampal neurons simply classify images, distinguishing between landscapes and other visual stimuli like objects and faces, or do they also evaluate images? Are they tuned to whether the landscapes are appealing or not? Such an experiment might teach us something important about the brain. Here, aesthetic objects are being used to probe properties of the brain, rather than the brain being used to probe the psychology of aesthetics.

A danger in experiments that relate inner and outer psychophysics is that one might think that they now know something about psychology without adequately investigating the behavior itself. This general problem in cognitive neuroscience is referred to as the reverse inference problem.[104] Thus, one takes the location of neural activation as an indication of underlying psychological process. For example, if one found activations in areas that control our motor systems in response to attractive stimuli, one might plausibly think that attractive stimuli encourage us to approach the stimuli. Such an inference is valid as a conclusion if and only if these motor regions are active in approach behaviors and none other. Such unique correspondences between regional activity and mental operation are rare in the brain.

The proposal that activations to attractive stimuli represent approach behaviors is better considered a hypothesis that is generated by the data rather than data that are confirming a hypothesis. The challenge for the investigator is to then design a follow-up experiment that would confirm or disconfirm this hypothesis.

3. WHAT IS THE ADDED VALUE OF NEUROSCIENCE?

This question, in my view, is the most important challenge for neuroaesthetics. If the goal is to understand aesthetics (as distinct from understanding the brain), what does neuroaesthetics deliver? When does neuroscience provide deeper descriptive texture to our knowledge of aesthetics, and when does it deliver added explanatory force? Knowing that the pleasure of viewing a beautiful painting is correlated with activity within very specific parts of the reward circuits adds descriptive texture to our understanding of aesthetic experiences. A new layer of description is added to how we think of this reward. However, such a study would not have taught us anything about the psychological nature of that reward.

To return to the question posed at the beginning of the chapter, does neuroscience have anything useful to say about aesthetics? To answer this question, we need to take the possibility of an inner psychophysics seriously. In other words, what is the relationship between the physiological properties of the brain and the psychology of aesthetics? But more specifically, when does neuroscience add something to the understanding of the psychology of aesthetics that cannot be discovered by behavioral studies alone?

These are early days in a field that may well generate considerable enthusiasm. As a field, neuroaesthetics is likely to draw interest from psychologists, philosophers, artists, art historians, art critics, and the lay public. It is up to neuroscientists to distinguish hype from hope. It is also up to neuroscientists to take seriously what art experts have to say about art when constructing their experiments and theories.

These cautionary notes should not be construed as causes for pessimism. Rather, they are laid out because neuroaesthetics is gradually coming of age. Neuroaesthetics may be ready to take itself seriously.

Acknowledgments

I profited greatly from discussions at the Neuroaesthetics conference held in Copenhagen, September 24–26, 2009, organized by Martin Skov and Jon Lauring. I also profited by comments made by Art Shimamura and Blake Gopnik. I would like to thank Bianca Bromberger for her careful reading of an earlier draft of this chapter.

Endnotes

1. Carroll, N., ed. (2000). *Theories of art today*. Madison-Wisconsin: The University of Wisconsin Press.

2. Weitz, M. (1956). The role of theory in aesthetics. *Journal of Aesthetics and Art Criticism, 15*, 27–35.

3. Dickie, G. (1969). Defining art. *American Philosophical Quarterly, 6*, 253–256.

4. Danto, A.C. (1964). The artworld. *Journal of Philosophy, 61*, 571–584.

5. Fechner, G. (1876). *Vorschule der Aesthetik*. Leipzig: Breitkopf & Hartel.

6. Berlyne, D. F. (1971). *Aesthetics and psychobiology*. New York: Appleton-Century Croft.

7. Rentschler, E., Herzberger, B., & Epstein, D. (Eds.) (1988). *Beauty and the brain: biological aspects of aesthetics*. Berlin: Birkhauser Verlag.

8. Zeki, S. (1999). *Inner vision: an exploration of art and the brain* (p. 224). New York: Oxford University Press.

9. Zeki, S. (1999). Art and the brain. *Journal of Consciousness Studies, 6*, 76–96.

10. Cavanagh, P. (2005). The artist as neuroscientist. *Nature, 434*(7031), 301–307.

11. Livingstone, M. (2002). *Vision and art: the biology of seeing*. New York: Abrams.

12. Conway, B. R., & Livingstone, M. S. (2007). Perspectives on science and art. *Current Opinion in Neurobiology, 17*(4), 476–482.

13. Ungerleider, L. G., & Mishkin, M. (1982). Two cortical visual systems. In *Analysis of visual behavior* (pp. 549–586). Cambridge: MIT Press.

14. Ramachandran, V. S., & Hirstein, W. (1999). The science of art: a neurological theory of aesthetic experience. *Journal of Consciousness Studies, 6*, 15–51.

15. Ramachandran, V. S., & Hirstein, W. (1999). The science of art: a neurological theory of aesthetic experience. *Journal of Consciousness Studies, 6*(6–7), 15–51.

16. Tinbergen, N. (1954). *Curious naturalist*. New York: Basic Books.

17. Chatterjee, A. (2002). *Universal and relative aesthetics: a framework from cognitive neuroscience*. In International Association of Empirical Aesthetics, Takarazuka, Japan.

18. Van Essen, D. C., et al. (1990). Modular and hierarchical organization of extrastriate visual cortex in the macaque monkey. *Cold Springs Harbor Symposium Quantitative Biology, 55*, 679–696.

19. Zeki, S. (1993). *A vision of the brain*. Oxford: Blackwell Scientific Publications.

20. Farah, M. (2000). *The cognitive neuroscience of vision*. Malden, MA: Blackwell Publishers.

21. Marr, D. (1982). *Vision. A computational investigation into the human representation and processing of visual information* (p. 397). New York: WH Freeman and Company.

22. Livingstone, M., & Hubel, D. H. (1987). Psychophysical evidence for separate channels for the perception of form, color, movement, and depth. *Journal of Neuroscience, 7*, 3416–3468.

23. Livingstone, M., & Hubel, D. (1988). Segregation of form, colour, movement, and depth: anatomy, physiology, and perception. *Science, 240*, 740–749.

24. Biederman, I., & Cooper, E. (1991). Priming contour-deleted images: evidence for intermediate representations in visual object recognition. *Cognitive Psychology, 23*, 393–419.

25. Grossberg, S., Mingolla, E., & Ros, W. D. (1997). Visual brain and visual perception: how does the cortex do perceptual grouping? *Trends Neuroscience, 20,* 106–111.

26. Vecera, S., & Behrmann, M. (1997). Spatial attention does not require preattentive grouping. *Neuropsychology, 11,* 30–43.

27. Ricci, R., Vaishnavi, S., & Chatterjee, A. (1999). A deficit of preattentive vision: experimental observations and theoretical implications. *Neurocase, 5*(1), 1–12.

28. Chatterjee, A. (2003). Neglect. A disorder of spatial attention. In *Neurological Foundations of Cognitive Neuroscience* (pp. 1–26). Cambridge, MA: The MIT Press.

29. Chatterjee, A. (2004). Prospects for a cognitive neuroscience of visual aesthetics. *Bulletin of Psychology and the Arts, 4,* 55–59.

30. Leder, H., et al. (2004). A model of aesthetic appreciation and aesthetic judgments. *British Journal of Psychology, 95,* 489–508.

31. Jacobsen, T. (2006). Bridging the arts and sciences: a framework for the psychology of aesthetics. *Leonardo, 39,* 155–162.

32. Russell, P. A., & George, D. A. (1990). Relationships between aesthetic response scales applied to paintings. *Empirical Studies of the Arts, 8*(1), 15–30.

33. Woods, W. A. (1991). Parameters of aesthetic objects: applied aesthetics. *Empirical Studies of the Arts, 9*(2), 105–114.

34. Locher, P., & Nagy, Y. (1996). Vision spontaneously establishes the percept of pictorial balance. *Empirical Studies of the Arts, 14*(1), 17–31.

35. Ognjenovic, P. (1991). Processing of aesthetic information. *Empirical Studies of the Arts, 9*(1), 1–9.

36. Motter, B. C. (1993). Focal attention produces spatially selective processing in visual cortical areas V1, V2, and V4 in the presence of competing stimuli. *Journal of Neurophysiology, 70,* 909–919.

37. Motter, B. C. (1994). Neural correlates of attentive selection for color or luminance in extrastriate area V4. *Journal of Neuroscience, 14,* 2178–2189.

38. Shulman, G. L., et al. (1997). Top-down modulation of early sensory cortex. *Cerebral Cortex, 7,* 193–206.

39. Watanabe, T., et al. (1998). Attention-regulated activity in human primary visual cortex. *Journal of Neurophysiology, 79,* 2218–2221.

40. Schultz, W., Dayans, P., & Montague, P. (1997). A neural substrate of prediction and reward. *Science, 275,* 1593–1599.

41. O'Doherty, J., et al. (2001). Abstract reward and punishment representations in the human orbitofrontal cortex. *Nature Neuroscience, 4,* 95–102.

42. Elliott, R., Friston, K., & Dolan, R. (2000). Dissociable neural responses in human reward systems. *Journal of Neuroscience, 20,* 6159–6165.

43. Delgado, M., et al. (2000). Tracking the hemodynamic responses for reward and punishment. *Journal of Neurophysiology, 84,* 3072–3077.

44. Breiter, H., et al. (2001). Functional imaging of neural response to expectancy and experience of monetary gains and losses. *Neuron, 30,* 619–639.

45. Berridge, K., & Kringelbach, M. (2008). Affective neuroscience of pleasure: reward in humans and animals. *Psychopharmacology, 199*(3), 457–480.

46. Shimamura, A. P. (2002). Muybridge in motion: travels in art, psychology and neurology. *History of Photography, 26,* 341–350.

47. Chatterjee, A. (2004). The neuropsychology of visual artists. *Neuropsychologia, 42,* 1568–1583.

48. Chatterjee, A. (2006). The neuropsychology of visual art: conferring capacity. *International Review of Neurobiology, 74,* 39–49.

49. Chatterjee, A. (2009). Prospects for a neuropsychology of art. In M. Skov & O. Vartanian (Eds.), *Neuroaesthetics* (pp. 131–143). Amityville, NY: Baywood Publishing Company.

50. Zaidel, D. (2005). *Neuropsychology of art.* New York: Psychology Press.

51. Chatterjee, A., et al. (2010). The assessment of art attributes. *Empirical Studies of the Arts, 28,* 207-222.

52. Jacobsen, T., et al. (2004). The primacy of beauty in judging the aesthetics of objects. *Psychological Reports, 94,* 1253–1260.

53. Etcoff, N. (1999). *Survival of the prettiest.* New York: Anchor Books.

54. Perrett, D. I., May, K. A., & Yoshikawa, S. (1994). Facial shape and judgments of female attractiveness. *Nature, 368,* 239–242.

55. Jones, D., & Hill, K. (1993). Criteria of facial attractiveness in five populations. *Human Nature, 4*(3), 271–296.

56. Langlois, J., et al. (2000). Maxims or myths of beauty: a meta-analytic and theoretical review. *Psychological Bulletin, 126,* 390–423.

57. Langlois, J. H., et al. (1991). Facial diversity and infant preferences for attractive faces. *Developmental Psychology, 27*(1), 79–84.

58. Slater, A., et al. (1998). Newborn infants prefer attractive faces. *Infant Behavior and Development, 21*(2), 345–354.

59. Cunningham, M., Barbee, A., & Philhower, C. (2002). Dimensions of facial physical attractiveness: the intersection of biology and culture. In G. Rhodes & L. A. Zebrowitz (Eds.), *Facial attractiveness. evolutionary, cognitive, and social perspectives* (pp. 193–238). Westport, CT: Ablex.

60. Kampe, K., et al. (2001). Reward value of attractiveness and gaze. *Nature, 413,* 589.

61. Aharon, I., et al. (2001). Beautiful faces have variable reward value: fMRI and behavioral evidence. *Neuron, 32,* 537–551.

62. O'Doherty, J., et al. (2003). Beauty in a smile: the role of orbitofrontal cortex in facial attractiveness. *Neuropsychologia, 41,* 147–155.

63. Ishai, A. (2007). Sex, beauty and the orbitofrontal cortex. *International Journal of Psychophysiology, 63*(2), 181–185.

64. Kranz, F., & Ishai, A. (2006). Face perception is modulated by sexual preference. *Current Biology, 16,* 63–68.

65. Winston, J., et al. (2007). Brain systems for assessing facial attractiveness. *Neuropsychologia, 45,* 195–206.

66. Senior, C. (2003). Beauty in the brain of the beholder. *Neuron, 38,* 525–528.

67. Wilson, M., & Daly, M. (2004). Do pretty women inspire men to discount the future. *Proceedings of the Royal Society of London, 271,* 177–179.

68. Grammer, K., & Thornhill, R. (1994). Human (*Homo sapiens*) facial attractiveness and sexual selection: the role of symmetry and averageness. *Journal of Comparative Psychology, 108*(3), 233–242.

69. Enquist, M., & Arak, A. (1994). Symmetry, beauty and evolution. *Nature, 372*(6502), 169–172.

70. Penton-Voak, I. S., et al. (2001). Symmetry, sexual dimorphism in facial proportions and male facial attractiveness. *Proceedings of the Royal Society of London: Series B, 268*, 1617–1623.

71. Chatterjee, A., et al. (2009). The neural response to facial attractiveness. *Neuropsychology, 23*(2), 135–143.

72. Palermo, R., & Rhodes, G. (2007). Are you always on my mind? A review of how face perception and attention interact. *Neuropsychologia, 45*, 75–92.

73. Olson, I., & Marshuetz, C. (2005). Facial attractiveness is appraised in a glance. *Emotion, 5*, 498–502.

74. Kenealy, P., Frude, N., & Shaw, W. (1988). Influence of children's physical attractiveness on teacher expectations. *Journal of Social Psychology, 128*, 373–383.

75. Lerner, R., et al. (1991). Physical attractiveness and psychosocial functioning among early adolescents. *Journal of Early Adolescence, 11*, 300–320.

76. Ritts, V., Patterson, M., & Tubbs, M. (1992). Expectations, impressions, and judgments of physically attractive students: a review. *Review of Educational Research, 62*, 413–426.

77. Dion, K., Berscheid, E., & Walster, E. (1972). What is beautiful is good. *Journal of Personality and Social Psychology, 24*, 285–290.

78. Grammer, K., et al. (2003). Darwinian aesthetics: sexual selection and the biology of beauty. *Biological Review, 78*, 385–407.

79. Di Dio, C., Macaluso, E., & Rizzolatti, G. (2007). The golden beauty: brain response to classical and Renaissance sculptures. *PLoS ONE, 2*(11), e1201.

80. Kawabata, H., & Zeki, S. (2004). Neural correlates of beauty. *Journal of Neurophysiology, 91*(4), 1699–705.

81. Vartanian, O., & Goel, V. (2004). Neuroanatomical correlates of aesthetic preference for paintings. *NeuroReport, 15*(5), 893–897.

82. Cela-Conde, C. J., et al. (2004). Activation of the prefrontal cortex in the human visual aesthetic perception. *PNAS, 101*(16), 6321–6325.

83. Jacobsen, T., et al. (2005). Brain correlates of aesthetic judgments of beauty. *Neuroimage, 29*, 276–285.

84. Hofel, L., & Jacobsen, T. (2007). Electrophysiological indices of processing aesthetics: Spontaneous or intentional processes? *International Journal of Psychophysiology, 65*(1), 20–31.

85. Nadal, M., et al. (2008). Towards a framework for the study of the neural correlates of aesthetic preference. *Spatial Vision, 21*(3), 379–396.

86. Tommaso, M. D., Sardaro, M., & Livrea, P. (2008). Aesthetic value of paintings affects pain thresholds. *Consciousness and Cognition, 17*, 1152–1162.

87. Rhodes, G., et al. (2002). The attractiveness of average faces: cross-cultural evidence and possible biological basis. In G. Rhodes & L. A. Zebrowotz (Eds.), *Facial attractiveness. Evolutionary, cognitive, and social perspectives* (pp. 35–58). Westport, CT: Ablex.

88. Symons, D. (1979). *The evolution of human sexuality*. Oxford: Oxford University Press.

89. Perrett, D. I., et al. (1998). Effects of sexual dimorphism on facial attractiveness. *Nature, 394*, 884–887.

90. Thornhill, R., & Gangestad, S. W. (1999). Facial attractiveness. *Trends in Cognitive Sciences, 3*(12), 452–260.

91. Zahavi, A., & Zahavi, A. (1997). *The handicap principle: a missing piece of Darwin's puzzle*. Oxford: Oxford University Press.

92. Dissanayake, E. (2008). The arts after Darwin: does art have an origin and adaptive function? In *World art studies: exploring concepts and approaches*.(pp. 241–263). Amsterdam: Valiz.

93. Brown, S., & Dissanayake, E. (2009). The arts are more than aesthetics: neuroaesthetics as narrow aesthetics. In M. Skov & O. Vartanian (Eds.), *Neuroaesthetics* (pp. 43–57). Amityville, NY: Baywood Publishing Company, Inc.

94. Rentschler, I., et al. (1999). Innate and learned components of human visual preference. *Current Biology, 9*(13), 665–671.

95. Martindale, C., & Moore, K. (1988). Priming, prototypicality, and preference. *Journal of Experimental Psychology: Human Perception and Performance, 14*, 661–679.

96. Smith, D., & Melara, R. (1990). Aesthetic preference and syntactic prototypicality in music: 'Tis the gift to be simple. *Cognition, 34*, 279–298.

97. Halberstadt, J., & Rhodes, G. (2000). The attractiveness of non-face averages: Implications for an evolutionary explanation of the attractiveness of average faces. *Psychological Science, 11*, 285–289.

98. Reber, R., Schwarz, N., & Winkielman, P. (2004). Processing fluency and aesthetic pleasure: is beauty in the perceiver's processing experience? *Personality & Social Psychology Review, 8*(4), 364–382.

99. Armstrong, T., & Detweiler-Bedell, B. (2008). Beauty as an emotion: the exhilarating prospect of mastering a challenging world. *Review of General Psychology, 12*(4), 305–329.

100. Moreland, R. L., & Zajonc, R. B. (1976). A strong test of exposure effects. *Journal of Experimental Social Psychology, 12*, 170–179.

101. Cutting, J. E. (2007). Mere exposure, reproduction, and the impressionist canon. In *Partisan canons* (pp. 79–93). Durham, NC: Duke University Press.

102. Kant, I. (1790/1987). *Critique of judgment* [W. S. Pluhar, translator]. Indianapolis: Hackett.

103. Wyvell, C., & Berridge, K. (2000). Intra-accumbens amphetamine increases the conditioned incentive salience of sucrose reward: enhancement of reward wanting without enhanced liking or response reinforcement. *Journal of Neuroscience, 20*, 8122–8130.

104. Poldrack, R. A. (2006). Can cognitive processes be inferred from neuroimaging data? *Trends in Cognitive Sciences, 10*, 59–63.

13

The Modularity of Aesthetic Processing and Perception in the Human Brain

FUNCTIONAL NEUROIMAGING STUDIES OF NEUROAESTHETICS

Ulrich Kirk

Functional Specialization of the Visual Cortex

Single-cell recording was pioneered by Edgar Adrian (1889–1977) and was applied to the visual system of mammals by Stephen Kuffler (1913–1980), the mentor of David Hubel and Torsten Wiesel. Hubel and Wiesel recorded from single cells in the visual cortex (area V1) both in the cat and later in the macaque monkey.[1] Hubel and Wiesel's basic findings were that different parts of the occipital cortex respond to the same stimulus at different levels of complexity. Specifically, in area V1 at the occipital pole of the cortex, they observed: "Each cell seems to have its own specific duties; it takes care of one restricted part of the retina, responds best to one particular shape of stimulus and to one particular orientation."[1] On closer observation they found that cells with similar orientation preferences grouped together in vertical columns that seemed to form a hierarchy of increasing receptive field complexity. This hierarchy, according to Hubel and Wiesel, consisted of simple and hyper-complex (end-stopped) cells. The simple cells showed linearity within their receptive fields so that the firing rate of the neuron could be predicted from its input. Thus, the more complex cells could then be built from the outputs of the simple cells. Upon summarizing these observations the subsequent proposal suggested that every aspect of the visual scene was processed in each area, but at a higher level of complexity.

Semir Zeki recorded from prestriate regions in the monkey[2] and came to a different proposal.[3] Zeki observed variation in responses relative to which area he was recording from. He observed that a region of cortex on the posterior bank of the superior temporal sulcus contained neurons that showed a strong preference for moving stimuli of certain directions over stationary stimuli. This area is today known as V5. In contrast to this area, Zeki found a region of cortex in the prelunate sulcus in the visual cortex containing neurons responding to color, but not motion. This area was named V4. From these observations Zeki proposed a theory of functional specialization that was different from Hubel and Wiesel's in that the visual system was organized according to multiple, parallel, functional specialized systems.

The final confirmation of functional specialization was made with the advent of neuroimaging techniques, first by positron emission tomography (PET) and later functional magnetic resonance imaging (fMRI), which would enable demonstrations of functional human activity at anatomical locations, such that functional specialization today has been documented beyond doubt.

Functional Specialization of Aesthetics

During evolution, the brain has devoted entire cortical areas to features that are of special use and importance. These functionally specialized attributes in relation to vision include, among others, color, motion, and form. According to Zeki these specialized processing systems also have a primacy in aesthetics.[4]

Based on the theory of functional specialization, Zeki has emphasized that a modularity of aesthetics can be deduced. The logic is that damage to area V4 in the human brain leads to the syndrome cerebral achromatopsia, where patients are unable to see the world in color. To see the colors of, for instance, a Fauvist painting requires an intact V4, and thus patients with cerebral achromatopsia are not able to aesthetically admire the coloration of such paintings. Another example: patients suffering from prosopagnosia have lesions in the human extrastriate cortex specialized for face perception.[5] These patients are unable to recognize familiar faces when visually presented, and thus these patients are impaired in appreciating the aesthetic qualities of portrait paintings. However, loss of one visual attribute does not necessarily entail a loss of the appreciation of another attribute, unless the lesion is in V1, which leads to total blindness. The argument is not that the aesthetic effect of Fauvist or portrait paintings is solely due to activity in these functional specialized visual areas, only that these areas are critical for recognition of these attributes. These examples suggest that there is not only one visual aesthetic sense, but many separate categories of aesthetics, with each one tied to activity of a functional specialized processing system.

Early Neuroaesthetic Studies

As the neurosciences reveal more about the functional organization of the brain, neuroscientists have become interested in exploring the fundamentals of subjective processes underlying aesthetics. Neuroaesthetics seeks to understand aesthetic judgments in the organization and functioning of the brain. In that sense neuroaesthetics is not a field that promises new insights to scholars of art history and artists themselves; rather, it is the opposite. Neuroscientists are in a position to take advantage of the artists, who show an instinctive knowledge of the brain, as I will advocate in this section.

To appreciate neuroaesthetics as a scientific discipline it is essential to discuss the origin and the underlying history of the discipline. Such a discussion will be addressed below in an overview of the development of experimental aesthetics. However, I will start by reviewing the early studies of neuroaesthetics. These studies are characterized by exploring specific artistic currents with implications for perception—for example, kinetic art, which has provided information about motion perception; Fauvism, with implications for color vision; and Surrealist art, which has implications for the saliency of object perception. These studies reflect a distinct category of neuroaesthetic studies that must be separated from the category of neuroaesthetics that explores the subjective processes involved in judgments of aesthetics.

Kinetic Art

Kinetic artists have found that the purpose of kinetic art is not simply to simulate motion, but rather to depict motion independently of other attributes, such as form and color. Indeed, it has been shown that when humans view an abstract colored pattern in motion, activity in area V5 increases, while activity in area V4 decreases. Zeki and Lamb[6] distinguish three stages in the development of kinetic art. In the first, artists expressed the importance of physical movement in manifestos, but represented motion in static form. In the second stage, physical objects that are actually in motion were incorporated into art. The third stage was an attempt to separate motion from form and color. Jean Tinguely designed a machine called *Homage to New York* (1960) that was explicitly built to self-destruct and thus liberate motion from form. Kinetic art never progressed further than this third stage. Zeki and Lamb studied the link between brain activity and perception of kinetic art. They tested the hypothesis that while viewing kinetic art, the brain responds as if the stimulus is an actual object in motion. While subjects viewed a static image that nevertheless gives a slight sense of movement, elevated activity was found in V5. When subjects viewed a visual stimulus that was actually in motion, activity was seen in area V1 and V5. Thus, it seems that V5 creates illusory motion.

Fauvist Art

The colorful artwork of another genre, Fauvism, is the optimal stimulus for area V4 of the visual cortex. Artwork that emphasizes a particular quality, such as motion or color, seems to de-emphasize all other qualities to produce the stronger effect. This is similar to neurons in area V4 and V5 that are finely tuned to respond to particular stimuli.

Fauvism arose from the attempt to distinguish the subjective aspects of vision from the mere reproduction of nature. Fauvist painters found it interesting to depict the relationship between the object and the subject, the artist, his personality and his ability to represent emotions. For this reason, the Fauvists tried to liberate form and color from the imitation of nature, adopting the solution of investing objects with unusual colors. Such compositions, abnormal or unnatural in color, also involve knowledge, to the extent that we learn to associate certain colors with certain objects. Zeki and Marini[7] therefore further explored not only the brain areas that were elevated when people view objects in their natural colors, but also those elevated when people enter a Fauvist world and view the same objects in abnormal colors. As expected, the naturally and abnormally colored objects activated visual areas known to be involved in color processing, V1 and V4. However, naturally colored objects (e.g., red strawberries) also engaged the fusiform gyrus and hippocampus located in the temporal lobe, which are related to object color knowledge. Interestingly, abnormally colored objects (e.g., purple strawberries) activated a region in the prefrontal cortex that is often involved in studies where deviations from sensory expectation occur. An example here would be "oddball" tasks where an abstract stimulus (e.g., a green color patch) is repeatedly presented, and on a subset of trials a red color patch is presented, thus violating sensory expectation. Such "oddball" effects seem to activate the identical region of cortex when the "oddball" belongs to a semantic category. This suggests that this region is a general mechanism involved in detecting when expectations are violated. Indeed, another artistic style, Surrealism, explored the effects of such sensory violations.

Surrealism, the Art of René Magritte

The Surrealist painter René Magritte (1898–1967) sought to give objects primacy by pursuing the relative relationship between the object and its context. This artistic experiment is interesting from a neuroscientific perspective. Objects and their properties, such as contextual information, are related to each other by relationships that get incorporated in the brain through experience. The co-occurrence of objects and contexts in natural scenes provides a contextual expectancy when perceiving objects. Magritte ignored convention by placing objects in very unusual settings. Such compositions challenge observers' previous understanding and experience of the relationship between object and context by letting the observer question the intention of these abnormal compositions.

A recent fMRI took advantage of the expressed artistic ambitions of Magritte.[8] By adopting stimuli inspired by Magritte scenarios, the researchers assessed whether the brain responds differently when a violation of the relationship between object and context occurs. This study sought to explore if brain areas that are activated when perceiving objects in normal conditions are also recruited when perceiving objects that are liberated from their expected and semantic context. A second aim of this study was to cast a new light on this artistic current from a neuroscientific perspective in order to further pursue the development of neuroaesthetic studies that take advantage of specific artistic currents with implications for the visual brain. Magritte developed a technique where he separated the pictorial objects from their conventional context and made the observer aware of the distance between the object and context (Fig. 13.1). Thus, Magritte's paintings sought to demonstrate the relative nature of the agreement between object and context. We thought it interesting to ask how this agreement is expressed in terms of brain activity. We expected that the work of Magritte where a perceptual conflict is present would activate the parts of the frontal lobe that were activated by the Fauvist stimulus material used by Zeki and Marini. In both these genres of paintings there is a conflict to resolve, which has to do with the record of past experience and the conventional relationship between color and object in the case of Fauvist paintings, and the relationship between object and context in the case of Surrealistic paintings.

In this neuroimaging study we were quite surprised to find an interesting activation pattern for the contrast (abnormal > normal) that included areas involved in theory of mind tasks. Theory of mind refers to the ability to attribute mental states about oneself and others in order to understand and predict behavior. It is called a *theory* of mind because each human can prove the existence of his or her own mind only through introspection and not through direct access to the mind of another. The assumption in theory of mind is that our ability to understand the behavior of others in terms of their goals and beliefs requires that we have some expectations as to what these goals and beliefs are likely to be. These expectations derive from our general knowledge of the world, from our specific knowledge of this person, and from our observations of what he or she is doing. When viewing images of Surrealist origin, where expectations of object–context relationships are broken, it presumably requires subjects to attribute a new semantic interpretation of the image in order to comprehend it. We found activation in regions such as the temporal parietal junction (between the temporal lobe and parietal lobe) and a region in the anterior cingulate overlapping with the medial superior frontal gyrus that has consistently been associated with theory of mind. These results are puzzling in that this study did not include attending to the mental state of the self and others. However, it has been argued that theory of mind is based on autobiographical experiences[9] and thus a self-referential process. It may be plausible to expand theory of mind to also be involved in the self-initiation of a cognitive process in the context of perceptual conflict that requires the active utilization of the subject's previous knowledge in order to interpret and comprehend the image. Indeed, Magritte has emphasized that his paintings were a visual instrument "by which people might, via shock and surprise, become aware of the lie behind conventions and be able to find the way back to the mysterious essence of things."[10] By "the

FIGURE 13.1 *(A)* La Reconnaissance Infinie *by René Magritte (1963; Leslie and David Rogath Collection). This work, among other Magritte paintings, served as inspiration for the stimulus development. Two examples of the stimuli used in the fMRI experiment are also presented: an object in its normal contextual setting and an object in an abnormal context. (B) Stimulus presentation paradigm. Subjects were asked to fixate (500 milliseconds) prior to a 3,500-millisecond stimulus presentation, followed by a rating period where subjects were required to make their aesthetic response via button press (2,000 milliseconds).*

mysterious essence of things" Magritte meant a relationship between objects and their contexts that was not obvious to the observer, but required an interpretation where the intentions of the paintings were hidden. It seems evident that Magritte, unknowingly, in this art took advantage of cerebral pathways that are distinct from those used by representational art, and unique to the movement of which Magritte was a protagonist, namely Surrealist art.

Fechner and the Foundation of Experimental Aesthetics

The foundation of an empirical investigation of aesthetics was initiated by Gustav Theodor Fechner (1801–1887), who was the co-founder of psychophysics. Fechner was the protagonist for a new empirical foundation of aesthetics, "aesthetics from below," as he called it, which should support the traditional "aesthetics from above" by a solid empirical and inductive approach. With his *Zur experimentellen Aesthetik*, a book published in 1871, and *Vorschule der Aesthetik*, a two-volume work from 1876, Fechner was the first to emphasize an experimental approach to aesthetics. Fechner aimed at deducing aesthetic principles from the empirical comparison of the aesthetic effect of geometric figures. Among the earliest accomplishments of experimental aesthetics put forward by Fechner was the "principle of the aesthetic mean." He exposed subjects to rectangles with sides of varying proportions and asked them which one they liked best. The rectangle closely approximating the Golden Section was selected by more subjects (see, however,[11,12] for experiments that do not find the Golden Section to be most preferred). The Golden Section is a number, approximately 1.618, that was studied by ancient mathematicians due to its frequent appearance in geometry, and thus was thought to reflect nature's balance between symmetry and asymmetry. Fechner concluded: "When an object of our contemplation undergoes random variation in size or shape, then, all other things being equal, the mean value seems to be preferred from the aesthetic point of view or appears with the character of predominant pleasantness as the normal value in comparison with the others, which, according to their degree of deviation from the mean, can appear less pleasing or, if certain limits are exceeded, even displeasing."[13] According to this statement the region of greatest pleasure is between the simple and the increasingly complex. It is interesting to note that since the Renaissance there have been attempts to specify the conditions for beauty and aesthetic pleasure. These have focused on the necessity of equilibrium between two factors. Descartes was among the first to do this in a statement that is strikingly close to that of Fechner: "among the objects of every sense, the one that is most agreeable to the soul is not the one that is perceived by it either very easily or with great difficulty but the one that is not so easy to become acquainted with, that it leaves something to be desired in the passion with which the senses are accustomed to approach their objects or so difficult that it makes the senses suffer in striving to become acquainted with it."[14]

Based on this century-long interest in the principles of aesthetic pleasure, it is difficult to believe that Fechner's approach was so ill received at the time. The disputes following the writings of Fechner reflect the contradiction between arguments based on empirical evidence and arguments based on rational ideas. Eduard von Hartmann, one of the most engaged critics of Fechner's empirical foundation of aesthetics, argued that "man takes more time over collecting empirical facts, the less he trusts the synthetic power of his speculative thinking."[15] This statement demonstrates that the claim for "aesthetics from below" hit a sensitive point of the self-consciousness of the academic aestheticians.

The novelty of Fechner's approach becomes evident only when considered in light of the philosophical thinking of his time. Fechner in 1871 defined his work as "aesthetics from below," which caused controversy in philosophical circles. It is this controversy that shows to what extent Fechner's academic approach was ahead of what was acceptable at the time. Before discussing this dispute it is useful to look more closely at Fechner's approach in the way he described it, especially in the preface of *Vorschule der Aesthetik*. In this book, Fechner characterizes his scientific approach by giving up "the attempt to define the objective nature of beauty, and to develop a system of aesthetics starting from this point."[16] Rather, he wanted to use "the concept of beauty as an auxiliary term to find a brief designation, in the sense of linguistic usage, of things that unite in themselves conditions that lead to general liking."[16] This turn away from the idealistic interpretation of "the true, good and beautiful" can be seen as a critique of a metaphysical concept of beauty. By trying to study the empirical conditions of liking, Fechner turns away from "conceptual developments on the basis of a definition of beauty." Thus, in his words, his approach takes a "direction opposite to the mainstream course." It is much more a bottom-up than a top-down approach, aiming at "clarification rather than intellectual elevation."[13]

Fechner saw the aim of his empirical research in aesthetics as "explaining aesthetical facts through laws" that could be proven only in an empirical way. In Fechner's eyes, this did not exclude the normative definition of true beauty. However, these high-level notions of beauty had to be constructed on the basis of precise knowledge of what was "likely to trigger a higher pleasure . . . directly from sensorial impressions and under which circumstances this was likely to occur with the probability of an intrinsic psychological law."[13] Fechner was convinced that without such an empirical foundation "all our systems of philosophical aesthetics" would be nothing but "giants with feet of clay."[13]

Fechner's "bottom-up aesthetics" is also very different from the conception of aesthetics held by others at the time. For example, Johann Friedrich Herbart reduced the aesthetic act to the perception of form through "cold expert judgment" and dismissed any related emotions as a psychological (side-)effect of aesthetics. In opposition to this, Fechner makes the emotional response to the aesthetic object the central focus of his research. Fechner defined beauty as everything that "had the property of immediately causing liking—not only after reflection or through its consequences."[16] Fechner establishes a direct link to the reality of experiencing beauty in everyday life, in a way that was taken for granted by the British philosophers of the Enlightenment, for example, but not at all by German philosophy. From this it is evident that Fechner's approach represents and stands in opposition to the aesthetic tradition in his academic environment. Shortly after Fechner's publications, Eduard von Hartmann made a critical review in his *Die deutsche Ästhetik seit Kant* published in 1886. "So-called experimental aesthetics," as von Hartmann puts it, "was therefore not yet aesthetics as such" but could "at the very best provide material for it."[17] Fechner also received criticism from Benedetto Croce, one of the most important philosophical minds of his time. Like von Hartmann, Croce dismissed the idea that Fechner's experimental studies had any relevance to aesthetics whatsoever. Croce thought that only where Fechner writes about the concept of the beautiful in a speculative way, he would come up with aesthetic statements, so that one had to wonder why Fechner, although already having a theory about beauty and also about art, went to all the trouble of making principles and drawing up charts. Despite the harsh critique that Fechner received for his "aesthetics from below," his ideas were studied, particularly by empirical psychologists from the 1970s and onwards.

This section has emphasized the similarities between experimental aesthetics founded by Fechner at the turn of the past century and the emerging field of neuroaesthetics. Fechner received criticism for approaching the area of aesthetics from the an empirical perspective, which in many ways is strikingly similar to a critique that has been made towards neuroaesthetics.[18] Neuroaesthetics uses an approach similar to that of Fechner, but neuroaesthetics is rather to be seen as a subdivision of system neuroscience that builds on the principle of functional specialization. Thus, artistic currents such as kinetic art, Fauvism, and the art of Magritte lend themselves to scientific queries that can provide important information about the organization and functioning of the brain.

Neural Correlates of Aesthetic Judgments

A separate category of neuroaesthetics is concerned with investigations of the higher faculties of aesthetics, such as aesthetic judgments and its interaction with emotional processes. The experiments I will describe in detail in this section represent a recent trend in cognitive neuroscience: investigating the subjective neural processes involved in decision-making. As aesthetic ratings represent a very subjective collections of responses (there are no right or wrong answers in forming a subjective aesthetic judgment), they are especially relevant to apply in probing the subjective processes engaged in decision-making. The experiments described in this section are particularly concerned with the hedonic or affective component involved in forming an aesthetic judgment from a visual stimulus. Early work[19] showed that when presented with a series of canonical paintings, the paintings found to be beautiful as opposed to those regarded as being ugly recruited the medial aspect of the orbito-frontal cortex (OFC). This early work served as a stepping stone to the question of whether it is possible to modulate the aesthetic preference of a painting by using semantic information presented alongside the painting. We designed a fMRI study to measure the influence of cognitive (semantic) information on aesthetic judgments of a stimulus consisting of abstract artworks.[20] The design consisted of presenting abstract artworks together with a word label at the bottom of the screen. The stimulus was labeled on different trials either as belonging to an art museum ("gallery" label) or as a computer-generated artwork ("computer" label) made by the experimenter. This was the instruction given to the subjects; however, the stimuli were all original non-canonical abstract artworks that were neither computer-generated replicas nor belonged to a specific art museum. Using this experimental design we wanted to learn if aesthetic perception and hedonic value can be altered and modulated by framing a painting as either "real art" or "fake art." Although it is likely that humans will rate aesthetically appealing stimuli highest and unappealing stimuli lowest, it remains a possibility that top-down influences are recruited and serve to influence coherent behavioral preference. Our hypothesis was that it is the subjects' conception of the object/stimulus, rather than the sensory properties of the stimulus, that primarily determine its hedonic value. This aspect also speaks to a longstanding question within philosophical aesthetics; indeed, the design was partially inspired by an argument first advanced by Arthur Danto. According to the so-called Art World[21] argument, there are no inherent properties that constitute an object as art. Instead, it is the object's institutional context (i.e., an art museum) that defines it as either art or non-art. In terms of this experiment this is tantamount to stating that objects must be labeled as art in order to be experienced as art. Our neural data provide an interesting renaissance to this debate.

The question addressed in this study was whether explicit contextual information influences activity in the OFC. Previous studies have demonstrated that activity in the medial aspects of the OFC is modulated by contextual information in experimental conditions where subjects evaluate their preference for liquids or odors. One study[22] demonstrated that human subjects will rate a test odor as significantly more pleasant when it is paired with a pleasant visual word than when it is paired with an unpleasant one. In this study they observed a neural correlate of this behavioral modulation in the medial OFC. This shows that high-level cognitive input such as word labels influences brain activity in the OFC. Similarly, McClure and colleagues[23] investigated the neural systems involved in generating preferences produced by two different brands of soft drinks (Coca-Cola and Pepsi) and found that the rated preference of unlabeled drinks (i.e., without cognitive influences) was reflected in activations of the ventromedial part of the prefrontal cortex (VMPFC). This result was recently extended by Plassman and colleagues,[24] who showed that knowledge of the monetary value of wine lead to an increase in subjects' reports of preference. They reported a neural correlate of this effect in the medial OFC.

We wanted to chart the neural correlates of contextual modulation of subjective preference for paintings. The aesthetic ratings collected during scanning for the two stimulus conditions (gallery vs. computer art) showed, surprisingly, that when a painting was labeled "gallery" the aesthetic rating was significantly higher than when a painting was labeled "computer." The neuroimaging results demonstrated that the medial aspects of the OFC were more activated when subjects rated a gallery-labeled painting as appealing as opposed to a computer-labeled painting. Furthermore, the frontal pole on the ventral aspect of the medial prefrontal cortex (VMPFC) was active. When looking at the neural effects of paintings labeled "gallery" as opposed to "computer," regardless of the specific aesthetic ratings we found increased activity in bilateral parahippocampal gyrus, visual cortex, and bilateral temporal pole, indicating that contextual processing are recruited differentially by the two labels. The activation of the medial OFC that was found to correlate with the aesthetic ratings given to the "gallery"-labeled conditions coincides with current evidence that the medial aspect of the human OFC represents the hedonic attributes involved in aesthetic judgments of various stimuli. This finding also provides evidence that this representation holds even when the attributed hedonic properties are modulated by cognitive and semantic input.

The study described here is similar to the study by de Araujo and colleagues,[22] who found more activation in the medial OFC when subjects were making hedonic judgments of a set of odors that were manipulated with a cognitive-positive label in contrast to a negative word label. It has been established by psychophysical studies that olfactory discrimination is inefficient in humans, such that successful odor identification is highly susceptible to factors such as familiarity and the semantic connection between an odor and its name.[25] Based on this evidence it may not be surprising that de Araujo and colleagues found that verbal or semantic information can strongly influence the perception of odor attributes. It is, however, not well documented that semantic labels can influence aesthetic and hedonic ratings of artworks. However, Russell[26] found an increase in the hedonic value from first to second ratings when abstract and semiabstract artworks were presented with title and the artist's name in the second phase. The results of Kirk and colleagues[20] extend that observation by showing that manipulated semantic labels influence hedonic judgments even when there is no difference in the stimulus material, and they furthermore found a neural correlate of this behavioral modulation in the medial OFC, a region that overlaps with that found by de Araujo and colleagues.[22] These results suggest that cognitive input, a word label, can influence brain activation in areas such as the medial OFC. A modulation of the medial OFC to objects of varying reward value has also been found in other studies. For example, Erk and colleagues[27] found that cultural objects such as sports cars versus small cars modulate the reward circuitry in regions such as the medial OFC. The VMPFC is strongly implicated in signaling basic appetitive aspects of reward. BOLD signal changes in this region scale with reward value.[28] The medial OFC and VMPFC have been shown to be strongly related and implicated in emotional processing,[29] with increased responses to rewarding outcomes. The implication is that these areas may be engaged under conditions when behavioral decision-making is required. This interpretation is compatible with the idea that the OFC and medial PFC are involved in integrating rewarding feedback for affective decision-making.

An interesting question is how the OFC result should be interpreted in relation to models of the neural mechanisms underlying aesthetic evaluation. The medial OFC might be involved in two functional sub-processes: (1) the evaluative categorization processes associated with making an aesthetic judgment (i.e., the subjective report) or (2) or the processes correlated with the coding of subjective pleasure (i.e., stimulus hedonic value). Results indicate a neural difference between making an active aesthetic judgment of the aesthetic value of some stimulus and attending to the same stimulus in other ways (passive viewing; symmetrical judgments). However, no involvement of the medial part of the OFC was found in a neuroimaging study investigating the processes involved in making aesthetic judgments compared to making symmetry judgments. The parametric modulation of the medial OFC in the present study is thus more likely to be related to the subjective coding of hedonic valence than mechanisms associated with the active act of making an overt judgment.

In the study by McClure and colleagues,[23] images of Coca-Cola versus Pepsi cans influenced activations in areas that are traditionally considered as more cognitive than flavor-related areas, including the hippocampus, primary visual cortex, and dorsolateral prefrontal cortex. We observed bilateral activation in the entorhinal cortex in the main effect (gallery vs. computer) irrespective of the actual aesthetic ratings. The entorhinal cortex adjoins and is interconnected with the hippocampus located in the temporal lobe, a region that has been consistently related to the processing of episodic memories. Hippocampal activation is associated with trials in which subjects correctly recollect contextual information compared to ones in which they do not.[30] Other findings suggest that midbrain dopaminergic systems involved in reward expectation could directly modulate declarative memory formation in the hippocampus.[31] This evidence is in line with our initial hypothesis that it is the subject's conception of the image, rather than its sensory properties, that primarily determines its hedonic value. One possible mechanism responsible for this effect might be due to subjects acquiring different prior expectations over future rewards evoked by the stimulus labels. The different expectations of hedonic value could be determined in different ways. The difference in context in this experiment straddles at least two possible factors. The first might be loosely described as a difference in prestige: the art gallery is more prestigious than the computer as a source of artworks. Accordingly, the prediction of higher reward for the gallery comes from a social prior. The more prestigious the art gallery, the more competition there is for artists to display works there; therefore, those who succeed will be more likely to reward viewers than those that fail. A second, closely related factor is the monetary value of the artwork. Artworks from a gallery are more likely to have a greater monetary value than those that are not (on average). Neglecting economic factors of supply and demand, one might have the simple prior that the more expensive the artwork, the more likely it is to have a higher hedonic value for a given observer.

Cognitive inputs such as semantic word labels can have a profound influence on the aesthetic ratings. The data summarized above raise the possibility that the entorhinal cortex and temporal pole may be engaged during recollection of art-related and cultural information that influences aesthetic judgments during gallery conditions, while the VMPFC and medial OFC are more involved in attaching hedonic properties to them. These two systems do not appear to function independently of each other but are modulated and cooperate to influence aesthetic judgments induced by semantic context. These data suggest that the (aesthetic) value of a stimulus can be modulated by the context in which is it presented.

A related question is if the degree of aesthetic expertise modulates the aesthetic value assigned to expertise stimuli. Numerous studies have demonstrated profound differences in the aesthetic preferences between experts and non-experts. In general, people without art training prefer simple and symmetrical visual elements, whereas people with art training prefer complex and asymmetrical visual elements.[32] Similarly, music novices prefer prototypical chord progressions, whereas experts do not show this preference.[33] It seems likely that two different processes contribute to these differential preferences. First, training in the arts is likely to increase the meaning of complex structures in paintings, poems, or music. Second, experts are more likely than novices to consider aesthetic value, the ideas behind the work, and the norms of "good" and "bad" taste.[34,35] As a result, preferences expressed by experts reflect a disposition to distance themselves from the popular taste of non-expert viewers. It seems that in the 20th century, recognition and understanding of individual style have become essential for aesthetic experience. Thus, an aesthetic experience involves processing of stylistic information. Cupchik[36] describes how style processing in abstract art depends on expertise when he states, "Even highly abstract paintings can be constrained by rules, although the underlying principles are not immediately evident to those outside the artist's circle." It is questionable if the artist is aware of the underlying rules of his or her art; it might be that the artist is simply intuitively grasping the most effective rules. However, it remains a fact that art critics are often aware of the preferred technique and rules used by the artist to distinguish one style from another. Based on empirical studies on expertise, mentioned above, it might be that the level of expertise in art affects the evaluation of works of art. In a neuroimaging study we sought to investigate the extent to which the neural correlates of aesthetic judgment vary as a function of expertise in architecture. In other words, it seemed likely that art experts pursue different strategies for determining aesthetic evaluation than non-experts; could such a putative difference in assessment strategies can be detected as a difference in neural activity using fMRI?

It has been shown by imaging experiments that acquired expertise is associated with changes in brain structures underlying perceptual and memory processes, even on a macro-anatomical scale. For example, in a study using voxel-based morphometry analysis, Maguire and colleagues[37] found that gray matter volume in the posterior hippocampus of London taxi drivers is greater than in age-matched controls, and that the size of this increase correlates positively with time spent driving a taxi. Furthermore, several experiments have demonstrated that musicians, after years of playing, respond differently to musical inputs compared to non-musicians. For example, in a recent fMRI study, Bangert and colleagues[38] compared brain activity in groups of musicians and non-musicians as they passively listened to a piano sequence and found elevated activity in the musicians in regions of the temporal lobe associated with auditory processing, and in frontal regions associated with motor control.

Several neuroimaging studies have investigated cortical areas that are recruited as subjects make aesthetic evaluations from a variety of stimulus modalities such as paintings, and the results suggest that the computation of aesthetic preferences for objects predominantly relies on the activity of areas implicated in the processing of reward, especially the OFC and anterior cingulate cortex (ACC). It is therefore an important question if expertise influences aesthetic evaluation through the modulation of neural activity in these areas. A key structure here appears to be the medial OFC, which not only is found to correlate with subjective value as mentioned above, but has also been demonstrated to be involved in coding stimulus value from a variety of other sensory modalities, including taste,[39,40] olfactory,[41,42] and somatosensory[43] stimuli. This suggests that the medial OFC is a crucial center for the tracking of reward value of different reinforcers independent of modality, and for relating this value to hedonic experience. To study the impact of expertise on aesthetic judgments we recruited control subjects (i.e., subjects professing to have no great interest or expertise in art or architecture) and expert subjects (i.e., graduate students in architecture and professional architects) and asked them to rate the aesthetic value of a series of images containing respectively architecture and faces during an event-related fMRI paradigm.[44] We hypothesized that the expert-specific condition (i.e., architectural images) would significantly affect both aesthetic ratings and neural activity differentially in the two groups. Since earlier psychometric studies have found that people in different cultures, and of both sexes, tend to agree as to which faces are attractive,[45] we predicted that aesthetic ratings and neural processing would not differentiate between the two groups for face images. Therefore, an expertise effect on the neural structures underlying the formation of an aesthetic judgment would be evident, if parts of the network mentioned above were activated differentially in the group of architects when judging buildings, but not when judging faces (Fig. 13.2).

The behavioral responses (i.e., aesthetic ratings) collected during scanning revealed no significant differences between groups. To test if architectural expertise modulated brain activity associated with making aesthetic judgments, an analysis was employed that focused on brain regions where the difference between the responses for the two stimulus conditions varied across the two subject groups. This analysis revealed significant activations in the bilateral ACC and bilateral medial OFC. Experts had greater activation in the ACC and medial OFC when making aesthetic judgments of buildings, while activation levels for the same voxels for face stimuli in both groups were essentially balanced, suggesting that the observed effect depends on acquired expertise of architecture.

The presented data suggest that architectural expertise modulates the neural response to buildings even in the absence of any aesthetic rating differences between experts and non-experts. Architectural expertise modulated the response only to buildings, but not to faces, indicating that the expertise effect is specific to the domain of their expertise (i.e., buildings).

The expertise-modulated areas, the ACC and the medial OFC, have been implicated in other studies of aesthetic judgment. Thus, the present experiment demonstrates that expertise may not only affect perceptual or cognitive system, but can also change the response profile of brain areas important for forming an aesthetic judgment.

The fact that the medial part of the OFC shows sensitivity to the magnitude of aesthetic value is in accordance with studies on reward processing showing that the relative reward value of stimuli is reflected by the amplitude of neural activity

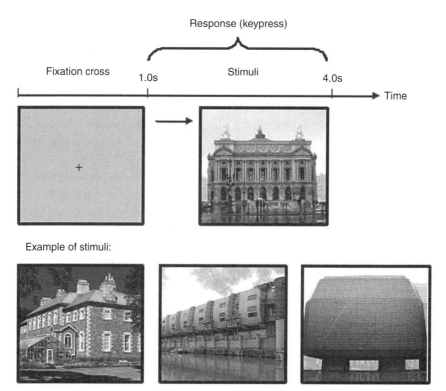

FIGURE 13.2 **Stimulus presentation paradigm.** *At the beginning of each trial a fixation cross was shown for 1,000 milliseconds, followed by stimulus presentation for 3,000 milliseconds, in which the subjects were instructed to press a key to indicate their aesthetic judgment (1–5). Examples of stimuli used during the scanning session are shown.*

in the OFC. For instance, in studies comparing subjects ingesting food in states of hunger and satiety, a contrast of these two states reveals different neural responses in the OFC, indicating that OFC neurons code rewarding aspects of a stimulus rather than sensory aspects.[46] The novelty of these results is that the representation of stimulus value, or possibly intrinsic motivation, in the medial OFC varies with expertise level such that the experts displayed higher activation to the building stimuli than the non-experts, but not to the control stimuli (i.e., faces). Activity in the ACC was also sensitive to expertise. It has been suggested that the ACC integrates affective drive and action strategies for the purpose of selecting appropriate motor responses (i.e., making decisions how to act).[47] One interpretation of the role of the ACC in aesthetic expertise might be that this region reflects the subjects' monitoring of their own emotional state, whereby architectural stimuli are more arousing to the experts than to the non-experts. The main result of this study indicates that separate reward regions involved with stimulus pleasure are differentially engaged as a function of expertise, but that the nucleus accumbens is equally activated in the two groups and thus seems to be a general response mechanism to salient stimuli that is not modulated by expertise.

Taken together, the findings described in this section have shown that the OFC is an important gateway to subjective conscious experience. The OFC could be viewed as having the role of evaluating the affective valence of stimuli. The reward value of a stimulus is assigned in the OFC, where it can be modulated by internal states such as hunger, and is recruited to influence subsequent behavior and made available for subjective hedonic experience. An aesthetic experience does not necessarily have a particular effect on our welfare and internal need state (as in contrast to primary rewards), but the data presented here suggest that different types of rewards such as aesthetic and hedonic experiences are coded in the OFC. However, as the OFC is a highly heterogeneous brain region, future neuroimaging and neuropsychological studies are likely to find more functional distinctions between its constituent parts.

Summary

The neuroaesthetic studies reviewed in this chapter were designed to expand our knowledge of the neurobiology of human hedonic experience by applying aesthetic stimuli to learn about the underlying neural mechanisms. The domain of motivation has been thought to be an area of neuroscience concerned with internal need states rather than with the processing of sensory information. But the representation of a visual aesthetic stimulus can be linked to the same neuronal mechanism that regulates the motivational state of an organism, thus connecting motivation to visual aesthetic inputs. When looking at neuroaesthetics from an empirical perspective, which has been the aim in this chapter, the prospects of the discipline are promising. The initial studies of neuroaesthetics presented in this chapter represent only a modest exploration of artistic styles and the underlying neurobiology of hedonic processes. In future studies one might investigate potential differences in sensory pathways in how artworks are processed and experienced as opposed to images of natural beauty such as a sunset. An equally interesting area of study is from the perspective of the artist, namely to investigate anatomical differences in visual areas such as area V4 in visual artists. From an empirical perspective neuroaesthetics is likely to continue to contribute new knowledge about the organization and functioning of the brain.

Endnotes

1. Hubel, D. H., & Wiesel, T. N. (1968). Receptive fields and functional architecture of monkey striate cortex. *Journal of Physiology, 195*, 215–243.

2. Zeki, S. (1973). Colour coding in the rhesus monkey prestriate cortex. *Brain Research, 53*, 422–427.

3. Zeki, S. (1978). Functional specialisation in the visual cortex of the rhesus monkey. *Nature, 274,* 423–428.

4. Zeki, S. (1999). *Inner vision.* New York: Oxford University Press.

5. Kanwisher, N., McDermont, J., & Chun, M. M. (1997). The fusiform face area: a module in human extrastriate cortex specilised for face perception. *Journal of NeuroScience, 17,* 4302–4311.

6. Zeki, S., & Lamb, M. (1997). The neurology of kinetic art. *Brain, 117,* 607–636.

7. Zeki, S., & Marini, L. (1998). Three cortical stages of colour processing in the human brain. *Brain, 121,* 1669–1685.

8. Kirk, U. (2008). Neural basis of object-context relationships on aesthetic judgment. *PLos ONE, 3,* e3754.

9. Vogeley, K., Kurthen, M., Falkai, P., & Maier, W. (1999). Essential functions of the human self model are implemented in the prefrontal cortex. *Consciousness Cognition, 8,* 343–363.

10. Hammacher, A. M. (1986). *Rene Magritte.* London: Thames & Hudson.

11. Weber, C. O. (1931). The aesthetics of rectangles and theories of affection. *Journal of Applied Psychology, 15,* 310–318.

12. Thompson, G. C. (1946). The effect of chronological age on aesthetic preference for rectangles of different proportions. *Journal of Experimental Psychology, 36,* 50–58.

13. Fechner, G. T. (1876). *Vorschule der Aesthetik* (Vol. I-II). Hildesheim: Olms.

14. Alanen, L (2003). *Descartes' concept of the mind.* Cambridge, MA: Harvard University Press.

15. Hartmann, E. (1924). *Philosophie des Schönen.* Berlin: Wegweiser.

16. Fechner, G. T. (1871). *Zur experimentalen Aesthetik.* Hildesheim: Olms.

17. Hartmann, E. (1886). *Die deutsche Ästhetik seit Kant.* Berlin: Ducker.

18. Ione, A. (2003). Examining Semir Zeki's Neural Concept Formation and art: Dante, Michelangelo, Wagner. *Journal of Consciousness Studies, 10,* 58–66.

19. Kawabata, H., & Zeki, S. (2004). Neural correlates of beauty. *Journal of Neurophysiology, 91,* 1699–1705.

20. Kirk, U., Skov, M., Hulme, O., Christensen, M. S., & Zeki, S. (2009). Modulation of aesthetic value by semantic context: an fMRI study. *Neuroimage, 44,* 1125–1132.

21. Danto, A (1964). The Artworld. *Journal of Philosophy, 61,* 571–584.

22. de Araujo, I. E., Rolls, E. T., Velazco, M. I., Margot, C., & Cayeux, I. (2005). Cognitive modulation of olfactory processing. *Neuron, 46,* 671–679.

23. McClure, S. M., Li, J., Tomlin, D., Cypert, K. S., Montague, L. M., & Montague, P. R. (2004). Neural correlates of behavioural preference for culturally familiar drinks. *Neuron, 44,* 379–387.

24. Plassmann, H. O., Doherty, J., Shiv, B., & Rangel, A (2008). Marketing actions can modulate neural representations of experienced pleasantness. *Proceedings of the National Academy of the Science U S A, 105,* 1050–1054.

25. Cain, W. S. (1979). To know with the nose: keys to odor identification. *Science, 203,* 467–470.

26. Russell, P. A. (2003). Effort after meaning and the hedonic value of paintings. *British Journal of Psychology, 94,* 99–110.

27. Erk, S., Spitzer, M., Wunderlich, A. P., Gally, L., & Waiter, H. (2002). Cultural objects modulate reward circuitry. *Neuroreport, 13,* 2499–2503.

28. O'Doherty, J. P., Critchley, H., Deichmann, R., & Dolan, R. J. (2003). Dissociating valence of outcome from behavioral control in human orbital and ventral prefrontal corti-ces. *Journal of Neuroscience, 23,* 7931–7939.

29. Lane, R. D. (1997). Neuroanatomical correlates of pleasant and unpleasant emotion. *Neuropsychologia, 35,* 1437–1444.

30. Cansino, S., Maquet, P., Dolan, R. J., & Rugg, M. D. (2002). Brain activity underlying encoding and retrieval of source memory. *Cerebral Cortex, 12,* 1048–1056.

31. Adcock, R. A., Thangavel, A., Gabrieli, A. W., Knutson, B., & Gabrieli, J. D. E. (2006). Reward-motivated learning: mesolimbic activation precedes memory formation. *Neuron, 50,* 507–517.

32. McWhinnie, H. J. (1966). Effects of a learning experience on preference for complex-ity and asymmetry. *Perception Motor Skills, 23,* 119–122.

33. Smith, J. D., & Melara, R. J. (1990). Aesthetic preference and syntactic prototypicality in music. *Cognition, 34,* 279–298.

34. Bourdieu, P (1979). *Distinction: a social critique of the judgment of taste.* Cambridge, MA: Harvard University Press.

35. Gombrich, E. H. (1995). *The story of art.* London: Phaidon.

36. Cupchik, G., & Laszlo, J (1992). *Emerging visions of the aesthetic process: psychology, semiology, and philosophy.* New York: Cambridge University Press.

37. Maguire, E. A., Gadian, D. G., Johnsrude, I. S., Good, C. D., Ashburner, J., Frackowiak, R. S., & Frith, C. D. (2000). Navigation-related structural change in the hippocampi of taxi drivers. *Proceedings of the National Academy of Sciences U S A, 97,* 4414–4416.

38. Bangert, M., Peschel, T., Schlaug, G., Rotte, M., Drescher, D., Hinrichs, H., Heinze, H. J., & Altenmuller, E. (2006). Shared network for auditory and motor processing in professional pianists: evidence from fMRI conjunction. *Neuroimage, 15,* 917–926.

39. Small, D. M., Zatorre, R. J., Dagher, A., Evans, A. C., & Jones-Gotman, M. (2001). Changes in brain activity related to eating chocolate: from pleasure to aversion. *Brain, 124,* 1720–1733.

40. Small, D. M., Gregory, M. D., Mak, Y. E., Gitelman, D., Mesulam, M. M., & Parrish, T (2003). Dissociation of neural representation of intensity and affective valuation in human gestation. *Neuron, 39,* 701–711.

41. Anderson, A. K., Christoff, K., Stappen, I., Panitz, D., Ghahremani, D. G., Glover, G., Gabrieli, J. D., & Sobel, N. (2203). Dissociated neural representations of intensity and valence in human olfaction. *Nature Neuroscience, 6,* 196–202.

42. Gottfried, J. A., Deichmann, R., Winston, J. S., & Dolan, R. J. (2002). Functional heterogeneity in human olfactory cortex: an event-related functional magnetic resonance imaging study. *Journal of Neuroscience, 22,* 10819–10828.

43. Rolls, E. T., Kringelbach, M. L., & de Araujo, I. T. (2003). Different representations of pleasant and unpleasant odours in the human brain. *European Journal of Neuroscience, 18,* 695–703.

44. Kirk, U., Skov, M., Nygaard, N., & Christensen, M. S. (2009). Brain correlates of aesthetic expertise: a parametric fMRI study. *Brain & Cognition, 69.* 306–315.

45. Langlois, J. H., Rubenstein, A. J., Larson, A., Hallam, M., & Smoot, M. (2000). Maxims or myths of beauty? A meta-analytic and theoretical review. *Psychological Bulletin, 126,* 390–423.

46. Kringelbach, M. L., O'Doherty, J. P., Rolls, E. T., & Andrews, C. (2003). Activation of the human orbitofrontal cortex to a liquid food stimulus is correlated with its subjective pleasantness. *Cerebral Cortex, 13,* 1064–1071.

47. Paus, T (2001). Primate anterior cingulate cortex: where motor control, drive and cognition interface. *Nature Reviews Neuroscience, 2,* 417–424.

14

Art Compositions Elicit Distributed Activation in the Human Brain

Alumit Ishai

"Indeed, the true miracle of the language of art is not that it enables the artist to create the illusion of reality. It is that under the hands of a great master the image becomes translucent. In teaching us to see the visible world afresh, he gives us the illusion of looking into the invisible realms of the mind—if only we know, as Philostratus says, how to use our eyes."[1]

With the advent of functional brain imaging techniques, especially functional magnetic resonance imaging (fMRI), a technique that permits the localization of regions that are activated during cognition, with fine spatial and temporal resolutions (millimeters and seconds, respectively), neuroscientists routinely investigate the neural mechanisms that mediate our experience of viewing and enjoying art. In order to "see the visible world afresh," we need to use not only our eyes, but, importantly, also our brain. In his book *Inner Vision*, Zeki suggested that both the nervous system and artists try to understand the essential visual attributes of the world. In the visual cortex, information is decomposed into such attributes as color, luminance, and motion. Similarly, many artists isolate and enhance such visual attributes in their work. Mondrian and Calder, for example, emphasized color and motion, respectively.[2] Although many artists have uncovered visual "modules" that are anatomically and functionally segregated in the brain, in my opinion Zeki's parallelism approach, although compelling, is oversimplified. When we view paintings, not only does our brain analyze the visual scene to identify familiar objects, but we also have an emotional reaction and we immediately assign aesthetic value to these paintings. Recent studies of art perception and memory suggest that when confronted with abstract or indeterminate art compositions, the human brain automatically solves the perceptual dilemma by generating predictions about their content based on familiar associations stored in memory. In this chapter, I will argue that viewing art is not a passive process, but rather a dynamic cognitive function that engages distributed cortical networks activated during the allocation of attention, mental imagery, and retrieval from memory. My fMRI studies provide, therefore, empirical evidence for Gombrich's suggestion that we use schemas when we view works of art—namely, we use stored structures of knowledge in order to form expectations (see also Chapter 1 by Shimamura).

Brain Evolution and the Origin of Art

The human brain has evolved over a period of 6 million years from the common ancestor of humans, apes, and other simians, to the appearance of *Homo sapiens sapiens* about 100,000 years ago.[3] Over that time, the architecture of the brain evolved to adapt to new functions and behaviors in response to complex encounters in the environment, while the mind formed an internalized model of this environment. Early humans made tools and socialized as the brain grew larger and its volume increased from 400 grams to 1,400 grams. Social interactions stimulated an ability to imagine the mind of others in order to predict their behavior. Language appeared about 250,000 years ago and its vocabularies and syntax became more sophisticated with time. Humans use language in distinctively different ways from the alarm calls used by animals because we have syntax—namely, we arrange words grammatically and embed qualifying clauses in sentences to demonstrate complex understanding of time, causation, connections, and relationships. Language is a sophisticated form of symbolic communication that allowed early humans to convey concrete, detailed information and abstract concepts and to cooperate and plan for the future, in order to ensure their survival.

It is unclear why, when, and how self-consciousness emerged, but around 135,000 years ago humans began to produce something different and exceptional: works of art. After using stones for tool-making for millions of years, humans started using bones and shells, which they fashioned into ornaments.[4] Some 30,000 years ago, cave paintings and ornamental sculptures began to appear at different sites across the world. Early visual art is surprisingly representational and informative. The famous Chauvet cave paintings are evidence of extraordinary figurative skill in depicting three-dimensional animals alive with movement, which were created with a distinctive individual style. Making sophisticated tools and using symbols both require the capacity to hold an abstract concept in one's mind and to impose a predetermined form on raw material based on an abstract mental template. In his book, Mithen proposes five properties for a definition of art in prehistory: like language, it contains symbols that are arbitrary in relation to their referents; it is created with the intention of communication; it operates outside the here and now of space and time; the meaning of symbols can be variable between individuals and cultures, or may carry multiple meaning; and the same symbols may vary as a result of individual mark-making.[3] Symbolic communication likely had an evolutionary advantage: it served as social glue that helped tribes of early humans to survive and reproduce. Art, from the prehistoric ornaments to Duchamp's *Fountain*, is therefore a medium intended to communicate meaning.[5]

Although it is widely accepted that art is a symbolic language, some challenge this notion. Based on the striking similarity in content and style of the cave art and the drawings of Nadia, an autistic girl who did not acquire spoken language but had an exceptional graphic ability, Humphrey argued that the naturalistic depictions are the result of lack of normal language development, in particular naming of animals and objects.[6] If indeed, as Humphrey suggests, language and graphic skills are partly incompatible, one would expect some anatomical and functional changes in the brain of children who can draw realistic animals from memory but cannot speak.

The Creative Brain

What is the neural basis of creativity? Do artists, with their unique ability to visualize and their imaginative and technical skills, have a "special" brain? With the advent of functional brain imaging techniques, such empirical questions can be routinely investigated. It is important to note, however, that most functional brain imaging studies of creativity have focused on creative problem-solving or on the brain of musicians, and only a very few have compared visual artists with non-artists. Converging evidence suggests that the creative brain is a result of right hemisphere specialization, which is manifested by anatomical changes in cortical thickness or volume of gray matter, and functional changes (i.e., differential patterns of neuronal activity). For example, when subjects solved verbal problems that required an insight, the "Aha!" moment was accompanied by increased activation, as measured with fMRI, in the anterior superior temporal gyrus, and a sudden burst of high-frequency (gamma-band) neural activity, as measured with EEG, in the same brain area, which was detected 0.3 seconds prior to the insight.[7] This distinct pattern of neural activity in the right anterior temporal region suggests that creative solutions require the integration of information across distant lexical or semantic relations, which enables seeing the problem in a new light.

The opportunity to scan the brains of living musicians revealed several structural and functional changes in their brain; musicians are therefore an excellent model for brain plasticity. Recent findings suggest that musicians have more gray matter than non-musicians in Heschl's gyrus, the region in the cerebral cortex that first receives auditory input.[8] Structural and functional specializations have been demonstrated across several sensory, motor, and higher-order association areas. These specializations are often instrument-specific and correlate with aspects of the training history, supporting the view that they are the result, rather than the cause, of skill acquisition.[9]

In some studies, artists were compared with non-artists while performing various cognitive tasks. Eye-movement recordings have shown that artists view pictures differently from laymen: they spend more time scanning structural and abstract features, whereas artistically untrained subjects look more at human features and objects.[10] A series of studies with the British portrait artist Humphrey Ocean have shown that when he draws, the fixations of his eyes are twice the duration of those when he is not drawing. Moreover, fMRI scans of his brain while he views faces revealed, relative to non-artists, decreased activation in the "fusiform face area," a region in the visual cortex that responds more to faces than to common objects, and increased activation in the prefrontal cortex. These findings suggest that the artist processes faces more efficiently and employs higher cognitive functions, such as associations and motor planning.[11]

It is important to emphasize that despite the accumulating evidence for neuro-anatomical changes, it is currently unknown what brain mechanisms enable gifted individuals to create art. The focus of my scientific research is not the artist, but, rather, the naïve observer. The main empirical question that interests me is how the brain interprets and experiences paintings, especially when the content is hardly recognizable. In my frequent visits to museums and art galleries across the world, when confronted with abstract and indeterminate paintings, I often find myself pondering the content of these paintings and search for familiar, recognizable visual forms. In an attempt to resolve the perceptual dilemma, I turn to the title, but alas many modern paintings come untitled or with meaningless titles. Inspired by my personal experience, I conducted a series of behavioral and fMRI studies in which the following issues were addressed: How does the brain process ambiguous paintings? Does aesthetic judgment depend on familiar content? Do titles affect the perception of art? Can training change our perception of art? In this chapter, I describe how visual information is represented in the brain, what happens in our brain when we imagine or retrieve from memory pictures of faces and objects, how the brain solves visual indeterminacy, and how training changes the way naïve observers view Cubist paintings.

How Do We Perceive and Imagine Faces and Objects?

The ability to recognize objects in the world is a highly developed visual skill in primates, and significant cortical resources are dedicated to the processing of visual information. Behavioral and electrophysiological studies in humans and monkeys suggest that object recognition is a rapid process that can be achieved within a few hundred milliseconds.[12] Moreover, identification of objects within natural scenes is facilitated when the context is meaningful—that is, it is more likely to find a teacup in the kitchen than in the shower.[13,14] The process of parsing the world into meaningful objects is mediated by activation in the ventral occipitotemporal cortex, the so-called "what" pathway, which is dedicated to object recognition.[15,16] Recent functional brain imaging studies in humans have shown that objects and faces elicit activation in a distributed cortical network that encompasses a wide expanse of the visual ventral stream.[17-19] Within the ventral stream, faces and animals evoke stronger activation in the lateral fusiform gyrus, a region along the ventral visual pathway (see Chapter 1), whereas houses and tools evoke stronger activation in the medial fusiform gyrus.[17,20-22] Interestingly, ambiguous figures,[23] illusory contours,[24] and binocular rivalry[25] also evoke activation in object-responsive regions in the visual cortex, suggesting that the visual system imposes top-down (namely prior knowledge) interpretations on ambiguous bottom-up (namely sensory) retinal input (some examples are illustrated in Chapter 1).

Visual imagery is the ability to generate percept-like images in the absence of retinal input and therefore is a vivid demonstration of retrieving pictorial information from memory. The subjective similarity of seeing and imagining suggests that perception and imagery share common internal representations. Psychophysical and brain imaging studies have demonstrated functional similarities between visual perception and visual imagery, to the extent that common mechanisms appear to be activated by both.[26-30] Numerous neuroimaging studies have shown that visual imagery, like visual perception, evokes activation in occipito-parietal and occipito-temporal visual association areas.[31] In some imagery studies, the primary visual cortex was activated,[32,33] suggesting that the generation of mental images may involve sensory representations at the earlier processing stages in the visual pathway. Studies of patients with brain damage have demonstrated a dissociation of visual–object and visual–spatial imagery,[34] indicating that different parts of the visual system mediate "where" and "what" imagery, a dissociation that parallels the two anatomically distinct visual systems proposed for visual perception.[15] Although many studies have focused on the overlap and similarities between perception and imagery, the subjective experience of imagining and seeing is clearly different. It has been shown that during visual imagery, deactivation in the auditory cortex is negatively correlated with activation in the visual cortex and with the score of subjective vividness of visual imagery. Thus, to generate vivid mental images, the brain needs to filter out irrelevant sensory information.[35]

In a series of fMRI studies we compared perception of faces and objects with visual imagery of faces and objects. Subjects viewed pictures of faces, houses, or chairs or imagined familiar faces, houses, and chairs. During visual imagery, object-specific patterns of activation were found, but this activity was restricted to small sectors of the regions that responded differentially during perception. The generation of mental images of familiar faces from long-term memory evoked activation within small subsets of the lateral fusiform gyrus, a face-responsive region, whereas generating mental images of houses and chairs evoked activation within subsets of the medial fusiform and inferior temporal gyri, respectively.[36] Similarly, studies in non-human primates indicate that the temporal lobe is the memory storehouse for visual representations of complex stimuli.[37] Visual imagery also evoked activation within a network of parietal and frontal regions, that include the precuneus, intraparietal sulcus, and inferior frontal gyrus, regions that were implicated in various attention and retrieval from episodic memory tasks.[38,39] These findings suggest that retrieval of content-specific memory traces, stored in the ventral pathway, is top-down controlled by a parieto-frontal network that mediates the generation and maintenance of mental images.[36]

We then asked how these visual, parietal, and prefrontal cortices are connected.[40] Analysis of effective connectivity among these cortical regions revealed that dynamic neuronal interactions between occipito-temporal, parietal, and frontal regions are task- and stimulus-dependent. Sensory representations of faces and objects in ventral extrastriate cortex are mediated by bottom-up mechanisms arising in early visual areas during perception, and top-down mechanisms originating in the prefrontal cortex during imagery. Additionally, non-selective, top-down processes, originating in superior parietal areas, contribute to the generation of mental images and their maintenance in the "mind's eye."[41]

Face recognition is a highly developed skill in primates and the cognitive development of face perception suggests a special status for face processing. The recognition of facial identity is based on invariant facial features, whereas animated aspects of the face, such as speech-related movement and expression, contribute to social communication. When looking at faces, we rapidly perceive the gender, expression, age, and mood. Processing information gleaned from the faces of others, therefore, requires the integration of activity across a network of cortical regions. Converging empirical evidence suggests that face perception is mediated by activation within a distributed neural system.[42–45] The cortical network for face perception includes regions along the ventral pathway (the inferior occipital gyrus and lateral fusiform gyrus), which process the identification of individuals;[20] regions along the dorsal pathway (the superior temporal sulcus), where gaze direction and speech-related movements are processed;[46] limbic regions (the amygdala and insula), where facial expressions are processed;[47,48] frontal regions (the inferior frontal gyrus), where semantic aspects are processed;[36,49] and regions of the reward circuitry, including the nucleus accumbens and orbito-frontal cortex, where facial beauty and sexual relevance are assessed.[50–53]

Famous faces represent a special class of stimuli because they are highly associated with rich pictorial and contextual information (e.g., Angelina Jolie's face elicits associations about her appearance in various movies, her liaison with Brad Pitt, her children, and her humanitarian work in Africa). When subjects view faces of contemporary Hollywood celebrities, activation is found in the inferior occipital gyrus, lateral fusiform gyrus, superior temporal sulcus, and amygdala, regions of the distributed network that mediates face perception.[42,43,54] Interestingly, when famous faces are compared with unfamiliar faces, activation is found in the parahippocampal cortex, a region that mediates contextual associations.[55] When subjects generate mental images of famous faces, activation is observed in small subsets of these face-responsive regions. Moreover, visual imagery of famous faces activates a network of regions that includes the calcarine, precuneus, hippocampus, intraparietal sulcus, and inferior frontal gyrus.[56] Taken collectively, these studies suggest that visual mental imagery is a multicomponent cognitive process that requires reactivation of specific representations stored in the visual cortex and their maintenance in the "mind's eye." It is therefore not surprising that the "imagery network" comprises parietal and frontal regions that also mediate attention and memory retrieval. We have recently discovered that viewing indeterminate art compositions also elicits activation within these imagery-related regions.[57]

Representational Paintings and Recognition Memory

Learning about a new category of stimuli requires experience with multiple instances that define that category. For example, encounters with very few paintings from Picasso's "Blue Period" is sufficient for the correct categorization of a new, never-seen-before Blue Period painting. As category learning and recognition memory require matching novel items with stored ones, we hypothesized that both are mediated by activation in a distributed cortical network, and used event-related fMRI to test whether matching between novel exemplars and familiar prototypes depends on their visual similarity. Our experimental approach combined explicit category learning with a recognition memory task, and an original set of stimuli, namely art compositions by painters with a unique style: portraits by Modigliani and Renoir, landscapes by Pissarro and Van Gogh, and abstract paintings by Kandinsky and Miro. In the training session, subjects were told that paintings from each artist belonged to a category of paintings with a characteristic signature and were instructed to learn and memorize these prototypes. Four days later, in the fMRI test session, subjects were presented with the familiar prototypes and with new exemplars and indicated whether they had seen these pictures before. The new exemplars were either visually similar to the prototypes, somewhat similar (ambiguous), or different. We predicted fast and accurate responses to the new, dissimilar exemplars, and slower, less accurate responses to the new, similar and ambiguous exemplars, due to their visual resemblance to the prototypes. Moreover, we predicted that activation in the visual cortex and in parietal and prefrontal regions would be modulated by the degree of visual similarity, and expected reduced activity with decreased visual similarity between the new exemplars and the familiar prototypes.

Our results show that, on average, 72% of the prototypes were correctly recognized and that responses to the novel items were faster and more accurate with decreased similarity to the prototypes.[58] In the visual cortex, the paintings evoked activation in face- and object-selective regions, where familiar prototypes elicited stronger activation than the new exemplars. Consistent with our hypothesis, in the intraparietal sulcus and superior parietal lobule, responses evoked by new exemplars were reduced with decreased similarity to the prototypes. In memory-related areas, two patterns of activation were observed: in the caudate, insula, and anterior cingulate cortex, the familiar prototypes elicited stronger activation than the new items, whereas in the precuneus, superior temporal, and superior frontal gyri the new, visually different exemplars evoked stronger activation. Finally, in the

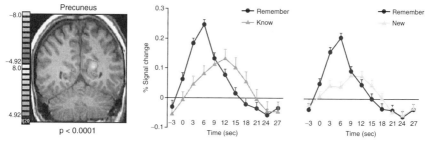

FIGURE 14.1 **Recollection and familiarity reflect memory strength.** *Subjects performed a flower detection task on portraits, landscapes, and abstract paintings, and 10 minutes later were surprised with a memory test. The previously seen paintings were presented with new paintings that were either visually similar to or visually different from the old ones. For each painting, subjects had to report whether they remember it, it looks familiar, or it is new. Activation in the precuneus showed that correctly remembered old paintings evoked stronger activation than both paintings that looked familiar and new, never-seen-before paintings. It therefore seems that recollection reflects strong memories, whereas familiarity reflects weak memories.*

hippocampus, the similar items evoked weaker activation than the other novel exemplars. These findings suggest that recognition memory is mediated by activation in a cortical network that includes regions in visual cortex where stimulus-specific representations are stored, attention-related areas where visual similarity to familiar prototypes is detected, and memory-related areas where new items are classified as a match or a mismatch based on their similarity to familiar prototypes.[58]

Our recognition memory task required subjects to simply report whether a painting was old or new. We did not address the issue of memory processes, namely to what extent the subject's decision was based on recollection, namely the retrieval of specific information about a past experience, or familiarity, namely a sense that an event has been previously experienced. We therefore designed a new event-related fMRI study to investigate whether recollection- and familiarity-based memory decisions are modulated by the degree of visual similarity between old and new paintings. Subjects viewed, in the MR scanner, portraits, landscapes, and abstract paintings and had to decide whether each painting contained a flower. Ten minutes later, they received a surprise memory test, in which the old paintings were randomly presented with new paintings that were either visually similar to or visually different from the old ones. Subjects had to decide whether they remember the picture, the picture looks familiar, or whether it's a new picture they've never seen before. Consistent with our prediction, subjects were significantly faster and more accurate at detecting new, visually different paintings than new, visually similar ones. The proportion of false alarms, namely "remember" and "know" responses to new paintings, was significantly reduced with decreased visual simi-larity. The retrieval task evoked activation in multiple visual, parietal, and prefron-tal regions, within which "remember" judgments elicited stronger activation than "know" judgments. New, visually different paintings evoked weaker activation than new, visually similar items in the intraparietal sulcus. Contrasting recollec-tion with familiarity revealed activation predominantly within the precuneus, where the BOLD response elicited by recollection peaked significantly earlier than the BOLD response evoked by familiarity judgments (Fig. 14.1). These findings suggest that successful memory retrieval of pictures is mediated by activation in a distributed cortical network, where memory strength is manifested by differential hemodynamic profiles. Recollection- and familiarity-based memory decisions may therefore reflect strong memories and weak memories, respectively.[59]

Visual Indeterminacy and the Brain

Visual indeterminacy occurs when we view apparently detailed and vivid images that resist object recognition. Indeterminate art compositions invoke an unusual state of awareness in which the formal aspects of perception (color, form, motion) become dissociated from the semantic aspects (association, meaning, memory). In contrast with the habitual mode of seeing, in which visual sensation is accom-panied by immediate recognition, the indeterminacy effect presents viewers with an apparently meaningful yet persistently meaningless scene, which they struggle to resolve. Robert Pepperell's paintings and drawings were designed to induce a disrupted perceptual condition: instead of a recognizable depiction, the viewer is presented with a "potential image"[60]—that is, a complex multiplicity of possible images, none of which ever finally resolves. Traditional abstract compositions, which do not depict natural objects, use purely visual forms of line, color, and shape to evoke emotional and aesthetic responses, whereas Pepperell's indeterminate paintings strongly imply natural forms, while at the same time resisting easy or immediate recognition (Fig. 14.2). The indeterminacy effect is achieved by omit-ting suggestively rendering forms, such as bodies, buildings, and mountains, from which visual cues might facilitate recognition.[61]

In collaboration with Pepperell, we designed a series of new studies in order to investigate the indeterminacy effect. In a behavioral study, subjects performed object recognition and judgment of aesthetic affect tasks while viewing represen-tational paintings by various artists and indeterminate paintings by Pepperell. Response latencies were significantly longer for indeterminate images, and sub-jects perceived recognizable objects in 24% of these paintings. Although the aes-thetic affect rating of all paintings was similar, reaction times for the indeterminate paintings were significantly longer. A surprise memory test revealed that more representational than indeterminate paintings were remembered and that affective strength increased the probability of subsequent recall, suggesting that meaningful

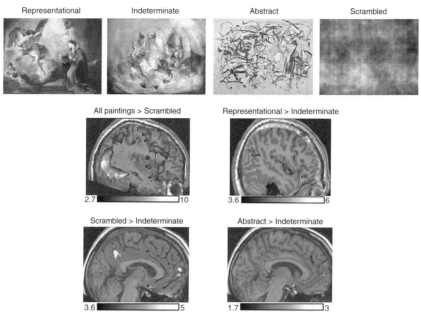

FIGURE 14.2 **Activation evoked by paintings.** *Viewing paintings as compared with scrambled pictures elicits activation in a distributed network of visual, limbic, parietal, and frontal regions. Comparing representational with indeterminate paintings revealed activation in the temporoparietal junction, a region that mediates the allocation of spatial attention across visual scenes. Comparing scrambled pictures with indeterminate paintings and abstract paintings with indeterminate ones revealed activation in the precuneus and medial frontal gyrus, regions that mediate the generation and maintenance of mental images from long-term memory. (Fairhall, Scott L., and Ishai, Alumit. (2008). Neural correlates of object indeterminacy in art compositions. Consciousness and Cognition. 17 (3), 923–932. doi: 10.1016/J.CONCOG.2007.07.005. Used with permission of the publisher.)*

content is critical for incidental memory. These findings show that perception and memory of art depend on semantic aspects, whereas aesthetic affect depends on formal visual features. The longer latencies associated with indeterminate paintings reflect the underlying cognitive processes that mediate object resolution. Indeterminate art works therefore comprise a rich set of stimuli with which the neural correlates of visual perception can be investigated.[62]

We then conducted an fMRI study in which subjects performed an object recognition task on three classes of paintings: representational, which explicitly depict complex scenes with familiar objects (people, animals, landscapes, still life); indeterminate, in which familiar objects are only suggestive; and abstract, which do not depict any familiar objects (Fig. 14.2). We hypothesized that subjects would rapidly recognize familiar objects depicted in representational paintings, but would be slower to report the presence or absence of recognizable objects in abstract and indeterminate paintings. Moreover, we predicted a posterior-to-anterior gradient of activation along the ventral visual pathway, such that with increased recognition of familiar content in the paintings, differential activation would be observed in more anterior, higher-tier, object-selective areas. Finally, we postulated that indeterminate paintings would invoke visual imagery-related activation in parietal and prefrontal cortices. Our subjects rapidly recognized familiar objects in representational paintings, but showed longer reaction times to indeterminate and abstract images. These differential response latencies suggest an automatic recognition of objects when they were explicitly depicted, but required more effortful cognitive processes when the objects were ambiguous or suggestive.[57] All paintings evoked activation within a distributed cortical network that included regions in the visual cortex, as well as parietal, limbic, and prefrontal regions (Fig. 14.2). Consistent with our hypotheses, representational paintings with meaningful content evoked stronger activation than abstract and indeterminate paintings in the fusiform gyrus, a region that responds to assorted common objects, including faces, houses, animals, and tools.[17,19,22] Our results are consistent with a recent study in which enhanced activation in the fusiform gyrus was observed when representational paintings were compared with filtered paintings.[63] The indeterminate paintings, when compared with the representational and the abstract compositions, evoked less activation in the right hippocampus.[57] This reduced activation may reflect the poor encoding of the indeterminate paintings, consistent with our previous study, in which subjects recalled significantly fewer indeterminate than representational paintings in a surprise memory task.[62]

To further identify the neural correlates of object indeterminacy, we compared activation evoked by scrambled paintings with activation evoked by the indeterminate paintings. We found that the scrambled paintings evoked enhanced activation in the precuneus and the medial frontal gyrus, regions of the "imagery network" that mediate the generation and maintenance of mental images from long-term memory.[36,38,41,56] Post-scanning debriefing revealed that most subjects used mental imagery during the perception of the scrambled paintings in order to decide whether the images contained any familiar objects. In contrast, to decide whether the indeterminate paintings, which were rich with suggestive objects, contained any recognizable objects, subjects relied on visual similarity and visual associations.

A direct comparison of representational and indeterminate artworks revealed significant activation in the temporo-parietal junction (TPJ), a region that has been implicated in exerting attentional control over switches from local to global processing,[64] and the allocation of spatial attention across the visual scene.[65] The enhanced activation within the TPJ for representational paintings reflects the binding of object form and spatial location within these cluttered visual scenes. Thus, the recognition of meaningful, familiar content in artworks is mediated by activation in the TPJ. Incidentally, the left TPJ was also activated by "beautiful" rather than "neutral" paintings.[66]

Our fMRI study shows that perception of art compositions evokes activation in multiple visual regions, the hippocampus, intraparietal sulcus, and inferior frontal gyrus. Content-related modulation in the fusiform gyrus reflects object perception, whereas hippocampal activation reflects memory consolidation. Imagery-related activation was observed for scrambled paintings. Finally, interpreting composite scenes relies on higher-order associations in the TPJ, which links the various elements of the visual scene. It therefore seems that the human brain is a compulsory object viewer, which automatically segments indeterminate visual input into coherent images. To resolve the visual indeterminacy, higher cognitive functions, such as attention, visual imagery, and memory retrieval, are recruited.

Object Recognition in Cubist Paintings

To the naïve observer, Cubist paintings contain geometrical forms in which familiar objects are hardly recognizable, even in the presence of a meaningful title. In Cubist artworks, objects are broken up, analyzed, and reassembled to produce abstracted forms, which often depict the same objects from different viewing points. We conducted a new study to test the extent to which a short training session about Cubism would facilitate object recognition in paintings by Picasso, Braque, and Gris (Fig. 14.3). We hypothesized that subjects who received training would recognize familiar objects faster than control subjects and would exhibit stronger activation in object-responsive and attention-related regions. Our subjects, students from the University of Zurich, had no formal art education and reported visiting art museums once a year or less. A meaningful title or the word "untitled" appeared before each Cubist painting, and subjects had to answer the question "Do you recognize any familiar objects?" by pressing one of two buttons (Yes/No), then the question "How many objects did you recognize?" by pressing one of four buttons to indicate "0," "1," "2" or "3 or more" objects. Thirty minutes before scanning, half the subjects received a short training session, during which they were presented with information about Cubism, viewed examples of Cubist paintings, and practiced recognizing familiar objects in these paintings.

Relative to the control group, trained subjects recognized significantly more objects in the paintings and their response latencies were significantly shorter. Moreover, trained subjects took longer to report not recognizing any familiar objects in the paintings. Cubist paintings evoked activation in a distributed cortical network that included extrastriate, parietal, and prefrontal regions. Within the parahippocampal cortex, trained subjects showed a significantly larger spatial extent of activation and a parametric increase in the amplitude of the fMRI signal as a function of the number of objects they recognized (Fig. 14.3). We also found that in trained subjects, the longer response latencies associated with failing to recognize familiar objects were correlated with activation in a fronto-parietal network that mediates spatial attention.[67]

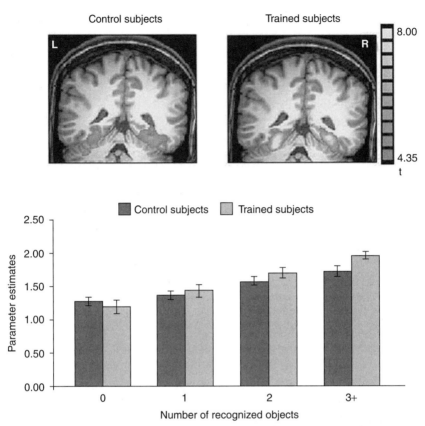

FIGURE 14.3 **Training facilitates object recognition in Cubist paintings.** *Subjects performed an object recognition task on Cubist paintings and indicated how many objects they recognized. Relative to the control group, the subjects who received a short training session on Cubism reported seeing more objects; activation in their parahippocampal cortex, a region that mediates contextual associations, was significantly stronger; and they showed a parametric increase in the amplitude of the fMRI signal as a function of the number of objects they recognized.*

The most surprising and intriguing finding in our study is the enhanced activation in the parahippocampal cortex of trained subjects. This region, implicated in the representation and processing of spatial navigation information,[68] episodic memory,[69] and remote spatial memories,[70] is a major node in the cortical network for contextual associations.[55] Associations are formed over time, when repeated patterns and statistical regularities are extracted from the environment and stored in memory. It has been recently suggested that the role of associations is to generate predictions about the immediate future in order to guide behavior.[71] It is highly likely that due to the short training session, our subjects used contextual associations to perform the tasks. Importantly, our findings provide empirical evidence for Bayesian analysis, which was proposed as a model for object perception[72] and evoked cortical responses.[73,74] According to the Bayes perspective, the short training session enabled our subjects to match the indeterminate visual input with their top-down predictions. It is reasonable to assume that trained subjects were more likely than control subjects to suppress errors and establish a consensus between the actual bottom-up input and the top-down prediction. Thus, minimizing prediction error resulted in faster recognition of more familiar objects in Cubist paintings.

The extent to which titles do or should influence the perception of meaning and the aesthetic impression of art compositions is contentious. In art theoretical terms, critics of a formalist persuasion claim that titles are merely "identification tags" that should not affect the viewer's reading of the work. Others, however, claim titles function as guides to interpretation and provide important contextual cues to engage the attention of the viewer.[1,75] Empirical evidence suggests that titles influence both the understanding and the appreciation of paintings.[76] In a compelling example of the top-down effects of titles on art perception, viewers' description of the content of paintings varied according to the title (e.g., "Agony" vs. "Carnival") they were presented with.[77] In our experiment, Cubist paintings were preceded by their meaningful title or by the word "Untitled." We found that meaningful titles facilitated object recognition, but only in trained subjects. Thus, relative to control subjects, trained subjects reported recognizing more familiar objects in paintings with meaningful titles. These findings suggest that meaningful titles can provide the top-down solution for ambiguous visual input, but only when prior knowledge or experience exists. Taken together, these observations suggest that recognition of familiar content in artworks is a skill acquired through training.

Summary

Using fMRI while subjects performed object recognition and memory retrieval tasks with various classes of paintings, we have shown that the perceptual experience of artworks is not a mere bottom-up process of visual analysis, but, rather, a higher cognitive function that requires top-down mechanisms such as mental imagery, memory retrieval, and contextual associations. The human brain is not a passive viewer of works of art, but a dynamic interpreter that constantly generates predictions about the content and its meaning based on previous encounters with similar visual input. Understanding the content of modern paintings is an acquired, context-dependent skill. It is perhaps not surprising that our emotional response to works of art is also influenced by knowledge and context, as suggested by recent studies of aesthetic judgment of paintings.[78] If indeed art was evolved as a medium for communication by symbols, it seems that with time, as these non-linguistic symbols become more and more detached from their referents, the human brain had to recruit additional cortical resources to comprehend their meaning.

Acknowledgments

The author is supported by the Swiss National Science Foundation grant 32003B–105278 and by the Swiss National Center for Competence in Research: Neural Plasticity and Repair.

Endnotes

1. Gombrich, E. (1960). *Art and illusion: a study in the psychology of pictorial representation*. London: Phaidon Press.

2. Zeki, S. (1999). *Inner vision: an exploration of art and the brain*. New York: Oxford University Press.

3. Mithen, S. (1996). *The prehistory of the mind: a search for the origins of art, religion and science*. London: Thames and Hudson.

4. Vanhaereny, M., d'Errico, F., Stringer, C., James, S. L., Todd, J. A., & Mienis, H. K. (2006). Middle Paleolithic shell beads in Israel and Algeria. *Science, 312*, 1785–1788.

5. Ede, S. (2005). *Art & science*. London, New York: I. B. Tauris.

6. Humphrey, N. (1998). Cave art, autism, and the evolution of the human mind. *Cambridge Archeological Journal, 8*, 165–191.

7. Jung-Beeman, M., Bowden, E. M., Haberman, J., Frymiare, J. L., Arambel-Liu, S., Greenblatt, R., Reber, P. J., & Kounios, J. (2004). Neural activity when people solve verbal problems with insight. *PLoS Biology, 2*, 500–510.

8. Schneider, P., Sluming, V., Roberts, N., Scherg, M., Goebel, R., Specht, H. J., Dosch, H. G., Bleeck, S., Stippich, C., & Rupp, A. (2005). Structural and functional asymmetry of lateral Heschl's gyrus reflects pitch perception preference. *Nature Neuroscience, 8*, 1241–1247.

9. Stewart, L. (2008). Do musicians have different brains? *Clinical Medicine, 8*, 304–308.

10. Vogt, S., & Magnussen, S. (2007). Expertise in pictorial perception: eye-movement patterns and visual memory in artists and laymen. *Perception, 36*, 91–100.

11. Solso, R. L. (2001). Brain activities in a skilled versus a novice artist: an fMRI study. *Leonardo, 34*, 31–34.

12. Thorpe, S., Fize, D., & Marlot, C. (1996). Speed of processing in the human visual system. *Nature, 381*, 520–522.

13. Biederman, I. (1972). Perceiving real-world scenes. *Science, 177*, 77–80.

14. Bar, M. (2004). Visual objects in context. *Nature Review Neuroscience, 5*, 617–629.

15. Ungerleider, L.G., & Mishkin, M. (1982). Two cortical visual systems. In: D. J. Ingle, M. A. Goodale, & R. J. W. Mansfield (Eds.), *Analysis of visual behavior*. Cambridge, MA: MIT Press.

16. Haxby, J. V., Horwitz, B., Ungerleider, L. G., Maisog, J. M., Pietrini, P., & Grady, C. L. (1994). The functional organization of human extrastriate cortex: a PET-rCBF study of selective attention to faces and locations. *Journal of Neuroscience, 14*, 6336–6353.

17. Ishai, A., Ungerleider, L. G., Martin, A., Schouten, J. L., & Haxby, J. V. (1999). Distributed representation of objects in the human ventral visual pathway. *Proceedings of the National Academy of Sciences U S A, 96,* 9379–9384.

18. Ishai, A., Ungerleider, L. G., Martin, A., & Haxby, J. V. (2000). The representation of objects in the human occipital and temporal cortex. *Journal of Cognitive Neuroscience, 12,* 35–51.

19. Haxby, J. V., Gobbini, M. I., Furey, M. L., Ishai, A., Schouten, J. L., & Pietrini, P. (2001). Distributed and overlapping representations of faces and objects in ventral temporal cortex. *Science, 293,* 2425–2430.

20. Kanwisher, N., McDermott, J., & Chun, M. M. (1997). The fusiform face area: a module in human extrastriate cortex specialized for face perception. *Journal of Neuroscience, 17,*: 4302–4311.

21. Aguirre, G. K., Zarahn, E., & D'Esposito, M. (1998). An area within human ventral cortex sensitive to building stimuli: Evidence and implications. *Neuron, 21,* 1–20.

22. Chao, L. L., Haxby, J. V., & Martin, A. (1999). Attribute-based neural substrates in posterior temporal cortex for perceiving and knowing about objects. *Nature Neuroscience, 2,* 913–919.

23. Kleinschmidt, A., Buchel, C., Zeki, S., & Frackowiak, R. S. (1998). Human brain activity during spontaneously reversing perception of ambiguous figures. *Proceedings of the Royal Society B: Biological Sciences, 265,* 2427–2433.

24. Stanley, D. A., & Rubin, N. (2003). fMRI activation in response to illusory contours and salient regions in the human lateral occipital complex. *Neuron, 37,* 323–331.

25. Tong, F., Nakayama, K., Vaughan, J. T., & Kanwisher, N. (1998). Binocular rivalry and visual awareness in human extrastriate cortex. *Neuron, 21,* 753–759.

26. Roland, P. E., Eriksson, L., Stone-Elander, S., & Widen, L. (1987). Does mental activity change the oxidative metabolism of the brain? *Journal of Neuroscience, 7,* 2373–2389.

27. Farah, M., Peronnet, F., Gonon, M. A., & Giard, M. H. (1988). Electrophysiological evidence for a shared representational medium for visual images and visual percepts. *Journal of Experimental Psychology: General, 117,* 248–257.

28. Ishai, A., & Sagi, D. (1995). Common mechanisms of visual imagery and perception. *Science, 268,* 1772–1774.

29. Ishai, A., & Sagi, D. (1997). Visual imagery facilitates visual perception: Psychophysical evidence. *Journal of Cognitive Neuroscience, 9,* 476–489.

30. Ishai, A., & Sagi, D. (1997). Visual imagery: effects of short- and long-term memory. *Journal of Cognitive Neuroscience, 9,* 734–742.

31. Mellet, E., Tzourio, N., Crivello, F., Joliot, M., Denis, M., & Mazoyer, B. (1996). Functional anatomy of spatial mental imagery generated from verbal instructions. *Journal of Neuroscience, 16,* 6504–6512.

32. Le Bihan, D., Turner, R., Zeffiro, T., Cuendo, C., Jezzard, P., & Bonnerot, V. (1993). Activation of human primary visual cortex during visual recall: A magnetic resonance imaging study. *Proceedings of the National Academy of Sciences U S A, 90,* 11802–11805.

33. Kosslyn, S. M., Alpert, N. M., Thompson, W. L., Maljkovic, V., Weise, S. B., Chabris, C. F., Hamilton, S. E., Rauch, S. L., & Buonanno, F. S. (1993). Visual mental imagery activates topographically organized visual cortex: PET investigations. *Journal of Cognitive Neuroscience, 5,* 263–287.

34. Levine, D. N., Warach, J., & Farah, M. (1985). Two visual systems in mental imagery: Dissociation of what and where in imagery disorders due to bilateral posterior cerebral lesions. *Neurology, 35,* 1010–1018.

35. Amedi, A., Malach, R., & Pascual-Leone, A. (2005). Negative BOLD differentiates visual imagery and perception. *Neuron, 48,* 859–872.

36. Ishai, A., Ungerleider, L. G., & Haxby, J. V. (2000). Distributed neural systems for the generation of visual images. *Neuron, 8,* 979–990.

37. Miyashita, Y., & Chang, H. S. (1988). Neural correlate of pictorial short-term memory in the primate temporal cortex. *Nature, 331,* 68–70.

38. Fletcher, P. C., Frith, C. D., Baker, S. C., Shallice, T., Frackowiak, R. S. J., & Dolan, R. J. (1995). The mind's eye: precuneus activation in memory-related imagery. *Neuroimage, 2,* 195–200.

39. Buckner, R. L., Raichle, M. E., Miezin, F. M., & Petersen, S. E. (1996). Functional anatomic studies of memory retrieval for auditory words and visual pictures. *Journal of Neuroscience, 16,* 6219–6235.

40. Mechelli, A., Price, C. J., Noppeney, U., & Friston, K. J. (2003). A dynamic causal modeling study on category effects: bottom-up or top-down mediation? *Journal of Cognitive Neuroscience, 15,* 925–934.

41. Mechelli, A., Price, C. J., Friston, K. J., & Ishai, A. (2004). Where bottom-up meets top-down: neuronal interactions during perception and imagery. *Cerebral Cortex, 14,* 1256–1265.

42. Haxby, J. V., Hoffman, E. A., & Gobbini, I. M. (2000). The distributed human neural system for face perception. *Trends in Cognitive Sciences, 4,* 223–233.

43. Ishai, A., Schmidt, C. F., & Boesiger, P. (2005). Face perception is mediated by a distributed cortical network. *Brain Research Bulletin, 67,* 87–93.

44. Ishai, A., & Yago, E. (2006). Recognition memory of newly learned faces. *Brain Research Bulletin, 71,* 167–173.

45. Ishai, A. (2008). Let's face it: it's a cortical network. *NeuroImage, 40,* 415–419.

46. Puce, A., Allison, T., Bentin, S., Gore, J. C., & McCarthy, G. (1998). Temporal cortex activation in humans viewing eye and mouth movements. *Journal of Neuroscience, 18,* 2188–2199.

47. Vuilleumier, P., Armony, J. L., Driver, J., & Dolan, R. J. (2001). Effects of attention and emotion on face processing in the human brain: an event-related fMRI study. *Neuron, 30,* 829–841.

48. Ishai, A., Pessoa, L., Bikle, P. C., & Ungerleider, L. G. (2004). Repetition suppression of faces is modulated by emotion. *Proceedings of the National Academy of Sciences U S A, 101,* 9827–9832.

49. Leveroni, C. L., Seidenberg, M., Mayer, A. R., Mead, L. A., Binder, J. R., & Rao, S. M. (2000). Neural systems underlying the recognition of familiar and newly learned faces. *Journal of Neuroscience, 20,* 878–886.

50. Aharon, I., Etcoff, N., Ariely, D., Chabris, C. F., O'Connor, E., & Breiter, H. C. (2001). Beautiful faces have variable reward value: fMRI and behavioral evidence. *Neuron, 32,* 537–551.

51. O'Doherty, J., Winston, J., Critchley, H. D., Perrett, D., Burt, D. M., & Dolan, R. J. (2003). Beauty in a smile: the role of medial orbitofrontal cortex in facial attractiveness. *Neuropsychologia, 41,* 147–155.

52. Kranz, F., & Ishai, A. (2006). Face perception is modulated by sexual preference. *Current Biology, 16,* 63–68.

53. Ishai, A. (2007). Sex, beauty and the orbitofrontal cortex. *International Journal of Psychophysiology, 63,* 181–185.

54. Fairhall, S. L., & Ishai, A. (2007). Effective connectivity within the distributed cortical network for face perception. *Cerebral Cortex, 17,* 2400–2406.

55. Bar, M., Aminoff, E., & Ishai, A. (2008). Famous faces activate contextual associations in the parahippocampal cortex. *Cerebral Cortex, 18,* 1233–1238.

56. Ishai, A., Haxby, J. V., & Ungerleider, L. G. (2002). Visual imagery of famous faces: effects of memory and attention revealed by fMRI. *NeuroImage, 17,* 1729–1741.

57. Fairhall, S. L., & Ishai, A. (2008). Neural correlates of object indeterminacy in art compositions. *Consciousness and Cognition, 17,* 923–932.

58. Yago, E., & Ishai, A. (2006). Recognition memory is modulated by visual similarity. *Neuroimage, 31,* 807–817.

59. Wiesmann, M., & Ishai, A. (2008). Recollection- and familiarity-based memory decisions reflect memory strength. *Frontiers in Systems Neuroscience, 2,* 1.

60. Gamboni, D. (2002). *Potential images: ambiguity and indeterminacy in modern art.* London: Reaktion Books.

61. Pepperell, R. (2006). Seeing without objects: visual indeterminacy and art. *Leonardo, 39,* 394–400.

62. Ishai, A., Fairhall, S. L., & Pepperell, R. (2007). Perception, memory and aesthetics of indeterminate art. *Brain Research Bulletin, 73,* 314–324.

63. Vartanian, O., & Goel, V. (2004). Neuroanatomical correlates of aesthetic preference for paintings. *Neuroreport, 15,* 893–897.

64. Fink, G. R., Halligan, P. W., Marshall, J. C., Frith, C. D., Frackowiak, R. S. J., & Dolan, R. J. (1996). Where in the brain does visual attention select the forest and the trees? *Nature, 382,* 626–628.

65. Corbetta, M., Kincade, M. J., Lewis, C., Snyder, A. Z., & Sapir, A. (2005). Neural basis and recovery of spatial attention deficits in spatial neglect. *Nature Neuroscience, 8,* 1603–1610.

66. Kawabata, H., & Zeki, S. (2004). The neurology of beauty. *Journal of Neurophysiology, 91,* 1699–1705.

67. Wiesmann, M., & Ishai, A. (2010). Training facilitates object recognition in Cubist paintings. *Frontiers of Human Neuroscience, 2:4,* 11.

68. Epstein, R., & Kanwisher, N. (1998). A cortical representation of the local visual environment. *Nature, 392,* 598–601.

69. Gabrieli, J. D., Brewer, J. B., Desmond, J. E., & Glover, G. H. (1997). Separate neural bases of two fundamental memory processes in the human medial temporal lobe. *Science, 276,* 264–266.

70. Spiers, H. J., & Maguire, E. A. (2007). The neuroscience of remote spatial memories: a tale of two cities. *Neuroscience, 149,* 7–27.

71. Bar, M. (2007). The proactive brain: using analogies and associations to generate predictions. *Trends in Cognitive Sciences, 7,* 280–289.

72. Kersten, D., Mamassian, P., & Yuille, A. (2004). Object perception as Bayesian inference. *Annual Review of Psychology, 55,* 271–304.

73. Friston, K. J., Harrison, L., & Penny, W. (2003). Dynamic causal modeling. *NeuroImage, 19,* 1273–1302.

74. Friston, K. (2005). A theory of cortical responses. *Philosophical Transactions of the Royal Society of London B Biological Sciences, 360,* 815–836.

75. Fisher, J. (1984). Entitling. *Critical Inquiry, 11,* 286–298.

76. Leder, H., Carbon, C. C., & Ripsas, A. L. (2006). Entitling art: influence of title information on understanding and appreciation of paintings. *Acta Psychologica (Amsterdam)*, *121*, 176–198.

77. Franklin, M. B., Becklen, R., & Doyle, C. (1993). The influence of titles on how paintings are seen. *Leonardo, 26*, 103–108.

78. Kirk, U., Skov, M., Hulme, O., Christensen, M. S., & Zeki, S. (2009). Modulation of aesthetic value by semantic context: an fMRI study. *NeuroImage, 44*, 1125–1132.

15

A Cognitive and Behavioral Neurological Approach to Aesthetics

Zachary A. Miller and Bruce L. Miller

Introduction

BEHAVIORAL NEUROLOGY

As a discipline, cognitive and behavioral neurology attempts to explain underlying mechanisms of cognition and behavior via the study of patients with neurological disease. Observations from patients with neurological disease have yielded critical understandings of both the structure and generation of many cognitive processes. Some of these processes, like memory and language production, have been rigorously studied and characterized as deficits in these processes can reveal themselves quite plainly.[1] Meanwhile, other behaviors, like musical and artistic abilities, are more challenging to study, as they likely represent a composite of cognitive processes and deficits per se may be harder to detect. Additionally, as individuals vary enormously depending on their exposure to the arts and their natural talents, it may be quite difficult to generalize the lessons learned in one person to another.[2] Yet, an underlying precept of behavioral and cognitive neuroscience is that the vast array of expression and production of humanity—no matter how sublime, elusive, or ephemeral—is derived from our central nervous system, and that with further study, we may be able to elucidate that which was previously thought to be inaccessible: aesthetics and the creative mind.

DEFINING AESTHETICS

Defining aesthetics and artistic ability is not a trivial endeavor, particularly when the definition depends on a subjective assessment based upon what the artist produces. What one person may classify as creative or engaging another may label as unremarkable or mundane. In the attempt to define aesthetics and artistry from a neurological perspective, Dr. Semir Zeki, professor of neurobiology at the Univeristy College of London, created the field neuroaesthetics. He and his colleagues approached the study of aesthetics from a neural basis ranging from appreciation to production of artwork, stating that:

> "the artist is in a sense, a neuroscientist, exploring the potentials and capacities of the brain, though with different tools. How such creations can arouse aesthetic experiences can only be fully understood in neural terms. Such an understanding is now well within our reach . . . neuroscientists would do well to exploit what artists, who have explored the potentials and capacities of the visual brain with their own methods, have to tell us in their works. Because all art obeys the laws of the visual brain, it is not uncommon for art to reveal these laws to us, often surprising us with the visually unexpected."[3]

Thus, artistic experience can be viewed as a continuum extending from sensory input to production. As a philosophical approach to the study of aesthetics, neuroaesthetics fits well with the clinical observations considered in this chapter. Measured changes in our patients' artworks, as evidenced by both the quantity and quality of their creative output, may actually represent changes in how they perceive and appreciate visual phenomenon—that is to say, their aesthetic sensibilities.

In this chapter, we present observations of individuals who developed new artistic impulses and modes of expression in the course of neurodegenerative disease. Through studying these patients we found that particular qualities of their disease appeared to predispose these remarkable individuals to altered aesthetic responses and increased desire to produce compelling works of art. We focus primarily on the skill sets and abilities necessary for the appreciation and production of the visual arts. In particular, we highlight the behaviors of a subset of patients suffering from left-sided frontotemporal degeneration and in whom altered artistic impulses emerge, despite the presence of progressive cognitive losses in other domains. However, prior to this discussion it may be helpful to appreciate some of the finding that neurologists have previously employed to explain these complex behaviors.

THE CULT OF ARTISTIC GENIUS

Historically, a significant amount of attention on aesthetics and artistry has focused on anecdotal observations of persons deemed by society as "creative geniuses." Famous examples include artists (Van Gogh and Picasso), musicians (Ravel), authors (Dostoevsky), and scientists (Einstein). Studies of their lives have revealed surprisingly similar histories of disease: childhood learning disabilities in Picasso and Einstein, manic depression in Van Gogh, epilepsy in Dostoevsky, and progressive aphasia in Ravel.[4,5,6,7,8] These initial anecdotal observations led to broader studies and surveys of artistic individuals—actors, musicians, writers, and visual artists—that found a higher incidence of psychological conditions like schizophrenia, bipolar disorder, or substance abuse than in the general population.[9,10] Conversely, other studies discovered that individuals with mental illness were more disposed towards expressive careers and endeavors.[11] These observations suggest a link between creativity and psychological disease, with certain individuals prone to heightened appreciation and abilities within the arts as a consequence of unique brain wiring that may be associated with psychological disease. Nevertheless, there are plenty of examples of artistic individuals of every sort who are the epitome of psychological fitness.

Other surveys have suggested that left-handed individuals may have greater aptitudes for visuospatial processing citing a higher percentage of left-handed individuals enrolled in art school or working as architects than in the general population.[12,13] However, with these enhanced abilities in left-handed individuals also comes greater likelihood of having verbal learning disabilities. In fact, it is theorized that the two processes are intrinsically connected. Norman Geschwind and colleagues proposed that in the process of developing left-handedness an underdevelopment of the left hemisphere, where language functioning tends to reside, necessarily facilitated development of right-sided brain functions, leading to greater sensitivity towards the visual experience.[14,15]

While these observations among conditions such as handedness, mood disorders, and artistry remain compelling within our popular consciousness, it is difficult to determine the exact nature and the significance of these relationships. Unlike these previous investigations, the examples we focus on in this chapter are of individuals who were not selected for their previous talents, aptitudes, or innate abilities, but rather were observed to have developed remarkable changes in behavior in the setting of known brain disease.

Behavioral Anatomy of the Brain

ANATOMY IMPLIES FUNCTIONALITY BUT FALLS SHORT

The human brain is composed of approximately 100 billion neurons, each of which has 7,000 synaptic connections.[16] The average human brain retains roughly the same configuration of sulci, gyri, and fissures. The human brain can be subdivided into three major structures: the brain stem, cerebellum, and cerebral hemispheres.[17] We will focus exclusively on the cerebral hemispheres, as in general the cerebral hemispheres are implicated in higher-level processing and integration of information. The hemispheres are comprised of the frontal, temporal, limbic, parietal, and occipital lobes. Classically, the frontal lobes are implicated in higher-level processing, the temporal lobes in processing auditory information and storing memory, the parietal lobes in processing somatosensory information, visuoconstruction, and musical skill, the occipital lobes in receiving visual information, and the limbic lobes in facilitating connections between the lobes and the other regions of the brain as well as emotional processing.[18,19,20] The frontal lobes can be divided further into three structural and functional units: the orbitofrontal, dorsolateral, and medial frontal cortices. These regions are respectively responsible for behavioral inhibition, executive functioning, and motivation.[21] As our discussion focuses on the integration, processing, and storage of visual information, we will focus our discussion on the connections among the frontal, temporal, and parietal lobes.

Much of our understanding of regional functionality derived from lesion observation and or experiment.[22,23] While this approach was critical in establishing a framework of neuroanatomical functionality, lesional based studies have fallen short of adequately explaining behavior and cognition. In particular, lesions are not restricted to boundaries of functionality and may result in mixed behavioral features. Furthermore, while brain lesions account nicely for what happens in the absences of a particular structure, they do not fully account for the normal functions of the untouched structure.

With the advent of functional MRI, however, the study of normal or even enhanced function was now possible. Observations of brain activity, in near real-time, revealed that vast and seemingly disparate areas of brain tissue were activated at the same time during particular tasks. Ultimately, the collection of these interconnections, or circuits, led to a model of the brain as a series of neural networks that together encompass all behavioral and cognitive processes.[24] A detailed network-based map of the brain is still in development, as new networks are being discovered all the time. At this time some of the best-characterized networks include:

"(1) a right hemisphere-dominant spatial attention network with epicenters in dorsal posterior parietal cortex, the frontal eye fields, and the cingulate gyrus; (2) a left hemisphere-dominant language network with epicenters in Wernicke's and Broca's areas; (3) a memory-emotion network with epicenters in the hippocampo-entorhinal regions and the amygdaloid complex; (4) an executive function-comportment network with epicenters in lateral prefrontal cortex, orbitofrontal cortex, and posterior parietal cortex; and (5) a face-and-object identification network with epicenters in lateral temporal and temporopolar cortices.[25]"

LATERALIZATION AS A MEANS OF FURTHER SUBSPECIALIZATION

In addition to these different anatomical regions of the brain, each structure is paired, with a left and a right side. The paired nature of our cerebral hemispheres allows for even greater subspecialization of function of within each particular region. The richest source of lateralized behavior research comes from Drs. Sperry and Gazzaniga's seminal observational studies of "split brain" patients in the 1960s. Drs. Sperry and Gazzaniga performed a series of neuropsychological tests on subjects who had undergone partial resections of their corpus callosum (effectively splitting their brains in half) with the intention of treating intractable epilepsy. Their results reveal that the left side of the brain is important for language, logical reasoning, grammar, verbal memory, and calculations, whereas the right side of the brain is generally more important for gestalt conceptualization, prosody of speech, visual manipulation, auditory processing, social cognition, and face and emotion perception.[26]

Beyond functional differences that exist between left and right there is also a great deal of evidence to show that each side may act in part to balance out or even antagonize the other side. For example, a seizure stimulating the left insula can cause symptomatic bradycardia (slowing of the heart) due to the hyperactivity of left-sided control of vagal tone. This effectively overrides the balance between left and right sides of the brain on the heart rate.[27] Meanwhile, patients with damage to that same region can develop tachycardia (racing of the heart) secondary to unopposed action of the right side on heart rate. Thus when working together left and right sides of the brain produce a buffered response. When one side is dominant this system may lean towards a tendency of behavior that the other side might normally dampen much like the actions of a seesaw.

THE RIGHT-SIDED AND POSTERIOR ANATOMY OF VISUOSPATIAL ABILITIES

Within the cerebral hemispheres, right-sided and posterior regions of the brain are most closely linked to the talents and abilities required to visually appreciate, encapsulate, manipulate, retrieve, and recreate: mental capacities necessary for the generation of a visual composition. These might also be implicated in a higher degree of sensitivity to and appreciation of artistic endeavors. Furthermore, there is reason to believe that left-sided and frontal activities may antagonize or inhibit these behaviors. This argument has been invoked in part to explain how substance abuse and mood disorders could facilitate artistic behavior (by reducing activity in the frontal lobes) and how being left-handed would provide easier access to creative endeavors given right-brain dominance, but again these observations are highly speculative.[28]

There are a handful of notable observations of artists who have suffered from either ischemic or neurodegenerative disease.[29,30] In one patient, right hemispheric damage completely abrogated previously attained skills in drawing or painting, whereas in a patient with similarly positioned but left-sided damage these abilities remained intact.[31] Further, a patient whose artistic style was highly symbolic, almost linguistic, lost the ability to create works of art in this previous style but retained the ability to copy and draw following a left-sided stroke.[32]

Similarly, there are accounts of famous artists suffering from neurodegenerative disorders who have developed significant changes in their artistic style with progression of disease. Cummings and Zarit observed that early in the course of Alzheimer's disease artistic and musical skills tended to deteriorate significantly.[33]

They postulated that Alzheimer's disease's known predilection for the parietal lobes that resulted in this rapid loss of ability.[34] This decline was famously detailed in the case of Willem de Kooning, a renowned Abstract Expressionist painter, who continued to produce artwork while suffering from a ravaging neurodegenerative condition presumed to be Alzheimer's disease. As his disease progressed, stylistic changes were noted. Over time, his paintings displayed simpler and freer forms of his characteristic approach.[35] It has been argued that de Kooning was able to maintain his artistic output only with great effort from his caregivers, who went so far as to place brushes with paint in his hand. Critics argue that without such a structured environment he would have likely followed the usual pattern of deteriorating production typical of Alzheimer's disease.[36]

Within the realm of neurodegenerative diseases there is an identifiable group of patients with reproducible patterns of disease who can serve as a model by which to explore more fully the multiple facets of artistry. Most of the observations have come in patients suffering from progressive deficits in speech due to left-sided temporal or frontal damage—leaving the right-sided and posterior regions intact, the exact regions previously implicated in artistic ability. And thus dementia has become perhaps our most significant model for understanding the behavioral and cognitive features of the artistic process.

Dementia as a Model for Understanding Behavior and Cognition

DEFINING DEMENTIA

Neurodegeneration refers to the death of nervous tissue; given enough burden of neuronal death, clinical symptoms will arise. When these clinical features involve cognitive and behavioral deficits, the syndrome is labeled a dementia.[37] Unlike the apoplectic presentations of stroke, neurodegenerative disease presents in an insidious manner and as such provides the unique opportunity not only to appreciate lesional aspect of deficits but also to see the evolution of functional changes in neural networks that are created by a particular lesion. Both the rate and the pattern of change can vary dramatically based on the type of neurodegenerative disease. In the majority of cases, neurodegenerative disease starts off focally and then expands diffusely, ultimately resulting in global deterioration of cognitive abilities and function and even death. This is the case in Alzheimer's disease, the most common from of dementia in persons age 65 and older, as well as other famous but less common conditions like Parkinson's disease and dementia with Lewy bodies.[38]

In stark contrast to this pattern of disease, there is a unique subset of neurodegenerative diseases that start off focally and generally remain focal, proceeding in a manner that respects those initial focal boundaries until quite late in the disease. This group of diseases has been named frontotemporal lobar degeneration (FTLD), derived from the anatomical locations the disease process attacks. Although at one time FTLD was thought to represent only a minor subset of all neurodegenerative conditions, it is believed to be either the most common or second most common form of neurodegenerative disease in persons younger than 65. Also, in contrast to the more global pattern of cognitive decline as seen in typical Alzheimer's disease, patients with FTLD generally develop more focal deficits, with sparing of function in unaffected brain regions.[39] Detailed neuropsychological testing has even revealed improvement of functions within the spared regions of brain tissue.[40] Even more striking are the reports of seemingly new and productive abilities in the setting of neurodegeneration, observations that a generation ago would have very likely been viewed as heretical when describing dementia.[41]

FRONTOTEMPORAL LOBAR DEGENERATION

FTLD actually represents a heterogeneous collection of different diseases, and as such FTLD is commonly considered an umbrella term referring to the underlying pathology of disease. Within the FTLD spectrum there are several clinical syndromes that selectively affect the frontal and temporal lobes. These syndromes include frontotemporal dementia (FTD) as well as other conditions like progressive supranuclear palsy and corticobasal degeneration. FTD can be further subdivided based on the clinical picture and pattern of brain atrophy. At this time there are three commonly accepted types of frontotemporal dementia: behavioral, non-fluent, and semantic variants.[42]

1. The behavioral variant of frontotemporal dementia (bvFTD) often presents with dramatic changes in personality and behavior: loss of empathy and disgust, hyperorality, poor personal hygiene, and significant disinhibition. These behaviors are as a result of bilateral atrophy in the frontal lobes (more so than temporal), most significantly the ventral and medial portions of the frontal lobes.

2. The semantic dementia variant (SD) leads to progressive loss of word meaning in the setting of preserved fluency. In addition to the prominent language symptoms, SD patients often display notable rigid behaviors and compulsions. They also have a tendency to manifest new-onset and prominent depression. SD is typically an asymmetrical process and generally affects the left side more so than the right. In contrast to bvFTD, SD tends to affect the temporal lobes more than frontal lobes. As such, in the past SD has been referred to as the temporal variant of FTD. SD may also involve structures like the insula, amygdala, and anterior hippocampus.

3. Lastly, the progressive nonfluent aphasia variant (PNFA) generally presents with progressive halting of speech that ultimately progresses to pure mutism. In contrast to bvFTD and SD, patients with PNFA tend to

have less severe behavioral presentations and in general are closer to patients with Alzheimer's than the other FTD variants in this respect.[43,44] PNFA is often caused by atrophy of the left frontal, insular, and parietal regions of the brain.

Overall, these disease conditions are caused by the abnormal accumulation of proteins, which can include tau, TDP-43, FUS, and even beta amyloid—the underlying pathological entity found in Alzheimer's disease.[45]

Left-Sided FTD and Art

FASTIDIOUS AND PRODUCTIVE: IMPLICATIONS OF SEMANTIC DEMENTIA FOR VISUOSPATIAL ABILITIES

In contrast to Alzheimer's disease, patients with FTD are able to maintain copying and drawing abilities due to the relative sparing of posterior structures.[46] Some of the first descriptions of new and/or heightened visual abilities in the setting of FTD came from Miller (1996) and Snowden (1996) and their associates.[47,48] Following up on this work, in a 1998 *Neurology* publication Miller and colleagues described a subset of FTD patients with predominant temporal lobe involvement, all of whom seemed to have developed new onset of visual art productivity in the setting of their FTD. Continuing with this line of investigation, in a 2000 publication in the *British Journal of Psychiatry*, Miller and colleagues described a total of 12 individuals suffering from FTD who developed new abilities or maintained their previous talents in musical and visual tasks, in contrast to 46 other FTD patients in whom these abilities were not witnessed. Of these 12 patients who had retained or developed nascent artistic abilities, 8 had common anatomical pathology, namely temporal disease. Seven were left-sided and the eighth had bilateral temporal involvement.[49] As such, while the majority of patients with FTD may not display increased interest in visuospatial tasks, there is a significant minority or subset of FTD patients with mainly left-sided temporal disease who may be compelled to show off their preserved and perhaps newfound talents.

These patients displayed striking similarities in the content and quality of their work. These similarities in content may speak directly to a change in the aesthetic sensibilities of these patients. In general, these patients' artworks tended to focus on detailed and photorealistic representations of landscapes, animals, and people. There was a notable absence of symbolic or abstract qualities in their work (Fig. 15.1). Further, most approached their creations with a surprisingly high degree of focus. Patients often became fixed on their compositions, obsessively working and reworking their creations, often to the detriment of all other aspects of life. The clinicians who observed these behaviors felt that these patients were displaying pathological obsessive and compulsive tendencies and noted other obsessive and compulsive behaviors, including coin collecting, spitting, picking teeth, and

FIGURE 15.1 *Three examples from Miller, B., Cummings, J., Mishkin, F., Boone, K., Prince, F., Ponton, M., & Cotman, C. (October 1998). Emergence of artistic talent in frontotemporal dementia.* Neurology, 51(4), 978–982.

copying the Bible, to name a few.[50] As opposed to minimizing the importance of compulsive behavior in the creative process, they argued that compulsion may play a vital role in explaining this differential of interest in patients with temporal disease, as it is often crucial to successful and skilled artistic endeavors. Indeed, the compulsion to paint or draw singularly focused subject matter has been hypothesized to be among the most likely mechanisms explaining the incredible talents displayed in artistic savants, and it certainly could play a major role in the abilities displayed by these FTD patients.[51,52]

PROPOSED MECHANISM OF ENHANCED ARTISTIC ABILITIES

To explain this surprising pattern of seemingly enhanced artistic abilities in the setting of known brain injury, Miller and colleagues postulated that these patients' lesions might be inducing a paradoxical functional facilitation. This term, coined by Kapur in 1996, describes the *paradoxical* observation of improvement in performance in a selective domain in the setting of neurological insult.[53]

Neurologically, observations are considered *paradoxical* when disease of the nervous system causes enhancement of function as opposed to worsening of abilities. For example, a focal ischemic stroke in the motor cortex will lead to paralysis of the contralateral limb. However, in this same example, in addition to paralysis, the affected limb also exhibits a release or enhancement of its deep tendon reflex activity.[54] In this scenario, if the neuroanatomy and circuitry were not already well characterized, this phenomenon of increased reflex activity might reasonably be interpreted as paradoxical. As such, while it may be surprising to see cognitive dysfunction in one region strengthening or releasing behavioral abilities in another region, it is certainly not unfounded.

Miller and colleagues speculated that the witnessed enhanced artistic abilities resulted from both intact right-sided and posterior functions (functional anatomy that accounts for visuospatial talents) and spared dorsolateral and medial frontal cortices (functional anatomy that could account respectively for the added organizational abilities and motivation needed to be able to appreciate, integrate, and ultimately create a composition).[55] This theory was based in part on the analysis of the atrophy patterns between the patients who were felt to display artistic abilities versus their non-artistic colleagues. Single photon emission computed tomography (SPECT) perfusion scans of these so-called artistic patients revealed a shared pattern of atrophy that was essentially limited to the temporal lobes with relative sparing of frontal lobes, whereas the non-artistic cohort tended to have widespread disease with extensive frontal and temporal hypoperfusion on SPECT analysis. To say that the artistic cohort of patients had relative sparing of disease in the frontal lobes is not to say that their frontal lobes were not involved: actually, this group of patients showed orbitofrontal atrophy with sparing of dorsolateral and anterior cingulate cortices. In fact, this differential involvement of the frontal lobes— isolated orbitofrontal involvement releasing dorsolateral and medial frontal activities—was thought to explain why the artistic patients were so capable or even driven to express themselves and perhaps why the non-artistic patients were not.

As to the aesthetic choices these artistic patients displayed, with similar subject matter and detailed photorealistic reproduction, it is difficult to speculate on an exact mechanism that led to such convergence. Nevertheless, it is well established that the frontal lobes play critical roles in both emotional processing and judging aesthetic value. In healthy patients, Zeki and colleagues performed analyses that revealed a direct correlation between orbitofrontal cortex activation and the extent of visual appeal an image carried for that particular individual.[56] Given the selective orbitofrontal disease of our artistic FTD patients, it is likely that their disease patterns affected the frontal lobe circuitry that is normally responsible for mediating aesthetic responses. As such, it is likely that frontal lobe disease either significantly contributed to or even directly resulted in these common features of expression.

Despite these patients' increased propensity towards creation, most experts felt that the quality of production in patients with FTD revealed diminished creativity. As the frontal lobes have been implicated in functions like abstract thinking, most researchers believed that decreased creativity should be the norm in patients with FTD.[57] Indeed, it may be that the diminished creativity noted in this group of patients is mediated by changes in their frontal lobe circuitry that in turn lead to changes in their aesthetic value judgment enhancing the drive toward realistic expression. An assertion like this is speculative and requires more testing, but becomes even more compelling when compared to the cases described below of similarly affected FTD patients in whom essentially the opposite behavioral phenomena occurs: changes in the frontal lobes that mediate diminished interest in representationalism and perhaps increased creativity.

CREATIVE AND INNOVATIVE: PROGRESSIVE NONFLUENT APHASIA'S ROLE IN THE ARTISTIC PROCESS

Miller and colleagues characterized a subset of patients with FTD who appeared to have actually become more creative in the setting of their disease.[58] These patients were also diagnosed with primary progressive aphasia, but as opposed to the semantic variant they were felt to have met criteria for the nonfluent subtype. The artworks produced by these patients with PNFA deviate away from realism and instead appear to be more expressive than their previous works. In fact, the extent to which their artistic style changed brought up the question as to whether or not these patients were actually developing novel means of aesthetic appreciation rather than just manipulating or releasing prior abilities.

In a 2003 case report in *Neurology*, Dr. Chang and colleagues followed a Chinese American woman who had studied painting in college, obtained an MFA, and worked as a high school art teacher. She subsequently developed primary progressive aphasia over the course of 15 years. During this process her artistic style changed dramatically from the calm, restrained, and measured traditional of Chinese Eastern brush paintings to wildly expressive, bold, and haunting figurative works (Fig. 15.2).[59] While it is difficult to speculate on the exact nature or reason for her stylistic change, there is no doubt that this patient displayed new interest in emotive and disturbing imagery and created works of haunting beauty in the context of her disease.

We can, however, speculate on the mechanisms behind another patient's remarkable stylistic changes. In the case of Anne Adams, Dr. Seeley and colleagues detailed the evolution of disease progression alongside the evolution of personal

FIGURE 15.2 *Two examples from Mell, J. C., Howard, S. M., & Miller, B. L. (2003). Art and the brain: the influence of frontotemporal dementia on an accomplished artist.* Neurology, 60, 1707–1710.

artistic style. Mrs. Adams suffered from primary progressive aphasia, developing nonfluent speech with poor grammar as her disease progressed. Importantly, in her case, the researchers had serial brain images chronicling the nature of change that took place (including an image serendipitously obtained, for unrelated reasons, many years prior to the onset of her disease) (Fig. 15.3). Analysis of these images revealed changes in both structural and functional brain images that documented left frontal atrophy that directly corresponded to localized growth of neural tissue in her right parietal lobe. For the first time in the liturgy of thought on artistic appreciation and production, the authors were able to correlate one patient's artistic production directly with the progression of left frontal disease; furthermore, they were able to show that this left frontal disease not only released right-sided posterior activity but actually appears to have potentiated or enhanced right-sided posterior activity, as evidenced by both the growth of neural tissue and increased perfusion of these regions.

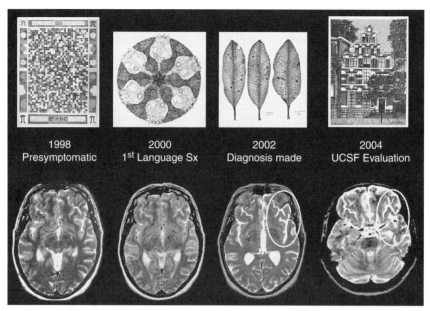

FIGURE 15.3 **The progression of the patient's artistic style and disease.** *The paintings are paired with brain MRIs from that same year. The circled area reveals the significant atrophy pattern, which is most evident in the widening of the left sylvian fissure. The brain MRIs are displayed in the usual radiographic manner with the left side of the page referring to the right side of the brain, as if you were looking at the patient lying in the scanner with her feet towards you and her head in the scanner. Of note, the first image was obtained for reasons unrelated to and before the onset of her cognitive complaints and as such is considered presymptomatic. The titles of the paintings across the top from left to right are pi, R, Arbutus, and* Amsterdam. *Gouache. (Seeley, W. W., et al. [2008]. Brain, 131, 39–49; doi:10.1093/brain/awm270)*

The authors hypothesized that these findings revealed the presence of a network involving connections between the left inferior frontal cortex and right parietal lobe. Based on the lesion-related increased volume of cortical gray matter in the right parietal lobe, they believed that in normal healthy individuals left-frontal activity was actually inhibiting right-sided posterior functions. They also felt that her remarkable stylistic changes not only were a consequence of released inhibition, or paradoxical facilitation, but might also be explained by the formation of new neuronal connections. This supposition was based on the statistically significant changes in perfusion and tissue volume found in her right parietal lobe (an area of brain tissue implicated in the processing and integration of sensory modalities). At the so-called creative peak of her artistic career Anne Adams began to create works of art that reflected an integration of auditory and visual stimuli (Fig. 15.4). The fact that her aesthetic experience rigidly adhered to a newfound internal logic—translating the qualities of an auditory process into a visual experience

FIGURE 15.4 **Unravelling Boléro.** *Gouache. (Seeley, W. W., et al. [2008].* Brain, *131, 39–49; doi:10.1093/brain/awm270)*

with aspects of tone and volume becoming color and form—was believed to be a consequence of the changes that had taken place during her disease. In particular, the quality of synesthesia she displayed, where one primary sensory modality automatically triggers another, might have been a direct consequence of this focal expansion of neural tissue in the parietal lobes engendering cross-modal connections and further bolstering her abilities to develop such a composition.

This painting was an ode to Ravel's famous composition *Boléro.* Ravel, unbeknownst to the patient, was believed to have suffered from primary progressive aphasia, the same condition as Anne Adams. Furthermore, the musical composition *Boléro* is seen as the best example of artistic style change associated with his disease. As her disease progressed, the quality of Anne Adams' artwork began to change again. During the more advanced stages of her disease, she began to create works that were photorealistic in nature, a pattern of stylistic change that is similar to that of our SD patients previously characterized (Fig. 15.5).[60] Her disease course and the associated changes in artistic style and aesthetic sensibilities provide the greatest evidence to date that left-sided frontotemporal atrophy affects networks that can engender both creativity and photorealistic compulsion, respectively. More importantly, in the example of Anne Adams, we see how the various facets of artistry, aesthetics, and creativity may exist within us all as a delicate balance of tendencies towards novel innovation and compulsions to create.

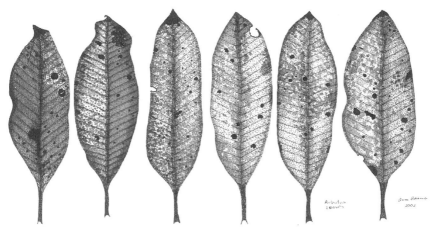

FIGURE 15.5 **Arbutus.** *Gouache. (Seeley, W. W., et al. [2008]. Brain, 131, 39–49; doi:10.1093/brain/awm270)*

Future Directions

DIAGNOSING ARTISTRY

In the past, neurological characterization of the artistic process has been undermined by both those who believe it is impossible to measure genius and by those whose explanations lacked academic rigor. As a field, cognitive and behavioral neurology has attempted to investigate the neural underpinnings of artistry and visuospatial abilities showing how the artistic process can be viewed as an aggregate of functions that can be broken down and targeted for systemic investigation. We believe that this aggregate exists on a spectrum that extends from appreciation to production and consists of a series of neural networks that have connections between the left frontotemporal regions and the posterior portions of the right hemisphere.

Clinically, we have witnessed and documented how various aspects of artistic ability can be manipulated by and evolve as a consequence of neurologic disease— revealing inherent modes or tendencies of expression. At this time, persons suffering from selective left frontal and temporal disease may represent the best model yet to study artistry, as these individuals can have sparing of other cognitive domains and even potentiation of new-onset artistic abilities. Further, depending on the pattern of left frontal and temporal disease, patients may be more likely to develop expressive and novel forms or may develop a tendency toward realistic representations. Investigations into these types of patients have already yielded major advances in our understanding. Now there is even evidence to suggest enhancement of right posterior parietal lobe activity as a direct consequence of left frontal lobe disease. Taken together, this implies neural circuitry in which the left frontal lobe, when functioning normally, inhibits contralateral parietal activity. With disease of the left frontal lobe, there is release of this inhibition, which leads to enhanced function of the right parietal lobe. The existence of this neural circuitry illustrates that these artistic abilities are not limited to geniuses but rather are readily available to and inherent in us all.

WHICH CAME FIRST, ARTISTRY OR DISEASE?

There were also some additional noteworthy features in the temporal-variant FTD patients. One third were left-handed, and more than half (n = 7) suffered from depression (depressive features are a well-known consequence of SD-related pathology). Again, while the associations between left-handedness, mood disorder, and artistry remain nebulous, their relationship remains strong. Actually, the strength of this relationship gives rise to the theory that there may be predisposing features that lead to increased vulnerability to selective types of neurodegenerative disorders, like primary progressive aphasia. There are clearly established risk factors that predispose individuals to neurodegenerative conditions, including genetic polymorphisms and repeated head trauma. Likewise, in FTD, it has been speculated that persons with left-sided frontotemporal disease may have unique predisposing vulnerabilities; as mentioned before, left-handed individuals have been shown on average to have higher rates of verbal learning disabilities, and as such they may be more susceptible to diseases that lateralize to the left side of the brain.[61] In several of the patients described by Miller and colleagues there was a known history of language dysfunction that well preceded the onset of their neurodegenerative disease. It remains a longstanding question as to whether the disease process is specific to particular networks, or rather particular networks are more susceptible to the disease process. Is it possible that language difficulties exhibited early in life (manifested by dyslexia, stuttering, or difficulty spelling) are facilitating the remodeling of posterior brain regions that enhance the ability to appreciate visual stimuli?

In conclusion, we have shown why we believe that patients with FTD provide us with the best chance to uncover the hidden process of artistic creation, from aesthetic impression to production. With further investigation into the abilities of these patients we may one day be able to address more pointedly the factors that predispose or lead to the formation of a creative and artistic individual. In the end we are left with much more work to do, but given our patients' generous donation of time and remarkable talents we are optimistic that further insights will follow soon.

Acknowledgments

Much of this work stems from the insights garnered from and discussion among members of the University of California San Francisco Memory and Aging Center.

In particular, the authors would like to thank Marie-Pierre Thibodeau and Matthew Growdon for their generous contributions.

Endnotes

1. Arbib, M. A. (1995). *The handbook of brain theory and neural networks.*

2. Mendez, M. (2004). Dementia as a window to the neurology of art. *Medical Hypotheses, 63,* 1–7.

3. Zeki, S. Statement on neuroesthetics. *Neuroesthetics.* http://www.neuroesthetics.org/statement-on-neuroesthetics.php.

4. Jamison, K. (1995). Manic-depressive illness and creativity. *Scientific American, 272*(2), 62–67.

5. Bogousslavsky, J. (2005). Artistic creativity, style, and brain disorders. *European Neurology, 54,* 103–111.

6. Heilman, K., et al. (2003). Creative innovation: possible brain mechanisms. *Neurocase, 9*(5), 369–379.

7. Chakravarty, A. (2009). Artistic talent in dyslexia—A hypothesis. *Medical Hypotheses, 73*(4), 569–571.

8. Seeley, W., et al. (2008). Unravelling Bolero: progressive aphasia, transmodal creativity and the right posterior neocortex. *Brain, 131,* 39–49.

9. Post, F. (1994). Creativity and psychopathology: A study of 291 world famous men. *British Journal of Psychiatry, 165,* 22–34.

10. Post, F. (1996). Verbal creativity, depression and alcoholism: An investigation of one hundred American and British writers. *British Journal of Psychiatry, 168,* 545–555.

11. Jamison, K. (1995). Manic-depressive illness and creativity. *Scientific American, 272*(2), 62–67.

12. Peterson, J. M., & Lansky, L. M. (1977). Left-handedness among architects: partial replication and some new data. *Perceptual and Motor Skills, 45*(3, Pt 2), 1216–1218.

13. Peterson, J. M., & Lansky, L. M. (1974). Left-handedness among architects: Some facts and speculation. *Perceptual and Motor Skills, 38*(2), 547–550.

14. Geschwind, N., & Behan, P. O. (1982). Left-handedness: Association with immune disease, migraine and developmental learning disorders. *Proceedings of the National Academy of Sciences U S A, 79,* 5097–5100.

15. Heilman, K., et al. (2003). Creative innovation: possible brain mechanisms. *Neurocase, 9*(5), 369–379.

16. Drachman, D. (2005). Do we have brain to spare? *Neurology, 64*(12), 2004–2005.

17. Nolte, J. (1998). *The human brain: an introduction to its functional anatomy* (4th ed.).

18. Nolte, J. (1998). *The human brain: an introduction to its functional anatomy* (4th ed.).

19. Arbib, M. A. (1995). *The handbook of brain theory and neural networks.*

20. Mesulam, M. (2000). *Principles of behavioral and cognitive neurology.*

21. Miller, B. L. (2007). *The human frontal lobes: functions and disorders.*

22. Arbib, M. A. (1995). *The handbook of brain theory and neural networks.*

23. Mesulam, M. (2000). *Principles of behavioral and cognitive neurology.*

24. Arbib, M. A. (1995). *The handbook of brain theory and neural networks.*

25. Mesulam, M. (2000). *Principles of behavioral and cognitive neurology* (p. 2).

26. Gazzaniga, M. S. (2005). Forty-five years of split-brain research and still going strong. *Nature Reviews Neuroscience, 6*(8), 653–659.

27. Tinuper, P. (2001). Ictal bradycardia in partial epileptic seizures: Autonomic investigation in three cases and literature review. *Brain, 124*(12), 2361–2371.

28. Heilman, K., et al. (2003). Creative innovation: possible brain mechanisms. *Neurocase, 9*(5), 369–379.

29. Chatterjee, A. (2004). The neuropsychology of visual artistic production. *Neuropsychologia, 42,* 1568–1583.

30. Bogousslavsky, J. (2005). Artistic creativity, style, and brain disorders. *European Neurology, 54,* 103–111.

31. Schnider, A., Regard, M., Benson, D. F., & Landis, T. (1993). Effects of a right-hemisphere stroke on an artist's performance. *Neuropsychiatry Neuropsychology Behavioral Neurology, 6,* 249–255.

32. Kaczmarek, B. J. (1991). Aphasia in an artist: a disorder of symbolic processing. *Aphasiology, 4,* 361–371.

33. Cummings, J. L., & Zarit, J. M. (1987). Probable Alzheimer's disease in an artist. *JAMA, 258,* 2731–2734.

34. Brun, A. (1993). Frontal lobe dementia of the non-Alzheimer type revisited. *Dementia, 4,* 126–139.

35. Espinel, C. H. (1996). de Kooning's late colours and forms: dementia, creativity, and the healing power of art. *Lancet, 347,* 1096–1098.

36. Chatterjee, A. (2004). The neuropsychology of visual artistic production. *Neuropsychologia, 42,* 1568–1583.

37. American Psychiatric Association (1994). *Diagnostic and Statistical Manual of Mental Disorders* (4th ed.).

38. Continuum, Lifelong Learning Neurology, 2007; *13*(2), 39–68.

39. Continuum, Lifelong Learning Neurology, 2007; *13*(2), 87–108.

40. Mendez, M. F., et al. (1996). Frontotemporal dementia vs. Alzheimer's disease: differential cognitive features. *Neurology, 47,* 1189–1194.

41. Miller, B. L., Cummings, J. L., Mishkin, F., et al. (1998). Emergence of artistic talent in frontotemporal dementia. *Neurology, 51,* 978–981.

42. Continuum, Lifelong Learning Neurology, 2007; *13*(2), 87–108.

43. Continuum, Lifelong Learning Neurology, 2007; *13*(2), 87–108.

44. Rosen, H. J., et al. (2006). Behavioral features in semantic dementia vs. other forms of progressive aphasias. *Neurology, 67,* 1752–1756.

45. Gorno-Tempini, M. L., et al. (2004). Cognition and anatomy in three variants of primary progressive aphasia. *Annals of Neurology, 55*(3), 335–346.

46. Brun, A. (1993). Frontal lobe dementia of the non-Alzheimer type revisited. *Dementia, 4,* 126–139.

47. Miller, B. L., et al. (1996). Enhanced artistic creativity with temporal lobe degeneration. *Lancet, 348,* 1744–1755.

48. Snowden, J. S., Neary, D., & Mann, D. M.A. (1996). *Fronto-temporal lobar dementia* (pp. 94–97). New York: Churchill-Livingstone.

49. Miller, B. L., Boone, K., Cummings, J., Read, S. L., & Mishkin, F. (2000). Functional correlates of musical and visual talent in frontotemporal dementia. *British Journal of Psychiatry, 176,* 458–463.

50. Miller, B. L., Boone, K., Cummings, J., Read, S. L., & Mishkin, F. (2000). Functional correlates of musical and visual talent in frontotemporal dementia. *British Journal of Psychiatry, 176,* 458–463.

51. Chatterjee, A. (2004). The neuropsychology of visual artistic production. *Neuropsychologia, 42,* 1568–1583.

52. Hou, C., et al. (2000). Artistic savants. *Neuropsychiatry, Neuropsychology, and Behavioral Neurology, 13*(1), 29–38.

53. Kapur, N. (1996). Paradoxical functional facilitation in brain-behaviour research: a critical review. *Brain, 119*(5), 1775–1790.

54. Brazis, P. W., Masdeu, J. C., & Biller, J. (2007). *Localization in clinical neurology.*

55. Miller, B. L., Boone, K., Cummings, J., Read, S. L., & Mishkin, F. (2000). Functional correlates of musical and visual talent in frontotemporal dementia. *British Journal of Psychiatry, 176,* 458–463.

56. Kawabata, H., & Zeki, S. (2004). Neural correlates of beauty. *Journal of Neurophysiology, 91*(1), 1699–1705.

57. Snowden, J. S., Neary, D., & Mann, D. M. A. (1996). *Fronto-temporal lobar dementia* (pp. 94–97). New York: Churchill-Livingstone.

58. Snowden, J. S., Neary, D., & Mann, D. M. A. (1996). *Fronto-temporal lobar dementia* (pp. 94–97). New York: Churchill-Livingstone.

59. Mell, J. C., Howard, S. M., & Miller, B. L. (2003). Art and the brain: the influence of frontotemporal dementia on an accomplished artist. *Neurology, 60,* 1707–1710.

60. Seeley, W. W., et al. (2008). Unravelling Boléro: progressive aphasia, transmodal creativity and the right posterior neocortex. *Brain, 131,* 39–49.

61. Miller, B. L., Boone, K., Cummings, J., Read, S. L., & Mishkin, F. (2000). Functional correlates of musical and visual talent in frontotemporal dementia. *British Journal of Psychiatry, 176,* 458–463.

16

Neurology of Visual Aesthetics

INDIAN NYMPHS, MODERN ART, AND SEXY BEAKS

Vilayanur S. Ramachandran and Elizabeth Seckel

What is art? Consider the following aphorisms.

The magic of the soul—Goethe[1]
  That which gives man his lost dignity—Schiller[2]
  (In) all true Works of Art wilt thou discern Eternity looking through Time . . . the Godlike rendered visible—Carlyle[3]
  The pleasure one takes in being who he is—Wagner[4]
  The accomplishment of our desire to find ourselves again among the phenomena of the external world—Wagner,[5] again
  And readers may wish to generate their own.

This is clearly a vast spectrum of opinions. It will be a long time before Science even scratches the surface of what we call Art, with a capital A. But we will argue in this chapter that one can indeed develop a scientific theory of aesthetics. Aesthetics is a broader term in many ways; it would include such things as fashion and design. But it also narrows the scope of enquiry by peeling off the encrustations of culture and allows us to get to the core of the matter. Traditionally, aesthetics has been the province of philosophers, but it is fair to say they haven't made much progress in understanding its basis (not for want of effort; they have been at it for 2,000 years). There's no evidence that neuroscience or psychology would do any better, but there's no harm in trying. What we offer is "a few hesitant steps in (hopefully) the right direction," to quote Semir Zeki.[6] In the rest of the article, we will use the terms *Art* and *Aesthetics* interchangeably, but in general we mean the latter, not the former. There is an arbitrariness to art, imposed by the auctioneer's hammer, art gallery proprietors, and art historians, that is hard to approach scientifically.

Let us begin with a challenge that, to my knowledge, no philosopher, neuroscientist, or psychologist has posed, at least not explicitly. What is the key difference between kitsch art and the real thing? How does one make such a distinction? Does one make the choice arbitrarily based on cultural influences; so that one man's kitsch is another's high art? We think not. Cultural factors unquestionably inspire what kind of art a person appreciates—be it a Monet, a Warhol, a Salvador

Dalí, a Picasso, a Chola bronze, a Moghul miniature, or a Ming Dynasty vase. But even if beauty is largely in the eye of the beholder, we believe there is a universal structure underlying all aesthetic experience. The details may vary from culture to culture and may be influenced by the way one is raised, but it doesn't follow that no genetic mechanism codes for the establishment of common denominators underlying all forms of art.

Secondly, one could argue that the decision about kitsch versus "real" can be settled by democratic vote, but that doesn't solve the problem either; in fact, more people like kitsch than the other way around. But many people, although still the minority, can evolve mentally to appreciate high art, but people rarely slide backward. Perhaps this could serve as an objective litmus test to distinguish real art versus kitsch. Without such a criterion one cannot claim to have objectively defined or measured the true worth of a work of art (or fashion design, for that matter).

Neuroaesthetics (a term coined by Semir Zeki)[7] is a relatively recent discipline devoted to the scientific study of the neurological bases for the contemplation and creation of a work of art. The concept at first appears as an oxymoron: science and art are seemingly fundamentally antithetical enterprises. Art involves celebrating individuality of expression, while science involves discovering conforming principles universal to all. C. P. Snow a long time ago spoke of these two polar cultures, humanities on the one hand and science on the other, and "never the twain shall meet."[8] We suggest that these two seemingly antipodal campaigns *do* meet, and they do so in the human brain. Art is a good place to start exploring this possibility.

Clearly, there is an immense diversity of artistic styles: there's Baroque art, Byzantine art, Gothic art, abstract art, Pop art, Dada (which is art parodying itself), Art Deco, and Art Nouveau, to list a few. In spite of this astounding diversity, are there underlying aesthetic universals? We believe there are. When sitting in the precincts of a temple in India, one of us (V. S. R.) came up with what we call the eight universal laws of aesthetics (Fig. 16.8). When we say there are universal laws of aesthetics, we're not saying that culture doesn't play a role. Obviously culture plays a huge artistic role; otherwise you would not have different artistic styles, nor could you put a Damien Hirst human skull studded with diamonds in an art auction and make $30 million.

These cultural influences and trends, however, are studied by art historians. Our focus is instead on the universal principles that transcend cultural boundaries. Remarkably, they even cut across phylogenetic lines.

Why would you find a peacock fanning its feathers or a bird of paradise beautiful? A peacock evolved to be beautiful to other peacocks, not to be found beautiful by your brain. And why, after 600 million years of parallel evolution, would you find a butterfly beautiful? We didn't evolve from butterflies. The real reason is that both organisms independently evolved and converged on the same aesthetic laws and principles. To emphasize that art transcends not only cultural boundaries but species boundaries, let's examine the bowerbird.

Bowerbirds are nondescript perching birds. The male bowerbirds, to attract potential mates, construct beautiful and incredibly elegant symmetrical bowers, sometimes 10 to 30 times taller than the bird itself, with wide entry archways and lawns. Amazingly, these diminutive architects garnish their bowers with pebbles or flower petals grouped according to similarity of colors, sometimes even with cigarette foils and berries. (If you put a bower in a Christie's art auction, it might fetch a fairly handsome sum of money!) You might argue that they're not really creating original works of art. Well, guess what: if you remove one berry and throw it away, the bowerbird will come back, take the berry, and replace it. These male bowerbirds are extremely compulsive and fastidious about it. Even within the same species, different males produce different bower styles. Perhaps these enticing bachelor pads are a "Freudian compensation" for such a dour appearance? (Similar to how human males will often compensate by sporting a Honda CRX.) This leads to sexual selection for the most beautiful bower.

Before we go through some of the principles common to aesthetically pleasing images, it would be useful to clear something up about visual processing. Many people have the common misconception that there is a picture on the retina in the eyeball that is transmitted along the optic nerve and displayed on a screen in the brain called the visual cortex. Of course this is nonsense; it sets up a problem of infinite regress. If you have a screen in the visual cortex, you must also have a little homunculus up there to watch the screen, and this doesn't solve the problem because then you need another little guy in his head, *ad infinitum*. There is no screen with a little homunculus watching it. Instead, you have to think in terms of symbolic descriptions that transform. For example, a Necker cube or Schroeder's staircase (Fig. 16.1) can be seen in one of two ways, but it can never be both at the same time. It flips mentally between these two percepts even though nothing is happening to the stimulus. This is evidence for the idea that every act of perception involves judgment by the observer. (In fact, there are not just two but an infinite set of different "distorted" staircases that can produce exactly the same image as Figure 16.1 on the retina, if tilted in the appropriate manner.) Yet the brain has

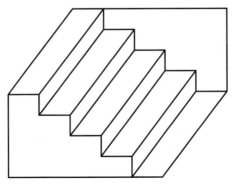

FIGURE 16.1 *Schroeder's staircase.*

built-in assumptions about the natural world that allow it to discard all of these and home in on just two unique interpretations. (The study of vision is the study of these assumptions/constraints and their neural implementation.) Given the incredible complexity and sophistication of human vision, over 30 cortical areas have evolved that are involved primarily with visual processing. The complexity of the visual system is good news for artists because if vision involved simply a homunculus viewing an image onto a screen, you couldn't have art.

The reason art works is because there are so many areas processing different aspects of the visual image and talking to each other. What the artist is doing is creating images that titillate these visual areas in the brain better than you could with a realistic image (and the titillations have to resonate with each other). So let's get rid of realism. The question is, how do you distort these images? You can't arbitrarily distort these images and call it art. So the question becomes, how do you create lawful distortions? Look at Figure 16.2. Initially seen as random splotches, there is an infinite number of possible groupings. Notice that as you scan the image for the hidden object, you can almost sense your visual system groping for an object, and once your brain has found the hidden image (a cow), it *locks* onto it, making it difficult to let go of this linked group of splotches. Like the pleasurable sensation of finishing a jigsaw puzzle, the linking of cow-relevant splotches triggers a reward jolt, an internal "aha!"

Let's take a more familiar example. When we go into our closets, we typically choose outfits that have similar bits of color (just like the bowerbird), although some of my colleagues seem to not follow this rule. For example, we select a red scarf if the skirt we'd like to wear that day is blue with red flowers. What are we doing here? Are we just responding to the aggressive hype and marketing put forth

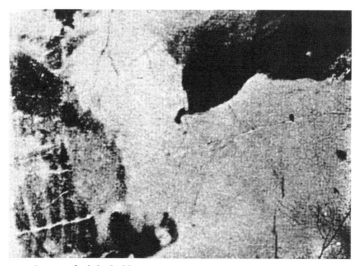

FIGURE 16.2 *Can you find the hidden image?*

FIGURE 16.3 *Illustration of color grouping.*

in advertisements? No, this is telling you something very deep about aesthetics and is tapping into brain circuitry involved in delineating objects from the background and especially in defeating camouflage.

Imagine one of your ancestor primates scurrying along the treetops. Your ancestor pauses, noticing splotches behind the trees. As soon as the splotches (a leopard!) start moving, the spots are seen as moving together and the brain says, "What's the chance those splotches are all moving together by chance? No, they're all one object, let me glue them together. Oh, wow, it's a single large object! It's a leopard, let me get out of here!" That "wow jolt" is absolutely critical. Discovering and associating multiple features into discrete clusters is expedited and reinforced by direct connections between these visual areas and the limbic system (and back from the amygdala to practically every stage in the visual hierarchy to allow " boot strapping"; we are talking about established pathways – not hypothetical ones).

Grouping can occur with color (Fig. 16.3). Imagine that through green foliage you see some yellow blotches. Your brain says, "What the hell is that? It can't be a coincidence that all these yellow blotches are unrelated; they must belong to the same object." You link them together, "Oh, wow, that's a lion! Let me get out of here!" So you are rewarded with an attention grabbing jolt, an "aha." (And there is a jolt for object boundary delineation, not just for recognition.) The knowledge that the act of picking out a matching tie for your jacket (before heading to the modern jungle known as the office) taps into the same circuitry that evolved to detect lions may add a whole new meaning to your morning dressing ritual.

We emphasize that the mini "aha" jolt doesn't necessarily have to produce immediate pleasure; attention grabbing can itself have an aesthetic effect and so can the act of recognizing and classifying an object even if it evokes displeasure. A horrifying painting of the devil can still elicit an aesthetic reaction at one level and fear at another. Aesthetics is almost certainly a multilayered process and a failure to recognize this has led to much confusion among some philosophers.

Speaking of the "aha!" experience, what we would like to suggest is that when you're looking at complex artistic images, what you get is an amplified "super-aha." The old model from MIT suggests that when you're looking at visual images, the information is processed sequentially along an assembly line, passing from one module to the next and the next, and finally you say, "Oh, wow, it' a lion!" This is the "serial hierarchical bucket brigade model of vision." Each module is autonomous and finishes computing and makes explicit some aspect of the information before delivering it to the next module. In fact, vision does not proceed in this unidirectional manner (whether for segmentation or recognition). At every stage in the hierarchy of processing (along with parallel processing), a partial solution to the visual problem is sent back to the earlier stages to bias subsequent processing. So you seem to get junior "ahas!" at every stage of visual processing.[9] These are subsequently sent to the limbic system (especially the amygdala). As previously noted, it has been shown that the amygdala (and possibly nucleus accumbens, septum, and habenula) sends connections all the way back to almost every visual processing area. Future research should pursue this connection further. We have previously suggested in many of our writings that these connections generate multiple mini-ahas, whose harmonious interplay results in a rich aesthetic experience.

Many grouping principles were also used by Renaissance artists (as well as almost every other school of art). For example, there are paintings in which the azure of the sky mimics the azure of the robes people in the painting are wearing. Similarly, the artist might choose to reiterate the same beige color throughout the painting. We do not believe this was due to a limited palette of colors; on the contrary, the artist was exploiting this desire of the visual system to group similar colors. Although grouping evolved for delineating a single object, the artist can exploit it by using like colors for different objects as well.[10] The point is the law works statistically in nature for discovering objects. The fact that an artist can exploit it by painting different objects the same color is beside the point, because evolution couldn't have anticipated this.

Another simple "law" is symmetry. The aesthetic allure of symmetry can be found in our reactions to naturally highly symmetric objects, such as butterflies, freshly formed crystals, or beautiful sea stars. Why is symmetry so satisfying to the eye? One theory that has been postulated is that this may be because parasitic infestation can lead a host to develop visible asymmetry. As a parasite species evolves, it labors unremittingly to match its surface antigens to those of its victim to evade immunological rejection. Concurrently, there is a strong selection pressure on the host to avoid mates with parasites, which reduce fitness and reproductive success. If parasitic infestation occurs sufficiently early in development it can result in minor deviations from symmetry. It would therefore be an adaptive advantage to use asymmetry as an indicator to avoid potential mates with poor health, weak genes, or a challenged immune system. Although this smacks of Ev Psych, it has a ring of plausibility.

We suggest a different explanation. The appeal of symmetry is universal; it's seen even in animals. In fact, most animals exhibit some form of symmetry, whether radial (around a central axis) or bilateral (arranged on opposite sides of a median axis). The attention-grabbing effect of symmetry, we suggest, evolved because most living things in nature (prey, predator, mate) are symmetrical, and there is a high premium on being able to detect living things. So it serves as an early-alert system, drawing your attention. And drawing and sustaining attention is the first minimum criterion for art, although hardly sufficient (Damien Hirst would disagree).

This is what you're tapping into when you look at a butterfly, or a human face, or even the monument to eternal love, the Taj Mahal. Of course monuments don't exist in nature, but the architect is tapping into the same circuitry that evolved to detect people, animals, and predators.

When coming up with these principles of visual aesthetics, ideally you must have three things in place: what, how, and why. By "what" we mean, what is the law? You must give a clear formulation of the particular principle, like peak shift, grouping, or symmetry. And if you can produce a clear statement of an " ill-posed" problem, all the better. Next, you must explain the evolutionary advantage for this law. Why is it useful to group things? To defeat camouflage. Why is it useful to detect symmetrical physiognomies? To detect animals in general and to detect healthy mates. Then you need to know how this law operates mechanistically—the neurophysiology. All three legs of the table must be in place before we can claim to have understood any complex biological concept such as art. (Imagine trying to understand digestion, looking at only the output!) The fourth leg, the ineffable, transcendental quality of great works of art, is unexplained (so far), which is why we use the word "neuroaesthetics" not "neuroart."

Another less obvious principle that can be applied to aesthetics is peak shift, which comes from studies of animal behavior. Imagine a hypothetical example: teaching a rat a simple discrimination between square and rectangle. (An easy way to do this is by rewarding selection of a rectangle with cheese, and giving no reward for a square.) Subsequently, you show the rat something it has never seen before: a longer, skinnier rectangle (Fig. 16.4). When given the choice between the original and this new longer, skinnier rectangle, the rat will prefer the novel stimulus. You may say that's stupid; why would it prefer that rectangle when it was trained that

FIGURE 16.4 *Example of the peak shift principle.*

the other resulted in food? The answer is that the rat isn't stupid; what it has learned is the rule "rectangularity"—the more rectangular, the better. This is called a peak shift effect.

What do sexy rectangles have to do with art? The same principle is used in caricature. If we were to ask you to create a caricature of Nixon, you take Nixon's big nose and shaggy eyebrows and subtract the average male face. You are left with what is characteristic of Nixon, and you amplify it. This results in a peak shift version of Nixon and you say, my God, that looks even more like Nixon than Nixon himself! (Rembrandt's portraits may be less extreme peak shifts; overdoing it or producing disproportionate deviations from prototype may result in caricature.) Peak shifts in "color-space" rather than "form-space" may have been used by Van Gogh and Monet. (They may also smudge outlines deliberately to make you focus on color at the expense of form; see below under law of "isolation.")

A caveat about the whole neuro-reductionistic aspect of art is in order. There have been many recordings from the brains of primates (and brain imaging in humans) to investigate the neural basis of aesthetic appreciation. For example, let us say you are a neuroscientist investigating the neural basis of kinetic art. You decide to put an electrode in MT (the middle temporal area, in which cells are sensitive to the direction of motion) in the human brain and show the person a great work of kinetic art, such as a Calder mobile. You record the MT cell's activity or do fMRI, producing pretty pictures that have a mesmerizing effect not just on a science journalist but on our neuroscience colleagues as well. Upon viewing the stimuli, the cell in MT starts firing and you say, my God, I've discovered the basis of kinetic art! This conclusion is silly because cells in MT will fire in response to any movement; they would fire in response to a swarm of bees or a running pig.

Or if you apply this methodology to face cells in the fusiform gyrus and show a subject paintings by Rembrandt, the cells will fire and you say, my God, I've discovered the basis of portraiture! But if you show the subject any face, the cells will fire. What actually needs to be shown is what is *special* about a Rembrandt face and how it is different from a regular photograph. We suggest that what the brain is doing here is similar to the rat's peak shift. If you show caricatures of an alpha male primate to a junior primate's face cell, we propose that will be more effective than the original non-doctored photo of the alpha male. One of us (V. S. R.) proposed this 10 years ago, and this has since been proven by a group at Harvard.

The same principle applies to "erotic" sculptures in Indian art, or any art for that matter. What you do is take the average woman and subtract the male from the female. You then accentuate and exaggerate this, and you're left with big breasts, hips, and a triple flexion poise, a posture unique to females. (This is due to the angle between the femoral shaft and the neck, and the width of the pelvis, and a woman can do this effortlessly and a man can't elegantly.) You've extracted the essence of feminine posture, what is woman-like about her (Fig. 16.5). Victorian art pundits found these sculptures repulsive partly because they were prudish, but also because the sculptures didn't look like real women.[11]

FIGURE 16.5 *A statue of Parvati, the essence of femininity.*

What about abstract art? What about Henry Moore, or Picasso for that matter? Let's go to ethology. Look at Figure 16.6. Here's a seagull with a spot on its beak. When a seagull chick hatches from the egg, it starts pecking at that spot. The mother then regurgitates the half-digested food into the gaping mouth of the chick. The chick swallows it and is satisfied. Tinbergen conducted a series of clever experiments to discover the answer. He found you don't need a mother (sorry, Mom). What you do is pluck the beak off and then you wave it in front of the chick. The chick will still peck at the beak! You say, "Well, that's stupid; why is the chick begging for food from a disembodied beak waved about by a scientist?" The answer is, it's not stupid at all. If you think about it, the visual system is trying to do as little work as possible for the job on hand (like some of our undergraduate students) and is saying, "What is the likelihood of my seeing a disembodied beak in nature? It's almost certainly attached to my mother, so why don't I simplify the computation

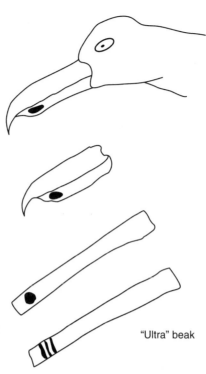

"Ultra" beak

FIGURE 16.6 *Tinbergen's discovery of peak shift in the seagull chick's pecking response to a spot on the mother's beak. Exaggerations of the stimulus, such as a stick with three stripes, induced an even greater pecking response than the actual beak.*

and go for that long thing with the spot, because I'm highly unlikely to encounter a mutant cow with a beak in nature?" Tinbergen[12] investigated further and found that you don't even need a beak: if you paint three red stripes on a stick and wave it in front of the chick, it fetishizes it. Going gaga over these stripes, the chick starts pecking at it ferociously, preferring this stimulus to its own mother! Why does the bird do this? We suggest that there are neurons in the tectum, hyperstriatum, wulst and other visual areas in the chick's brain that are specialized for extracting and responding to certain "form primitives." (We don't know the coding scheme—the basic alphabet—used by these circuits, but the "beak detector" may be wired in such a way that it adventitiously embodies the rule "more colored outlined, the better" as an accidental by-product of the wiring). Therefore, when you paint three stripes together, you are creating an ultrabeak that is *even more beak-like than the real beak*, and the chick goes, "My God, what a beak!" We make a distinction between supernormal and ultranormal stimuli. The former refers to things like the peacock tail or the sparrow incubating a giant cuckoo egg, and one knows what dimension the exaggeration is along. The latter taps into idiosyncrasies of wiring, and it's not obvious what parameter is being "exaggerated" (e.g., three stripes versus a spot).

So if the seagulls had an art gallery, what we're suggesting is that they would hang this multi-striped stick up on the wall, worship it, idolize it, even pay millions of dollars for it. You may say, "This unnatural stick doesn't even look like a real thing; how could this possibly be pleasing?" But that's exactly what you're doing when you buy abstract art: you're behaving like a seagull chick. (Could Van Gogh's sunflowers or Monet's water lilies be our super-beaks in the domain of color rather than form?)

On the other hand there's another principle, which we call isolation, the art of understatement. Sometimes a little doodle by Picasso of a bull or little nudes drawn by Klimt using only a suggestive outline are wonderfully evocative and beautiful. As the aphorism in Art goes, "less is more." But wait, you say: are we not contradicting ourselves? We just finished saying how exaggeration and peak shift and hyperbole were conducive to art. Now we're telling you that what is aesthetically pleasing is minimalism and understatement. Is this not a contradiction? Often science progresses by resolving contradiction. We would argue that these principles are not necessarily antagonistic. For example, when you see a three-dimensional colored photo of a nude, you're given all sorts of irrelevant information that clutters the image and has nothing to do with her outline or form. Even though you have over one billion nerve cells, your brain has a limited attentional capacity, and only one set of neurons can be active at any single moment representing an object in the visual world; you can't have overlapping sets. Given that attentional bottleneck, cluttering an image with all sorts of irrelevant information distracts your attention away from where the peak shift has been added: contours and outlines.

For a good illustration of this, take a look at Figure 16.7a. This horse is drawn by a normal 8-year-old and is not aesthetically pleasing at all. In fact, it looks hideous. On the other hand, Figure 16.7b is a great work of art by the great Renaissance artist Leonardo da Vinci. Everyone would agree this is very aesthetically pleasing. Figure 16.7c is a figure drawn by an 8-year-old autistic child named Nadia. Many people naïve to which figure was created by which artist remark that Nadia's figure is far more aesthetically pleasing than da Vinci's, conveying more animation, energy, and movement. How can an 8-year-old autistic child produce a figure more pleasing than one drawn by Leonardo da Vinci? The answer is again the principle of isolation. The autistic child, with many modules malfunctioning, may only have one brain region (mainly in the right parietal, involved in the sense of artistic proportion) that is especially active. All of her attentional resources may spontaneously be deployed in this functioning module. This makes Nadia more adept at extracting what is unique about the image and disregarding all the irrelevant details much more effectively than you or we can. Hence the savant syndrome.[13]

A principle mistaken for isolation is the principle of "perceptual problem solving," or the peek-a-boo principle. This can explain why pin-ups are less enchanting than a nude hidden behind a shower curtain. You might say that's kind

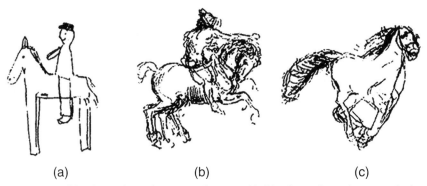

(a)   (b)   (c)

FIGURE 16.7 *(a) A horse drawn by a normal 8-year-old. (b) A horse drawn by Leonardo da Vinci. (c) A drawing of a horse by Nadia at age 8.*

of weird—hitting dozens of visual areas in the brain, the stark naked pin-up contains a lot more information than a woman (or man) hidden behind a shower curtain. When the brain is faced with an image with a built-in challenge, the image is actually more pleasing to the eye than an obvious one. (Just as intellectual problem solving is rewarding because there's a small "aha" jolt at each step in solving a puzzle.) Otherwise, if you were to see a woman or a man in a fog, you would give up the chase immediately instead of pursuing her or him. This "aha" reinforcement makes the hunt in itself rewarding, going to the visual areas in the brain back to the limbic system saying, "Pursue further! This is exciting!" (Sometimes the pursuit itself becomes a substitute reward, even if there is no possibility of consummation.)[14] We propose that visual art and aesthetics is *visual foreplay before the climax of object recognition.* Just as foreplay can be annoying but at the same time delightful and pleasing, the same is true of art.

Indeed, peek-a-boo in children may be enjoyable for precisely the same reason. In early primate evolution on treetops, baby monkeys most often would have become temporarily occluded completely by foliage, and it had to be visually reinforcing for offspring and mother to periodically glimpse each other to keep the child safe and within a reasonable distance. Additionally, the smile and laugh of parent and offspring mutually reinforce each other.

Another law of aesthetics is visual punning or metaphor; examples can be seen both in design (and draftsmanship) and in high art, as in the dancing Shiva bronze called *nataraja*, from India, whose dance symbolizes the cyclical nature of time and the dance of the cosmos itself. A more mundane example would be the word "tilt" depicted with actually tilted letters or "tremble" or "shiver" or "ice" with wavy lines.

There are several other laws too, on our list, but one of us (V. S. R.) has considered them in some detail in other publications,[15] so we will omit them here (they are listed in Fig. 16.8). But we will add a new one, which we'll call harmony, by which we mean the use of multiple laws within a single image harmoniously so

Universal Laws of Aesthetics

1 Peak shift
2 Grouping
3 Contrast
4 Isolation
5 Perceptual problem solving
6 Symmetry
7 Abhorrence of coincidence/generic viewpoint
8 Repetition, rhythm and orderliness
9 Balance
10 Metaphor

FIGURE 16.8 *Suggested universal laws of aesthetics.*

that they don't clash. For example, in many Indian sculptures, a sexy nymph is languorously standing beneath the arched branch of a tree, which has ripe fruits dangling from it. There are the peak shifts (in form and posture) that make her exquisitely feminine and voluptuous. Additionally, the fruits are a visual echo of her breasts, but they also symbolize the fecundity and fertility of nature just as the nymph's breasts do; thus, the perceptual and conceptual elements resonate. The sculptor will also often add baroque ornate jewelry on her otherwise naked torso to enhance, by contrast (one of the "laws" on our list) the smoothness and suppleness of her youthful estrogen-charged skin. (We mean contrast of texture rather than luminance.)

In addition to these theoretical ideas on art, the experimental work needs to proceed in parallel, a tradition ushered in by Gestaltists like Rudolf Arnheim and pursued more recently by Steve Palmer. For example, it is astonishing that we should find as simple a thing as a beauty spot alluring, even though it's a blemish. We recently moved around a beauty spot on a photograph of a model and asked naïve subjects to rate the faces' attractiveness (Fig. 16.9). By doing so we were able to obtain what psychologists refer to as a " psychometric function" (which in plain English simply means "graph"). A spot looks pretty if placed on or near the labial crease (the crease from the outer rim of the nostril to the lips, in case you are wondering) or just above or below where the lips meet or near the outer canthus of the eye—but it looks hideous on the tip of the nose (and not because it is centrally placed: a dot on the center of the chin looks OK). Placement on the nasal bridge or even to its side is bad. The fact that aesthetics can't yet explain as simple an observation as this tells us how far we still have to go before neuroaesthetics deserves the lofty designation of "Science."

With the principles we have outlined, can we re-address the question raised earlier about the difference between kitsch art and the real thing? We think the idea that the distinction is arbitrary or entirely cultural is nonsense. As we said, there is a genuine difference because you can graduate from kitsch art to the real

FIGURE 16.9. *When a beauty spot is placed near the labial crease or near the canthus of the eye it is pleasing, while on the tip of the nose or to the side of the nasal bridge it isn't.*

thing, but you can't slide backwards. For example, compare two works of art, a Monet and a Thomas Kinkade (the latter's paintings often hang on the walls of hotel lobbies and law offices). The first is a great work of art extremely pleasing to the eyes. The other is kitsch and sets the absolute zero of art (not to offend Kinkade collectors). Perhaps kitsch artists blindly follow the principles we've outlined without a gut-level understanding of them. We are tempted to suggest that true "understanding" taps into the aesthetic sensibilities of the right hemisphere, whereas kitsch results from the left hemisphere's attempts to usurp this and replace it with an (inevitably superficial) intellectual deployment of the same principles. And of course it fails. In addition, aesthetically pleasing works might help dissolve the commication gap between the neural "languages" of the two hemispheres. In theory, one could show a volunteer non-kitsch works of art and then subtract the activation produced by kitsch works of art to see what lights up. Will you then have discovered the art center of the brain? You would need to further subtract signals generated by some other form of pleasure (e.g., viewing a tasteless but arousing pin-up) to ensure that you have homed in on the brain regions concerned with purely aesthetic pleasure rather than pleasure in general.

One of us (V. S. R.) has also suggested recently that in addition to evolution driving the emergence of aesthetic laws, the laws of aesthetics (e.g., the gull chick principle) can drive the evolution of quirky and otherwise inexplicable external traits of morphology and color (e.g., we predict the future emergence of a race of seagulls with very long, thin, striped beaks[16,17]). This has nothing to do with Darwinian fitness; it's an adventitious byproduct of visual principles that were evolved for other reasons entirely (e.g., object segmentation aided by grouping and object recognition enhanced by peak shift).

We will conclude by answering a question that is frequently raised. Would this kind of purely neuro-reductionist/psychophysical analysis of art diminish the aesthetic joy or higher metaphysical implications of art? The answer is no, and I'll illustrate with an analogy. Imagine a Martian neuroscientist gives you a complete analysis of what's going on in your lover's brain—neurons activated, transmitters released, etc.—when she is making love to you. If you were to ask her, "You mean that's all there is to it? It's just nerve cells firing—not real?" she would (should) answer, "On the contrary, my dear, it is additional objective proof that it's real and I am not faking it."

Or to quote Richard Feynman: "Poets say science takes away from the beauty of the stars—mere globs of gas atoms. I, too, can see the stars on a desert night, and feel them. But do I see less or more?"[18]

Acknowledgments

This chapter is based on a lecture given at the Center for Academic Research and Training in Anthropogeny (CARTA) at the University of California, San Diego, March 20, 2009. We thank Eric Landrum and Beatrix Krause, who worked with us on beauty spots.

Endnotes

1. Jinarajadasa, C. (1996). *Art as will and idea* (pp. 31, 65). Montana: Kessinger Publishing.

2. Hempel, C. (Ed.). (1879). *Schiller's complete works* (p. 514). Philadelphia: Sherman & Co.

3. Carlyle, T. (1896). *Sartor Resartus* (p. 203). Boston: Ginn & Co.

4. Jinarajadasa, C. (1996). *Art as will and idea*. Montana: Kessinger Publishing.

5. Jinarajadasa, C. (1996). *Art as will and idea*. Montana: Kessinger Publishing

6. Zeki, S. (1999). *Inner vision: an exploration of art and the brain*. Oxford: Oxford University Press.

7. Zeki, S. (1999). Art and the brain. *Journal of Conscious Studies, 6*, 76–96.

8. Snow, C. P. (1959). *The two cultures and the scientific revolution*. The Rede Lecture 1959. New York: Cambridge University Press.

9. Ramachandran, V. S., & Rogers-Ramachandran, Diane (May 2008). The neurology of aesthetics. *Scientific American, 18*, 74–77.

10. Arnheim, R. (1974). *Art and visual perception: a psychology of the creative eye* (pp. 79–80, 92). Berkeley: University of California Press.

11. Srinivasan, R. (1999). *Facets of Indian culture*. Mumbai: Bharatiya Vidya Bhavan Press.

12. Tinbergen, N. (1954). *Curious naturalists*. New York: Basic Books.

13. Ramachandran, V. S. (2004). *A brief tour of human consciousness* (pp. 53–54). New York: Pi Press.

14. Anstis, Stuart. Personal communication, June 1, 2010.

15. Ramachandran, V. S., & Hirstein, W. (1999). The science of art. *Journal of Consciousness Studies, 6*(6–7), 15–41.

16. Ramachadran, V. S. (2011). *The tell-tale brain*. W. W. Norton.

17. Ramachandran, V. S. (2003). *The artful brain, lecture 3*. Available at http://www.bbc.co.uk/radio4/reith2003/lecture3.shtml

18. Feynman, R. (1994). *Six easy pieces* (p. 59). Boston: Addison-Wesley.

INDEX

Abramovic, Marina, 152
abstract art
  brain activity response to, 306
  content of, 140
  fMRI during recognition of, 346–48, 346f
  peak shift effect in, 385
  personality in appreciation of, 181
  size effect on aesthetic experience of, 172
  style processing in, 330
  visual processing of, 301
Abstract Expressionism, 9
ACC. *See* anterior cingulate cortex
achievement, art as, 117–18
achromatopsia, 319
Adams, Anne, 366–69, 368f, 369f, 370f
Adams, Ansel, 11
adjective-matching studies, 33–34
aesthetics
  definition of, 3–4, 25–26, 31–32, 189, 299,
    356–57, 376
  functional specialization of, 319
  as probe for understanding brain, 311–12
  science, nature of art, and, 132–36
Aesthetica (Baumgarten), 31
aesthetic appreciation of artifacts, 111–14
  art definitions and, 123–24
  as extension of agency, 121–23
  openness in, 109–11
  philosophy and, 114–18
  as traces of human activity, 118–21
aesthetic attitude, 308–9
aesthetic culture, 71
aesthetic experience, 47–48, 163–84, 250–71. *See
    also* triangulation of aesthetic experience
  appraisal approach to, 260–71, 262f, 267f
  artwork as stimulus, 165–73
  balance and power of center, 167–70
  criticism in, 81
  diversity in, 262–63
  focal exploration as second phase of, 164,
    175–79
  global impression as first phase of, 164, 173–75
  information processing involved in, 17–18, 17f,
    23, 91–92, 92f
  information-processing model of, 164
  label effect on, 174–75, 328

line perception, 165–67
neurobiological proposal for value of, 307–9
picture format influences, 170–73
poles of, 251–53
psychobiological model of, 254–57, 256f
psychological theories of, 253–60, 256f
psychophysiological approaches to, 183–84
subjectivity in, 260–62, 262f
unwrapping of, 270–71
viewer contributions to art
  experience, 179–81
visual exploration as second phase of aesthetic
  experience, 164, 175–79
aesthetic experimentalism, 47–48
aesthetic fluency, 179–80
aesthetic judgment, 65
  in art experts, 177–78
  brain and, 303
  color preferences in, 190–202, 195f, 197f, 198f,
    200f, 217
  fMRI of participants making, 34
  imagination in, 44
  instability of, 142–43
  Kant's definition of, 7–8
  neural correlates of, 326–33, 332f
  prestige effects in, 239
  spatial composition in, 202–18,
    204f, 205f, 207f, 209f, 210f, 214f, 215f
  in study of art, 133–36
Aesthetic Measure (Birkhoff), 229
aesthetic norms, 71–72
aesthetic oblique effect, 166–67
aesthetics philosophy, 31–58
  literature, 35–41
  music, 41–47
  visual art, 47–57, 50f, 52f, 55f
aesthetic pleasure, 64–66, 223–41
  art and fluency theory, 235–41, 237f
  challenges to fluency theory, 230–38, 237f
  consequences of fluency, 226–28
  culturally shared taste, 238–41
  definitions of, 224
  determinants of fluency, 225–26
  fluency theory of, 211–14, 214f,
    216, 224–30
  processing fluency defined, 225

aesthetic preference, 64
  color preferences, 190–202, 195f, 197f,
    198f, 200f
  complexity relationship with, 232–33, 324
  effect of exposure and rule of thirds on, 70–72
  line contribution to, 165–67
aesthetic primitives, 51
aesthetic processing. *See* information processing
aesthetic response, 189–90
  affective, evaluative, and interpretative
    components of, 76–77
  art v., 67–69
  combining contributions from humanities
    and scientific approaches to, 72–75
  fragility of, 69–72
  fundamental disagreement in research into,
    63–66
  moving towards integrating explanations of,
    75–77
  philosophical theories of, 66–69
  in study of art, 133–36
  visual processing and, 72–75
aesthetic science, 3–26, 129–54
  brains, perception, and stuff in world, 136–37
  changes in art, 143–46
  cognitive science approach to, 16–18, 17f
  combining contributions from humanities
    and scientific approaches, 72–75
  conceptual approach to, 11–14, 22–24, 24f
  conceptual art, 148–52, 150f
  content and art history, 140–41
  content-based approach of lay reactions,
    141–42
  defining phenomenon of interest, 25–26
  development of empirical analysis framework,
    22–24, 24f
  elite and expert guidance, 146–48
  empirical approaches to, 14–22, 17f, 20f
  expressionist approach to, 7–9, 9f, 22–24, 24f
  formalist approach to, 9–11, 12f, 22–24, 24f
  fragility of aesthetic response, 69–72
  inconstancy of beauty, 142–43
  integration of, 63–66
  integration of aesthetic sciences, 63–66
  issues for, 22–26, 24f
  mimetic approach to, 4–7, 6f, 22–24, 24f
  moving towards integration, 75–77
  neuroscience approach to, 19–22, 20f
  object features v. art features, 137–40
  philosophical approaches to, 4–14, 6f, 9f, 12f
  philosophical theories of aesthetic
    response, 66–69
  place for science, 152–54
  psychological science approach to, 14–16
  science, aesthetics, and nature of art, 132–36

  science and artistic expertise, 130–32
"aesthetics from below." *See* bottom-up
    processing
aesthetic theory, 63–77
  of art, 68–69
  combining contributions from humanities
    and scientific approaches, 72–75
  fragility of aesthetic response, 69–72
  integration of aesthetic sciences, 63–66
  moving towards integration, 75–77
  philosophical theories of aesthetic response,
    66–69
affect-as-information framework, 228
affective response. *See also* emotion
  art features v., 137–40
  to music, 42–43
affordance space, 205–7
Africa: Art of a Continent, 114
Afternoon at the Island of the Grande Jatte
    (Seurat), 135–36
agency, art as extension of, 121–23
The Alarm Clock (Léger), 178–79
alienation effect, 237–38
Alzheimer's disease, artistic talent in
    response to, 360–61
The Ambassadors (James), 39
amygdala activity, 100, 305, 379–80
Anderson, Sherwood, 260–61
anger, 268–69
angularity, of line, 165–66
anomalous suspense, triangulation for
    tracking of, 90–92, 92f
anterior cingulate cortex (ACC), 330–33
anterior superior temporal gyrus, 339
anthropology in art, 107–24
  applying philosophy to artifacts, 114–18
  argument for openness, 111–14
  art as extension of agency, 121–23
  artworks as traces of human activity, 118–21
  biological artifacts, 107–9
  definition of art, 123–24
  universal art, 108–11
appearance properties, aesthetic appreciation
    based on, 116–18
Appiah, Kwame Anthony, 114
appraisal approach to aesthetic
    experience, 260–71
  diversity in aesthetic experience, 262–63
  emotions, 263–70, 267f
  subjectivity in aesthetic experience,
    260–62, 262f
appraisal structure, 265
appreciation. *See* aesthetic appreciation
approach signals, color preferences and, 191
Arbutus (Adams), 368f, 370f

architectural expertise, brain activity
modulation by, 331–33, 332*f*
Aristotle, 5
Arnheim, Rudolf, 15–16, 204
arousal, in aesthetic experience, 255–57
art. *See also specific types*
applying philosophy to artifacts, 114–18
argument for openness in, 111–14
art as extension of agency, 121–23
audience of, 146–48
beauty in, 3, 7–8, 223–24
biological artifacts, 107–9
bistability in, 54–55, 55*f*
brain evolution and origin of, 338–39
brain parallels with, 299–301
changing conceptualization of, 67–68
as conceptual statement, 11–14, 22–24, 24*f*
cultural/contextual approaches to, 283–91
definition of, 123–24, 278, 376
education in, 277–78
as emotional expression, 7–9, 9*f*, 22–24, 24*f*
emotional response to, 16, 22–24, 24*f*,
260–63, 262*f*
fluency theory and, 235–41, 237*f*
framework for conceptualizing
experience of, 22–24, 24*f*
imaging studies of, 306–7
individual differences in, 285–91
integration of spheres, 286–91
language and, 338–39, 371
left-sided FTD and, 363–70, 364*f*, 367*f*, 368*f*,
369*f*, 370*f*
memory of, 345–46
as mimesis, 4–7, 6*f*, 22–25, 24*f*
neuroscience contributions to, 299
object features *v.* features of, 137–40
as perceiving significant form, 9–11, 12*f*,
22–24, 24*f*
psycho-historical theory of, 236–38
science, aesthetics, and nature of, 132–36
as search for enduring features, 72–75
spheres essential for psychological
explanations of, 278–86
as stimulus, 165–73, 253, 264
theories of, 67–69
as trace of human activity, 118–21
universal approaches to, 279–83, 286–91
universal art, 108–11
variability of, 143–46
viewer contributions to, 179–81
art about art, 13–14
Art and Illusion (Gombrich), 17–18
Art and Visual Perception (Arnheim), 15
art criticism. *See* criticism
art-elicited brain activation. *See* brain activation

art expertise. *See* expertise
art forgeries, aesthetic value of, 182
art history
aesthetics throughout, 132–36
content and, 140–41
evolutionary theories and, 282
artifacts, 111–14
art definitions and, 123–24
biological artifacts, 107–9
as extension of agency, 121–23
openness in, 109–11
philosophy and, 114–18
as traces of human activity, 118–21
artificial laboratory research, 252–53
Art in a New Key (Langer), 13
artist, eye movements of, 339–40
artistic development, 276–92
cultural/contextual approaches to art, 283–91
in digitally mediated participatory cultures,
288–91
individual differences in art, 285–91
integration of spheres, 286–91
spheres essential for psychological
explanations of art, 278–86
universal approaches to art, 279–83, 286–91
U-shaped curve in, 287–88
artistic genius, 357–58, 371, 385, 386*f*
artistic knowledge, 129–54
brains, perception, and stuff in world, 136–37
change in art, 143–46
conceptual art, 148–52, 150*f*
content and art history, 140–41
content-based approach of lay reactions,
141–42
elite and expert guidance, 146–48
inconstancy of beauty, 142–43
object features *v.* art features, 137–40
place for science, 152–54
science, aesthetics, and nature of art, 132–36
science and artistic expertise, 130–32
artistic value, 65
artistry, neurological characterization of, 370–71
art philosophy, 31–58
literature, 35–41
music, 41–47
visual art, 47–57, 50*f*, 52*f*, 55*f*
art reproductions, aesthetic adequacy
of, 170–73, 182
Art World argument, 327
Asmat shields, 113, 121–22
aspect ratio, measurement *v.* experience
of, 81–82, 82*f*
attentional inhibition account of
positive affect, 234–35
attentional strategy, art as, 55–57

attitude, aesthetic, 308–9
attractiveness. *See* beauty
audience, of art, 146–48
audiovisual experience, film's
    creation of, 87*f*, 88, 89*f*
auditory imagery, 43–47
auditory splitting, 84–85, 87*f*, 88, 89*f*
autism, artistic genius and, 385, 386*f*
avant-gardism, 148–52, 150*f*
Avatar (Cameron), 81
avoid signals, color preferences and, 191

Bach, Johann Sebastian, 240
balance, 167–70
Barry, Robert, 123
Baselitz, Georg, 236
Bathers at Asnières (Seurat), 49–51, 50*f*
Batteux, Charles, 68
Baumgarten, Alexander, 3, 7, 31
The Beautiful in Music (Hanslick), 42
beauty
    achievement and, 117
    aesthetic response and, 65
    in art, 3, 7–8, 223–24
    complexity relationship with, 232
    definitions of, 7–8, 224
    drive for, 307–8
    in environmental adaptation, 308–9
    Fechner's definition of, 325
    fluency and, 223, 228
    imaging studies of, 303–5
    inconstancy of, 142–43
    neural correlates of, 303–7
    power derived from, 121–23
    in study of art, 133–36, 139–40
Beethoven, Ludwig van, 3, 42
behavior, dementia as model for
    understanding of, 361–63
behavioral anatomy, of brain, 358–61
behavioral neurology. *See* cognitive and
    behavioral neurology
behavioral variant of frontotemporal
    dementia (bvFTD), 362
behaviorism, neural, 97–100
Bell, Clive, 10
Berkeley Color Project, 196–200, 197*f*,
    198*f*, 200*f*
Berlyne, Daniel, 16, 254–57, 256*f*
bias
    center, 203–6, 208, 212, 217–18
    ecological, 206–12, 209*f*, 210*f*, 217–18
    inward, 170, 203–6, 211–12, 217–18
    perspective, 207–10, 218
    rightward, 170
    symmetrical center, 170

violation of, 214–16, 215*f*
biological artifacts, 107–9
biopsychological approaches to art, 279–83,
    286–91
Birkhoff, George, 229
bistability, in art, 54–55, 55*f*
Boas, Franz, 109
body
    in aesthetic processing of artworks, 163,
    183–84
    aesthetic sensibility based on, 118–21
    beauty of, 305
    neural mapping of, 94–97, 98*f*
Boléro (Ravel), 369
Bonnar, Lizann, 54–55, 55*f*
bottom-up processing, 17–18, 17*f*, 323–26
    in explaining anomalous suspense, 91–92, 92*f*
    in object recognition, 350
    top-down processing influences on, 178–79
    top-down processing *v.*, 233–34
Bourdier, Jean-Paul, 213, 214*f*, 216
Bourdieu, Pierre, 223, 238–40
bowerbirds, "art" of, 377
brain. *See also* mind; *specific structures*
    art parallels with, 299–301
    behavioral anatomy of, 358–61
    body mapping by, 94–97, 98*f*
    cerebral cortex, 19–21, 20*f*, 45–46
    functional studies of, 20–22
    information processing by, 19–22, 20*f*
    lesion studies of, 303, 304*t*
    perception, stuff in world, and, 136–37
    PFC, 19–21, 20*f*
    as probe for understanding aesthetics, 311–12
brain activation, 318–33, 337–51
    art neuroimaging studies, 306–7
    beauty neuroimaging studies, 303–5
    brain evolution and origin of art, 338–39
    early neuroaesthetic studies, 319–20
    Fauvism, 320–21
    Fechner and foundation of experimental
    aesthetics, 323–26
    functional specialization of aesthetics, 319
    functional specialization of visual cortex,
    318–19
    kinetic art, 320
    neural basis of creativity, 339–40
    neural correlates of aesthetic judgments,
    326–33, 332*f*
    object recognition in Cubist paintings,
    348–50, 349*f*
    perception and imagination of faces and
    objects, 340–43
    representational paintings and recognition
    memory, 343–45, 344*f*

Surrealism, 321–23, 323*f*
  visual indeterminacy, 345–48, 346*f*
brain injury, 370–71
  artistic talent in response to, 360–61
  dementia as model for understanding
    behavior and cognition, 361–63
  left-sided FTD and art, 363–70, 364*f*, 367*f*,
    368*f*, 369*f*, 370*f*
Brakhage, Stan, 88, 89*f*
Braque, George, 184, 348, 349*f*
Brodmann, Korbinian, 19
Brodmann areas, 19
Brunelleschi, Filippo, 5
bvFTD. *See* behavioral variant of
  frontotemporal dementia

Cage, John, 68–69
Calder, Alexander, 73, 75, 337
Calling of Saint Matthew (Caravaggio), 154
Cameron, James, 81, 90–91
canonical neurons, 119
canonical orientation, 211
canonical perspective, 210–12, 211*f*
canonical size, 211
Caravaggio, Michelangelo Merisi da, 146, 151, 154
caricature, peak shift effect in, 382
Carroll, Noël, 67
category learning, 343–45, 344*f*
cattle, as art, 107–9
cave paintings, 279, 338
center
  bias, 203–6, 208, 212, 217–18
  gaze fixations on, 177–78
  power of, 167–70, 177–78, 204
cerebral achromatopsia, 319
cerebral cortex, 19–21, 20*f*, 45–46. *See also*
  specific structures
Cézanne, Paul, 10, 174–75, 281–82
change blindness, 18, 84
Chauvet cave paintings, 338
chiaroscuro, 5–7, 6*f*, 18
child art, 287–91
Child With Doll (Ensor), 142
chimerical color experience, 87–88
Christus, Petrus, 171–72, 182
Churchland, Paul, 86–88
The Clarinet (Picasso), 349*f*
Clark, T. J., 145
class, taste developed
  within, 238–41
cognition
  artist manipulation of, 282
  dementia as model for
    understanding of, 361–63
  disfluency affect on, 237–38

eye movement studies of, 175–79
fluency effect on, 227–28
imagination and, 44
influence on aesthetic judgment, 326–29
limitations in, 81–82
mirror system and, 94
of music, 43
pupillary response during, 184
skills of, 91–92
in understanding art, 143–46
cognitive and behavioral neurology, 356–71
  artistic genius, 357–58, 371
  behavioral anatomy of brain, 358–61
  defining aesthetics, 356–57
  dementia as model for understanding
    behavior and cognition, 361–63
  future directions, 370–71
  left-sided FTD and art, 363–70, 364*f*, 367*f*,
    368*f*, 369*f*, 370*f*
cognitive monitoring, of emotional
  response, 39–41
cognitive neuroscience. *See* neuroscience
cognitive science, as approach to aesthetic
  science, 16–18, 17*f*
cognitive theories
  of aesthetic response, 66
  of emotions, 35–41
collaborative art, digitally mediated, 288–91
collative variables, 16, 255–56
color
  balance of, 168–169
  brain disorders and, 319
  emotional content of, 192–93, 198–200, 200*f*
  perception of, 86–88, 89*f*
  processing of, 320–21
color appearance theory, 192, 198
color grouping, 379–80, 379*f*
color preferences, 190–202, 217
  color WAVEs, 198–202, 200*f*
  culture and, 195–96, 201
  idiosyncratic effects in, 196, 201–2
  subculture and, 196, 201
  theories of, 191–96, 195*f*
  in United States, 196–98, 197*f*, 198*f*
communication, art as, 338–39
complexity
  aesthetic preference relationship
    with, 232–33, 324
  interest and, 266, 267*f*
  inverted-U curve of, 255–56
composition
  balance, 167–70
  color preferences, 190–202, 195*f*, 197*f*,
    198*f*, 200*f*
  line, 165–67

composition (*Cont'd*)
  power of center, 167–70, 177–78, 204
  processing of, 302
  spatial, 202–18, 204f, 205f, 207f, 209f, 210f,
    214f, 215f
Composition with Red, Yellow and Blue
    (Mondrian), 174–75
compulsion, in left-sided FTD and art, 363–64
computer-generated animation, cognitive
    approach applied to, 18
conceptual approach, to aesthetic
    science, 11–14, 22–24, 24f
conceptual art, 148–52, 150f
conceptual fluency, 225, 236–38
cone-contrast model, 198
confusion, 266–68
consciousness
  of art, 136–37
  triangulating evidences of, 83–90
contempt, 268–69
content, 129–30, 135–39
  in aesthetic processing of artworks, 163, 165
  art history and, 140–41
  fluency as cue to, 236–38
  form *v.*, 304t
  influence on aesthetic judgment, 326–29
  lay reactions to, 141–42
  in perception and memory of art, 345–46
  processing of, 302
  spatial composition preferences and, 213–16,
    214f, 215f
  Surrealist violations of, 321–23, 323f
context
  aesthetic experience in response to, 181–83
  influence on aesthetic judgment, 326–29
  parahippocampal cortex and, 348–50, 349f
  Surrealist violations of, 321–23, 323f
  as variable in aesthetics research, 252–53
contextual approach
  to art, 283–91
  to artifacts, 116–18
Contrast of Forms (Léger), 178–79
Coote, Jeremy, 108
coping potential appraisal, 266, 267f
costly signal proposal, 307–8
creation, imagination and, 44
creativity
  cultural influence on, 284–85
  genius in, 357–58, 371
  neural basis of, 339–40
  personality associated with, 285
  PNFA and, 366–69, 367f, 368f, 369f, 370f
  semantic dementia and, 366
Creed, Martin, 68–69
criticism, 67
  in aesthetic experience, 81

  in aesthetic response, 67, 74–75
  aesthetic science in, 129–30
  in lay understanding of art, 148
  role of, 145–46
Critique of Judgment (Kant), 7, 115
Critique of Pure Reason (Kant), 7
Croce, Benedetto, 325
Cubism, 153
  object recognition in, 348–50, 349f
  processing fluency and, 184
cultural approaches to art, 283–91
culture, 107–24, 376–77
  aesthetic, 71
  applying philosophy to artifacts, 114–18
  argument for openness, 111–14
  art as extension of agency, 121–23
  art as trace of human activity, 118–21
  biological artifacts, 107–9
  color preferences and, 195–96, 201
  definition of art, 123–24
  digitally mediated participatory, 288–91
  museum, 182
  of psychology, 251–53
  in understanding art, 143–46
  universal art, 108–11
Cutting, James, 70–71, 146

Dadaism, 13
  changing view on, 152
  content of artworks of, 140
Dalí, Salvador, 54–55, 55f
dance, fMRI of participants making aesthetic
    judgments of, 34
Danto, Arthur, 116, 327
David (Michelangelo), 3
da Vinci, Leonardo, 5–6, 6f, 385, 386f. *See also*
    Mona Lisa
Davis, Stuart, 174–75
Death in the Woods (Anderson), 260–61
De Bont, Jan, 90–91
*Deeper than Reason: The Emotions and their
    Role in Literature, Music and Art*
    (Robinson), 35
default preferences, 213, 214f
de Kooning, Willem, 361
dementia
  defined, 361–62
  FTLD, 361–63
  left-sided FTD and art, 363–70, 364f, 367f,
    368f, 369f, 370f
  as model for understanding behavior and
    cognition, 361–63
Demoiselles d'Avignon (Picasso), 146
Descartes, René, 324
development. *See* artistic development
Dewey, John, 230

diachronia, 163, 179–81
Dickie, George, 32–35, 235
Die deutsche Ästhetik seit Kant
(von Hartmann), 324–25
digitally mediated participatory cultures, 288–91
dilation, pupil. *See* pupillary response
dimensionality, measurement *v.* experience of, 81
Dinka art, 107–9
disfluency, 236–38, 237*f*
disgust, 268–69
disinterested interest, 309
diversity, in aesthetic experience, 262–63
diversive exploration, 177–78
Dolce, Ludovico, 135
dorsal visual processing pathway, 300
Dostoevsky, Fyodor, 357
Drapery for a seated figure (da Vinci), 6*f*
drive
in aesthetic experience, 255–57
for beauty, 307–8
Duchamp, Marcel, 11–13, 148–49, 152, 154
duration, measurement *v.* experience of, 81–82

ecological biases, 206–7, 209*f*, 210–12, 210*f*
ecological valence theory
(EVT), 191–96, 217
color WAVEs, 198–202, 200*f*
cultural commonalities and differences, 201
individual differences, 201–2
object association task, 199
object-color match ratings, 199–200, 200*f*
object valence ratings, 199
subcultural differences, 201
education in art, 277–78
Ehrsson, Henrik, 96
Einstein, Albert, 357
Ekman, Paul, 37
Elemente der Psychophysik (Fechner), 14, 311
embarrassment, 269
emotion
aesthetic emotion *v.*, 263
artist manipulation of, 282
brain processing of, 20–22
cognitive theories *v.* non-cognitive
theories of, 35–41
color and, 192–93, 198–200, 200*f*
hostile emotions, 268–69
knowledge emotions, 265–68, 267*f*
Lyons' theory on, 40–41
positive emotions, 268
processing fluency and, 226–28
in response to music, 41–43
Robinson's neo-Jamesianism
approach to, 35–41
self-conscious emotions, 269–70
emotional contagion, 37

emotional learning, 39–40
emotional response, 250–71
appraisal approach to, 260–71, 262*f*, 267*f*
to art, 16, 22–24, 24*f*, 260–63, 262*f*
to beauty, 304–5
brain and, 303
diversity in, 262–63
Fechner's focus on, 325
poles of aesthetic experience, 251–53
psychological theories of aesthetic
experience, 253–60, 256*f*
pupillary response during, 184
subjectivity in, 260–62, 262*f*
unwrapping of, 270–71
empathy
neural body maps in understanding
of, 94–97, 98*f*
triangulation for understanding of, 93–94
empirical aesthetics, 14–22, 17*f*, 20*f*, 47–48,
163–84, 250–71. *See also specific disciplines*
appraisal approach to aesthetic experience,
260–71, 262*f*, 267*f*
art as stimulus, 165–73, 253, 264
balance, 167–70
development of framework for, 22–24, 24*f*
diversity in aesthetic experience, 262–63
foundation of, 323–26
global impression as first phase of aesthetic
experience, 164, 173–75
imaging studies of art, 306–7
imaging studies of beauty, 303–8
lesion studies, 303, 304*t*
line perception, 165–67
music, 42–43
picture format influences, 170–73
poles of aesthetic experience, 251–53
power of center, 167–70, 177–78, 204
psychological theories of aesthetic experience,
253–60, 256*f*
psychophysiological approaches to aesthetic
experience, 183–84
subjectivity in aesthetic experience, 260–62, 262*f*
unwrapping of aesthetic experience, 270–71
viewer contributions to art experience, 179–81
visual exploration as second phase of aesthetic
experience, 164, 175–79
empirical challenges, to fluency theory of
aesthetic pleasure, 230–33
Enlightenment, 135
Ensor, James, 142
entorhinal cortex, 329
environment
in aesthetic processing of artworks, 163, 181–83
beauty in adaptation to, 308–9
color preferences and, 191–96, 217
spatial preferences and, 206–12, 209*f*, 210*f*, 217–18

erotic sculpture, peak shift effect in, 382, 383*f*
evaluation. *See* aesthetic judgment
evolution
    aesthetic attitude, 308–9
    aesthetic laws arising from, 376–77, 380–81, 388
    of brain and art, 338–39
    color preferences and, 191–92, 194
    in drive for beauty, 307–8
    spatial composition and, 217–18
    in understanding art, 279–80, 282, 286–91
EVT. *See* ecological valence theory
executive control, 19
expectations
    in music, 233–34
    surprise and, 265
    violation of, 213–16, 214*f*, 215*f*, 321–23, 323*f*
experience. *See* aesthetic experience
experience seeking, 181
experimental aesthetics, 252–53, 323–26
experimental psychology, 280–81
expertise
    aesthetic judgment in response to, 177–78,
        329–33, 332*f*
    aesthetic science and, 130–32
    appreciation and, 285–86
    art experience in response
        to, 179–80
    interest and, 266
    line angularity preference and, 166
    perception in response to, 177–78
    in psychobiological model, 256–57
    as variable in aesthetics research, 253
exploration, as second phase of aesthetic
        experience, 164, 175–79
exposure effect, 65, 70–71, 211–14, 214*f*,
        225–27, 259
    attentional inhibition account and, 234
    in culturally shared taste, 239–41
    as fluency determinant, 229–30
Expressionism, 9
expressionist approach, 7–9, 9*f*, 22–24, 24*f*
expression theory of art, 68
expressive development
    left-sided FTD and, 363–70, 364*f*, 367*f*, 368*f*,
        369*f*, 370*f*
    U-shaped curve in, 287–88
eye movement studies
    of artists *v.* laymen, 339–40
    of processes underlying aesthetic
        experience, 175–79
Eysenck, Hans-Jürgen, 229

face
    beauty of, 304–5
    imagery of, 340–43
    profile perception, 85–86

recognition of, 340–43
facial expressions
    emotional response to, 37
    empathy evoked by, 97, 98*f*
facing direction, of objects in artworks, 169–70,
        203–6, 204*f*, 205*f*
facsimile accommodation, 173
fake artwork, aesthetic value of, 182
familiarity, boredom due to, 231–32
Fauvism, processing of, 320–21
fear, neurological response associated with, 100
Fechner, Gustav, 14–16, 229, 311, 323–26
Femme et Pot de Moutarde (Picasso), 184
Feynman, Richard, 389
fictional literature
    learning from, 39–40
    paradoxical emotional response to, 36, 39
Figgis, Mike, 87*f*, 88
film
    aesthetic experience *v.* measurement
        of, 81–82, 82*f*
    anomalous suspense in, 90–92, 92*f*
    appreciation for, 286
    audiovisual experience created by, 87*f*, 88, 89*f*
    empathy evoked by, 97, 98*f*
first impression, as first phase of aesthetic
        experience, 164, 173–75
Fishing Boats (Braque), 184
Fishkin, Samantha, 21
fit, representational, 213–16, 214*f*, 215*f*
fit hypothesis, 211–14, 214*f*
fixations, in study of aesthetic experience, 175–79
Flanagan, Owen, 83–86
flatness, of modern art, 10
flicker, 88, 89*f*
fluency. *See also* processing fluency
    aesthetic, 179–80
    conceptual, 225, 236–38
    known *v.* unknown source of, 231–32
    perceptual, 65–66, 225, 231
    proper measurement of, 231, 233
    pupil response and, 184
fluency theory of aesthetic pleasure, 211–14, 214*f*,
        216, 224–30, 258–60, 308
    alternatives to, 233–35
    art and, 235–41, 237*f*
    beauty and aesthetic pleasure, 224
    consequences of processing fluency, 226–28
    culturally shared taste and, 238–41
    determinants of processing fluency, 225–26
    empirical challenges to, 230–33
    evidence for, 228–30
    outside of art realm, 230
    processing fluency defined, 225
fMRI. *See* functional magnetic resonance
        imaging

focal exploration, as second phase of aesthetic experience, 164, 175–79
forgeries, aesthetic value of, 182
form
  content *v.*, 304*t*
  primitives, 384
  processing of, 302
formalist approach
  to aesthetic science, 9–11, 12*f*, 22–24, 24*f*
  to art, 68
  to artifacts, 116–17
formal structure of artworks, visual system operations coupled to, 48–57, 50*f*, 52*f*, 55*f*
format. *See* picture format
Fountain (Duchamp), 11–13, 149, 154
4´ 33″ (Cage), 68
foveal vision, in sfumato technique, 52–53, 52*f*
frequency-specific adaptation, 54
Frith, Francis, 11
frontal cortex, 304, 306, 358–59, 370–71. *See also* orbitofrontal cortex
  left-sided FTD and art, 363–70, 364*f*, 367*f*, 368*f*, 369*f*, 370*f*
  in perception and imagination of faces and objects, 342
frontotemporal dementia (FTD), 362–63
  in art, 363–70, 364*f*, 367*f*, 368*f*, 369*f*, 370*f*
frontotemporal lobar degeneration (FTLD), 361–63
FTD. *See* frontotemporal dementia
FTLD. *See* frontotemporal lobar degeneration
Fugue No. 1 in C-major (Bach), 240
functionality, brain anatomy and, 358–59
functional magnetic resonance imaging (fMRI), 21–22, 337, 359
  of abstract art, 346–48, 346*f*
  of art response, 306–7
  of bodily beauty, 305
  of cognitive information influence on aesthetic judgment, 326–29
  of creative brain, 339–40
  of expertise role in aesthetic judgment in response to, 330–33, 332*f*
  of object recognition in Cubist paintings, 348–50, 349*f*
  of participants making aesthetic judgments, 34
  of perception and imagination of faces and objects, 341–43
  of recognition memory and category learning, 343–45, 344*f*
  of response to Super Bowl ads, 99–100
  of Surrealist art processing, 321–23, 323*f*
  of visual indeterminacy, 346–48, 346*f*
functional specialization
  of aesthetics, 319
  of visual cortex, 318–19
fundamental disagreement, in research into aesthetic response, 63–66
fusiform gyrus, 347–48

Gage, Phineas, 20–21
Gallese, Vittorio, 86, 119–20
Garden at Saint-Adresse (Monet), 174–75
Gauguin, Paul, 10
gaze fixations, in study of aesthetic experience, 175–79
Gell, Alfred, 113, 121–23
gender, color preference based on, 191–92
genius. *See* artistic genius
Géricault, Théodore, 8, 9*f*
Gestalt psychology, as approach in aesthetic science, 15–16
gesture, empathy evoked by, 97, 98*f*
global impression, as first phase of aesthetic experience, 164, 173–75
Godard, Jean-Luc, 88, 89*f*
Golden Section, in Fechner's studies, 324
A Goldsmith in His Shop, Possibly St. Eligius (Christus), 171–72
Gombrich, Ernst, 18, 51, 53
Goodman, Nelson, 13, 277–78
Gosselin, Frédéric, 54–55, 55*f*
Greenberg, Clement, 10, 116
Greengrass, Paul, 91
Gris, Juan, 348, 349*f*
grouping principle, 378–80, 378*f*, 379*f*
Guernica (Picasso), 285
guilt, 269
Guitar and Flowers (Gris), 349*f*

Haacke, Hans, 148
habitat preference, in explaining art existence, 280
Halpern, Andrea, 45–47
Hanslick, Eduard, 42
Harlow, John Martyn, 21
harmony principle, 386–87
health, color preferences and, 193
hedonic fluency model. *See* processing fluency
hedonic response, 4, 25–26
  cognition influence on, 326–29
Herbart, Johann Friedrich, 325
hidden knowledge in aesthetic judgments, 189–90
  color preferences, 190–202, 195*f*, 197*f*, 198*f*, 200*f*, 217
  conjectures and conclusions, 217–19
  spatial composition, 202–18, 204*f*, 205*f*, 207*f*, 209*f*, 210*f*, 214*f*, 215*f*

hippocampal activation, 329, 347–48
Hirst, Damien, 152, 376
history. *See* art history
Hitchcock, Alfred, 92, 92*f*, 97, 98*f*
Homage to New York (Tinguely), 320
horizontal line preference, 166–67
horizontal object placement, 203–6, 204*f*, 205*f*
hostile emotions, 268–69
Hull, Clark, 254
Hume, David, 7–8, 44
Humphrey, Nicholas, 117, 191
Huron, David, 233–34
Hurvich-Jameson opponent-process
    theory, 86–87
Hutcheson, Francis, 7–8

Iacoboni, Marco, 99–100
idealism, Plato's view of, 4–5
identity theory, 86, 88
idiosyncratic effects, color preferences
    and, 196, 201–2
image format, aesthetic experience
    response to, 170–73
imagery
    auditory/musical, 43–47
    perception and, 44–47
    visual, 44–45, 340–43
imagination
    musical, 43–47
    senses of, 44
imitation theory of art, 68
implicit movements, in aesthetic
    appreciation, 119–20
Impressionism, 10, 70–71, 282–83, 300
indeterminacy effect, 345–48, 346*f*
Indian erotic sculpture, peak shift
    effect in, 382, 383*f*
individual differences. *See* personal
    differences
infants
    color preferences in, 194, 195*f*
    stimuli preferences in, 281
information processing, 318–33. *See also*
    processing fluency; visual processing
    of aesthetic experiences, 17–18, 17*f*, 18*f*, 23,
        91–92, 92*f*
    brain mechanisms of, 19–22, 20*f*
    early neuroaesthetic studies, 319–20
    Fauvism, 320–21
    Fechner and foundation of experimental
        aesthetics, 323–26
    functional specialization of aesthetics, 319
    functional specialization of visual cortex,
        318–19
    kinetic art, 320

model of, 164
neural correlates of aesthetic judgments,
    326–33, 332*f*
    in neuroaesthetic framework, 301–2, 302*f*
    Surrealism, 321–23, 323*f*
inner psychophysics, 311
Inner Vision (Zeki), 337
insula, 305
integration within aesthetic science
    combining contributions from humanities
        and scientific approaches, 72–75
    fragility of aesthetic response, 69–72
    integration of aesthetic sciences, 63–66
    moving towards integration, 75–77
    philosophical theories of aesthetic response,
        66–69
interest, 266, 267*f*
interestingness, 256, 258–60
Internet, artistic development and, 288–91
inward bias, 170, 203–6, 211–12, 217–18
ipsichronia, in aesthetic processing of artworks,
    163, 182
irradiation, 49–51, 50*f*
Isenberg, Arnold, 145
I-SKE framework, 23–24, 24*f*
isolation principle, 385
"Is Psychology Relevant to Aesthetics?"
    (Dickie), 32
It Takes a Nation of Millions to Hold Us Back
    (Public Enemy), 261

Jacobsen's framework for psychological study of
    aesthetic processing of artworks, 163–64
    body, 163, 183–84
    content, 163, 165
    diachronia, 163, 179–81
    ipsichronia, 163, 182
    person, 163, 179–81
    situation, 163, 181–83
James, Henry, 39
James, William, 35–36
Janaway, Chris, 109
Jaws (Spielberg), 100, 101*f*
Johns, Jasper, 13, 145
Judd, Donald, 152
judgment. *See* aesthetic judgment
judgmentalism, in literature
    philosophy, 36–38

Kant, Immanuel, 7–8, 44, 115
kinetic art, 320
King Lear (Shakespeare), 138–39
Kinkade, Thomas, 261, 269, 388
kitsch art, 282, 375–76, 387–88

Kivy, Peter, 42
knowledge. *See also* artistic knowledge; hidden
    knowledge in aesthetic judgments
    art influence on, 23–24, 24*f*
    art production of, 140–41
    Kant's definition of, 7
    Positivist approach to, 32
    in processing of aesthetic experiences, 17–18,
        17*f*, 18*f*, 23
knowledge emotions, 265–68, 267*f*
Koffka, Kurt, 15
Köhler, Wolfgang, 15
Kosuth, Joseph, 14, 123

label
    aesthetic experience in response to, 174–75,
        328–29
    exploratory behavior in response to, 178–79
    perception of meaning and, 350
laboratory research, defense of, 252–53
Landesman, Peter, 21
Langer, Suzanne, 13–14
language, art and, 338–39, 371
Languages of Art (Goodman), 13
La Reconnaissance Infinie
    (Magritte), 323*f*
Lascaux cave paintings, 279
Las Hilanderas (Velazquez), 149–50, 150*f*
lateral inhibition, in retina, 50–51
lateralization, 359–60
Latto, Richard, 49–51, 50*f*
law of inverse ratios of areas, 168
lay reactions
    to content in art, 141–42, 148
    eye movements during, 339–40
Lazarus, Richard, 37
learning. *See also* artistic development
    category, 343–45, 344*f*
    emotional, 39–40
Lectures in Aesthetics (Wittgenstein), 32
LeDoux, Joseph, 38
left frontal lobe, 370–71
    left-sided FTD and art, 363–70, 364*f*, 367*f*,
        368*f*, 369*f*, 370*f*
left-handedness, artistic genius and, 358, 371
left hemisphere specialization, 359–60
Léger, Fernand, 178–79
Levinson, Jerrold, 68–69
Lewin, Kurt, 252
Lichtenstein, Roy, 13
liking, wanting *v.*, 309
limbic system, in visual processing, 379–80
line, as perceptual primitive of art, 165–67
linear perspective, 5–7
literature

aesthetics of, 138–39
psychology and neuroscience applied to
    philosophy of, 35–41
Livingstone, Margaret, 52–54, 52*f*
Logical Positivism, knowledge and, 32
Louis, Morris, 140–41
Lyons, William, 40–41

Macbeth (Polanski), 91
Mach, Ernst, 49
Mach bands, 49–51
Made in USA (Godard), 88, 89*f*
magnetoencephalography, for imaging
    response to art, 306
Magritte, René, 321–23, 323*f*
Manet, Édouard, 10, 141
Marc, Franz, 233–34
Martindale, Colin, 146
Masaccio, 5
mate selection, 307–8
    cultural modulation of, 284
    in explaining art existence, 279–80
    visual aesthetics and, 376–77, 380
Matisse, Henri, 9
McCleary, Robert, 37
McDowell, John, 109
*Meditationes Philosophicae de Nonnullis ad
    Poema Pertinentibus* (Baumgarten), 31
memory
    of art, 345–46
    recognition, 343–45, 344*f*
mental illness, creativity associated
    with, 285, 357–58, 371
mental phenomena, triangulating
    evidences of, 83–90
mere exposure. *See* exposure effect
meta-art, 13–14
metacognition, 20
metaphor principle, 386
Michelangelo, 3
Middle Ages, 134
mimetic approach, 4–7, 6*f*, 22–24, 24*f*
mind, in aesthetic processing of
    artworks, 163
Minimalist sculptures, 152
mirror neurons, 86
    in aesthetic appreciation, 119
    in explanations of empathy, 93–94
    during Super Bowl ads, 99
modern art
    bias and fit violations in, 216
    child art in, 287–88
    disfluency in, 236–38, 237*f*
Modernism, 10
Modernist Painting (Greenberg), 10

modularity of aesthetic processing and
    perception, 318–33
  early neuroaesthetic studies, 319–20
  Fauvism, 320–21
  Fechner and foundation of experimental
    aesthetics, 323–26
  functional specialization of aesthetics, 319
  functional specialization of visual
    cortex, 318–19
  kinetic art, 320
  neural correlates of aesthetic judgments,
    326–33, 332f
  Surrealism, 321–23, 323f
Mona Lisa (da Vinci)
  instability of reading of, 142–43
  scientific study of, 132
  sfumato used in, 51–54, 52f
Mondrian, Piet, 167–69, 174–75, 337
Monet, Claude, 10, 174–75
mood disorder, artistic genius
    and, 285, 357–58, 371
Morris, Robert, 152
motion processing, 320
motivation, in aesthetic experience, 255–57
museum
  aesthetic experience in response to, 181–83
  aesthetics of artifacts in, 114
music
  brain activation and, 339
  expectations in, 233–34
  psychology and neuroscience applied to
    philosophy of, 41–47
  shared taste in, 239–41
musical imagery, 43–47
musical imagination, 43–47

Nadia, 385, 386f
narrative, empathy in, 93
nativist fallacy, 260–61
Natural Color System, 192, 196
"natural method," for explaining aesthetic
    experience, 83–90, 87f, 89f
natural selection. *See* evolution
Nature's Writing (Bourdier), 213, 214f, 216
negative stimuli, processing fluency
    and, 232–33
neo-Jamesianism approach to emotions, 35–41
neural behaviorism, 97–100
neural body maps, 94–97, 98f
neural correlates, 337–51
  of aesthetic judgments, 326–33, 332f
  of beauty, 303–7
  brain evolution and origin of
    art, 338–39
  of creativity, 339–40
  neural basis of creativity, 339–40

object recognition in Cubist paintings,
    348–50, 349f
perception and imagination of faces and
    objects, 340–43
representational paintings and recognition
    memory, 343–45, 344f
visual indeterminacy, 345–48, 346f
neural networks, 359
  individual subjectivities arising from, 137
neural processing, 19–22, 20f
  aesthetic response and, 72–75
Neurath, Otto, 83
neuroaesthetics, 22, 183–84, 299–312, 318–33,
    356–57, 375–89, 387f
  cautions for, 309–12
  early neuroaesthetic studies, 319–20
  early studies in, 319–20
  empirical evidence from imaging studies of
    art, 306–7
  empirical evidence from imaging studies of
    beauty, 303–5
  empirical evidence from lesion
    studies, 303, 304t
  Fauvism, 320–21
  Fechner and foundation of experimental
    aesthetics, 323–26
  framework of, 301–3, 302f
  functional specialization of aesthetics, 319
  functional specialization of visual
    cortex, 318–19
  grouping principle, 378–80, 378f, 379f
  harmony principle, 386–87
  isolation principle, 385
  kinetic art, 320
  neural correlates of aesthetic judgments,
    326–33, 332f
  neurobiological proposal for value of aesthetic
    experiences, 307–9
  parallels between art and brain, 299–301
  peak shift effect, 64, 381–85, 381f, 383f, 384f
  peek-a-boo principle, 385–86
  punning principle, 386
  Surrealism, 321–23, 323f
  symmetry principle, 380–81
neurobiological mechanisms
  of aesthetic response, 65
  for value of aesthetic experiences, 307–9
neurodegenerative disease, 370–71
  artistic talent in response to, 360–61
  dementia as model for understanding
    behavior and cognition, 361–63
  left-sided FTD and art, 363–70, 364f, 367f,
    368f, 369f, 370f
neuroimaging, 21–22, 318–33. *See also* functional
    magnetic resonance imaging
  of art response, 306–7

of beauty, 303–5
early neuroaesthetic studies, 319–20
Fauvism, 320–21
Fechner and foundation of experimental
    aesthetics, 323–26
functional specialization of aesthetics, 319
functional specialization of visual cortex,
    318–19
kinetic art, 320
neural correlates of aesthetic judgments,
    326–33, 332*f*
Surrealism, 321–23, 323*f*
neurological evidence
in explaining anomalous suspense, 91–92
in explaining empathy, 93–94
in explaining neural body mapping, 96–97
of mental phenomena, 83, 85–86, 88–90
neural behaviorism and, 97–100
subpersonal processing and, 100–101, 101*f*
neurology. *See* cognitive and behavioral
    neurology
neuron
canonical, 119
mirror, 86, 93–94, 99, 119
neuropsychological investigations, 20
neuroscience
added value of, 312
as approach to aesthetic science, 19–22, 20*f*
brains, perception, and stuff in world, 136–37
in literature, 35–41
in music, 41–47
object features *v.* art features, 137–40
role in understanding art, 152–54
in visual art, 47–57, 50*f*, 52*f*, 55*f*
neuroticism, creativity associated with, 285
Nilitic art, 107–9
Ninth Symphony (Beethoven), 3
Noë, Alva, 136, 147
non-cognitive approach to emotions, 35–41
norms, aesthetic, 71–72
novelty appraisal, 265
nucleus accumbens, 332–33

object
art features *v.* features of, 137–40
imagery of, 340–43
recognition of, 340–43, 348–50, 349*f*
Surrealist violations of, 321–23, 323*f*
as variable in aesthetics
    research, 252–53
objectivist approach to aesthetic
    experience, 260–62
oblique effect, 166–67
occipital lobes, 306
occipitoparietal cortex, 341
occipitotemporal cortex, 304–5, 340–41

Ocean, Humphrey, 340
oddball effects, 321
OFC. *See* orbitofrontal cortex
Of the Standard of Taste (Hume), 7
On Criticism (Carroll), 67
One and Three Chairs (Kosuth), 14
Onians, John, 137
openness, 109–11
argument for, 111–14
art definitions and, 123–24
to experience, 180–81
philosophical theory and, 114–18
orbitofrontal cortex (OFC), 20–22, 304, 306–7,
    326–28, 330–33
disease in, 365–66
orientation
canonical, 211
of line, 165–67
Osborne, Peter, 134
outer psychophysics, 311

P$_2$ potentials, 309
pain, beauty and, 309
paradoxical functional
    facilitation, 365, 368
parahippocampal cortex, 348–50, 349*f*
parietal cortex, 341–42, 358–59, 367–71, 368*f*
participatory art cultures, digitally mediated,
    288–91
peak shift effect, 64, 301, 308, 381–85, 381*f*, 383*f*,
    384*f*
peek-a-boo principle, 385–86
Pepperell, Robert, 236, 345
Pepper No. 30 (Weston), 11, 12*f*
perception, 14–16, 318–33
in art experts, 177–78
art features *v.*, 137–40
artist manipulation of, 282, 300–301
artwork as stimulus, 165–73, 253, 264
audiovisual, 87*f*, 88, 89*f*
of balance, 167–70
bistability, 54–55, 55*f*
brain damage effect on, 303
brains, stuff in world, and, 136–37
of color, 86–88, 89*f*
early neuroaesthetic studies, 319–20
eye movement studies of, 175–79
of faces and objects, 340–43
Fauvism, 320–21
Fechner and foundation of experimental
    aesthetics, 323–26
functional specialization of aesthetics, 319
functional specialization of visual
    cortex, 318–19
imagery and, 44–47
irradiation, 49–51, 50*f*

perception (*Cont'd*)
  judgment involved in, 377–78, 377*f*
  kinetic art, 320
  of left and right face profiles, 85–86
  limitations in, 81–82, 84
  of line, 165–67
  neural correlates of aesthetic judgments,
    326–33, 332*f*
  pictorial, 153–54
  of power of center, 167–70
  semantic aspects of, 345–46
  sfumato, 51–54, 52*f*
  skills of, 91–92
  Surrealism, 321–23, 323*f*
  Surrealist violations of, 321–23, 323*f*
  of visual art, 48–57, 50*f*, 52*f*, 55*f*
perceptual fluency, 65–66, 225, 231
perceptual organization, 165
perceptual primitives, 165–67
perceptual problem solving, 385–86
Pericolo, Lorenzo, 154
peripheral vision, in sfumato
    technique, 52–53, 52*f*
person, in aesthetic processing of
    artworks, 163, 179–81
personal differences
  in aesthetic experience, 261–62
  in art, 285–86
  integration with other psychological
    theories, 286–91
personality
  aesthetic experience and, 180–81
  creativity associated with, 285
perspective
  bias, 207–10, 218
  canonical, 210–12, 211*f*
Petkova, Valeria, 96
PFC. *See* prefrontal cortex
Phantoms in the Brain (Ramachandran), 95
phenomenological evidence
  in explaining anomalous suspense, 91–92
  in explaining empathy, 93–94
  in explaining neural body mapping, 96–97
  of mental phenomena, 83–85, 88–90
  neural behaviorism and, 97–100
  subpersonal processing and, 100–101, 101*f*
philosophical approaches, 4–14, 6*f*, 9*f*, 12*f*, 31–58
  to aesthetic response, 66–69
  conceptual approach, 11–14, 22–24, 24*f*
  expressionist approach, 7–9, 9*f*, 22–24, 24*f*
  formalist approach, 9–11, 12*f*, 22–24, 24*f*
  to literature, 35–41
  mimetic approach, 4–7, 6*f*, 22–24, 24*f*
  to music, 41–47
  to visual art, 47–57, 50*f*, 52*f*, 55*f*
philosophy, artifacts distorted by, 114–18

photography
  art and, 11
  as trace of artist activity, 120–21
Picasso, Pablo, 146, 153, 184, 285, 287
  content of, 140
  genius of, 357
  object recognition in paintings of, 348, 349*f*
pictorial perception, 153–54
picture format, aesthetic experience response
    to, 170–73
Pissarro, Camille, 282
Piss Christ (Serrano), 261, 262*f*
Plato, 4–5, 42
pleasingness, 255–56, 258–60
pleasure
  aesthetic, 64–66
  in study of art, 133–36, 139–40
PNFA. *See* progressive nonfluent aphasia variant
The Poetics (Aristotle), 5
Polanski, Roman, 91
Pop Art, 13
positive affect
  attentional inhibition account of, 234–35
  processing fluency and, 226–28
positive emotions, 268
Positivism, knowledge and, 32
posterior anatomy, of visuospatial abilities,
    360–61
post-modernism, 13
power
  beauty adding to, 121–23
  of center, 167–70, 177–78, 204
The Power of the Center (Arnheim), 204
Prägnanz, 15
preference. *See* aesthetic preference
preference-ordering studies, in aesthetics, 33–34
prefrontal cortex (PFC), 19–21, 20*f*, 306–7
  in perception and imagination of faces and
    objects, 341–42
  VMPFC, 327–28
prehistoric art, 279, 338
presentation format, aesthetic experience
    response to, 170–73
prestige effects, 239
pride, 269
primary visual cortex, 19
Primitive Art (Boas), 109
primitives, 51, 165–67, 384
principle of aesthetic mean, 324
prior exposure. *See* exposure effect
processing fluency, 223–41, 258–60, 308
  in art, 235–41, 237*f*
  challenges to fluency theory, 230–38, 237*f*
  consequences of, 226–28
  in culturally shared taste, 238–41
  definition of, 225

determinants of, 225–26
fluency theory of aesthetic pleasure, 211–14,
    214*f*, 216, 224–30
progressive nonfluent aphasia variant (PNFA),
    artistic talent in patients with, 362–63,
    366–69, 367*f*, 368*f*, 369*f*, 370*f*
Project Zero, 277–78, 287
prosopagnosia, 319
prototype preference theory, 257–58, 308
prototypicality, 64, 226
Psycho (Hitchcock), 92, 92*f*
psychobiological model, 254–57, 256*f*
psycho-historical theory of art, 236–38
psychological approach, 14–16, 31–58
    to aesthetic experience, 253–60, 256*f*
    to aesthetic processing of artworks, 163–64
    cultural/contextual approaches to art, 283–91
    culture of, 251–53
    individual differences in art, 285–91
    integration of spheres, 286–91
    to literature, 35–41
    to music, 41–47
    spheres essential for psychological
        explanations of art, 278–86
    universal approaches to art, 279–83, 286–91
    to visual art, 47–57, 50*f*, 52*f*, 55*f*
psychological disease, creative genius and, 285,
    357–58, 371
psychological evidence
    in explaining anomalous suspense, 91–92
    in explaining empathy, 93–94
    in explaining neural body mapping, 96–97
    of mental phenomena, 83–85, 88–90
    neural behaviorism and, 97–100
    subpersonal processing and, 100–101, 101*f*
psychophysics, 14–15, 17–18
psychophysiological approaches, 183–84
Public Enemy, 261
punning principle, 386
pupillary response, during aesthetic
    experience, 184
The Raft of the Medusa (Géricault), 8, 9*f*
Rage Net (Brakhage), 88, 89*f*
The Railway (Manet), 141
Ramachandran, V. S., 95–97
Raum-Zeit-Materie (Weyl), 230
Ravel, Maurice, 357, 369
Ray, Man, 152
Raymond, Jane, 234
realism, of art, 135
Reber, Arthur, 225
recognition
    of faces, 340–43
    of objects, 340–43, 348–50, 349*f*
    of representational *v.* indeterminate *v.* abstract
        art, 346–48, 346*f*

recognition memory, representational paintings
    and, 343–45, 344*f*
rectangle, structural skeleton of, 204, 205*f*
reductionism, neuroaesthetics use of, 310–11, 382
Rée, Jonathan, 136, 139–40
"refined" taste, 238–39
Renaissance, 134–35, 380
Reni, Guido, 143
Renoir, Pierre-Auguste, 10
repetitive transcranial magnetic stimulation
    (rTMS), 45
Report from Rockport (Davis), 174–75
representational art
    brain activity response to, 306
    fMRI during recognition of, 346–48, 346*f*
    recognition memory and, 343–45, 344*f*
representational fit, 213–16, 214*f*, 215*f*
reproductions, aesthetic adequacy of, 170–73, 182
Republic (Plato), 4–5, 42
response. *See* aesthetic response
retina, lateral inhibition in, 50–51
reverse inference problem, 311
reward, in aesthetic experience, 255–57, 256*f*
right hemisphere specialization, 360
    creativity and, 339
    visuospatial abilities and, 360–61
right parietal cortex, 367–71, 368*f*
rightward bias, 170
Robinson, Jenefer, 35–41
Rogoff, Irit, 140
Romanticism, 8, 9*f*
Rosa, Salvator, 143
rTMS. *See* repetitive transcranial magnetic
    stimulation
rule of thirds, 70–72

saccades, in study of aesthetic
    experience, 175–79
samples, for research in empirical aesthetics,
    252–53
Santayana, George, 224
Sara Nader (Shepard), 17–18, 17*f*
savant syndrome, 385, 386*f*
scanpath, in study of aesthetic experience,
    175–79
schemas, 18
schlock, 282
Schroeder's staircase, 377, 377*f*
Schyns, Phillipe, 54–55, 55*f*
Scruton, Roger, 43
SD. *See* semantic dementia variant of
    frontotemporal dementia
seagull chicks, peak shift effect
    in, 383–85, 384*f*
Sekula, Alan, 140–41
self-conscious emotions, 269–70

selfhood
    spatial containment of, 94–97, 98f, 101
    unity of, 101
semantic dementia variant of frontotemporal
    dementia (SD), artistic talent in patients
    with, 362–64, 364f
semantic meaning. *See* content
sensation, art influence on, 23–24, 24f
sensory processes, 14–16
sensory violations, 321–23, 323f
Serrano, Andres, 261, 262f
Seurat, Georges, 49–51, 50f, 135–36
sex selection, 307–8
    cultural modulation of, 284
    in explaining art existence, 279–80
    visual aesthetics and, 376–77, 380
sfumato, 51–54, 52f
Shakespeare, William, 138–39
shame, 269
Shannon, Joshua, 145
Sharits, Paul, 88, 89f
Shepard, Roger, 17–18, 17f
Shutter Interface (Sharits), 88, 89f
significant form, 10
simulated movements, in aesthetic appreciation,
    119–20
simulation theory, 93–94
situation, in aesthetic processing of artworks,
    163, 181–83
size
    aesthetic experience in response to, 172
    canonical, 211
Skov, Martin, 143
*Slave Market with the Disappearing Bust of
    Voltaire* (Dalí), 54–55, 55f
Snow, C. P., 376
Snow Storm (Turner), 236–37, 237f
social class, taste developed within, 238–41
social construction, of aesthetic response, 71
social context, aesthetic experience in
    response to, 181–83
social interaction
    art role in, 308
    in digitally mediated participatory cultures,
    288–91
Solomon, Robert, 36
spatial composition, 202–16, 214f, 215f
    bias violation, 214–16, 215f
    ecological biases, 206–7, 210–11, 210f, 217–18
    ecological biases in vertical position,
    208–10, 209f
    exposure, fluency, and fit, 211–14, 214f
    horizontal object placement, 203–6, 204f, 205f
    representational fit, 213–16, 214f, 215f
    vertical object placement, 206–10, 207f, 209f

spatial-frequency information, in
    bistability, 54–55, 55f
spatial resolution, in perception of
    artworks, 51–54, 52f
specialization
    of aesthetics, 319
    creativity and, 339
    lateralization as means of
    subspecialization, 359–60
    of visual cortex, 318–19
    visuospatial abilities and, 360–61
species, art transcendence of, 376–77
specific exploration, 177–78
Speed (De Bont), 90–91
Spielberg, Steven, 100, 101f
split brain, art and, 359–60
square, structural skeleton of, 204, 205f
startle response, 38
Still Life with Apples (Cézanne), 174–75
stimulus. *See also* perception
    artwork as, 165–73, 253, 264
    as fluency determinant, 229
    infant preferences for, 281
    supernormal and ultranormal, 384–85
Stork, David, 154
Strangers on a Train (Hitchcock), 98f
structural organization, of artwork, 165
structural skeleton, of square or
    rectangle, 204, 205f
style processing, 330
"subception" experiments, 37
subculture, color preferences and, 196, 201
subjectivity, in aesthetic experience,
    260–62, 262f
sublime feelings, 8, 310
subpersonal processing, 100–101, 101f
Super Bowl ads, neurological evidence on,
    99–100
supernormal stimuli, 384–85
surprise, 233–34, 265–66
Surrealism, 321–23, 323f
suspense, 90–92, 92f
Sweet Anticipation (Huron), 233
symmetrical center bias, 170
symmetry principle, 380–81
    brain activity and, 307
    evolution and, 280
Symphony No. 3 (Beethoven), 42
synesthesia, in PNFA, 368–69, 369f

taste
    culturally shared, 238–41
    definitions of, 7–8
temporal lobe, 358–59
temporo-parietal junction (TPJ), 347–48

three-dimensional (3-D) space, two-dimensional
depictions of, 5–7, 6f
Timecode (Figgis), 87f, 88
Tinguely, Jean, 320
Titanic (Cameron), 90–91
Titian, 151
title
aesthetic experience in response
to, 174–75, 328–29
exploratory behavior in response to, 178–79
perception of meaning and, 350
Tolstoy, Leo, 9
top-down processing, 17–18, 17f
bottom-up processing interactions
with, 178–79
bottom-up processing v., 233–34
in explaining anomalous suspense, 91–92
in object recognition, 350
PFC in, 19–20
TPJ. *See* temporo-parietal junction
training. *See* expertise
A Treatise of Human Nature (Hume), 44
triangulation of aesthetic experience, 80–101
brain mapping of body, 94–97, 98f
as "natural method" for explaining aesthetic
experience, 83–90, 87f, 89f
neural behaviorism, 97–100
physical measurement v.
experience, 81–82, 82f
subpersonal processing and, 100–101, 101f
for tracking suspense, 90–92, 92f
for understanding empathy, 93–94
The Triumph of the Egg, Horses and Men
(Anderson), 260–61
truth judgments, exposure effect
on, 227–28
Turner, Joseph Mallord William, 236–37, 237f

ultranormal stimuli, 384–85
United 93 (Greengrass), 91
United States, color preferences
in, 196–98, 197f, 198f
universal approaches to art, 279–83, 286–91
universalism. *See also* openness
in art, 108–11
art definitions and, 123–24
universal laws of aesthetics, 375–89, 387f
grouping, 378–80, 378f, 379f
harmony, 386–87
isolation, 385
peak shift effect, 64, 381–85, 381f, 383f, 384f
peek-a-boo principle, 385–86
punning, 386
symmetry, 380–81
Unravelling Boléro (Adams), 369, 369f

Valéry, Paul, 145
value
aesthetic, 65, 182, 307–9
artistic, 65
Van Gogh, Vincent, 10, 357
van Meegeren, Han, 182
Varèse, Edgar, 43
variability
of art, 143–46
of beauty, 142–43
variables
collative, 16, 255–56
for research in empirical aesthetics, 252–53
Vasari, Giorgio, 135, 151
Velazquez, Diego, 149–50, 150f
ventral visual pathway, 300, 306–7, 340–41,
346–47
ventromedial part of the prefrontal cortex
(VMPFC), 327–28
Verfremdungseffekt, 237–38
Vermeer, Johannes, 153–54
changing views on, 142, 146
forgeries of, 182
vertical line preference, 166–67
vertical object placement, 206–10, 207f, 209f
ecological biases in, 208–10, 209f
viewer contributions, to art experience, 179–81
View of Delft (Vermeer), 153–54
visual art, psychology and neuroscience applied
to philosophy of, 47–57, 50f, 52f, 55f
visual cortex, 304–7, 337, 347
color processing in, 320–21
functional specialization of, 318–19
motion processing in, 320
in perception and imagination of faces and
objects, 340–43
visual exploration, as second phase of aesthetic
experience, 164, 175–79
visual imagery, 44–45, 340–43
visual indeterminacy, 345–48, 346f
visual processing, 19–20, 20f, 301–2, 302f,
375–89, 387f
of abstract art, 301
aesthetic response and, 72–75
artist manipulation of, 300–301
of color, 86–88, 89f
film's use of, 87f, 88, 89f
grouping principle, 378–80, 378f, 379f
harmony principle, 386–87
isolation principle, 385
limitations of, 84
peak shift effect, 64, 381–85, 381f, 383f, 384f
peek-a-boo principle, 385–86
perception and imagination of faces and
objects, 340–43

visual processing (*Cont'd*)
  punning principle, 386
  simplification of, 383–84
  symmetry principle, 380–81
visual stimuli, art features *v.*, 137–40
visual system, formal structure coupled to, 48–57, 50*f*, 52*f*, 55*f*
visuospatial abilities
  posterior anatomy of, 360–61
  right-sided anatomy of, 360–61
  semantic dementia and, 363–64, 364*f*
VMPFC. *See* ventromedial part of the prefrontal cortex
von Hartmann, Eduard, 324–25
Vorschule der Aesthetik (Fechner), 15, 323–25

wanting, liking *v.*, 309
Warhol, Andy, 13
Watkins, Carleton, 11
WAVEs. *See* weighted affective valence estimates
web design, cognitive approach applied to, 18–19
The Wedding (Léger), 178–79
weight, of color in artworks, 169

weighted affective valence estimates (WAVEs), 198–202, 200*f*
Wertheimer, Max, 15
Weston, Edward, 11, 12*f*
Weyl, Hermann, 230
What is Art? (Tolstoy), 9
Winesburg, Ohio (Anderson), 260–61
Wittgenstein, Ludwig, 32–34
woman reading (Braque), 349*f*
Work No. 227, the lights going on and off (Creed), 68
world, brains, perception, and stuff in, 136–37
The Yellow Cow (Marc), 233–34

Zajonc, Robert, 37
Zeki, Semir
  art and aesthetic response described by, 72–75
  on artists, 282, 300, 337, 356–57
  on function of art, 136
  on Picasso's *Demoiselles d'Avignon*, 146
  visual cortex studies of, 318–19
Zmijewski, Artur, 140–41
Zur experimentellen Aesthetik (Fechner), 323